PREHAB EXERCISE BOOK FOR RUNNERS

FOURTH EDITION

Michael Rosengart, CPT, CES, CSCS

Prepare to perform.

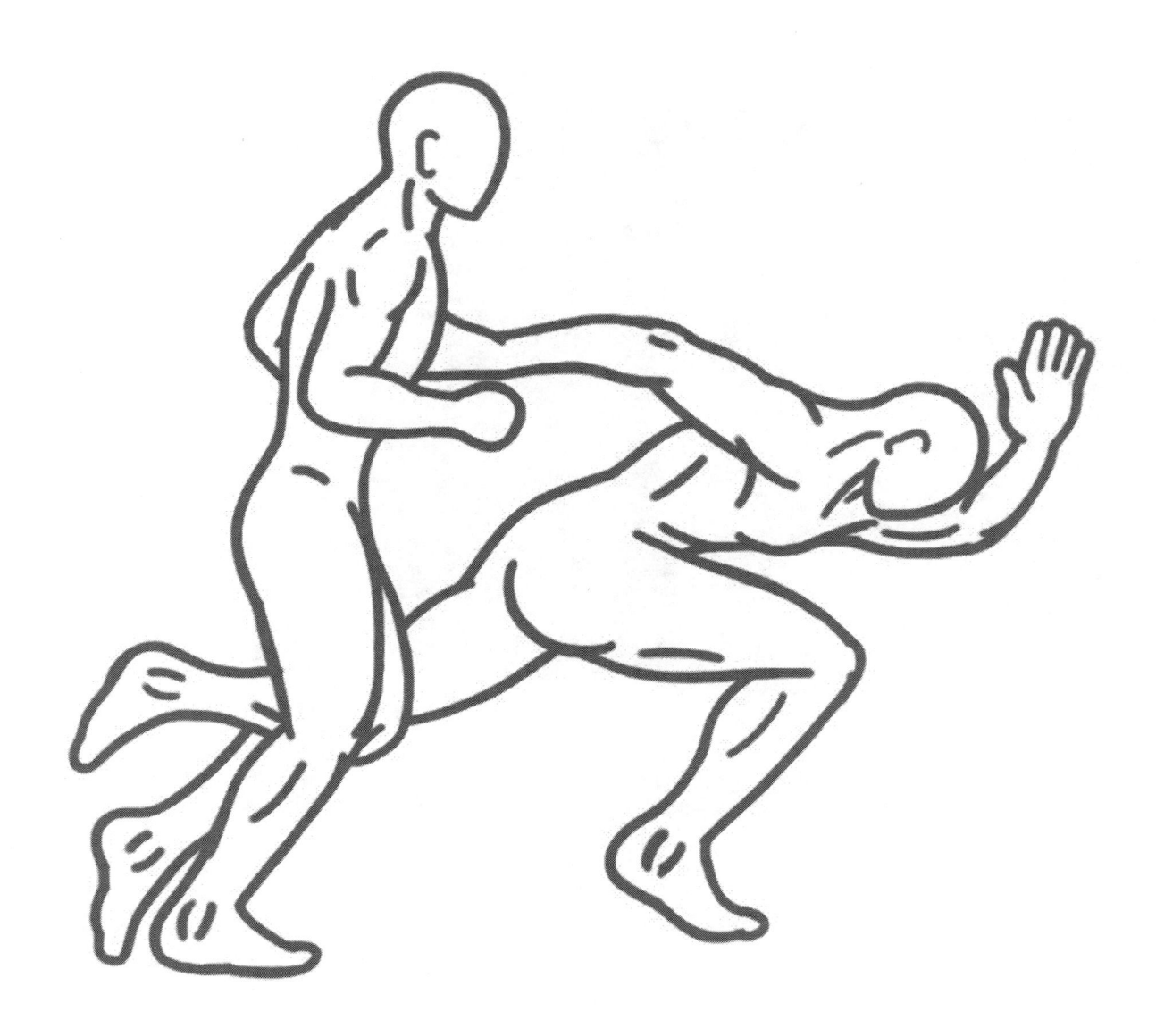

PreHab Exercises
Hagerstown, MD - USA
© 2016

To my friends and family,

Thank you for supporting me every step of the way!

To the Coaches and Athletes,

Keep getting better!

-Michael

TABLE OF CONTENTS

PREHAB EXERCISE BOOK FOR RUNNERS
By Michael Rosengart, CPT, CES, CSCS

- **Introduction to PreHab** 5
  - **Personal Journey:** 9
  - ***How I found PreHab*** 9
    - A Foot Perspective 13
    - The Functional Movement Screen 15
    - Proper Preparation Techniques 16
  - **What to Expect from PreHab** 19
  - **A.M.A.S.S. Method** 21
  - **The Habit of Preparation** 25
  - **Address Pain First** 27
- **Common Injuries for Runners** 33
  - **Hamstring Pulls** 35
  - **Runner's Knee** 38
  - **Iliotibial Band Syndrome (ITBS)** 40
  - **Achilles Tendinitis** 46
  - **Plantar Fasciitis** 49
  - **Shin Splints** 53
  - **Ankle Sprains** 54
  - **Stress Fracture** 55
    - Strength Training Guidelines 58
- **Alignment** 59
  - What is alignment? 59
  - Living in a Modern World 61
  - **Assessing Alignment** 65
    - Front View 65
    - Profile View 67
    - Plank Alignment 69
  - **Movement Evaluations** 73
    - MOVEMENT EVALUATION - Kneeling Lunge and Reach ... 74
    - MOVEMENT EVALUATION - Single-Leg Bridge Off Roller ... 74
    - MOVEMENT EVALUATIONS - Single-Leg Box Squat 75
  - The Joint-by-Joint Approach 79
- **Mobility** 87
  - MOBILITY ASSESSMENT: Wall Slide 89
  - MOBILITY ASSESSMENT: Wall Squat 90
  - MOBILITY ASSESSMENT: Hip Hinge 91
  - Mobility Changes 92
- **Soft Tissue Therapy** 93
  - Soft Tissue Therapy Techniques 96
- **Biotensegrity** 99
- **Foam Rolling** 101

TABLE OF CONTENTS

Forward Head 111
    The Biomechanical Cost 112
    Top Down Rx 113
Thoracic Spine Mobility 119
Shoulder Mobility 131
Hip Mobility 145
    Types of Rollers 148
    Balling 150
Ankle & Foot Mobility 163
    A Foot Perspective 163
    Big Toe Test 164
Posterior Chain Mobility 173
    Power and Speed 173
    Supine Mobility Sequence 181
Combination Exercises for Mobility 195

Activation Exercises 211
    Activation Techniques 215
    Ankle & Foot Activation 223
    Hip Activation 231
        Band Walks 239
        Practice Standing 244
    Core Activation 245
    Shoulder Activation 253
        Shoulder Girdle Activation 259
    Posterior Chain Activation 267
        Compensation Strategies 267
        Use the Whole Chain 268
    Combination Exercises for Activation 289

Stability 317
    STABILITY ASSESSMENT: Single-Leg Heel Lift 319
    STABILITY ASSESSMENT: Single-Leg Rotation 320
    STABILITY ASSESSMENT: Hip Hinge 320
    STABILITY ASSESSMENT: Single-Leg Box Squat 322
    STABILITY ASSESSMENT: Lateral Lunge to Single-Leg Balance ... 323
    STABILITY ASSESSMENT: Trunk Stability Push-up 324
    STABILITY ASSESSMENT: Ipsilateral Rotary Stability Test 325
Shoulder Stability 327
Core Stability 343
    One Powerful Lever 343
    Broken Chain 344
Hip Stability 361
    Need for Hip Stability 361
    HIP STABILITY TEST 362
Ankle Stability 371
    Eye Test 372
Combination Exercises for Stability 385

TABLE OF CONTENTS

Strength Training for Runners **405**
    Repetitive Stress 405
    Perceived Exertion (PE) 407
    Programming 408
    Periodization 409
    Law of Diminishing Returns 412
    Designing your Program 413
  Strength Exercises **417**

RUNNING DRILLS **429**
  Gait Efficiency Drills **431**
    Exercise Progression 432
  Running Technique **445**
    Improve your Technique 445
    Ground Contact 446
    Heel Strike - Oh, no! 446
    Stepping in the Right Direction 450
    Forward Lean 451
    Slope and Speed 453
    PreHab in Sports 454
    Forefoot Strike 454
    Mid-Foot Strike 456
  Form Running Drills **458**
    ANKLE HOP 459
    HEEL STRIDE 460
    LATERAL SHUFFLE 461
    KNEE TUCK STRIDE (HIGH KNEES) 462
    HEEL PULL STRIDE (BUTT KICKERS) 463
    STRAIGHT-LEG STRIDE 464
    BACKPEDAL 465
    CARIOCA 466
    A-SKIP 467
    B-SKIP 468
    TRIPLE A-SKIP 469
    ALTERNATING BOUNDING SKIP 470
    FORWARD LEAN POSITIONING 471

Recovery **473**
  Yoga **475**
    The Practice of Yoga 476
    Breathing in Yoga 477
    Breathing to Energize and Calm 478
  Inversions **497**
  Sleep **503**

INDEX **505**

BASIC ASSESSMENTS AND MOVEMENT EVALUATIONS **513**

TABLE OF CONTENTS

Introduction to PreHab

Sun Tzu said that every war is won before it's ever fought.

PreHab brings that belief alive in your training by physically prepare the body to perform the best that it can in every workout and run.

How does PreHab bring better results?
The main goal of PreHab is to restore function and integrity to your biomechanics in order to optimize efficiency in every movement pattern and improve the performance of each run.

To understand how to use PreHab within the context of your training program, it's advantageous to look at where many exercises and techniques come from: Rehab.

Rehab, or rehabilitation to be formal, intentionally aims to restore function to the human body by realigning a person's body mechanics, or biomechanics, and optimizing how a person moves.

Consequentially, the concept of rehab infers that there is a misalignment or dysfunction in how a person moves, usually associated with an acute injury or chronic stress.

**The truth is: everyone will endure faults in their biomechanics.
No one is immune.**

Repetitive movements found in sports or exercises as well as your lifestyle will lead to the distortion of your natural movement patterns. In other words, if you run on a consistent basis or if you sit at a desk for work all day, these repetitive movements will slowly warp and distort your natural alignment and biomechanics.

Add some minor injuries, like a sprained wrist or twisted ankle, to a series of random circumstances, such as helping a friend move, and some not-so-random activities, like going to the gym or playing basketball, and soon enough your body is changing in a negative way, and you may not even realize it.

In fact, Katy Bowman, M.S., a well-known biomechanist and author of *Alignment Matters*, tells us that our bodies are actually shifting and changing with how we live our lives – not figuratively, but literally. Our bones reshape themselves and our muscles can lose their length due to how we live our lives, which is the very reason why we should look at "how" we physically live our lives.

INTRODUCTION

Unless we actively look for it, we will not see how we cheat in the way that we move. We will not be aware of how we compensate for inefficiencies or weaknesses every time we move. Yet, we will still compensate one way or another.

PreHab is a way of looking at 'how' we move in order to move better. And with better movement, we can then create better performances in all that we do: whether it's running a marathon, playing football, working out to lose weight, or just carrying the groceries in from the car.

PreHab helps to improve Movement Quality, enhance performance and prevent injuries.

Tim Ferriss was one of the first people to talk about PreHab in his book, *The 4-Hour Body*. Since then, it has steadily crept into the Strength and Conditioning world as coaches keep looking for better ways to train their athletes and prevent injuries. Now, it is proliferating through cyber space as people share PreHab exercises and techniques in podcasts, blogs, and all over YouTube.

But what is PreHab and how do I do it?
Believe it or not, this is an easier question to answer than the first one. Let's look at the root word of rehabilitation.

Habilis, in Latin, means to "fit, equip or make skillful."

Everything you do in PreHab is designed to make you more skillful in the way you move with your body. From loosening up to strengthening up, anything is PreHab if there is an intention of making the body move better.

PreHab are those preparatory habits, such as practicing mobility exercises, that help you achieve specific goals through movement.

Dr. Kelly Starrett, a well-known physical therapist and owner of San Francisco CrossFit, created his popular Mobility WOD series and his book, *Becoming a Supple Leopard*, as a way to help people develop daily maintenance on their bodies and perform better.

Practice daily maintenance as a way to perform better.

Can you accomplish goals without PreHab?
Of course, you can. People are amazingly resilient and adaptable, as Dr. Starrett puts it, which is a good thing because we strive to accomplish some amazing feats in sports and in life. Remember when Mary Lou Retton won the gold medal in the 1984 Olympics on a sprained ankle? When we put our minds to it, we can overcome a lot.

INTRODUCTION

The argument for PreHab is best expressed in a combination of thoughts from two men; Gray Cook, physical therapist and creator of the Functional Movement System and the philosopher Aristotle.

Cook teaches coaches and trainers to address all dysfunctions in movement first and foremost because they will eventually lead to an injury or some form a breakdown in the movement system – it is just a matter of when and not if.

For example, let's look at a 30-something office worker ready to cross running a marathon off of his bucket list. For 20-plus years, this person has been spending eight or more hours a day sitting and developing a limited range of motion in his entire body, especially his hips. As soon as he starts his marathon training, his body will modify and change his gait to compensate for the lack of mobility in his body. Strange movement patterns will appear. And won't be too long until his body starts breakdown in certain areas.

Worse off, this man may have the will of Alexander the Great and resolve to finish his training and compete in a marathon. It's at this point that his own passion and determination may become his very own enemy.

One of the goals of PreHab is to prevent future injuries through addressing dysfunctions in our movement.

Optimizing movement to improve performance and achieve specific results is another goal of PreHab that can be best expressed through the sentiment laid out in the following words:

'We are what we repeatedly do.
Excellence, then, is not an act, but a habit.'
-Aristotle

If we develop a personal system of preparatory habits to performance our best and avoid injury, we have PreHab.

This book will help create habits that restore biomechanics, optimize movement and improve performance.

Do you need to do PreHab to run?
No. Running is just putting one foot in front of the other to move through space at an elevated effort or pace. It's one of the most primal attributes of the human species.

However, if you are looking to optimize your running in terms of speed and distance, then keep reading because PreHab will help you.

INTRODUCTION

INTRODUCTION

Personal Journey:
How I found PreHab

I had a long journey to finding PreHab. And I believe that if certain things didn't happen the way that they did, I would never have found PreHab.

Growing up, I was really into sports. I played with all the kids in the neighborhood back in good old Verona, New Jersey. We were very unorganized. Our sporting events basically consisted of me calling each person in the morning to meet at Forest Avenue Elementary School or my backyard, where we would pick teams and play until we were too tired to play anymore.

I went on to play Little League and Pee-Wee football as well. I don't recall much instructing going on in either one, but then again maybe I was just not listening to the coaches. Regardless, I soon found myself becoming a student of form and technique because it led to success.

In football, I would pay close attention to my leverage when participating in tackling and blocking drills. I learned to stay low and I also learned how to be fast out of my stance. In baseball, I learned to hit by watching the alignment of the pitcher's shoulder and elbow. I saw 'form' in movement.

Then I got my first gym membership the summer before seventh grade- yes, seventh grade. I joke to friends that: kids in New Jersey start going to the gym earlier than most kids. The truth is that the school nurse reported me as obese at the end of sixth grade and my mother sat me down for a talk. Consequentially, I joined a gym, started Weight Watchers and lost 30 pounds that one summer.

After losing all that weight, my life was never the same. I kept my gym membership and slowly began evolving into a 'gym rat.' I also assume that one of the reasons this lifestyle change really took a hold over me was because once I lost weight and started working out, girls were finally interested in me. And what 13-year-old wouldn't like that?

So, to keep getting attention from girls, I kept working out and tried to learn more. I religiously read *Muscle & Fitness* magazine and watched how other people in the gym worked out. I thought I knew a lot, and every year I would learn more.

After I graduated from college, I got certified as a personal trainer in a weekend course, and I thought I was done with "school" forever. Boy, was I wrong.

Personal Training-
I was hired to be a trainer at Equinox Fitness in New York, which was one of the best things that ever happened to me. At that time, Equinox was one of the only gyms that had continuing education classes for their trainers – and I loved them!

INTRODUCTION

The Equinox Fitness Training Institute was taught by Dr. Paul Juris, who was a very passionate and creative man. He taught me the principals of periodization and functional movement, aka functional training. For two years, I sat in the front row, scribbled down notes and drove Dr. Juris crazy with my questions.

I loved all the work we did in those EFTI classes because I began to understand the matrix of human movement even more. I would pair exercises in workouts and create programs for my clients with the same zeal that a kid would have while enjoying putting together a puzzle. It was thrilling in a way!

In my time with Equinox, I accumulated over 20 different certifications of various disciplines and emphases. However, the two certifications that left the biggest impact on my training were:

Certified Strength and Conditioning Specialist
Functional Movement Screen

These two certifications made me realize how little I truly had learned by being a 'gym rat,' reading all those fitness magazines and talking 'bro-science.' I had missed out on how important biomechanics are to movement and performance.

Experience is the Ultimate Teacher
I really set myself up for the biggest lesson of my life when I went back to grad school. I chose the University in England because I wanted to study abroad. Plus they actually had an American Football team, and I really wanted to play again.

I was not a star on my high school football team. If anything, I was an unsung hero. I played tight end on a running team. However, we ran the veer option and did very well because I was the one setting the edge and designating the option man in the blocking scheme. I was smart, physical and reliable. Yet, I always believed I had more potential that I displayed in the game and I longed to prove it – at least to myself.

I got my chance to be a star in England. I helped the University's team to its first winning season ever, as well as a playoff berth. I took over as the quarterback half way through the season, when we were 1-3, and started a winning streak that took us into the playoffs.

I had such an experience that year with my teammates in England that I choose to stay one more year and play more football.

'Greed is Good'- the famous quote from the movie: Wall St.

I enrolled in a Creative Writing class at the University in order to be eligible to play one more season of football. I figured why not? Would I ever play again? No. I was 30 years old and everyone else was 19 to 22 years old on average. So, I saw this as a chance in a lifetime and I took it.

INTRODUCTION

And even though I had kept myself in great condition my entire life – at 30 years old I was playing football with college kids. I felt pretty lucky to still be playing college football with younger players, but my luck would run out.

I was running '18 Option' when two enormous opposing players jumped on my back. I resisted as much as I could, but my foot sank into the mud and a bone in my lower leg gave out. It broke. I was done for the season.

The doctor showed me the fracture in the X-ray, and all I thought about was what I would need to do in order to get back to playing. About a thousand different movie montages flashed through my mind. I was ready to be Rocky Balboa. I was ready to work hard to get back to football. I was not ready to let this opportunity slip away.

As soon as I could, I was back in the gym – crutches and all. I worked out every day, got my cast off, reported to rehab a few times, and then gathered some teammates and started training together.

It was less than a few weeks later when my Achilles ruptured. My left leg was over compensating for the newfound weakness of my right leg, the broken leg.

Greed may not be so good, Mr. Gecko.

Protection from Myself
What I really needed was not rehab, but a straightjacket to protect me from myself. I was too passionate about playing football one more time. I wanted to end my playing days in a different way, and I just simply was not ready to give up a game that I love. However, I was too determined for my own good.

Not only did I re-injure myself once – I did it twice. All in all, I had three injuries that year, which put me on crutches and in a cast for a total of 36 weeks in a consecutive 52-week span.

I went from a broken leg to training for football. Then I ruptured my Achilles in practice. Then I recovered and returned to practicing football again. I was running Jet Sweeps and Go-Routes at full speed (and beating the coverage too.) Yet, on my first play back in a real game, my Achilles ruptured again as I tried to turn the corner and a defender dragged me down.

Back to Reality
I returned to the States to resume my personal training career. I was rather excited to be helping people again. However, I was shocked with what I saw when getting back to the gym as a trainer.

After spending two years training and competing with college-aged athletes, I was astounded to see the coordination and fitness level of an average commercial gym member. The physical decline was obvious.

INTRODUCTION

I could see how distorted people's movements were and I tried to change in vain to correct these dysfunctions. I was creating "functional" training programs along with many of my colleagues. However, I was still disappointed in the results with my clients.

> *Disappointed with my own results too-*
> Even though I had 8 percent body fat at age 35, and I still ate pizza for lunch, I was not happy with the results I was getting in my own training.
>
> Even since my injuries, I had trouble running further than 50 yards at any given time. I would feel unstable and weak. Running became my Achilles Heel – with pun intended. Worse off, I really missed running.

INTRODUCTION

A Foot Perspective

In 2010, I attended a seminar through the Equinox Fitness Training Institute called "The Foot: The First Link in the Kinetic Chain" with Lenny Parracino, CMT, NTP, FAFS, a well-known Integrative Practitioner in Los Angeles. The seminar was amazing, as I learned the simple understanding that the Glutes will fire if the ankle plantar flexes (aka point the toes down into the floor.)

Then I looked down at my feet and started to wonder if I was moving correctly due to my Achilles injuries. The truth was no, not even close. When I asked Lenny for his advice, he chuckled in a friendly, non-B.S. way and told me that I had a lot of work to do. And he was right. I did have a lot to do, and I would keep that moment fresh in my head for a long time afterwards.

During this seminar, we all took off our shoes and socks to look at the bottom of our feet. The soles of our feet reveal the sole of our movement patterns. A person who has well-balanced movement patterns and alignment would have callused imprints on their forefoot and heels.

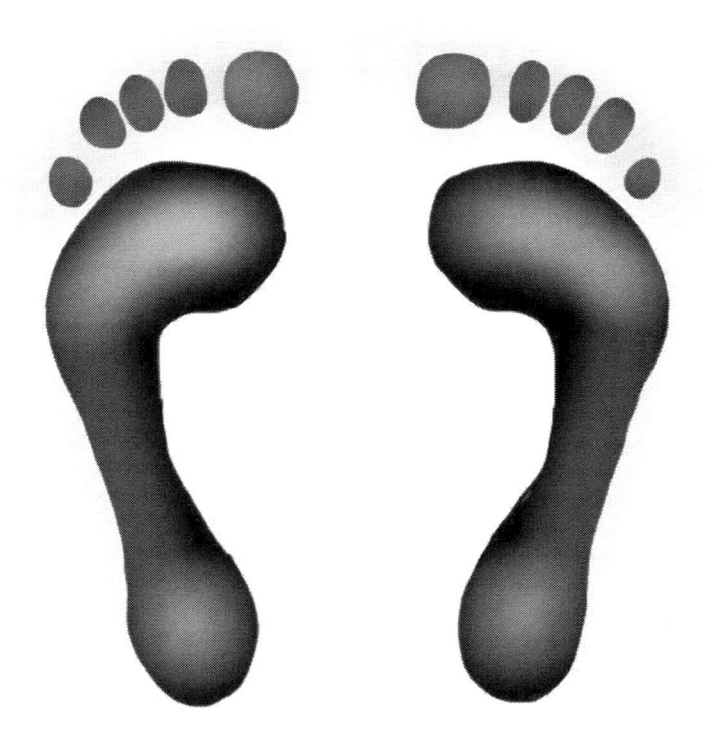

Ideal Pressure Distribution on Feet

INTRODUCTION

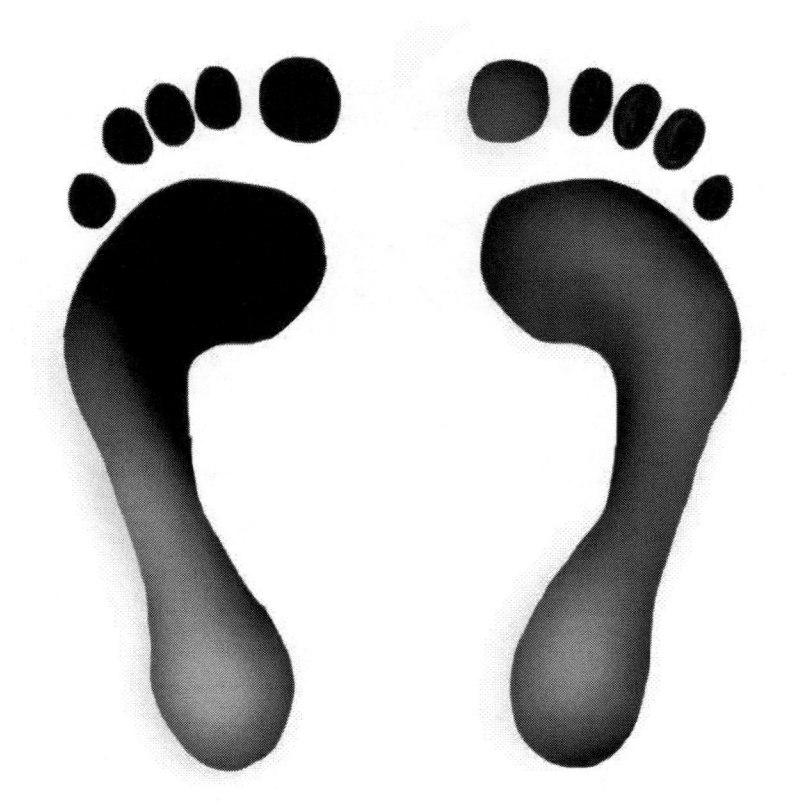

Pressure Distribution after my Achilles Tendon Ruptures

On the leg with the torn Achilles, I had a heavy, dense imprint on my heel with a lighter callus on the outside ridge of my foot and almost nothing on the forefoot, while my other foot had an imprint that was only slightly balanced.

In other words, I was misaligned in my body and moving with dysfunctions in my movement patterns. Yet, I thought I was functionally training myself.

INTRODUCTION

The Functional Movement Screen

When Gray Cook and Lee Burton rolled out the Functional Movement Screens, I was one of the first trainers to have a personal orientation to the method all the way back in 2007. I learned how to evaluate and score people's movement patterns that led to a new trend in training called "Assess and Correct."

The FMS provided me with a way to look at movement that was quantifiable and systematically manageable. I could now show a client where dysfunctions occurred and by how much. I literally had numbers on a sheet of paper and a process to get those numbers that was repeatable, which meant that I would know if what I was doing was effective or not.

> **Getting Up to Speed**
> When FMS first came out, assessing the Corrective Exercise library was a bit cumbersome. On top of that, impatient clients were not very receptive to "learning corrective exercises." Most people were still just waiting to get to the workout.
>
> Unfortunately, Correcting Biomechanics and Movement Patterns was losing out to adding weights and spiking heart rates as clients believed that was the essentials of a good workout.
>
> I personally had more than just a few clients tell me that they didn't want to do these corrective exercises. They just wanted to work out, and I did not have the right words to convince them otherwise. In fact, I lost a few clients when I stuck to a firm line on correcting movement.
>
> I am sure I am not the only trainer who faced resistance from clients when it came to teaching corrective exercises.

New Solution
I kept looking for better answers and more techniques in training because I was not satisfied with the results I was getting – for myself and my clients. I still wanted to run again, which was not happening. Coincidently, I also had a client, who was also determined to run.

Ann was a 40-year-old lawyer, who weighed 108 pounds and wanted to get down to 106 by running. However, she had horrible form when she ran. Her foot slapped the ground, her head bobbed from side to side, and she shrugged her shoulders the entire time. Consequentially, she would get severe pain on the bottom of her feet and in her shins to the point of limping. Yet, she would still limp into the gym and climb up on the treadmill to run for her warm up.

INTRODUCTION

First and foremost, I wanted to stop the pain from occurring. Luckily, I found an answer for Ann in an unexpected place.

Proper Preparation Techniques

In 2011, I took a NSCA seminar with Shannon Turley, the Head Strength Coach for the Stanford University football team called "Proper Preparation Techniques for Training" and learned the importance of "how."

Turley looked at how football players moved and devoted a large portion of the training time to develop maximum efficiency in these movement patterns. In fact, the detail and specificity of these exercises and techniques were very exacting and precise compared to what I regularly saw in the gym.

In the seminar, Turley introduced the concept of *PreHabilitation* in correlation to mobility exercises and a heavy dose of soft tissue therapy techniques that he employed to achieve improved form and function on the football field.

Impressed with the seminar as well as the performance of the Stanford football team, I started to incorporate Turley's philosophy into my own training.

At the time I was coaching semi-pro football in Los Angeles and I coached by 'doing' a lot. After a few weeks of adding Turley's exercises into my own training, I saw a difference as I was running fast enough to keep up with many of the players. Now, I promise you that I do not think we were running at an elite speed, say sub 4.5, but it was very thrilling for me to know that at 36 years old, I could turn and burn for 40-50 yards in practice with the players once again.

Furthermore, regaining my speed on the football field with Turley's techniques gave me insight to working with my client, Ann.

PreHabbing Ann
I started to introduce a heavy dose of soft tissue therapy and mobility techniques into Ann's training program along with a series of activation and stability exercises for running. Ann was very quad-dominant and had tight hip Flexors due to sitting so much. This inhibited her Glutes from being as active as they should be when she moved – let alone run. On top of that, Ann loved to wear high heels and consequentially had numerous knots or adhesions in her calves. Each day, we would apply a heavy dose of soft tissue therapy to her quads and calves as well as the rest of her body before targeting her mobility with a series of active flexibility exercise. Then we would focus on activating and stabilizing her core and glutes before we redefined her gait mechanics and running technique.

Again PreHabilitation worked as Ann was up and running in her workouts with no pain in only a few weeks.

INTRODUCTION

Aiming Higher
After I helped Ann to run again and I recaptured some of my speed, I looked at conquering longer distances. I set my aim on completing a 5K once again – a feat that eluded me ever since I broke my leg and ruptured my Achilles.

On September 11, 2011, I completed my first 5K since August 2004.

I was thrilled but not satisfied. My time was 25:11, which was far off of my 19:46 time I set before my injuries. Still I wanted to do better. I wanted to know that I could return to form and be that guy who raced through the Manhattan streets years before. So, I created my PreHab Challenge.

I saw how PreHab helped Ann run again and helped me to gain some of my speed back as well as complete a 5K, but I still had some doubts. Did PreHab really make a difference? And if it did, how could it be replicable on a consistent basis?

> ***Answering the Challenge***
> I created a 30-Day PreHab training program for a 5K that included no conditioning. In other words, I only focused on the biomechanics and movement patterns of running, and I did not run once in 30 days.
>
> ***After 30-Days I ran another 5K and lowered my time by 3 minutes using only these PreHab exercises.***

Even though I had a VO2 Max of 63, a body composition of 10 percent, and a resting heart rate of 48 at the time of this Challenge, I wanted to make sure that any difference in my time was not a result of metabolic conditioning, which is why I did not run once during the 30 days.

Instead, I believe that I was able to retrain and condition my biomechanics to support more efficient movement patterns for a longer amount of time, which consequentially resulted in a lower overall time.

Seeing the Light
Completing this Challenge gave me a new direction to explore with my training. I continued to incorporate PreHab exercises (mobility, activation, stability and strength exercises) into my training programs with a heavy dose of soft tissue therapy as well, and I continued to see great results.

A month later, I ran the Bay to Breakers 10K course in San Francisco in 68:03 despite the mega hill in the middle of the course. Another month later, I hiked to the Colorado

INTRODUCTION

River and back in the Grand Canyon on Hermit's Trail, a course that transverses 18 miles and ascends/descends another mile, in a little over six hours. Two months after that, I completed a 10-mile in 1:36:29. One month after that, I clocked a 5:57 mile. Another month later, I ran a 6:15 mile after a 5x5 WOD of Clean and Presses at 135lbs. at a CrossFit box.

I was happy with the results I was getting and confident that PreHab was contributing to my success.

INTRODUCTION

What to Expect from PreHab

The main goal of PreHab is to restore function and integrity to your biomechanics in order to optimize movement and thus improve performance.

> *PreHab's ROI:*
> **Restore Biomechanics**
> **Optimize Movement Quality**
> **Improve Performance**

Many exercises and much of the knowledge base for PreHab comes from the world of physical therapy and that is fittingly so. The purpose of PreHab is to equip you to perform. In other words, it's a sequence of preparatory habits for movements in sports and your life.

> **Unfortunately, most of us need rehab from our lifestyle.**

In one-way or another, life has messed you up from a biomechanically point of view at least. Whether you tore your Achilles twice like myself or you just sat in a chair while going to school like everyone else, your body has learned different strategies of compensation in your movement.

Yes, some people are more messed up than others. So, count your blessings – especially since you're reading this book. You are a lot closer to restoring your biomechanics than before.

'Rehabbing' from our lives and lifestyles, including sitting, deskwork, inactivity and injuries, is all a very important part of PreHab.

Your goal in PreHab is to restore functionality in your movement through creating a higher level of integrity in your biomechanics, which essentially parallels the course work in rehab and physical therapy.

Let's break down PreHab into smaller segments and work our way to mastering the habit of preparing ourselves to move well in steps.

INTRODUCTION

INTRODUCTION

A.M.A.S.S. Method

Over the last couple of years, I have analyzed all the PreHab exercise and techniques that I use and categorized them in relation to their intention or objective. Many times, as you will later see, I use the same exercise but in a different way in order to accomplish two or more specific goals. For example, many Activation exercises can double as Mobility or Stability exercises as well as an evaluation of someone's Alignment. Yet, the way that these exercises are executed will be different. However, the objective of each exercise always needs to be clear and intentional.

> *Every exercise serves a specific objective and goal.*

I have created the following A.M.A.S.S. acronym to help guide you through the various training objectives and their specific intentions.

> **PreHab Training & Development Goals**
>
> A. = Assess
> M. = Mobility
> A. = Activation
> S. = Stability
> S. = Strength

A.M.A.S.S. is an integral foundation for an effective training program as it properly prepares the body for any workout or run and addresses the essential components of Human Movement in regards to biomechanics and physiology. Without it a comprehensive training system such as A.M.A.S.S., you may be placing unrealistic demands on your body.

For example:
Here I am sitting at my computer, writing this book about PreHab. My Hip flexors are getting tighter by the moment as I search my brain for the next words to write. At the same time, I want to run a 5K later on today. I need a way to physically prepare my body, which is what A.M.A.S.S. will provide.

PreHab Thought Process: *The A.M.A.S.S. Method in action.*

Assess- In addition to 'watching' my form while I exercise, I will also continuously check

INTRODUCTION

my alignment and posture (my form in Daily Life Activities) all day long in all that I do because it will tell me what I am working with and without. For example, if I find myself slouching over my keyboard, I know that my Upper Trapezius and Pectorals muscles are overactive while my Rhomboids and Lower Trapezius are turned off.

Action- walk away from my computer for at least ten minutes, find a wall and stretch out my chest, neck and shoulder muscles.

Mobility- Since I love to run, I am continuously loosening up my hips, specifically lengthening my hip flexors. I focus a lot on the hip flexors because I know how important they are to the length of my stride as well as reducing any "pulling" stress on my lumbar spine that I may feel after sitting for a while.

Action- practice several different stretches, such as a Kneeling Lunge and Reach stretch, throughout the day and especially when I get down to the track later to run.

Activation- Having the essential muscle groups fire when you need them to fire is important in any sport. However, if I have been sitting for a long time, my Glute muscles had no reason to be active and will be slow to fire when I start to run. Yet, I need them when I run because the Glutes are my prime movers. So, I will do a series of exercises that will specifically stimulate and activate my Glutes.

Action- practice some Single-Leg Toe Touches and Bridges when I get to the track to help fire up my Glutes (Hip muscles) and turn on that neurological connection.

Stability- In my case, I am looking to develop some more Core Stability because when I sit a lot, my abdominals do not need to do any work at all. Yet, when I am trying to run fast, I need my Abdominals and the rest of my Core to help stabilize the position of my Spine and channel the Kinetic flow of energy through my body on every single step!

Action- I can pop down onto the ground for some Dead Bugs, Side Planks and Dog Pointers before I run or grab some weights and combine some Single-Leg Deadlifts with a Tall Cable Chop as another option.

Strength Training- Truth be told, I don't need much strength to survive in this modern world. Civilization has made survival very convent for many people out there. However, I do need strength if I want to optimize my health and my performance.

Simply put: strength training is a deliberate plan to stress the body in a strategic way to make it grow stronger, use more nutrients and fortify the essential physiological structures of the body. In other words, if I want to keep a large portion of my muscles well into my 50's, 60's and 70's, I need to do some strength training.

Action- schedule at least one or two strength training sessions each week and perform these strength exercises with the appropriate amount of weight and proper form.

INTRODUCTION

Correcting Movement
PreHab exercises will also serve as evaluations that can assess your alignment and movement patterns to detect any biomechanical faults in your movement.

There is a natural blueprint to how your body moves that is very evident when you look at a toddler. However, as we get older, our ability to hold this natural form of movement diminishes due to injuries, lack of use and several other reasons.

One of the intentions of PreHab is to re-align the body with the natural form of Human Movement. The first step is to assess how you move, one movement pattern at a time. Then whenever you find a limitation in how you move, you then have an opportunity to correct that movement pattern and restore functional integrity to the biomechanics involved.

Now, there are many different ways to evaluate movement – just ask a physical therapist. At the same time, if you don't have a physical therapist handy right now, try this quick movement evaluation:

Stand on one leg for 20 seconds. Now, the other leg.

How'd you do? If you lost balance before 20 seconds was up on either leg, try balancing on that leg more throughout the day and re-test yourself every day until you can stand on one leg for 20 seconds.

Injury Prevention-
One great benefit of exercising and performing with proper biomechanics is a surmountable reduction to the risk of injury. When the body moves the way it is designed to move, there is adequate stability and integrity to one's movement. However, when a person attempts to perform or exercise with dysfunctions or imbalances in their body mechanics, injury is inevitable. Gray Cook, creator of the Functional Movement Screen, will tell you that it's not a question of "if" an injury will occur when improper body mechanics are applied, but it is a matter of "when" the injury will occur.

In addition to injury prevention, cultivating proper body mechanics will also lead to peak performance in any sport or activity. When you are pushing yourself to new limits, success will depend on a concentrated effort of limited resources in exact direction. Conversely, dysfunctions of imbalances in body mechanics will misdirect your efforts and waste your energy. So, if you are going for a personal record in the mile or just trying to improve your waistline, improving your body mechanics will deliver better results.

Use the A.M.A.S.S. Method to be objectively clear and intentional with every exercise that you use.

INTRODUCTION

INTRODUCTION

The Habit of Preparation

In his book, *Power of Habit*, Charles Duhigg states that people generally succeed more than others in life because of a few keystone habits, which are responsible for shaping their entire decision-making tree and thus behavior.

In football, I had one habit, one mantra if you will, that helped shape my entire career. It was simply, "keep your feet moving."

I learned all the way back in Pop Warner football, where a bunch of local police officers volunteered as coaches and religiously worked us hard every day. From hitting the sled to bear crawls to the Oklahoma tackling drill, and on and on, they repeatedly screamed "keep your feet moving." Of course there is a part of me today that realizes that that there really is not that many other choices to yell during practice when you are coaching a bunch of fifth graders.

In football, you gain more opportunities to overpower your opponent or outmaneuver them by chopping your feet more, because every step literally yields more force. Therefore, keeping your feet moving more than your opponent gives you the leverage and the freedom to explore other options, such as spinning off your opponent, swimming over them or pushing them away from you.

Nonetheless, I always keep my feet moving on every play – in every practice and every game, which rewarded me so many more opportunities. My coaches relied on me more. I won in more drills. I got more playing time and inevitably also made more plays by always keeping my feet moving.

How to Build PreHab as a Habit
To leverage the most success from PreHab, focus on creating a high frequency of awareness on your alignment and movement patterns. As much as you can, look at how you are using or positioning your body. Stop in front of mirrors and look at your reflection. Set reminders in your calendar or phone that tell you to stand up at your desk and move around. Prepare your gym bag the night before. Put your foam roller in front of your TV.

Awareness on your Alignment is key to optimizing the way that you move.

Improve your Mobility
Practicing soft tissue therapy and mobility exercises is a great way to help develop a keen awareness of Alignment and Movement. Chances are that your mobility has been limited in some form or another due various movement habits that you've created over the years. Don't worry; you're not alone. We all have movement habits that we hardly ever notice.

Deliberating working to improve your mobility will help you to break and distinguish

INTRODUCTION

many movement habits that are biomechanical deficient or liable.

Mobility Improves Physiology and More
Improving your mobility will create more opportunities for you to improve in other areas of Movement and Alignment. For example, there are muscle fibers (sarcomeres) in your body that are not being used due to your stiffness and tightness. Worse off, they will never be activated if the physiological room in which they need to operate in is not restored. In fact, they may actually be absorbed by the body due to the lack of inactivity. This why restoring your mobility is important. It is the keystone habit in PreHab.

In addition to ability, having the proper mobility and range of motion of your body will also help you recover faster. Increased mobility improves the circulation of blood and carries more nutrients to needed cells for repair while also extrapolating unwanted metabolic waste and inducing deep, restful bouts of sleep.

Develop Awareness
In terms of habits, the ultimate goal of PreHab is to develop a keen awareness of your Alignment and Movement, which will enable you to cultivate and maintain functional biomechanics that will help optimize your Movement Patterns and improve the way you perform while also reducing the risk of injury.

Use Mobility Exercises and Techniques to help develop Awareness and cultivate an effective habit of PreHabilitation.

INTRODUCTION

Address Pain First
Before Getting Started

Before looking to improve performance, you should address any and all pain that you have first and foremost. Simply put, pain is your body's way of telling you that there is something wrong in the way that you move.

Please understand that no one is immune to pain. So, it's not wise to put on your "man up" shirt and train through the pain. You are only going to make it worse.

Repetitive Stress Syndrome
Everyone is destined for some kind of injury in his or her life at some point. The human body is not invisible. You are mortal and if you're not actively working to maintain proper function of your biomechanics, the mere nature of repeating movements over time weakens your body and eventually leads to a break down.

Repeating the same movement over time – weeks, months and years, leads to gross imbalances in the biomechanics and over stresses the soft tissue until injury occurs.

What are repetitive movements?
Any movement that you do frequently on a habitual basis such running, sitting and moving your mouse across the computer screen. Another way to look at it is to imagine you are watching yourself in a silent film. This way you can concentrate on the actual movements of your body and see how many times you move your arm in a certain way or see the way you hold yourself as you sit and stand or watch how your legs swing as you walk. All of these movements have specific qualities to them and create a finite impact on your biomechanics and your body due to the frequency or repetitive nature that you use these movements.

What's the danger?
Over time, these movements build up a large cause-and-effect influence on your biomechanics – no matter how small the movement. Biomechanist Katy Bowman has discovered that our bodies will be remolded and reshaped more dramatically by the movements that we employ move frequently as opposed to movements that we employ more enthusiastically. In other words, how you move throughout the day (frequency), will impact your body more than what you do in a workout (enthusiastically). Therefore, focusing on correcting your biomechanics and the way that you move can positively shape how you move throughout the day as well as in your workout.

Spoiler Alert
In the movie, *Shawshank Redemption*, Tim Robbin's character slowly digs his way out of prison one pocketful of dirt each day. He quietly dug this long tunnel under the prison walls and out to freedom by only digging enough dirt each day to fill his pants pocket. The beauty in this example is that it was such a small action, but he repeated it so much that it made a huge difference! This is what happens to your biomechanics over time.

INTRODUCTION

> ***What you do repeatedly will have more effect on the shaping your body and directing the evolution of your biomechanics than anything else.***

So, you want to look at the movements you perform most frequently on a daily basis and start to address them or counter them. For example, try opening doors with your left hand or switch up the way your cross your legs when you sit.

The Different Ways that Breakdowns Occur
Repetitive movements can create a breakdown in the soft tissue and cause injury by stressing the body in a compensation strategy. For example, some people will excessively pronate at the ankle while running. This pronation causes the ankle to collapse to the inside more than it is biomechanically intended to do. It's an added strain on the surrounding soft tissue, which can later manifest into plantar fasciitis or Achilles tendinitis.

Another way repetitive movements can cause injuries is through the creation of strength/tension imbalances around a specific joint. A classic example of this is "mirror muscle" syndrome.

Mirror muscle syndrome refers to people, typically men, who will only work to strengthen the muscles that they can see in the mirror, mainly the chest, anterior shoulders and biceps. The more that they train and strengthen these anterior or pushing muscles, the more of a structural imbalance will develop in the body. It's caused by a disproportionate amount of strength and tension on either side (front vs back) of the body. Over time, the shoulder is pulled forward and consequentially loses functional stability, as the posterior muscles are not able to counter the forces produced by the anterior muscles. This imbalance can and eventually will lead to shoulder impingements, sprains or injury.

Lastly, the stress of repetitive movements can just wear away at the body – the soft tissue and the bone. It is common for professional or collegiate athletes to suffer stress fractures from the amount of training that they perform over time. The constant pounding of running has been known to create fractures in metatarsals (bones in the foot) and all the way up to the pelvis.

A Lesson in Economy
The economic principal, the Law of Diminishing Returns, applies to training and exercise as well. Simply put, the Law of Diminishing Returns predicts that the reward that you generate from a specific action will lessen each and every time you repeat that action until the point that the reward turns from positive to negative. In other words, the more that you perform any act, such as a specific exercise like the bench press, the less reward or gain you will receive from it.

INTRODUCTION

To further elaborate, if a person bench presses for the first time, they will notice a large increase in their strength due to more neural activation of formal muscle fibers. Yet, the more often that this person bench presses, the less benefit they will gain. In fact, this person will eventually start to create negative 'rewards' if they continue bench press too much. Their chest muscles will become tight and eventually pull their shoulders forwards into a protracted posture, which is an unstable position for the shoulder. Then the person's overall posture will begin to change as well to compensate for these protracted shoulders. Meanwhile, this person has now increased the risk of a shoulder impingement or injury, especially if they decide to start throwing a football around with some friends, all because they continued to bench press too much. In short, the more that you repeat a specific action, the less your body will benefit from it unless you are proactively protecting and nurturing proper biomechanics.

An Effective Solution
Creating an effective intervention or 'remedy' for repetitive movements can be achieved by integrating "Counter Movements" and "Corrective Exercises" into your training that will help to protect and positively shape your biomechanics. Counter Movements and Corrective Exercises will help maximize all of the gains that one can get from consistent training.

Counter Movements are synergistic compliments to repetitive movements and an easy tool to include in your training program. Simply look at all the repetitive movements you employ and see what direction your joints are using in these specific movements. Then incorporate new movements and exercises in which the joint action is in a different direction from that in these repetitive movements. For example, if you frequently run, then take some time in your training to lateral shuffle or carioca. Or if you are doing crunches, flip over onto your stomach and perform some back extensions. In other words, you want to 'Cross Train' and diversify your exercise selection in order to get counter movements into your training program.

Corrective Exercises, on the other hand, are more specific exercises used to address known dysfunctions in your biomechanics and are very effective tools to use in a training program. Corrective Exercises will help to bring your biomechanics back to their proper positioning and alignment. For example, the previous example of a person that bench presses so much that their shoulders begin to form a protracted or forward posture would gain a lot from a few Corrective Exercises. Protracted shoulders lose stability and are an increased risk for injury. However, performing a series of Corrective Exercises that will help to retract and stabilize the shoulders would limit the risk of injury and also revert the protracted posture. Scapulae retraction, eternal rotation, shoulder depression, rows and pulls are all suitable examples of Corrective Exercises for protracted shoulders as they will help restore alignment, improve mobility, activation of essential muscles, mechanical stability and adequate strength into this person's movement patterns.

As for the skill of running, this book will offer numerous Corrective Exercises for specific dysfunctions and compensation in your biomechanics.

INTRODUCTION

> ***Fundamental Movement Principals***
> When addressing dysfunctions and compensation strategies in your own biomechanics, these are five movement principals to address into your PreHab.

Assess - How are the specific parts of your body positioned in relation to the other parts? Are they in the right position? If they are not in the correct **alignment**, believe it or not, there are specific reasons that they are positioned the way that they are. These reasons are the clues that allow you to see exactly how your body is compensating in how it moves. Now, don't feel bad, all humans start to compensate early on in life and unless you were fortunate enough to grow up with trainers and coaches all your life, chances are that you compensate to some degree in how your move.

Mobility- since the body moves in patterns, the lack of flexibility of any muscle can affect how well a person can move in any given pattern. Mobility refers to how well the body can move through a specific pattern. It does not just mean how far you can stretch your hamstrings.

For example, let's say an office worker who sits for 8-plus hours a day decides to take up running. The prolonged shortening of their hip Flexors caused by sitting will create a limited mobility of the hip and effectively change that person's stride (gait pattern) for the worse. Yet, improving the mobility of their hip will help to restore their natural gait.

Activation— our muscles work together in an orchestrated effort to produce movement. When you raise an arm, a whole host of muscles in your body plays a role in the movement pattern. There are muscles that rotate the Scapula, brace the spine, neck and head, engage the Core and ground the pelvis. A deficiency in any of these muscles will affect the entire movement pattern and once this deficiency is observed, we can then find out which muscles are under acting in the process.

Activation exercises are designed to get the 'under acting' or inhibited muscles to fire in order to restore our biomechanics.

Stability- after the ability to execute a movement pattern is established through improving mobility, the next step is to focus on how well you can move through that pattern, specifically, how much control do you have over how your body moves? This is an aspect of Stability.

Back to our office runner: once they have created adequate mobility, the next step is to make sure that they can control how their body executes the gait pattern. More specifically, does the leg swing forward in a straight line, does the ankle collapse to the inside when the foot strikes the ground, is their head and shoulders steady and level with the ground? These are all aspects of Stability in the larger movement pattern of running.

INTRODUCTION

Stability exercises will help you to address the quality and control of your movement. If you cannot control how you move your arm, you cannot control the quality and benefits of moving your arm.

Strength Training- most people view strength as an upward, linear progression that streams from weak to strong. However, strength is truly relative based on the corresponding activity. Do you need a certain level of strength to bench press 400 lbs.? The answer is yes. At the same time, what is the level of strength needed to hold a plank for 60 seconds? It's different from the previous example because strength is relative.

Strength is the degree to which you have the ability to perform a specific action. The amount of strength will differ from task to task. The important concept to embrace is: knowing what amount of strength is needed to perform the task you want to perform. Once you know how much strength you will need, you can train your body to achieve that strength by following some simple strength training protocols.

The Permanent Solution
The most effective course of action to take to securing better performance over a long period of time is to focus on your alignment, mobility, activation of essential muscles, stability in movement and applying the appropriate amount of strength. Taking on this approach will also develop an awareness of your biomechanics and increase your fluency in the language of human movement.

Rome Was Not Built in a Day
Your biomechanics and your movement habits were not created in one moment on any specific day. They were created over time just as your training and maintenance of your body can improve over time.

Pain First
The first place to start is by adding any immediate pain in your body. Down below is a list of common injuries in running. If you experienced any of these in the past, it is wise to keep an "eye"' out for the effects it may have had on your biomechanics as well as start to explore and undo the causes of your injury.

Listen to your Body
I am well aware of the mantra of "push through it" and the code of being tough enough, but this does not serve your body. This may build character and create some memories. Yet, this does not serve the body in the long run.

Plain and simple, pain is an indication that there is something wrong with your body and that change is necessary.

INTRODUCTION

Be smart, deal with your pain first-
Just because you don't feel your knee once you start running, doesn't mean the problem corrected itself. It just means that you don't feel pain while you run because the signals won't get through to your brain.

The techniques in this book, starting with soft tissue therapy, will help correct what causes the pain in your body. If it doesn't you should see your doctor and speak with a physical therapist or certified personal trainer.

Ignoring pain will not correct your problems.

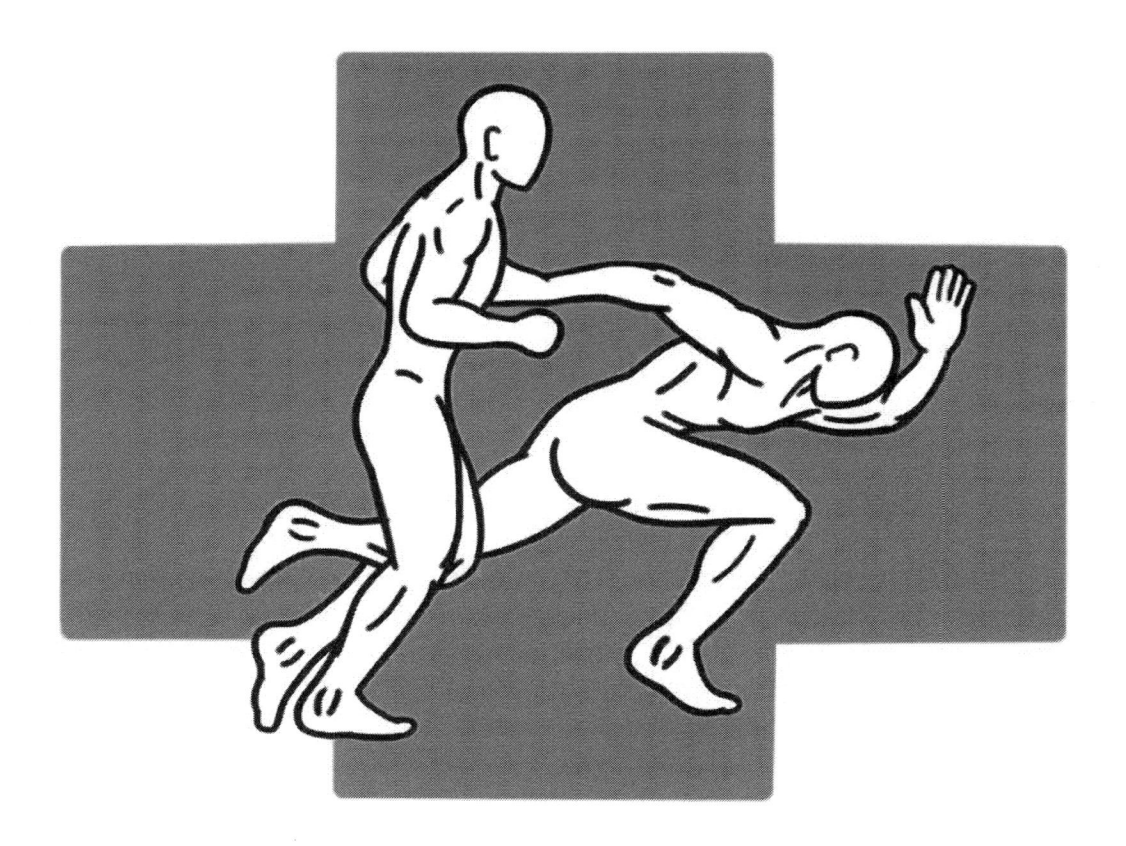

Common Injuries for Runners

There are statistics that say about 80 percent of runners will suffer a running-related injury each year and based on the repetitive nature of running, I can see how that stat can hold up. Yet, whether that stat is accurate or not, there is a high chance that you will suffer some kind of injury if you are a runner. It's the dangerous combination of repetitive movements mixed with an unflappable desire to run and feel alive which makes the risk of injury so high.

Here are some of the most common injuries that runners endure, along with some recommendations to revert the cause, calm the symptoms and get you back to running.

COMMON INJURIES

COMMON INJURIES

Hamstring Pulls

I was in the middle of playing flag football in my weekend league when I spirited after an over thrown ball on a "Go" route. I felt a ping in the back of my leg between my knee and hip. I strained my hamstring because I was trying to cover too much ground too fast. I over-strided in order to make up ground for a ball I was never going to catch. Ironically, I "pulled" my hamstring because I was trying to "pull" the ground back under me as fast as possible.

Our hamstrings are not the primary movers (main muscles producing the force needed in the movement) when we run. Our hips and core will start generating the necessary force and our hamstrings assist in the process. However, many people will start to overuse their hamstrings when they run for two reasons.

> They are trying to cover more ground by over-striding.
> They customarily employ a "Heel Strike" when running.

Heel Strike vs Forefoot and Mid-foot Strike
When running, the foot will contact the ground using the heel first. This is a learned technique, or better put: a compensating strategy. We are designed to run by striking the ground with the forefoot or mid-foot, which employs the ankle joint to absorb some of the gravitational contact forces on each stride.

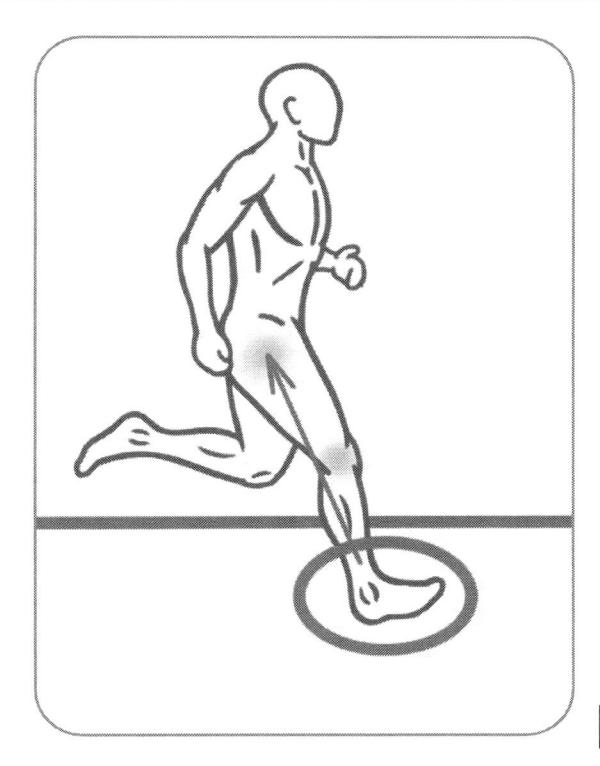

Heel Strike

COMMON INJURIES

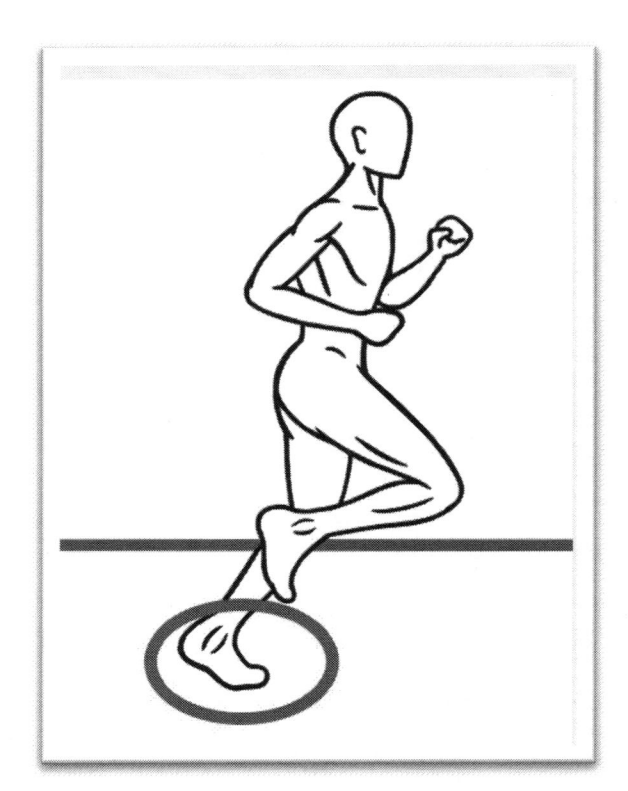

Forefoot Strike *Mid-foot Strike*

The biomechanics of the Forefoot and Mid-foot strike has a great engineering structure that allows the body to be very economical when running. The Forefoot and Mid-foot strikes load the ankle joint with torque that quickly transitions up the Deep Longitudinal Muscles Sub-set system and ignites (facilitates) the glutes and Core to absorb and elastically revert the power and force back out into our stride.

Developing a Forefoot or Mid-foot Strike
Changing your stride from a Heel Strike to a Forefoot or Mid-foot Strike will take time and focus. If you have a Heel Strike, you learned it over time. It will take some time to replace this movement pattern, but it will help you avoid more hamstring issues and improve the economy of your running technique.

The Right Course of Action
One of the first steps to take is to develop a forward lean while you run. Dr. Nicolas Romanov created the POSE Technique in the former Soviet Union during the 1970s as a method to train athletes, mainly sprinters, to run faster. This technique encompasses several specific exercises to develop the forefoot strike, including the Forward Lean.

What is the Forward Lean?
While running, practice leaning forward with your chest as if you are on the verge of actually falling forward over your own feet. Then shorten your stride and quicken your foot turnover as you run. Make sure that you are not flexing too much in your hips as a

COMMON INJURIES

compensation strategy. To avoid this mistake, push your hips forward on every stride and run with a tall spine.

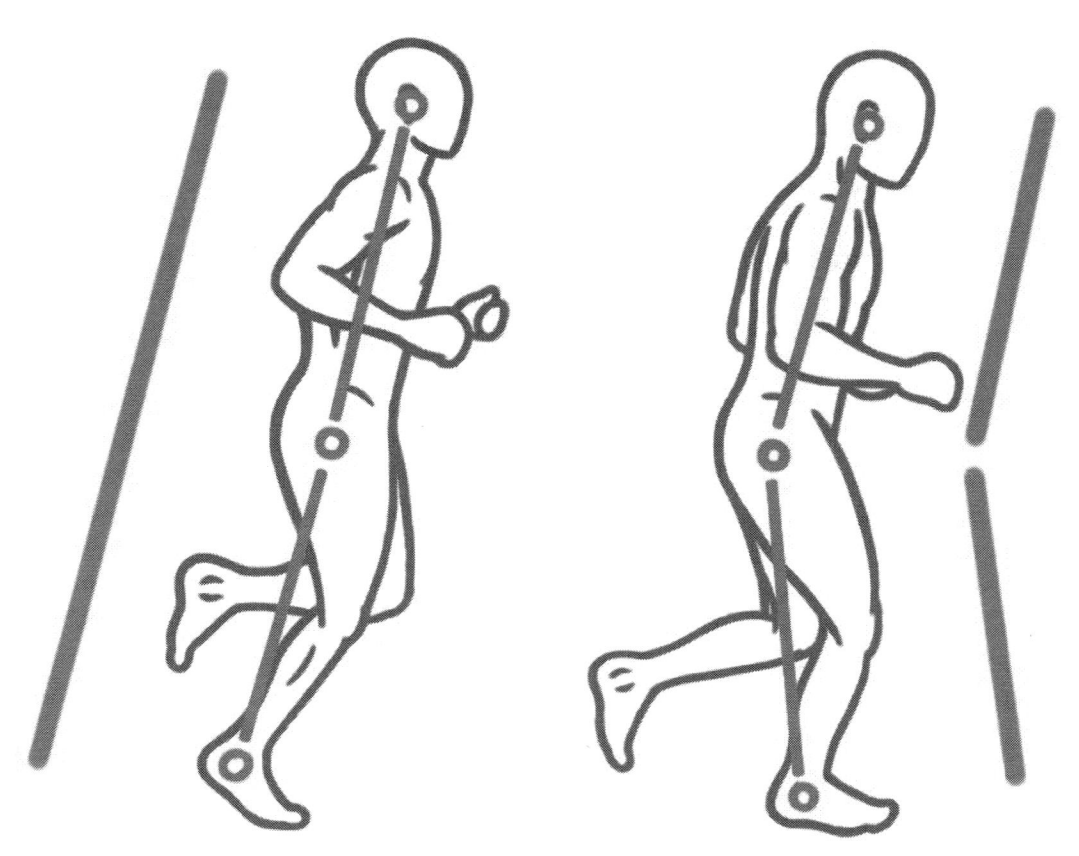

Build the Forward Lean in your Running Technique:
*Draw an imagine line from ear to hips to ankle on a slant when you run.
Do not let the hips fall out of alignment.*

The Next Step – Relax

Once you can feel yourself leaning forward, take a page from Danny Dreyer's *Chi Running* book and relax. All too often, people are trying to gaggle up ground to make faster times and run farther distances, and they lose the natural economy of running. The legs become tense and prohibit the natural flow of kinetic energy from the body. Sooner or later, the leg muscles will get tired and grow tighter, both of which will lead to more compensations in your stride and probably lead you back to a Heel Strike.

Instead, learn to relax the body, especially the legs, and feel a flow of energy through your body as you run. Initially, making these changes will reduce your speed and distances. Yet, in the long run, all pun intended, relaxing your legs and adding a forward lean will economize your stride and save your hamstrings.

There are several exercises that will further help you transition from a Heel Strike to a Forefoot/Mid-foot Strike in the Running Technique section of this book.

COMMON INJURIES

Runner's Knee

Do you ever feel pain in your knee? Does it hurt to go up or down stairs? Perhaps you have a burning sensation under the kneecap as if the pain is inside the knee? Chances are that you are experiencing Patellofemoral pain syndrome (PFPS), or "runner's knee."

Believe it or not, the source for all of this disdain lies above and below your knee at the hip and the ankle. A lack of both mobility and stability in the hip and ankle will create large sheering forces in the knee as the femur (thigh bone) is driven against the back of the patella (kneecap) and pressurizes the soft tissue, especially the knee cartilage, patella tendon and surrounding fascia.

The Right Course of Action
- Start with a heavy dose of soft tissue therapy (foam rolling and trigger point techniques) on the legs and hips.
- Increase the mobility of both the ankle and the hip
- Strengthen the hip muscles, especially your lateral stability by using a variation of Side Plank exercises as well as Gait Marches and walking exercises with Thera Bands.
-

Thera Band Walks: Stand in an athletic stance or a high-squat position with a Thera Band wrapped around your legs just above your ankles. Spread your feet to shoulder width or wider and point your feet forward, no duck feet please. It's important to train your body to move with your toes pointed forward as it will protect your ankles and knees in the long run.

Starting Position   *Sagittal (Forward and Backwards)*

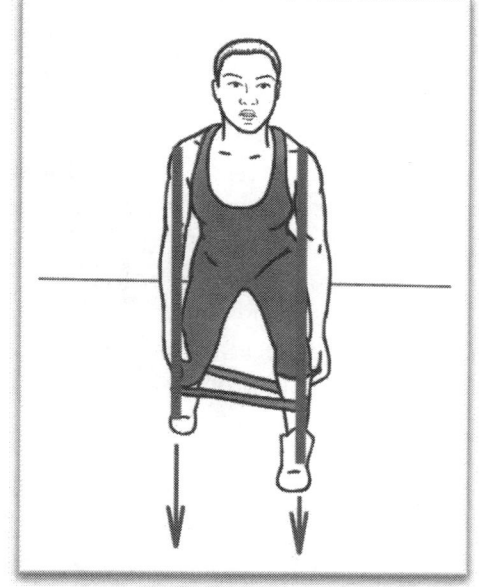

COMMON INJURIES

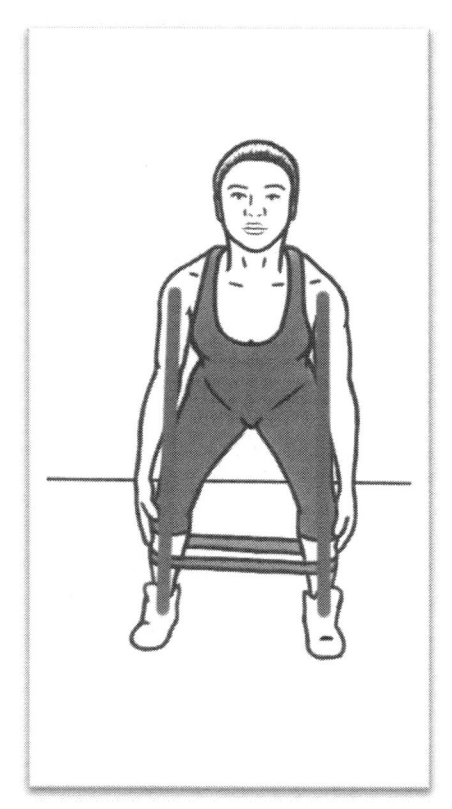

Starting Position   Lateral (Side to Side)

Sagittal Walks: Walk forward for 10-15 steps. Keep your feet shoulder width or wider as you walk and stay in an athletic stance. Attempt to keep your hips level with the floor as you walk. Next, walk backwards for 10-15 steps.

Lateral Walks: Now, walk sideways in both directions for another 10-15 steps.

You want to feel your hips working and if the tension of the band diminishes, that means you have brought your feet too close together. Keep your toes pointed straight and your feet at least shoulder width apart. *See page 233*

COMMON INJURIES

Iliotibial Band Syndrome (ITBS)

You probably have heard of the IT Band, as it is commonly referred to. It's a long tendon that stretches down the outside of your thigh from the hip to the knee.

For many people, the IT Band is easily irritated. Too much strain on the tendon while running may cause the outside of your thigh and knee to flare up and become painfully inflamed. An IT Band injury may sideline you for a few weeks, and if you're not careful enough, this irritation may not go away fast.

The true source of your problem is your biomechanics. Your IT Band is forced to work much harder than it's supposed to for stabilizing and maintaining good alignment through your knee. Chances are that while you run, you are too reliant on your quadriceps to break your fall and keep the knee from collapsing inwards (with excessive pronation at the ankle).

The Right Course of Action

First treat the IT Band with plenty of soft tissue therapy to reduce the irritation and inflammation. This will also help to spur on the natural healing of the tendon. So, don't be too quick to get back up on your horse to run.

Take your time to smooth out the IT Band and let the soft tissue heal.

Train Proper Biomechanics

While abstaining from running, take on a heavy dose of corrective exercises. First, make sure that you have adequate ankle and hip mobility. You want to be sure that you have adequate range of motion in your hip extension and dorsiflexion at the ankle.

Next, you want to focus on activating the Gluteus Medius and Gluteus Maximus. If you are having irritation in your IT Band, chances are that these two muscles are not firing as much as they should while you run.

Perform the following circuit of PreHab Exercises:

Clams
Bridge March
Quadruped Hip Abduction
Single-Leg Bridge
Side Plank Hip Hike
Side Plank Hip Abduction

COMMON INJURIES

Clams

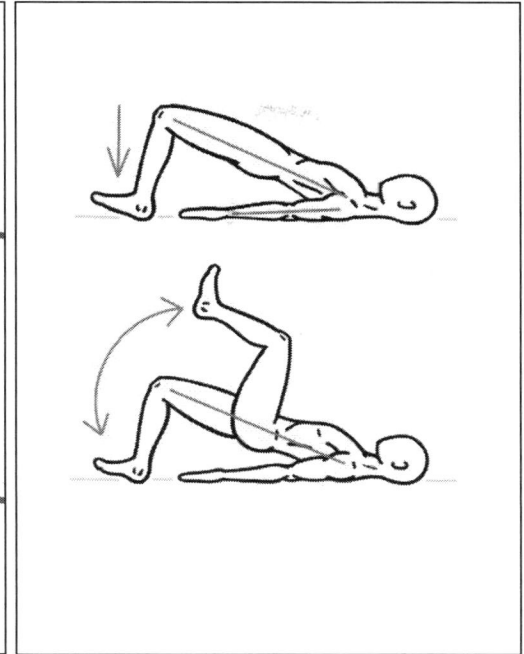

Bridge March

Quadruped Hip Abduction

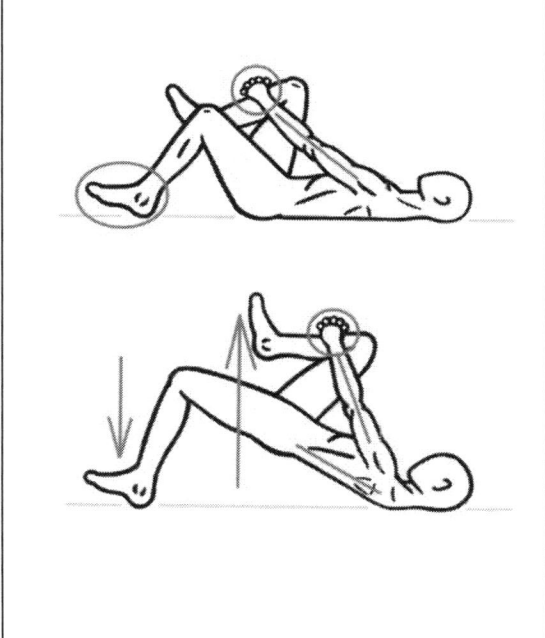

Single-Leg Bridge

COMMON INJURIES

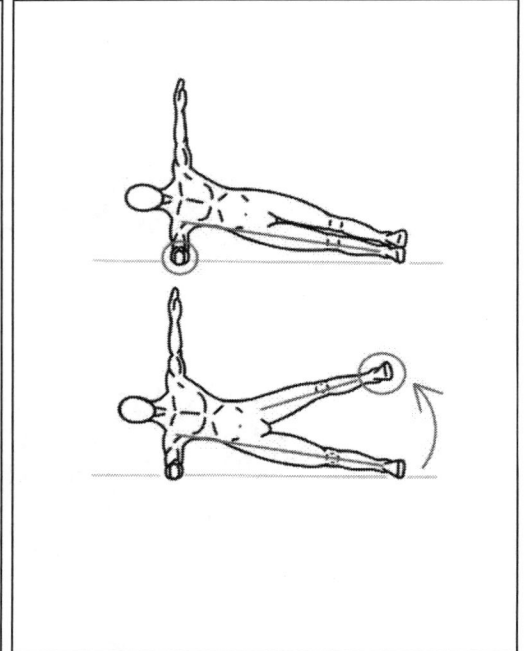

Side Plank Hip Hike   Side Plank Hip Abduction

Note: You want to feel these glute muscles firing. If not, there is not guarantee that what you are doing will help. Isometric holds for 3-5 seconds in the midpoint of each exercise will help you to feel if you are effectively activating these muscles or not.

Not Done Yet
There is one more muscle that you want to activate and that is your Gastrocnemius, also referred to as your calf muscle. Perform a series of Heel Lifts with a slow Eccentric Contraction (negative) to help activate the muscle.

Here's how:
Press up onto your forefoot and lift the heels as high off the ground as possible. Next, slowly lower the heels back to the floor. Count to 5 or 10 each time that you lower and see if you can feel the calf muscles turn on.

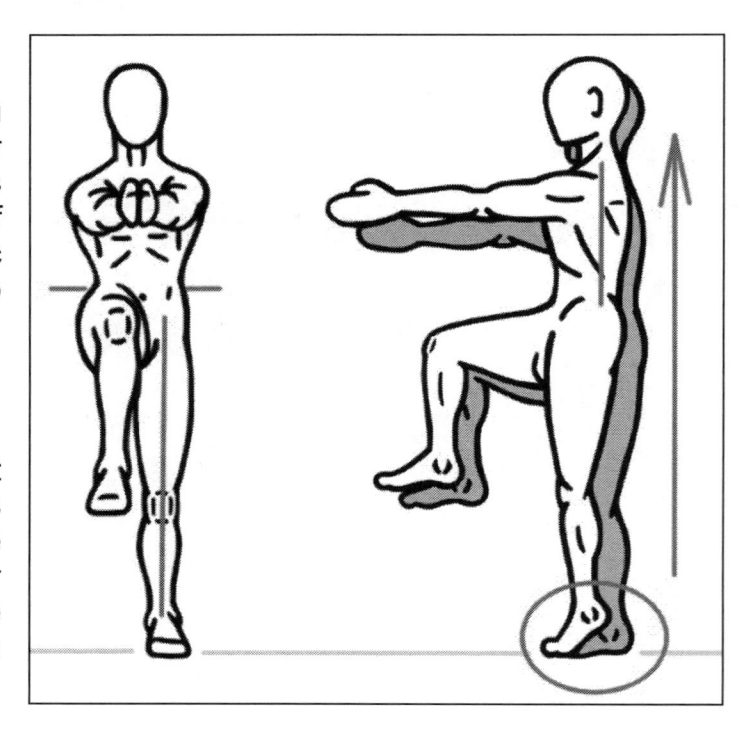

COMMON INJURIES

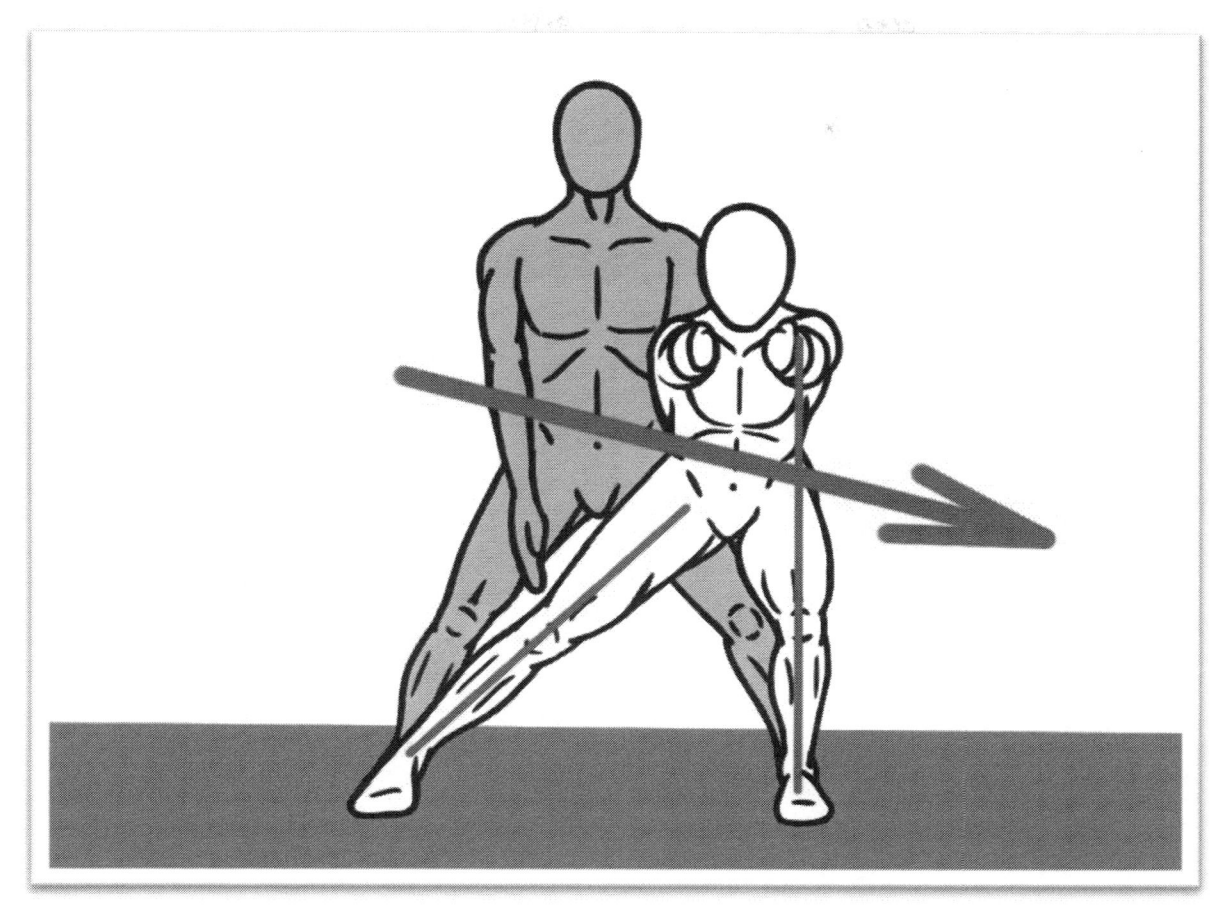

Lateral Lunge to Activate the Hip

Next, Stabilize the Knee
After activating the Glutes and your Gastrocnemius, you will want to perform larger movements with your bodyweight and resistance bands to help develop more knee stability.

It may be weird to think that focusing on the hips and ankle will help to stabilize the knee, but that's how the body works. The knee is a joint that has very little lateral or rotational range of motion. Therefore, it cannot adequately control the forces and torque placed on it. It is up to the ankle and the hip to help direct the flow of kinetic energy through the knee.

Perform these Stability Exercises:

Single-Leg Rotations
Compass Reaches
Single-Leg Squat to Bench
Single-Leg Deadlifts

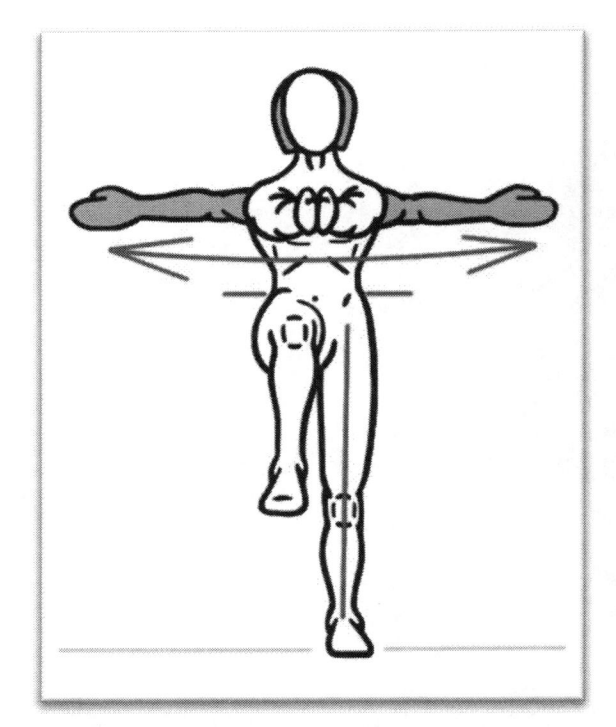

COMMON INJURIES

Single-Leg Rotation

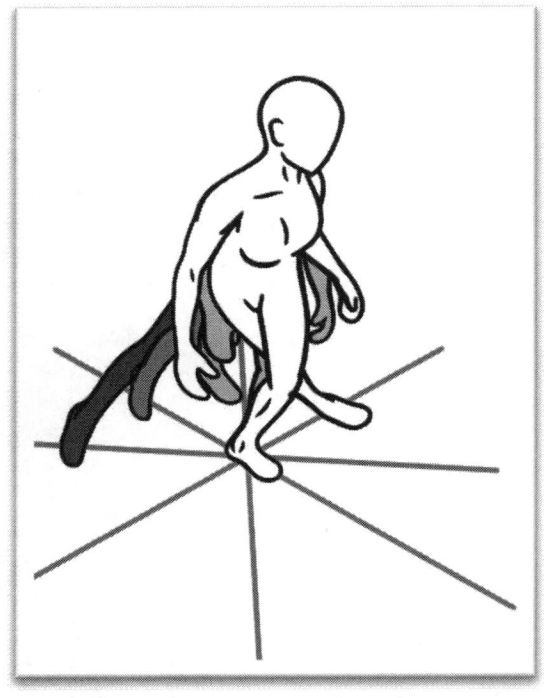

Compass Reaches

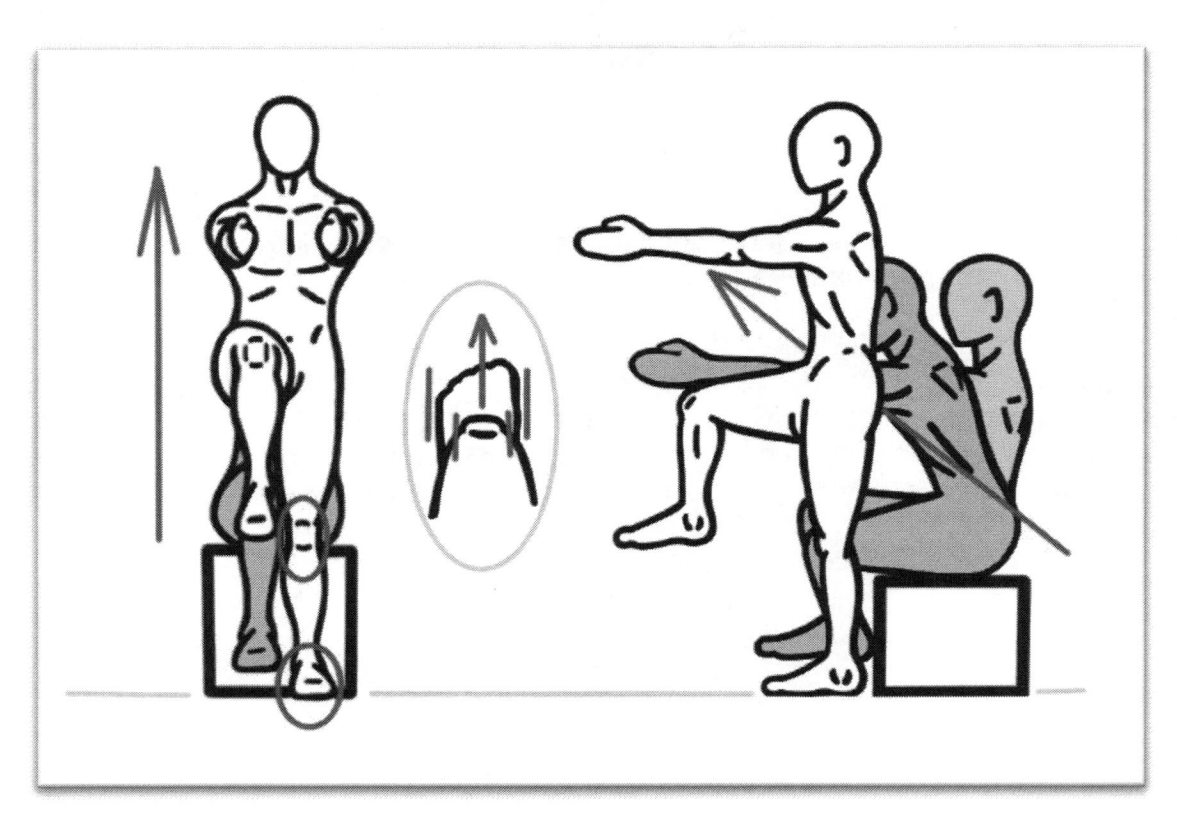

Single-Leg Box Squat

COMMON INJURIES

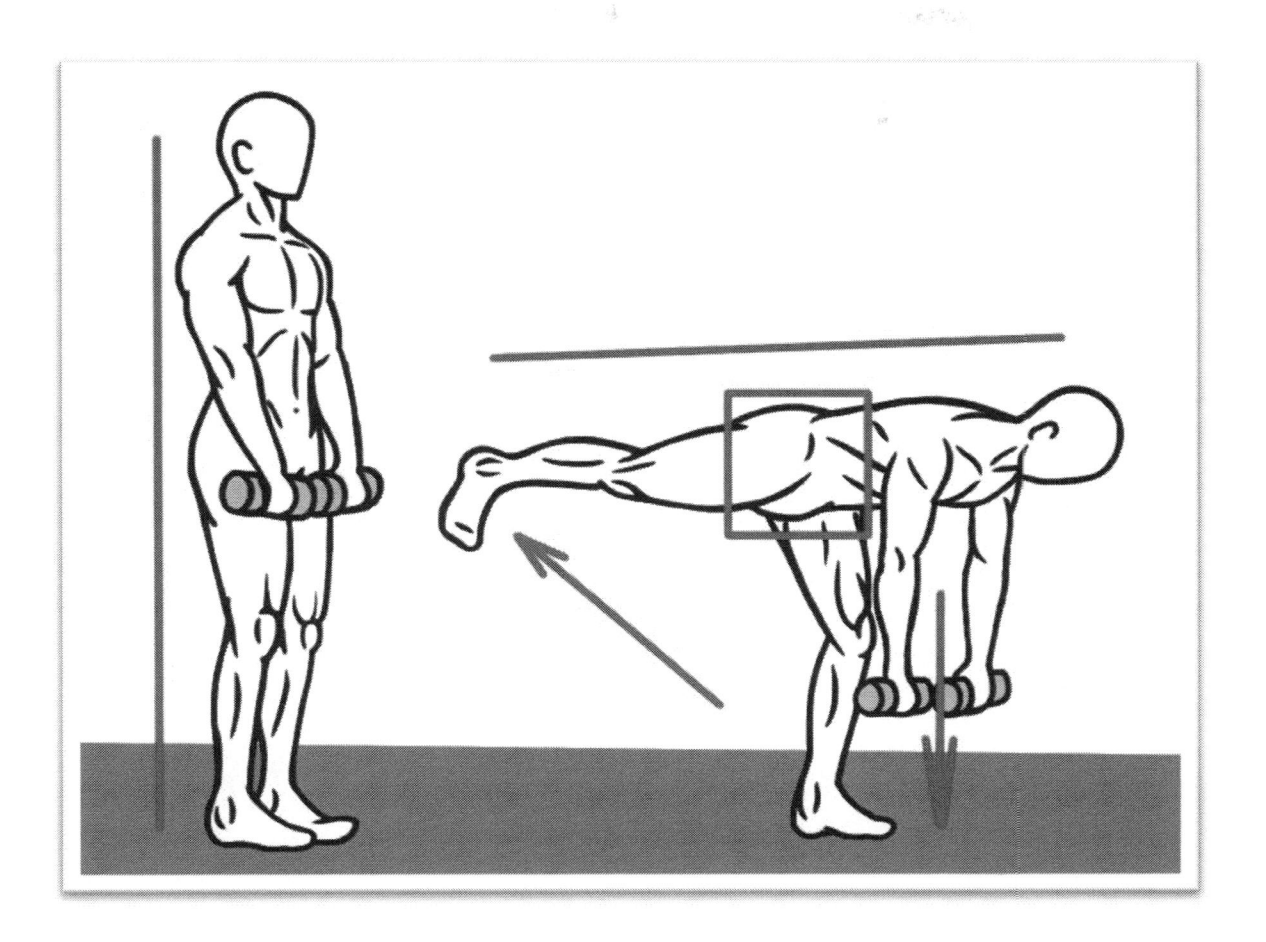

Single-Leg Deadlift

COMMON INJURIES

Achilles Tendinitis

Do you feel pain or discomfort in your calves – the back of your lower legs? Perhaps a prolonged soreness that does not easily go away? Chances are you may have or be flirting with Achilles Tendinitis.

What is tendinitis?
Whenever you move, you place tension on your tendons, the tissue that attaches muscle to bone. When this tension stresses or strains the tendons, inflammation will occur as part of the healing and adaption process.

Tendonitis is a state of prolonged inflammation or irritation due to repetitive stress. In other words, you are using the tendon too much and it needs more time to heal.

Tendonitis is not something to work through! It is something that needs to be addressed correctly or you run a huge risk of injuring yourself down the road.

The Right Course of Action
Soft Tissue Therapy is very important because it will help reduce the inflammation and acute irritation. Effective soft tissue therapy will also induce the parasympathetic nervous system that will accelerate the healing process.

Rest is also very important. Tendonitis is a sign that your Work-Recovery ratio is unbalanced and that you have not allowed your body adequate recovery. So, it's wise to examine your nutrition, lifestyle and eating habits in order to cut out habits that are not working for you because recovery is not just time off from training. Recovery is creating the best environment, in regards to activity, lifestyle, nutrition and sleep, for your body to adequately heal itself.

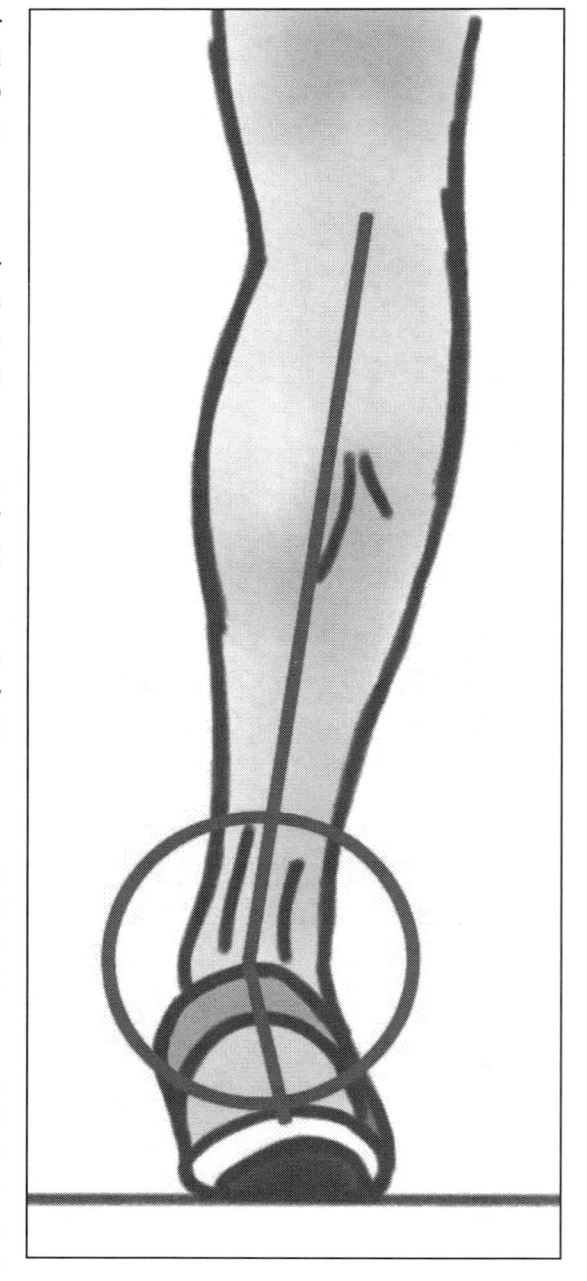

Lastly, it's time to evaluate your biomechanics. Tendonitis may be caused by how you move and whether or not you are compensating with your Achilles for a limited range of motion in your hip extension or ankle mobility.

COMMON INJURIES

Test Hip Range of Motion: Hip Extension

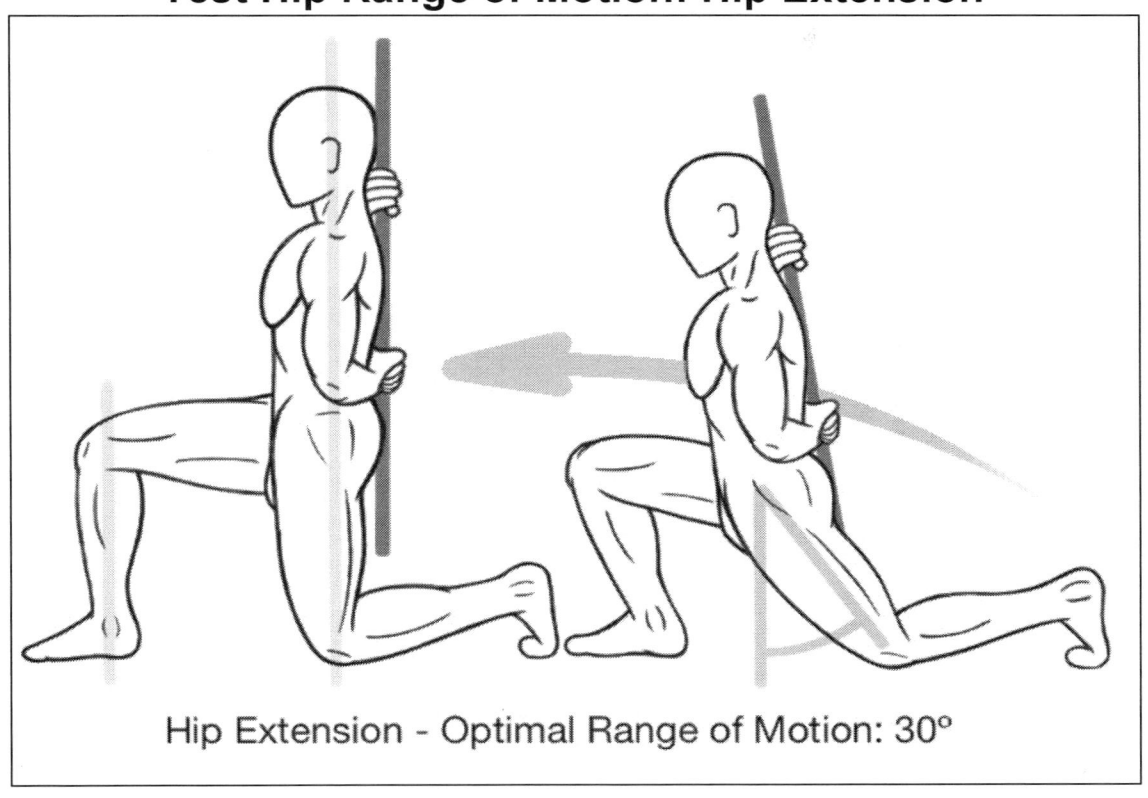

Hip Extension - Optimal Range of Motion: 30°

Test Ankle Range of Motion: Dorsiflexion & Plantar Flexion

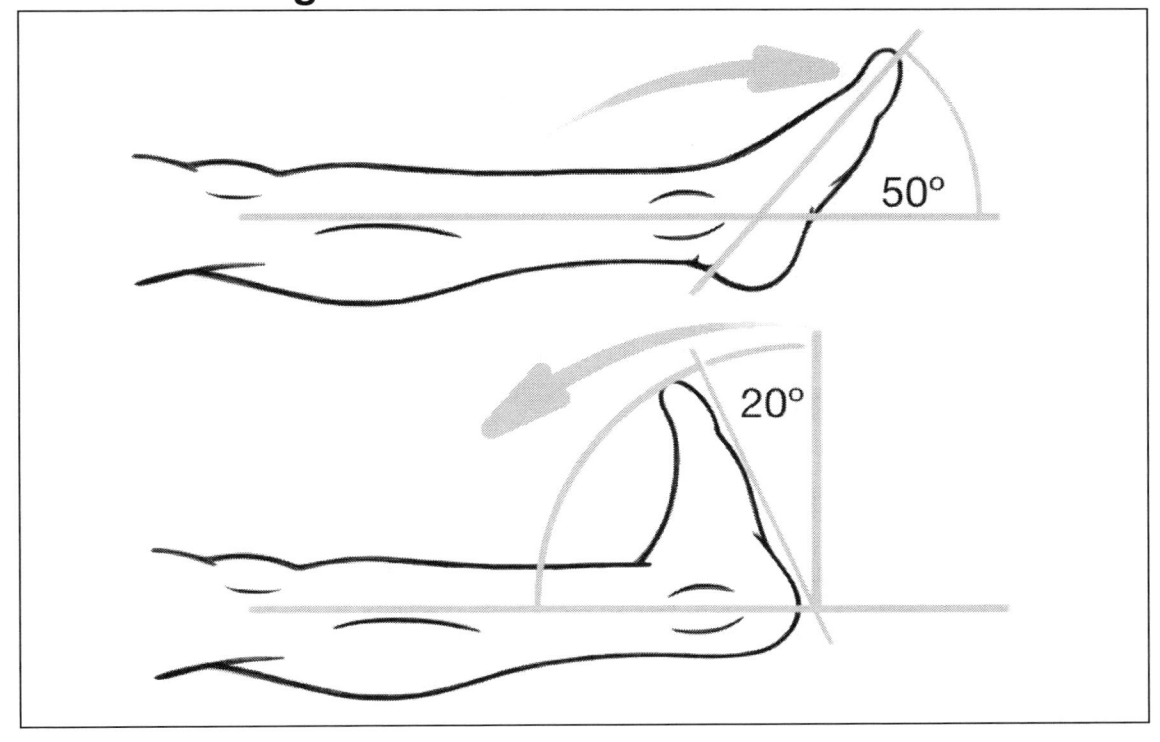

50°

20°

COMMON INJURIES

Train the Toes to Point Forward

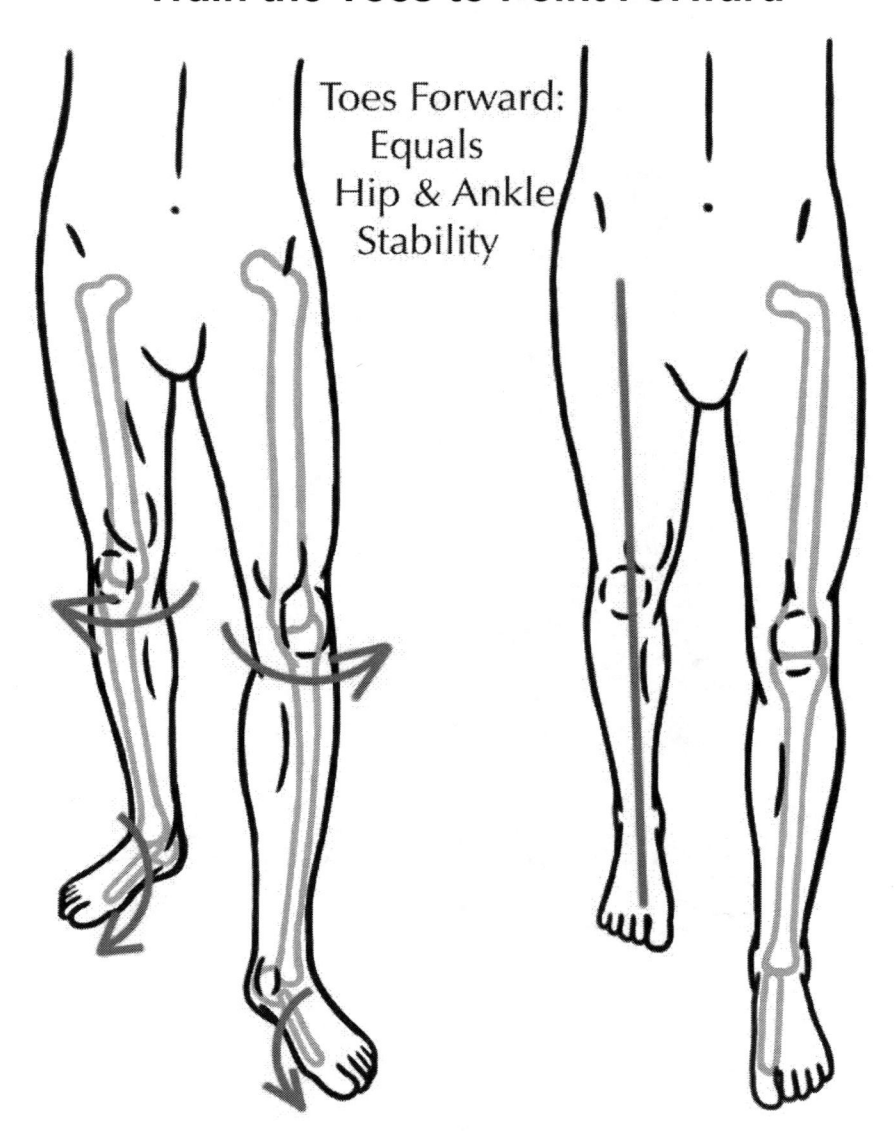

Toes Forward: Equals Hip & Ankle Stability

Plan of Action
First and foremost, work to eliminate any limitations in your range of motion as these restrictions will add more tension and stress to your Achilles tendon. Also, focus on improving the alignment of your feet as the 'toes out' deviation will not only place more stress on your ACL, but it will also create a slanted line of action in the Achilles, which will stress the tendon more.

If you are suffering from Achilles Tendonitis, take some time off from running to improve your mobility and alignment. Start to include Soft Tissue Therapy into your training routine as well as a healthy dose of mobility exercises. However, don't just focus on ankle mobility. You will need to address the mobility of your entire body, including the hips, posterior chain, thoracic spine and even the shoulders and neck.

COMMON INJURIES

Plantar Fasciitis

In 2009, the New York Giants' quarterback, Eli Manning, suffered from plantar fasciitis, not because he ran a lot – he's not Michael Vick. Manning was simply pushing off his foot too much to throw the ball and the soft tissue underneath his foot became extremely inflamed and irritated.

Essentially, fasciitis is the same as tendonitis in terms of too much stress applied to the soft tissue of a specific area that leads to a prolonged inflammation or irritation to occur.

People who experience bouts of plantar fasciitis are simply moving with irregularities in their biomechanics and making their feet compensate for other dysfunctions. The end result is that the soft tissue of their feet gets torn up.

The Right Course of Action
Evaluate your foot when you walk or run and specifically look to see if your foot rolls inwards or outwards too much. Does the anklebone seem to collapse towards the floor on either side?

You want to keep your anklebones from dropping to either side when you walk. More often than not, the anklebone will want to drop inside towards the floor, which is called pronation.

Too much pronation, places a heavy load onto the soft tissue of the foot – stretching it from toe to heel and side to side. Over time, the stress of this load will cause too much stretching and the soft tissue will break down and become inflamed.

You can easily buy shoes or put extra padding in your shoes to help make the pain go away, but it will not make the problem go away. Excessive pronation and supination is a sign of instability in the ankle and hip.

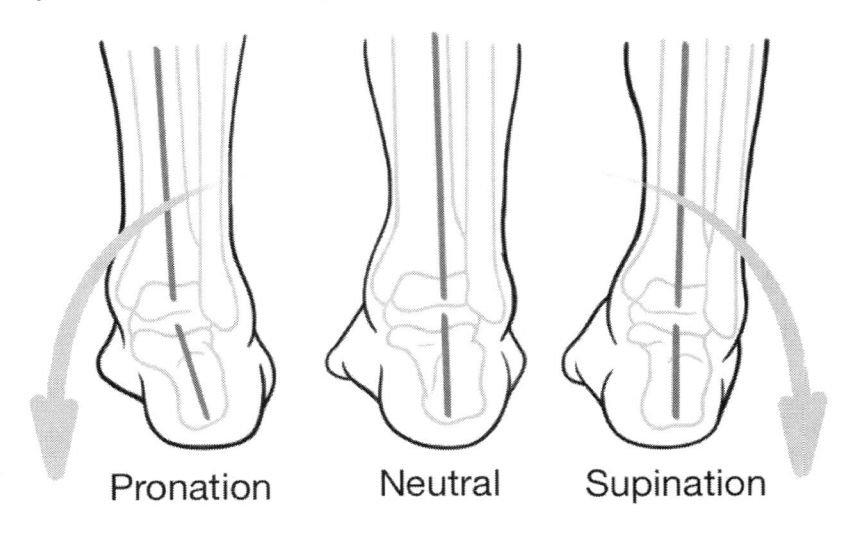

Pronation   Neutral   Supination

Posterior View of Ankle

PreHab Exercise Book for Runners

COMMON INJURIES

Soft Tissue Therapy
The first course of action is to tend to the soft tissue (muscles, tendons and fascia) of the entire leg-hip complex with the goal of restoring appropriate length and responsive to all of the tissue. Soft tissue therapy will help the healing and recovery process, thus allowing the tissues to repair and strengthen.

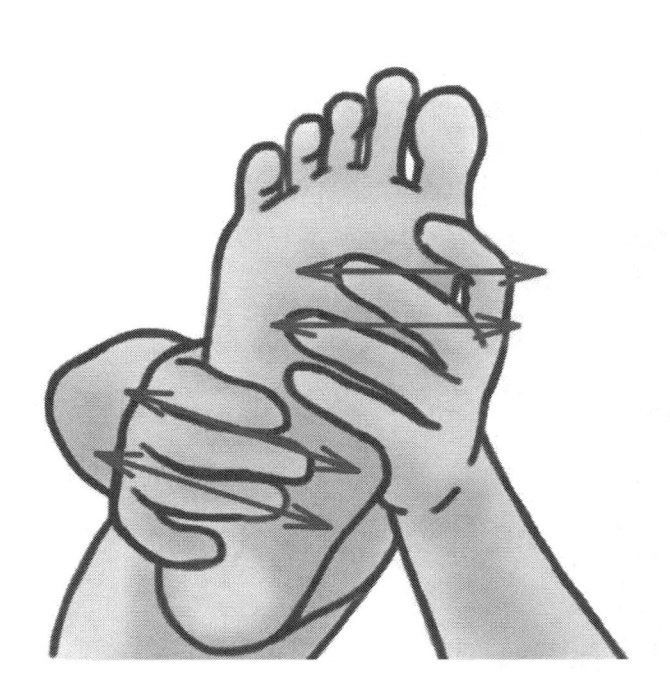

Soft tissue therapy will also help to restore the appropriate range of motion to your functional movement patterns, specifically your gait. Somewhere along the way, your body started to compensate in this movement. Maybe you have tight hip flexors from sitting a lot. Or tight calf muscles from wearing a heel in your shoe – yes, even if it's only a one-inch heel in your sneakers. In any case, plantar fasciitis is a sign that there is a certain dysfunction in your movement patterns.

One of the best soft tissue therapy techniques to use for plantar fasciitis is rolling your foot over a couple of golf balls after you place them in a freezer for a few hours.

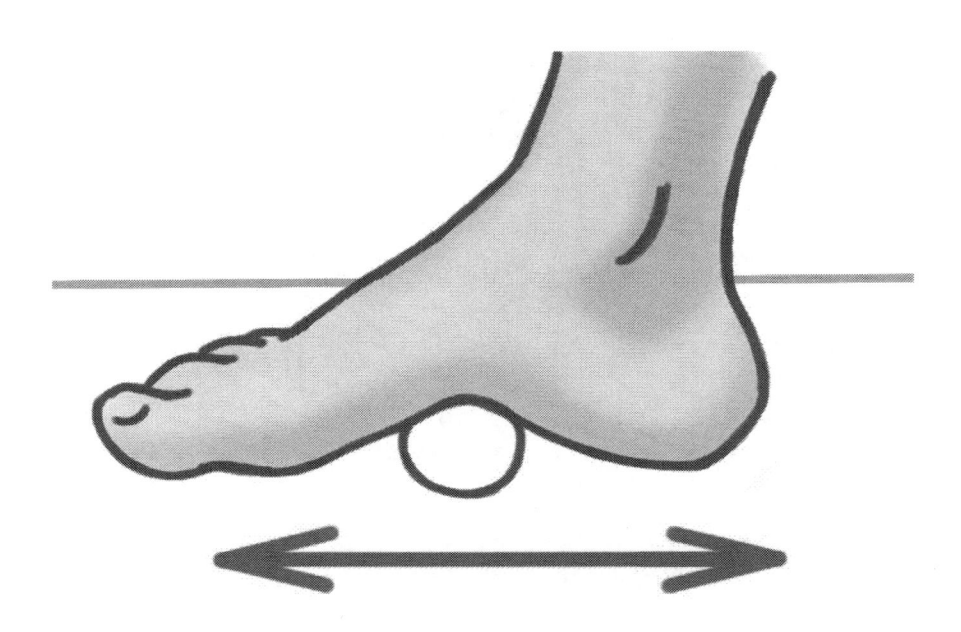

Soft Tissue Therapy: Rolling the Foot with a Golf Ball

50   PreHab Exercise Book for Runners

COMMON INJURIES

Mobility then Stability

After performing a heavy dose of soft tissue therapy, it's time to restore the proper mobility and stability to your foot, ankle and your hip. First test to see if you have the proper range of motion in your ankle and hip with the Hip Extension and Ankle Dorsiflexion tests on page 47.

Here are some Mobility exercises:

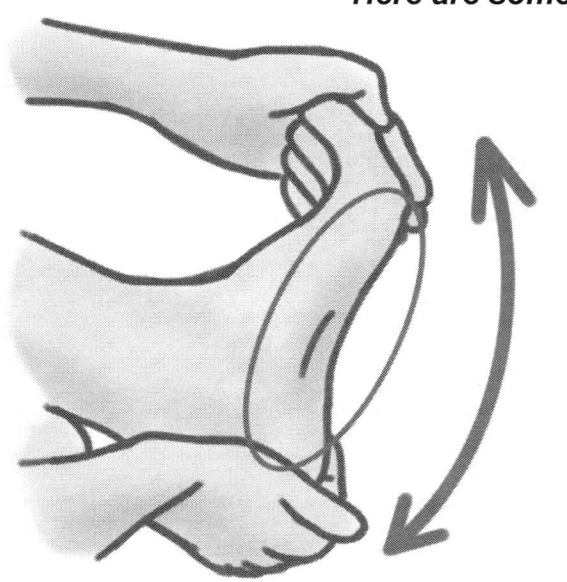

Plantar Fascia Stretch with Hands

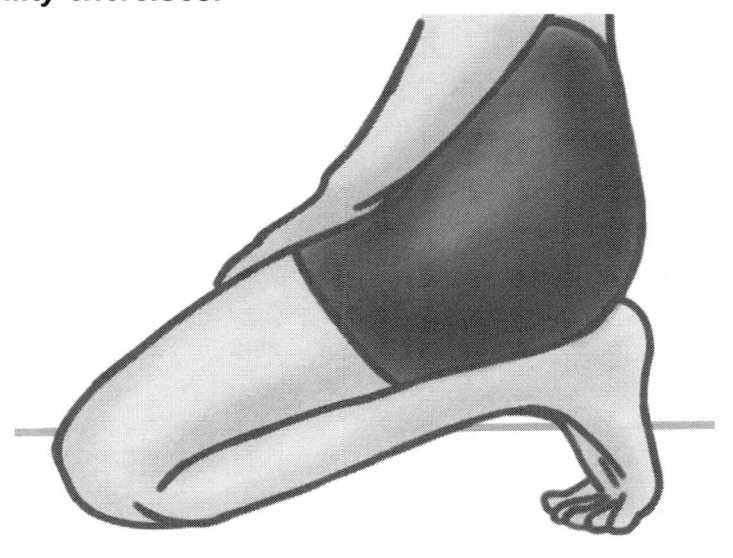

Sitting Plantar Fascia Stretch

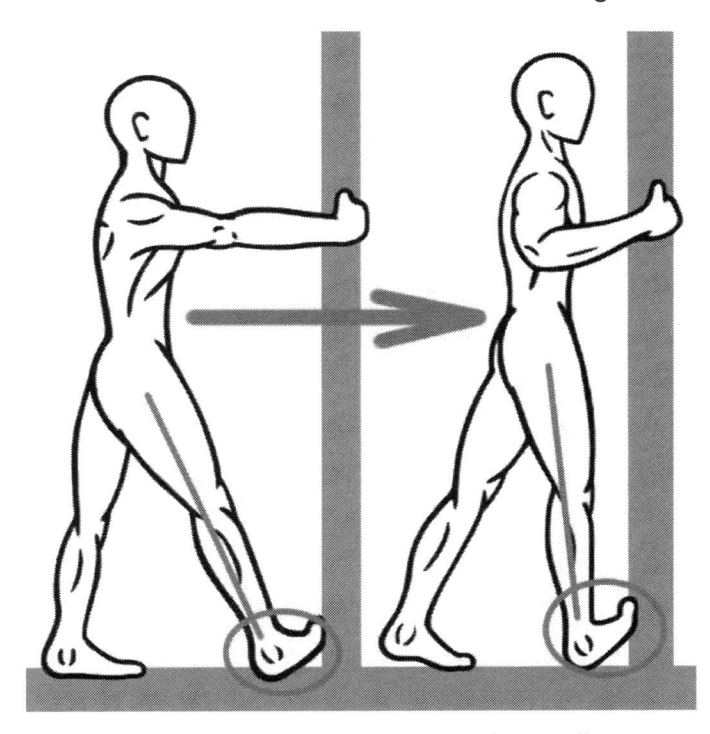

Calf & Foot Stretch against the wall

PreHab Exercise Book for Runners

51

COMMON INJURIES

Next, develop the appropriate stability at the ankle and hip to help keep the proper alignment when standing, walking or running. Here are a couple of movement evaluations to test your ankle and hip stability.

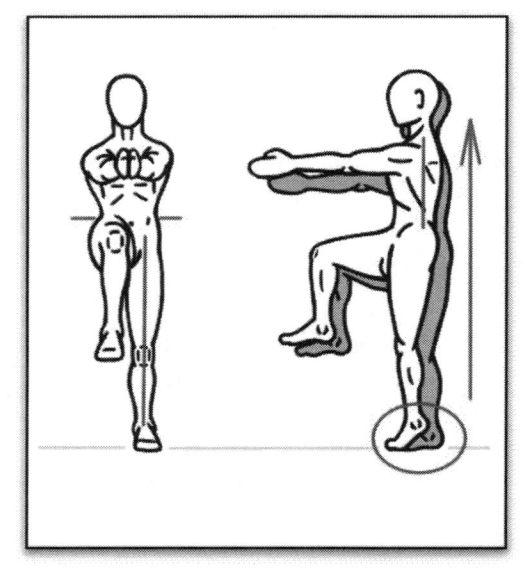

Single-Leg Heel Lift

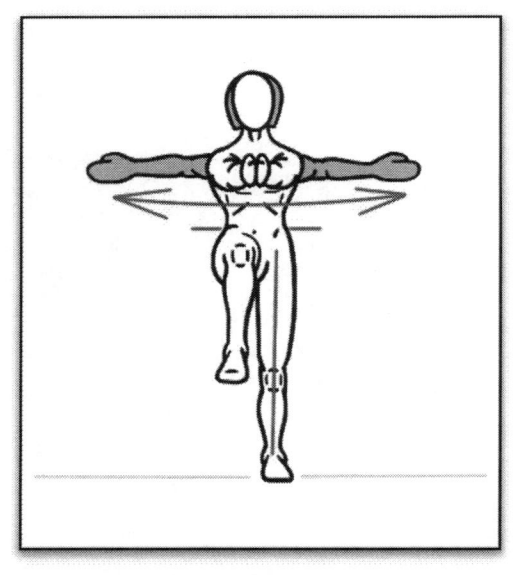

Single-Leg Rotation

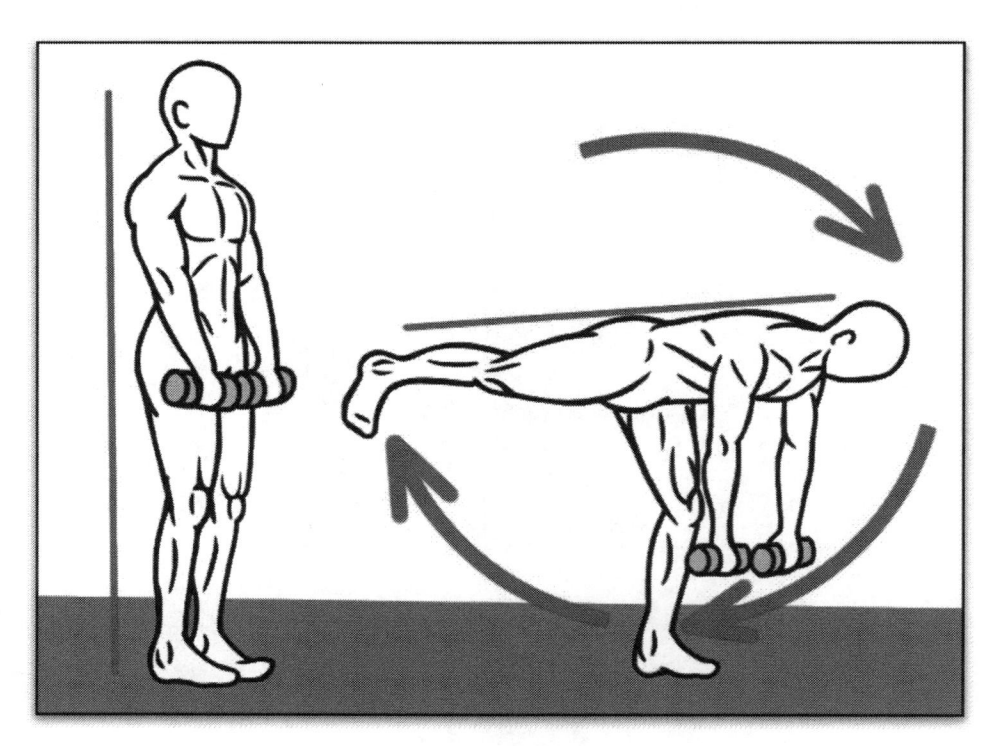

Single-Leg Deadlift

If you are failing any of these tests, refer to the plethora (many) of exercises in the Hip and Ankle Stability Sections.

COMMON INJURIES

Shin Splints

Ouch! You have pain in your calves and it feels as if your shins are breaking. Well, you have Shin Splints, which is very common to newbie runners or those starting back up again after a prolonged break.

A Lesson in Functional Anatomy

Your shins are shock absorbers. Like the shocks on your car, they work to absorb the force of impact from striking the ground when you run. Your shins are made up of two bones that will bend slightly each time you land on the ground. Over the course of running, these two bones are vibrating as if you're continuously hitting a tuning fork. The more you run, the more your shins vibrate and the less you feel the impact of each step.

The De-conditioned Runner

Now, as your shins vibrate and absorb a great deal of force from the impact of running, the soft tissue, muscles, fascia and tendons that wrap around these two bones are working very hard to minimize the vibration as much as possible.

A conditioned runner will have the appropriate strength and endurance within this soft tissue to handle the amount of force that is bouncing around inside the shins. However, a de-conditioned runner, such as a newbie or a returner, will not have this same ability because the soft tissue in their shins has been on a vacation.

The Right Course of Action

If you are experiencing shin splints right now, take some time off from running and perform a heavy dose of soft tissue therapy, as well as evaluate your biomechanics. You can also help to improve your conditioning by working with the mobility, stability and strength exercises in this book.

If you are still experiencing shin splints after taking this whole course of action, it's time that you evaluate your lifestyle and nutrition as well because your body's Work-Recovery ratio is not adequately balanced.

COMMON INJURIES

Ankle Sprains

Just as Hip-Hop artist Drake proclaims the song, *Forever*, a sprained ankle is nothing to play with. So, don't.

A sprained ankle is an acute injury where the joint is suddenly forced beyond its functional alignment. The injury varies in degree of severity, from ligament damage that may require surgery to just inflammation and more types in between.

The Right Course of Action
First, you want to assess the severity of your sprain. Ideally, you should seek out some professional evaluation for your injury. Yet, if that is not plausible, you can play the "wait and see" game with the increased risk of making things worse for you.

> *Don't be the Hero*
> Stay off of it. Seek help and live to run another day. There is very little to gain from soldiering on. At best, you teach your body how to compensate in specific movement patterns and at worse, you can turn a sprain into a tear.

Once a professional clears you to train or run after a sprain, be sure to apply plenty of soft tissue therapy to the leg upon return. Then gently restore your functional range of motion with some mobility exercises and test your ankle stability before you resume running at max speeds or prolonged distances. Practice caution for several weeks after the onset of the sprain. Be smart.

A sprain is really not something that you want to play with.

COMMON INJURIES

Stress Fracture

Believe it or not, you can experience a fracture in one of your bones from repetitive stress. In running, these stress fractures typically occur in one of the following areas:

Metatarsals (Foot Bones)
Calcaneus (Heel Bone)
Tibias (Shin Bone)
Pelvis (Hip Bone)

The constant pounding from running can literally splinter any one of these bones over time – especially if the body is not recovering enough between runs.

Stress Fractures Affect All Ages
I worked with a 23-year-old woman who was diagnosed with a stress fracture in her pelvis while doing cross-country for a Division I University. Developing a stress fracture is not uncommon to both high school and college student athletes, as their bodies take a large pounding in their training and then they burn the midnight oil preparing for their exams.

The Right Course of Action
If you have a lifestyle similar to a student athlete, where you balance heavy loads in both your sport and your work, make sure that you are recovering properly. Test your biomechanics to make sure that your body is able to perform proper movement patterns and then assess your stress levels with the Shavasana Test on page 494. If you experience pain, either sharp or burning-throbbing, deep within your body, reduce your workload in training, prioritize more recovery time for yourself and speak with a professional as soon as possible.

Strength Training
In the long run, adding strength exercises to your training program will reduce your risk of stress fractures. Strength exercises will positively stress your body and lead to the fortification of your bones as well as tendons and ligaments.

Barometer of Strength
Here are a few baseline metrics to use when assessing your own strength and conditioning. Ideally, you should be able to perform each of these exercises with proper form for the prescribed weight and rep scheme:

COMMON INJURIES

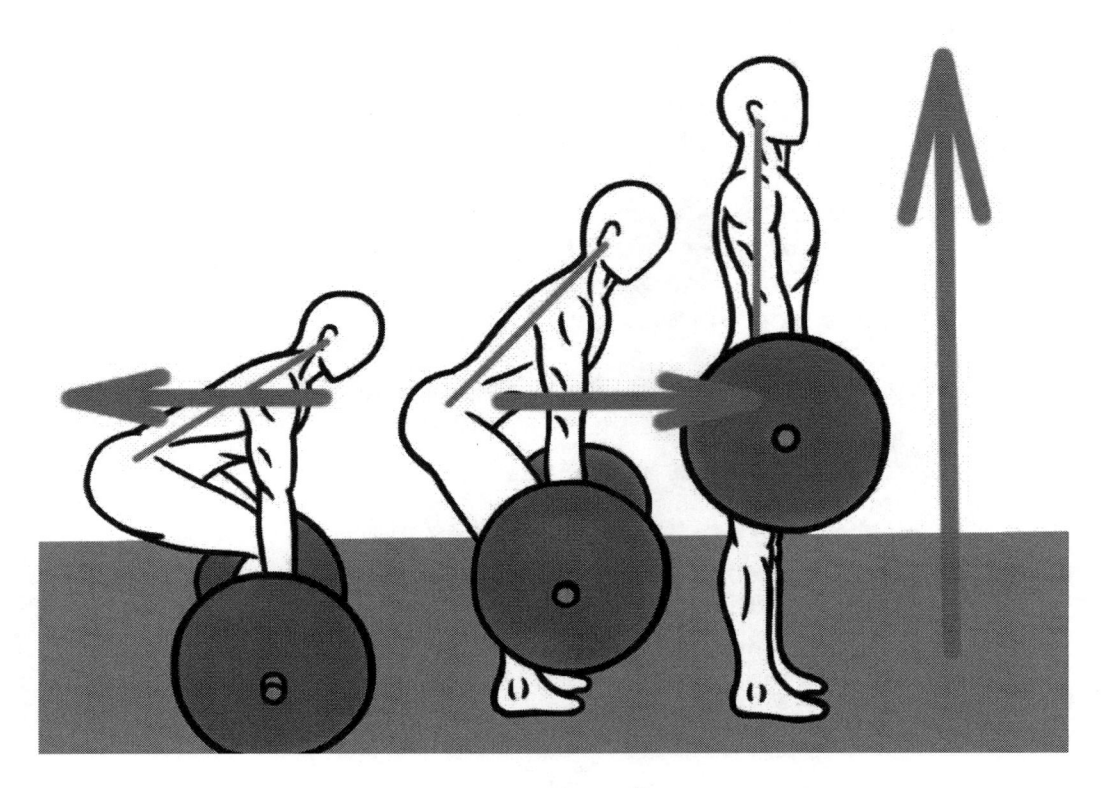

Deadlift 1.5x your Bodyweight for One Rep

Perform 20 consecutive Push-ups

COMMON INJURIES

Squat your own Bodyweight for One Rep

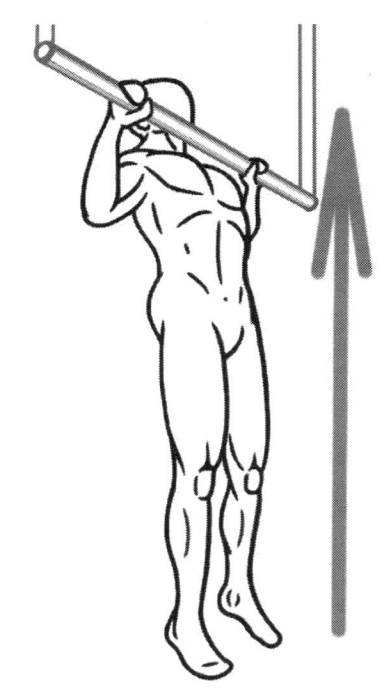

Perform one complete Pull-up

Strength Training Guidelines

- Start with the load (weight) that you can perform each repetition with proper form through a full Range of Motion.

- Gradually increase the load (weight) as you progress through sets and workouts.

- Don't perform reps with a load (weight) that compromises your form in the exercise.

- Perform strength sets at a load (weight) that rates as a 7 or 8 on your own 1-10 Perceived Effort scale.

- Trust that your body will grow stronger over time. Strength gains will be a gradual progress.

- Record your progress in your training journal.

- Move through a full Range of Motion (ROM) and practice proper exercise form on each repetition.

Alignment

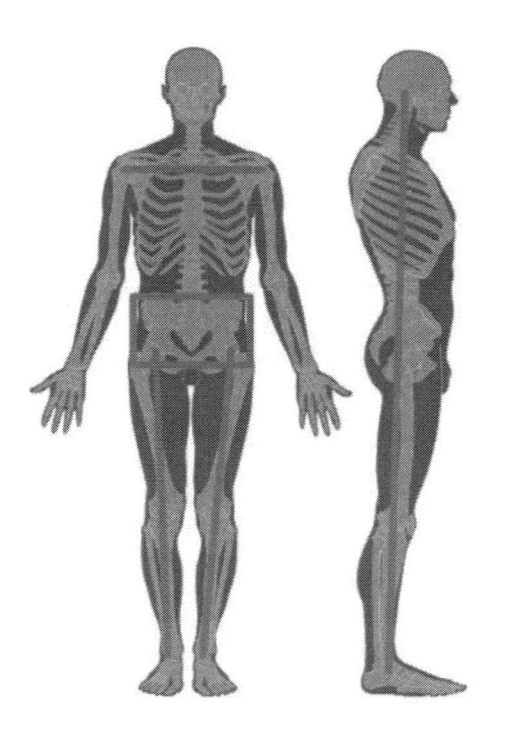

Classic moving arts, like yoga and qigong, have honored the body's health by carefully cultivating the flow of life's energy, respectively called prana and qi. Both of these moving arts practices cure disease and promote longevity simply base on alignment or the continual positioning of the body.

The East and the West-
Today, many practitioners in Western culture are embracing these ancient philosophies of the East as we can easily find a yoga class on any gym schedule. However, achieving effectiveness in these practices requires more than just wearing the hot new yoga pants or chugging down a shot of wheat grass before your workout.

Improving your health and fitness involves improving your movement and that requires developing an awareness of your alignment – in all positions.

Stop and take a look at yourself. Look at the position of your body. Where are your shoulders in relation to your hips? What is your spine doing? Is it bending or curving in a particular direction? Yes, this is a pop quiz. You were not ready for it, I know. So, it doesn't really count – or does it?

What is alignment?
In layman terms, alignment in the human body refers to how we move and hold ourselves together – literally and figuratively. There is "alignment" in both your posture and your movements.

ALIGNMENT

Katy Bowman, MS, a biomechanist and the author of *Alignment Matters* and *Move Your DNA*, will tell you that your body is continuously subjected to a combination of forces, such as torque, leverage and gravity, every second of every day and that your alignment is a major tool to safeguarding a long and biological, functional future.

Why does alignment matter?
Bowman is one of the first people in the world who will tell you that not only does your alignment affect your current state of Wellness, it will eventually also dictate your future diseases and health predicaments, including injuries.

> *Alignment is the continual positioning of the body wherein 'form equals function.'*

Bowman believes that if we do not correct our alignment, then other parts of our body will become prematurely wore down from absorbing an inappropriate amount of stress (torque or force) produced by our movements.

Alignment Affects Performance-
The transitive law in mathematics postulates that in order to perform well in anything we have to move well because movement is the basic component of performing. Then in order to move well, we would need to know (and practice) the correct form and alignment of specifics movements. In other words, I can't throw a curve ball for a strike if I do not know (nor practice) the mechanics involved.

> *Alignment is the mechanical foundation of movement and a key ingredient in every performance.*

This goes for performance in life too. Look, if you went into a job interview or met with an investor and you sat in your chair all slumped down and sliding off the chair, do you think you would be successful? Try it right now to find out for yourself.

Find an office like chair and sit in it. Now, drop your chest down, thrust your chin forward, slide your hips forward and turn your feet onto their sides. Stay there for 60 seconds or so and then answer these questions: Do, you feel confident? Do you feel grounded? Do you feel smart?

Now, get up and stand tall. Toes pointed forward, squeeze your glutes and push the hips forward. Now, pull the belly button in towards your spine and slide your hips back over your anklebones. Pull the shoulders down and away from your ears and imagine that you are parking your shoulder blades into your back pockets while tiny strings pull

ALIGNMENT

your armpits down towards your front pockets. Firm up your abdominals and press the very top of your head up towards the sky as you tuck your chin back in towards your Adam's apple. Now, relax your jaw and easily gaze at the horizon, which should intersect perfectly with the midpoint in your line of sight.

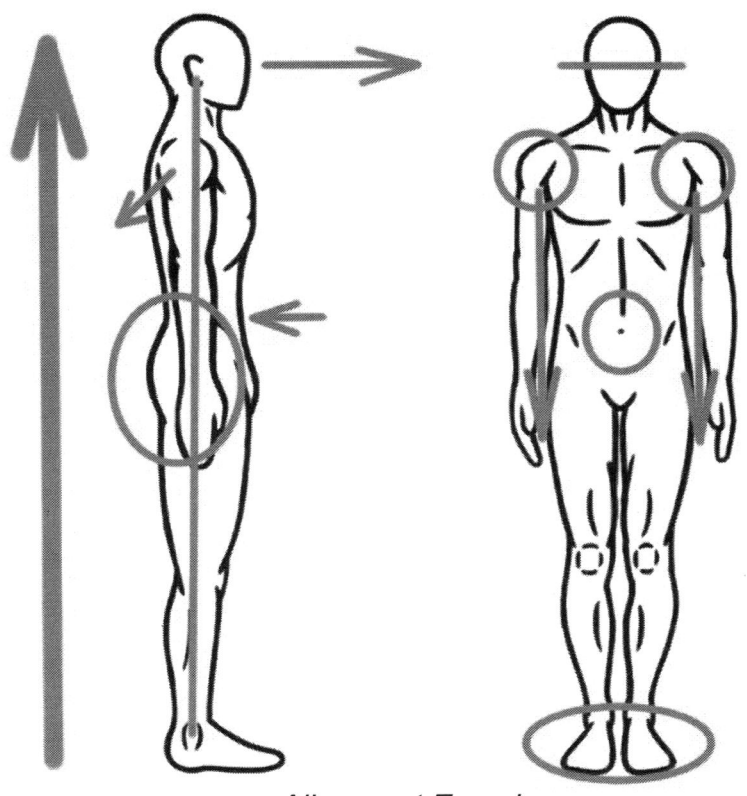

Alignment Exercise

Do you feel confident? Do you feel grounded? Do you feel smart?

Alignment makes a difference, which is why you will need to develop an awareness of it if you are looking to perform better in your life and your sport. It is more than just geometry and physics, and it's more than just the accumulation of joint angles and load or torque forces on them. Alignment is a map of how you move collectively – the accumulation of your movement patterns and lifestyle habits.

Looking at your body's alignment is an excellent start to developing functional movement that will fulfill task-oriented performance in life with optimal efficiency.

Living in a Modern World
Chances are if you work on a computer and sit at a desk your head protrudes forward. The muscles at the base of your skull and back of your neck are tight from overuse. The detailed movements that allow you to read what is on your computer screen interfere with proper alignment of your head and neck.

ALIGNMENT

Using alignment to see what your movement habits and lifestyle has done to you is an effective way to identify biomechanical problems. Once you know where your alignment is off, you can plot an effective course to bring you closer to natural movement patterns and better performance in life.

Our modern-world lifestyle is full of solutions and devices that have reduced the quantity of movement, as Bowman says. In other words, humankind has continuously been looking for new ways to move less to make life easier. Without even knowing it, this has actually made our lives much harder by diminishing our ability to move well and properly function.

Assessing our alignment is the first step to restoring the functionality of our biomechanics and optimizing movement.

You can set forth a large precedence for change through cultivating an ongoing awareness of your alignment. The more that you can check in with how you are positioned and how you are moving, the more chances you have to correct your alignment.

Yet, alignment is not a one-and-done with kind of game. You don't just check in with you alignment at noon every day, make a few corrections and be good for the rest of the afternoon. It's continual…

How do you sit?
How do you sit and text?

According to Bowman, your alignment is a living compilation of your lifestyle behaviors and what you do more often is more impactful than what you may do deliberately.

For example, say you are looking to improve your 10K time and you were told to develop a longer stride length. All of the stretches for your hip flexors will do very little if you are still sitting at your desk for eight hours a day, driving for another hour and a half and watching TV on the couch at home. The accumulative time you spend with your hip flexors in a shorten position will have more impact on your alignment despite how deep you push yourself in any stretch.

The best solution in this example is to get a stand-up desk and take regular walk breaks throughout the day to develop more lifestyle habits that promote length in the hip flexors.

62   PreHab Exercise Book for Runners

ALIGNMENT

Where to start? Start at your feet.
You have to start somewhere, right? Start with the feet as they are the platform in which to operate from and you can learn a lot from your feet.

In an EFTI seminar with Lenny Parracino, *The Foot: The First Link in the Kinetic Chain*, I learned to evaluate our habitual alignment by looking at the bottom of the feet.

Here's how it works:
Take off your shoes and socks and examine the bottoms of the feet. Next, look at where the calluses are located and compare the densities. The denser the callus, the more pressure that part of the foot receives over time, which points to where your true center of gravity is. Ideally, you want to have an even amount of density across all five balls of the feet and the heel, with some lighter calluses running along the outside ridge of the foot. You can compare the ideal Foot Perspective below on the left to my results at the time of this seminar. I have since then changed the location of the calluses on my feet – thankfully!

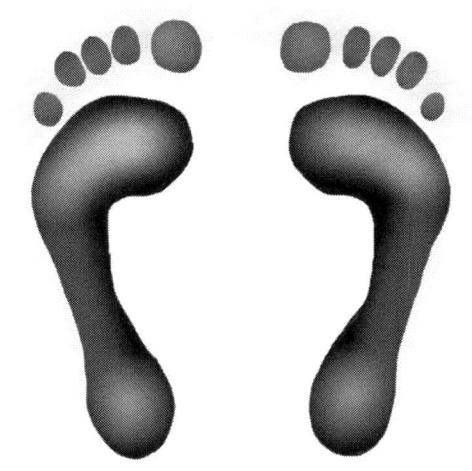

Ideal Pressure Distribution on Feet

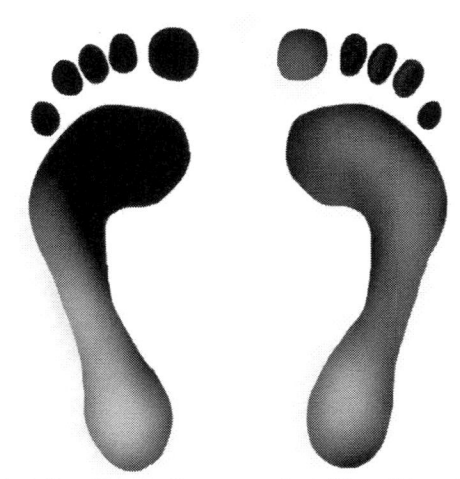

Pressure Distribution after my Achilles Tendon Ruptures

ALIGNMENT

ALIGNMENT

Assessing Alignment

It's time to get practical again and assess your alignment in a couple of primary, static positions. This will allow you to assess your movement habits and any dysfunctional or compensating strategies. It's wise to take some notes and put them in a safe place for future comparison because if there is no change over time, the actions you think you are taking are not being effective.

Assess from the ground up:
Feet to hips to ribs to shoulders to head.

If you still have your shoes on, take them off. You may also want to consider switching to minimalist shoes if you have not all ready. In her book, *Every Woman's Guide to Foot Pain Relief*, Bowman explains the pitfalls of wearing a shoe that has a heel and that goes for men as well. Even a one-inch heel in your basic running shoe will create an angled platform in which your entire body will operate from. So, start to consider switching to minimalist footwear – both men and women.

Front View
Do you think you have level shoulders? Most people that I ask smirk and confidently nod their heads "yes." Some even ask whose shoulders wouldn't be level, huh? The odd thing is that a large number of people have left-right asymmetry issues and do not even know it. Here's a quick way to see where you stand – or better yet, to see how you stand with left-right asymmetries.

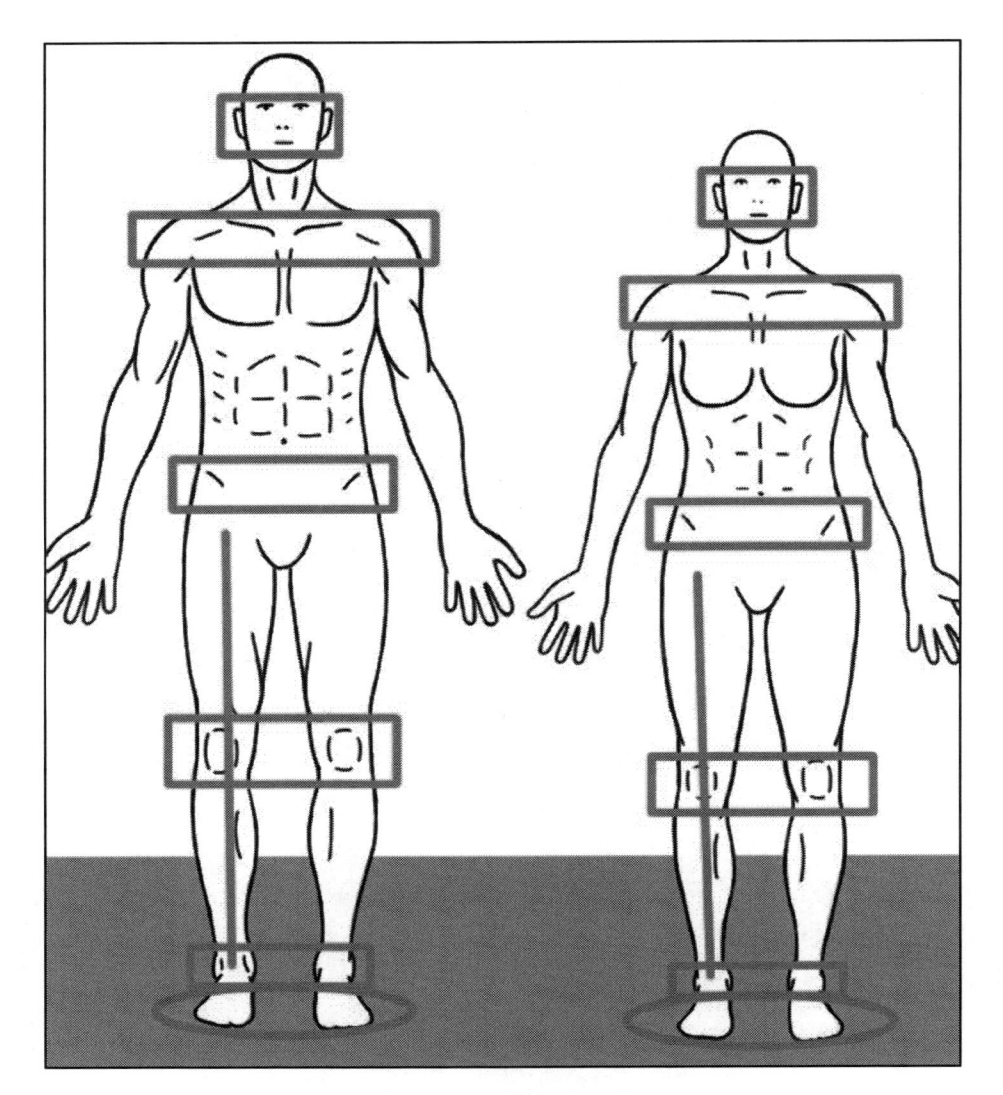

ALIGNMENT

Alignment Diagrams

Stand in front of a mirror or take a photo of yourself.
Relax your shoulders and look at the horizon.
Now, march in place for 10 seconds and then stop.
Now, examine your standing alignment with these cues:

Is your head vertical straight? Look to see if your ears are level.
It's better if they are.
Are your shoulders even with one another?
It's better if they are.
Are your collarbones parallel to the floor?
It's better if they are.
Are your hips even?
It's better if they are.
Are your kneecaps even? Do your feet point straight ahead?
It's better if they do.

ALIGNMENT

Profile View

For this you need some help. You will need a ruler, a pen and someone to take a photo of you from the side.

Set up the camera on one side of your body. The camera needs to capture your profile exactly. If you can see either the far hip, buttock or shoulder, you are not in an exact profile position.

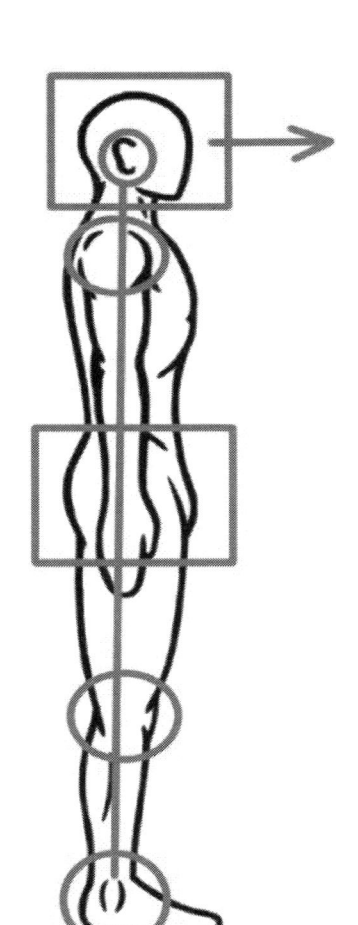

Relax the shoulders, look at the horizon and then close your eyes. March in place for 10 seconds and then stop.

Now, stand still and take a photo of your standing alignment in profile.

Print out the picture and grab your ruler. Place the ruler right at the anklebone and square it with the floor at 90 degrees. Next, draw a line from the anklebone straight up through the top of the head.

Does the middle of the knee stack directly over the anklebone? *It's better if it does.*

Does the hip socket stack directly over the middle of the knee? *It's better if it does.*

Does the shoulder joint stack directly over the hip socket? *It's better if it does.*

Does the ear hole stack right over the shoulder joint? *It's better if it does.*

Does the horizon land directly in the middle of your field of vision as you look ahead? Do you see an equal amount of sky and floor? *It's better if you do.*

How to find the hip socket and shoulder joint-
When performing these alignment evaluations, you need to know exactly what you are lining up, especially when it comes to your shoulder joint and hip socket.

Hip Socket: place the hands on the sides of your hips and press your thumbs into the indentation of the Glutes. Gently shift your hips forward and backwards as well as left to right. You will be able to feel where the hip socket is located through the juxtaposition of movements.

Shoulder Joint: place your hand over the opposite shoulder and move that arm around in small circles. Feel with your fingers where the arm bone intersects with the shoulder

ALIGNMENT

girdle. That's the shoulder joint.

Now, if your alignment is not what it should be, there is no need to panic. Instead, take on a new practice of aligning yourself with the first step of cultivating more awareness to your alignment on a daily basis.

It took years for your alignment to become what it is and it will take time to change it. However, it will not change if you do not develop a more focused attention on what your alignment is in how you move.

With a committed practice to develop mobility, activate essential muscles and create stability in your movement, PreHab will help you to cultivate better alignment over time.

ALIGNMENT

Plank Alignment

Lie on your stomach and place your palms flat on the ground along your rib cage. Align the heel of your palms with the bottom of your chest and pull the shoulders down and away from the ears. Tuck the toes under and fully extend the arms.

It's important to evaluate your plank alignment. There are so many exercises and activation techniques that are employed in this position that doing this will help develop stability in the shoulders and core.

First make sure that your elbows are straight and that your hands are shoulder-width apart. Pull your hands inwards if they are too wide and spread your fingers on the floor.

Next, stabilize the shoulders by squeezing the armpits down towards your front pockets and parking your shoulder blades into your back pockets. Pull the shoulders down and away from your ears.

Now, power up your plank hold even more by adding external rotation in the shoulder joint. Roll the belly of your biceps to face forward and screw your hands into the ground. Try to rotate the fingers towards the outside without lifting your hands off the ground. You should feel your shoulders tighten and widen.

Next, lengthen the entire body from head to toes. Reach the top of the head away from the tailbone while also pulling the jaw into your throat to make you feel as if you have a double chin. Feel the back of your neck becoming long and straight.

Squeeze the glutes and drive the hips towards the ground while you lift your kneecaps up towards the sky. Pull the belly button into towards the spine to engage the abdominals.

ALIGNMENT

The natural "S" curve of your spine should transform into a "Hollow" position – an arch-like alignment with a shallow curvature. If the curve of your spine is too large or exasperated, you are compensating by creating torque and sheer on your spine. The curve is a minimal curve – approximately 5-10 degrees from head to hip.

Side Plank

Start in a plank position on your elbows with your arms folded over one another and the elbows directly beneath the shoulder joints. Position your feet at shoulder width and lengthen from head to heel.

Next, rotate over into a side plank by rolling the hips and shoulders 90 degrees and lifting one arm completely off the floor. Turn the feet as well and press the heels into the floor.

Use a partner or mirror to make sure that the bottom ankle, hip and shoulder are aligned in a straight line and that your shoulders are also stacked over one another.

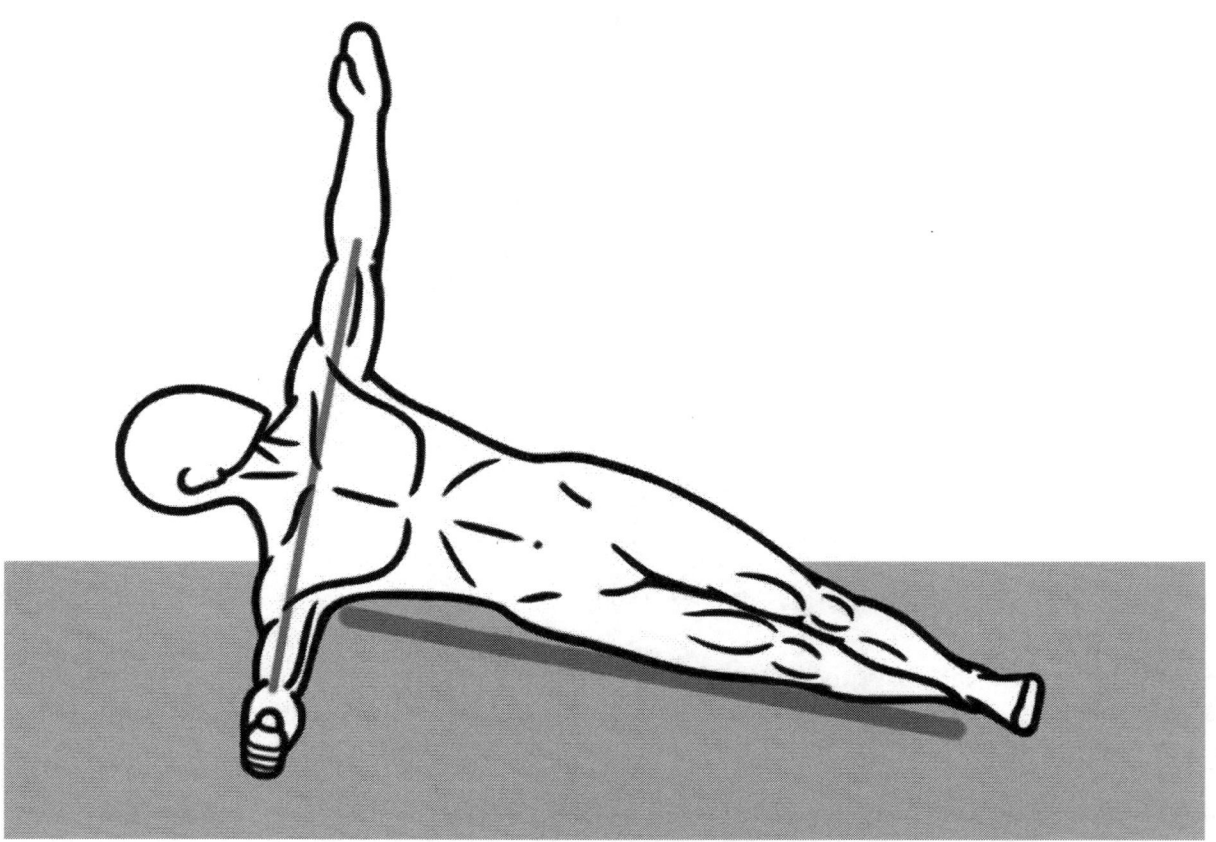

Stabilize the bottom shoulder by pulling the armpit down towards the hips and parking your shoulder blades into your back pockets.

ALIGNMENT

Common miscues:
Elevated shoulders cause tightness in the trapezius muscles and place extra strain on the cervical spine. Make sure that the shoulder joint is pulled down and away from the ear.

Misalignment with the bottom ankle, hip and shoulder may occur and look as if the hips bow up into the air or sag down towards the floor. In either case, there is excess torque place on the spine and it represents a dysfunction in this pattern, which can affect your lateral stability in other movements.

Shoulders or hips may fail to rotate and stabilize at 90 degrees due to tightness or weakness in this pattern. Make a personal note about this and refer to it for future assessments.

Lastly, compare the length of time that you are able to hold this position on either side. If the times do not match, it represents an asymmetry in your biomechanics and you will want to improve this over time as asymmetries increase your risk for injury.

ALIGNMENT

ALIGNMENT

Movement Evaluations

PreHab exercises and techniques are intended to prepare your body to perform task-oriented goals, such as throwing a football, running a marathon, or just carrying the groceries in from the car.

Now, people are fully capable of completing many tasks, if not all tasks, with poor biomechanics and dysfunctional movement patterns. In his book, *Becoming a Supple Leopard,* physical therapist Kelly Starrett salutes the resiliency that people have in regards to completing movements with gross dysfunctions or extreme limitations in their mobility. Starrett acknowledges that people can be very strong-willed and adaptable when it comes to movement. Yet, any movement with poor biomechanics and dysfunctional patterns will eventually take its toll on your body.

Why are Movement Evaluations important?
Physical Therapist and Strength Coach Gray Cook created the Functional Movement Screen with Lee Burton to help people correct their alignment and functional movement patterns. "It's not a question of if they will break down, it's a question of when," Cook stated at a NSCA Tactical Strength and Conditioning Conference,

Evaluate to Improve
If you want to be at your best when you cross the finish line of your next marathon, throw the winning touchdown pass in your flag football league, or complete your daily boot camp workout to look great for summer, 'good' biomechanics will help as will a practice of PreHab.

Human Movement is task orientated in nature. Therefore, it's an important investment to examine how you do things and how you move in these task-oriented activities to reduce the risk of injuries and create better results.

How do you accomplish this? Evaluate your movement. It's as simple as that. Evaluating your movement provides valuable information about how you perform in the gym, on a run and everywhere in between.

Where to Start?
Aaron Li, Physical Therapist at Select Physical Therapy in Los Angeles, uses this approach. He says he is constantly using an array of Movement Evaluations to find out where to start the corrective phase with his clients. If he's not evaluating, he won't know where to start. On top of that, if he doesn't keep evaluating, he will never know what works and what doesn't work.

ALIGNMENT

MOVEMENT EVALUATION - Kneeling Lunge and Reach
Possible results and limitations-
Front Heel coming off the ground indicates a limited range of motion in the ankle and calf muscles. Chest dropping or fingers not reaching vertical or backwards with straight arms indicates limited range of motion in the thoracic spine, hip flexors or shoulders.

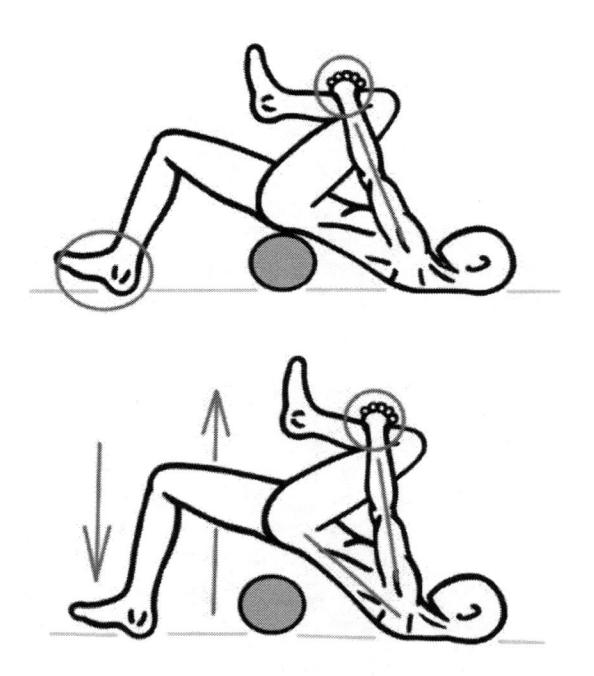

MOVEMENT EVALUATION - Single-Leg Bridge Off Roller
Possible results and limitations-
Not being able to bridge off of the foam roller indicates an inhibited connection to the glutes and a lack of force production and range of motion in the hip extension.

ALIGNMENT

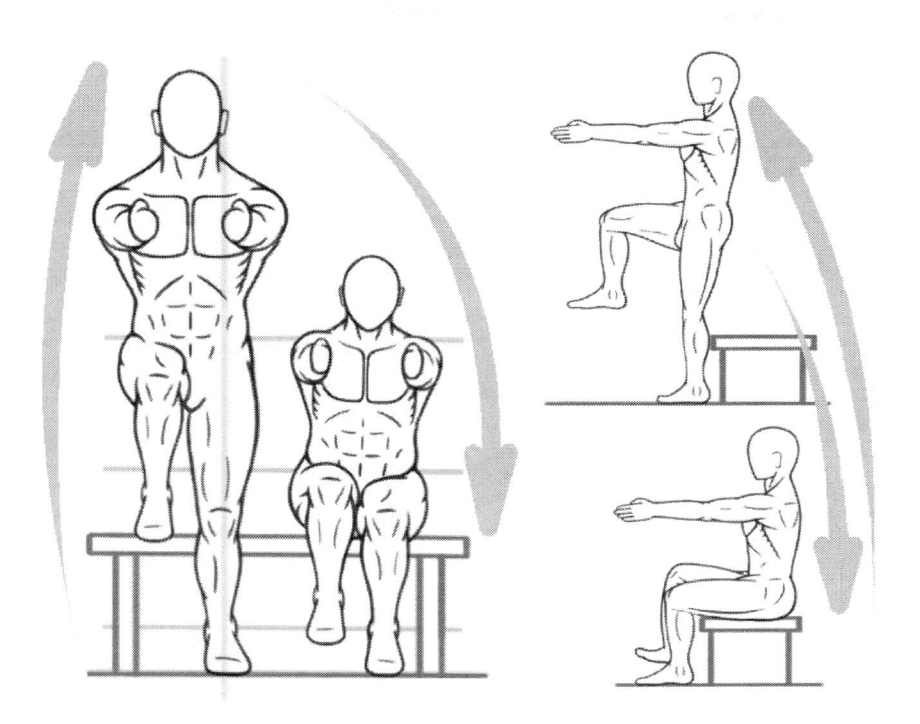

MOVEMENT EVALUATIONS - Single-Leg Box Squat
Possible results and limitations-
A lack of control over the directional path of the kneecap indicates a lack of stability in either the hip or the ankle.

Self-performed movement evaluations is what Rehab Technician Christopher Trinih uses with patients in order to help them better understand their own biomechanics. And it's a form of applied knowledge that can serve them in the future to help prevent injuries, improve their fitness and manage their wellbeing.

Benefits to Movement Evaluations:
- Reduce the risk of injury while performing or exercising
- Create larger gains in performance through moving with more efficiency
- Improve overall health through the reduction of stress on your body caused by the disproportionate accumulation of forces on your joints and soft tissue from running, jumping, lifting weights or playing sports.

The Functional Movement Screen (FMS)

There are already some incredible methods out there in terms of evaluating how your body moves. One renowned resource is the *Functional Movement Screen* created by Gray Cook and Lee Burton. The screen uses seven different exercises that are incrementally graded to diagnose ability and quality of a person's movement. FMS is used by many professional and college athletic programs in addition to thousands of private practitioners due to its ease of use and effectiveness. A movement screen can be completed in as little as 10 minutes and provide much valuable information.

ALIGNMENT

What if I am not a professional, what do I do?
If you didn't spend three years of graduate school to become a physical therapist and you're not a professional strength coach or certified trainer, that's still okay. As long as you can move, you can still evaluate your movement.

Physical Therapist Craig Liberson of LA Sport and Spine offers a valuable tip to anyone looking to use exercise to improve their fitness or health. He says:

> *"Make every exercise an evaluation."*

Simply put, Liberson is saying that every exercise has a specific alignment or form to it and the degree to which you can properly perform the exercise will provide much insight into your biomechanics and movement habits.

Air Squat
Let's take the squat as an example. Here's how to evaluate your movement for this exercise. Stand with feet shoulder-width apart and parallel, or turned out to 5-10 degrees. Lower the hips down below the height of the knees while keeping a neutral spine. Press the thighs wider as you squat to allow more space for the hips and torso to lower. Also, extend the hands towards the horizon to help keep a neutral spine.

Now, did you accomplish the squat in the correct form? If you did, congratulations! If you didn't, you now know that you have some issues to address.

ALIGNMENT

Advanced Evaluations: Add Weight or Speed
When you add weight or speed to any exercise, not only do you get insight into your biomechanical ability, you also gain insight into your capacity of strength, endurance and motor control (stability and coordination). Performing exercises with weight or speed, or even both added, will answer more questions of strength and conditioning and certainly give you great insight in how to adjust your training program to accomplish specific results.

Evaluating Before, After and During Workouts
For example, a runner training for a marathon is evaluating hip and ankle stability by performing the single-leg squat test before running. Yet, after an eight-mile run in her fourth week of a 16-week program, she is feeling pain in her knee. Re-testing the single-leg squat after the eight-mile run will help her understand if she has the hip and ankle strength to maintain an efficient gait throughout the rest of her training. If she fails to perform this exercise successfully, the failed exercise proves to be a negative indication of her strength, which allows her to adjust her training program to correct the lack of ankle and hip strength without suffering a setback in her marathon training program.

How do I know what the correct form of an exercise is?
This is a great question to ask and bigger solution for the health and fitness world to create. There are thousands, if not millions, of different exercises that a person has a choice of performing at any moment. Unfortunately, there is no all-encompassing lexicon of human movement or exercise library for people to access. Until there is, become a student in the language of human movement.

Your first lesson in Human Movement Studies:
Learning how the body moves Joint-by-Joint.

ALIGNMENT

ALIGNMENT

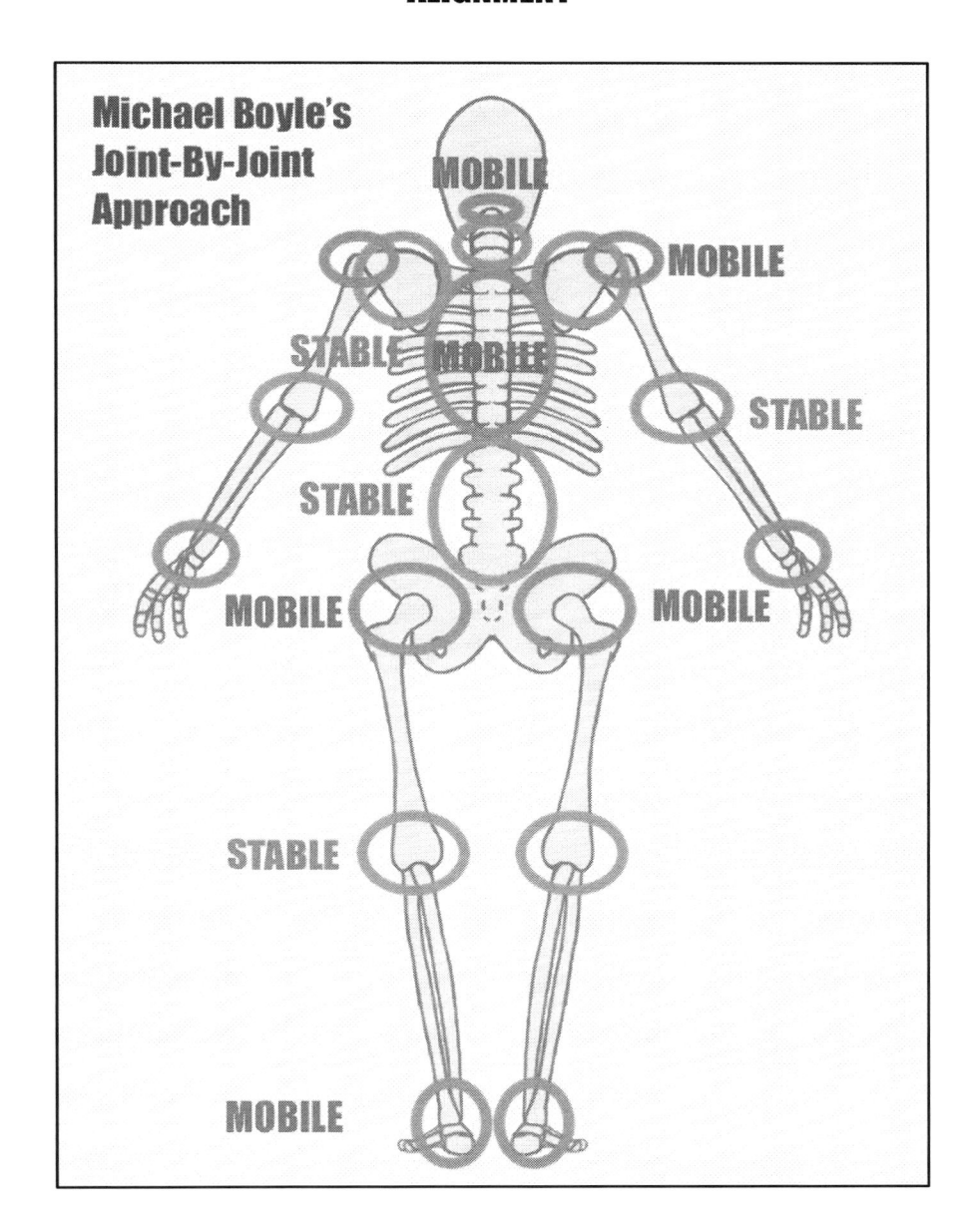

Michael Boyle's Joint-By-Joint Approach

- MOBILE (head/neck)
- MOBILE (shoulders)
- MOBILE (thoracic spine)
- STABLE (scapula)
- STABLE (elbows)
- STABLE (lumbar spine)
- MOBILE (wrists)
- MOBILE (hips)
- STABLE (knees)
- MOBILE (feet/ankles)

The Joint-by-Joint Approach
Assessing Human Movement

Michael Boyle is a well-known strength coach who is rather famous for sharing his wisdom and techniques with millions via his blog and presentations at fitness seminars around the world. One of his most influential contributions to the strength training community is his *Joint By Joint Approach*, a simplistic analysis of the body that helps to evaluate movement and identify dysfunctions.

The *Joint By Joint Approach* provides insight to how a person moves and where the limitations exist in movement patterns. In other words, Boyle's approach is a portable compass that helps you navigate through the science of human movement.

ALIGNMENT

The Basis Behind the Approach
Boyle recognized an alternating pattern of mobility and stability in the joints. Meaning each joint in the body was functionally designed for either: mobility, a wide range of possible movement, or stability, a minimal range of movement.

Starting from the ankle and working up through the rest of the body, the movement expression of each joint would alternate from mobility to stability and back again. See the illustration for a depiction of this approach.

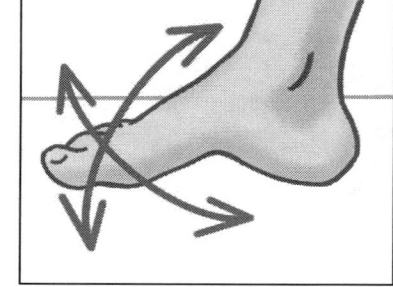

The Ankle is a Mobile Joint-
Watch to see how well the ankle can flex or extend as well as pronate and supinate. It is a multi-directional joint. If there is limited movement in the ankle, this will create compensation elsewhere.

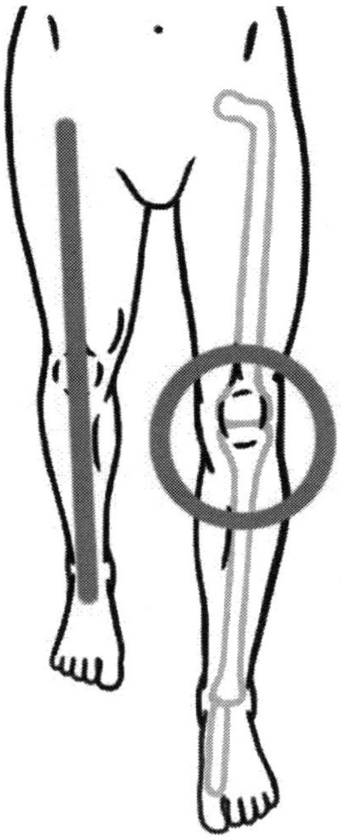

The Knee is a Stable Joint-
There is one main function of the knee and it's to bend or extend, as it is a unidirectional joint. Therefore, seeing any other kind of movement at the knee joint besides front-to-back Flexion and extension is a red flag!

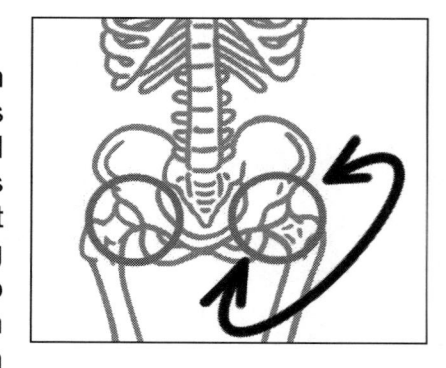

The Hip is a Mobile Joint-
Believe it or not, the range of motion of your hips should be very large as this ball and socket joint is designed to be multi-directional. The hips serve many different movement functions from squatting to lifting something to running or walking to sitting on the floor in lotus position (crossed legged). However, sitting in chairs for extended periods of time will rob this joint of much of its mobility.

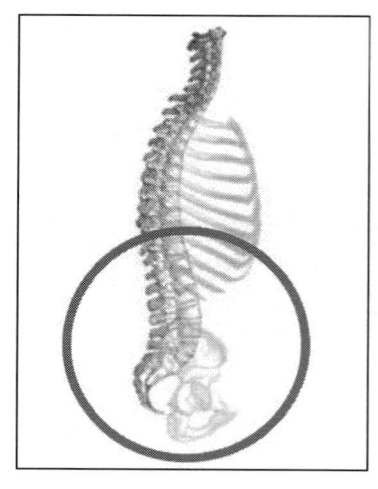

Note: Be sure to watch how well the hip socket functions by watching the thigh in relation to the Pelvis and Lumbar Spine.

The Lumbar Spine is a Stable Joint-
Every vertebra in your spine is an actual joint. The five vertebrae between your pelvis and rib cage make up the Lumbar Spine. This joint complex is precariously created with no structural support except for the core muscles. At the same time, the range of motion for this joint complex is very limited in design. However, due to the lack of core strength found in those who sit a lot, the Lumbar Spine becomes too mobile in many people.

ALIGNMENT

Note: Watch for minimal change in the spatial relationship between the lowest ribs and the pelvis.

The Thoracic Spine is a Mobile Joint-
The 12 vertebrae that run through the rib cage make up the Thoracic Spine and should account for the majority of movement in the entire torso. Oddly enough, the Thoracic Spine and the rib cage are designed to bend, extend and rotate much the way an accordion does to make music. The tough part is that driving and using computers tend to restrict the natural mobility of the Thoracic Spine.

Note: Watch the spatial relationship between the top ribs and the bottom ribs to evaluate the mobility of the Thoracic Spine.

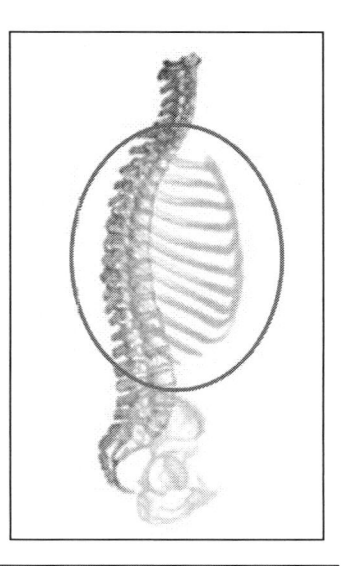

Now from the top of the Thoracic Spine, our chain of joints splits into two separate paths: towards the head and out to the arms.

Towards the Head...

The Cervical Spine is a Stable Joint-
Many people find this hard to believe, but the seven vertebrae that make up the Cervical Spine, aka neck, are a stable joint system. The perceived mobility from the neck is actually designed to come from the Thoracic Spine and the Skull-Spine Junction. However, the lack of Mobility in the Thoracic Spine leads to compensation in movement and changes in alignment.

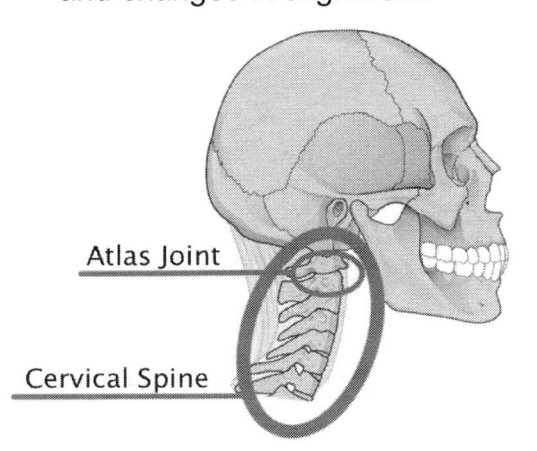

The 'Atlas' Joints are Mobile Joints-
The functions of the Atlanto-occipital and Atlanto-axial joints can be best described by the Greek myth Atlas, a Titan who held the celestial sphere up on his shoulders. (Yes, Atlas held up the stars in the sky, not the world on his shoulders, but that's really not important.) Let's use the image of Atlas standing on top of a mountain holding this large planet-like object on his shoulders to represent how your Cervical Vertebrae supports your skull- a mass weighing 10-12 pounds. Just as the celestial sphere was rather stable on Atlas' shoulders, your head does not move much on top of the C1 vertebra, fittingly called Atlas. This juncture is the Atlanto-occipital joint, which is actually a gliding joint with limited movement. The real mobility for the head comes from the Atlanto-axial joints, which is a pivot joint located between C1 and C2. Just like in the Greek Myth, it is Atlas's footing on the mountain that could make the heavens shake or the stars move across the sky.

ALIGNMENT

More important, it is wise to know that many people lose the mobility of the head in relation to the Cervical Spine due to a poor alignment and the prolonged action of sitting and staring at a computer screen. Restoring the mobility to this region is very beneficial to your health, as it will greatly help to restore your natural alignment in your entire body.

Practice these mobility movements if you find yourself working on a computer or driving a lot.

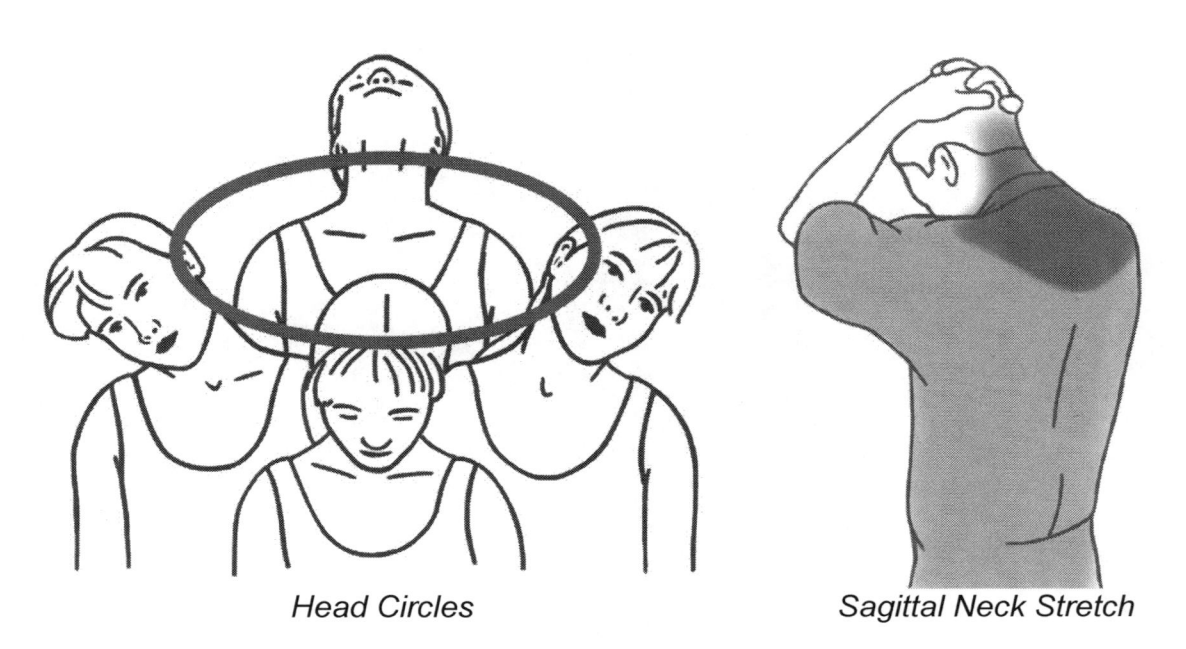

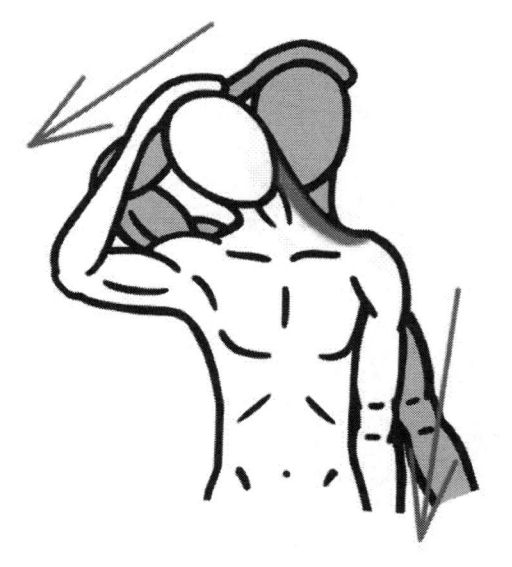

Head Circles

Sagittal Neck Stretch

Lateral Neck Stretch

Rotated Neck Stretch

PreHab Exercise Book for Runners

ALIGNMENT

Out to the Arms…

The Scapula & Sternoclavicular Joints are Stable Joints-
Do you know where your arms connect to the rest of your skeletal system? It's where your collarbone meets your sternum. Yes, that is a joint. If you're like a lot of guys who do Chest three times a week in the gym, you may not know that there is supposed to be movement at that juncture. It's not large movements because this joint, the Sternoclavicular Joint, is a stable joint as is the Scapula.

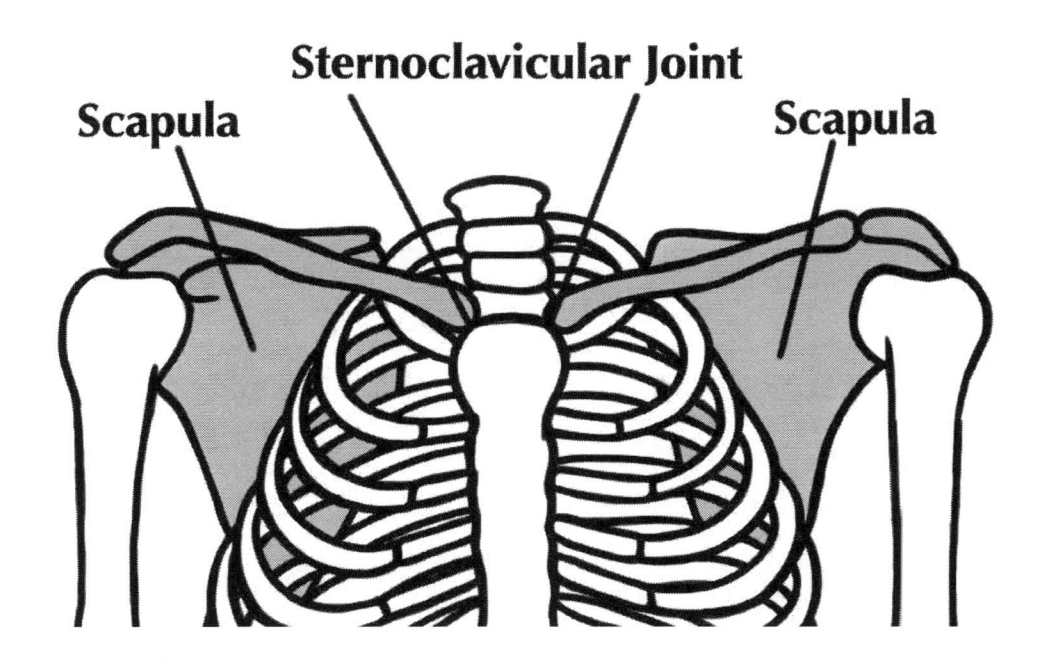

Now, did you know that the Scapula is a floating bone? It is only supported by muscular action and tension of the soft tissue, which makes it seem very mobile. However, the Scapula's role is to function as a movable platform to stabilize the shoulder. The Scapula will rotate, elevate, protract, retract and depress all in an effort to get the shoulder joint into a better position to move and create a greater range of motion. However, despite all of this movement, the Scapula is designed to be stable. How so? With a lot of muscular force and tension.

Imagine that someone is trying to tickle you under your armpit and you clamp down with your arm to block the attempt. It would seem as if there is no way someone can tickle you now, and you are invisible to the tickle. It's because of the muscular force that is produced greatly in part to the muscles connected to the Scapula.

However, most people are losing the ability to stabilize the Scapula due to lifestyle factors and unbalanced exercise programs. So, if you think you may be one of these people, try out these two exercises to help develop more stability for the shoulder by learning how to retract and depress the Scapula.

ALIGNMENT

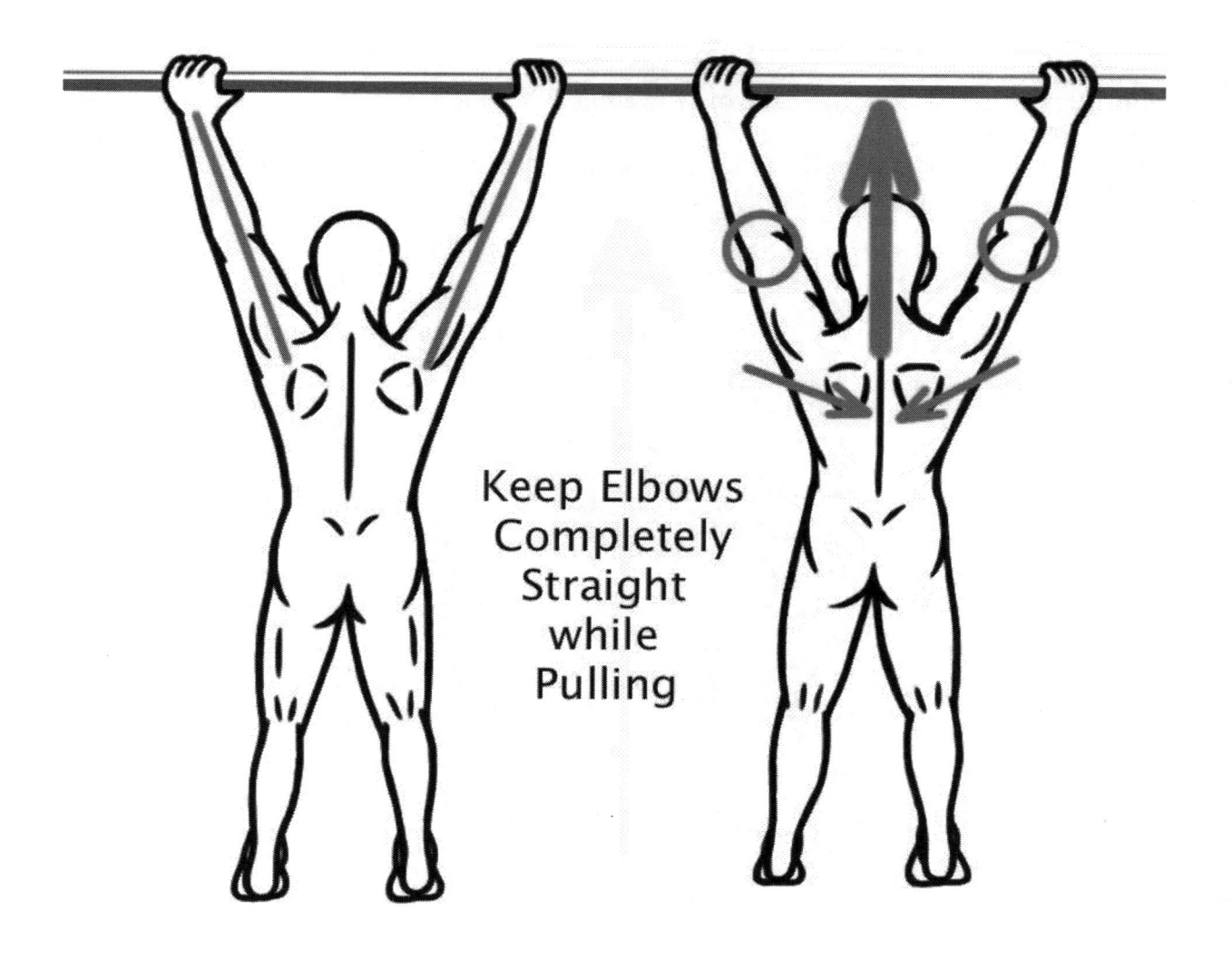

Keep Elbows Completely Straight while Pulling

The Faux-Pull-Up
Hanging Scapula Depression Exercise

Hang from a pull-up bar, with or without assistance, and attempt to perform a pull-up while keeping the elbows fully extended. That's right; try to do a pull-up with straight elbows – that's the exercise.

This exercise will train your body to depress the Scapula. The movement may be minimal at first, but keep working on it until you can really notice an increase in mobility. Eventually, you will want to easily reverse shrug your bodyweight.

ALIGNMENT

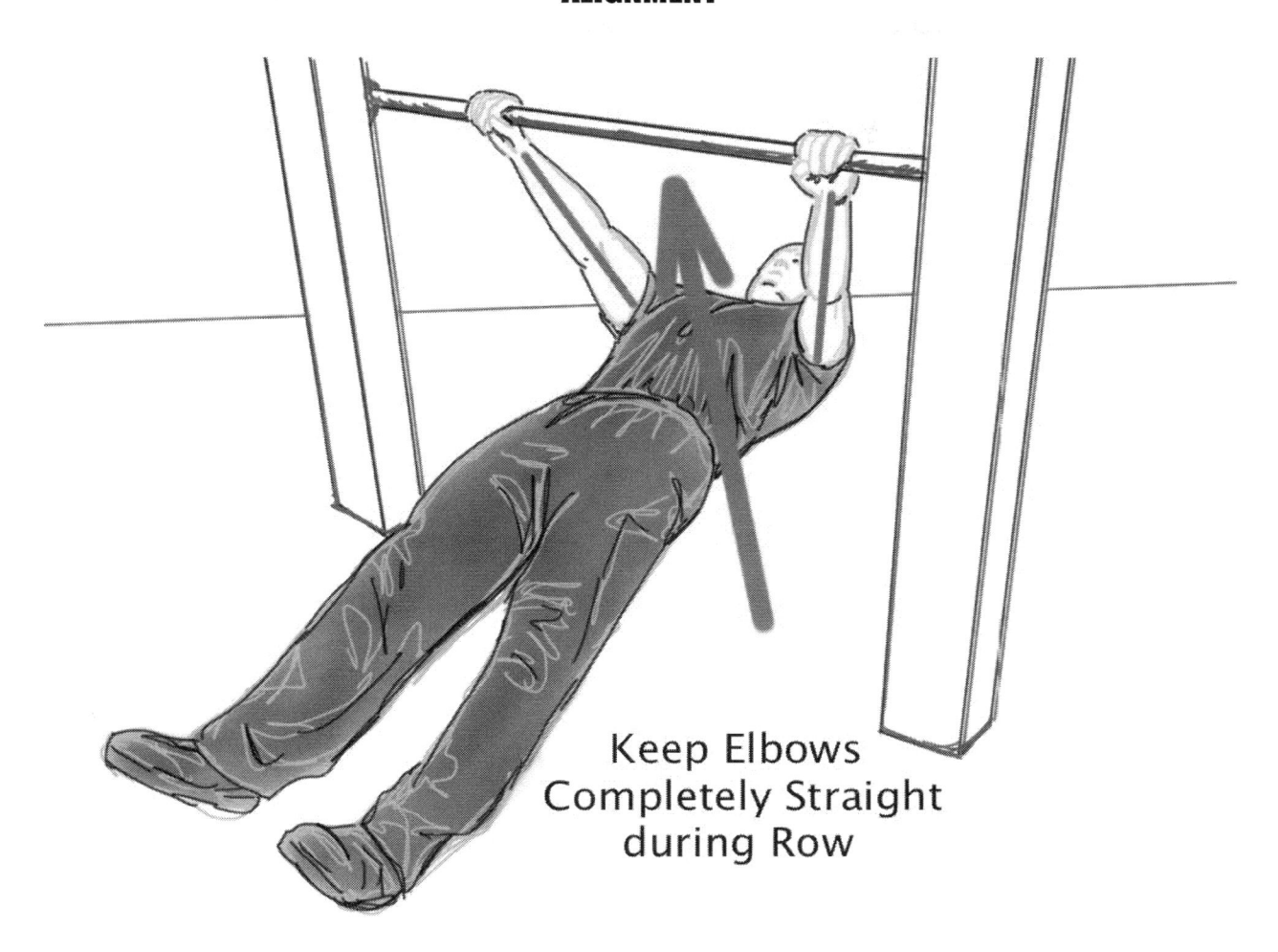

Keep Elbows Completely Straight during Row

The Recline Retraction Pull
Scapula Retraction Exercise

Hang from a bar in a horizontal position or use a cable row machine and practice pitching your shoulder blades together. Ask someone to spot you or have them place a finger in the center of your back while you pull. If you touch their finger, then you've retracted through a full range of motion.

You want to be able to fully retract the scapula with your bodyweight in an inverse row or with the amount of weight that you use in a cable row.

You can also practice retracting your shoulder blades without any weight. See illustration for an example.

Simply, squeeze your shoulder blades together and pull your belly button in towards your spine to stabilize your lumbar spine as you lift your chest up like Superman.

PreHab Exercise Book for Runners

ALIGNMENT

The Arms: Just Like the Legs
The joints in the arms emulate the same structure of the legs.

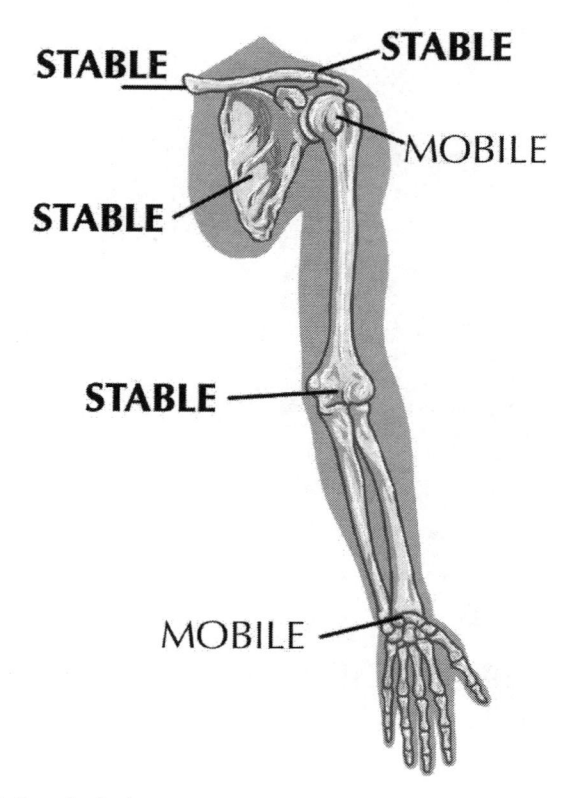

The Shoulder is a Mobile Joint
Just like the Hip, the Shoulder is a ball-in-socket joint that have a wide range of motion and is a very mobile joint.

The Elbow is a Stable Joint
Just like the Knee, the Elbow is a very stable joint that primarily moves in only one direction.

The Wrist in a Mobile Joint
Just like the Ankle, the wrist is a mobile joint that is multi-directional.

A Tool to Use
The Joint By Joint Approach is a great tool that anybody can use to help evaluate how a person moves. It's relatively simplistic to follow and will generate a world of benefit in anyone's health and fitness as it can act a simplistic translator and dictionary in the language of human movement. And the more versed that you can become in evaluating movement, the more effective you can become in fulfilling the intentions and goals that you have with movement.

Mobility
Bodies in Full Motion

When Ethiopian runner Kenenisa Bekele blazed his way to a record-setting 5K finish in 12:37:35 for a new world record in 2004 that still stands, he beat the six-year-old time for the distance by only two seconds. The same year, the legendary NFL football player Jerry Rice closed his 19-year career with an unmatched 1,549 receptions.

Whether you're a pro athlete, new to fitness, or somewhere in between, the training principles for success are essentially the same. To run fast, catch footballs, or perform well in any other sport you need sustainable Mobility.

When I was first introduced to PreHab a few years ago, I saw the importance of Mobility show up in my own personal 5K Challenge. I created this challenge to see if "PreHab" would make a difference in my running. Like a lot of runners and athletes, I was constantly looking for ways to improve, run faster, and reduce recovery time and the risk for injury. But for years, my usual routine was to just head outside and start running.

Then I learned about PreHab in Shannon Turley's presentation, "Proper Preparation Techniques in Training" with the National Strength and Conditioning Association. Shannon shared clips of the techniques that he uses with the Stanford University football team – of which Mobility was a big factor. So, I figured I'd apply the "PreHab" method to my running.

MOBILITY

I set up this 5K PreHab Challenge by doing the following:
I ran a 5K and recorded the time. I then followed a PreHab program that emphasized Mobility in specific movement patterns for running for 30 days and I did not run once. Finally at the end of the program, I ran another 5K and recorded my time. The final result was that I lowered my 5K time by 3 minutes without running once and I have PreHab to thank for that.

> *So, what is Mobility?*
>
> *The quick answer is:*
>
> **Mobility is our ability to move.**
>
> *The long answer is:*
>
> Mobility is the degree to which a person is able to execute specific Movement Patterns with naturally prescribed biomechanics, neuromuscular coordination and mechanical efficiency.

There is a natural blueprint to human movement, just look at a toddler moving. They are instinctively moving in alignment with how their body is designed to move. In terms of mobility and range of motion, toddlers are flawless.

So, where do the flaws come in?
Over time we begin to lose the capacity to maintain complete and full mobility due to injuries, lifestyle and other factors. We tend to kill off certain movement patterns in our life through the lack of use, while over-using other movement patterns. In the end, we lose our ability to move the way we are intended to move and we replace that with different strategies of compensation.

For example: try picking a pen up off the floor. Do you bend with your knees and hinge your hips? Or do you fold over by bending the spine forward. If you did the later, you're using your spine more to complete the movement, probably to compensate for a lack of mobility through your hips, legs and feet.

> *So, what is "good" Mobility?*
> Mobility is evaluated in relation to movement patterns. Mobility is not just flexibility, which is how long a muscle and tendon can lengthen. And though, flexibility is a part of mobility, attaining "Good Mobility" is determined per individual movement pattern.

MOBILITY

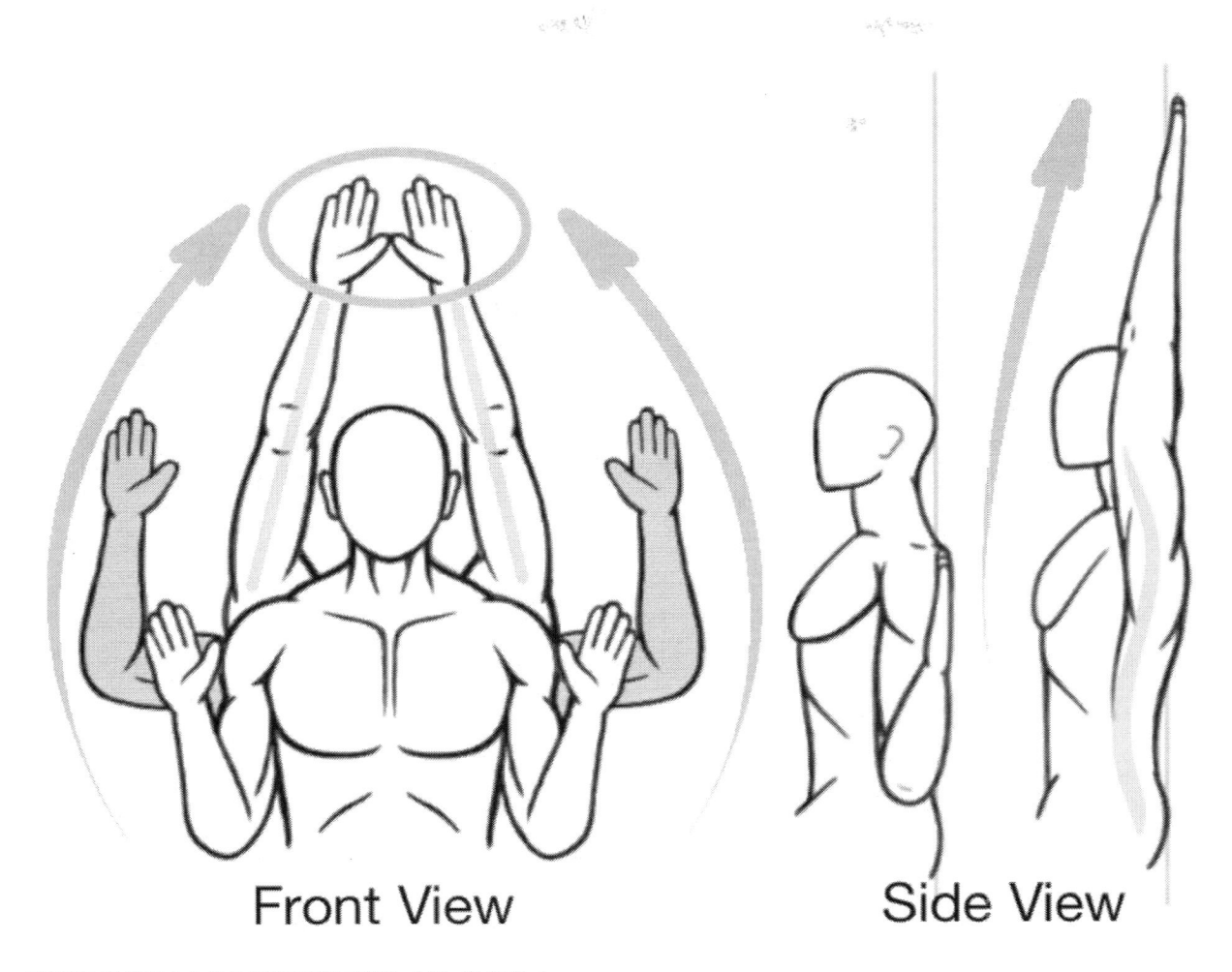

Front View   **Side View**

MOBILITY ASSESSMENT: Wall Slide

POSITION: Align your back up against a wall or lie flat on the ground. Hold the arms out to the side with the fingertips matching the height of the top of your head. Position the forearms parallel with one another and press the elbows and wrists flush against the wall or floor.

ACTION: Slide your arms against the wall or floor until the thumbs touch overhead with fully extended elbows.

        SQUAT AGAINST WALL
        PRESS ARMS INTO WALL
        ELBOW AND HANDS TOUCH WALL CONTINOUSILY
        FULLY EXTEND ARMS OVER HEAD

If you can touch the thumbs together with straight elbows while keeping the backs of the hands and the elbows flushed against the wall or floor, then you have "good mobility" in this movement pattern.

If not, practice this movement pattern religiously over the course of the next two weeks and watch it change.

MOBILITY

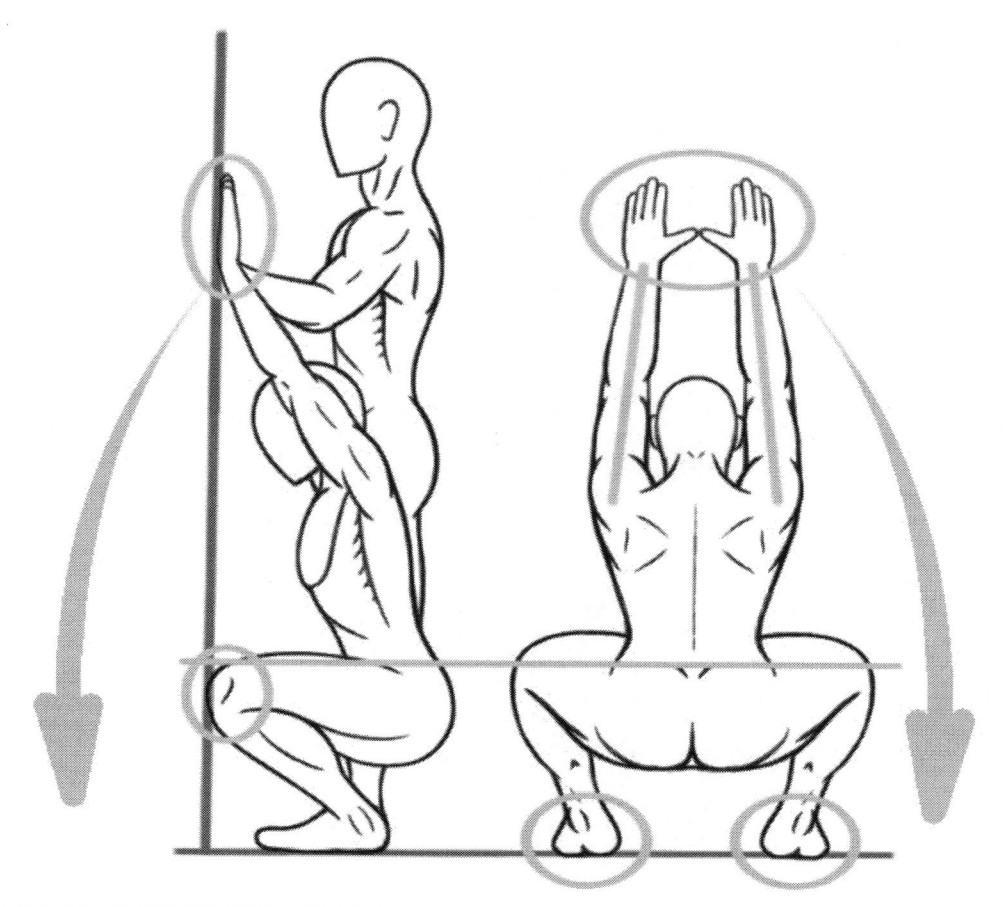

MOBILITY ASSESSMENT: Wall Squat

POSITION: Stand with the feet shoulder-width or slightly wider and place the hands on the wall with both of the thumb tips touching one another. Point the toes forward

ACTION: Squat down until the hips lower beneath the height of your kneecaps and press your thighs out wide to allow more space to squat. Keep the heels flat on the floor and extend the arms straight up. Place the palms on the wall and touch the thumbs together while keeping the elbows straight.

> LOWER HIPS TO KNEE HEIGHT
> HEEL FLAT ON FLOOR
> TOES POINTED FORWARD
> THUMB TOUCHING THUMB
> ELBOWS FULLY EXTENDED

If all the requirements are met, you have the appropriate amount of mobility in this movement pattern and can translate over in many other functional movement patterns.

If not, practice this movement pattern religiously over the course of the next two weeks and watch it change.

MOBILITY

MOBILITY ASSESSMENT:
Hip Hinge

POSITION: Stand with feet together and grasp the pole behind the back with two hands. One hand is placed at the small of the back with the palm facing out while the other hand is placed directly behind the neck with palm facing the body. Next, align the body against the pole so that the head, the spine (just between the shoulder blades) and the hips are all in contact with the pole.

ACTION: Now, slide the hips directly backwards while bending at the knees, keeping the hips, spine and head in contact with the pole. Keep the shins vertical to the floor. The primary movement in this exercise is the flexion in the hip socket, not a flexion or bending of the spine. Attempt to align the thighs and torso into a 90-degree angle or smaller while maintaining the head, spine and hips in complete contact with the pole.

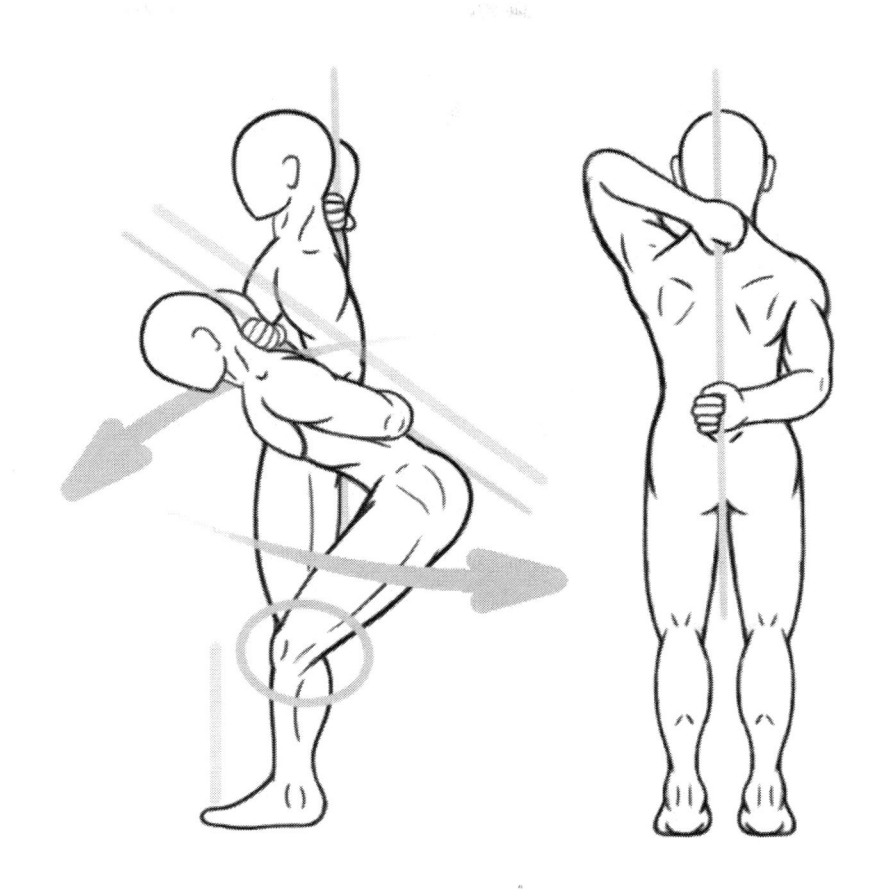

ALIGN HEAD, UPPER BACK AND HIPS AGAINST POLE
KEEP SHINS VERTICAL
PRESS HIPS BACK
LOWER TORSO FORWARD
MAINTAIN 3 POINTS OF CONTACT WITH POLE
MAKE 90-DEGREE ANGLE WITH TORSO AND THIGHS

If all requirements are met, you have the appropriate amount of mobility in this movement pattern to allow your hips to hinge and avoid using spinal flexion as a compensation strategy. This evaluation also indicates the ability you have to maintain a stable spine throughout dynamic movement patterns, which is very instrumental to channeling the flow of kinetic energy through your body while running or lifting weights.

If you do not meet all of the requirements in this assessment, then your body will use compensation strategies in all movement patterns, such as a deadlift, that relies on a hip hinge sequence.

MOBILITY

Mobility Changes
It is possible to radically change your mobility within minutes if you know what techniques to use – and there are many. So, stay tuned, as I'll cover a lot of them over time!

Learning to be a Star
As a training method to prevent injuries and improve performance, PreHab has many ties to physical therapy, especially when it comes to mobility work. And if you want to meet the rock star of physical therapy trends and best practices, you don't have to look any further than San Francisco-based physical therapist Kelly Starrett, also known as K-Starr.

The foundational mobility principles and techniques that Dr. Starrett demonstrates in his book, *Becoming a Supple Leopard*, as well as on his website **www.MobilityWOD.com** are very effective in improving a person's alignment, biomechanics and performance.

Test and Retest.
There is one single phrase that Starrett echoes in his Mobility WOD videos that quintessentially sums up the intention of practicing all of these techniques. The phrase is, "test and retest."

Effective mobility work will present visual evidence of success. You will see a difference in your range of motion if you are doing the techniques and exercises well enough.

Starrett's catch phrase, "test and retest,'" is the simplest principal that you can employ in your training that will yield the largest gain. This practice helps you know if you have made a positive difference in your mobility or not. If you have not, change your technique style or execution because it is simply not working.

It's important that your mobility work be effective as it sets the premise and guidelines for which your movement and performance will be based on.

MOBILITY

Soft Tissue Therapy

Just about everyone has some experience with scar tissue, adhesions and knots. You might not be familiar with the clinical definition of these conditions. But there's no mistaking muscle pain, a strained tendon, or a bruise from a kick in the leg during a game of soccer. Your first inclination might be to head to the medicine cabinet and pop some ibuprofen, but that's not the ideal fix for a soft tissue injury or the discomfort. PreHab will provide a better way to deal with the soft tissue damage that can help you heal and get back to being active.

If you really want move better and improve your performance in your workouts as well as your life, you will need to learn about soft tissue and its role in movement.

Soft tissue consists of your muscles, tendons, fascia, skin and everything in between – virtually the entire body except for your bones and internal organs.

Most people know what a muscle is, but not many truly understand how it works and in many more cases, how to make a muscle work that you don't use often. Try to move just your pinkie toes, nothing else. Hard, right? Chances are that if you don't take yoga or train in bare feet, you've lost the capability to activate the muscles that controls your pinkie toe.

Muscles contract because there is a neurological charge sent to a motor neuron that elicits a chemical stimulus in the muscle fiber that will create a contraction. However, if this neurological charge does not visit that specific motor unit often, the charge may get lost somewhere along the way.

Have you ever forgotten how to get somewhere? Perhaps you were driving to visit an old friend and you couldn't remember if you took the first left or the second left after the light. That's more or less what happens in our bodies. Your neurological system forgets how to get that charge down to the muscles that control the pinkie toe and after a while it doesn't want to move.

Good thing though, if you keep trying, you can reconnect those neurological charges to the muscles that move the pinkie toe. It may take some time and effort though.

Muscles Contractions
Some people may understand the physiology of a muscle contraction and the sliding filament theory. For those who don't, try this on for size:

Extend your arm out straight and then slowly bend the elbow. Now, as you watch the biceps contract, imagine you could see the billions of microscopic arms pulling the protein structures of the muscles fibers closer to one another like how the legs of a caterpillar pull the body forward along a surface.

MOBILITY

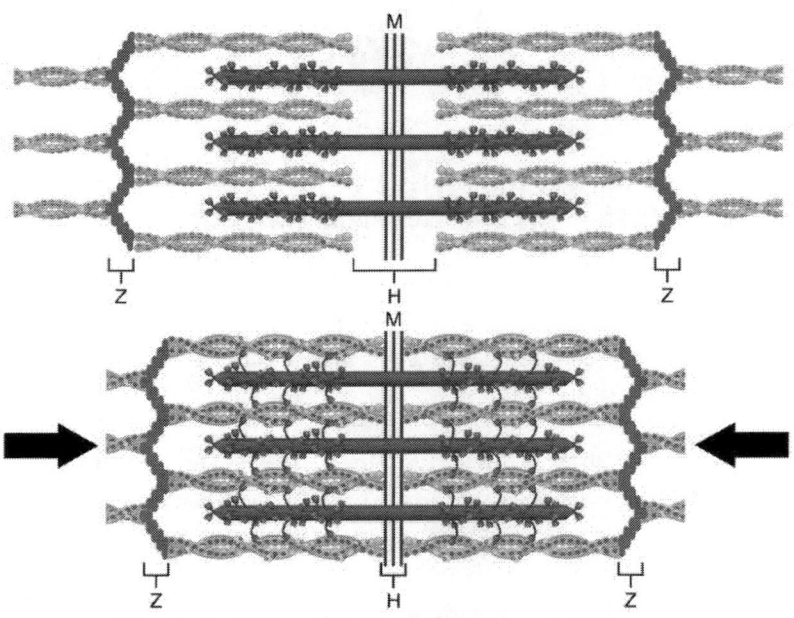

Model of the Sliding Filament Theory
Photo: OpenStax College

Inside your body, there are millions of muscles fibers with billions of microscopic myosin arms that attach, pull and shorten the muscle as a whole. It's that simple.

The complicated part is whenever a muscle fiber is shortening under a load that is too great for it, these little "arms" begin to break and micro tears form inside the muscle.

When these little arms break, or the myosin and actin experience micro tears, the body will induce a process called protein synthesis and rebuild the tears in as little as 24-48 hours.

What happens if I push too hard?
If you are working out at a high intensity, chances are you are creating micro tears galore. The real problem occurs when you don't relent and continue to push yourself too hard.

In addition to creating compensation in your movement patterns, your body will try to prevent further damage by laying down collagen fibers known as scar tissue to protect the injured areas as well as tighten or restructure the local fascia that surrounds the area.

Micro tears will either heal when you stop working out or be protected by formation of scar tissue and fascia realignment.

Fascia
Everything in your body is connected by fascia. This web-like substance is made of very strong and elastic proteins that surround and penetrate every part of your body. Fascia connects, supports and moves your body.

MOBILITY

Tom Myers, the author of *Anatomy Trains*, has enlightened the training world with an understanding of how fascia works in the body. Through dissection exercise, Myers has discovered that fascia exists in large patterns throughout the body that seemingly connect various joints together, such as the right shoulder and left hip.

Fascia can be malleable and flexible, which promotes mobility of the body. It also can get so sticky and tight that movement can become severely limited and restrictive.

The goal of PreHab is to develop and cultivate healthy fascia in order to keep your body moving well.

> *There are various ways to help maintain healthy fascia and are essential to any effective PreHab Training Program.*

Breathing and Stretching- fascia serves as a biomechanical structure, or more pointedly noted, a biotensegrity structure. This connective tissue will contract and establish enough tension in a line-of-action to support movement around the joints as well as just keeping the body together.

Stretching will help the fascia to restore its length and also help open up pathways for new nutrients to enter into the soft tissue and metabolic waste to exit. Yet, before you just nod and start stretching, you must realize that there is a certain way to stretch – with large exhalations.

Deep breathing, with a concentration on the exhalation, will help to activate the parasympathetic nervous system as opposed to the sympathetic nervous system, which is the fight-or-flight mechanism.
The parasympathetic nervous system induces healing and rejuvenation of the body. It ignites anabolic hormonal reactions that will help to repair damaged tissues. Meanwhile, the sympathetic nervous system is more like the gas pedal in your body. It will induce catabolic hormonal reactions while getting you going.

Each one of these nervous systems has their time and place of use: sympathetic gets you up and going while the parasympathetic helps you recover and heal. We just want to make sure to activate the parasympathetic nervous system when we are intending to make a healing difference with our soft tissue.

Hydration
Our soft tissue, especially the fascia, will lose its elastic capacity when it is not adequately hydrated. However, drinking water alone will not hydrate all of your soft tissue and fascia. Physiological restrictions, i.e. knots, adhesions, and tightness due to scar tissue, will negatively affect the body's hydration levels.

Think of a river. Now, imagine that river has a dam on it. What happens? The water can't get pass the dam and the rest of the riverbed dries up. Well, knots, adhesions, scar tissue and chronic tightness in the soft tissue can easily act as a dam and prevent your body from hydrating itself completely. That's why the practice of implementing various soft tissue therapy techniques will help you in the long run.

Common Soft Tissue Therapy Tools:
Rollers and The Myo-fascial Stick

Soft Tissue Therapy Techniques
There are many different ways that we can attend to the health and function of our soft tissue. Soft tissue therapy techniques also referred to as Self-Myo-fascial Release Techniques and SMR, can be applied with a variety of tools including our hands. Here are the most traditional soft tissue therapy tools and techniques:

Foam Rolling: for broad application over the entire body, rollers are very effective and practical. On top of that, rollers come with a variety of different textures that help to penetrate and smooth out adhesions and knots. In case you are wondering, some days I use a barbell as my roller.

Rolling is simple to do: Just lay your body over the roller and use your body weight as the source of pressure. Also, be sure to add variety into how you roll – add in joint manipulation (bending and extending) and oscillate (rotating or twist) to break up sticky areas.

Myo-fascial Stick: more or less a roller that fits into your hands, the Stick is a great tool to work deeper into the soft tissue at a specific area because it is more acute than an average roller. Plus, the Stick is easy to control in terms of pressure and direction,

MOBILITY

which is great when in the hands of a skilled user such as your personal trainer. However, all the pressure that is applied needs to be manually generated by the person holding the Stick.

Balls: from the Posture Ball to tennis balls to lacrosse balls, using these acute round surfaces can really help to break up scar tissue, adhesions and knots. On top of that, there is a lot of room to be creative in how you apply pressure or budget for your soft tissue therapy. I still use a baseball that I found at a park to this day and rolling your feet over a couple of golf balls may be the cheapest reflexology massage of your life.

Trigger Point Tools: there are more devices out there, some elaborate and some simple, that can help break up the stickiness and turn trigger points, areas of high neurological activity, into friends. These tools may look like little rolling pins, large hooks, dull blades, small boomerangs, or even large hooks like the TheraCane.

Hands, Fingers and Elbows: there is nothing to stop you from creatively applying pressure with your own body. In fact, you might just find ways to make your significant other feel good too.

Massage Tips: Start with the pads on your fingers tips and gently jostle the soft tissue to see if you can smooth it out. If some stickiness and tightness persists, try using your knuckles or elbows to press and slide through the knots and adhesions as well as pressing and twisting the soft tissue.

Just remember when using Soft Tissue Therapy tools, if you can help make the skin able to easily slide and see noticeable improvement in mobility, then your method works and makes a difference.

The importance of Soft Tissue Therapy-
Aaron Li, a Doctor of Physical Therapy in Los Angeles, warns against training or performing without intervening with soft tissue therapy. Li says that the body will begin to surround these micro-tears with scar tissue and form knots in the soft tissue if there is continuous pressure or force applied to the area. This will prohibit blood flow into the injured area, which would bring in nutrients to help proteins synthesis and the rebuilding process.

When knots appear in the soft tissue, the body begins to compensate in its movement patterns both geometrically and physiologically. We will begin to move differently and inefficiently. On top of that, fascia, this net of collagen and fibers that wrap around everything, will form new holding patterns around prolonged knots, adhesions and micro-tears in the soft tissue.

It's important to remove as many knots and adhesions as possible to help restore proper form and function to the soft tissue.

MOBILITY

MOBILITY

Biotensegrity

Why is soft tissue therapy even important? The simple answer is "biotensegrity." Illustrating this complex structural system in the body, on the other hand, is rather complicated. Regardless, your body is a biotensegrity structure.

What is tensegrity?
Did you ever build a blanket fort in your bedroom as a kid? I used to build a lot of blanket forts with my brother and one way that we would do it was to use a bed sheet as a wall or a ceiling. We would anchor one end of the sheet to the floor with a pillow and then drape it over a chair and anchor it on the other side with another pillow. This was a tensegrity structure!

If we didn't use the pillow to hold down the sheet at a distance to create an angled roof, the sheet would just fall down on us. Yet, the adequate tension to hold the sheet in place was provided by the pillow and we were free to play in our fort.

The tensegrity that exists in our bodies is much more complex and much more real than my pretend blanket forts. The following photo is an example of a tensegrity structure. In the photo, you will be able to see how the bands and strings suspend solid objects in space while helping to maintain the overall shape and design of the entire structure.

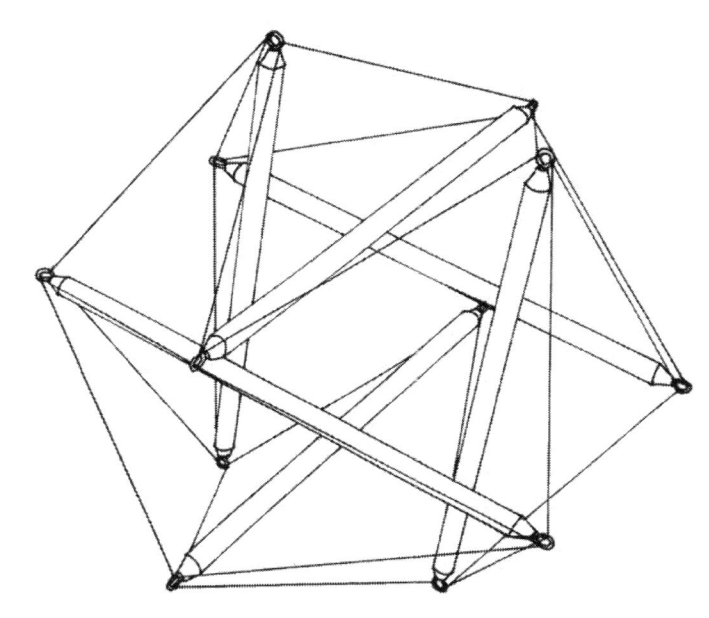

Tensegrity Model by Bob Burkhardt

> Our bodies are very much like this tensegrity structure; in as far as the bands and strings can represent muscles and soft tissue, while the solid objects can emulate our skeletal structure.

Soft Tissue and Biotensegrity:
Once you can start to view your body as a tensegrity structure and know that your soft tissue is responsible for keeping it together and creating movement, you will grow in ways that help you maintain your health, performance in your workouts, as well as in your life.

MOBILITY

Scar Tissue, Adhesions and Knots
The world of soft tissue, scar tissue, adhesions and knots are usually thought of as the unwanted bad boys or repulsive criminals, and in many ways this is spot on. Scar tissue, adhesions and knots can bind and restrict the soft tissue from sliding and expanding, which consequentially will restrict movement and cause the body to compensate in some way or another.

At the same time, scar tissue, adhesions and knots can inform us a lot about the tensegrity of our bodies, just as caught criminals can be flipped by a good detective and turned into informants.

What are Knots?
Myofascial Trigger Points, commonly referred to as a knot, are the result of a sarcomere(s) involuntary binding of the myofilaments, Actin and Myosin. Knots usually occur in Slow Twitch (Endurance and Postural) Muscles Fibers due to either: a drop in the cell's pH level towards acidity with a corresponding drop in oxygen levels, a flood of Calcium and Acetylcholine or a combination of both causes, which are usually caused by Repetitive Movement Patterns and overuse of the soft tissue.

How to eliminate knots?
The main way to eliminate or release a knot (Myofascial Trigger Point) is to replenish the blood flow to that specific sarcomere (Muscle Fiber) through either movement, such as stretching and general movements, or through the use of Soft Tissue Therapy techniques, including foam rolling, which will mechanically replenish the blood flow to the affected sarcomere and help release the knot.

What are adhesions?
The body is designed to protect itself on a cellular level by wrapping damaged areas with small collagen fibers and binding them (sticks like glue) to nearby cells for structural support. When this occurs, the buildup and accumulation of these individual cells into sticky groups becomes what we know as a adhesion.

How to break up adhesions-
Using applied pressure, either directly like in a massage or indirectly such as in breathing exercises, will help to break these adhesions and knots. Sometimes they don't go away easily, and sometimes they do. They are like snowflakes, as in every adhesion is different.

Hydration helps to limit knots
Photo by Jenny Downing

PreHab Exercise Book for Runners

MOBILITY

Foam Rolling
A Basic Blueprint for Soft Tissue Therapy

The first time I foam rolled, I moaned in agony because it was so painful. I had spent my entire life playing sports, beating myself up, and creating a load of adhesions in my soft tissue. That first foam-rolling session made me realize my body was like a street full of speed bumps. Yet, when I placed my head on my pillow that night, I fell asleep in a heartbeat.

The very next day, I went right back to foam rolling, and I've used it repeatedly ever since. In fact, there have been nights where I have fallen asleep on my foam roller in my living room as I was massaging out the stressful knots in my body from a very long day.

Foam Rolling is a form of **Soft Tissue Therapy** and it is commonly referred to as a *Self-Myofascial Release* technique (SMR). It uses applied pressure to help break up knots and adhesions in the soft tissue as a way to restore functionality.

The benefits of foam rolling are tremendous. For athletes, foam rolling can provide the edge that can help you move quicker, reach further and recover faster.

> *More specifically, foam rolling will help to:*
>
> **Improve Soft Tissue Flexibility and Responsiveness**
> **Increase Joint Range of Motion**
> **Optimize Movement Efficiency**
>
> You will be able to do more with less effort too!

As mentioned before, foam rolling is a Soft Tissue Therapy technique and one of the easiest ones to learn. Here is a basic blueprint to get started with foam rolling.

MOBILITY

Target Area: Neck
Place the back of your head on the foam roller as you lay on the ground. Gently press your neck into the roller as you slowly turn your head from side to side. Focus on applying pressure to the area where your skull connects to your neck. In this area of the neck there are a couple of small muscles that are responsible for moving your head. These muscles tend to hold a lot of tension, especially if you are habitually looking at a computer screen, driving a car, or just looking around the room. Furthermore, if you have a Forward Head alignment, where your ears vertically align in front of your hip sockets, the soft tissue in this target area will be experiencing an inappropriate amount of physiological stress on a daily basis.

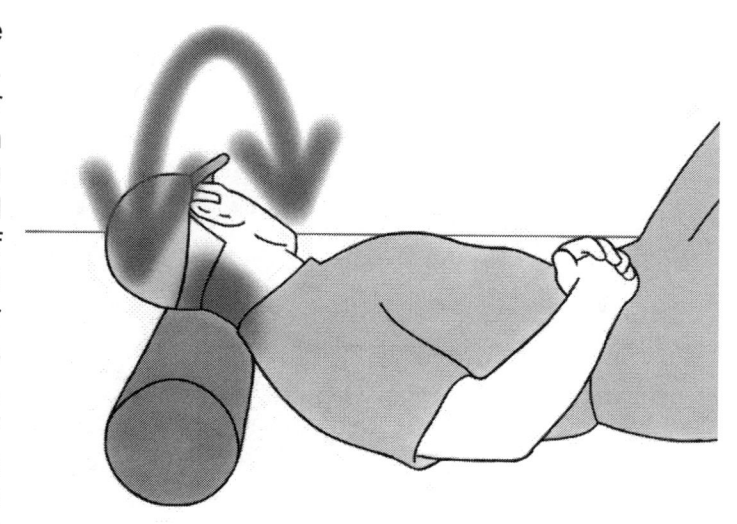

Pain in the Neck
This is an example of a Forward Head alignment. Notice how the ears line up vertically in front of the hip sockets and create an elongated curve of the neck. This alignment stresses the back of the neck. Gently foam rolling this area can help reduce the tension in soft tissue and can help relieve pain or discomfort.

Target Area: Trapezius & Shoulders
Place the tops of the shoulders on top of the foam roller where part of your Trapezius muscle is located, also known as your Trapz. Next, bridge your hips up in the air as far as you can to help create more pressure on the Trapz. Once you have created adequate pressure on the Trapz, start to slowly roll back and forth in small increments. Remember to breathe and relax.

While rolling back and forth, start to oscillate or rotate the torso in order to change the angle of pressure on the Trapz. You want to explore and search for tense areas or knots in your soft tissue. Once you find a sensitive area, practice gently rolling through and oscillating on top of that knot or adhesion until you can feel it release and smooth out.

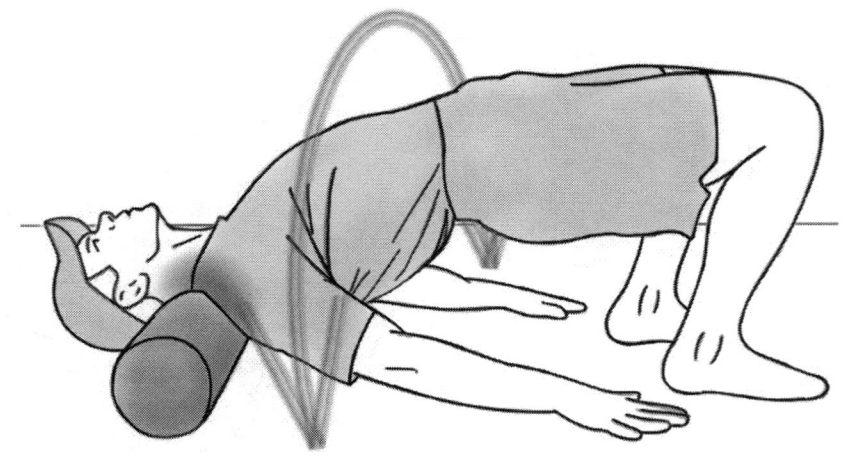

MOBILITY

Oscillate-
If you are unfamiliar with this technique or term, think of a room fan that turns from side to side. It's oscillating. This is the motion that you will want to apply to your soft tissue in addition to just rolling over the target area. Oscillating will help to break up knots and adhesions more by emulating a massage technique known as Cross Fibering.

Note-
The higher you lift your hips, the more weight you can direct down onto your Trapz, which will apply more pressure. This is a helpful cue because the Trapz get very tight and overworked in many people who do not have adequate shoulder stability. The Trapz can be especially exasperated in people who work at a desk, drive a lot and spend more time on developing their chest and shoulders with "Pushing" or "Pressing" exercises in the gym, such as a Bench Press or Military press.

The goal is to smooth out and lengthen the Trapezius muscle as much as possible.

Target Area: Back & Thoracic Spine
Interlace the hands behind your head and squeeze your elbows towards each other. This position will spread your shoulder blades and allow you to foam roll the rest of your Trapezius muscle as well as your Rhomboids, Latissimus (Lats) and Erector Spinae muscles, which collectively span over your rib cage, spine and shoulder blades.

Roll over the entire back of the rib cage and shoulders while oscillating or rotating in order to help break-up the tightness that may exist between the individual ribs and vertebras as well as around each shoulder blade. If you come across an area that is too painful or sensitive to roll over, gently roll the tissue in the surrounding vicinity instead as you breathe deeply and relax.

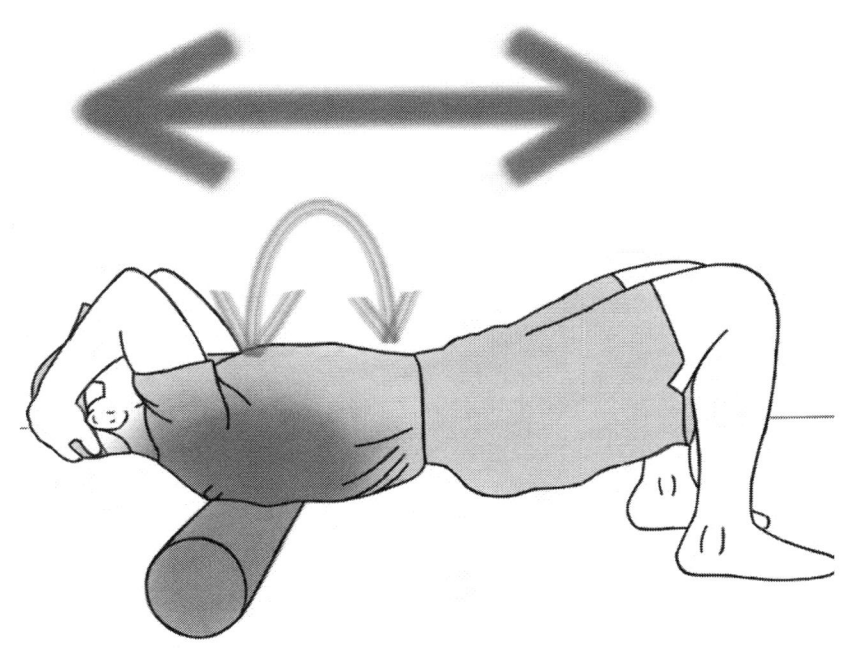

Essentially, you are treating all of the muscles that are responsible for your upper body's alignment and posture as well as mobility and stability of the shoulders and arms. On average, these muscles have a tendency of being under-developed, turned-off and sticky due to repetitive lifestyle factors of deskwork, driving and too much emphasis on "pushing exercises" in the gym, such as bench pressing and push-ups.

MOBILITY

Trigger Points-
Somewhere in your soft tissue, you come across specific spots of high neuromuscular activity, which may radiate pain and discomfort. These are Trigger Points and they become sensitive due to a high frequency of tension in the area because of repetitive movement. In other words, these trigger points are neuromuscular junctions that are over worked and physiologically over stressed.

Treating Trigger Points is extremely important to restore functionality back to the area in terms of mobility and strength. However, the damage to these areas may already be very severe. If this is the case, it is wise to apply soft tissue therapy techniques, such as foam rolling, to the tissue in the surrounding area in a combination with other restorative techniques, such as stretching, mindfulness, relaxation and sleep.

Target Area: Chest, Shoulders & Thoracic Spine
Place the foam roller under your heart and set your hips flat on the ground as you interlace your hands and support your head. Reach the top of your head back towards the floor as you keep the hips on the ground.

Use the foam roller as a fulcrum to bend your Thoracic Spine over and open up the front of your rib cage. Breathe deeply and release all tension from your body as you lengthen the spine.

Keep the back of your neck long and pull the belly button into the spine to engage the abdominals. This helps maintain the natural alignment of the Lumbar Spine- the vertebrae that connect your rib cage to your pelvis. It is common for people to bend or manipulate the Lumbar Spine as a way to compensate for a lack of mobility in the Thoracic Spine. Avoid this compensation by activating your abdominals.

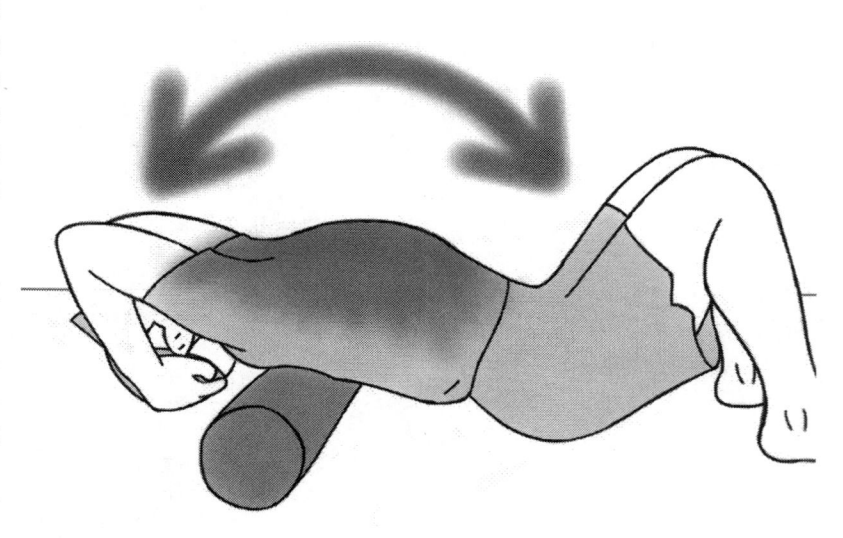

Gently oscillate or rotate the rib cage in this exercise and re-position the foam roller under another part of the Thoracic Spine. This will shift the fulcrum and change the angle of flexion in the spine and rib cage.

Also, use this exercise in combination with other soft tissue therapy techniques that you can apply to the chest and shoulders.

MOBILITY

Target Area: Hips
Sit and gently roll over the top of the foam roller. You want to cover the entire area of the hips, from the top of the pelvis to all the way under the "Sit Bones" or where your hamstrings and thighs connect to the pelvis.

When rolling over the hips, slowly turn the knees towards one side to rotate the angle of the hips on the roller. Incrementally changing the position of knees will help apply pressure to different areas of the hip's soft tissue, which increases the effectiveness of this technique.

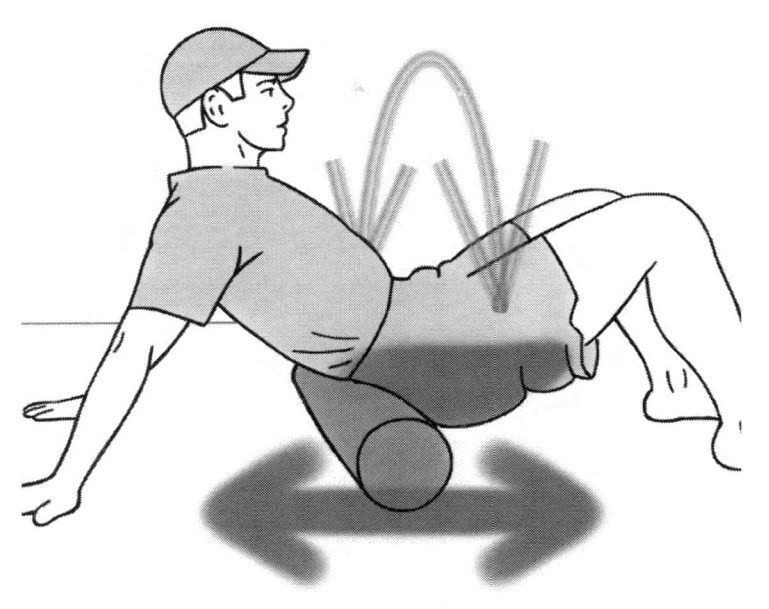

Prime Movers-
The hips, and more specifically the Gluteus Maximus, Gluteus Medius and Gluteus Minimus, are the true engines of the body. These muscles are primarily responsible for creating all locomotive forces, i.e. walking, running, jogging, squatting, jumping and so forth.

Applying soft tissue therapy techniques to the hips will only enhance your ability to perform any movement with more power and strength as well as help the body maintain proper alignment while moving.

Red Flag for Compensation-
People who have sedentary lifestyles are at a higher risk for having the Glutes become inhibited or "Turned-Off" because of the lack of frequency in use of these muscles. In other words, the axiom of "use it or lose it" is fittingly appropriate.

Foam rolling over the hips will help to create more neuromuscular responsiveness in the hips and help to activate the Glutes before exercising or competing.

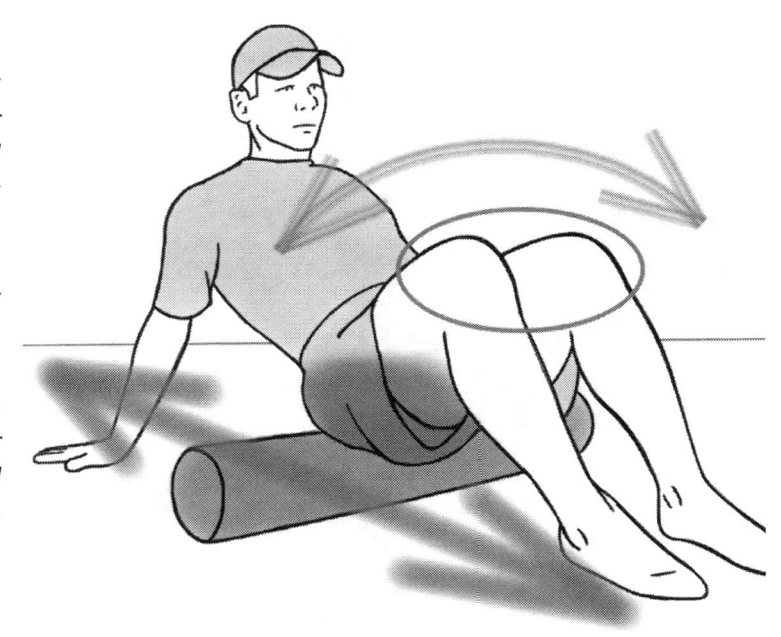

PreHab Exercise Book for Runners 105

MOBILITY

Target Area: Piriformis
Deep within the hip socket is the Piriformis muscle also known as the walking muscle. This is a small muscle that connects the Femur (thigh bone) to the Pelvis and initiates hip extension or the backwards stride phrase when you walk and run.

Sit on the roller and place one ankle on top of the opposite knee. Then rotate the hips slightly on an angle while rolling back and forth. Your body is angled towards the side that has the foot off of the ground. You should feel the roller pressing into the soft tissue deep within the hip, near the actual hip socket.

Target Area: Lateral Side of the Hips & Legs
Lie on top of the foam roller and turn your hips 90 degrees onto their sides. Slowly roll down the side of your body from your hips down to your knees while gently oscillating or rotating along the way.

You will be applying pressure to the Vastus Lateralis, a muscle on the outside of your thighs, as well as to the Iliotibial Band, commonly referred to as your IT Band. Both of these soft tissue structures will get over-worked and stressed due to instability and the lack of mobility in the corresponding hip and ankle. Therefore, it's important to include more exercises in your PreHab routines for Hip and Ankle stability and mobility if this area of your body is very sensitive or experiences discomfort while foam rolling.

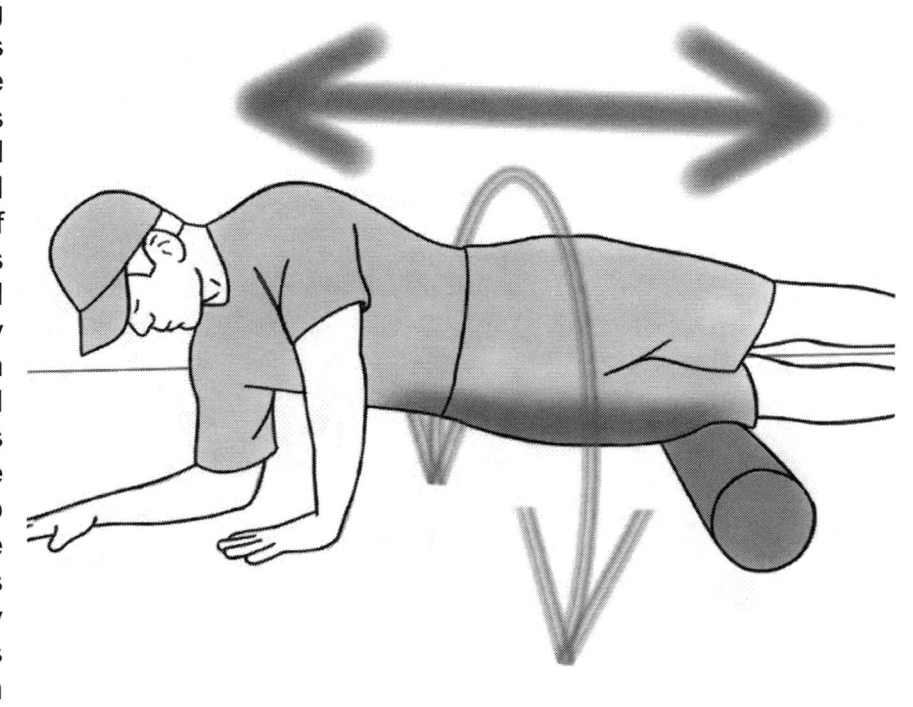

MOBILITY

Target Area: Quadriceps and Hip Flexors
Lie on top of the foam roller with your hips facing the floor. Slowly roll over the front of your thighs and the hips while gently oscillating or rotating along the way.

You will be foam rolling your Quadriceps and Hip Flexor muscles, which both tend to be tight and inflamed in people with sedentary lifestyles as well as for those who wear high heels. The Quads and the Hip Flexors will commonly be overworked and stressed as they attempt to compensate for the lack of Glute activation in many activities including running and lunging.

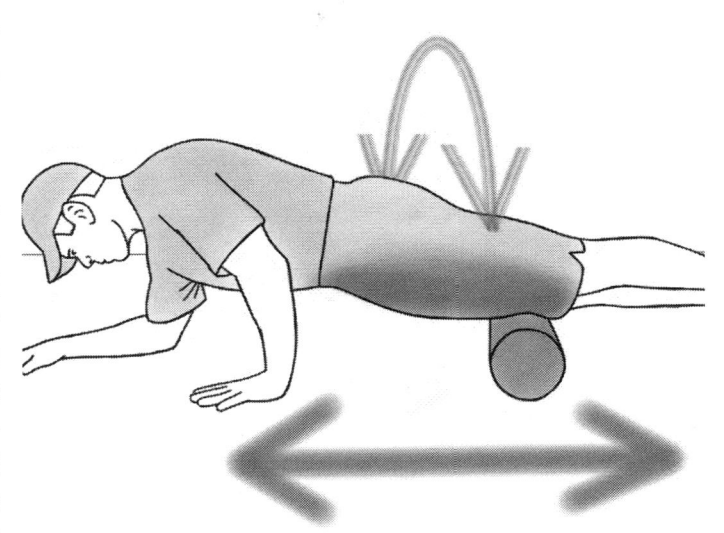

> *Re-Train Compensation Strategies*
> Foam rolling the Quadriceps and Hip Flexors will help to lengthen these tissues and restore proper range of motion. The improved mobility of the hips will help you to activate the Glutes and re-train the way that you run, squat and lunge.
>
> If you experience sensitivity or discomfort in this area while foam rolling, include other mobility techniques, such as the Couch Stretch or Kneeling Hip Flexor Stretch with a combination of activation exercises for the Glutes.

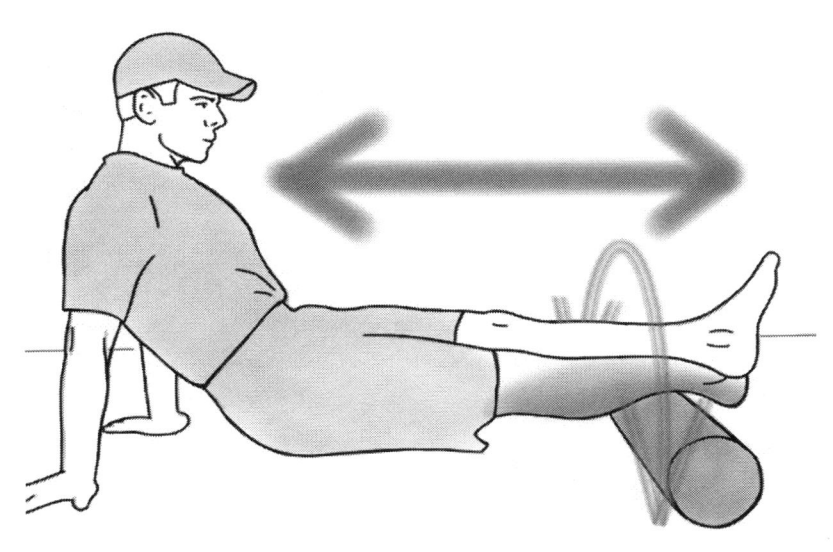

Target Area: Calves
Place one leg on top of the foam roller just behind the knee. Start to roll down towards the ankle as you gently oscillate or rotate your legs.

Use your arms to lift your hips off the ground to create more pressure on the calves while rolling. You can also use the top leg to squeeze the bottom calf into the roller if you keep your hips on the floor.

MOBILITY

Articulate the Ankle
You can help to break up more of the knots, adhesions and scar tissue in your calves by slowly pointing and flexing the foot as you foam roll. The simple articulation of the ankle joint will combine with the applied pressure of foam rolling to help release more tightness or stickiness in the calf.

Target Area: Lats & Shoulders
Lay an arm over the foam roller and slowly roll the sides of body where your Latissimus muscles are located. Oscillate or rotate the rib cage as you roll up into your armpit and over the backs of your shoulders.

There are a couple of muscles, the Teres Major and Teres Minor, that connect your arm to your shoulder blade. As part of a compensation strategy, these muscles will become over-worked and stressed in people who do not have adequate shoulder and scapula stability.

It is very beneficial to foam roll this area in your PreHab routine and combine this work with a series of shoulder and scapula stability exercises, in particular Scapula Retraction and Scapula Depression.

Target Area: Arms
Lay your arm over top of the foam roller and gently oscillate or rotate the arm as you roll back and forth. You can also articulate the elbow joint by bending and extending your arm to help create more release within the soft tissue of the arm.
It's important to foam roll the arms as well as the rest of the body because the soft tissue will experience the formation of knots and adhesions in it, especially for those who work out with weights or play throwing sports.

MOBILITY

> **Navigating through Soft Tissue Therapy**
> The purpose of foam rolling, as well as all soft tissue therapy techniques, is to prepare the body to move by breaking up knots and adhesions that cause restrictions in our movement. These techniques will help to restore the full range of motion in joints, increase flexibility and ultimately improve overall mobility. Foam rolling offers a way to treat our soft tissue in broad strokes while also including some fine details.

How to Approach Foam Rolling

Since it's possible to address the entire body in as little as 10 minutes, foam rolling is a great place to start. It's also a form of therapy that can help you learn more about your soft tissue and movement tendencies. Here's how to maximize the effect of foam rolling:

- Foam Roll the entire body with as much fluidity and speed as possible.
- Combine other mobility techniques to the areas in which you experience any discomfort or sensitivity.
- For example, include passive stretching and mindful relaxation for the shoulders and neck if you experience pain or tension in these areas.
- Coordinate corresponding Activation and Stability exercises for your trouble areas.
- For example, combine exercises to activate the glutes when experiencing tightness and sensitivity in the Quads and Hip Flexors.

> **Feel the Difference.**
> It's important that you actually feel a difference after you have foam rolled as a way of knowing that you are improving the functionality of your soft tissue. If you do not notice an improvement in how you move and how you feel, then it is best to switch to a different kind of technique to help prepare you to move.
>
> *If you are new to soft tissue therapy, foam rolling is the perfect place to start! And don't worry, the more that you practice, the better you will get at foam rolling and the more results you will see in how you train and exercise!*

MOBILITY

MOBILITY

Forward Head
Neck Mobility and Alignment

Is the positioning of your head, neck and shoulders important to running? A lot of people might be quick to assume that the head, neck, and shoulders are only marginally involved when you're running. But that's just not the case. The position of your head, neck and shoulders has a great influence on how you run and how you move in general.

The Top Down Approach
I remember watching this one street performer in New York's Central Park. Perhaps you've seen him too – he's the guy who balances a slew of chairs on top of one another until they look like a tree blossoming and it's all possible because of geometric alignment. And in some ways, the design of our bodies looks kind of like this.

Our bodies have a unique design to it that is unlike all other creatures. We stand on two feet, also known as bipedal. And we expend less energy than every other creature that is positioned on four feet or more. This biomechanical designed was advantageous to the survival of our species. And it's something author Chris McDougal spends a fair amount of time talking about in his book, *Born to Run: A Hidden Tribe, Superathletes, and the Greatest Race the World Has Never Seen*. In the book, he discusses the unique ability of early humans to hunt by outrunning their prey based on our bipedal alignment. He attests that four-legged animals would over heat as they fled from humans and eventually succumb to capture, as we were able to run further and expend less energy.

> ***The alignment of our head is important to the mechanics of running.***

The Forward Head
Unfortunately for our biomechanics, we live in a world where we sit often and constantly respond to an environment overloaded with stimulation. This phenomenon is the recipe for the "Forward Head" as our eyes and ears race to make sense of the digital or real stimulates and our hips and spine slowly fall asleep in a chair. Altogether, this leads to compensation patterns in our movement, more precisely, our head and neck begin to protract forward beyond their natural alignment and the rest of the body pays the price.

MOBILITY

The Biomechanical Cost

There is a simple ratio that summarizes the Biomechanical Cost of a Forward Head. It is:

Add 12lbs to the head for each inch that it protracts forward.

Over time, those pounds can really add up and account for a lot of physiological energy wasted on just holding up your head alone. Worst yet, the Biomechanical Cost of a Forward Head doesn't stop there. It will affect your running mechanics immensely too. In fact, you lose speed, longevity and distance with a Forward Head alignment because your body cannot properly align into a forward lean position, which is the foundation of bipedal running.

The Forward Head alignment will create too much of an angular displacement between the head and thoracic spine. This forces the pelvis and lumbar spine as well as the feet and knees to compensate in various ways. And it can overload the quads, and lead to heel striking, curling of the spine, poor hip movement and more.

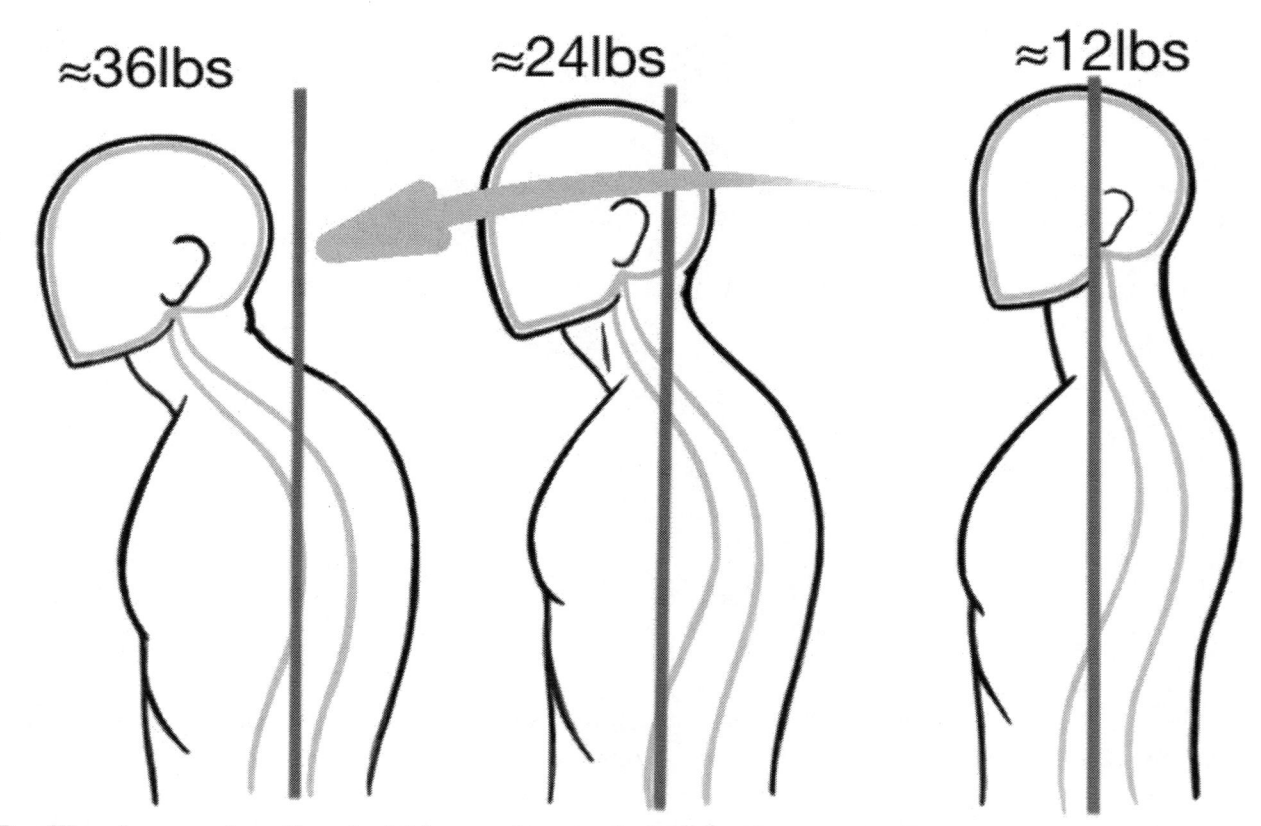

Profile view and estimated biomechanical disadvantage in terms of weight of the Forward Head Posture.

MOBILITY

Top Down Rx
Fortunately, you can remodel the Forward Head alignment, if you have it, with a series of soft tissue therapy techniques and mobility exercises. This remodeling process will take some time, in the ranger of 7-18 months, but it will be worth it for sure!

A journey of a thousand miles starts with a single step.
-Loa Tzu

First Step: Soft Tissue Therapy
Grab a lacrosse ball (advanced), tennis ball (intermediate) or use your fingers (beginner) to dig into your soft tissue and break up the tightness as well as the knots and adhesions that are looming in there somewhere.

Roll the ball in different patterned ways, such as horizontal, vertical, circling and even gently twisting or just press down on triggers until they release.

**The ultimate goal is to restore 'softness' to these tissues.
So, wherever you feel hardness or tightness, work to loosen up those tissues until they are soft once again.**

Here are several illustrations that demonstrate strategies to address the quality of your soft tissue in the neck and trapezius region.

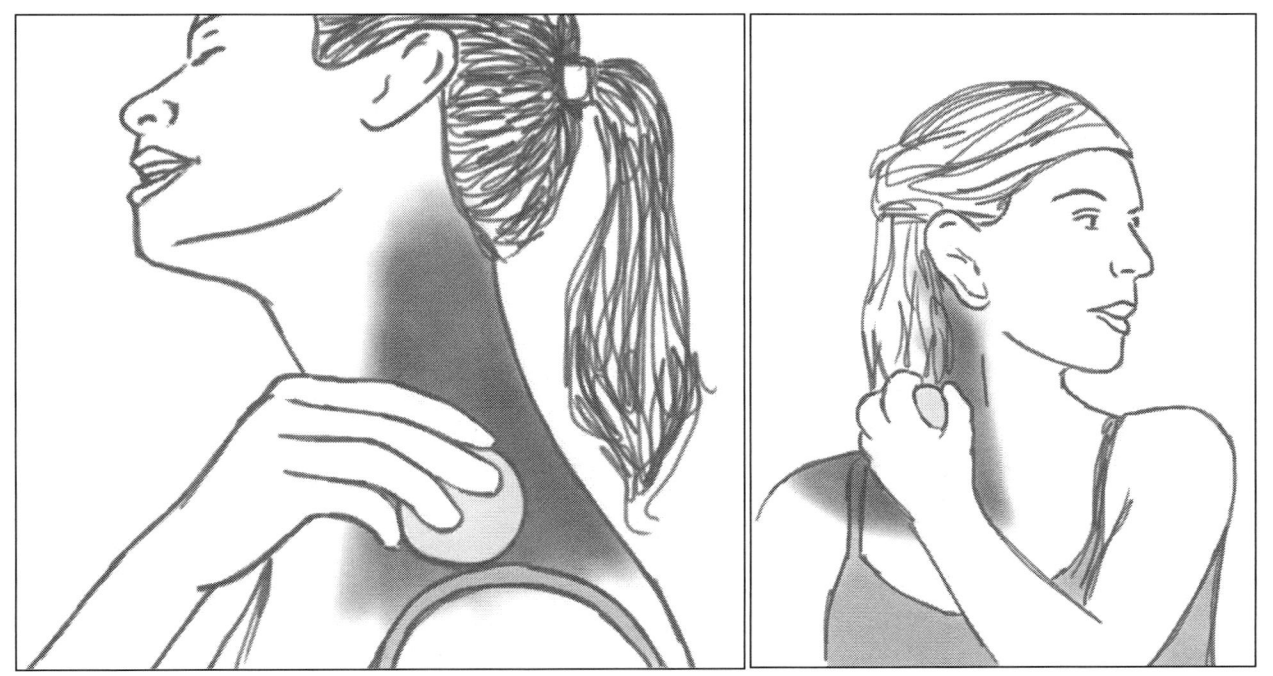

Use a Ball to Roll Out the Trapezius and Scalenes (Neck Muscles)

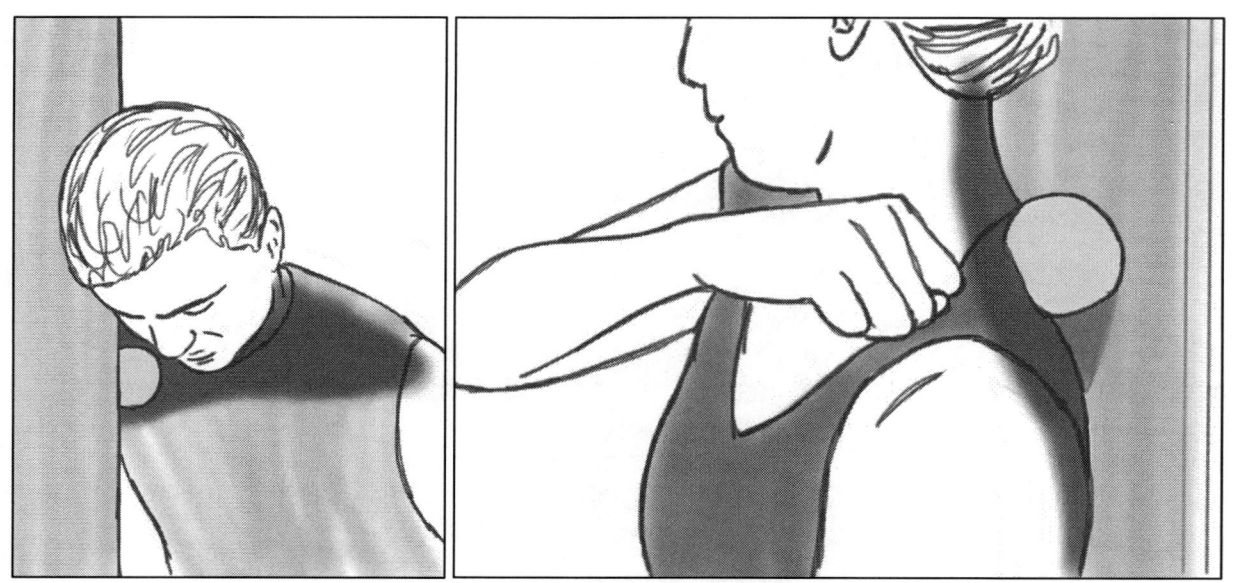

MOBILITY

Use a ball up against a wall to help roll out the Neck and Shoulder Muscles.

You can also use the Thera Cane or a Myofascial Stick shown below.

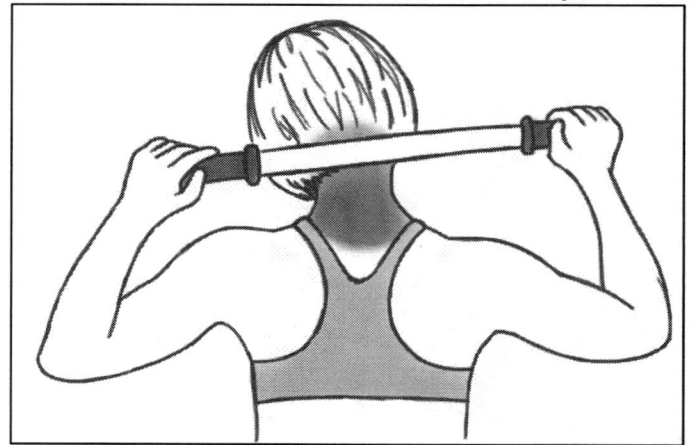

Myofascial Stick

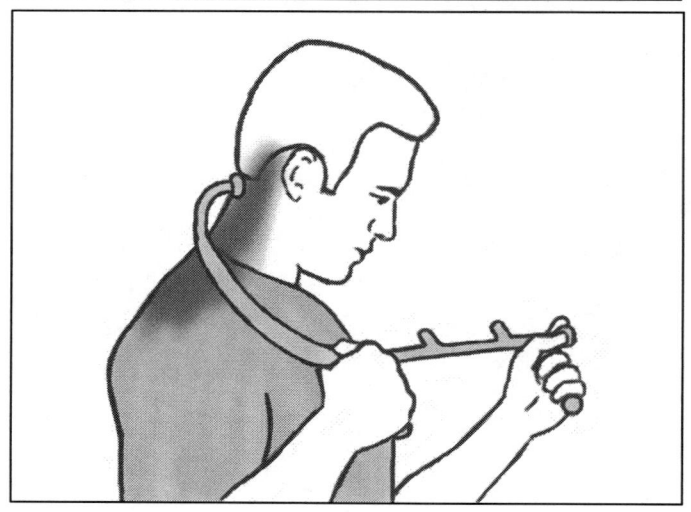

The Thera-Cane

MOBILITY

Next Step: Mobility
Once you have loosened the soft tissue and prepped your neck for movement, restore proper range of motion with these mobility exercises. Employ any stretching technique you prefer:

Static Stretch – Dynamic Movement – Active Flexibility – PNF Stretching

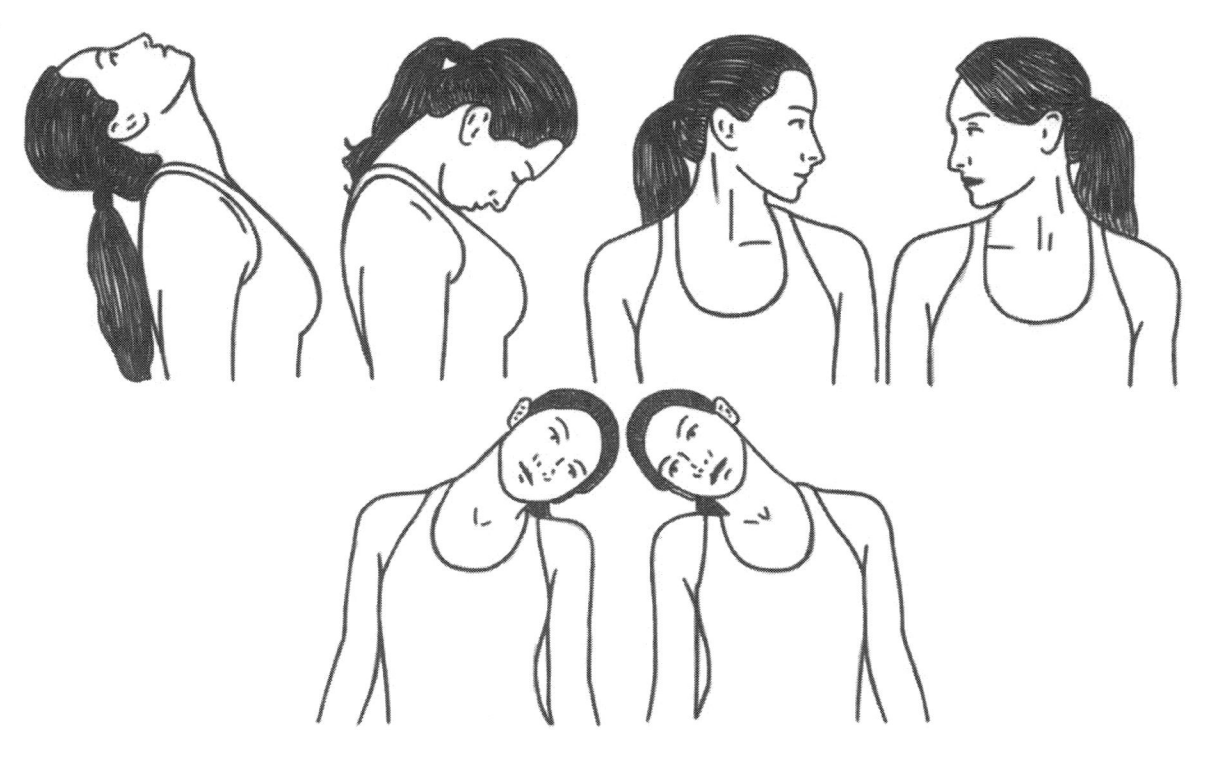

Range of Motion for the Neck

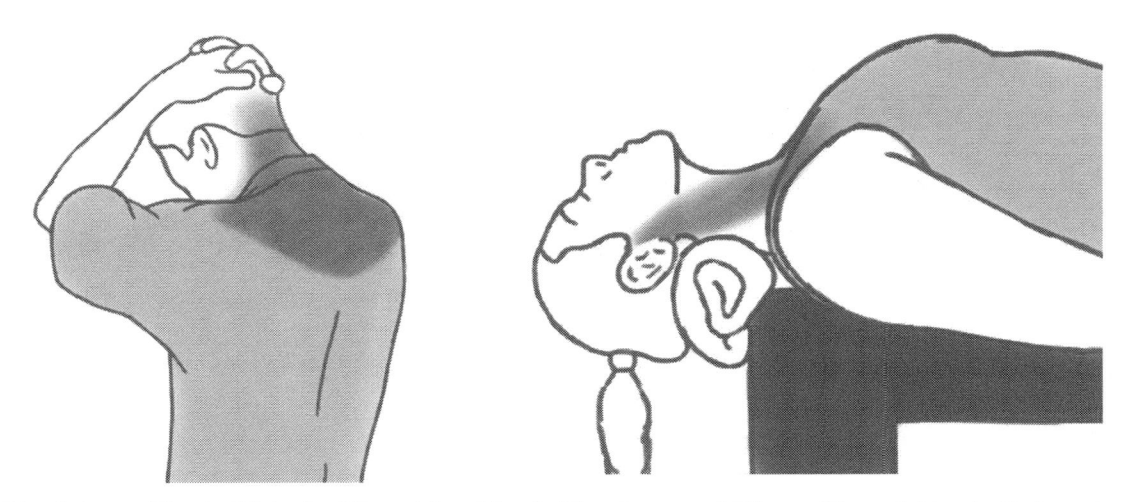

Static Stretches: Tuck Chin to Chest for Neck Flexion and Place Towel Neck Extension

PreHab Exercise Book for Runners

MOBILITY

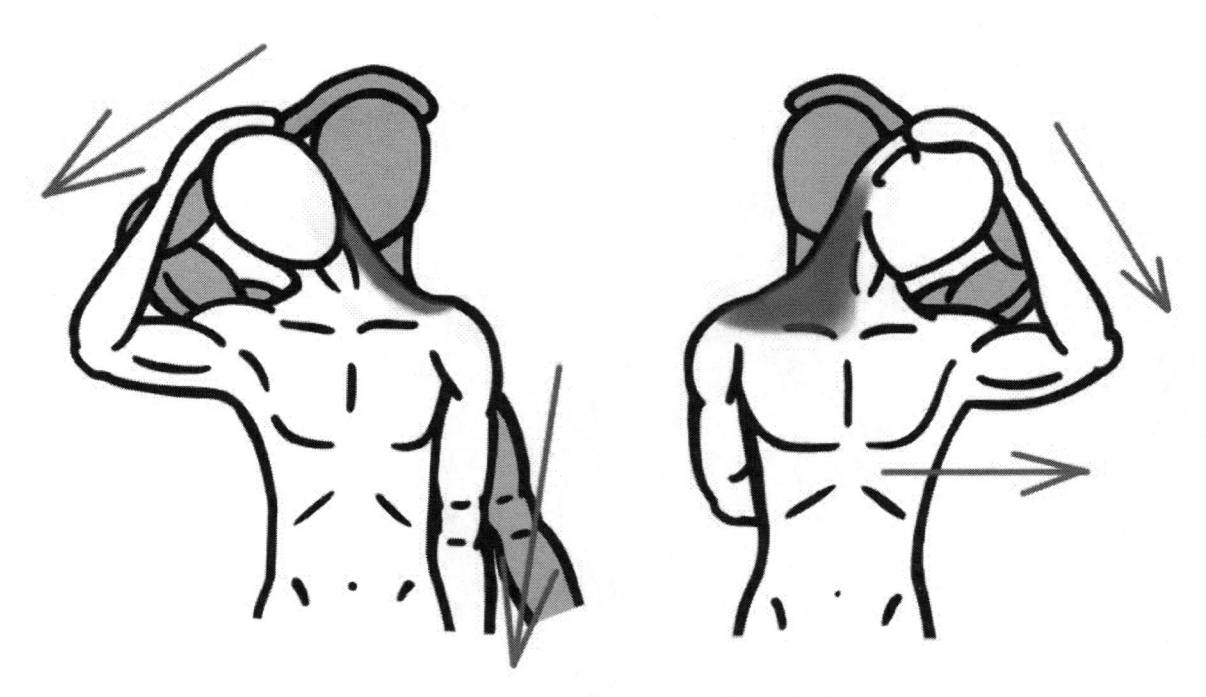

Static or PNF Stretches: Lateral Neck Flexion and Rotated Neck Flexion

Active Stretch: Head Circles

MOBILITY

Last Step: Stabilizing the Neck
Now that your soft tissue is loosened up and stretched out, it will be easier to realign your head and neck into proper positioning. Here are two simple exercise techniques:

Tucking the Chin
Place your fingers on your chin as you gaze at the horizon. Next, use your fingers and press your chin back in towards your throat as if you are intentionally giving yourself a double chin.

It is a common mistake to drop the head forward when you push your chin in towards your throat. Keep your eyes on the horizon and lengthen the back of the neck as you grow tall through the spine.

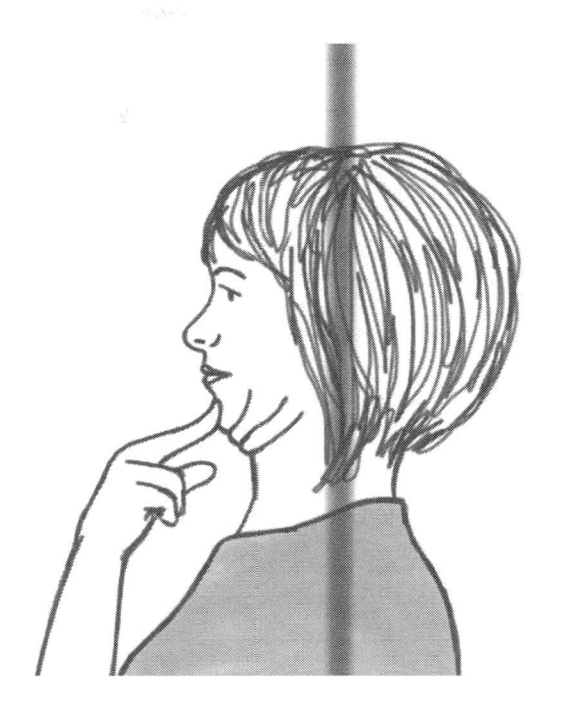

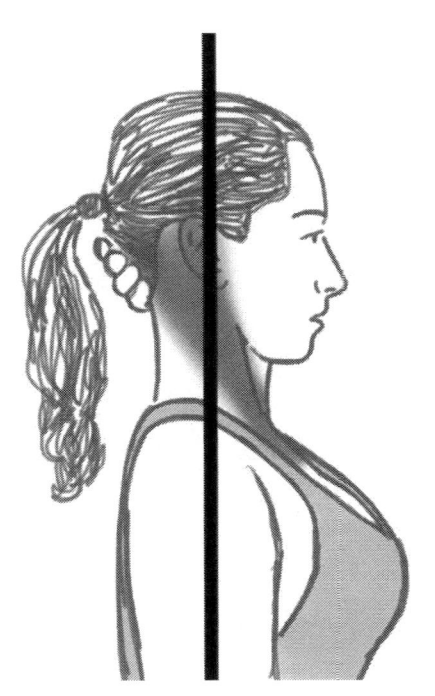

Hand on Back of the Head
Place a hand on the back of your head so it covers the rear bulge of your skull. Next, lift the bulge of the skull up toward the sky to lengthen the back of the neck as you tuck your chin in towards your throat.

Again, don't let your head dip forward. Keep your eyes on the horizon and stay tall through your spine.

PreHab Exercise Book for Runners

MOBILITY

Modern Day Alignment
A portrait on how our lifestyle and cultural traditions are shaping our bodies.

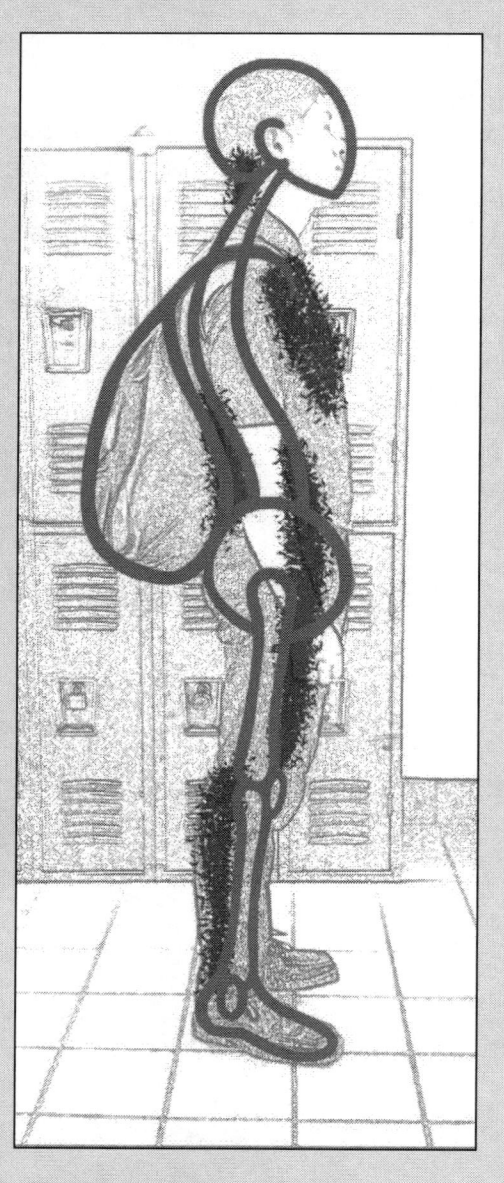

The Alignment of a Modern Student

These illustrations demonstrate the compensation patterns that many students endure due to the habitual lifestyle patterns of sitting and carrying backpacks. The alignment of the spine, head and pelvis, including Forward Head, is outlined in the second illustration along with the muscle groups that hold this position and thus become tight and restricted.

MOBILITY

Thoracic Spine Mobility

The thoracic spine, also referred to as the T-Spine, is the mobile joint complex that tends to be very tight and restricted in many people. It's especially prevalent for those who were accustomed to wearing heavy backpacks full of books all throughout school. Now, I am not saying that books are a bad thing. I am saying that it's time to take up a daily practice of mobilizing your thoracic spine in order to move well and feel good.

What is the Thoracic Spine?
The T-Spine covers all of the vertebrae that connect with the rib cage. In fact, the rib cage is specifically designed with individual ribs to move in correspondence with the thoracic spine, which is important to remember because when you work to improve the mobility of the T-spine you will need to address the soft tissue that connects the ribs together.

The rib cage is made to move like an accordion. The thoracic spine is the thread that connects the ribs and orchestrates the global movement of the upper body.

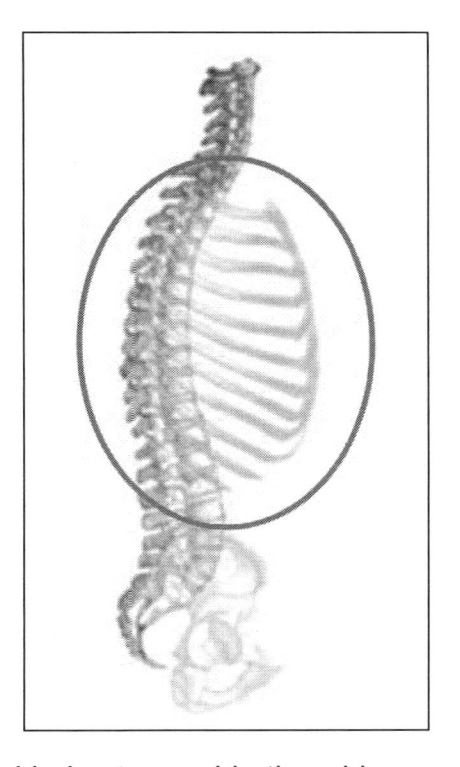

The thoracic spine is the mobile platform for the shoulders and helps to provide the wide range of motion of the arms and hands. Without the mobility of the thoracic spine, the arms' range of motion would be cut in half or more. Therefore, developing the mobility of the T-spine will help to improve all that you do with your arms directly.

Top Down Approach Continued
It may be obvious how the thoracic spine affects the mobility of the arms, but it also influences how the rest of the body also moves. Any tightness or limitations in the thoracic spine will restrict the flow of kinetic energy through the body. This can also inappropriately shift your body's center of gravity in specific movement patterns. The ultimate result is changes in how you move and creates patterns of compensation, such as a shortened hip extension or an overworked calf muscle while running.

What to do?
The first step in restoring mobility to the thoracic spine is applying soft tissue therapy techniques to the entire body, especially the torso and arm areas. Feel up the tissues for any restrictions, which means addressing all adhesions, knots and tightness that exist in that area.

If you sit, work on a computer, or habitually carry a heavy backpack in school or in the armed forces, you most likely have tightness along your thoracic spine.

MOBILITY

Step One: Foam Roll
Foam rolling will help to break up some tightness in the thoracic spine. More importantly, it helps to invigorate the neuromuscular connections and restore circulation to this area. So, starting with foam rolling is ideal.

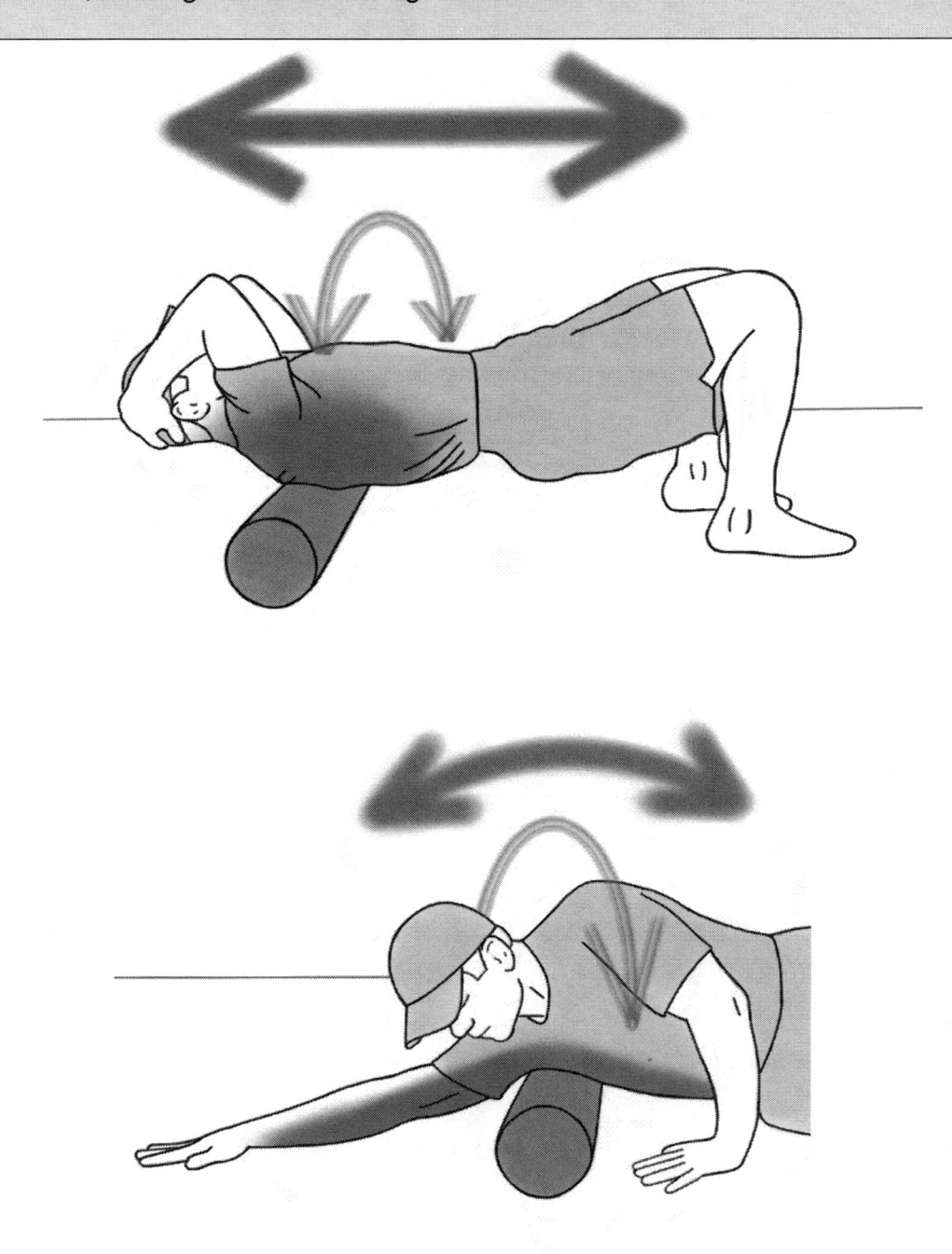

Oscillate (Rotate) as you Foam Roll for better results and target all the soft tissue that covers the rib cage and connects through the shoulders.

MOBILITY

Step Two: Balling and Massage
After rolling, you want to start exploring all of your tissue for any tight areas. Then work out those knots and adhesions with either a lacrosse ball, tennis ball or your fingers.

Find a knot or some stiffness in your soft tissue and start to apply pressure from a multitude of directions until you can feel the area begin to release and to smooth out.

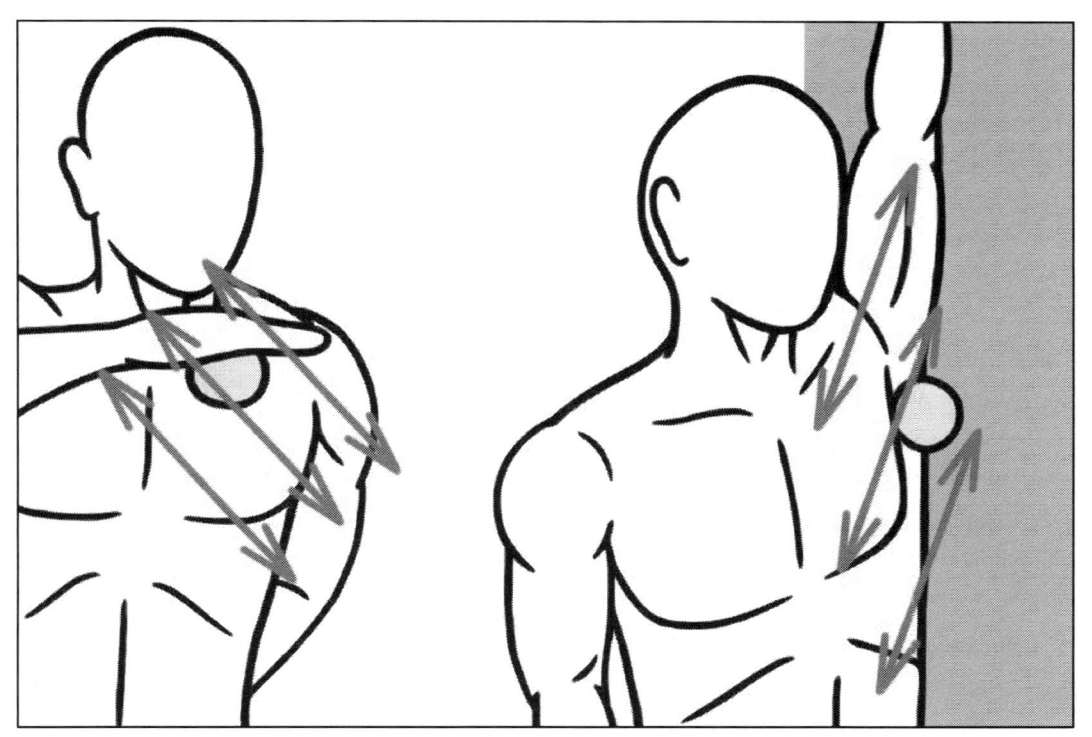

Roll a ball over your chest, shoulders and lats in several directions. Use a wall or the floor to provide more support too.

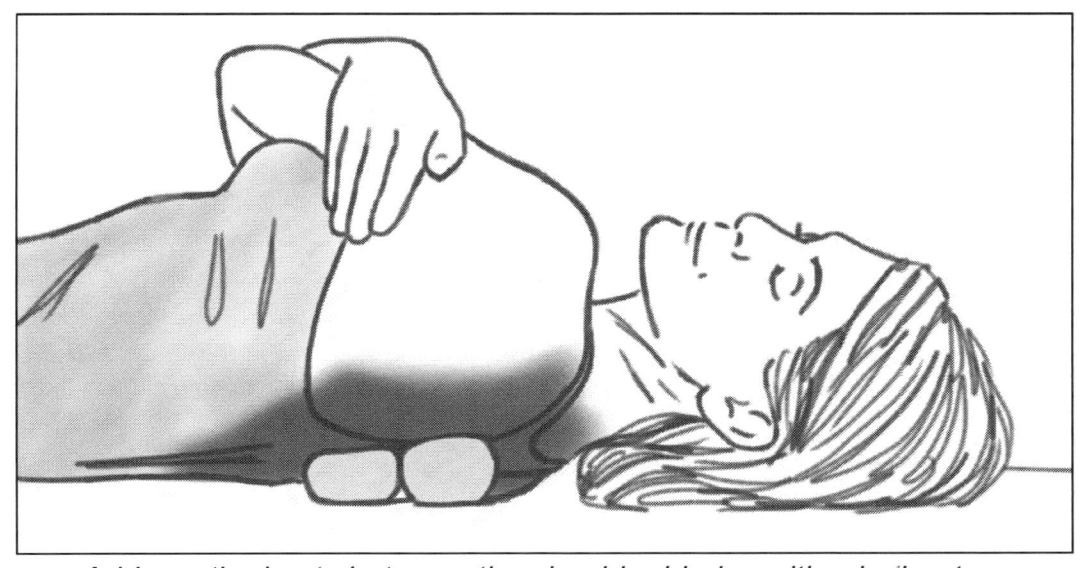

Address the knots between the shoulder blades with a ball or two.

MOBILITY

Rolling the Erector Spinae with a 'Peanut'
Tape two balls together into a Peanut shape that you can roll over on the floor or against a wall.

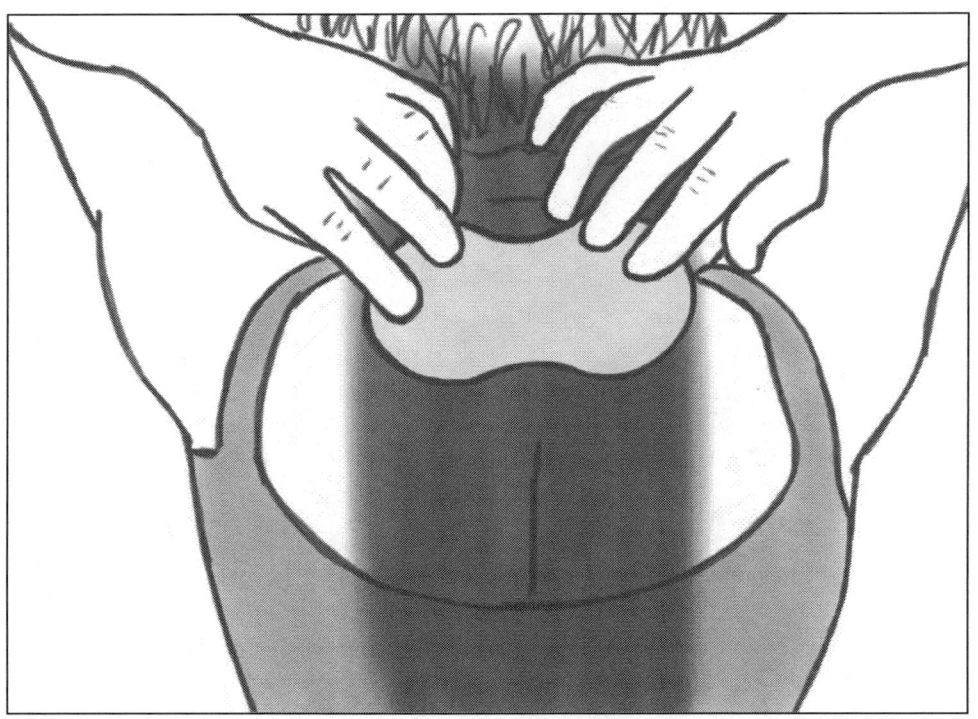

Place the 'Peanut' across the Spine.

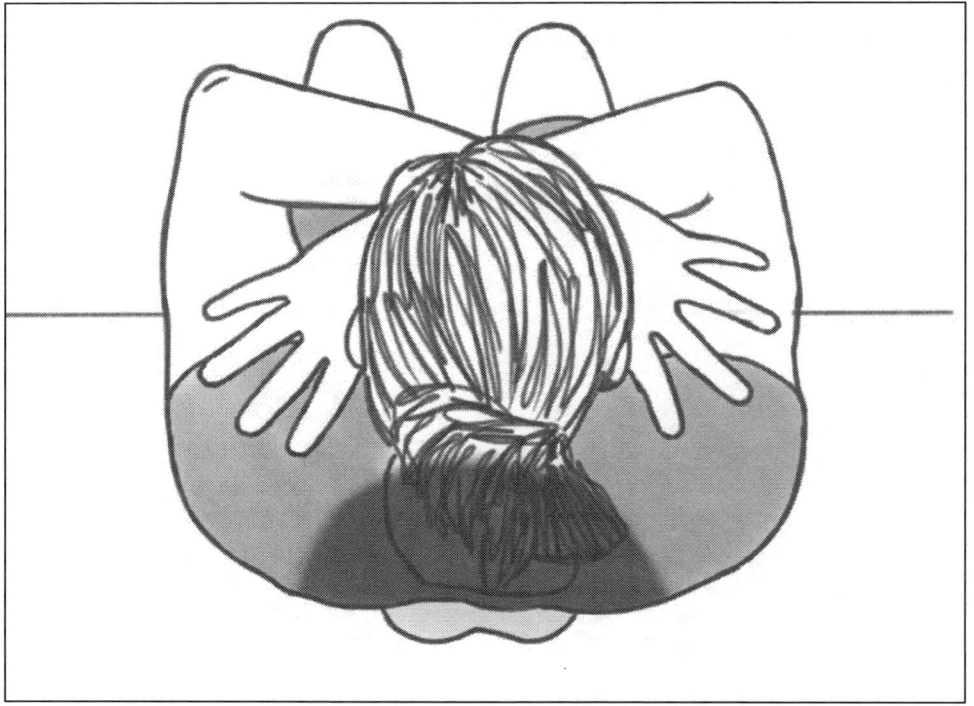

Slowly roll up and down the entire Spine on the 'Peanut.'

MOBILITY

Roll with No Pain
Don't cause yourself too much pain, as that will only excite your sympathetic nervous system and create more tension in your soft tissue. Gently work through the tissue and massage the area until you can feel a difference.

Again, it's important to make a practice of soft tissue therapy because knots and adhesions will continue to redevelop over time.

Here are some illustrations of how to apply soft tissue therapy to the thoracic spine area using a lacrosse ball or tennis ball. Feel free to just substitute your fingers for the ball if you do not have a ball handy.

Step Three: Mobility Exercises
After applying a healthy dose of soft tissue therapy, you want to restore length to the tissue and a full range of motion to the entire thoracic area. Here is a series of mobility exercises to start with, and please feel free to improvise.

Thoracic Expansion on Roller
This exercise will use either: a foam roller, yoga block, or a firm pillow to help mobilize the thoracic spine.

Place the foam roller directly behind the heart as you lay over it on your back. Make sure that your hips are firmly planted on the ground and interlace your hands together behind your head.

Now, extend backwards over the roller while you keep the hips on the ground. Reach the top of the head down towards the floor and pull the chin in towards your throat in order to keep the neck in neutral alignment. Feel the front of your rib cage and your chest expanding as your squeeze your elbows towards one another. At the same time, pull your shoulder blades away from one another on your back. Pull the belly button in towards the spine to engage the abdominals and anchor the lower ribs. Focus on several rounds of deep exhales while stretching.

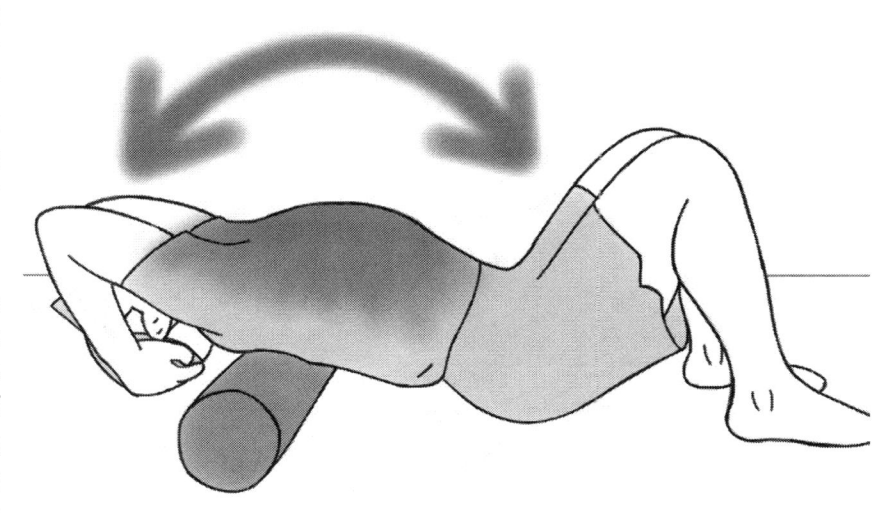

MOBILITY

STANDING ROTATION
This is another mobility exercise that addresses the rotational aspect of the thoracic spine. The only difference in this exercise compared with the Rotated Reach in Tabletop, is that the torso produces all the rotational movement and there is no assistance from the arm that is bracing on the floor.

POSITION: Stand with the feet in a comfortable, wide stance and place one palm directly on top of the opposite shoulder joint while threading the other arm around the back of the rib cage.

ACTION: Pull the covered shoulder backwards and rotate the entire body as much as possible while continuing to thread the other hand deeper around the rib cage. Lengthen through the spine and attempt to look directly behind the body. Rotate several times in both directions.

Modes of Application:
- Hold this position for approximately 30 seconds as you mentally imagine your upper torso rotating more and focus on deep exhalations.
- Smoothly perform several reps of this movement as you breathe deeply and relax.
- Hold the end position and perform several PNF Contract/Relax sequences by gently trying to counter-rotate or unwind the spine on the Contract phase before releasing more on the Relax phase.

STANDING LATERAL FLEXION
This mobility exercise addresses the lateral portion of your thoracic spine, including your Latissimus muscles and shoulders. Unfortunately, many runners will overlook this movement pattern. Yet, any tightness in this entire area can create restrictions and compensation in how you run. Don't overlook this movement pattern!

POSITION: Stand with the feet in a comfortable, wide stance and straight knees.

MOBILITY

ACTION: Laterally fold the torso to the side and reach the top arm overhead towards the horizon as the bottom arm extends towards the opposite horizon. Lengthen through the spine and attempt to position the head parallel to the ground if possible. Breathe deeply and relax. Repeat several times in both directions.

Modes of Application:
- *Hold this position for approximately 30 seconds as you mentally imagine your spine lengthening and focus on deep exhalations.*
- *Smoothly perform several reps of this movement as you breathe deeply and relax.*
- *Hold the end position and perform several PNF Contract/Hold sequences by reaching each set of fingers further towards the horizon on the Contract phase and relaxing on the Hold phase.*

FORWARD BEND

POSITION: Stand with the feet in a comfortable, wide stance with straight knees.

ACTION: Fold the torso forwards and reach both arms through the legs towards the horizon. Keep the knees fully extended and lengthen through the spine by pulling the top of the head away from the tailbone. Breathe deeply and relax. Repeat several times.

Modes of Application:
- *Hold this position for approximately 30 seconds as you mentally imagine your spine lengthening and focus on deep exhalations.*
- *Smoothly perform several reps of this movement as you breathe deeply and relax.*
- *Hold the end position and perform several PNF Contract/Hold sequences by reaching each set of fingers further towards the horizon on the Contract phase and relaxing on the Hold phase.*

SIDE-LYING CHEST EXPANSION

This exercise will help mobilize your thoracic spine in a horizontal direction and help stretch out the infamously tight chest muscles that many people have.

POSITION: Lie on your side with your hips and shoulders stacked vertically over one another. Reach the top leg out in front as far as possible to help anchor the hips in a 90-degree angle to the floor. Then reach the top arm out in front as well.

MOBILITY

ACTION: Reach the top arm up towards the sky and over backwards towards the floor behind you while you keep your hips completely still. Roll the shoulders backwards and attempt to touch the floor with the upper shoulder blade as you reach the hand towards the horizon. Pull the belly button in towards your spine to engage the abdominals and anchor the lower ribs as much as possible. Continue to hold the position as you deeply exhale several times.

You can also perform the PNF (proprioceptive neuromuscular facilitation) technique of Contract/Relax in this stretch to help create more mobility. Simply, extend the arm backwards and perform several rounds of light contractions in your chest and shoulder followed by a few seconds of deep relaxation.

RIB CAGE PEEL
This mobility technique can help lengthen the soft tissue that connects the ribs together and restore more range of motion to the entire upper body movement system.

POSITION: Place your arm up against a wall and turn your hips in order to create a rotation through your torso.

ACTION: Start to cycle through several deep exhalations as you use your other hand to literally peel your ribs away from the wall. Remember to be gentle with the peel in this exercise. If you are too forceful in this manual manipulation technique, your soft tissue will reflexively tighten. Relax as you peel and focus on deep exhalations.

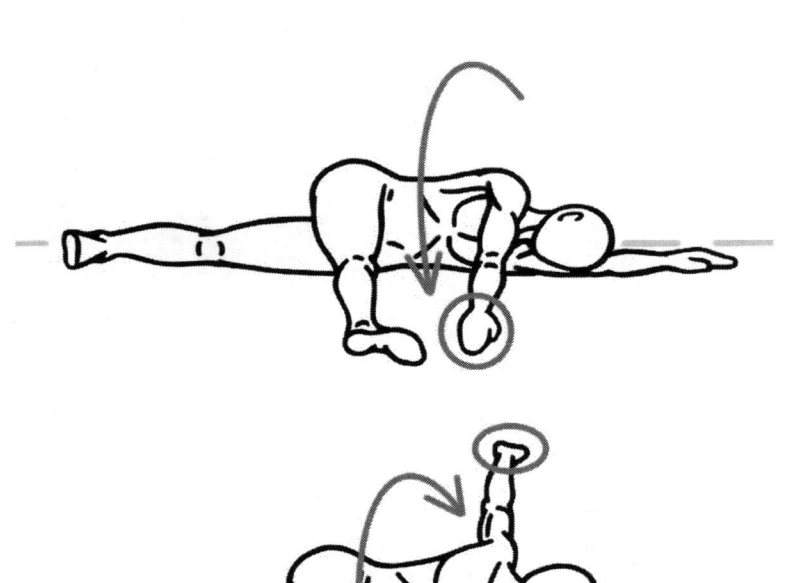

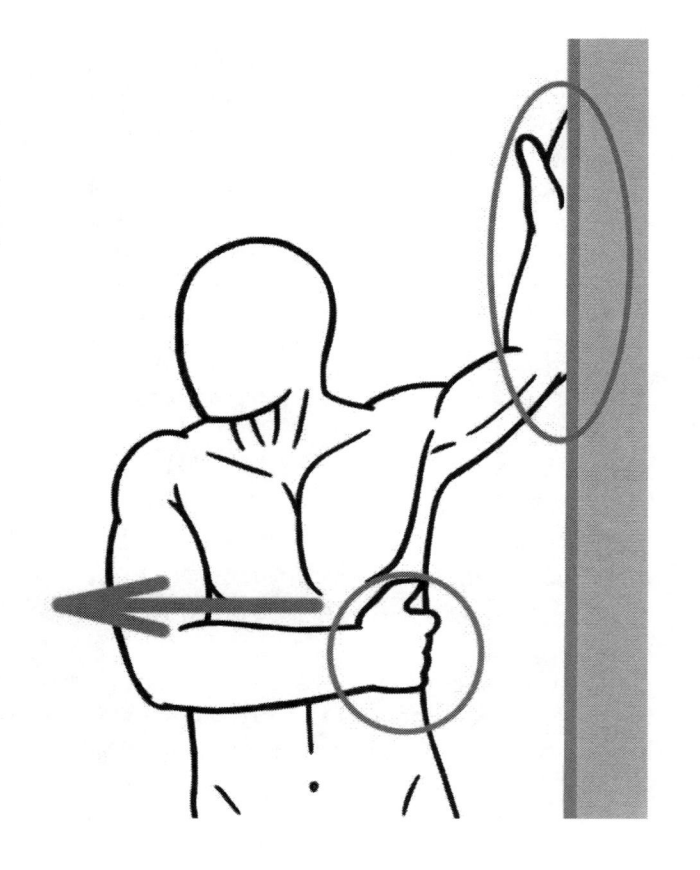

MOBILITY

CAT-COW

This mobility exercise will help reintroduce your spine to its full range of motion while flexing and extending. It's a reintroduction because you were originally born with full mobility of the spine, but lifestyle factors, especially sitting, slowly begin to rob us. Therefore, this exercise is great to incorporate in your mobility work as it prepares your body for larger movement patterns.

POSITION: Align the wrists under the shoulders and the knees under the hips. Lengthen the spine and look down at the floor. Keep the elbows fully extended.

ACTION: Drop the stomach towards the ground and press the top of the head up to the sky. Next, pull the bellybutton directly up to the sky and drop the top of the head towards the floor as the toes uncurl from the floor. Repeat several times in each direction

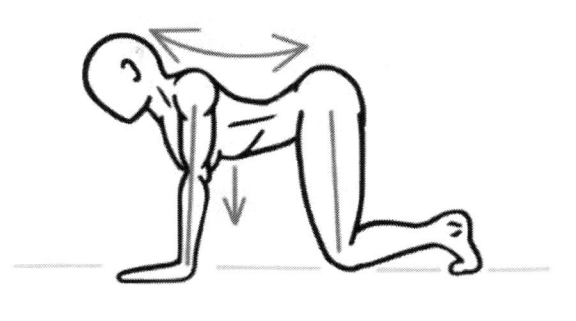

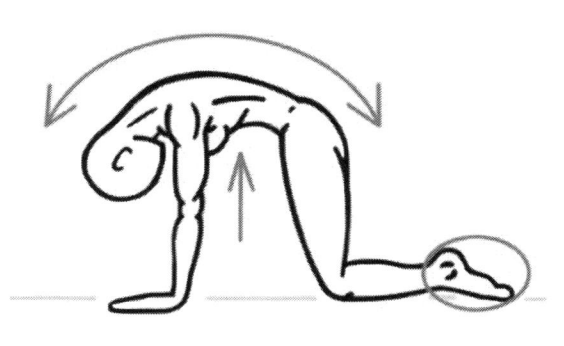

Modes of Application:
- *Hold this position for approximately 30 seconds as you mentally imagine your entire spine lengthening and focus on deep exhalations.*
- *Smoothly perform several reps of this movement as you breathe deeply and relax.*
- *Hold the end position and perform several PNF Contract/Hold sequences with the reciprocal muscles, i.e. when targeting your posterior side, contract your abdominals to help your back release.*

ROTATED REACH

This mobility exercise will focus on enhancing the rotational movement aspects of the thoracic spine. The thoracic spine tends to become restricted from excessive tension in the shoulders or chest by working on computers and driving.

POSITION: Align the wrists to shoulder width and sit the hips onto the heels to keep them stable. Lengthen the spine and look down at the floor. Keep the elbows fully extended.

MOBILITY

ACTION: Reach one arm under the opposite armpit and touch elbow to elbow before rotating the torso to reach the arm up into the sky. Keep both elbows straight and press into the floor to extend higher into the sky. Repeat several times on each arm.

Modes of Application:
- *Hold this position for approximately 30 seconds as you mentally imagine your upper torso rotating and focus on deep exhalations.*
- *Smoothly perform several reps of this movement as you breathe deeply and relax.*
- *Hold the end position and perform several PNF Contract/Hold sequences by activating your upper back muscles to help expand your chest and rotate deeper.*

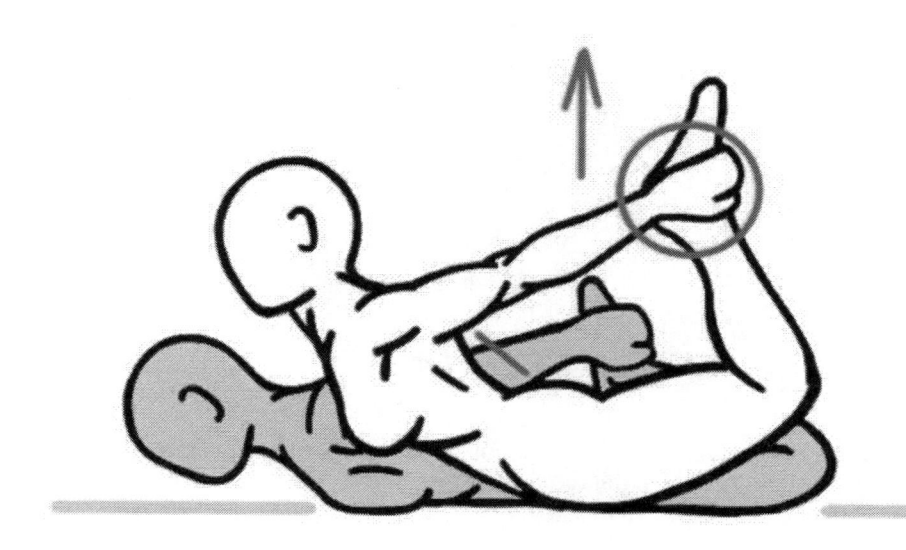

BOW POSE
POSITION: Reach back with both hands and take hold of the ankles. If the hands are unable to reach, use a towel wrapped around the ankles to hold on to.

ACTION: Hold the ankles and gently kick the hands and feet up towards the sky, lifting the chest and thighs off the ground. Keep the spine long and squeeze the thighs together as the chest and shoulders open up. Breathe deeply and stay relaxed through the entire body.

Modes of Application:
- *Hold this position for approximately 30 seconds as you mentally imagine your chest and shoulders expanding and focus on deep exhalations.*
- *Smoothly perform several reps of this movement as you breathe deeply and relax.*
- *Hold the end position and perform several PNF Contract/Relax sequences by gently contracting your chest on the Contract phase before releasing more on the Relax phase.*

MOBILITY

More Important than you may think!
It may seem counter-intuitive that runners should care about the mobility of their thoracic spine, but it really is not. The alignment of your thoracic spine has a large influence on the construction of all of your movement patterns. Therefore, the mobility of your thoracic spine needs to be taken seriously because it will help shape how you run!

More importantly, if you spend much of your time working at a computer, sitting at a desk or even driving a car, take the time to restore the full range of motion to your thoracic spine and improve your mobility overall!

MOBILITY

MOBILITY

Shoulder Mobility

I never knew what a difference mobility exercises could do for the shoulders until I actually did them. I grew up punching a heavy bag, bench pressing a lot, and throwing a football countless times –all shoulder-centric activities. However, I hardly paid any attention to maintaining my shoulder's range of motion and alignment until I started practicing yoga.

When I was new to yoga, every single class was such an intense workout. It was hardly a relaxing, meditative experience, but it took me some time to figure out why. The reason was that I had horrible shoulder mobility and I could not get into the correct position for Down Dog. So, every vinyasa flow was more like I was doing upside-down push-ups. And when the teacher would tell us to "rest" in Down Dog and breathe, I would simply laugh to myself and feverishly try not to collapse onto the floor. I would sweat so much in those yoga classes that my mat would be as slippery as ice and my shorts would be completely soaked.

Then I started to apply PreHab mobility techniques and exercises to my shoulders and a world of difference opened up. The first major change was that I could reach the back of my heart with each hand (we all should be able to do that). Then I noticed a difference in how I throw a football. I had more control over the flight of the ball and I could make those throws where the ball seems to float over the defender and then drop in perfectly on a dime. Yet, my biggest improvement was how I did yoga. I could actually flow through a vinyasa and hit Down Dog and Up Down effortlessly!

Our shoulders are the most agile joint and can create finely tuned and articulated movements when we have proper mobility. Without shoulder mobility, we are left to create compensations in our movements and alignment in everything we do – even running.

Shoulder Mobility for Running?
Just like the head and neck, the shoulder's alignment and mobility will affect the way that you run, let alone the way that you throw, catch, press or pull. If your shoulders are restricted in their full range of motion, you will lose your capacity to create torque (produce force) in your stride.

When you run, your shoulders will semi-rotate around your spine and reciprocally pair up with the opposite leg. The ensuing pendulum action of the arm and opposite leg creates kinetic energy in the form of torque around the spine, which reactively propels the body forward. The longer the arc in this pendulum swing, the more force is transferred from the shoulders into the legs. In other words, if you run with stiff shoulders, you make your legs work even harder. You want your arms to move freely with every single step.

MOBILITY

Range of Motion: Arm Swing
Now, there are different ranges of motion for the arms while you run that correlate to your speed. Simply put, the faster you want to go, the larger swing you want in your arms.

Sprinting: Full Swing
'Cheek to Cheek'
You want to generate as much torque through your arms to transfer as much power into every single step when you are sprinting. Use the following phrase as a guide, "Cheek to Cheek", which refers to the path of your hands. You want to swing your hand up to the cheek on your face and then back down to your butt cheek, i.e. "Cheek to Cheek."

Long Distances: Moderate Swing
'Front to Back'
On long distances, you will utilize a forward lean to help economize your effort and conserve energy for the entire run. Therefore, your stride will also become shorter. Yet, the biomechanics of reciprocal torque is still important though the legs and arms and will not travel an elongated path. You want to minimize the arm swing to "Front to Back," meaning that the elbows will swing out just in front of the rib cage and then just behind the rib cage. Another way of looking at this modification is that the hand will swing up to shoulder height and then back down to the front of the rib cage, i.e. "Shoulder to Ribs."

Shoulder Alignment
Another important reason to address your shoulder mobility is its effect on your alignment while running. If the chest is tight, the shoulder head is pulled forward and interferes with the "Forward Lean" technique when running because the center of gravity is also pulled forward by the shoulder and creates a bowing in the spine or a piking of the hips that breaks the kinetic flow of energy.

Additionally, if the shoulders are chronically

MOBILITY

elevated due to tight trapezius muscles, the biomechanics of running are also thwarted. Elevated shoulders will influence the center of gravity and also compromise hip and ankle stability because the core muscles are over extended and may not fire fast enough in reflexive movement patterns. This could make the hips and legs attempt to overcompensate in their stability strategies. Therefore, you want to employ a healthy dose of mobility exercises and techniques to the shoulders in order to restore their proper alignment.

Top Down Approach Continued
Our shoulder's alignment and mobility will have an effect in every movement pattern. As part of the Top Down approach, use these exercises and techniques to help mobilize and align the shoulders, neck and thoracic spine.

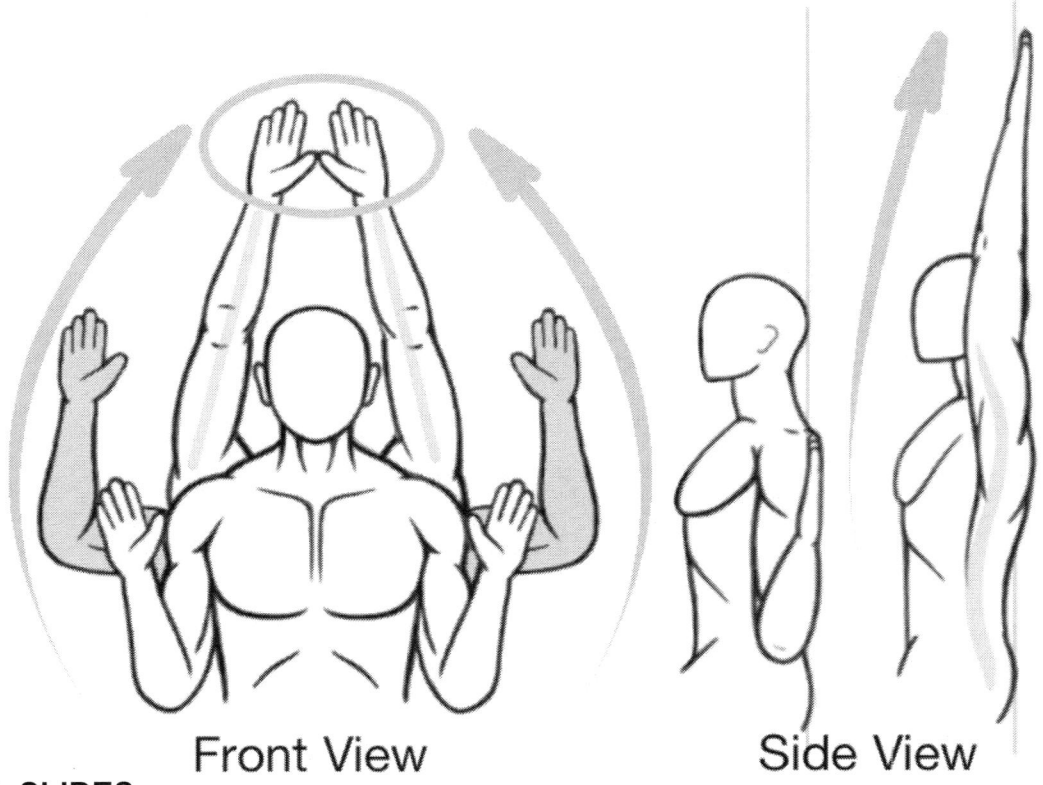

Front View   Side View

WALL SLIDES
POSITION:
Squat or sit up against a wall with the entire spine, both elbows and wrists pressed completely flat to the wall. Align the fingertips with the top of the head.

ACTION:
Slide both arms up to touch overhead while keeping the forearms and spine completely flat against the wall.

If the arms can fully straighten overhead and the thumbs touch, while the spine, especially the lower back, remains completely flat with the wall, then you have adequate shoulder mobility. If you were unable to complete this movement with proper form, then it's time to work on your shoulder mobility.

MOBILITY

Soft Tissue Therapy
In addition to foam rolling all of the regions that connect directly to the shoulders, you can improve your mobility greatly by working with a lacrosse ball or tennis ball in the following areas.

Use the ball to smooth out the knots and adhesions in your soft tissue by rolling the ball across the muscles and applying enough pressure. These tissues are meant to be smooth and soft. So, if you feel any tightness or bumps, those are the areas that you want to work on until you can feel a noticeable change.

Do your best to make a difference in each soft tissue session that you have and more importantly, make it a long-term practice. Keep applying these soft tissue therapy techniques for years to come, as they will truly make a positive difference in how you move and perform.

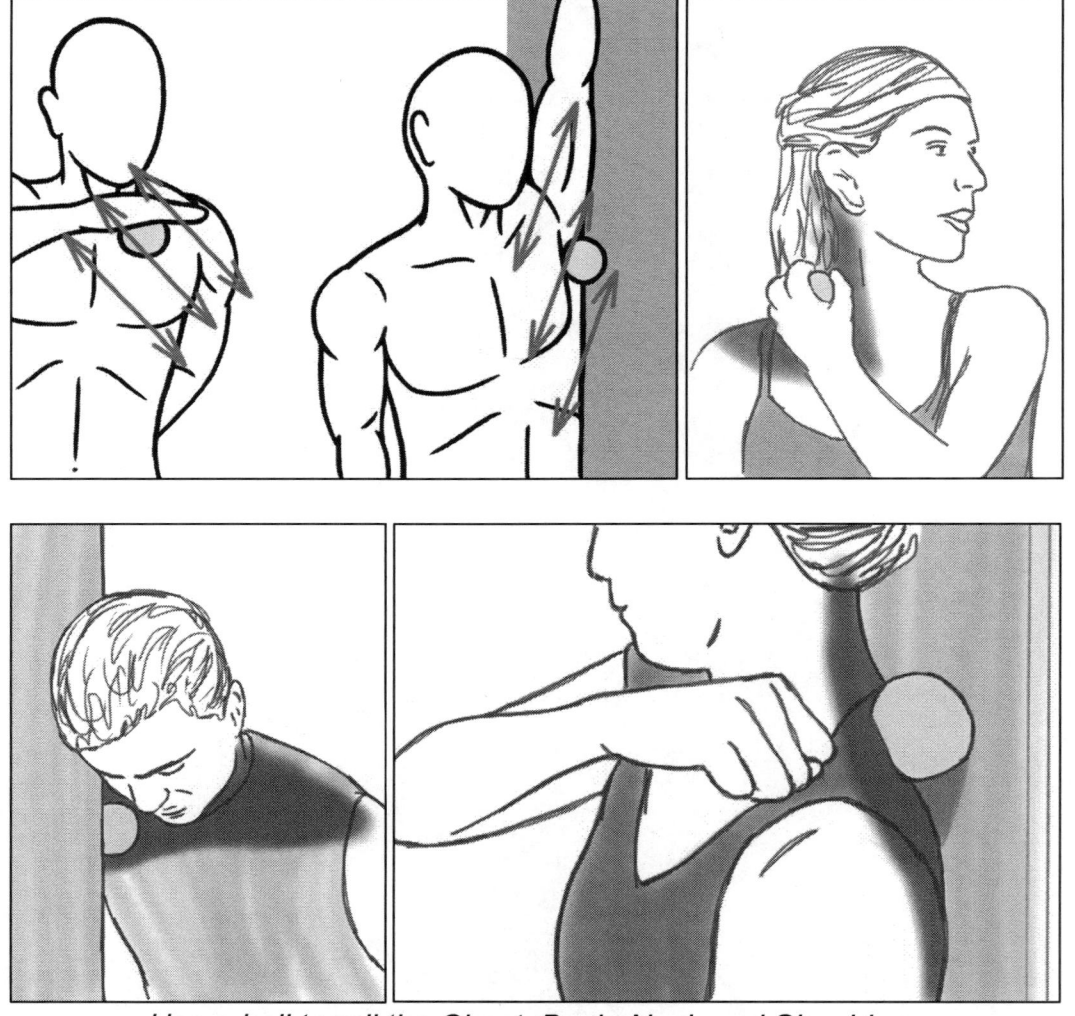

Use a ball to roll the Chest, Back, Neck and Shoulders.

MOBILITY

> **Mobility Exercises**
> Once you have treated the soft tissue and made a difference in its composition, use these mobility exercises to restore length and range of motion.

SIDE-LYING ARM CIRCLES

POSITION: Lie on your side with your hips and knees folded 90 degrees in a chair position.

ACTION: Reach your top arm forward as far as possible and then slowly trace your fingers on the floor and draw a large circle around your body.
Repeat 5-10 on each side.

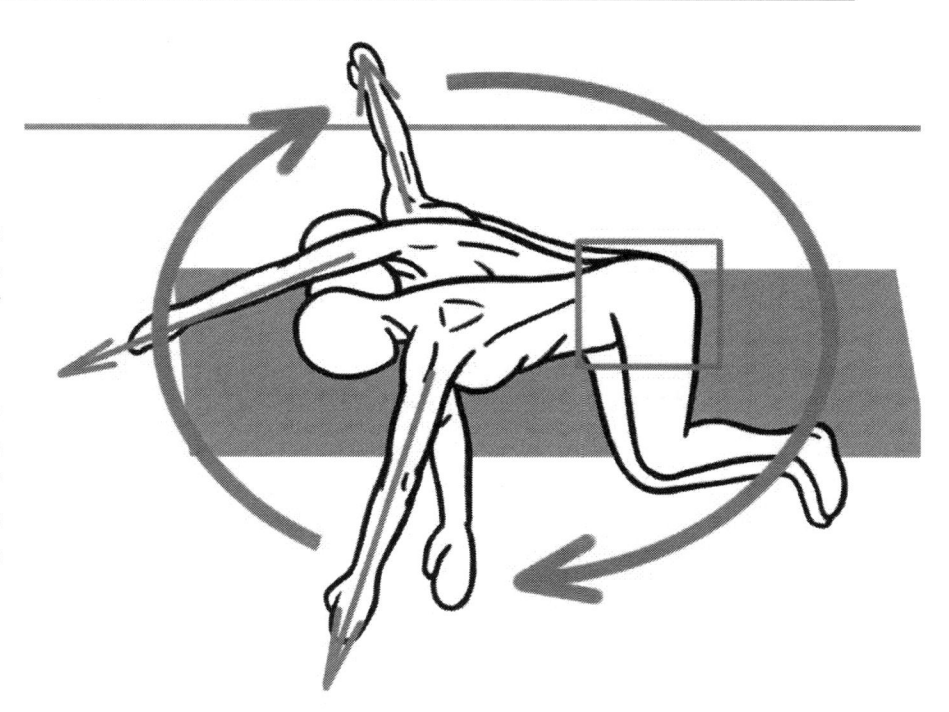

ARM CIRCLES on Foam Roller

POSITION: Lie on top of a foam roller with your spine vertically aligned with the roller.

ACTION: Reach your arms out to the side and touch the floor with your hands if possible. Next, slowly circle your arms up overhead while keeping your elbows straight and continuing to press the hands into the floor.
Circle the arms 5-10 times.

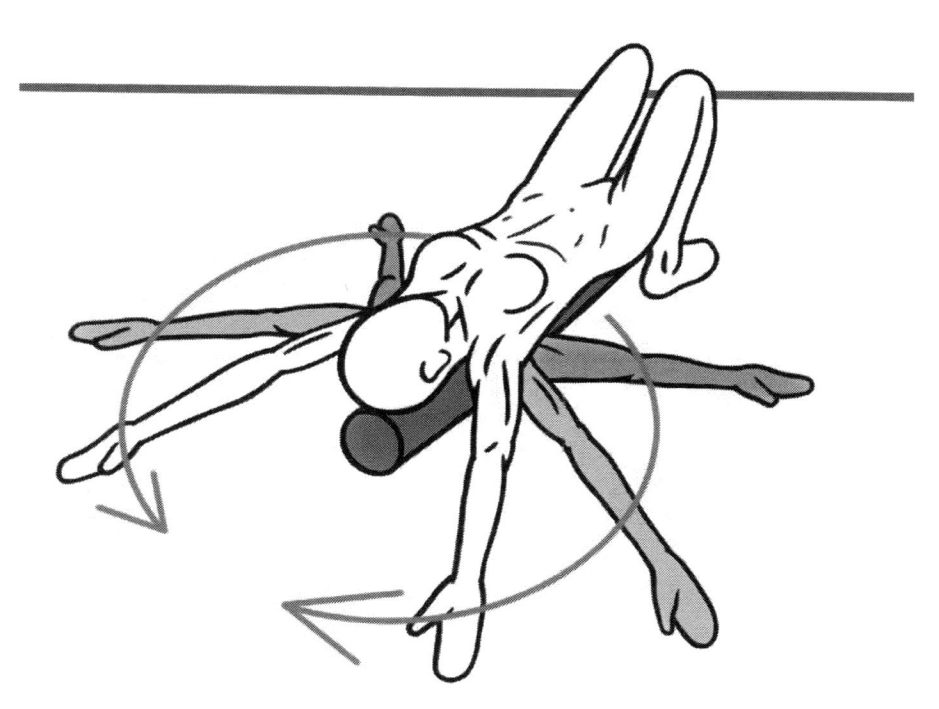

MOBILITY

INTERLACED ARM SWINGS - MOBILITY SEQUENCE:

ANTERIOR
POSITION: Kneeling on the floor, interlace the fingers with the palms together in front of the body. Engage the abdominals to support a straight and upright spine.

ACTION: Reach both arms up and overhead as far as possible while engaging the abdominals to keep the back from arching. Attempt to touch the biceps to the back earlobe.

Perform 5-10 lifts and then switch all fingers over one position and repeat.

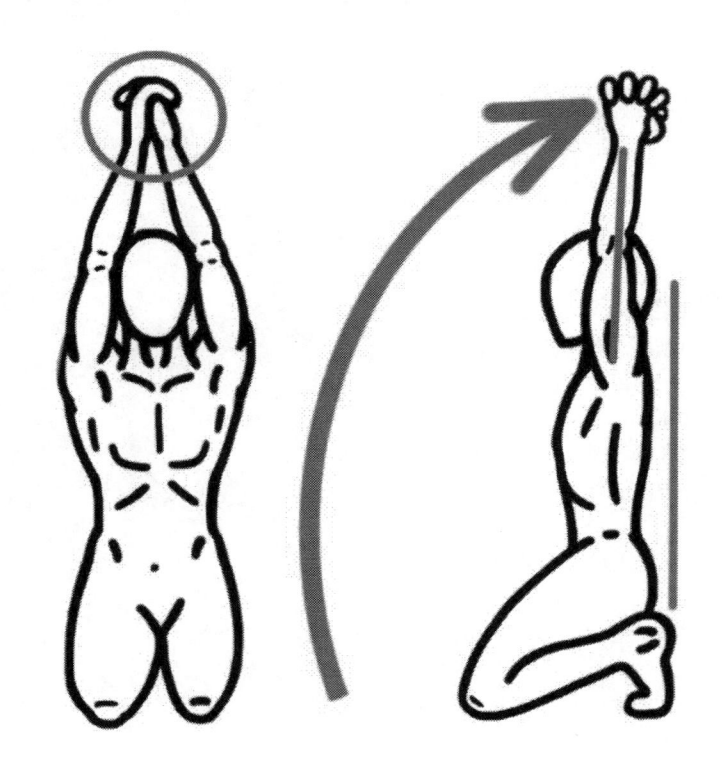

POSTERIOR
POSITION: Kneeling on the floor, interlace the fingers behind the body with the palms together. Engage the abdominals to support a straight, upright spine.

ACTION: Lift the hands back and away from the body as far as possible with fully extended elbows. Engage the abdominals to keep the lower back from arching.

Perform 5-10 swings and then switch all fingers over one position and repeat.

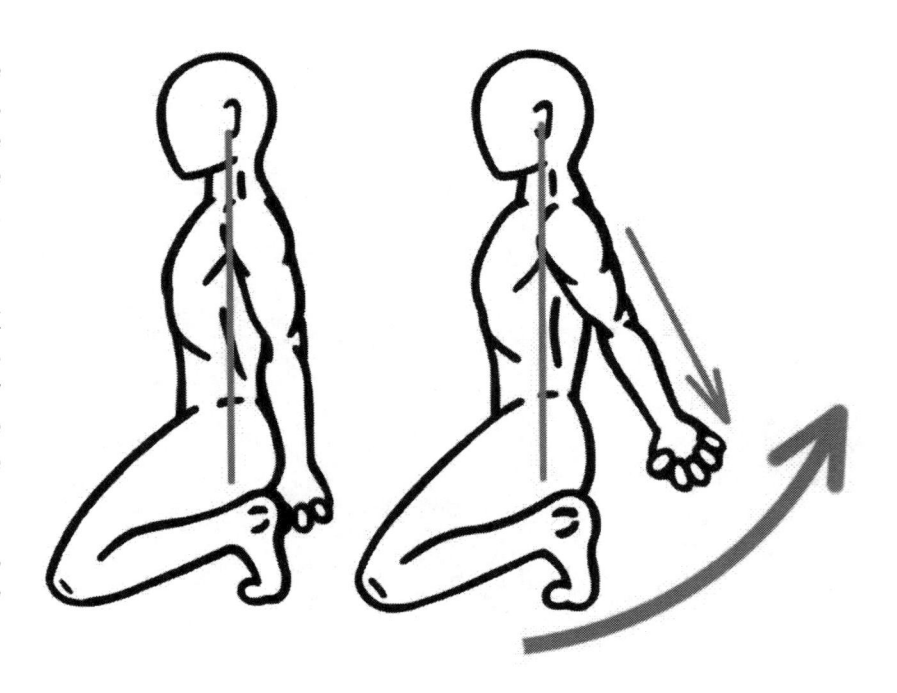

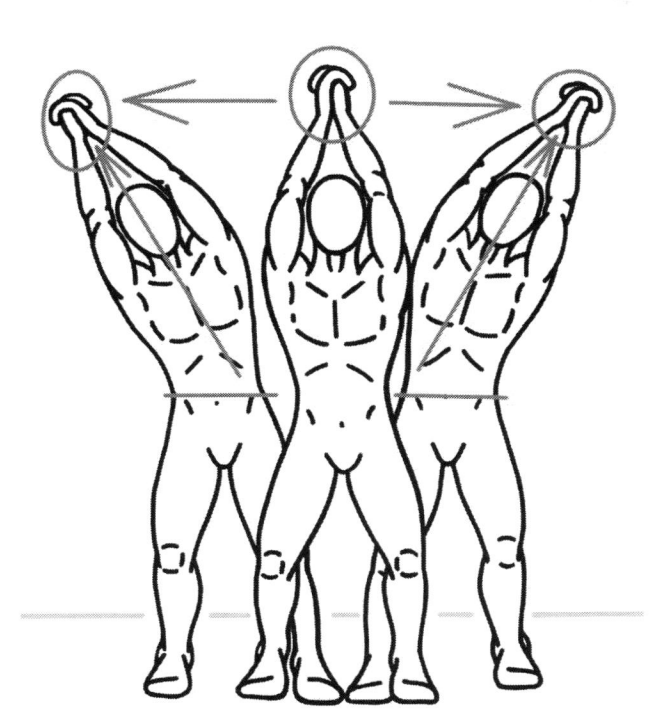

MOBILITY

OVERHEAD

POSITION: Stand with the feet just outside shoulder-width and interlace the hands. Lift the arms overhead with straight elbows. Reach the top of the head to the sky and pull the belly button into the spine to engage the abdominals.

ACTION: Laterally reach both arms out to the side as far as possible while keeping the hips level. Keep the shoulders and the chest square to the front and keep the elbows straight. Breathe into the sides of the torso and lengthen through the spine.
Repeat 5-10 times in each direction and then switch all fingers over one position and repeat.

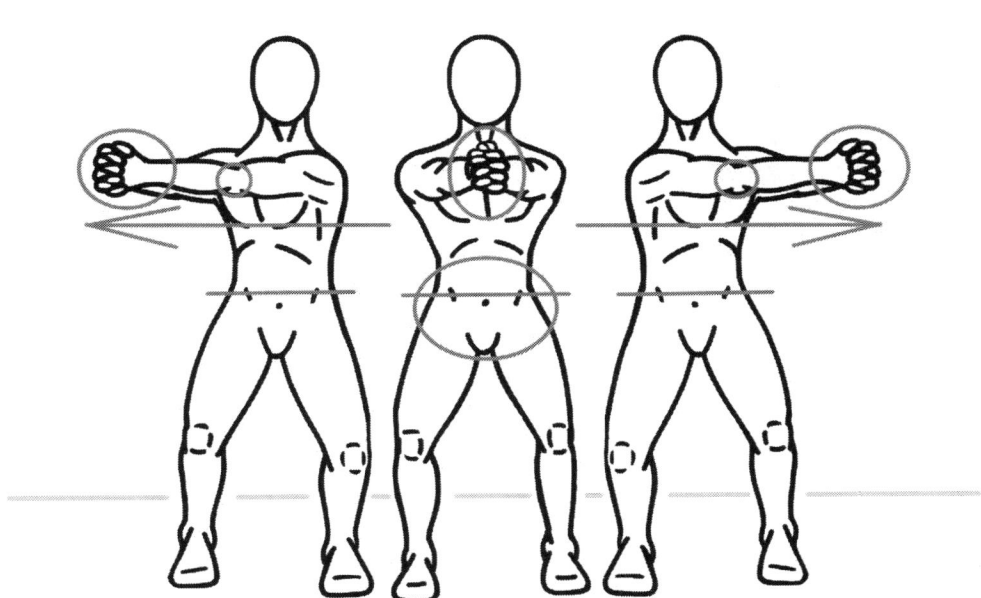

HORIZONTAL

POSITION: Stand with the feet just outside shoulder-width and interlace the hands. Lift the arms parallel to the floor with straight elbows. Reach the top of the head to the sky and pull the belly button into the spine to engage the abdominals.

ACTION: Laterally reach both arms out to the side as far as possible while keeping the arms parallel to the floor and the hips squared off to the front. Keep the eyes focused forward and maintain straight elbows.
Repeat 5-10 times in each direction.

MOBILITY

REVERSE-PALM ARM SWING – MOBILITY SEQUENCE:

TRANSVERSE
POSITION: Kneeling on the floor, interlace the fingers in front of the heart with the palms facing away from the chest. Engage the abdominals to support a straight, upright spine.

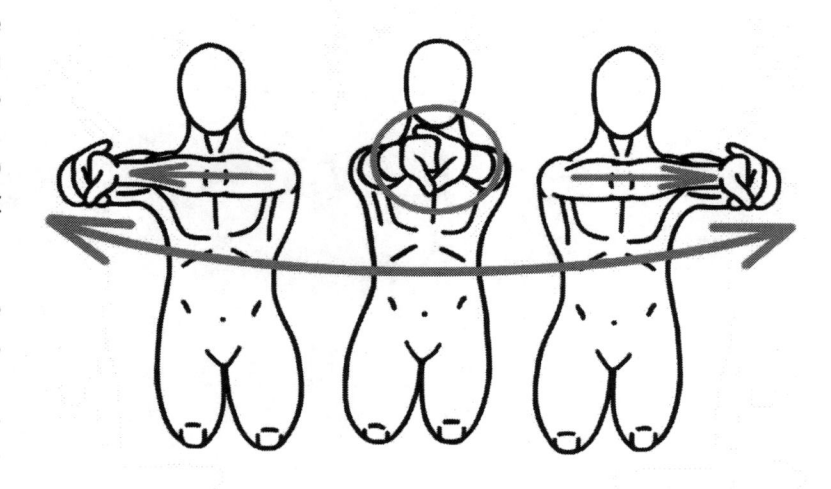

ACTION: Depress the shoulders by pulling the armpits away from the ears and horizontally slide both hands from side to side as far as possible with straight elbows.
Perform 5-10 swings and then switch all fingers over one position and repeat.

SAGITTAL
POSITION: Kneeling on the floor, interlace the fingers in front of the body with the palms facing out and keep a straight, upright spine.

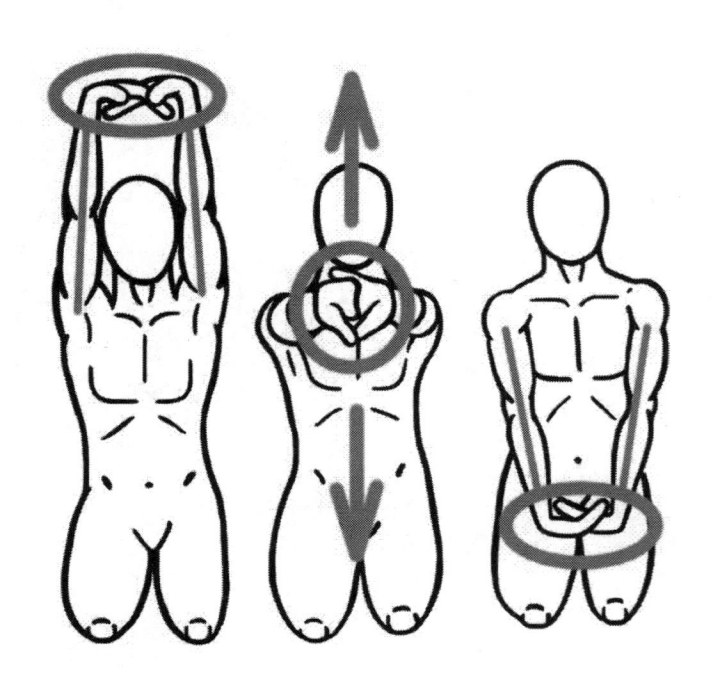

ACTION: Contract the abdominals to eliminate arching in the lower back and lift both hands up and over the top of the head as far as possible with elbows fully extended. Attempt to touch the biceps to the ears with a neutral spine.
Perform 5-10 swings and then switch all fingers over one position and repeat.

MOBILITY

WALL-ASSISTED MOBILITY EXERCISES
Find a wall to use as support in the following stretches.

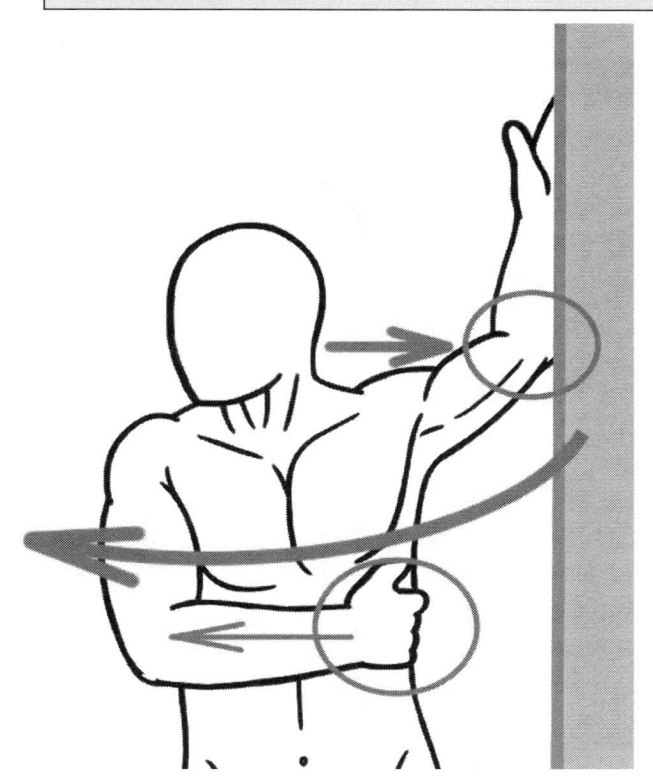

HORIZONTAL ABDUCTION
POSITION: Place your palm against the wall at or slightly below the height of your shoulder.

ACTION: Press the chest forward while pulling the shoulder down and away from the ear. This movement will help lengthen your chest muscles as well as your anterior shoulder muscles. Also, imagine squeezing your armpit down towards your front pocket. This will help lengthen the trapezius muscle.

Modes of Application:
- *Hold this position for approximately 30 seconds and focus on deep exhalations.*
- *Optional: Hold the end position and perform several PNF Contract/Relax sequences.*

SHOULDER EXTENSION
POSITION: Place your hand on the wall at shoulder height with the fingers pointing up.

ACTION: Turn your front away from the wall and keep your chest lifted. This movement will lengthen the chest muscles as well as the anterior shoulder muscles. Pull the ear down and away from the ear by imagining that you are squeezing your armpit down to your pockets. This movement will help lengthen the trapezius muscle.

Modes of Application:
- *Hold this position for approximately 30 seconds and focus on deep exhalations.*
- *Optional: Hold the end position and perform several PNF Contract/Relax sequences.*

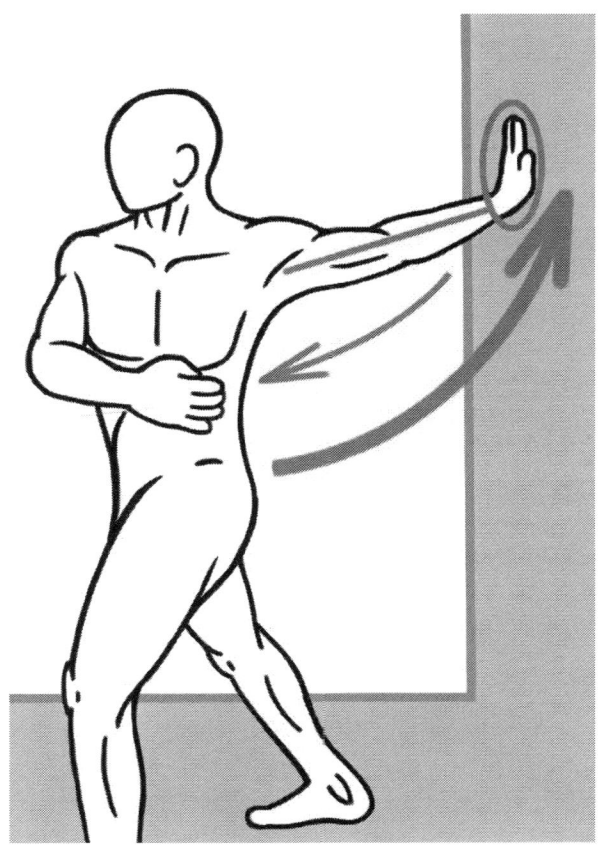

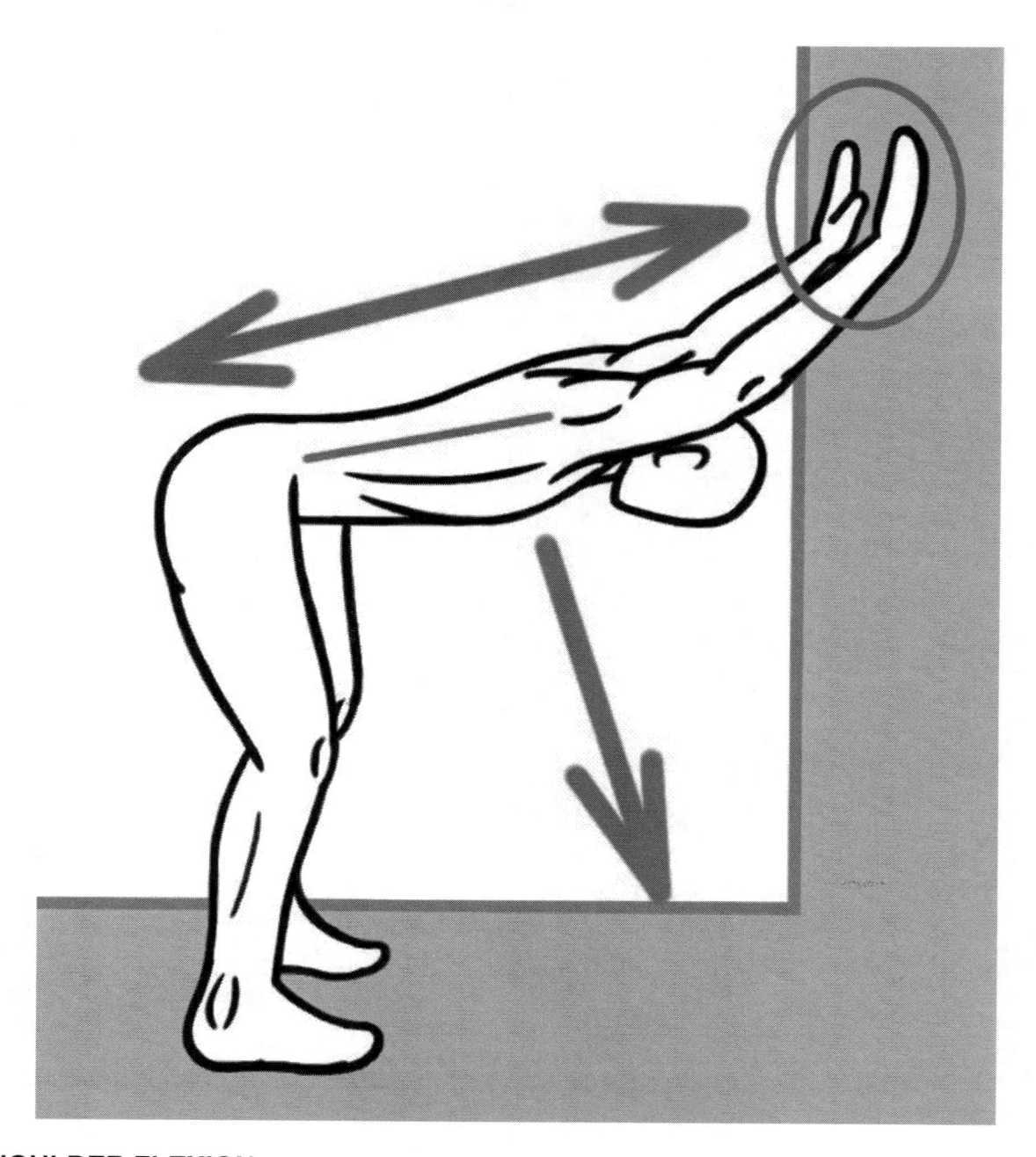

MOBILITY

SHOULDER FLEXION
POSITION: Place both hands on the wall with the fingers pointing up.

ACTION: Drop your chest down towards the floor and push your hips away from the wall. This movement will help lengthen the Lats and the chest muscles. Attempt to twist the belly of your biceps up towards the sky by externally rotating the shoulders. This movement will create even more length through the shoulders, Lats and chest muscles.

Modes of Application:
- *Hold this position for approximately 30 seconds and focus on deep exhalations.*
- *Optional: Hold the end position and perform several PNF Contract/Relax sequences.*

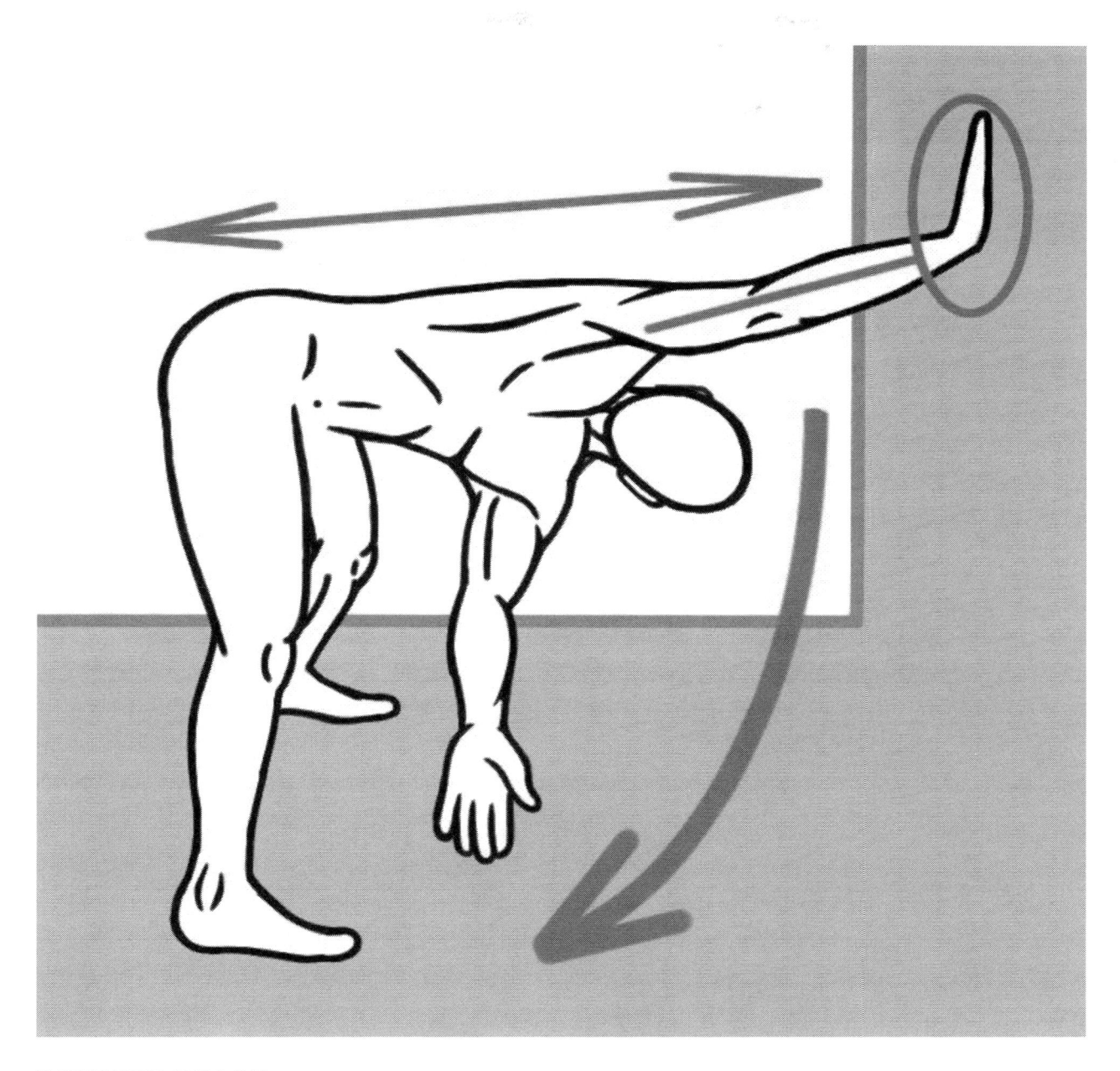

MOBILITY

ROTATED REACH

POSITION: Place both hands up against the wall at hip height with the fingers pointed up towards the sky. Walk the hips backwards until the spine is parallel to the floor. Vertically aligned the feet with the hips in a profile view and wider than shoulder width in a frontal view. Roll the belly of the biceps up towards the sky.

ACTION: Take one hand off the wall and reach under the opposite armpit and towards the horizon as far as possible. Keep the spine long and the hips square as you attempt to reach your head under your armpit as well. Exhale deeply as you extend the reach.

Modes of Application:
- Hold this position for approximately 30 seconds and focus on deep exhalations.
- Optional: Hold the end position and perform several PNF Contract/Relax sequences.

MOBILITY

> **POLE-ASSISTED MOBILITY EXERCISES**
> The following mobility exercises use a pole to help lengthen the muscles that connect to the shoulders.

ARM CIRCLES (SHOULDER DISLOCATES)
POSITION: Gently hold the pole in front of your body with your hands wider than shoulder width.

ACTION: Lift your arms up and circle the pole back overhead until you touch your hips with the pole. Then circle the pole backwards and forwards and repeat several more times while sliding the hands closer together as much as possible. Also, keep your spine and elbows straight when you are circling the pole overhead.

Modes of Application:
- *Repeat several times in a relaxed manner and attempt to reposition the hands closer together after each circle. Once you have found the limit on your range of motion in relation to the width of your hands as you circle your arms, hold the arms behind your back for approximately 30 seconds and focus on deep exhalations.*
- *Optional: Hold the end position and perform several PNF Contract/Relax sequences.*

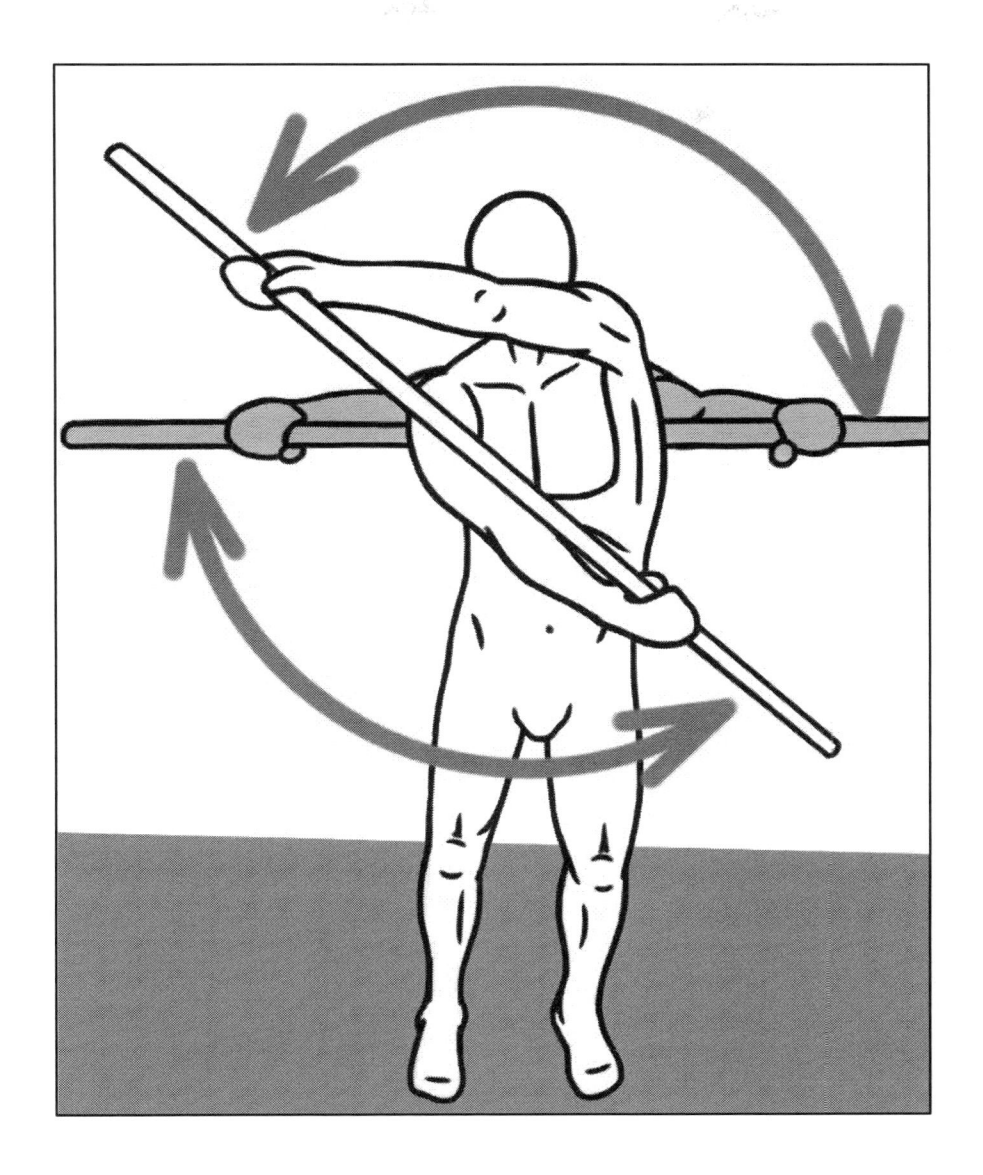

MOBILITY

ARM TWIST

POSTION: Hold the pole out in front of your body with the hands just wider than shoulder width.

ACTION: Twist the pole either clockwise or counterclockwise as far as possible while pulling the shoulders down away from the ears. Keep your spine and elbows straight and remember to breathe and relax as you twist your arms around with the pole. Work in both directions, as this movement will help lengthen your Lats as well as your upper back muscles.

Modes of Application:
- *Repeat several times in a relaxed manner before holding your arm back in the reached position for approximately 30 seconds and focus on deep exhalations.*
- *Optional: Hold the end position and perform several PNF Contract/Relax sequences.*

MOBILITY

> ***Summary-***
> If you want to run farther and perform better, your shoulders need to be aligned and mobile. Any restrictions in how your shoulders can move will ultimately have an effect on everything that you can do. I am not saying that you can't do things with poor shoulder mobility. In fact, if you want to make yoga into a 90-minute shoulders and chest workout, by all means feel free. What I am saying is that improving your shoulder mobility and alignment will lead to improvements in all of your workouts.
>
> Shoulder mobility is far from overrated. It's essential if you are really looking to have great performances!

MOBILITY

Hip Mobility

Mobilizing the hips is extremely important because any tightness in these prime movers will only limit how you move, period! Full Stop – pun intended.

In all seriousness though, if you are going to run or workout, the mobility of your hips will play a big role in how well you do everything. And when I say "how well you do everything," I am not referring to whether or not you ran as far as you said you would run or if you did all of the sets and reps that you said you would. I am referring to the quality of your workouts. I am specifically referring to whether or not you had full range of motion in your movement or if your body started compensating in one way or another.

Protect your Knees and Spine
When you lack full range of motion in your hips, any one of the various compensation strategies that your body will employ will add stress and sheering forces to either your knees or spine or both. It is simply not worth the risk to neglect your hip mobility.

Butt Wink
There is an unofficial term used to describe a biomechanical fault when someone is squatting. It's called the "Butt Wink." What happens is fairly simple to describe, yet not ideal for the spine and your disks, especially if you are squatting heavy weights. On the other hand, developing adequate hip mobility can help prevent the Butt Wink.

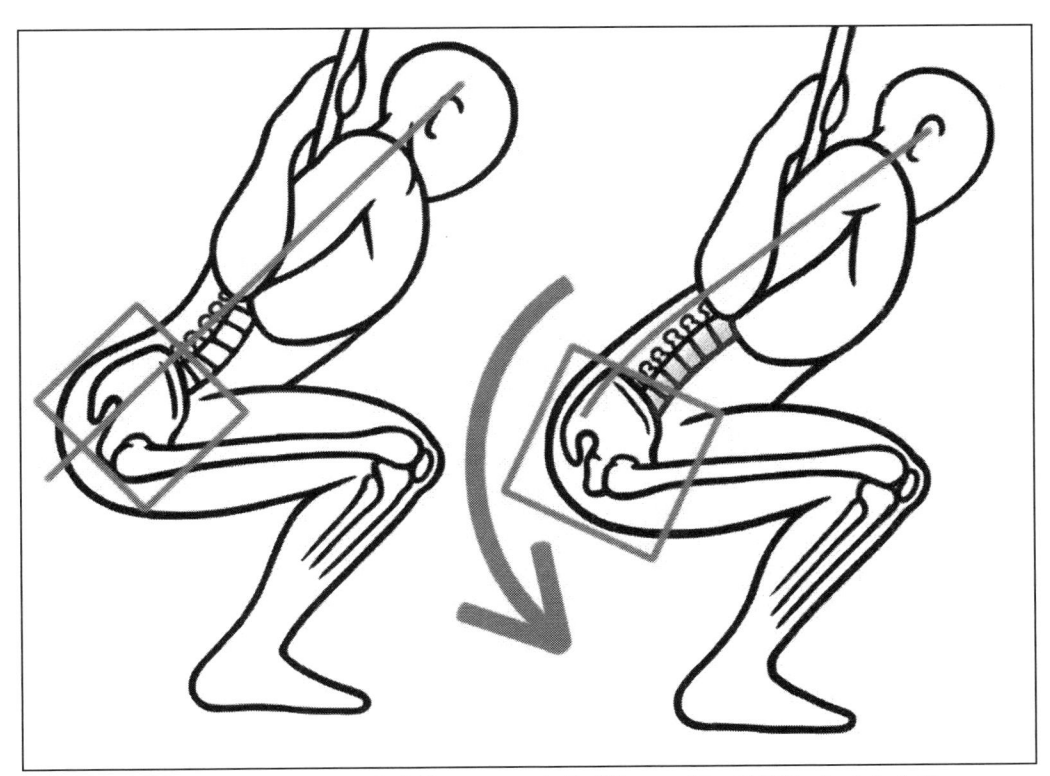

Diagram: Neutral Alignment (left) vs. Butt Wink (right)

MOBILITY

What is the Butt Wink?
If you watch the pelvis as someone lowers down towards the bottom of a squat, there may suddenly be a posterior rolling of the pelvis – it looks as if their butt just gave someone a wink. Yet, what is really happening is that the hips run out of room in flexing and the pelvis needs to compensation by rotating backwards in order to continue lowering down into the squat.

Once the pelvis rolls backwards into the Butt Wink, the disks of the lumbar spine are suddenly compressed in an uneven way, which can lead to a herniated disk or worse if repeated numerous times under heavy load.

One of the easiest ways to prevent the Butt Wink and to protect your spine is to develop sufficient hip mobility and practice proper range of motion when you are squatting.

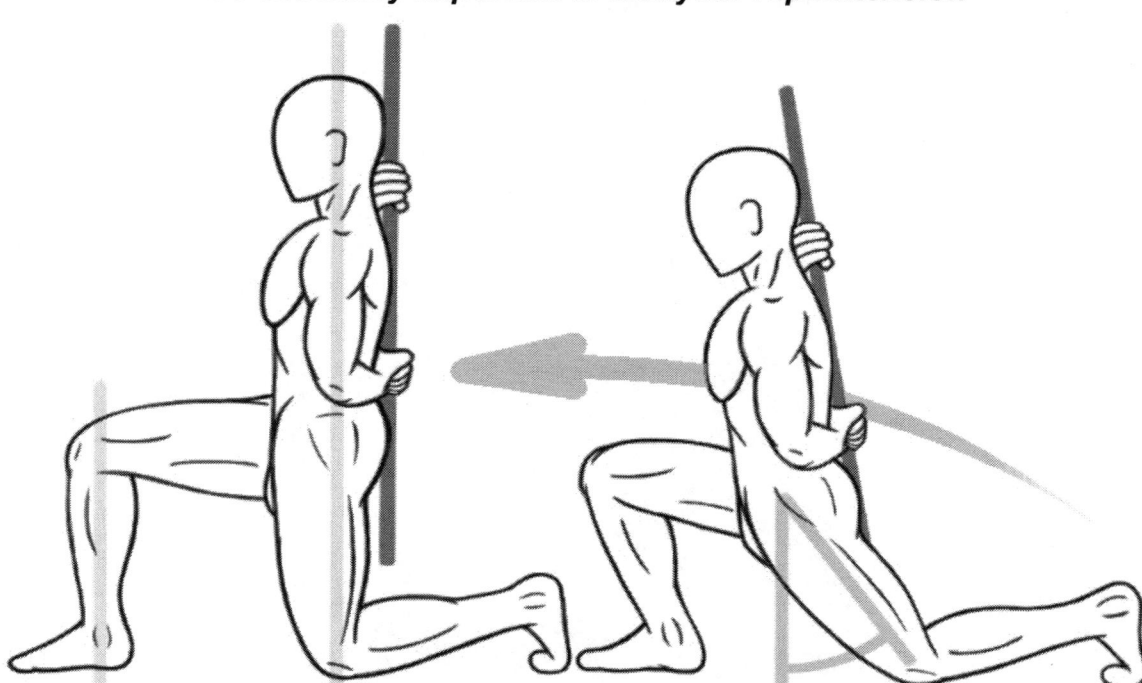

It's extremely important to test your Hip Extension

Hip Extension - Optimal Range of Motion: 30°

The Flip Side
While the Butt Wink is a perfect example of how the body compensates for a lack of adequate hip flexion, there are many other examples of how the body compensates for a lack of hip extension, especially in running.

In running, you need at least 10 degrees of extension in the hip socket in order to have the glutes act as the driving force of your stride. This means that the femur (thigh bone) needs to reach backwards at least 10 degrees from vertical, as the pelvis remains unmoved or not tilting.

MOBILITY

Use a pole to brace your spine and pelvis as you lunge forward to test the range of your hip extension. Can your knee clear your hips as the small of the back and your hand remains touching the pole? If not, please work on your hip mobility!

The lack of hip extension can make your calves and quadriceps attempt to compensate because of the lack of push off from the glutes due to a limited range of motion in the hip socket. This ultimately leads to the glutes becoming underworked, your stride becoming shorter and your quads and calves working harder than they are supposed to.

Advocate for Stand Up Desks
I believe that everyone in the world is entitled to a stand up desk because it will truly help our biomechanics. See, I am truly amazed that I ever wrote one book, let alone two, while sitting down at a desk. Sitting in a chair is unnatural and it warps our bodies!

So, the first thing I believe that you should do is to get yourself a stand up desk. Or at least consider getting one and limit your time sitting dramatically until you finally do get a stand up desk. When we sit, our hip flexors and quads both grow tighter and tighter while our glutes actually begin to turn off. This is a terrible combination for anyone who wishes to exercise after work, let alone be active in his or her life. You begin to walk different. You begin to stand different. You begin to do everything different.

I used to squat down to instruct my clients and my knees would crack because my quads were tight and compressed my patella into my knee joint. Not good! However, once I got a stand up desk, my hips now feel looser and my knees never crack when I squat down to help people. So, please get a stand up desk.

Basic Hip Mobility Sequence
As with all mobility work, you want to treat the soft tissue first. Feel free to start with the foam roller and then move on to using a lacrosse ball or tennis ball to smooth out your muscles and fascia. Here are some illustrations to follow:

Soft Tissue Therapy
Before you start stretching, you may want to dive into some soft tissue therapy to help prep your muscles and fascia to lengthen. Your hips are your prime movers and need to be able to operate with full range of motion and proper biomechanics if you want to move well and perform your best.

Foam Rolling
Since the hips have a lot of musculature on them, foam rolling is a great place to start your soft tissue therapy. You can address the hips with a roller in broad strokes and identify specific areas to come back to with a ball that are more tender or tighter than other areas. Additionally, a foam roller will help to excite a large number of neuromuscular connections, which will only add to the effectiveness of the other mobility exercises, especially the dynamic stretches.

MOBILITY

Types of Rollers

Styrofoam Rollers

Padded Rollers

Textured Rollers

MOBILITY

Foam Rolling Sequence for the Hips

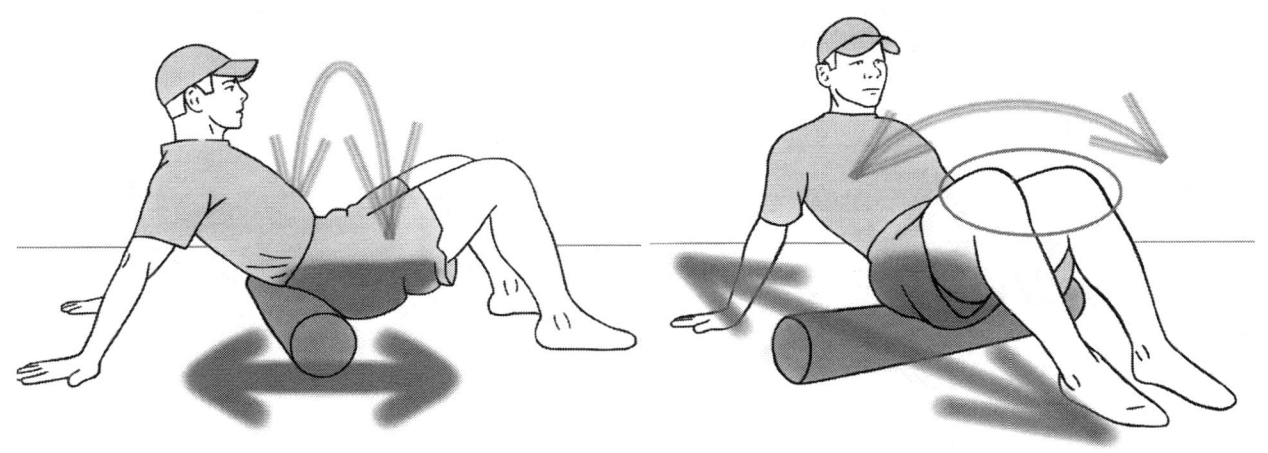

Basic Rolling Pattern

Variation: Angle the Knees

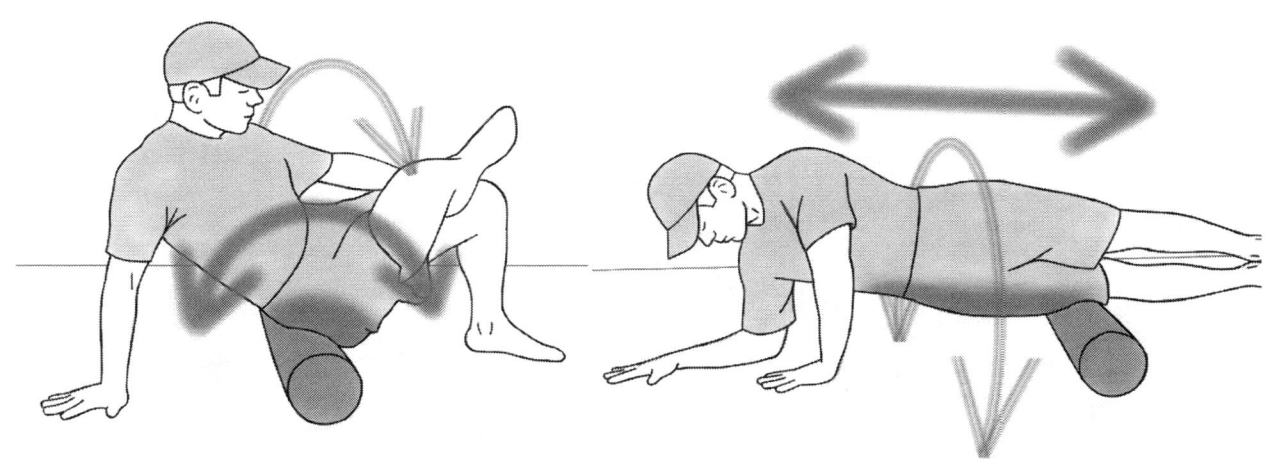

Variation: Cross the Legs

Basic Lateral (Side) Rolling Pattern

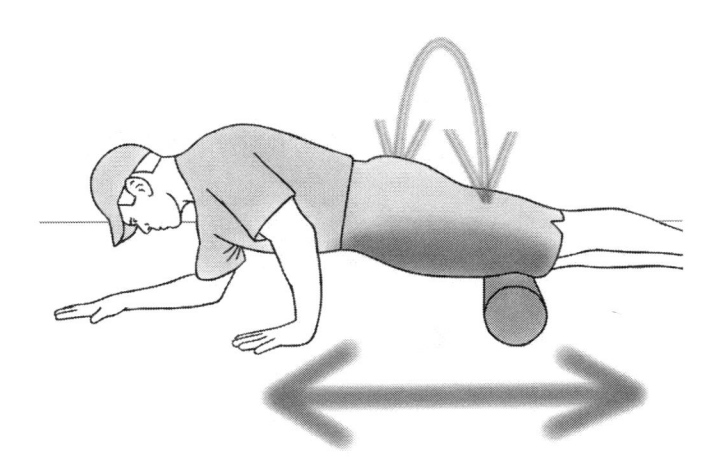

Basic Anterior (Front) Rolling Pattern

MOBILITY

Balling
Now, you can take your soft tissue therapy to a deeper level by using a lacrosse ball or even a tennis ball to help separate adhesions and break up knots that are rather resistant to foam rolling. Keep in mind the main goal of these soft tissue therapy techniques is to make the tissue soft again. Therefore, any tightness or hardness in your soft tissue is an area to address with these techniques.

A Few Types of Balls to Use for Soft Tissue Therapy:

Lacrosse Ball *Tennis Ball*

Golf Ball *Softball*

Massage Balls *The Peanut: Two Balls Taped Together*

How to Ball?
There are a lot of different ways to practice soft tissue therapy with a ball because the shape of the ball allows you to work in many different directions almost simultaneously. You can circle around knots, roll over them, tap on them or even twist right through. You just want to make sure whichever method you use that you can tell that you are making a difference in the texture of your soft tissue.

MOBILITY

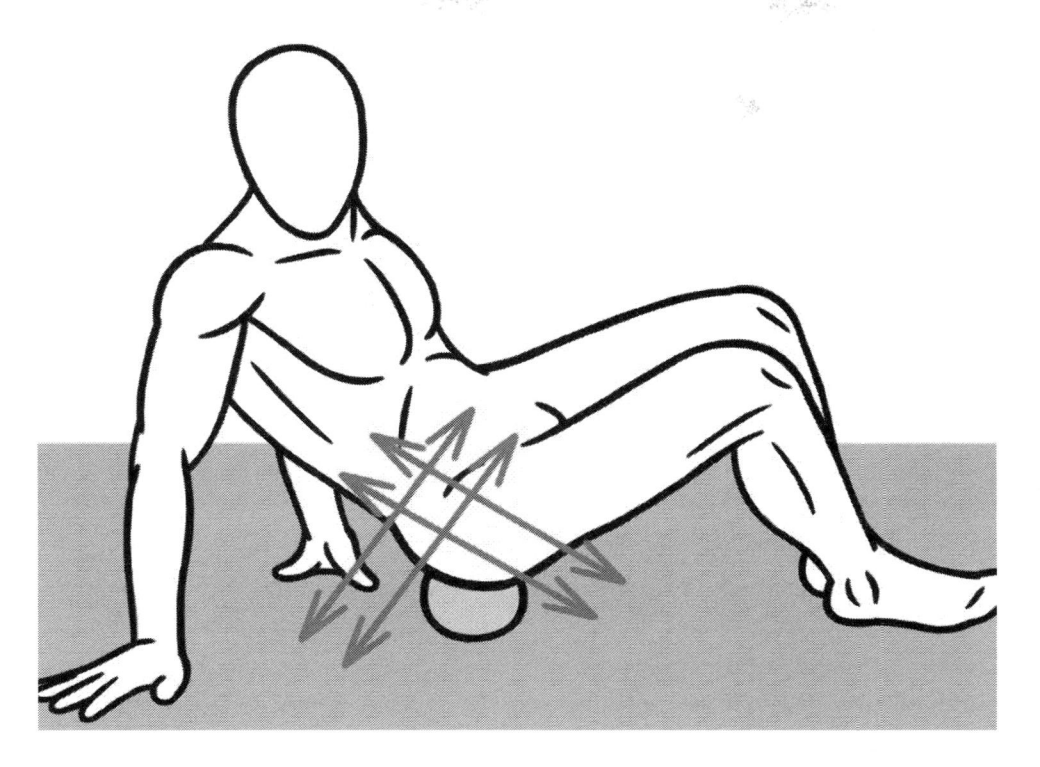

Soft Tissue Therapy: Balling the Hips (Posterior)
Simply sit on the ball and roll in different directions seeking out any knots or tightness that you may feel in your hip's soft tissue. You can use any of the following: Softball, Posture Ball, Lacrosse Ball, Tennis Ball

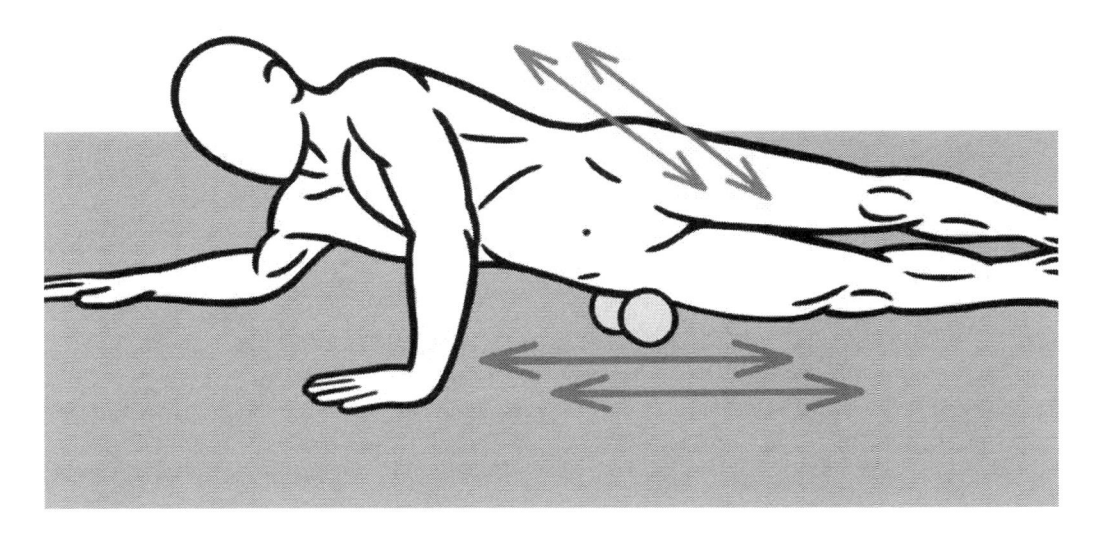

Soft Tissue Therapy: Balling the Hips (Anterior)
Lay over the ball or balls and roll in every direction. Also, be sure to include the Quadriceps and IT Band as well when addressing the front and sides of the hips because these tissue all connect through the hips.

MOBILITY

> **Mobility Exercises**
> After soft tissue therapy, use these stretches to restore length to your tissues and full range of motion to your movement patterns. Remember that your hip mobility will help protect your spine and knees when you move!

GROUNDED WINDSHIELD WIPERS

POSITION: Lie down on the floor with both knees bent and the feet planted on the ground shoulder width apart. Place the arms along the sides of the body.

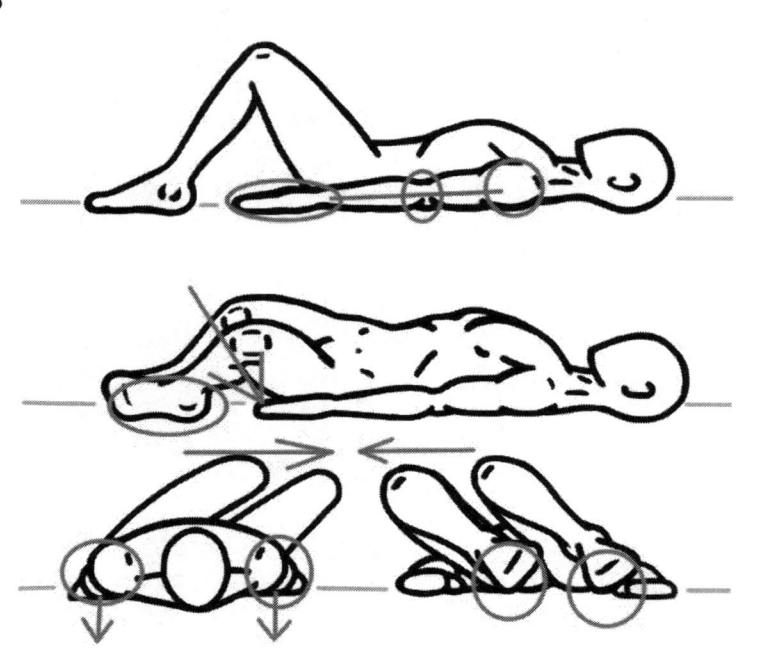

ACTION: Slide the knees from side to side while rolling over the edges of the feet and pressing into the floor with straight arms. Feel the hip sockets rotate and release along with the thighs, torso and shoulders. Breathe deeply and begin to vary the width of the feet as the repetitions progress.

Time: Approximately 15 seconds but longer if you are very tight.

SUPINE DOUBLE KNEE HUG

POSITION: Lie down on the floor and hug both knees into the chest with the arms.

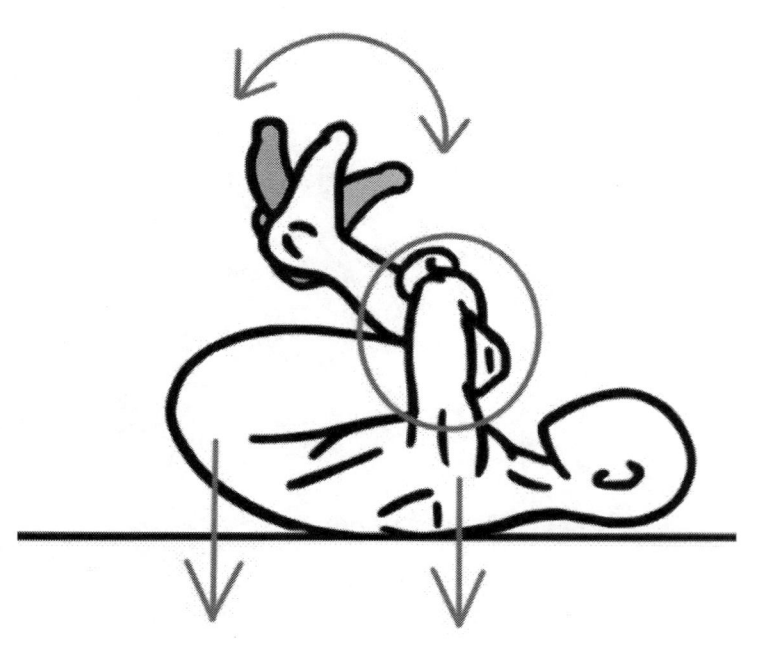

ACTION: Flex, extend and rotate the ankles in every direction as the arms squeeze the knees into the chest. Press the shoulders and hips into the floor to create more release in the hips and legs and work through the largest range of motion available in the ankles. Breathe deeply and relax.

Time: Approximately 15 seconds but longer if you are very tight.

MOBILITY

Kneeling Lunge Sequence
These mobility exercises use different torso positions to effectively lengthen the hip flexors and restore range of motion to your hip extension, which is essential when running.

KNEELING LUNGE & VERTICAL REACH

POSITION: Kneel on the ground with a kneecap directly beneath the hip socket and the opposite foot directly below the "up" knee. Square the hips, lengthen the spine and hold the arms parallel to the ground.

ACTION: Drive the hips forward and reach both arms up and back, extending through the rib cage, shoulders and hip flexors before returning back to the starting position.

Modes of Application:
- Hold this position for approximately 30 seconds as you mentally imagine your hip flexors lengthen and focus on deep exhalations.
- Smoothly perform several reps of this movement as you breathe deeply and relax.
- Hold the end position and perform several Contract/Relax sequences with the targeted hip flexor.

MOBILITY

KNEELING LUNGE & CONTRALATERAL REACH

POSITION: Kneel on the ground with a kneecap directly beneath the hip socket and the opposite foot directly below the "up" knee. Square the hips, lengthen the spine and hold the arms parallel to the ground.

ACTION: Drive the hips forward and reach the arm that is opposite of the "up" knee, forward to the horizon while the other arm reaches backwards to the opposite horizon twisting the torso. Lengthen the spine and open up the chest as the hands reach in opposite directions.

Modes of Application:
- Hold this position for approximately 30 seconds as you mentally imagine your hip flexors lengthen and focus on deep exhalations.
- Smoothly perform several reps of this movement as you breathe deeply and relax.
- Hold the end position and perform several Contract/Relax sequences with the targeted hip flexor.

KNEELING LUNGE & IPSILATERAL REACH

POSITION: Kneel on the ground with a kneecap directly beneath the hip socket and the opposite foot directly below the "up" knee. Square the hips, lengthen the spine and hold the arms parallel to the ground.

ACTION: Drive the hips forward and reach the arm that is opposite of the "up" knee back towards the horizon as the other arm extends forward. Keep the front knee aligned over the front toes and lengthen the spine. Open the chest to the side as the hands reach in opposite directions.

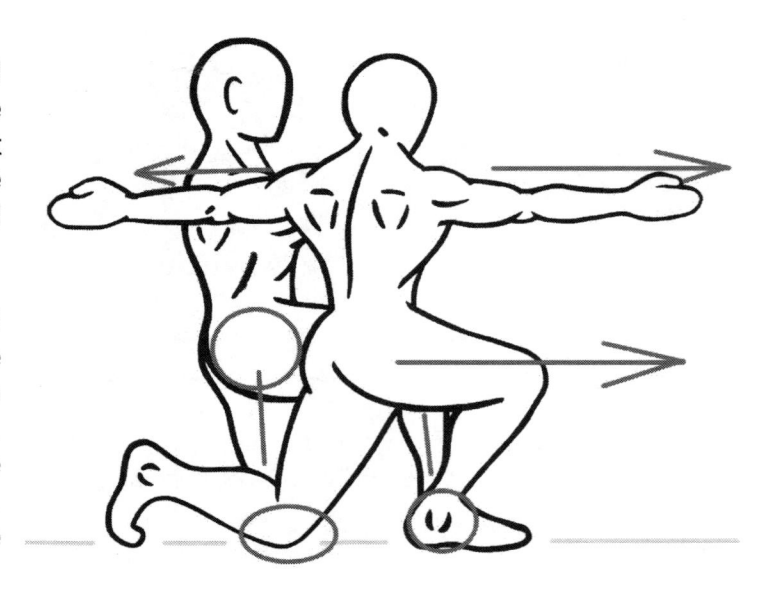

Modes of Application:
- Hold this position for approximately 30 seconds as you mentally imagine your hip flexors lengthen and focus on deep exhalations.
- Smoothly perform several reps of this movement as you breathe deeply and relax.
- Hold the end position and perform several Contract/Relax sequences with the targeted hip flexor.

MOBILITY

KNEELING LUNGE & LATERAL REACH

POSITION: Kneel on the ground with a kneecap directly beneath the hip socket and the opposite foot directly below the "up" knee. Square the hips, lengthen the spine and hold the arms parallel to the ground.

ACTION: Drive the hips forward and reach the arm that is opposite of the "up" knee over top of the head and towards the horizon. As the torso laterally folds over the front leg, keep the front knee tracking over the front toes. Allow the head to fall towards the ground in a controlled manner.

Modes of Application:
- *Hold this position for approximately 30 seconds as you mentally imagine your hip flexors lengthen and focus on deep exhalations.*
- *Smoothly perform several reps of this movement as you breathe deeply and relax.*
- *Hold the end position and perform several Contract/Relax sequences with the targeted hip flexor.*

MOBILITY

SPIDERMAN

This mobility exercise will help to loosen up the posterior hip musculature, namely the glutes. It will also help to restore range of motion to your hip flexors, which are essential in performing squats and lunges.

POSITION: Start in a plank position with the arms in a 90-degree angle to the spine. Align the body in a straight line from head to heels and fully extend the elbows. Pull the belly button into the spine to engage the abdominals.

ACTION: Step one foot forward to the outside of the hand and align the toes and fingers in a straight line if possible. Press the floor away with the arms and keep the straight-line alignment from head to heel. Breathe deeply and relax while alternating feet on each forward-lunge step.

Modes of Application:
- *Hold this position for approximately 30 seconds as you mentally imagine your hip flexors lengthen and focus on deep exhalations.*
- *Smoothly perform several reps of this movement as you breathe deeply and relax.*
- *Hold the end position and perform several Contract/Relax sequences with the targeted hip.*

MOBILITY

PIGEON POSE with Contralateral Reach
POSITION: From a push-up plank position, fold one leg under the torso and align the shin in a 90-degree angle with the spine if possible. Lower the hips down onto the ground and reach back through the rear leg. Keep arms straight.

ACTION: Take the *arm opposite from the folded leg* and reach under the opposite armpit as far as possible while keeping the supporting arm straight. Then lift and reach the arm up towards the sky and rotate through the torso. Allow the hip muscles to release and open.

Modes of Application:
- *Smoothly perform several reps of this movement as you breathe deeply and relax.*
- *Next, hold this position for approximately 30 seconds as you mentally imagine your glutes and posterior hip muscles lengthen and focus on deep exhalations.*
- *Optional: Hold the end position and perform several Contract/Relax sequences with the targeted hip.*

PIGEON with Ipsilateral Reach
POSITION: From a push-up plank position, fold one leg under the torso and align the shin in a 90-degree angle with the spine if possible. Lower the hips down onto the ground and reach back through the rear leg. Keep arms straight.

ACTION: Take the *arm on the same side from the folded leg* and reach under the opposite armpit as far as possible while keeping the supporting arm straight. Then lift and reach the arm up towards the sky and rotate through the torso. Allow the hip muscles to release and open.

Modes of Application:
- *Smoothly perform several reps of this movement as you breathe deeply and relax.*
- *Next, hold this position for approximately 30 seconds as you mentally imagine your glutes and posterior hip muscles lengthen and focus on deep exhalations.*
- *Optional: Hold the end position and perform several Contract/Relax sequences with the targeted hip.*

MOBILITY

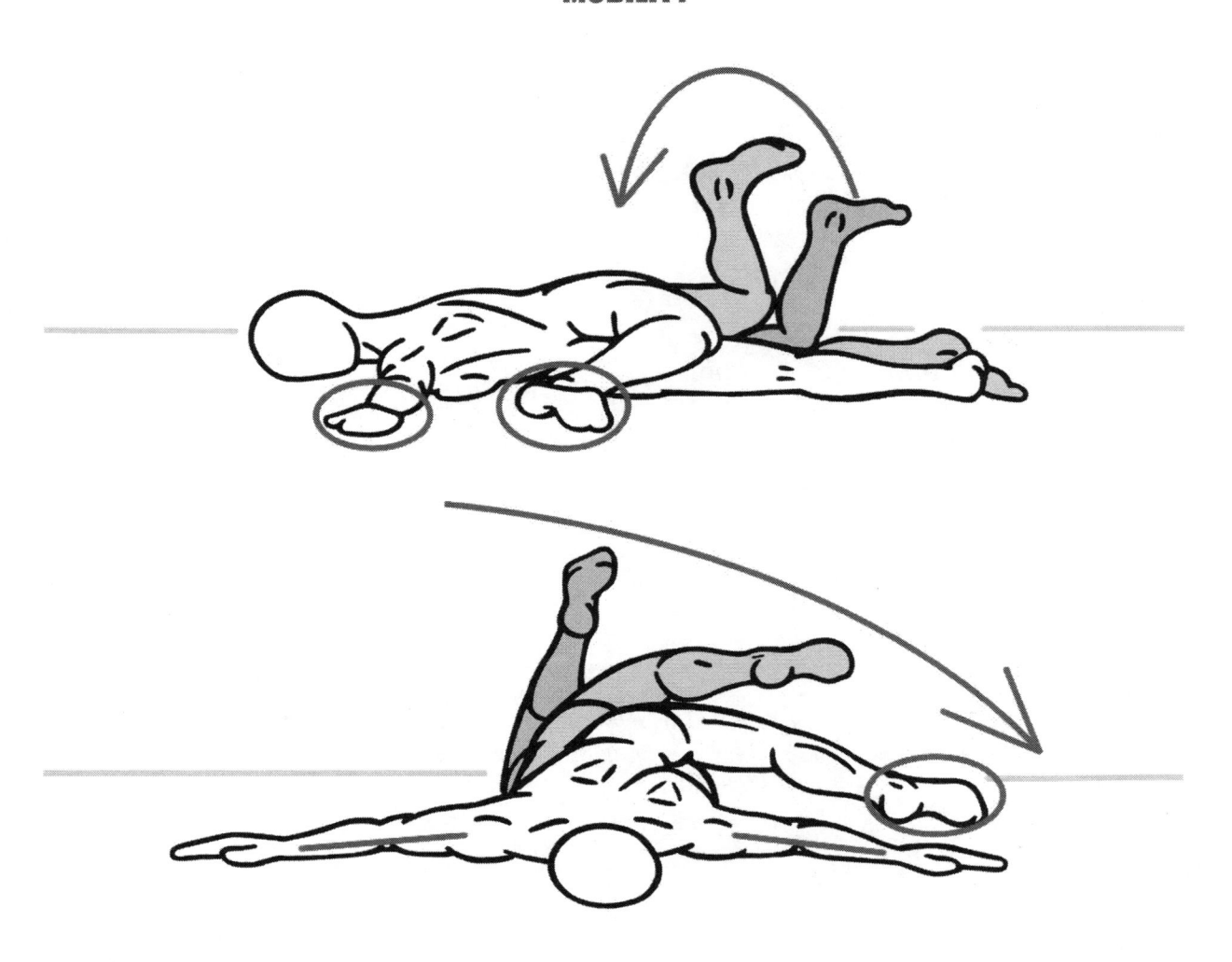

SCORPION

This mobility exercise will help lengthen the hip flexors and restore range of motion to hip extension as well as thoracic rotation and knee flexion. This movement will greatly benefit running and jumping.

POSITION: Lie on the ground with the arms fully extended out to each side, making a "T" formation with the spine. Turn the head to one side and place the cheek on the ground.

ACTION: Lift a foot off the ground and reach the heel towards the opposite hand while lengthening through the spine and the opposite leg. Keep the arms, shoulders and chest flat on the ground and lower the leg back to the floor with control before switching sides.

Modes of Application:
- *Smoothly perform several reps of this movement as you breathe deeply and relax.*
- *Next, hold this position for approximately 30 seconds as you mentally imagine your hip flexors lengthen and focus on deep exhalations.*

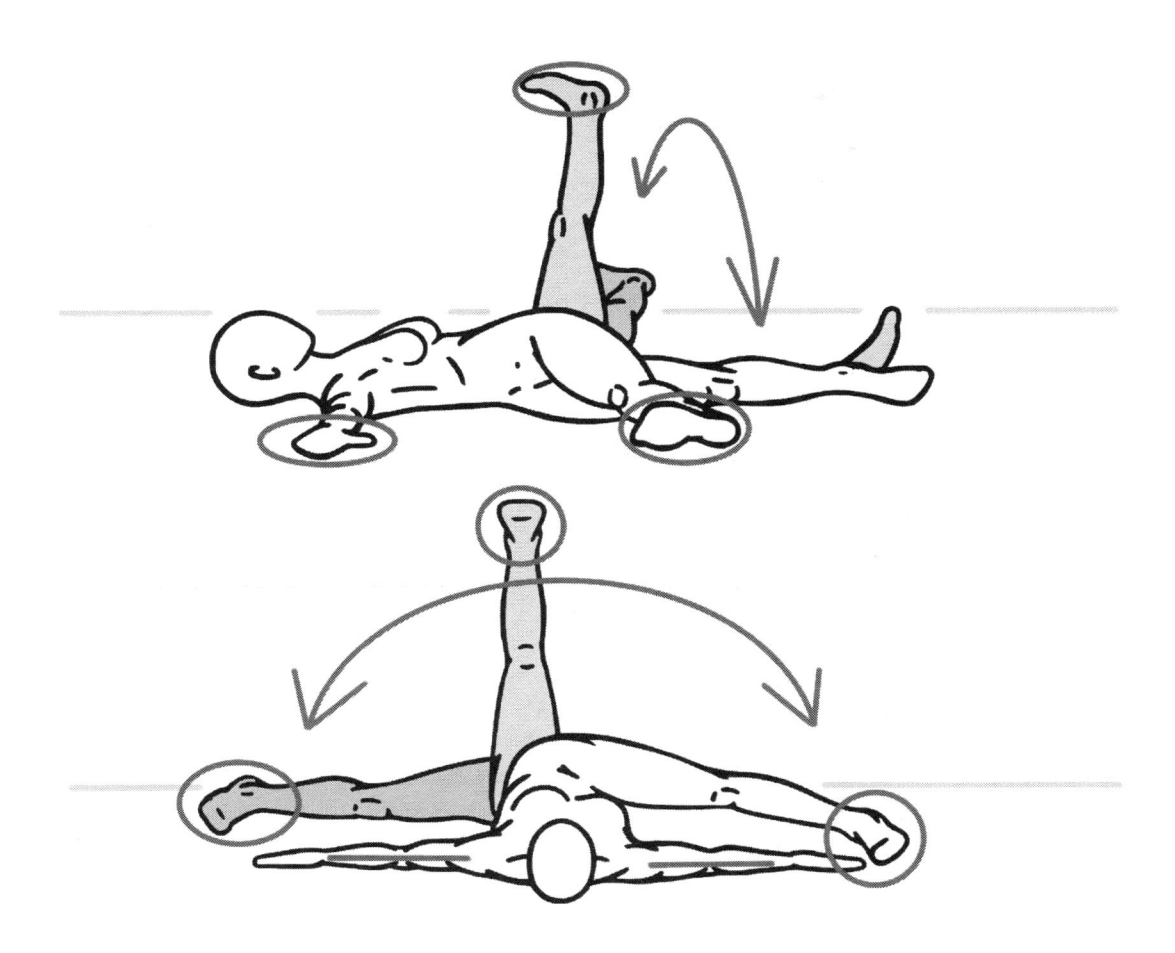

REVERSE SCORPION

POSITION: Lie on the floor with one foot lifted up into the sky and both arms extended into a "T" formation with the spine. Palms flat on the floor.

ACTION: Pull the leg across the body and lower the foot to the floor before reversing directions and touching the floor on the other side of the body. Keep the arms flat against the floor and roll the hips over and back as the torso rotates. Move the leg with control and reach as far as possible.

Modes of Application:
- *Smoothly perform several reps of this movement as you breathe deeply and relax.*
- *Next, hold each end position for approximately 30 seconds as you mentally imagine your hip flexors, adductors and hamstrings lengthening and focus on deep exhalations.*

MOBILITY

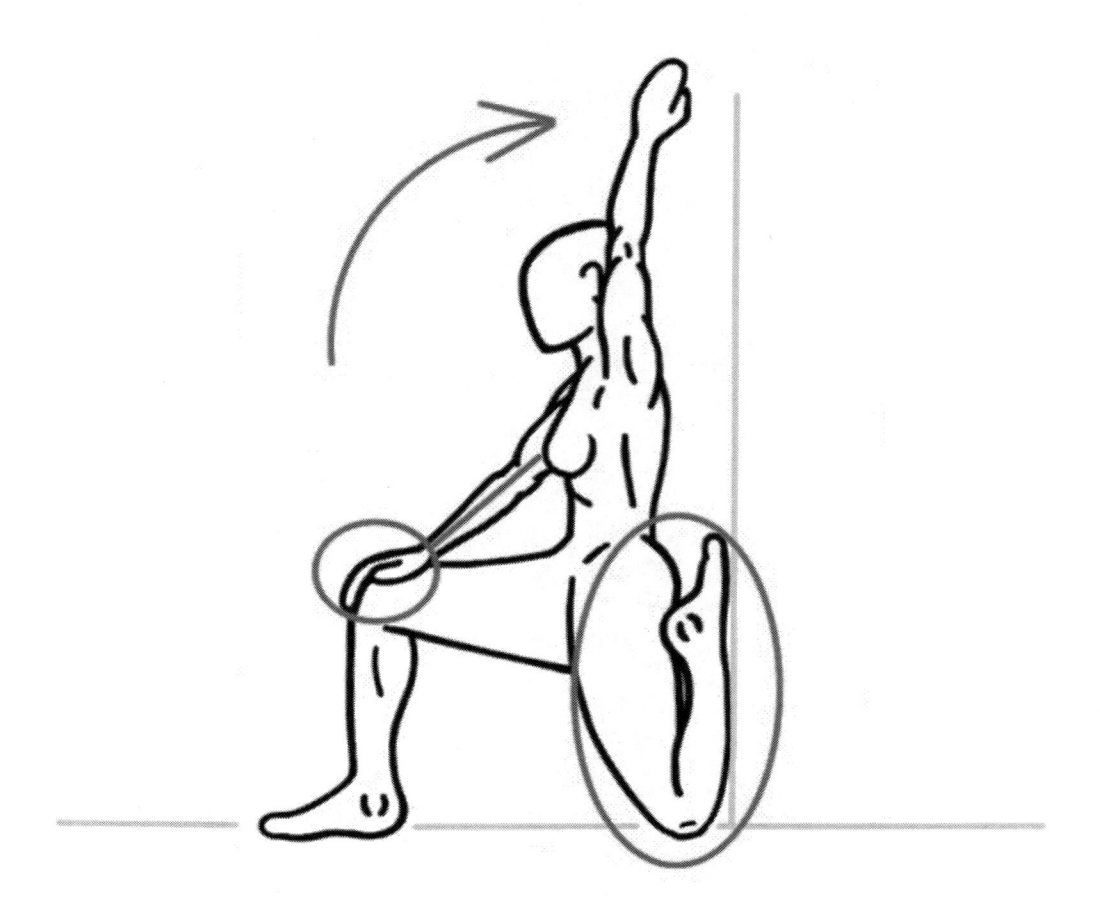

COUCH STRETCH

In addition to demonstrating the optimal range of motion in the Hip Flexors and Quadriceps, this exercise is an indicator of movement tendencies, i.e. habits, when it comes to running. Severe tightness in this pattern usually correlates with a 'Quad Dominant' stride with the absence of the Forward Lean technique. In other words, this exercise may tell you if your running technique is holding you back. If you happen are very tight in this exercise, make a commitment to loosening up your Hip Flexors and Quads as well as emphasizing Hip Activation exercises.

POSITION: Kneel on the ground with the rear shin pressed against a wall.

ACTION: Place both hands on the forward knee and gently slide the rear knee closer to the wall. Press against the front knee with both hands and press the hips back towards the wall, attempting to touch the rear heel. Once the hips are back far enough, take the arm that is on the same side of the braced knee, and reach up to touch the wall. Breathe deeply and relax

Modes of Application:
- *Hold this position for approximately 30-60+ seconds as you mentally imagine your hip flexors lengthen and focus on deep exhalations.*
- *Hold the end position and perform several Contract/Relax sequences with the targeted hip and quadriceps.*

MOBILITY

Linked to the Posterior Chain

If you have gotten this far with all of these mobility exercises for your hips, that's tremendous! You've done a great job of prepping your prime movers to move. But you're not done yet.

The hips are an important part of the Posterior Chain, which is a very large neuromuscular system that spans the entire backside of your body. The Posterior Chain is a very interdependent tensegrity structure. In other words, every muscle as well as every bit of soft tissue from head to toe will affect the biomechanics of the Posterior Chain and how you run.

Fortunately, you have just cleaned up the mobility of the biggest and most important muscles in the Posterior Chain! So, when you take on mobilizing the entire Posterior Chain as a system, you have a perfect opportunity to develop efficient movement patterns and some great biomechanical habits.

MOBILITY

MOBILITY

Ankle & Foot Mobility

The foot is the very first link in the kinetic chain as it literally connects us to the ground in most movements. However, the importance of the foot and ankle is very underrated, as it is rare to see people taking the time to practice foot and ankle mobility. Yet, those who do, certainly have an edge over all those who don't in regards to mechanics, balance, reflexes and agility.

A Foot Perspective
What does proper ankle/foot alignment and mobility look like? Well, there are a few things we need to consider, and we can start by looking underneath the foot first.

Even Distribution
In a seminar with foot and ankle specialist, Lenny Parracino, we all took off our shoes and socks to look at the calluses on the bottom of our feet because they tell us how we stand and use our feet. Ideally, we want to have calluses evenly dispersed across the balls of our feet, lightly down the outside edge of the foot, and evenly on the heel.

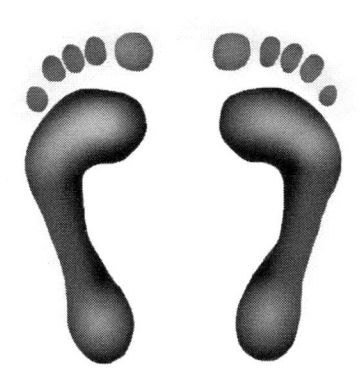

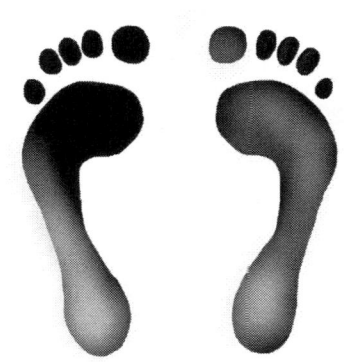

Ideal Pressure Distribution on Feet vs. Pressure Distribution on my Left Foot after tearing my Achilles Tendon – twice.

Work to do.
When I took my shoes and socks off, my training partner dropped his jaw in surprise. The calluses on my left foot heavily covered only my heel and back half of my foot. Since I had torn my Achilles tendon attached to this foot, I grew accustomed to standing on my heel because I was lacking the endurance and strength in my Gastrocnemius (Calf muscle). I quickly showed Lenny my foot and told him my story to which he softly chuckled and said, "You have a lot of work to do. " And work I did. I spent hours upon hours retraining the alignment and mobility of my ankle/foot complex, which is why I noticed how many other people neglect to do the same.

Look at the bottom of your feet to see how you stand.

MOBILITY

The Toes
Next, we want to focus on the toes- two in particular. Let's start with the little toe. Stand up with your shoes and socks off and try to laterally move your pinkie toe. In other words, attempt to move it out to the side as far as possible. If you can, great! The tissues in your feet are mobile enough in this pattern to allow your toes to move independently as they are designed too. In fact, the pinkie toe is partially responsible for creating lateral stability in all of your movements.

If you cannot independently move the pinkie toe out to the side, this is a sign that the tissues of your feet are not sliding the way that they should. They have grown a stickiness to the surrounding tissues as a compensation. This usually happens to those who sit often and don't practice moving a lot in bare feet.

Start applying soft tissue therapy techniques to your feet and use the following mobility exercises as well as make a practice of getting out of your shoes as often as possible.

Big Toe Test
Stand in your bare feet and try to lift just the big toe up off the ground. This exercise will test an important joint in your gait that can dramatically affect how you walk and run.

If your big toe cannot lift up to a 30-degree angle, then your entire gait will be compromised, as its range of motion is limited. Tightness in this big toe will not allow the foot to roll over as it is meant to in your stride. If this is you, start right away with applying soft tissue therapy to your feet and practice these mobility exercises until you can see noticeable improvement.

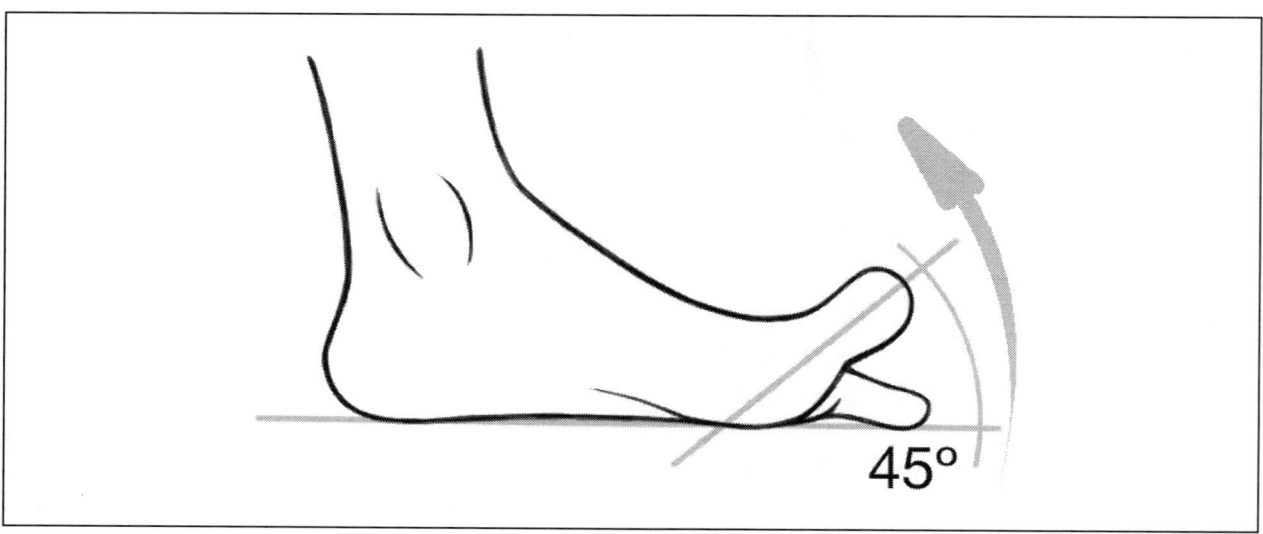

Big Toe Test:
Lift the Big Toe Off the Floor

Does the Big Toe Extend to at least 45°?
If not, practice some Soft Tissue Therapy on your Foot and Ankle.

MOBILITY

Soft Tissue Therapy
The foot is a very intricate and complex system of joints, which connects tissues together in a multitude of ways. Performing soft tissue therapy techniques with a golf ball, tennis ball, lacrosse ball or even just your fingers and hands can get into the small areas of the foot and help smooth out the knots and adhesions.

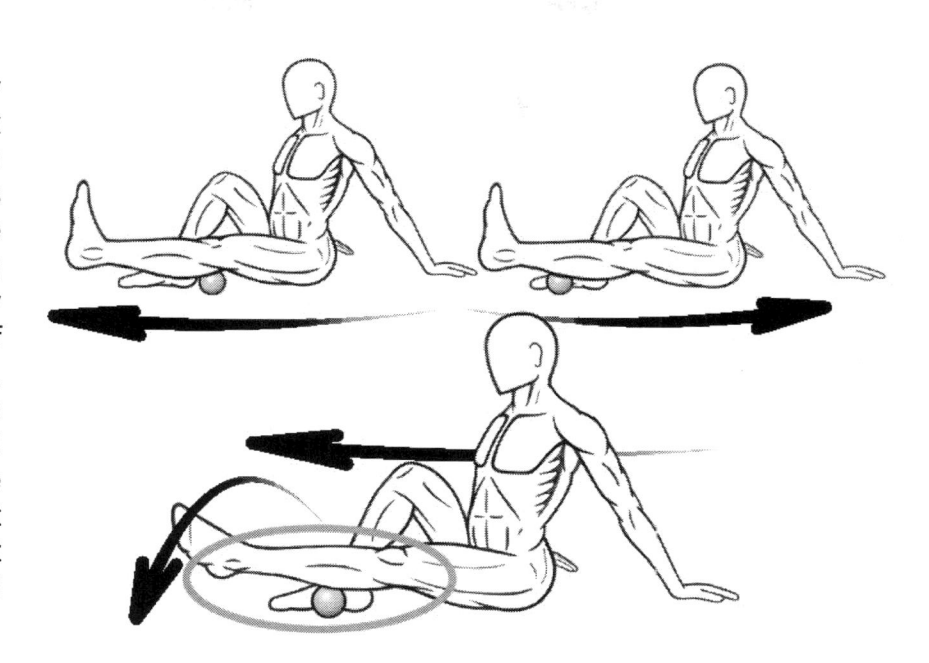

Balling Your Calf
Using a foam roller on your calves is helpful to stimulate your neuromuscular connections and smooth out some lingering knots. However, elevating your soft tissue therapy to the next level can really help to mobilize your ankles and calves. Use either a Posture Ball, Lacrosse Ball or tennis ball to explore deeper into the soft tissue of your calves and really help separate adhesions and remove built up scar tissue.

The calves can endure much neuromuscular strain, especially in runners with all of the force absorption that occurs in every step. Be smart and start to tend to the soft tissue in this area, as it will only add more spring back into your step.

My personal recommendation is to ball your calves at least one minute for every mile you run each day and if you are an athlete who runs a lot in your sport, then I recommend at least five minutes of ball work on your calves each day. Yet, feel free to do more if it pleases you!

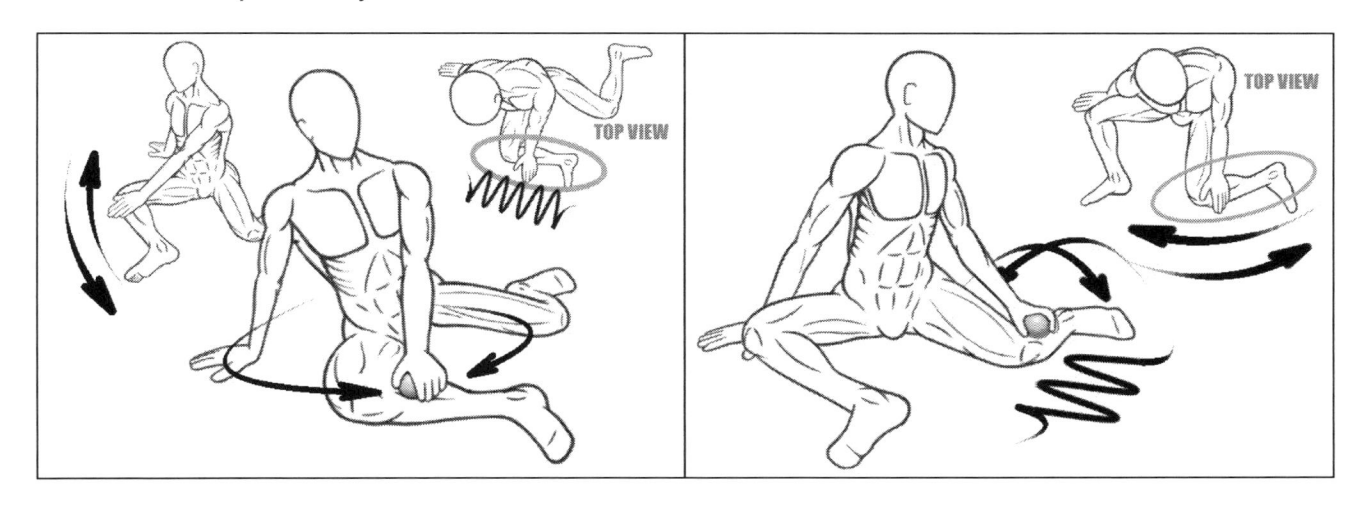

PreHab Exercise Book for Runners

MOBILITY

Use a Golf Ball
Place a golf ball on the floor and roll your foot back and forth over it while applying pressure. The acute curvature of the golf ball will be useful in separating soft tissue and smoothing out the knots and adhesions under the foot. Roll in a multitude of directions to be more effective.

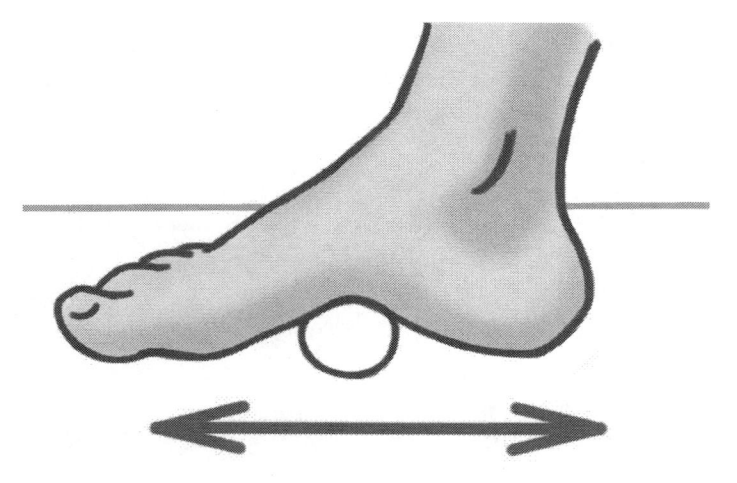

Grab, Pull and Twist
Use your hand to help separate and smooth out the knots in the foot by grabbing the foot and pulling or twisting the soft tissue. Squeeze and apply pressure with the pads of your fingertips on and around any sticky or hard areas. Keep a limit to how hard you squeeze, but keep working on the knots until you can feel a noticeable difference in your soft tissue.

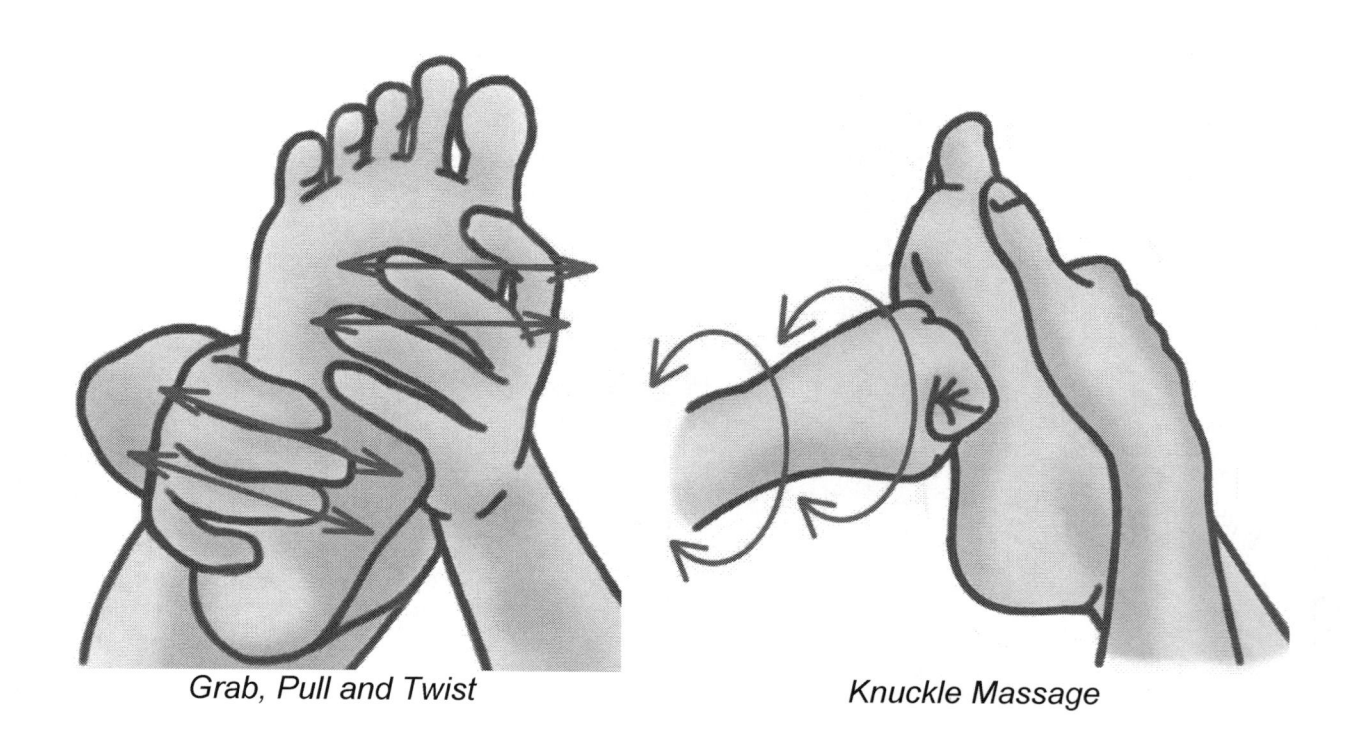

Grab, Pull and Twist   Knuckle Massage

MOBILITY

Mobilize and Lengthen the Plantar Fascia
Pull your heel away from the balls of your foot while you emphasize deep exhales. This stretch will help to lengthen your Plantar Fascia as well as the muscles and tendons underneath.

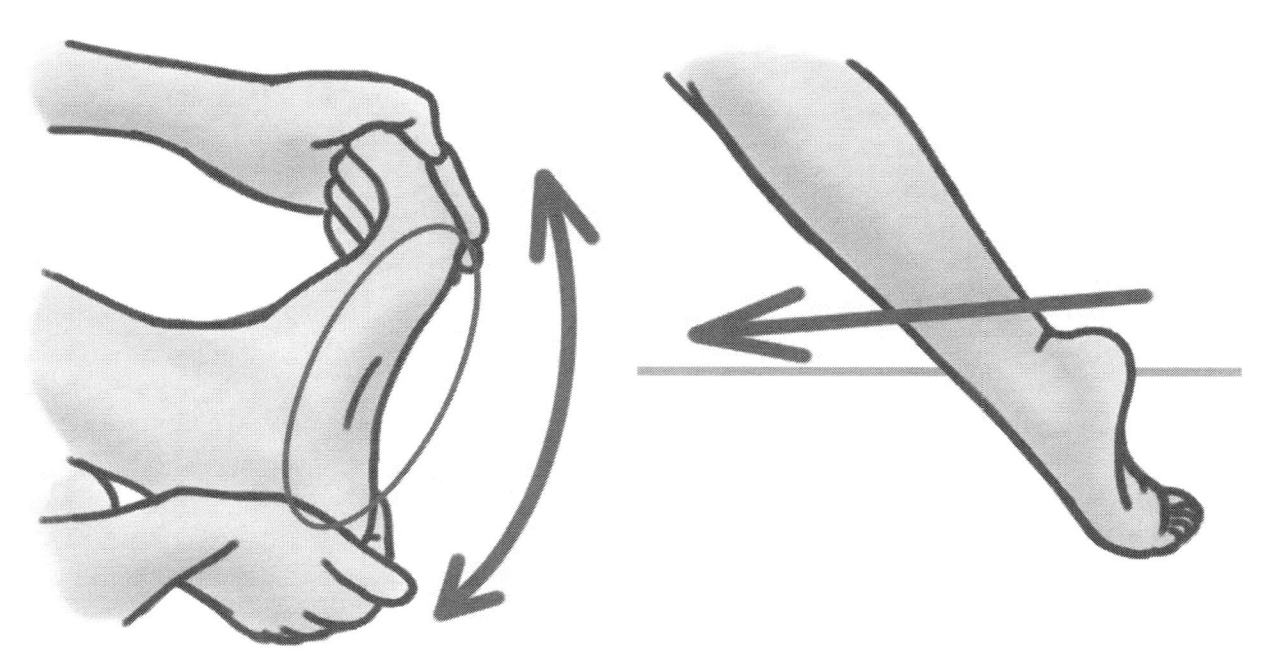

Stretching the Plantar Fascia   **Plantar Flexion of the Ankle**

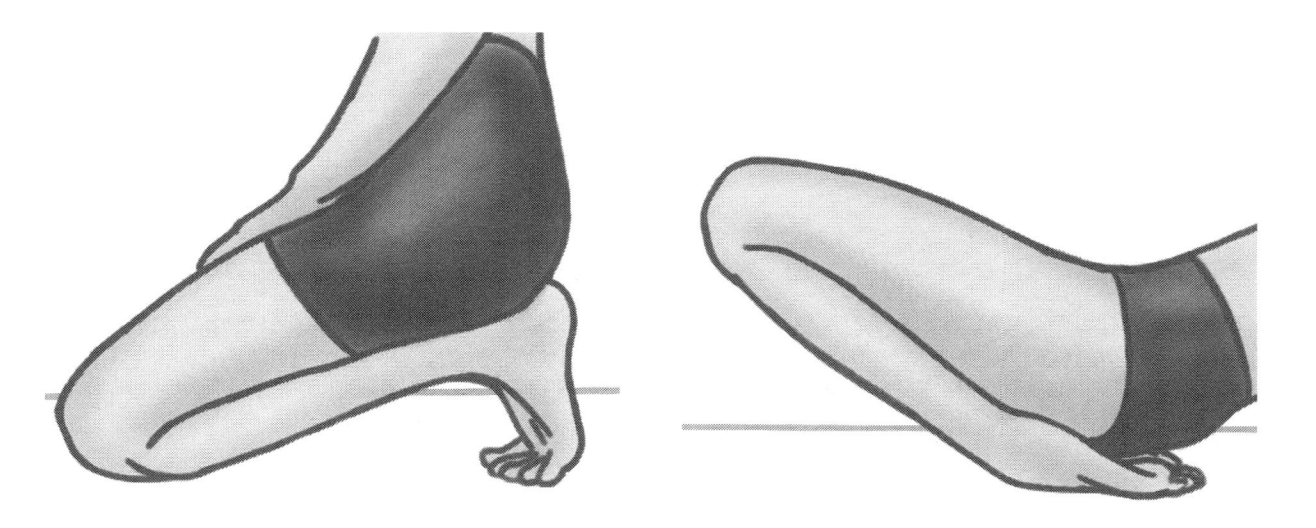

Static Dorsiflexion Stretch and Static Plantar Flexion Stretch

MOBILITY

Mobility Exercises

Here are several different active flexibility exercises that you can perform in a static position, a dynamic flow, or apply a Proprioceptor Neuromuscular Facilitation (PNF) technique, such as Contract/Relax.

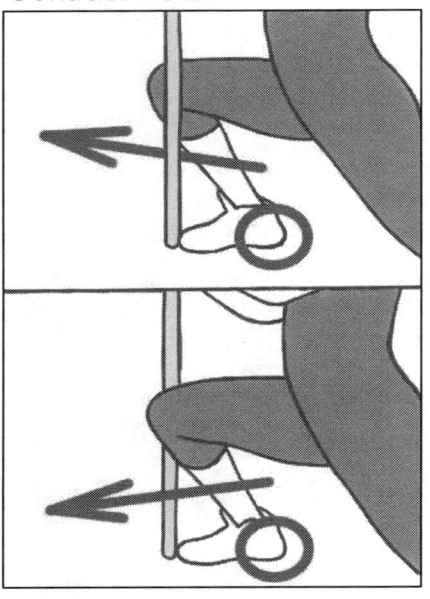

KNEELING CALF STRETCH with Pole
This mobility exercise will help you to loosen up your ankle and foot complex while also providing a visual measurement to gauge the amount of mobility that you have in your lower leg system.

POSTION: Kneel on the ground and vertically hold a pole at the front of your foot. Make sure the pole is straight and not drifting to the side. If you do not have a pole, you can simply use a wall instead.

ACTION: Drive your knee forward and to the side of the pole while keeping your heel completely flat on the ground. Use one of the following three stretching techniques:

Modes of Application-
- Hold this dorsiflexed position in a static stretch and generate large exhalations to elicit a parasympathetic tone in your nervous system that will help the neuromuscular system release.
- Perform several reps of this action with smooth and controlled movements as you relax and breathe.
- Apply the PNF technique of Contract/Relax while in the stretched position. Contract the calf and foot muscles for 5 seconds by pressing your forefoot into the floor, then relax for 10 seconds or three deep exhalations. Repeat contract release cycle 3-5 times or until you can feel a release in the musculature of your lower leg and foot.

Your knee should be able to pass the pole or touch the wall if you are not using a pole with your heel on the ground. If your knee cannot pass the pole, you have limited mobility in your ankle and foot, which will create compensation in other movement patterns. Practice these stretches in combination with the recommended soft tissue therapy above until you can establish full range of motion in your ankle and foot.

MOBILITY

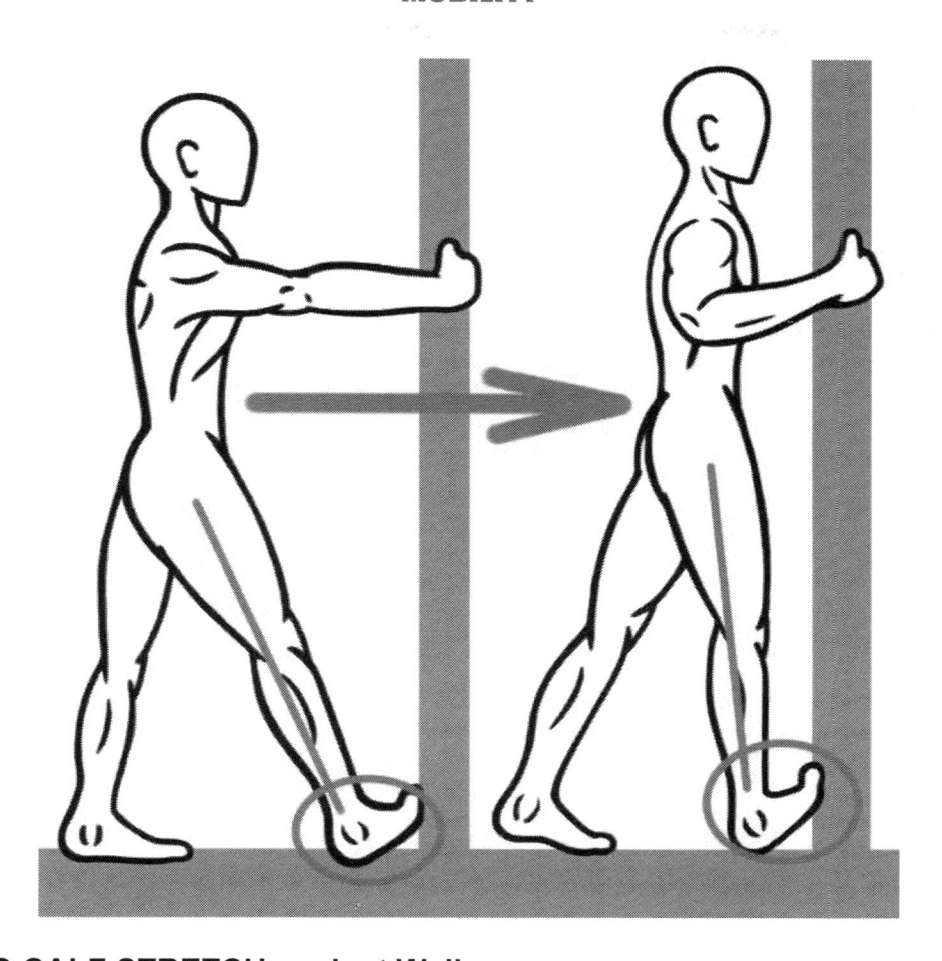

STANDING CALF STRETCH against Wall

We get to focus on lengthening the Gastrocnemius (Calf Muscle) in this mobility exercise. The focus is different from the kneeling calf stretch because the Gastrocnemius, that bubble muscle in your calf, attached at about the knee, will not be affected to a great degree if the knee is bent.

POSITION: Place your forefoot flush up against a wall and wedge the heel into the floor. Try to make an equilateral triangle with your foot, wall and floor. Then straighten your knee and press your hips towards the wall.

ACTION: Press your hips towards the wall and then slide from side to side, looking for any tight sensations in your foot or calf. Once you have found a line of action through your musculature that is tight, use one of the following three stretching techniques:

Modes of Application-
- Hold in a static stretch and generate large exhalations to elicit a parasympathetic tone in your nervous system that will help the neuromuscular system release.
- Perform several reps of pressing your hips towards the wall with smooth and controlled movements as you relax and breathe.
- Apply the PNF technique of Contract/Relax while in the stretched position. Contract the calf and foot muscles for 5 seconds by pressing your forefoot into the floor, then relax for 10 seconds or three deep exhalations. Repeat contract release cycle 3-5 times or until you can feel a release in the musculature of your lower leg and foot.

MOBILITY

ANKLE MATRIX
This PreHab exercise uses a dynamic flow of movement to help mobilize the ankle/foot complex. It is useful in a group-training situation when there are limitations in providing effective instructions for PNF stretching.

POSITION: Use your arms to brace your body against the wall on an angled slope with straight-line alignment from ear to hips to ankle. Slope the body approximately 30-45 degrees, but make sure that the standing heel is flush on the ground. Lift one leg off the ground and hold with a flexed position of the hip.

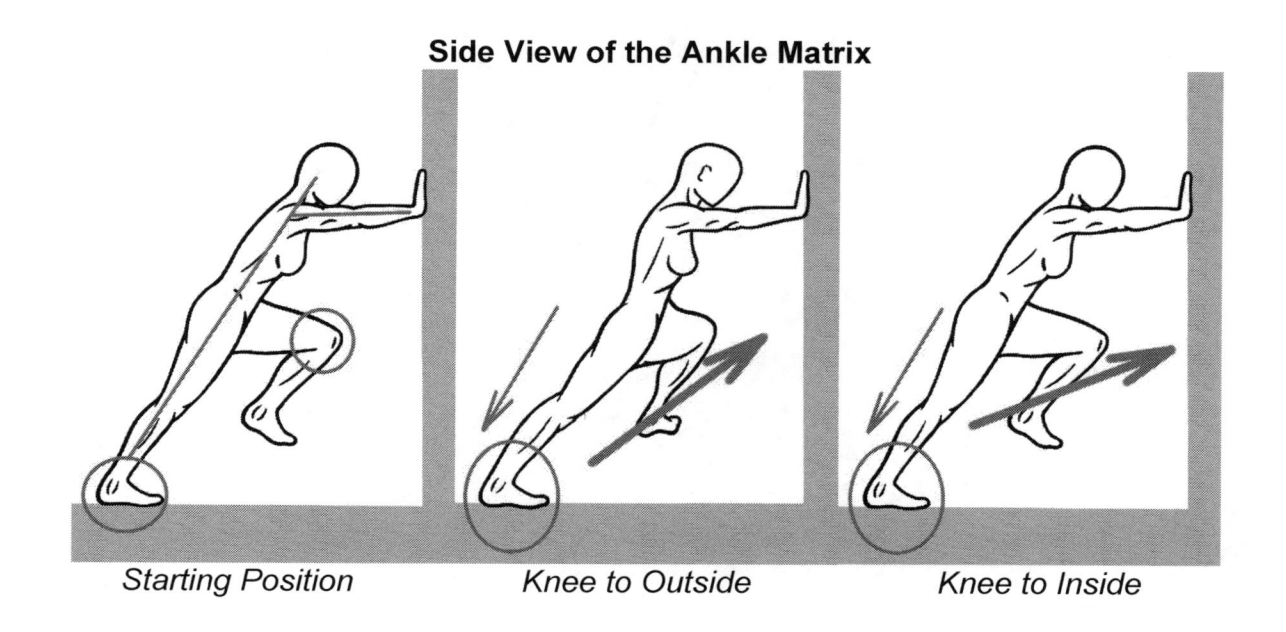

Side View of the Ankle Matrix

Starting Position   *Knee to Outside*   *Knee to Inside*

ACTION: As you keep the standing heel flat on the ground, drive the raised knee towards the wall in several directions: forward, right and left.

Driving the hips forward will stretch the standing calf and foot, while changing the angle of the raised knee can change the stretching emphasis on the calf and foot. Perform these movements in a smooth and controlled manner. Stay relaxed and breathe deeply. Find the directions and areas that work to release the most tension in your calf or foot and focus on those areas more.

Keep the back heel pressed into the floor throughout all of the movements. The back heel is the ankle that is being targeted. If the heel begins to lift from the floor as you drive the knee in the different directions towards the wall, it is an indication that you are tight and have restrictions in that movement pattern.

Revisit the other stretches and soft tissue therapy techniques for the calf and foot if you are not able to keep the back heel completely flat on the ground while performing this Ankle Matrix.

MOBILITY

Rear View of Ankle Matrix

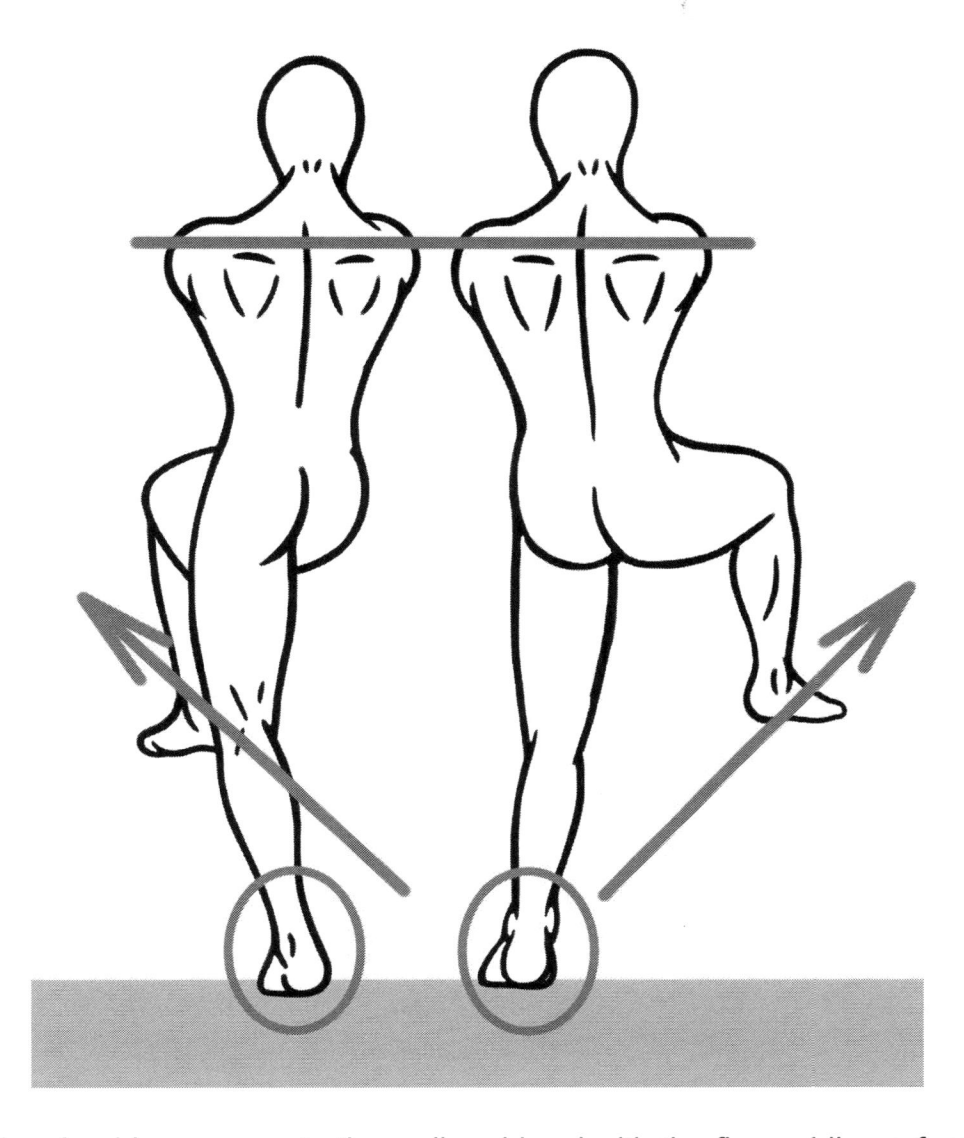

Also, keep the shoulders square to the wall and level with the floor while performing the different variations of this stretch.

Modes of Application:
- Smoothly perform several reps of this movement in each direction as you breathe deeply and relax. Next, hold this position for approximately 30 seconds as you press your knee towards the wall and keep the rear heel flat on the ground. Focus on deep exhalations.
- Optional: Hold the end position and perform several Contract/Relax sequences with the targeted ankle/foot.

MOBILITY

STANDING ANKLE CIRCLES

The simplest mobility exercise for the ankle is the standing ankle circles. Well, it is conceptually easy. However, you may find that it is not as easy as it looks, and that is in part to the tensegrity of your body. As you hold your leg in a different position, the lines of tension in your body will change. This exercise helps you to gauge what positions or line of action have the most tension or limitation in your body.

POSITION: Place the hands on the hips and hold one leg out into three different positions.

ACTION: Flex and extend the ankle several times before rotating the ankle in both directions for several more times. Keep the hands on the hips and focus the eyes on the horizon to develop balance. Move the foot through the largest range of motion on each repetition as much as possible while maintaining balance.

Repeat several times with each leg in the three positions.

Go in the Right Direction
When it's all said and done, if you want to get the results you desire from training, you need to make sure that your ankle and foot mobility will send you in the right direction. It may be easy to overlook, but if you do neglect your ankle and foot mobility, there is no telling where you will end up.

MOBILITY

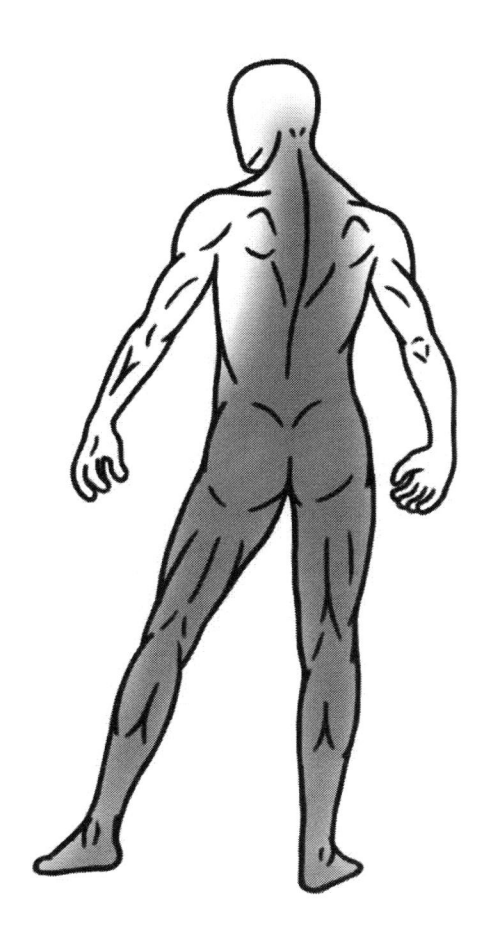

Posterior Chain Mobility

You've heard the saying, "only as strong as the weakest link." Well, when it comes to running, your stride is only as fluid as your tightest link in your posterior chain.

Posterior Chain
Our bodies are tensegrity structures that perform movements in designated patterns. The posterior chain is the neuromuscular system that spans the entire backside of our bodies, from underneath the big toe to the base of the skull. This expansion system is also very interdependent, meaning what happens under the foot can affect what happens all throughout this chain in certain movement patterns, such as running, walking or jumping – to name a few.

The Posterior Chain is the large neuromuscular system along the backside of our bodies that is biomechanically responsible for how we walk, run, and jump.

For runners, as well as athletes who run, properly maintaining adequate range of motion and tending to the health of your soft tissue in your posterior chain will reap many benefits, including increased speed, endurance and longevity.

Power and Speed
The posterior chain is the most powerful neuromuscular system in the body. It has produced world records like a 1,268-pound squat, a 2:03-marathon finish, and a 9.58-second 100-meter sprint. Yet, none of these records would have ever been created if these athletes who set these records did not develop strength through their entire range of motion. That's why developing and maintaining mobility in your posterior chain is so important.

Full and functional mobility in your posterior chain provides the biomechanical foundation on which you can create impressive power and speed.

MOBILITY

In addition to creating full range of motion, the following mobility exercises and soft tissue therapy techniques will help to develop neuromuscular responsiveness in your posterior chain. Doing this will help your reflexes and timing as you run, lift weights and play sports.

National Glory
What would you think if I told you the fate of an entire nation depends on the health of the posterior chain in a few elite athletes? You might think I'm crazy. However, the hopes and strategies of the U.S. Men's National Soccer Team competing in the 2014 FIFA World Cup both took a hit because of injuries that occurred to some of the players' posterior chain. Both Jozy Altidore and Matt Besler suffered hamstring pulls that kept them from competing in the 2014 World Cup, and consequentially hurt Team USA's chances in the Sweet 16 knockout round.

Photo by Steve Evans

More than ROM
Developing and maintaining adequate mobility is important to practice for more reasons than just having proper range of motion in your movement patterns. Establishing mobility will allow you to avoid various compensations by developing strength throughout an entire movement pattern. Pulled hamstrings are an example of how restricted mobility will create an uneven strength distribution in a given movement pattern, specifically in your gait or stride. During a hamstring pull, the hamstring is either too weak to contract through the ground's resistance or it is attempting to help overcome weak glutes and produce more speed in the stride. In either case, the uneven development of strength throughout the movement pattern eventually leads to a compensation strategy if not an injury.

> ***Practice and maintain adequate mobility in order to fully develop strength and power throughout an entire movement pattern.***

MOBILITY

Step One: Soft Tissue Therapy
Start with foam rolling and then progress to applying additional soft tissue therapy techniques with a lacrosse ball, tennis ball, posture ball or hands.

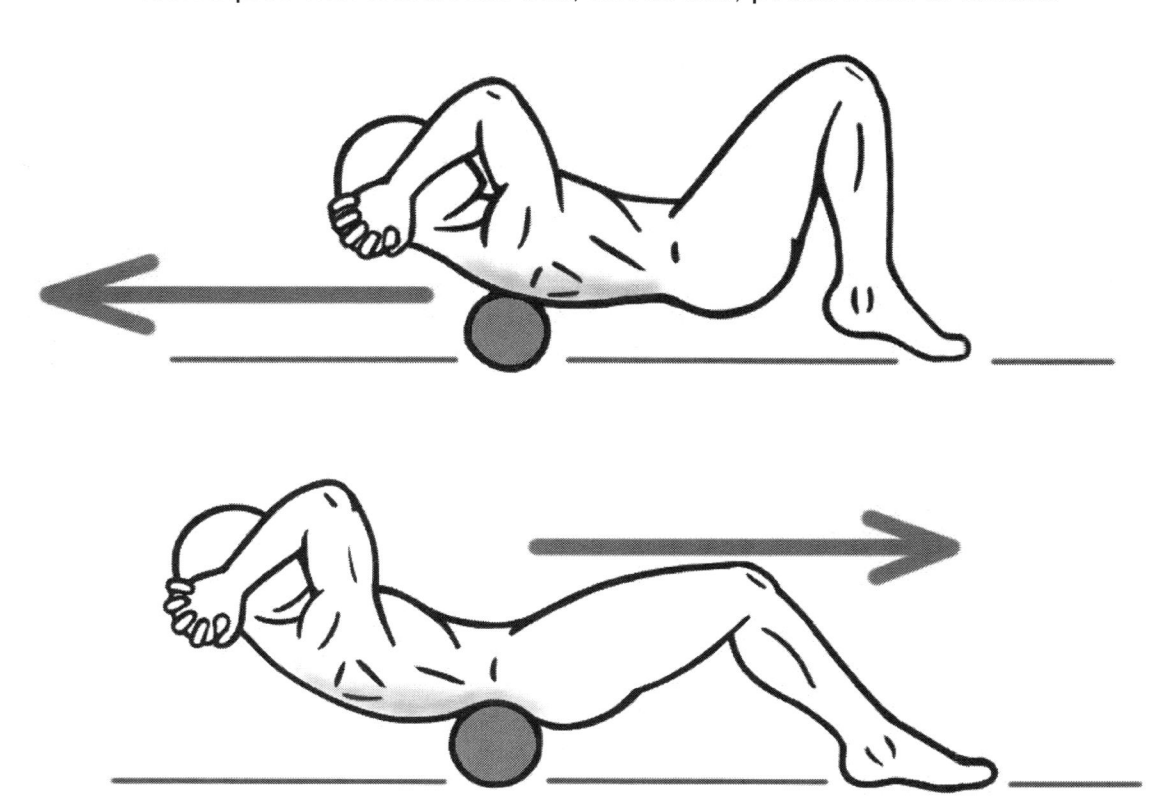

Rolling the Spine

Rolling the Hips (Posterior)

PreHab Exercise Book for Runners

MOBILITY

Rolling the Legs (Posterior)

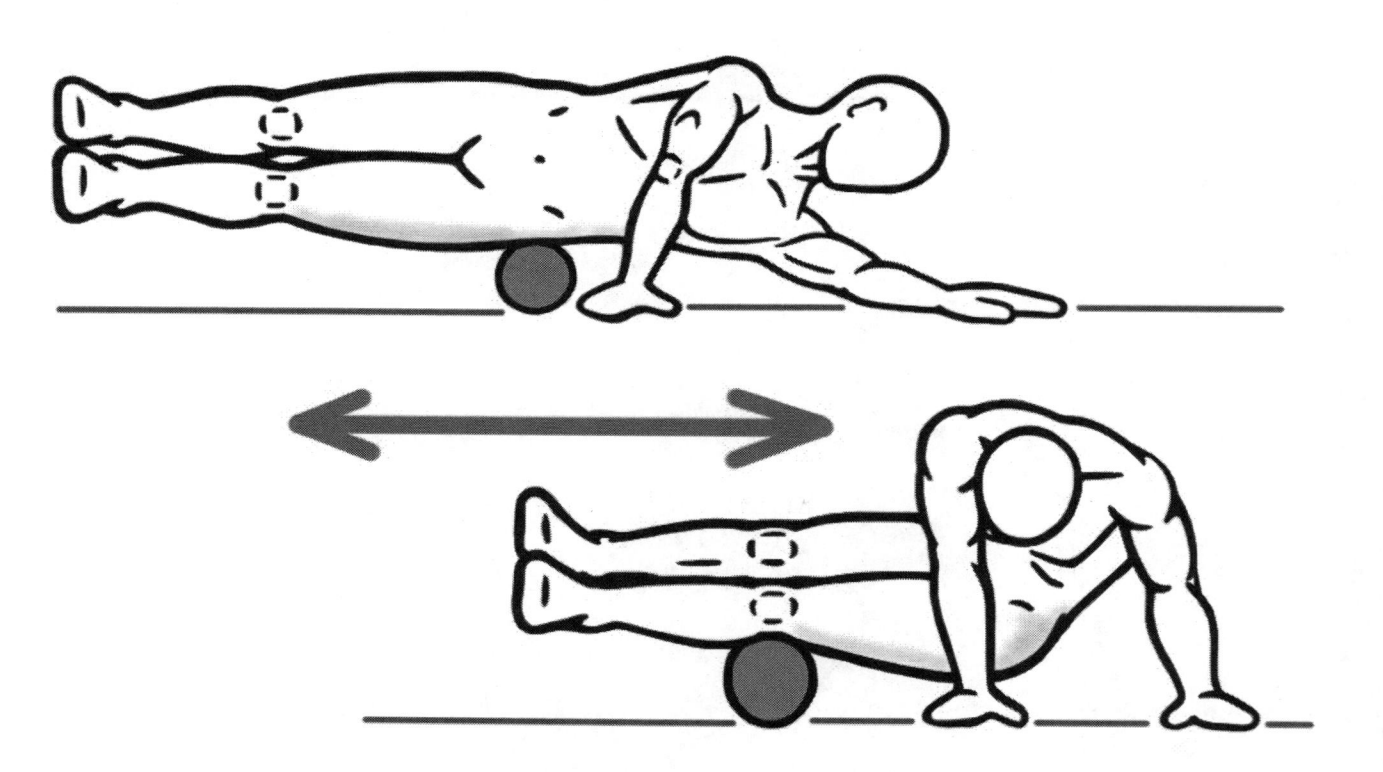

Rolling the Hips and Legs (Lateral)

PreHab Exercise Book for Runners

MOBILITY

Step Two: Mobility Exercises
After you have practiced your soft tissue therapy, move on to these mobility exercises to restore the full range of motion of essential movement patterns.

PNF Contract/Relax Stretches with a Strap

Grab either a yoga strap or a long towel and lie down on your back for some Proprioceptor Neuromuscular Facilitation (PNF) stretches. The PNF Contract/Relax technique is very simple to use. Here's how:

Contract/Relax Technique

Get into a static stretch position

Contract the muscle that you intend to stretch for 5 seconds

Relax that muscle for 10 seconds

Contract again for another 5 seconds

Relax again for another 10 seconds

Contract again for another 5 seconds

Relax again for another 30-plus seconds

If you don't feel the muscle release more after the last contraction, evaluate the alignment of your body in the stretch and make sure that you have the appropriate amount of tension on the target area while relaxing. Adjust and try again. You will know when it works because you will feel the release and see the lengthening occur.

MOBILITY

PNF Autogenic Inhibition

CONTRACT
3-5 Seconds
3-5 Seconds
3-5 Seconds

RELAX
5-10 Seconds
5-10 Seconds
10-30+ Seconds

Supine PNF Contract/Relax Stretch for the Posterior Chain

SUPINE SAGITTAL STRETCH-
TARGET: Glutes, Hamstrings, Calf and Foot in a Sagittal (Forward) line of action, which is greatly responsible for the push-off phase of your gait.

POSTION: Lift one leg straight up towards the sky with a strap or towel wrapped around the arch of the foot. Position the heel directly over the hip socket if possible. If not, keep the leg vertically aligned with the hip socket and the shoulder.

ACTION: Contract for a 5-count with one-fourth of your strength and attempt to pull the heel back to the floor as you hold it in place with the strap. Next, relax for a 10 count as you hold the leg. Repeat this Contract/Relax sequence two more times and continue to hold the stretch until you can feel the muscles release.

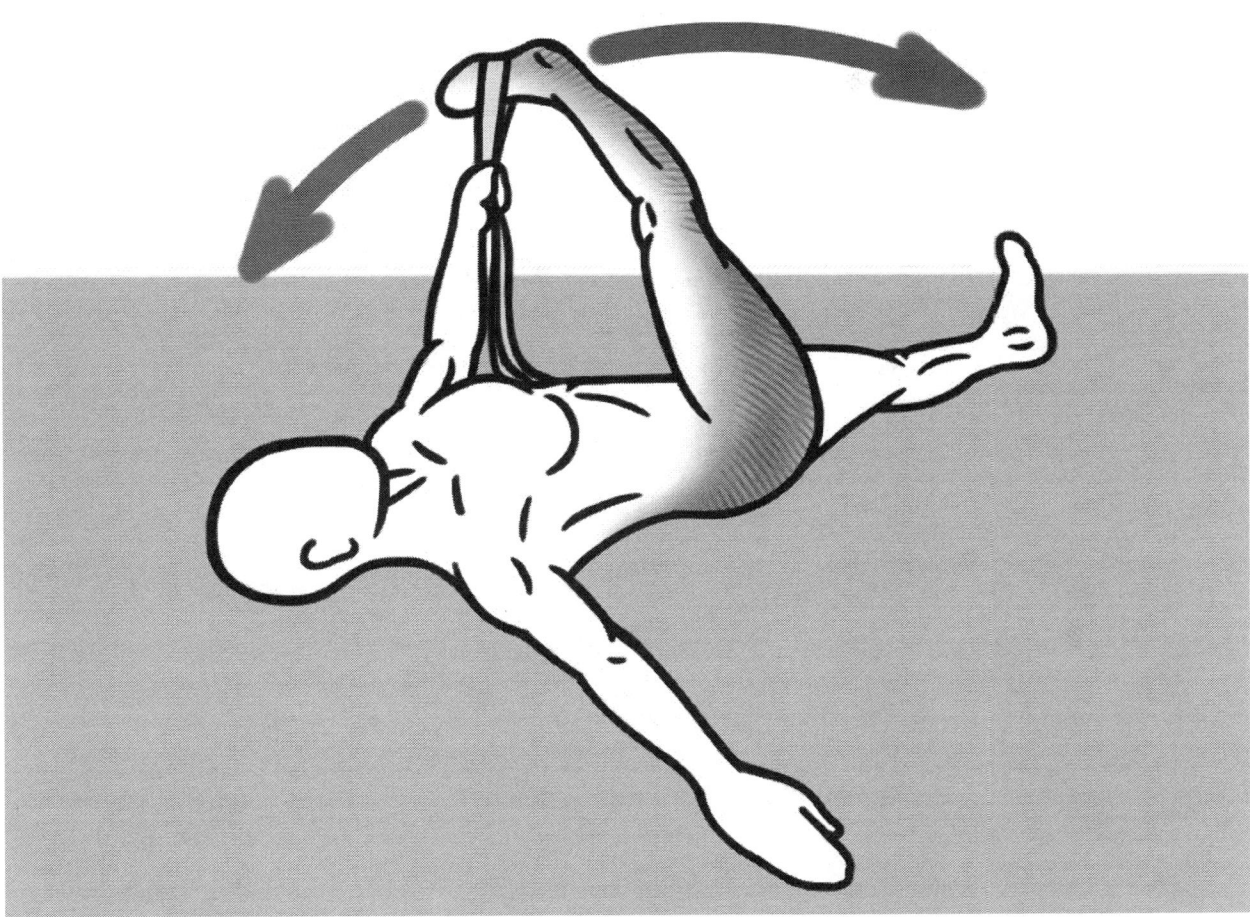

MOBILITY

Supine PNF Contract/Relax Stretch for the Posterior Chain and Abductors

SUPINE ABDUCTOR STRETCH-
TARGET: Lateral aspect of the Glutes, Hamstrings, Quadriceps, IT Band, Calf and Foot in a Transverse (Rotational) line of action, which is greatly responsible for the pulling (backward) phase of your gait and stabilizing the planted leg while running.

POSTION: Lift one leg straight up towards the sky with a strap or towel wrapped around the arch of the foot. Pull the heel across the body and down towards the floor while you keep the same side shoulder flat on the ground. Attempt to align the foot at hip height or as close as possible in order to affect more of your soft tissue on the lateral side of your hamstrings, quadriceps and glutes.

ACTION: Contract for a 5-count with one-fourth of your strength and attempt to pull the heel back up towards the sky as you hold it in place with the strap. Next, relax for a 10-count as you hold the leg. Repeat this Contract/Relax sequence two more times and continue to hold the stretch until you can feel the muscles release.

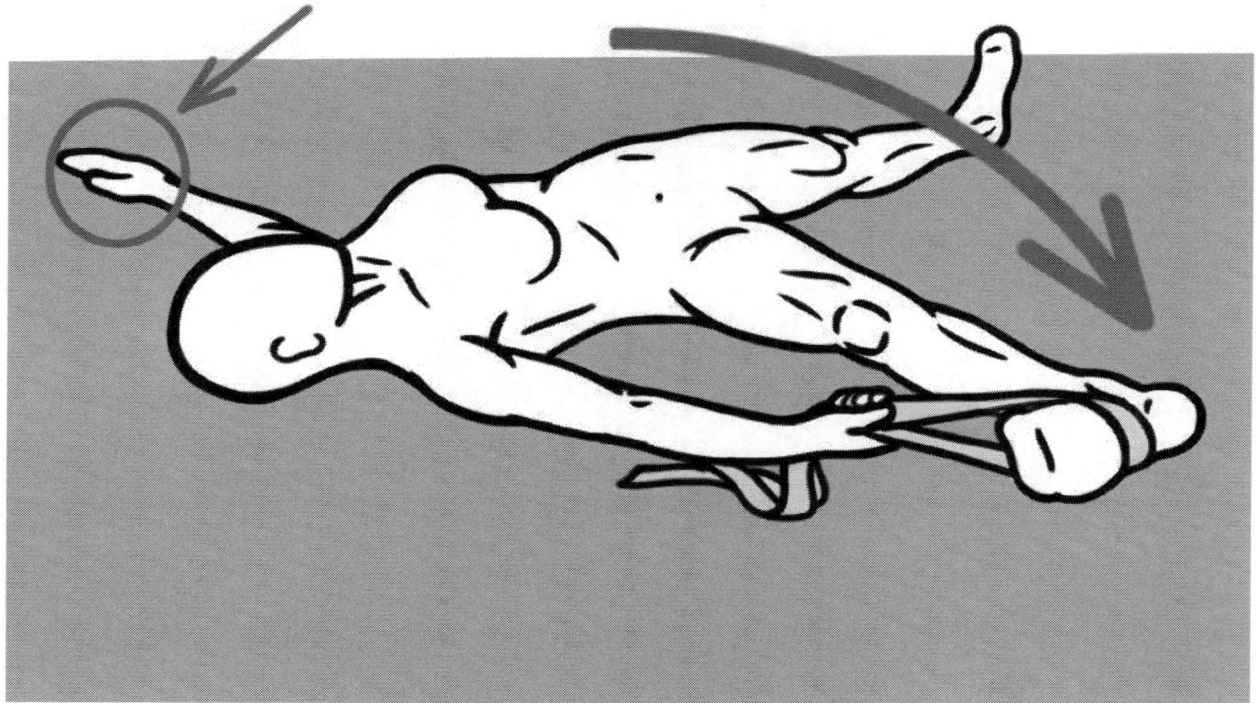

MOBILITY

Supine PNF Contract/Relax Stretch for the Posterior Chain and Adductors

SUPINE ADDUCTOR STRETCH-
TARGET: The Medial (Inner) aspects of the Hamstrings, Quadriceps, Calf and Foot as well as the Hip Flexors and Adductors. These muscles, which are positioned on the inner thigh and groin, are partially responsible for the pulling (forward) phase of your gait and the stabilization of the planted leg.

POSTION: Lift one leg straight up towards the sky with a strap or towel wrapped around the arch of the foot. Position the heel directly over the hip socket if possible. If not, keep the leg vertically aligned with the hip socket and the shoulder.

ACTION: Contract for a 5-count with one-fourth of your strength and attempt to pull the heel up towards the sky as you hold it in place with the strap. Next, relax for a 10 count as you hold the leg. Repeat this Contract/Relax sequence two more times and continue to hold the stretch until you can feel the muscles release.

MOBILITY

> **Active Flexibility Exercises**
> The following exercises, also referred to as Dynamic Stretches, will help lengthen the soft tissue and prep the neuromuscular connections of the posterior chain.

Supine Mobility Sequence

This sequence of dynamic stretches is very beneficial for runners for a couple of reasons. First, the supine position unloads the body and changes the gravitational pull on the body, which helps to elicit more of a parasympathetic tone in your nervous system. The Parasympathetic nervous system will help the body facilitate its own natural healing process and help the soft tissue release or lengthen. In contrast, the Sympathetic nervous system, also known as the "Fight or Flight" mechanism, creates more tension in the body and elevates the heart rate as well as stimulates a host of other biochemical reactions that are geared to help the body take action.

Another way runners will benefit from this Supine Mobility Sequence is the opportunity to stimulate specific neuromuscular connections while coordinating the actual movements of these exercises. Simply by performing these stretches, a host of neuromuscular connections are activated and since these movements are the primitive movements found within running, the body is essentially being prepped to run while experiencing an increase of Parasympathetic activity in your nervous system. In a way, this sequence can help you find the Zen in your running mechanics if that is one of your goals.

SUPINE LEG LIFT

POSITION: Lie down with one leg extended straight out on the floor with the opposite foot planted flat on the ground with a bent knee. Extend the arms alongside of the body.

ACTION: Lift the extended leg straight up to the sky and flex the ankle. Keep the knee fully extended throughout this entire movement. Press the arms into the floor and draw a straight line across the sky with the heel on each lift.

Repeat several times on each side.

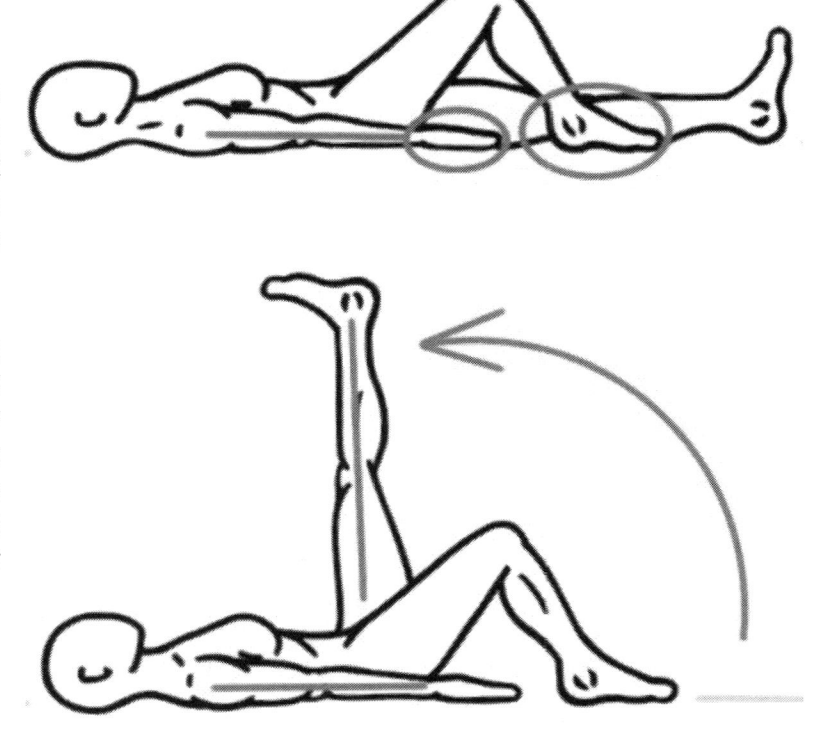

PreHab Exercise Book for Runners

MOBILITY

SUPINE LEG-LOCKED KNEE EXTENSION

POSITION: Lie down on the ground with the hands locked around one thigh and the opposite leg fully extended out on the floor. Interlace the fingers and hold the leg tightly.

ACTION: Gently kick the foot up into the sky while pressing the opposite leg down into the floor. Press the heel up into the sky as far as possible and attempt to fully extend the knee on each repetition. Pull the toes back down towards the nose.

Repeat several times on each leg.

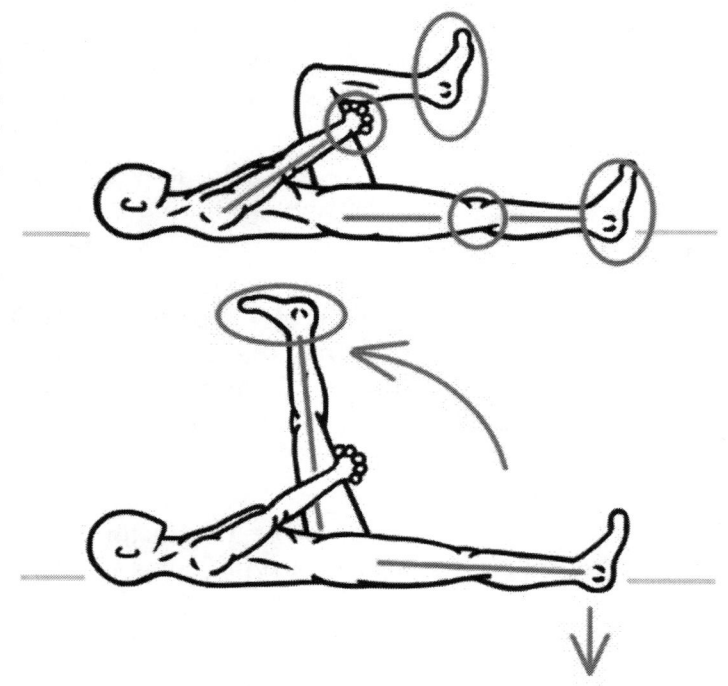

SUPINE ANKLE CIRCLES

POSITION: Lie down on the ground and extend one leg into the sky. Hold the lifted leg with both arms and interlace the fingers while extending the opposite leg straight on the floor.

ACTION: Flex and extend the ankle as far as possible several times in each direction. Next, rotate the ankle as far as possible several times in each direction. Draw tiny circles with the heel and keep the knee fully extended if possible.

Repeat this sequence on each leg.

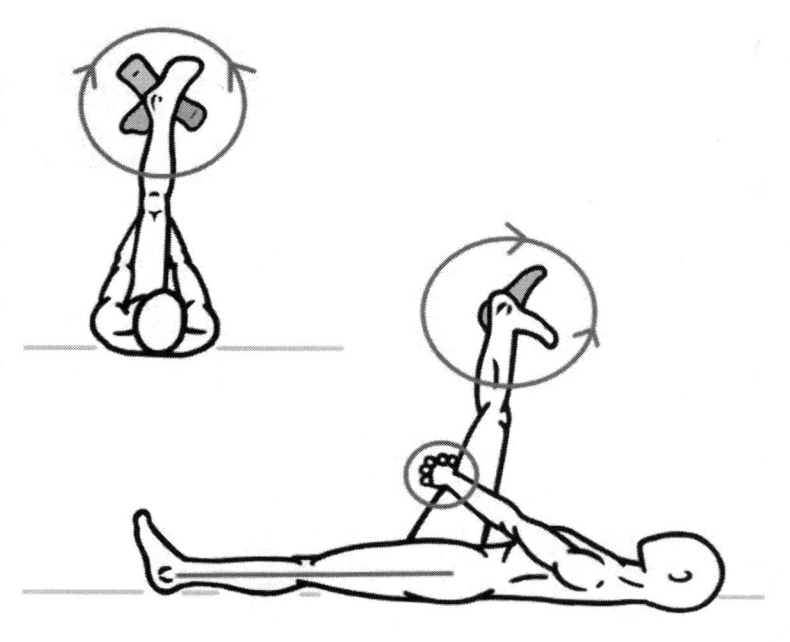

MOBILITY

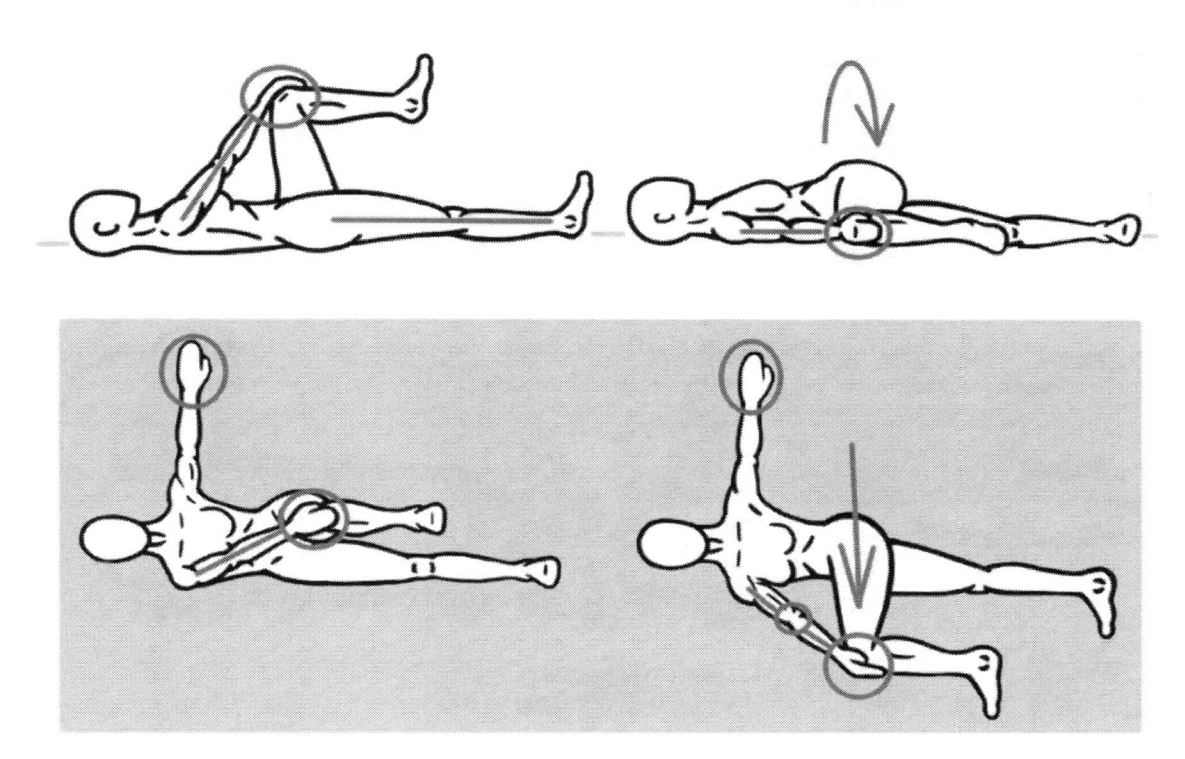

SUPINE LOCKED ROTATION

POSITION: Lie down on the floor and place a hand on top of the opposite knee with the palm covering the kneecap while the other arm and leg extend straight on the floor.

ACTION: Pull the locked-palm-and-knee across the body and rotate the hips while the shoulders stay flat on the ground. Press the opposite hand into the ground, lengthening through the spine by pressing the top of the head away from the extended heel. Keep the elbow straight on the rotating arm throughout the movement. *Repeat several times on each side.*

SUPINE ROTATED KNEE EXTENSION

POSITION: Lie down in a rotated position with one hand on top of the opposite knee. Press the other hand into the floor as the top of the head lengthens away from the other heel.

ACTION: Flex and extend the knee of the rotated leg several times. Drive the heel away from the hips and pull the toes back towards the nose on each extension. Press the opposite arm into the ground and lengthen through the spine.
Repeat this movement with the opposite leg as well.

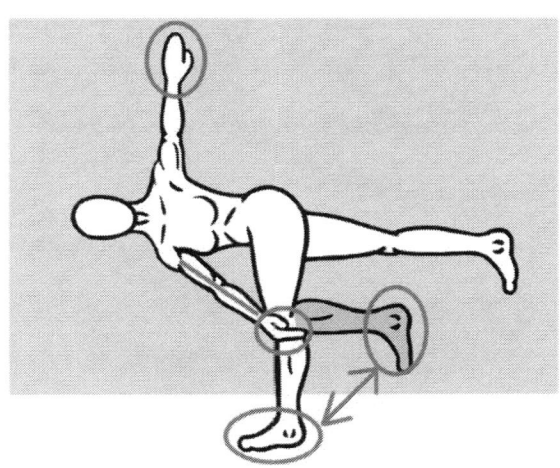

PreHab Exercise Book for Runners

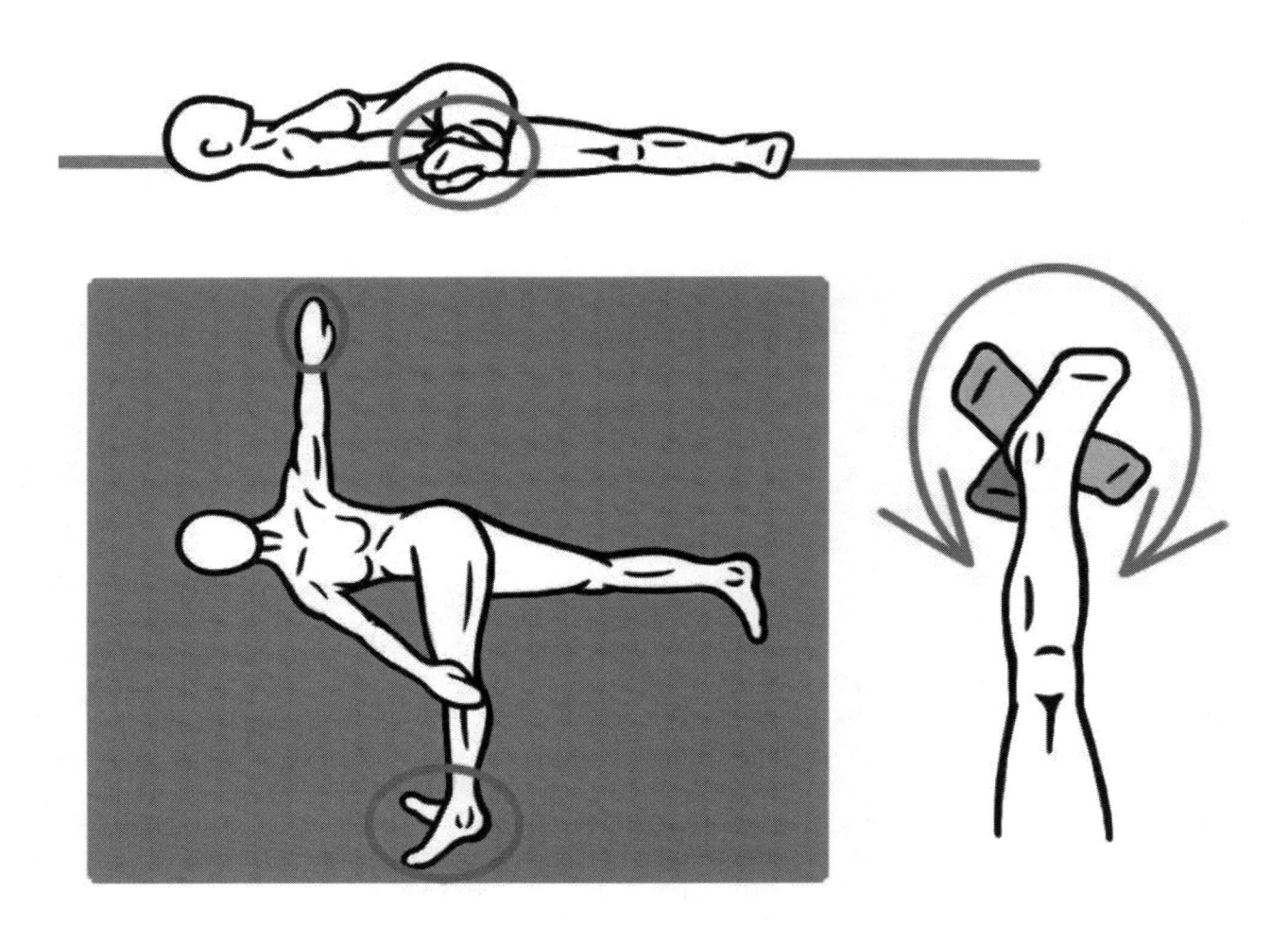

MOBILITY

ROTATED ANKLE CIRCLES

POSITION: Lie down in a rotated position with one hand on top of the opposite knee, which is fully extended. Press the other hand into the floor as the top of the head lengthens away from the other heel.

ACTION: Circle the ankle of the rotated leg several times in each direction. Focus on circling the heel as oppose to circling the toes. Stay long through your entire body and remember to breathe as you stretch as you press the opposite arm into the ground.

Repeat this movement with the opposite leg as well.

MOBILITY

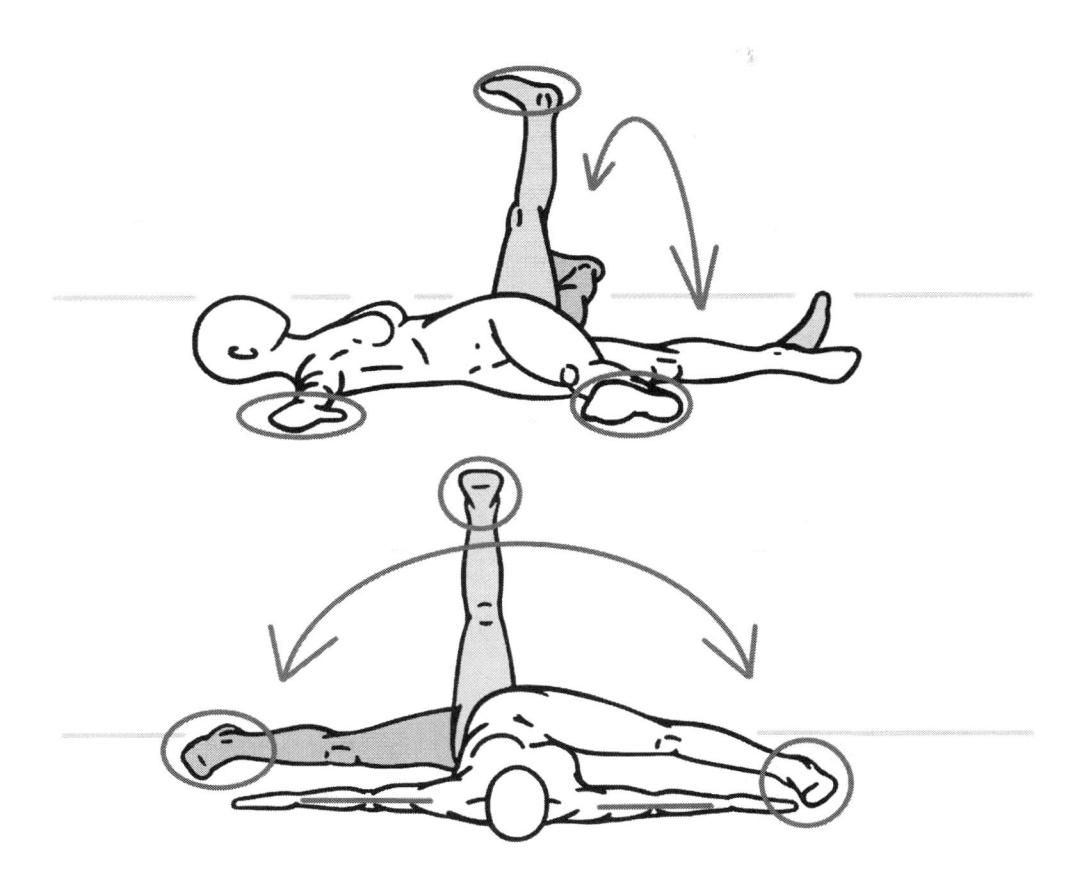

REVERSE SCORPION

POSITION: Lie on the floor with one foot lifted up into the sky and both arms extended into a "T" formation with the spine. Palms flat on the floor.

ACTION: Pull the leg across the body and lower the foot to the floor before reversing directions and touching the floor on the other side of the body. Keep the arms flat against the floor and roll the hips over and back as the torso rotates. Move the leg with control and reach as far as possible.

Time: Approximately 15 seconds but longer if you are very tight.

MOBILITY

> **Seated Mobility Sequence**
> *These two mobility exercises use specific movement patterns of the spine and torso to help address any limitations or restrictions that may linger in these areas and affect the rest of the posterior chain.*

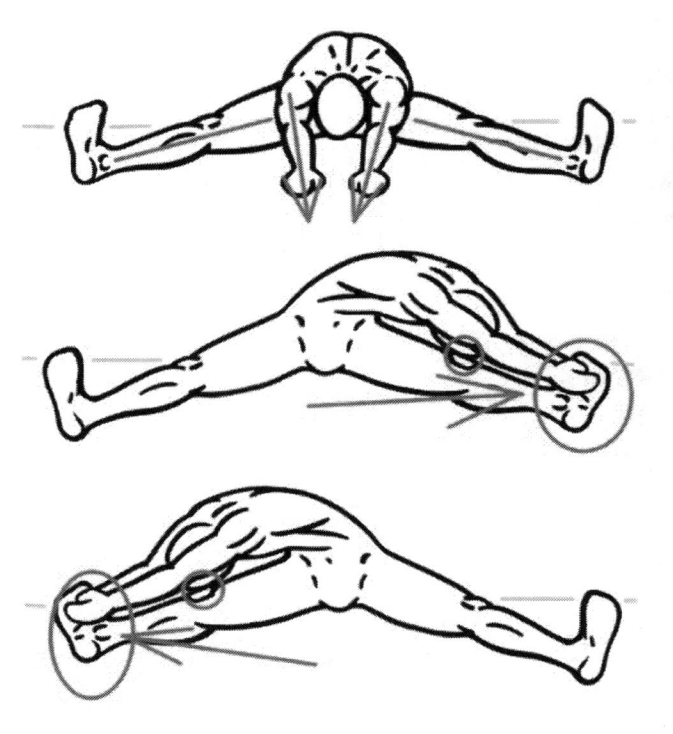

WIDE-LEGGED HAND WALK

POSITION: Sit on the floor with the legs separated far apart from one another. Reach both hands out in front as far as possible and fold forward while pulling the toes back to the hips.

ACTION: Walk the hands over to one foot and attempt to touch the forehead to the knee. Square the shoulders with the floor and alternate sides.

Repeat several times to each side.

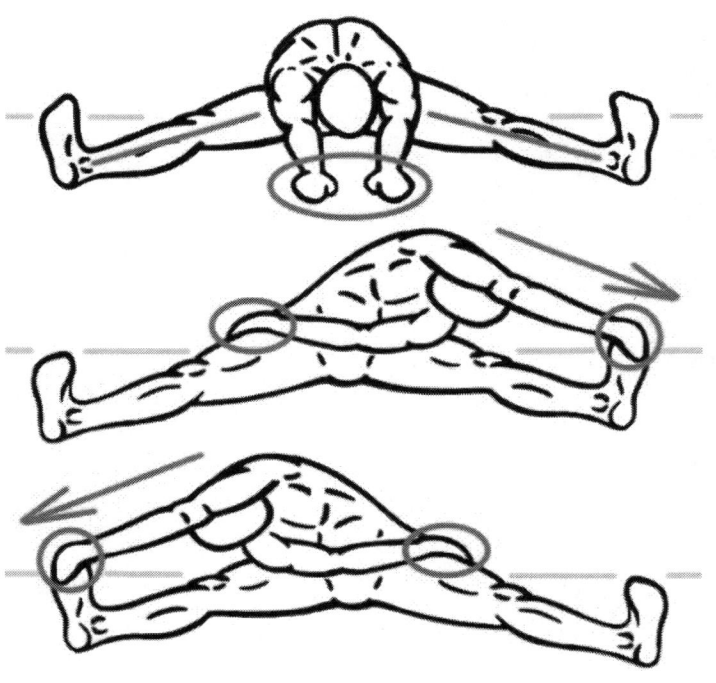

WIDE-LEGGED ROTATION

POSITION: Sit on the floor with the legs separated far apart from one another. Reach both hands out in front as far as possible and fold forward while pulling the toes back to the hips.

ACTION: Reach one hand towards the opposite foot and hold onto the opposite hip with the other hand. Rotate through the torso, twist the shoulders and lengthen the spine as much as possible. Attempt to touch the top of the head to the kneecap and keep the hips flat on the floor.

Repeat several times to each side.

MOBILITY

> **Getting Off the Ground**
> *It's important to practice mobility exercises while supporting your own body in space. You coordinate and strategize movement differently when you are responsible for your own stability and alignment. At the same time, you don't want to rush to get off the ground too fast either. When you were little, it took a while to learn how to crawl before you could walk. You can tap into some primitive movement strategies by taking your time to get fully off the ground!*

LOW-LUNGE & ROTATION

POSITION: Kneel down and place both hands on the ground. Align the fingertips with the front toes and the front knee directly over the ankle. Slide the rear knee back as far as possible.

ACTION: Fully extend the back knee and rotate the torso towards the front leg to reach the arm up to the sky. Lengthen from head to heel and exhale as the torso rotates. Keep the back knee straight and press into the floor to reach higher. Repeat several times on each side.

Modes of Application:
- Smoothly perform several reps of this movement as you breathe deeply and relax. Next, hold this position for approximately 30 seconds as you mentally imagine your Posterior Chain lengthen and focus on deep exhalations.
- Optional: Hold the end position and perform several PNF Contract/Relax sequences throughout your hips and legs, including pressing your big toe down into the floor.

MOBILITY

DOWN-DOG
POSITION: Start on floor with hands tucked into the ribs.

ACTION: Push the palms and feet into the ground and press the hips up into the sky. Sink the heels down to the floor and straighten the elbows. Lengthen through the spine and pull the shoulders away from the ears while pushing the heart towards the ankles. Repeat several times.

Modes of Application:
- *Smoothly perform several reps of this movement as you breathe deeply and relax. Next, hold this position for approximately 30 seconds as you mentally imagine your Posterior Chain lengthen and focus on deep exhalations.*
- *Optional: Hold the end position and perform several PNF Contract/Relax sequences throughout your hips and legs, including pressing your big toe down into the floor.*

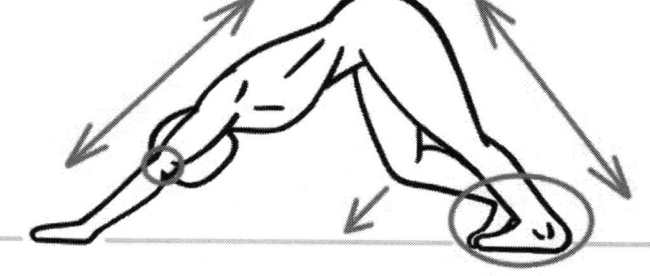

DOWN-DOG FOOT PEDAL
POSITION: Start in the Down-Dog position with the elbows straight and the hips lifted to the sky. Sink the heels to the floor and lengthen through the spine and legs.

ACTION: Bend and straighten one knee at a time while pressing the hips up into the sky. Stay long in the spine and keep the elbows fully extended.

Pedal the feet several times (10-30 each).

MOBILITY

DOWN-DOG WITH HIP EXTENSION
POSITION: Start in the Down-Dog position with the elbows and knees fully extended. Press the hands and feet into the ground and lift the hips high into the sky.

ACTION: Lift one leg up and reach the heel high into the sky. Keep the hips square with the floor and press the floor away with the hands and opposite foot. Lengthen through the entire body as much as possible. Alternate legs and repeat several times.

Modes of Application:
- *Smoothly perform several reps of this movement as you breathe deeply and relax. Next, hold this position for approximately 30 seconds as you mentally imagine your Posterior Chain lengthen and focus on deep exhalations.*
- *Optional: Hold the end position and perform several PNF Contract/Relax sequences throughout your hips and legs, including pressing your big toe down into the floor.*

DOWN-DOG WITH ANKLE TOUCH
POSITION: Start in the Down-Dog position with the elbows and knees fully extended. Press the hands and feet into the ground and lift the hips high into the sky.

ACTION: Reach one hand towards the opposite foot while pushing into the floor with the feet and opposite hand to press the hips into the sky. Keep the elbows and knees straight and attempt to touch the ankle with the fingers. Alternate sides and repeat several times.

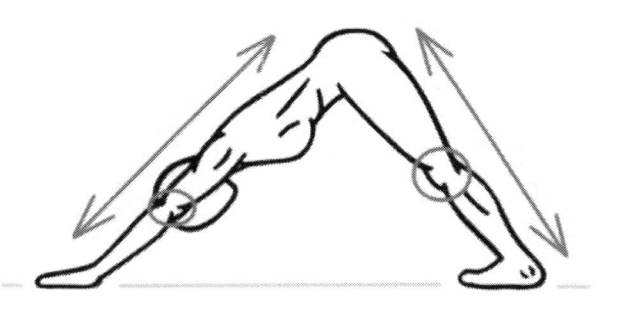

Modes of Application:
- *Smoothly perform several reps of this movement as you breathe deeply and relax. Next, hold this position for approximately 30 seconds as you mentally imagine your Posterior Chain lengthen and focus on deep exhalations.*
- *Optional: Hold the end position and perform several PNF Contract/Relax sequences throughout your hips and legs, including pressing your big toe down into the floor.*

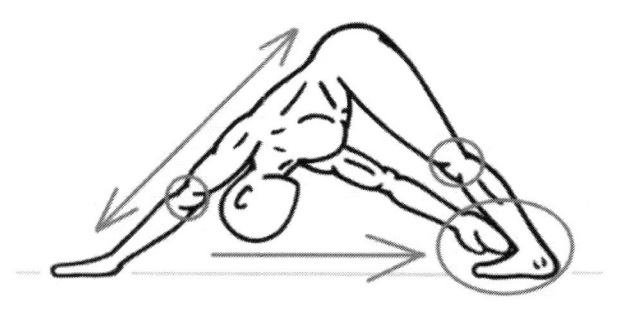

PreHab Exercise Book for Runners

MOBILITY

WIDE STANCE FORWARD BEND

POSITION: Stand with the feet in a comfortable, wide stance and straight knees.

ACTION: Fold the torso forwards and reach both arms through the legs towards the horizon. Keep the knees fully extended and lengthen through the spine by pulling the top of the head away from the tailbone. Breathe deeply and relax. Repeat several times.

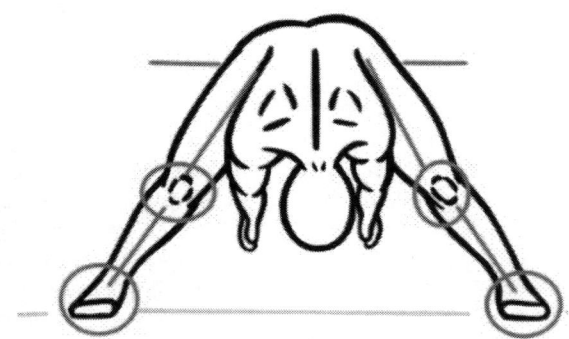

Modes of Application:
- *Smoothly perform several reps of this movement as you breathe deeply and relax. Next, hold this position for approximately 30 seconds as you mentally imagine your Posterior Chain lengthen and focus on deep exhalations.*
- *Optional: Hold the end position and perform several PNF Contract/Relax sequences throughout your hips and legs, including pressing your big toe down into the floor.*

WIDE STANCE ROTATED FORWARD BEND

POSITION: Stand with the feet in a comfortable, wide stance and straighten the knees.

ACTION: Fold the torso forward over one leg and reach both hands for the foot. Then rotate the torso to fold over the opposite leg and reach for the respective foot. Keep the knees straight and lengthen through the spine. Attempt to touch the forehead to the kneecap while aligning the heart and belly button with the thigh. Breathe deeply, relax and alternate between sides. Repeat several times to each side.

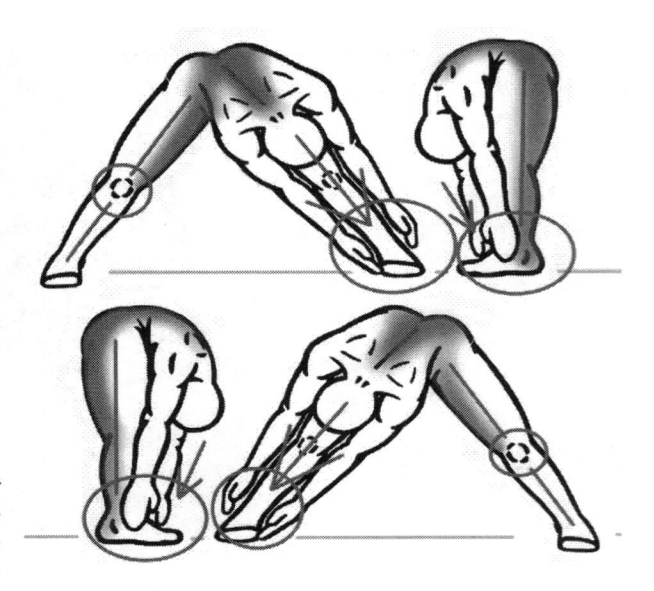

Modes of Application:
- *Smoothly perform several reps of this movement as you breathe deeply and relax. Next, hold this position for approximately 30 seconds as you mentally imagine your Posterior Chain lengthen and focus on deep exhalations.*
- *Optional: Hold the end position and perform several PNF Contract/Relax sequences throughout your hips and legs, including pressing your big toe down into the floor.*

MOBILITY

> **Wall Assisted Exercises**
> As a runner, this is one of my favorite mobility exercises as it addresses the entire posterior chain, including the underside of the feet. Plus, this exercise also includes an emphasis on the lateral aspect of your gait, which is an important synergist (assistant) to the Posterior Chain.

WALL-ASSISTED TOE TOUCH

POSITION: Align the body in a straight line from wrists to heels on a 45-degree angle between the wall and the floor. Wedge a foot into the corner with the crease evenly dividing the foot.

ACTION: Rotate forward and attempt to touch the front toes with the opposite hand. Keep the arms and legs straight and twist through the hips. Relax the bottom of the feet and press into the floor and the wall while reaching forward. Stay long through the body and repeat several times. Repeat several times on each leg.

Modes of Application:
- Smoothly perform several reps of this movement as you breathe deeply and relax. Next, hold this position for approximately 30 seconds as you mentally imagine your Posterior Chain lengthen and focus on deep exhalations.
- Optional: Hold the end position and perform several PNF Contract/Relax sequences throughout your hips and legs, including pressing your big toe down into the wall.

MOBILITY

LEG SWING - SAGITTAL

POSITION: Stand tall and hold the arms out to the side or hold on to a wall for more support.

ACTION: Gently swing one leg forwards and backwards in a straight line with a fully extended knee and a loose ankle. Gradually increase the height of each swing and keep the spine long and upright by lifting the chest. Relax as much as possible when swinging to help the muscles release and increase the range of motion.

Smoothly swing your legs several times with little or no tension.

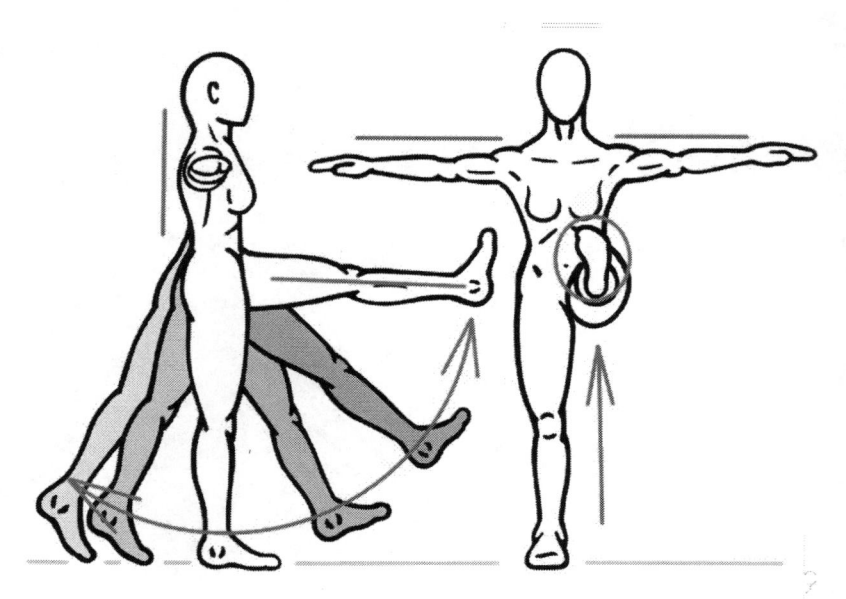

LEG SWING - LATERAL

POSITION: Stand tall and hold the arms out to the side or hold on to a wall for more support.

ACTION: Gently swing one leg from side to side in a straight line with a fully extended knee and a loose ankle. Gradually increase the height of each swing and keep the spine long and upright by lifting the chest. Relax as much as possible when swinging to help the muscles release and increase the range of motion.

Smoothly swing your legs several times with little or no tension.

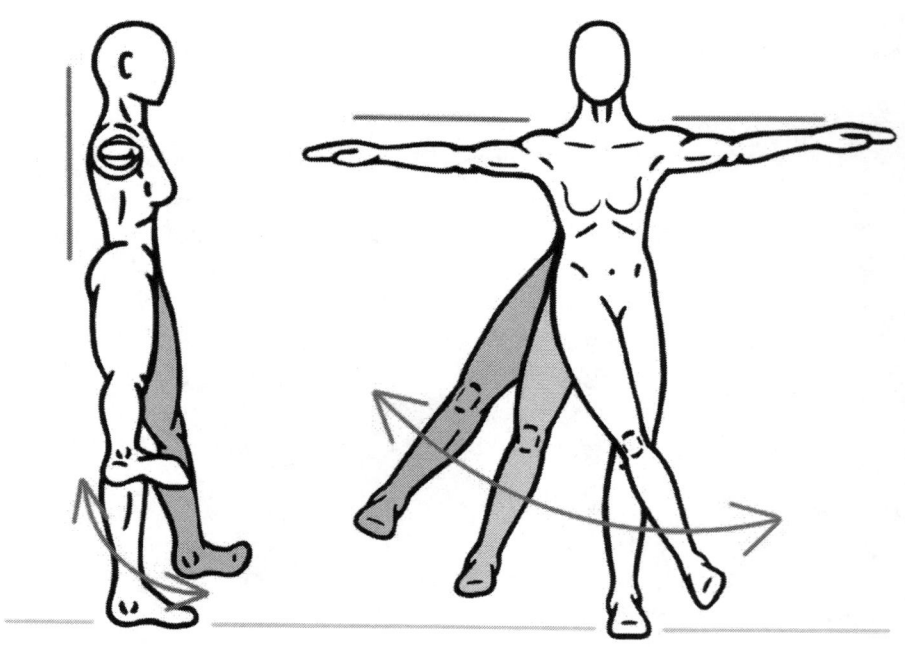

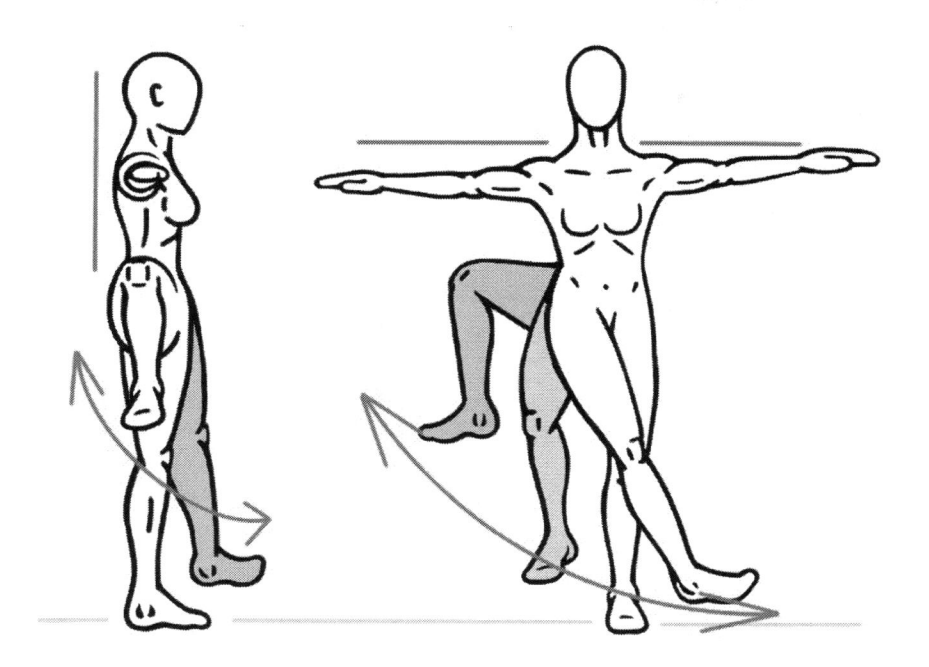

MOBILITY

LEG SWING - TRANSVERSE

POSITION: Stand tall and hold the arms out to the side or hold on to a wall for more support.

ACTION: Tuck one knee towards the elbow and then gently swing one leg around the standing leg with a loose ankle. Fully extend through the knee when wrapping around the standing leg and stay fluid as the rotation of the hips prepares the standing leg for coordinating balance while running in a reflexive manner. Repeat several times before alternating legs.

Smoothly swing your legs several times with little or no tension.

The Way to Get Ahead
Remember that all of your forward movement depends on your Posterior Chain and any restrictions in your range of motion can lead to some form of compensation, if not injury. Don't get sidelined in your training. Be sure to mobilize your posterior chain and keep moving forward!

MOBILITY

MOBILITY

Combination Exercises for Mobility

Developing adequate mobility and a proficient range of motion through larger movement patterns that incorporate various joints and soft tissue functions across the spectrum of the entire body will enhance performance in your training, sport and life activities.

The following mobility exercises will target various joints and combine local movement into larger, interrelated patterns, which can translate into workout or sports-specific skills. In other words, these exercises will help bridge movement for maintenance and mobility into a foundation of skill and performance.

The following mobility exercises intend to bridge various local or individual joint movements into larger and more expansive movement patterns that will help create a base of mobility that translates easier in sports-specific or life skills.

In other words, these combination exercises are looking to develop mobility patterns that are more applicable to the goals of your workouts and training. It is a progression in training that needs to be scrutinized and assessed just as much as the biomechanics around individual joints are evaluated and corrected.

"Golden Rule"
Evaluate each complete movement and assess the functionality of every joint involved in order to effectively address the specific faults or dysfunctions in your biomechanics.

Mobility Progression
Here is a sequence of mobility exercises that will gradually progress in the level of complexity and difficulty. Use the exercises that are appropriate for your level of mobility.

MOBILITY

SQUAT AND ROTATE

> This mobility exercise will help restore the range of motion for: *Hips, Thoracic Spine, Ankles, Shoulders & Posterior Chain*
>
> Use in PreHab routines for: *Running, Jumping, Squatting, Pulling, Rotation, Throwing & Spinal Extension*

POSITION: Stand with feet shoulder-width apart and in neutral alignment from head to heel.

ACTION: Squat down by driving the hips backwards and bending in the knees. Keep the shins as vertical as possible and press the thighs wide to create room for the torso and hips to lower down. Extend the arms backwards and reach the fingers towards the horizon while lifting the chest and lengthening the spine.

Next, drive into the heels and stand up while reaching one arm up and over the opposite shoulder.

Push the hips forward as you stand and pull the belly button in towards your spine to engage the abdominals and stabilize the core.

Rotate through the shoulders as you lift one arm up and reach over the opposite shoulder. Reach the fingers back towards the horizon and lengthen through the entire body as much as possible.

Pivot on the big toe of the foot on the same side as the reaching arm. Rotate the hips and turn the knee in towards the middle as you peel the heel up off the ground. Create an internal rotation in the hip socket and press the balls of the foot into the ground. Reach and lengthen as far as possible and then return to standing before performing the entire sequence to the other side of the body.

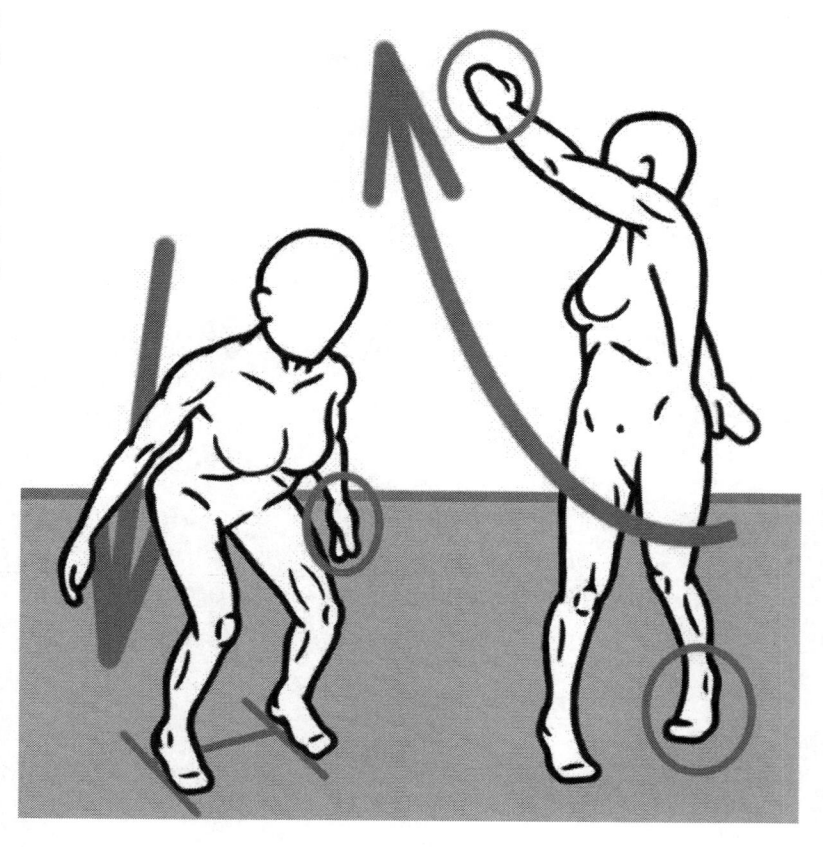

Perform several reps on each side in a smooth, controlled and relaxed manner.

MOBILITY

LATERAL LUNGE AND REACH

This mobility exercise will help restore the range of motion for: *Posterior Chain, Ankle, Hip, Thoracic Spine & Shoulders*

Useful in PreHab routines for: *Running, Agility, Jumping, Squatting, Hip Hinging (Deadlifts), Lunges & Throwing*

POSITION: Extend your arms out to the side and parallel to the ground to measure your foot position. Step each foot out and vertically align them with your elbows. Next, turn both feet parallel with one another and point the toes forward.

ACTION: Bend on one leg and slide the hips backwards and to that side as you reach an arm forward. Press the hips back towards the horizon as you bend your knee. Attempt to align the shoulder, hip, knee and ankle of the lunging side all in the same vertical plane. Use a mirror or a partner to spot you on this alignment.

Next, press your foot into the ground and drive your hips forward to return to the starting position.

- *Perform several reps of this movement on each side with each arm.*
- *Pause at the bottom of the stretch or at the top and perform the PNF Contract/Relax technique with any of the muscles that feel tight or restricted.*

MOBILITY

KICK STAND - Mobility for the Adductors, Hips & Posterior Chain

> This mobility exercise will help restore range of motion for:
> *Adductors (Groin), Hips & Posterior Chain*
>
> Use in PreHab routines for: *Running, Agility, Jumping, Squatting, Hip Hinging & Lunging.*

POSITION: Start in a tabletop or quadruped position where your wrists are aligned directly beneath your shoulder capsule, your kneecaps are directly beneath the hip sockets and your spine is long and in neutral alignment. Squeeze the armpits into the ribs, park the shoulder blades in the back pockets and pull the shoulders down and away from the ears to stabilize the shoulders. Also, pull the belly button in towards your spine to engage the abdominals and stabilize the core.

Next, extend one leg out directly to the side with a straight knee while not disrupting the rest of you tabletop or quadruped alignment. Place the heel in line or in front of the hips and lift the forefoot up off the ground. Pull the toes back towards the shin as much as possible while maintaining a straight knee.

ACTION: Shift backwards and slide your hips towards the horizon behind you as far as possible while maintaining a neutral spine and straight arms. Keep the shoulders and core stable as your slide backwards.

You will feel your glutes, hamstrings, Adductors (groin) and calf muscles all lengthen and stretch as you press your hips backwards.

- *Repeat this movement several times as you exhale deeply and relax.*
- *Also, perform the PNF Contract/Relax technique while deep in this stretch to create more release in the soft tissue.*

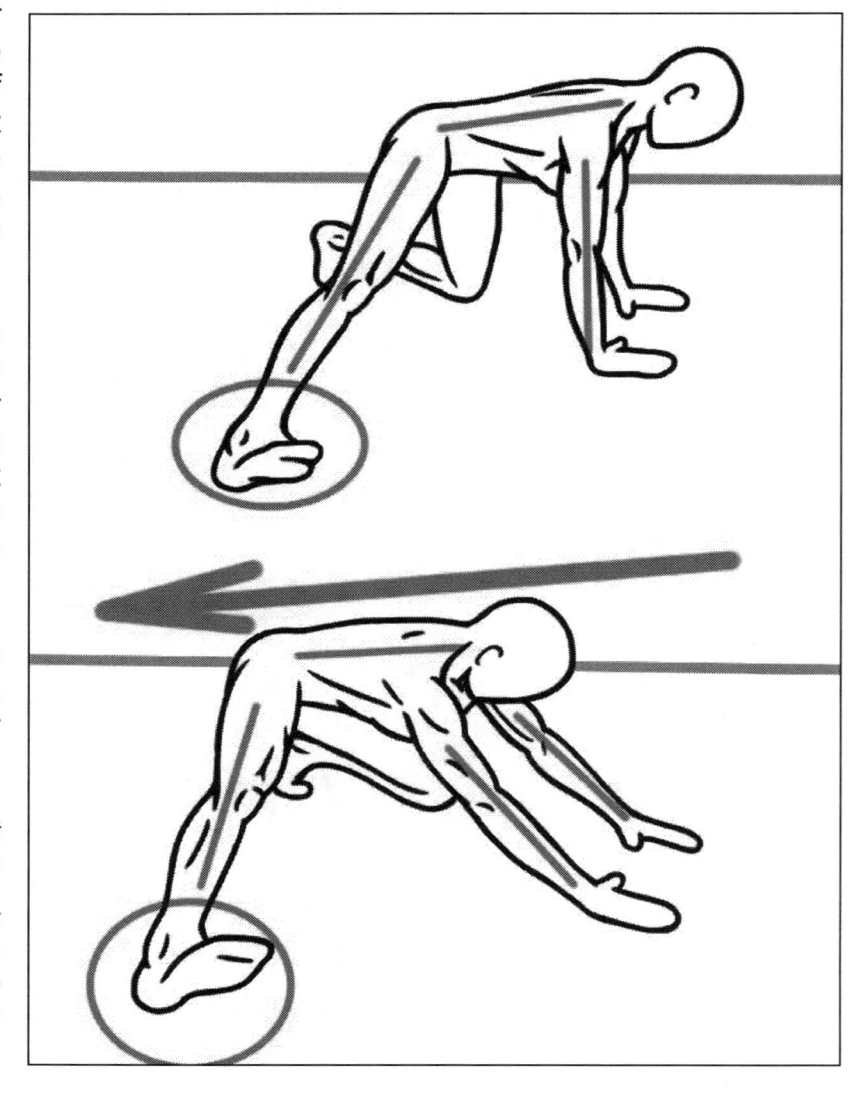

PreHab Exercise Book for Runners

MOBILITY

QUADRUPED PIGEON REACH

This mobility exercise will help restore range of motion for: *Hips, Thoracic Spine & Shoulders.*

Use in PreHab routines for: *Running, Agility, Jumping, Squatting, Rowing, Pressing/Pushing, Pulling, Rotation & Spinal Extension.*

POSITION: Start in a tabletop or quadruped position where your wrists are aligned directly beneath your shoulder capsule, your kneecaps are directly beneath the hip sockets and your spine is long and in neutral alignment. Squeeze the armpits into the ribs, park the shoulder blades in the back pockets and pull the shoulders down and away from the ears to stabilize the shoulders. Also, pull the belly button in towards your spine to engage the abdominals and stabilize the core.

Next, thread one leg under the torso and turn the shin perpendicular to the spine as much as possible as your brace the ankle against the front of the opposite knee. Attempt to widen the threaded knee to reach beyond the width of your hips if possible.

ACTION: Press your hips backwards until you feel a stretch in the hip of the threaded leg. It's important to keep your spine in neutral and aligned with your hips. Do not let your pelvis roll under. Instead, reach the tailbone back towards the horizon as far as possible.

Now, lift up the arm that is opposite of the threaded leg and reach under your torso and through the armpit as far you possibly can. Keep your braced arm completely straight as you reach under your body and exhale.

Next, pull the extended arm back out from underneath the body and reach the hand up into the sky as high as possible. Rotate the shoulders and press into the floor with the braced arm.
You may feel stretching occur in your shoulders, thoracic spine, hips or thighs as you perform this movement. Continue to reach under and back up in smooth motions as you breathe and relax.

- *Perform several reps of this movement on each side with each arm.*
- *Pause at the bottom of the stretch or at the top and perform the PNF Contract/Relax technique with any of the muscles that feel tight or restricted.*

MOBILITY

Hip Matrix Variations
These mobility exercises will help to lengthen the hip flexors and the adductors (inner thigh muscles). Additionally, the multi-dimensional increased range of motion will improve your agility, which is your ability to change direction.

> These mobility exercises will help restore the range of motion for: *Hip Flexors, Thoracic Spine & Shoulders.*
>
> Useful in PreHab routines for: *Running, Jumping, Squatting, Hip Hinging, Lunging, Pressing/Pushing, Pulling (Pull-ups), Spinal Rotation and Extension.*

HIP MATRIX – LUNGE & REACH

POSITION: Kneel on the ground with 90-degree angles in both knees. Square the hips, place the hands together and lengthen the spine.

ACTION: Slide the hips forward and drive the front knee over the front toes as the arms lift and reach off to the side, rotating in the torso and the hips. Keep the hands touching and the arms straight when reaching. Pull the belly button into the spine to engage the abdominals and return to start.

- Perform several reps of this movement on each side.
- Pause at the bottom of the stretch or at the top and perform the PNF Contract/Relax technique with any of the muscles that feel tight or restricted.

MOBILITY

HIP MATRIX – DIAGONAL LUNGE & REACH

POSITION: Kneel on the ground with one foot placed out on a 45-degree angle. Square the hips, place the hands together and lengthen the spine.

ACTION: Slide the hips forward and drive the front knee over the front toes as the arms lift and reach off to the side, rotating in the torso and the hips. Keep the hands touching and the arms straight when reaching. Pull the belly button into the spine to engage the abdominals and repeat.

- *Perform several reps of this movement on each side.*
- *Pause at the bottom of the stretch or at the top and perform the PNF Contract/Relax technique with any of the muscles that feel tight or restricted.*

MOBILITY

HIP MATRIX – LATERAL LUNGE & REACH

POSITION: Kneel on the ground with one foot placed out on a 90-degree angle. Square the hips, place the hands together and lengthen the spine.

ACTION: Drive the hips forward and drive the front knee over the front toes as the arms lift and reach off to the side, rotating in the torso and the hips. Keep the hands touching and the arms straight when reaching. Pull the belly button into the spine to engage the abdominals and repeat.

- *Perform several reps of this movement on each side.*
- *Pause at the bottom of the stretch or at the top and perform the PNF Contract/Relax technique with any of the muscles that feel tight or restricted.*

MOBILITY

Spiderman Lunge with Touch and Reach
These Mobility exercises build upon the Spiderman Lunge and are much more complex as they address each and every joint from head to toe. Using these versions can help you to be more time efficient in your PreHab routines. However, only include these variations if you are proficient enough in the basic movement patterns: Hip Extension, Hip Flexion and Thoracic Rotation.

> These mobility exercises will help restore range of motion for: *Hips, Thoracic Spine, Posterior Chain, Shoulders & Hip Flexors.*
>
> Use in PreHab Routines for: *Running, Jumping, Agility, Squatting, Hip Hinging, Lunging, Spinal Rotation & Extension.*

SPIDERMAN LUNGE with Contralateral Touch and Reach

POSITION: Step into the Spiderman Lunge position with the fingers and toes aligned in a straight line. Press the floor away with the arms and fully extend the elbows. Maintain a straight-line alignment from head to heel and pull the belly button into the spine to engage the abdominals.

ACTION: Lower the inside elbow down and attempt to touch the forearm to the ground. Next, rotate the torso and reach the arm up into the sky. Twist as much as possible in the shoulders and torso and extend the fingers high into the sky. Maintain a fully extended elbow in the supporting arm and lengthen through the entire body. Open the chest and vertically align the shoulders over one another if possible. Breathe deeply and relax.
- *Perform several reps of this movement on each side with each arm.*
- *Pause at the bottom of the stretch or at the top and perform the PNF Contract/Relax technique with any of the muscles that feel tight or restricted.*

SPIDERMAN LUNGE with Ipsilateral Touch and Reach

POSITION: Step into the Spiderman Lunge position with the fingers and toes aligned in a straight line. Press the floor away with the arms and fully extend the elbows. Maintain a straight-line alignment from head to heel and pull the belly button into the spine to engage the abdominals.

ACTION: Lower the outside elbow down and attempt to touch the forearm to the ground. Next, rotate the torso and reach the arm up into the sky. Twist as much as possible in the shoulders and torso and extend the fingers high into the sky. Maintain a fully extended elbow in the supporting arm and lengthen through the entire body. Open the chest and vertically align the shoulders over one another if possible. Breathe deeply and relax.
- *Perform several reps of this movement on each side with each arm.*
- *Pause at the bottom of the stretch or at the top and perform the PNF Contract/Relax technique with any of the muscles that feel tight or restricted.*

MOBILITY

Spiderman Lunge with Contralateral Touch and Reach

MOBILITY

Spiderman Lunge with Ipsilateral Touch and Reach

PreHab Exercise Book for Runners

205

MOBILITY

SQUAT AND REACH

This mobility exercise will help restore range of motion for:
Hips, Thoracic Spine & Ankles.

Use in PreHab routines for: *Running, Agility, Jumping, Squatting, Hip Hinging, Lunging & Spinal Extension.*

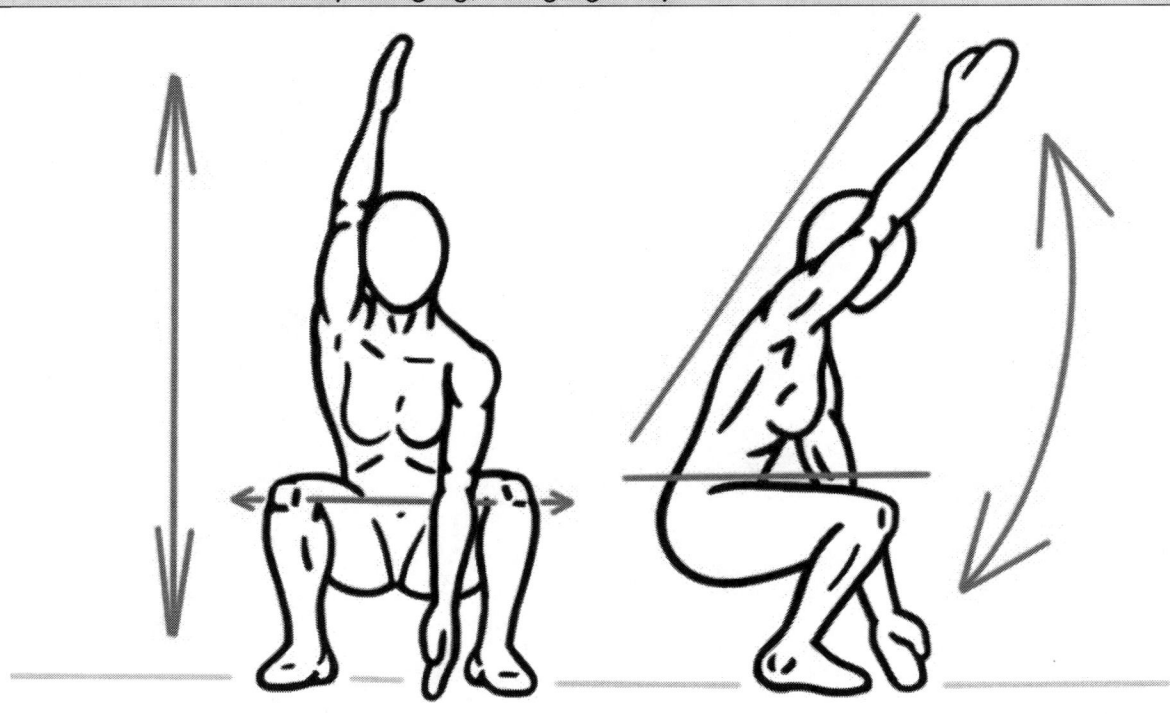

POSITON: Stand with feet shoulder width apart or even closer, which is preferred. Make sure that the feet are pointed straight ahead. You can allow a slight turn out, but keep the big toes parallel at least. Sit back with the hips and lower down as far as possible into a squat. Keep the heels on the ground and the shins as vertical as possible. Press your thighs wide to make room for your torso to lower down and also keep your chest lifted.

ACTION: While in a deep squat position, lift one arm up towards the sky as far as possible with a straight elbow as you reach the opposite arm down towards the floor. Keep the spine long and the heels on the ground. Do not allow your toes to turn out and pull your toes back up towards your shins to further the Dorsi Flexion of the ankles. Continue to press the thighs wide and keep the knees from passing out in front of the toes. Allow the knees to widen past the width of your feet instead.

- *Hold the stretch position of one arm lifted and relax for 30+ seconds.*
- *Focus on your exhales and relax.*
- *Optional: Perform the PNF Contract/Relax Technique*
- *Contract the chest, back and hip muscles without disrupting your stretched position for 5 seconds. Then relax these muscles for 10 seconds. Repeat the Contract/Relax cycle 3 times and then remain relaxed for 30 seconds or until you can feel your chest and shoulders release more.*

MOBILITY

DOWN-DOG with Ankle Touch

This mobility exercise will help restore range of motion for: *Hips, Thoracic Spine, Shoulders & Ankles.*

Use in PreHab routines for: *Running, Agility, Jumping, Squatting, Hip Hinging, Rowing, Pressing/Pushing, Spinal Rotation & Extension.*

POSITION: Start in the Down-Dog position with the hips lifted into the sky, both elbows fully extended and the shoulders pulled away from the ears. Straighten the legs and sink the heels into the ground.

ACTION: Reach a hand back to touch the opposite ankle while maintaining the length in the entire body. Keep the hips at the same height and allow the torso to twist when reaching. Alternate sides and breathe.

- *Perform several reps of this movement on each side with each arm.*
- *Pause at the bottom of the stretch or at the top and perform the PNF Contract/Relax technique with any of the muscles that feel tight or restricted.*

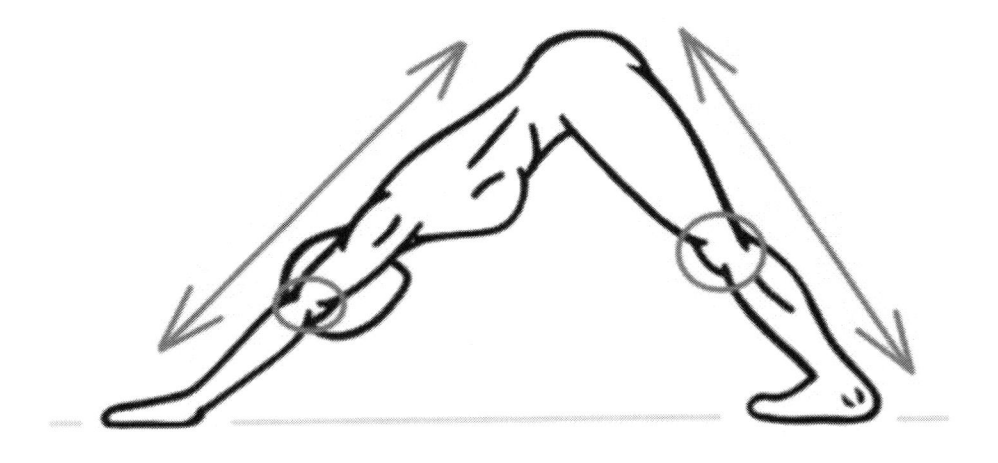

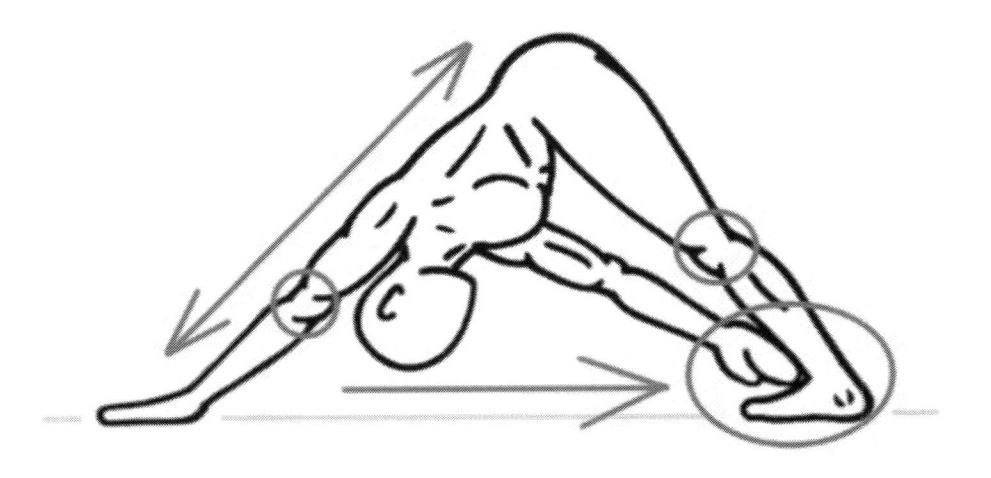

MOBILITY

SCORPION SHOULDER ROLL

This mobility exercise will help restore range of motion for: *Shoulders, Thoracic Spine & Hip Flexors.*

Use in PreHab routines for: *Running, Lunging, Rowing, Pulling, Pressing/Pushing, Thoracic Rotation & Extension.*

POSITION: Lie on your stomach and reach the arms out to the side to form a "T" with the spine. Then lift one leg and reach the heel towards the opposite hand. Roll the hips onto their side and pull the belly button in to engage the abdominals and stabilize the core. Establish a stable position and lengthen your entire spine before progressing onto the next phase.

ACTION: Lift up the arm that is on the same side of the raised leg and extend it backwards towards your opposite hand. Walk the raised foot further away, backwards from the hips, to help stabilize the body while rotating through the shoulders.

Reach the hand back as far as possible while you squeeze the armpits into the ribs. Park the shoulder blades in the back pockets and pull the shoulders down and away from the ears to help lengthen the trapezius muscle and open the shoulders.

- *Hold the stretched position and breathe deeply for 30+ seconds.*
- *Focus on large exhales as you relax.*
- *Optional: Perform the PNF Contract/Relax Technique*
- *Contract the chest and shoulders muscles without disrupting your stretched position for 5 seconds. Then relax these muscles for 10 seconds. Repeat the Contract/Relax cycle 3 times and then remain relaxed for 30 seconds or until you can feel your chest and shoulders release more.*

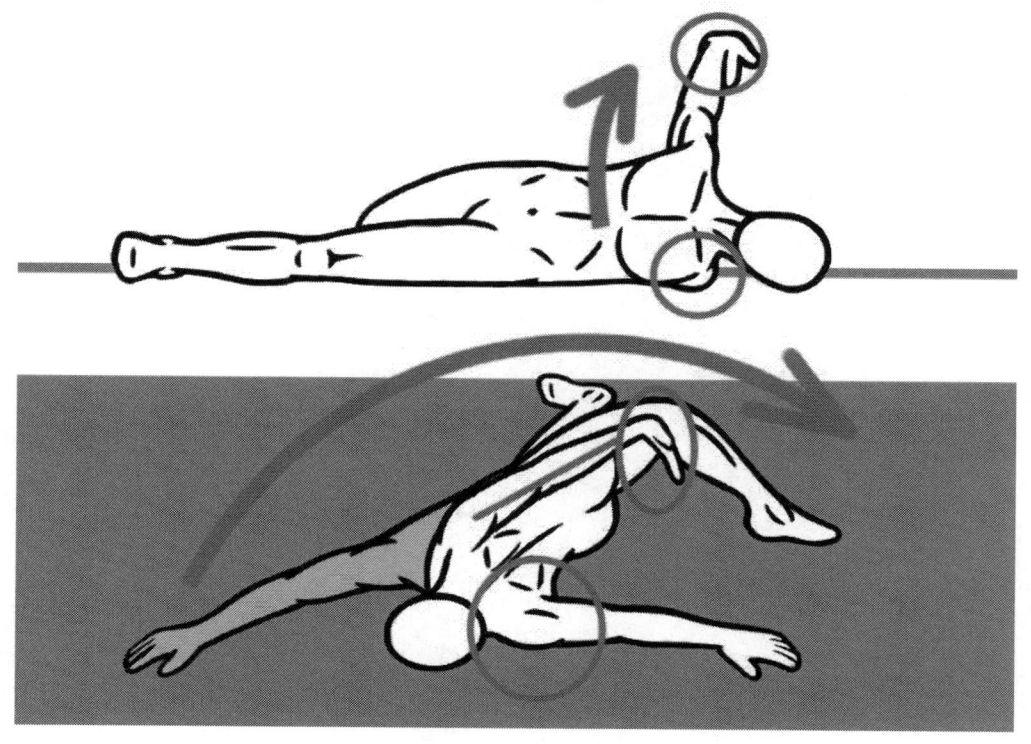

MOBILITY

HUMAN PRETZEL

This complex Mobility Exercise will help open up your hips and Thoracic Spine as well as address any tightness in your Quadriceps and Shoulders. It is recommended to progress through other exercises before performing this Pretzel.

> This mobility exercise will help restore range of motion for:
> *Thoracic Spine, Shoulders & Hips.*
>
> Use in PreHab routines for: *Running, Jumping, Squatting, Lunging, Rotation & Spinal Extension.*

POSITION: Lie on your side and reach the bottom leg back behind your body, pushing the heel up towards the back of your shoulder. Bend the knee and point the toes as much as possible.

Pull the opposite leg, the top leg, forward and position the knee in line with the hips or belly button if possible. Bend the knee deeply and rest the leg on the ground without letting your hips to rotate forward too much.

Reach the bottom arm forward and place the hand on top of the knee of the top leg. Keep the elbow straight and attempt to cover the kneecap with the palm.

Extend the top arm backwards and take hold of the bottom foot with the top hand. Attempt to hold the toes with the fingers in a parallel alignment. If this is not possible, modify the hold by grasping the top of the foot or the ankle.

ACTION: Rotate the top shoulder backwards and down to the floor in an attempt to touch the shoulder blade to the ground.

Extend the top knee forward towards the horizon and pull the bottom shoulder into a forward rotation as the head relaxes on the floor.

Lengthen through the entire spine and attempt to keep the back foot and front knee on the floor while your arms remain completely

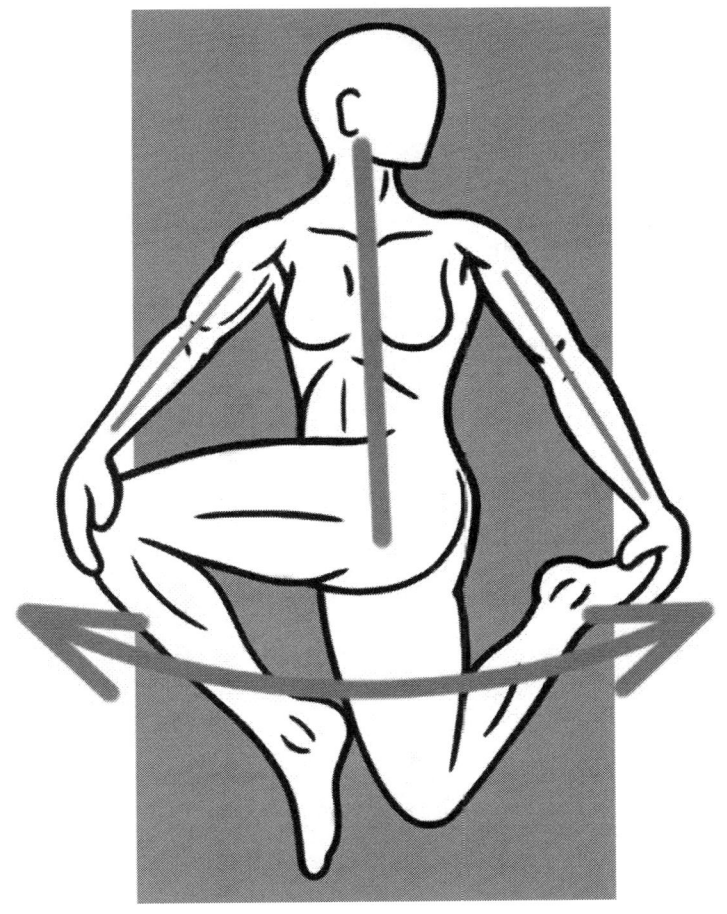

PreHab Exercise Book for Runners

MOBILITY

straight.

- *Hold this stretch position and breathe for 30+ seconds*
- *Focus on the exhales and relax.*
- *Optional: Perform the PNF Contract/Relax Technique*
- *Contract the muscles in various areas without disrupting your stretched position for 5 seconds. Then relax these muscles for 10 seconds. Repeat the Contract/Relax cycle 3 times and then remain relaxed for 30 seconds or until you can feel your chest and shoulders release more.*

Keep Your Eye on the Prize

As you start to put all of these exercises together and increase your mobility, you want to honor the reason that you are doing all this work in the first place. In other words, keep your eye on the prize and stay focused on your ultimate goal – moving well and performing to the best of your capability in any activity you choose.

It's easy to get lost in the details of these mobility exercises to the point of fixating too much on the little things. Don't get lost. Keep everything in perspective.

PreHab is a practice and a way to improve how you move. If you struggle with these advanced progressions of mobility exercises, go back to the joint specific exercises and focus on improving the areas that are most restricted.

Don't rush through your work. Your movement will not improve if you continue to move with faults or dysfunctions in your biomechanics. Remember that it will take 10,000 hours to be world class, and you can't cheat your way to the end. Do the work and the work will change how you move for the better.

Activation Exercises

When Luke Skywalker learns he's destined to become a Jedi Knight in the iconic blockbuster movie *Star Wars*, the wise Jedi Master Yoda begins to teach him about the Force. "A Jedi's strength flows from the Force," Yoda says, and soon enough Luke can levitate objects, control people's minds, and even heal people...

If you want to harness Jedi-Knight powers to improve your athletic performance, move faster, and be stronger, you need to train the connection from your brain to your muscles.

> **Learn to use Activation Exercises as part of your PreHab routines and soon enough you'll have The Force on your side too.**

Activation Exercises are designed to stimulate, facilitate and hard-wire the neuromuscular connections to specific muscles that will make the body mechanics function properly and create efficient movement patterns.

ACTIVATION

Do I need to make a new neuromuscular connection? The answer is no, unless you unfortunately injured the connection. All of our muscles are connected to our nervous system, and thus connected to our brain. However, some of these connections get lost in the shuffle somewhere because of lack of use and the overuse of other connections, which relates back to our lifestyles.

Over the course of our lives, we develop neuromuscular habits based on the dominant movements of our lifestyle. We will use certain muscles repeatedly through the course of the day, of which we develop a stronger neuromuscular connection in that movement.
Conversely, there are many muscles in our bodies that we neglect or do not use as often. This again is based on our lifestyle. For example: a person who has an office job and works at a desk will not being utilizing their glutes a lot during the day because they sit a lot. This lifestyle factor will lead to a weaker neuromuscular connection to the glutes over time.

Sparks in a flame, photo by Debivort

> ***Facilitated (Turned On) Muscles have a strong and active neuromuscular connection.***
>
> ***Inhibited (Turned Off) Muscles have a weak and inactive neuromuscular connection.***

Try this:
Take off your shoes and socks and sit on the floor with your feet out in front of you. Now, try to wiggle just your pinkie toe and no other toes. Unless you are an active Yogi, chances are that the neuromuscular connection to your pinkie toe is Inhibited or Turned Off. The end result is compensation.

As you try to wiggle your pinkie toe, chances are that all of your other toes begin to wiggle instead because our bodies will rely on the most Turned On (Facilitated) neuromuscular connections first and foremost.

> **Unfortunately, humans are compensating geniuses.**

The drawback is that every strategy of compensation will ultimately create a dysfunction in human movement and cause an injury or breakdown somewhere down the line.

ACTIVATION

Use the Force-
Activation Exercises deliberately work to restore proper functioning to all body mechanics by strengthening specific neuromuscular connections that weaken over time because of injury or lifestyle.

Activation exercises help to 'turn on' a muscle in the warm up, so the muscle will fire when you need it in the workout.

Additionally, Activation Exercises will help create efficiency in movement through restoring the proper function to specific body mechanics. They will also help to pave the way for developing "functional" movement habits.

Let's look at an example-
Sue is an accountant, who works in an office and sits a lot. She sits while she works on her computer, and she also sits during numerous meetings throughout the week. On the weekend, she visits with friends and goes out to eat –where, you guessed it, she sits more.

Her lifestyle creates certain movement habits that will influence the creation of specific Facilitated (Turned On) and Inhibited (Turned Off) neuromuscular connections in her body mechanics.

Then one day, Sue joins her friend's Tough Mudder campaign because it seems like fun! Unfortunately, Sue does not realize that she is about to start training 2-3 times a week for the Tough Mudder with a bunch of imbalances in her body mechanics.

Unfortunately, Sue is primed for a breakdown somewhere down the line.

Photo by Candice Villareal

ACTIVATION

Move to Act

Activation Exercises will help restore proper function to all your movement patterns and they do not take a lot of time. They just take a certain amount of concentrated effort on each repetition.

Activation Exercises:

Reduce Compensation
Prevent Injuries
Improve Performance

Go back to your pinkie toe and you will see that if you concentrate hard enough, you can re-learn how to wiggle that single toe in just a few minutes. Activation Exercises do not need to take up a lot of time if your concentration and effort are guided in the right direction.

Training

It's why Luke went to find Yoda – to learn to use The Force.

Be your own Yoda

ACTIVATION

Activation Techniques

Growing up, I was a huge fan of *Star Wars* – the original trilogy. The fight scenes, spacecraft, and good vs. evil storylines fueled my imagination for hours. My brother and I spent a lot of time role-playing scenes from the movies with *Star Wars* action figures and the X-Wing Star Fighter. We even taped up Whiffle Ball bats to use as light sabers and battled it out as Obi-Wan Kenobi and Darth Vader.

When summer thunderstorms crawled across New Jersey when I was a kid, my brother and I happily spent the entire day playing with those Star Wars action figures with the air conditioning cranked up. It was fun to imagine taking down the evil Galactic Empire, but it was even more fun to pretend I had The Force.

I always thought that The Force was the best part of Star Wars, and I was a little baffled that Luke didn't know that he had it before Obi-Wan told him about it. I am thinking that his life would have been much different if he knew. In fact, I don't think he'd complain about doing all those farmhand chores if he knew he had The Force.

Oddly enough, many of us are all a lot like the young Luke Skywalker. We don't realize that we possess a certain kind of Force too.

Star Wars Actions Figures by Richard Lewis

Most of us, even professional athletes, compensate when we move. We routinely substitute muscle groups for other muscles without even knowing it. Of course, we get away with it – for a while – because as humans, we are a lot more resilient than we give ourselves credit for – just like Luke Skywalker.

Luke did not realize that he had the power to destroy Darth Vader's Empire. And many of us do not realize how much we compensate in our movement.

Activation exercises are our way to restore correct movement patterns by powering up the muscles that have been turned off or inhibited. Master correct movement patterns, and you'll tap into a Force that can help you run faster, be more competitive, and lower your risk for injury. Techniques to improve your biomechanics and activate your muscles include:

- *Using different modes of muscle contractions*
- *Positioning your body to facilitate a specific muscle*
- *Adding resistance or load to invigorate inhibited muscles*

ACTIVATION

Muscle Contractions
Do you know how you can contract a muscle? Most likely, you just sense it or feel the contraction. In other words, you flex your muscles, perhaps in the prototypical biceps pose, and bang!...You say, "There. I contracted my muscle." But did you know that there are different modes of contracting?

Varying Modes
Your muscles have three different types of contractions: concentric (shortening), eccentric (lengthening) and isometric (holding the same length under tension). Now, we will apply a few varying modes to these different types of muscle contractions in order to successfully activate the targeted muscle.

> **Modes:**
> Pulsating
> Sustained
> Holding
> Loaded
> Slow
> Positioned

We use these varying modes to help activate muscles because our bodies have a tendency to develop compensation strategies on movement and our neuromuscular system can "forget" how to contract specific muscles.

Weak Connections
The neuromuscular system will not "forget" how to fire any muscle but specific neural connection can weaken over time due to the lack of use. Conversely, other neuromuscular connections can grow stronger over time due to use, which presents problem to Human Movement. Our neuromuscular system prefers to use the neural connections that are strongest, which is why habits rule people's lives and compensation strategies so dangerous to the way we move.

Interrupt Bad Habits
When we develop compensation strategies in our movement patterns, they can become a habit over time. Therefore, Activation Exercises and these varying modes of contraction are our attempt to interrupt the habitual neuromuscular loops for these compensation strategies.

Many Ways to Die
We use a variety of modes in these activation exercises because every person's body, as well as every muscle, will respond differently. Not every mode will work, and many times they all work. What's important is that we are successful in activating the targeted muscle group.

ACTIVATION

PULSATING
In this mode, we will send a string of pulsing contractions to the targeted muscle. This will help further the frequency of use in the neuromuscular connection to develop a stronger connection.

KNEELING LUNGE STRETCH
Position yourself in a half-kneeling position and push your hips as far forward as possible. Next, activate the Glutes in a string of pulsing contractions- on/off, on/off, on/off, etc.

If you are successfully activating the Glutes, the Hip Flexors will release and lengthen.

ANKLE HOPS
Another example of pulsing is Ankle Hops. Start by standing on your forefeet with your heels off the ground. Next, hop in place and do not let the heels touch the ground. This action will activate the calf muscles as well as the Proprioceptors sensors of the lower leg.

SUSTAINED
The next mode of activation is sustaining a contraction at the end of the full range of motion in order to further develop the neurological impulse and connection to the target muscle group. This technique also helps you develop a kinetic sense in how to contract the targeted muscle group.

SINGLE-LEG BRIDGE to Activate the Glutes
Lie on your back and pull one knee into your chest with both arms. Place the opposite foot on the ground with the knee bent 90 degrees or greater. Lift the forefoot up off the ground so that the lower leg does not compensate for any loss of power from the Glutes.

Next, drive the heel into the ground and press the hip up into the sky. At the top of the bridge, sustain the contraction by continuing to press the hips up into the sky. Keep contracting for an additional 1-3 seconds before coming down from the bridge and repeating the sequence 5-10 more times.

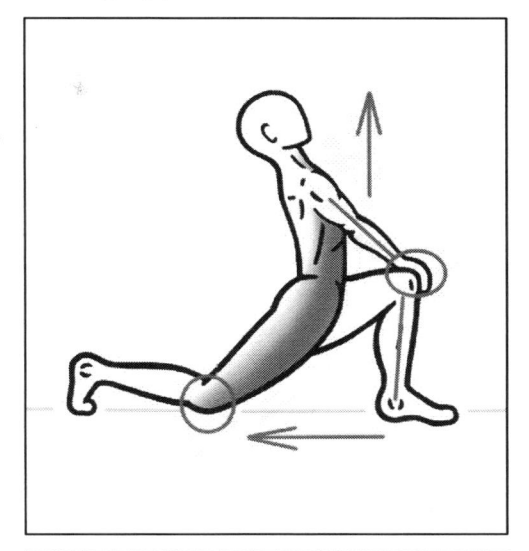

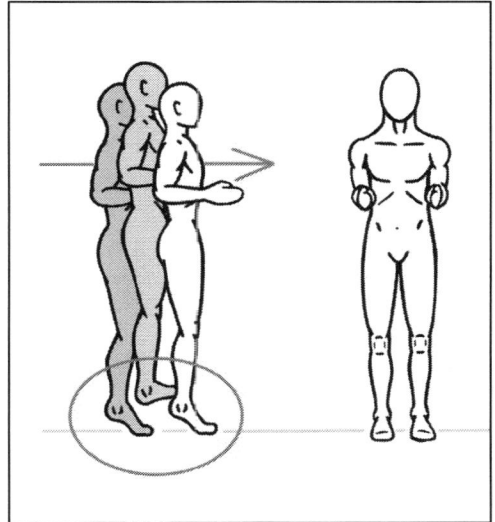

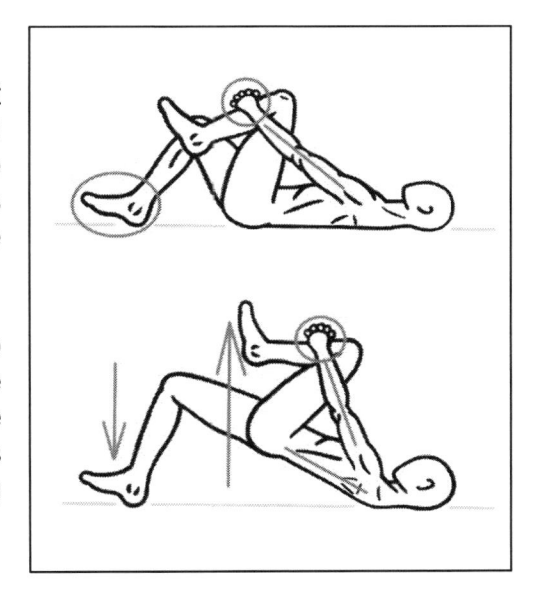

PreHab Exercise Book for Runners

ACTIVATION

HOLDING
This activation mode uses an isometric contraction to strengthen a neuromuscular connection like in a plank hold or a wall squat. First, it requires precise positioning to illicit a contraction and then utilizes duration to strengthen the connection. Save plank exercises for later and try this exercise instead.

ABDOMINAL ACTIVATION
Lie on your back with both arms and legs extended straight up to the sky. Press your lower back firmly into the floor so that there is absolutely no space between your back and the floor.

Better yet, have a friend place a strap under the small of your back and tell them to try to pull it out as you press your back into the floor and hold the strap in place.

Next, slowly begin to lower your arms and legs towards the floor, but do not let your lower back come up off the floor. Keep pressing your back flush against the floor and lower the arms and legs as far as possible.

Now, hold for as long as you can. If your abdominals start to tremble or spasm, then you are doing it right. If you start to feel pain in your lower back, you are doing it wrong. Hold the arms and legs at a height that creates a lot of tension in your abdominals and still don't let your friend pull that strap out from beneath you.

Afterwards, you should really feel your abdominals are turned on.

SLOW
Another way to activate the muscles is by performing a movement pattern very slowly and fully. Weaken neurological connections can hide if there is too much momentum in a movement pattern. Going slow will expose a lot of muscle fibers that are hiding out on purpose. Those are the ones you want to get.

SIDE PLANK ROTATION for
Lateral Core and Shoulder Stability
Bridge up into a side plank with the bottom shoulder, hip and ankle aligned in a straight line. Place the top hand behind your head and stabilize your lower shoulder by squeezing the armpit towards the hips

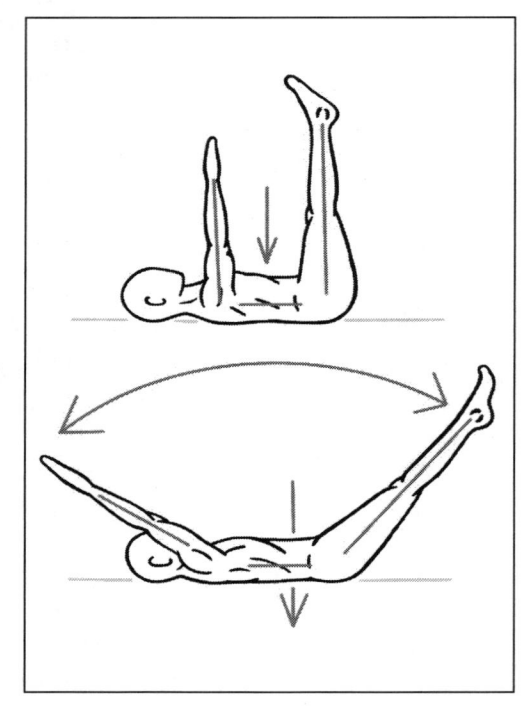

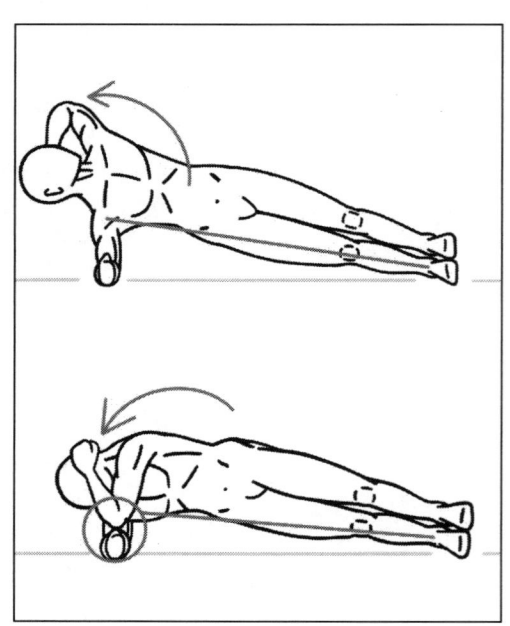

PreHab Exercise Book for Runners

ACTIVATION

and pull the shoulder down away from the ear.
Next, slowly rotate the shoulders and touch the top elbow to the bottom fist as you keep the hand behind your head and maintain a straight line alignment of the bottom shoulder, hip and ankle.

Rotate to touch on a three- to five-count in both directions. The repeats 5-10 more times before switching to the opposite side.

You should be able to feel the muscles that stabilize your shoulders and the lateral side of your core are much more active after this exercise.

POSITIONED
This technique aims to activate the targeted muscle with strategic positioning of the body that may require props such as a roller, block, strap, wall or more. The goal of this technique is to position the body in such a way that it forces the targeted muscle group to become activate in order to perform a movement.

SINGLE-LEG BRIDGE Off Roller to Activate the Glutes

This is a classical exercise that can stimulate very deep and underworked muscle fibers in the Glutes. Here's how to do it:

Get into position for a single-leg bridge by lying on the floor and grabbing hold of one knee with both arms. However, before doing that, place a foam roller or a six-inch yoga block directly under the hips.

Now, press the hips up as high as possible into the sky by driving the heel into the floor. Chances are your body will want to cheat. So, don't let it. Attempt to smoothly lift the right and left hip off the roller at the same time, as this will really make the Glutes work hard.

Repeat this exercise 5-10 times before switching sides.

This exercise is ideal to do before running, squatting or competing in any sport. It will surely help activate the glute muscles and develop more efficiency in all your movement patterns because the hips are your prime movers.

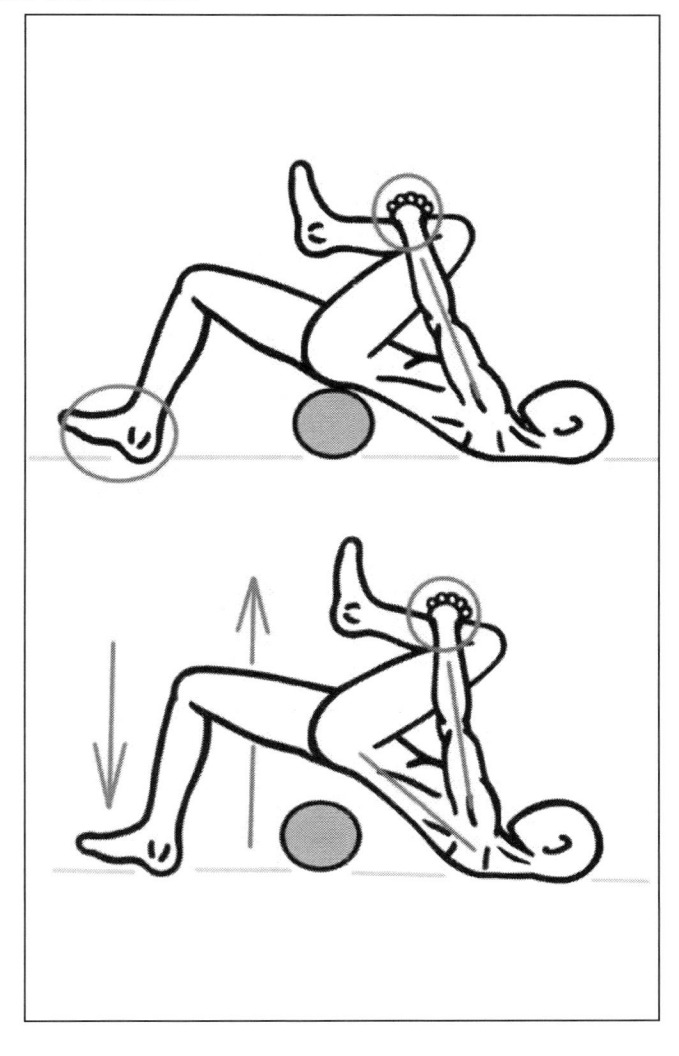

ACTIVATION

LOADED

Sometimes referred to as neural activation exercise, this technique uses load, such as weights, or other forms of resistance, such as tubes, bands or even opposing muscles, to help activate the targeted muscles. It works well because the body is conditioned to recruit all the muscles fibers in a specific vicinity if the firing threshold is high enough. In other words, if there's enough resistance, every muscle fiber will turn on.

Note: performing loaded activation exercises can be risky depending on your level of stability in specific movement patterns. If you know that you have pre-existing stability issues, such as the inability to stand on one leg for 20 seconds or a lack of core strength, it is recommended to use the other activation techniques as you develop more stability in all your movement patterns.

BARBELL BACK SQUAT

This exercise can help activate virtually all of the muscle fibers in your body, especially your hips, back and legs. It can be a quick fix if pressed for time or looking to break a personal record. I believe one of the reasons I clocked a 6:15-mile after five rounds of clean-and-presses was because so much of my total musculature had been activated in the workout and I felt so strong as I ran, almost effortlessly in fact.

POSITION: Stand with your feet shoulder-width a part or just slightly wider as the

ACTIVATION

loaded barbell rests on your back, atop of your shoulder blades and off of your neck. Keep your chest lifted, abs engaged and toes pointed forward.

LOAD: Start with a warm-up of light jogging, lightweight squats, or some other activity to engage your muscles. After a proper warm-up, load the bar with a weight that is 80 percent of your one rep max (1RM). You'll increase the weight to 85-90 percent of your 1RM when you develop more experience with this technique.

REPS: With this loaded technique, aim for 1-5 reps on one or two sets. This is just to activate your musculature for another performance. This is not a strength training or power-building technique. The goal is to get stimulated and get out. So, stick with low reps and low sets.

SQUAT ACTION: Lower down until your hips match the height of your knees and then drive your feet into the floor and return to standing. Keep your chest lifted throughout the entire movement and press your thighs wide as you lower to make more room to lower your torso closer to the floor.

Gaze at the horizon the entire time. Inhale as you lower, and exhale when you stand.

Get It Right!
Technique Summary

Activation Exercises are designed with the intention of preparing your body for a designated work period, i.e. workout, game or a run. More specifically, these exercises are to be used to just help your body make neuromuscular connections come alive and get your muscles ready for the upcoming activity.

You need to know which muscles you are targeting as well as knowing if you were successful or not at activating the intended muscles.

Inhibited muscles, or 'turned-off' muscles, tend not to be easy to activate. If there were, you wouldn't need these exercises in a PreHab routine. However, we all have Inhibited muscles to some degree. So, we need Activation Exercises to help restore our biomechanics.

Additionally, you may have to try 'new' ways to activate the intended muscles, which is why there are 'varying modes' of application for these exercises. Activating muscles depends on the neuromuscular system, which means this part of your PreHab is about exercising the Mind-Body connection.

Be willing to use all the different techniques and find the one that works best for you!

ACTIVATION

ACTIVATION

Ankle & Foot Activation
Fast Track Your Training

Image that you are on your way out of a crowded theater and there are only two exit doors opened. A long line will surely form, and you will need to exercise patience as you slowly shuffle along and wait to exit.

Yet, if the theater chooses to open more doors, including the emergency exit doors, the outpouring of people would surely multiply and your wait time would clearly diminish. And that is kind of how your biomechanics will function depending on your Proprioceptor recruitment and development. Your Proprioceptors are a network of sensory neurons that reflexively work to communicate and control how your body moves in space.

If you were trying to exit a crowded theater, opening more doors will help the crowd disperse a lot faster. Increasing the Proprioceptor activity around your feet and ankles can have a similar effect on neuromuscular output and reaction time.

Balance, Agility and Coordination all improve when the neuromuscular systems of the ankle and foot are activated. And when it comes to athletic performance, speed, and agility, the Proprioceptors make all the difference when millimeters and nanoseconds matter.

The neurological responsiveness of your ankle and foot can help you stay in bounds when trying to save an errant basketball pass or keep you upright after you stumble over a rock on your trail run. Yet, there are other benefits too.

In addition to improving your balance, coordination and agility, developing the responsiveness and articulation of the Proprioceptors in your ankle and foot complex can also help to increase your speed and power in running, lifting weights and playing sports.

Activating these neuromuscular sensory neurons will allow more muscle fibers and fascia sheathes to contribute in the force production mechanism. Eventually, well-conditioned Proprioceptors provide more power in less time, which ultimately provides a platform for new movement patterns to be formed in terms of coordination and timing.
Essentially, activating your ankle and foot will help create a faster turnover rate in running, a higher power output in your triple extension or power extension while performing Olympic lifts, and a quicker reaction time in sports.

Use It or Lose It
Maybe you are scratching your head wondering why activation exercises are even necessary. It seems that if we have all of these Proprioceptors that we would use them all. Unfortunately, our bodies do not use what we have, unless we need to, which is why we can either practice to use our Proprioceptors in how we move, or just move without them.

ACTIVATION

More specifically, our modern lifestyle of sitting for hours every day has decreased the necessity of eliciting Proprioceptor activation to assist with balance, coordination and agility. However, if we flash back a few hundred years when people were stealthily hunting in forested mountainsides out of necessity, the physiological demands on the body are tremendously different. Centuries ago, there was a real daily need for balance, coordination and agility. Today, we need to supplement this physiological demand, but just playing sports isn't enough. Our bodies can't activate these Proprioceptors if the neurological connection is dormant due to the influence of our modern lifestyle.

> *Start Here*
> Here is a progression of PreHab exercises that will help to activate the neuromuscular connections surrounding your ankle and foot.

PNF CALF STRETCH
This mobility exercise can also serve to activate the musculature of the ankle and foot when you apply the PNF technique of Autogenic Inhibition, also referred to as Contract/Relax.

POSITION: Place your forefoot flush up against a wall and wedge the heel into the floor. Try to make an equilateral triangle with your foot, wall and floor. Then straighten your knee and press your hips towards the wall.

ACTION: Press your hips towards the wall and then slide from side to side, looking for any tight sensations in your foot or calf. Address tight areas first and apply the Contract/Relax technique.

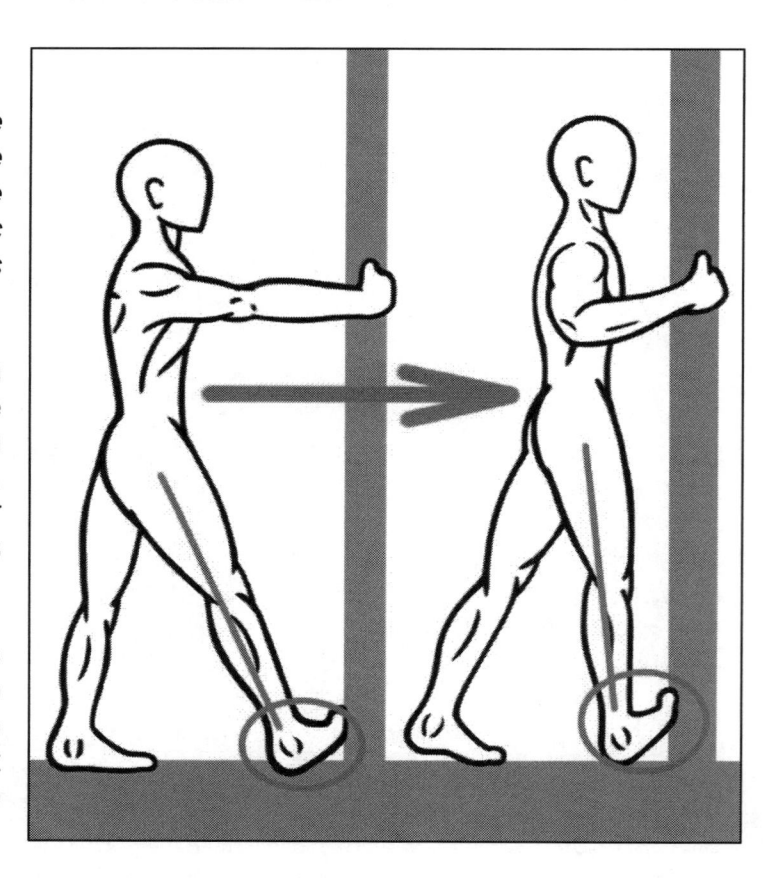

Contract and Relax

Press your forefoot into the wall with about 1/4 of your strength and then relax. Continue to cycle through these 'contract and relax' phases without losing the tension in the stretch. Also, make sure to breathe and focus on the exhalations as this will help elicit a stronger parasympathetic tone of your nervous system and make the soft tissue release more.

Use this Contract/Relax technique on each leg and feel the musculature of your calf and foot 'turn on' as your range of motion also increases.

ACTIVATION

TOE TOUCH PROGRESSION
This exercise will place your feet in different loaded positions and will help elicit more neuromuscular activation. You will need a Half Dome exercise ball and a towel for this exercise.

POSITION 1: Stand with your feet shoulder width apart and your forefoot on top of a Half Dome as your heels are anchored on the floor. Squeeze a towel between your thighs to help your knees track in line with your ankles.

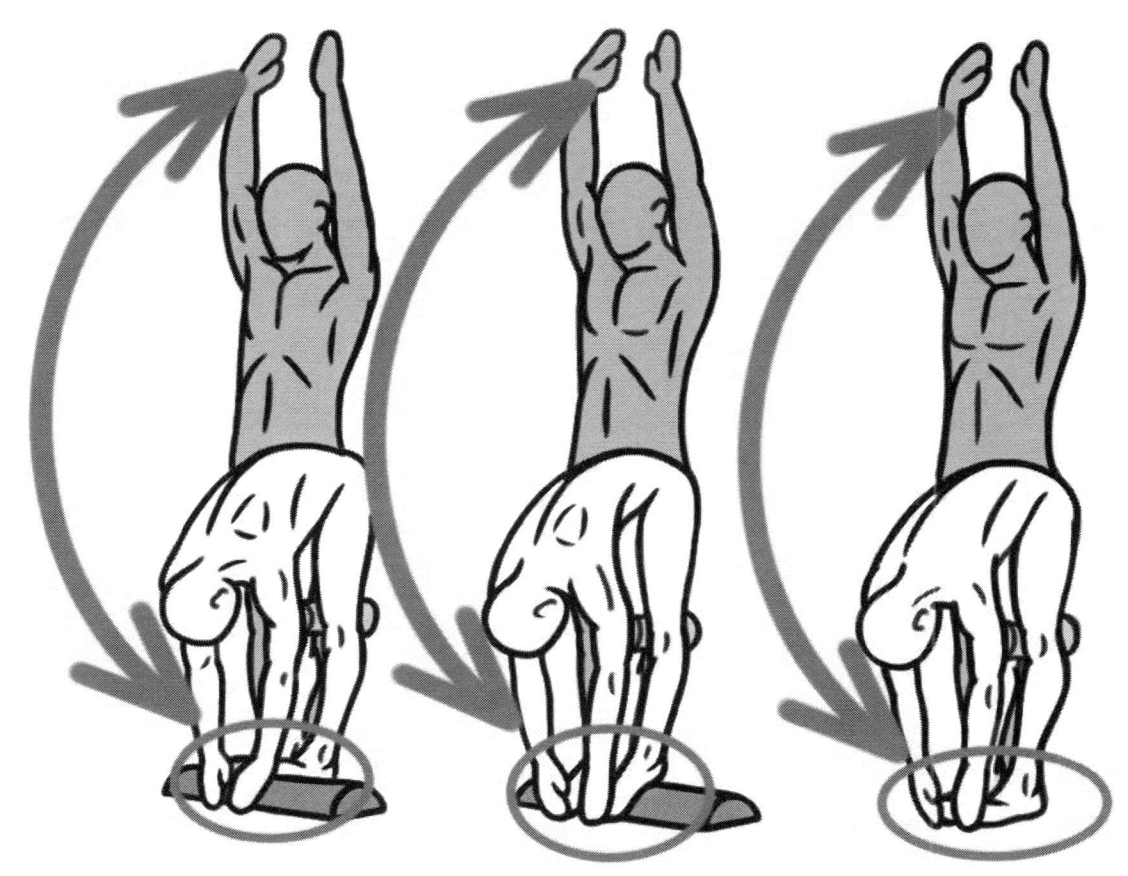

Toe Touch Progression: Position 1, 2 & 3

ACTION: Press the hips backwards and hinge in the hip socket as you reach your arms down to touch your toes. Keep your shins vertical and bend through the knees. After you touch your toes, return to standing by driving your hips forward and lifting the chest.

POSITION 2: Stand with your feet shoulder width apart and your heels on top of a Half Dome as your forefeet are anchored on the floor. Squeeze a towel between your thighs to help your knees track in line with your ankles.

ACTION: Press the hips backwards and hinge in the hip socket as you reach your arms down to touch your toes. Keep your shins vertical and bend through the knees. After you touch your toes, return to standing by driving your hips forward and lifting the chest.

ACTIVATION

POSITION 3: Stand with your feet shoulder width apart and your feet flat on the floor. Squeeze a towel between your thighs to help your knees track in line with your ankles.

ACTION: Press the hips backwards and hinge in the hip socket as you reach your arms down to touch your toes. Keep your shins vertical and bend through the knees. After you touch your toes, return to standing by driving your hips forward and lifting the chest.

Smoothly perform several reps in each of the three positions.

SINGLE-LEG HEEL LIFT

POSITION: Lift one knee to hip height and stand with arms parallel to the ground with palms pressed together. Focus the eyes on the horizon and lengthen the spine.

ACTION: Press into the forefoot and lift the standing heel off the ground while maintaining focus on the horizon. Drive the top of your head straight up into the sky and pull the belly button in towards the spine to engage the abdominals and maintain alignment over the standing heel.

- Practice one of the different Activation Techniques:
- Perform each rep slowly, on a 3 or 5 count.
- Add pulsating contractions at the top of the lift.
- Hold at the top in an isometric contraction.

Advanced Version: Eyes Closed- for further stimulation of the Proprioceptors in the lower leg and foot, try this exercise all over again with the eyes closed.

SINGLE-LEG ROTATION

POSITION: Stand on one leg with arms parallel to the ground and palms pressed together. Lift the opposite knee to hip height and establish balance. Focus the eyes on the horizon and lengthen the spine.

ACTION: Rotate the arms 45 degrees to the left and right and keep your eyes on your hands throughout the entire movement. Pull the belly button in to engage the abdominals and attempt to maintain alignment over the standing heel. Do not protract your shoulders forward. Relax your trapezius muscles and turn your sternum

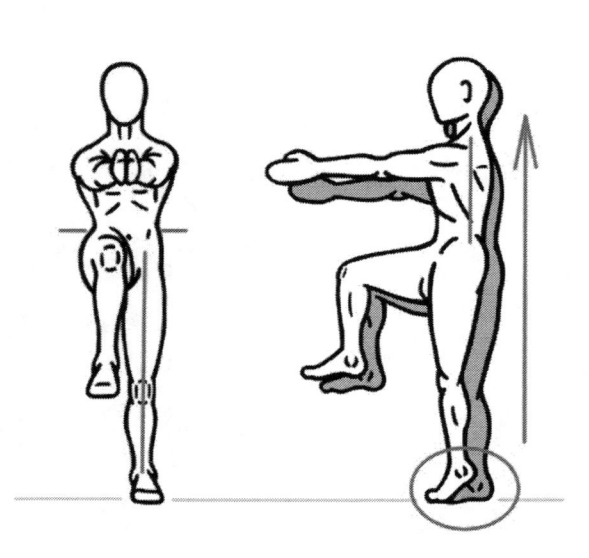

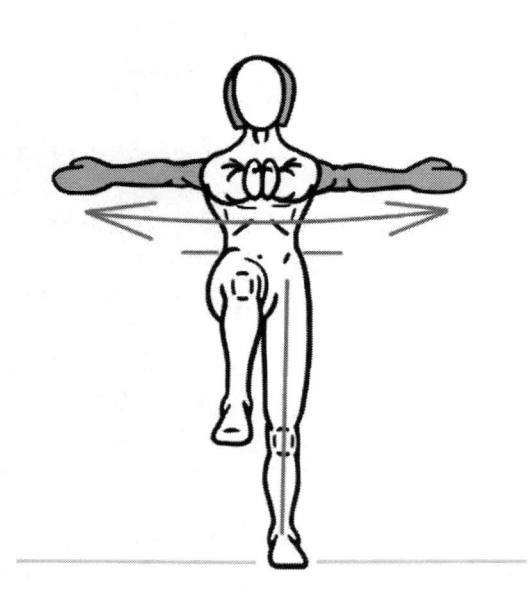

ACTIVATION

towards each side as you rotate. Also press your pinkie toe into the ground to help create more lateral stability in the standing leg.

- *Practice one of the different Activation Techniques:*
- *Perform each rep slowly, on a 3 or 5 count.*
- *Add pulsating contractions at the top of the lift.*
- *Hold at the top in an isometric contraction.*

Advanced Version: Eyes Closed- for further stimulation of the Proprioceptors in the lower leg and foot, try this exercise all over again with the eyes closed.

TOWEL SCRUNCH
This PreHab exercise will develop dexterity and activate the intricate muscle actions of the foot, which will provide a foundation for improved coordination and agility while helping reduce the risk of plantar fasciitis. The Towel Scrunch will benefit those who run barefoot, practice yoga or compete in gymnastics in addition to helping improve your posture and balance.

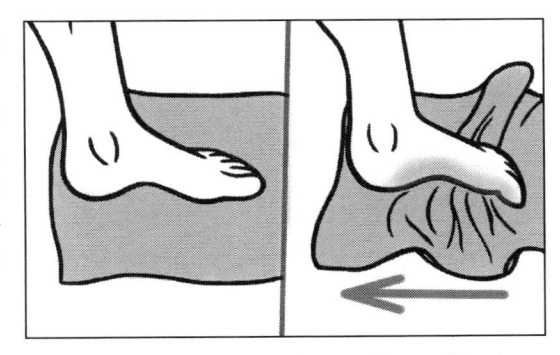

POSITION: Place your foot on a towel with the forefoot just across the edge. First attempt this exercise while sitting, then attempt it while standing.

ACTION: Pull the towel under the foot by scrunching or curling the toes and foot. Attempt to spread the toes wide to pull the towel in from the sides and use the forefoot to push the towel further back towards your heel.

Practice the Towel Scrunch for either time or reps on each attempt.

FOREFOOT MARCH
This PreHab exercise can help activate the musculature in the lower leg and foot while also developing stability in the ankle complex and assist in training a person to run with a forefoot strike.

ACTION: Stand tall; focus the eyes on the horizon and walk forward using only the forefoot to make contact with the ground. Fully extend through the ankles, lift the chest and swing the arms as the heels stay lifted off the ground. Also, pull the belly button in towards the spine to engage the abdominals and reach the top of the head up to the sky to lengthen through the spine. This exercise will help develop proper forefoot position when running.

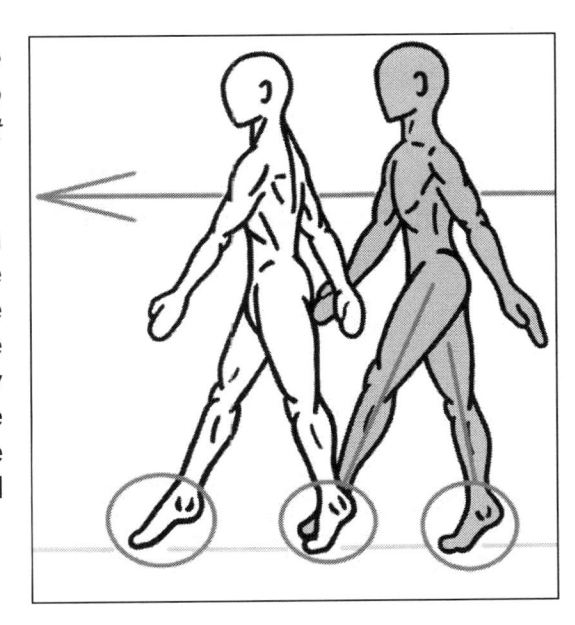

Repeat 10-20 times on each side for 1 or 2 sets.

ACTIVATION

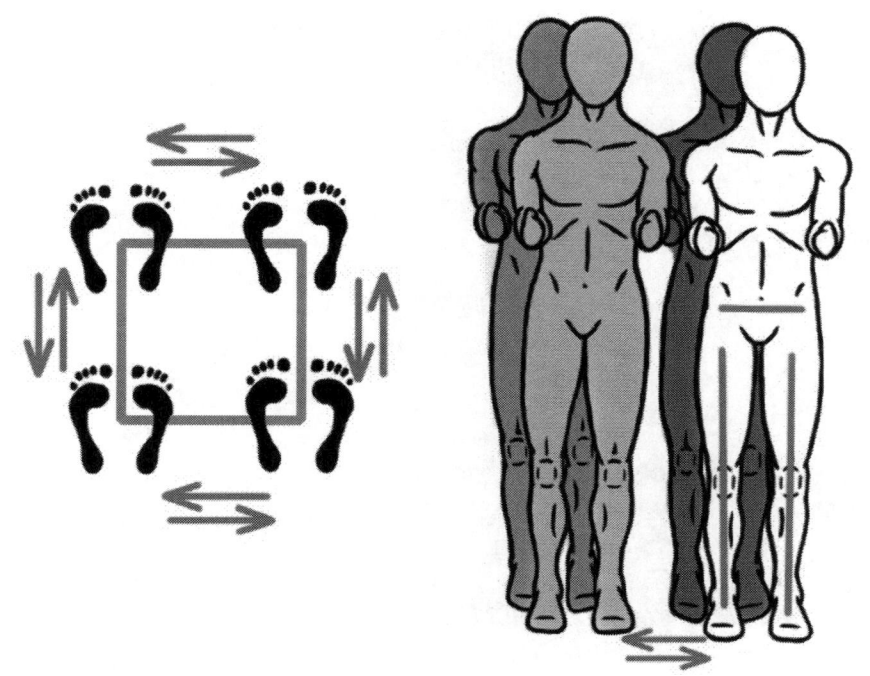

ANKLE BOX HOP

This PreHab exercise will activate the entire neuromuscular system of the lower leg and ankle/foot complex, which is very beneficial for runners and athletes who compete in activities that demand a high level of agility and acceleration, such as basketball, lacrosse, boxing and other sports.

Before starting, it is best to draw a box on the floor with the sides approximately 6-12 inches long. An alternate option is to place a cone on the floor and hop around the cone.

This exercise will help you to develop the ability to change direction and move in the four basic directions (forwards, right, left and backward) with reactionary forces generated by the ankle and foot complex. This exercise will help create greater levels of agility when combined with larger movement patterns.

POSITION: Stand with the pelvis in neutral, the abdominals engaged, spine tall, and the shoulder blades pulled towards the hips. Keep the eyes focused on the horizon, and the heels off the ground while balancing on the forefoot.

ACTION: Hop around the box the best that you can only using the ankles. Do not let your knees or hips bend too much and absorb or generate force. Focus solely on using your ankles to hop around the box.
Forcefully extend through the ankles to push the ground down and away. Land only on the forefoot and keep the heels off the ground while engaging the abdominals, staying tall through the spine with the eyes focused on the horizon.

- *Hop around the box for 3-5 times in each direction or for time (approximately 30 seconds)*
- *Be intentional about your form and keep your heels off the ground.*

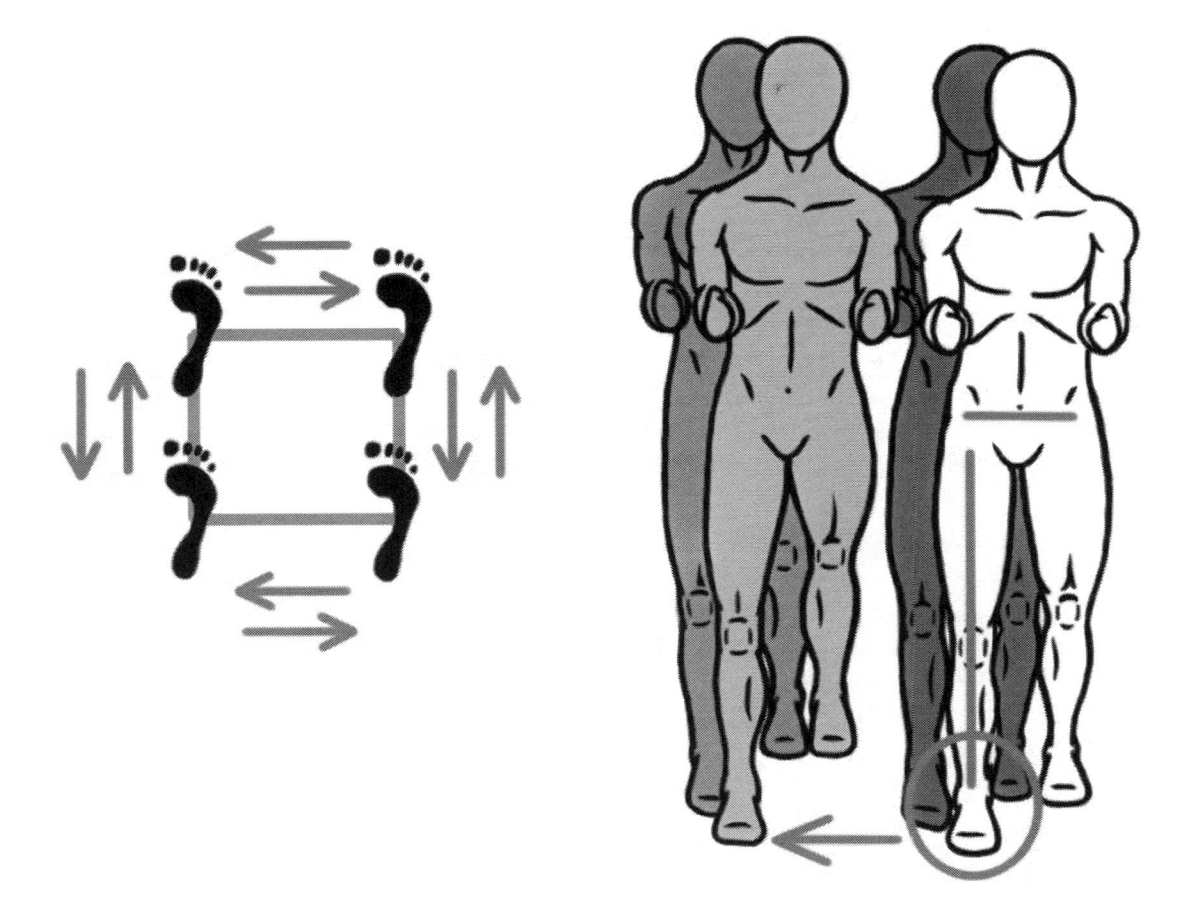

ACTIVATION

SINGLE-LEG ANKLE BOX HOP
This PreHab exercise is an advanced version of the Ankle Box Hop, which is designed to stimulate the neuromuscular connections surrounding the ankle and foot. Performing the Box Hop on one leg raises the physiological demands on the ankle/foot complex and will further develop agility and power.

POSITION: Stand on one leg with the pelvis in neutral, the abdominals engaged, spine tall, and the shoulder blades pulled towards the hips. Keep the eyes focused on the horizon, and pull the standing heel off the ground.

ACTION: Hop around the box the best that you can only using the ankles. Do not let your knees or hips bend too much and absorb or generate force. Focus solely on using your ankles to hop around the box.

Forcefully extend through the ankles to push the ground down and away. Land only on the forefoot and keep the heels off the ground while engaging the abdominals, staying tall through the spine with the eyes focused on the horizon.

- *Hop around the box for 3-5 times in each direction or for time (approximately 30 seconds)*
- *Be intentional about your form and keep your heels off the ground.*

ACTIVATION

Emphasized Turn Over Run
Another way to activate the neuromuscular system of the lower leg and foot is to run with an emphasis on the turnover rate of your foot in your stride. In other words, attempt to pull the foot off the ground as quick as possible on each step.

In many cases, emphasizing the turnover will shorten your stride or interrupt your normal rhythm. Yet, the benefit of pulling your foot off the ground as fast as possible will help develop a faster stride in the long run as the foot and lower leg will adapt to an increase in elastic energy that is created in this exercise. When the foot is deliberately pulled up from the ground, additional ground reaction forces will be absorbed by the foot and calf as there is a kinetic cost at pulling the foot up before the natural cycle of your stride is complete. This exercise uses that kinetic cost of additional force to recruit more neuromuscular support, and thus activate more of the musculature in the foot and lower leg.

ACTION: While running, turn your feet over as fast as you can and deliberately attempt to spend as little time with your foot in contact with the ground. Do not place concern on how fast you can run in terms of distance. Instead, focus on increasing the speed in which you lift your feet and turn your feet over as quickly as possible.

Practice a quick Turn Over stride for a specific number of strides (50), a set distance (400m) or time (30 seconds).

Making It Count
If you want a good time in your run or if you want to perform well in any sport or activity that requires agility, make time for Proprioceptor training. Be very intentional about the results that you want and make sure that you activate the musculature that surrounds your foot and ankle joints. This area is the first link in your kinetic chain, and it can make all the difference when millimeters and nanoseconds are important.

Take the time to activate this link and leave all the excuses behind.

ACTIVATION

Hip Activation
Turn On your Engine

When I train at UCLA, I cringe when I watch hordes of co-eds run laps at Drake Stadium because their biomechanics are so restricted. And I have a pretty good guess why I see so many students on the track with warped biomechanics. UCLA is one if the best schools in the nation and all of these co-eds have certainly put their time in studying. Unfortunately, that probably means that they were hunched over a desk for hours upon hours doing homework. That's all good, except too much sitting causes the Hip Flexors to grow tight, the glutes to turn off and the thoracic spine to collapse forward. So, when these coeds choose to run some laps and get exercise, an array of compensation shows up in their biomechanics.

Activate the Glutes
The glutes are your prime movers and you want them to be ready to fire whenever you move, especially when you walk or run.

10 Degrees of Hip Extension
When you are walking, as well as running, your body is designed to use 10 degrees of hip extension. This means that your femur bone (thigh) needs to pass behind the midline of the pelvis while having a neutral and stable spine. A common compensation is that people will start to bend through their lumbar spine and break a stable spine position in order to help the leg pass behind the hips in the push-off phase of our walking or running gait. A compromised spine will do no good for anyone!

Activating the glutes is a way to help biomechanically restore hip extension to your gait as you walk or run.

Compensation
Unfortunately, the importance of hip extension is not a testable topic on the SAT's. If it were the nightly scene at UCLA's Drake Stadium would look very different.

I can still see how many of these coeds run in my head: shoulders slouched forward, necks protruding forward like tired geese, hips bending as if they are doing a hundred shallow squats and their feet slapping on the ground with every step as they grimace and listen to their music through their headphones.

The real amazing aspect of this picture is that these coeds will tough out hundreds of laps a year with horrible form but a lot of determination. At least it gives me some assurance that they will put forth a lot of devotion in their future careers as engineers, doctors, visionaries and more! These coeds are a testimony of the resiliency of human beings. However, there's at least one lesson I hope they can learn before graduation. Exercise, let alone movement, does not need to be punishing.

ACTIVATION

PreHab Prescription
The more that you include Glute activation exercises into your daily routines, the stronger that neuromuscular connection will grow. It will take time to create a high level of proficiency, but it worth the effort.

First Stage
Repetition will be key to enhancing this neuromuscular connection to activate the hips. Simply start by incorporating at least two Glute activation exercises to your daily routine, and in a matter of weeks, you'll turn this into a habit.

Second Stage
Once you develop a habit of including Glute activation into your daily routine, raise your standards and get creative. You will soon find that whenever you are, sitting in a meeting, having a conversation with someone, or stretching out your Hip Flexors, you can easily activate the glutes.

The glutes are your prime movers, so practice activating them often and thoroughly. Don't settle for trying. Feel them turn on and know that your glutes are activated. You'll see a difference in how you perform in everything.

Basic Glute Activation Sequence
Here is a sequence of PreHab exercises to get stated with that will help activate your Glutes in the Sagittal plane as well as the frontal plane, which translates to locomotion actions and lateral stability.

> *Activating the hip muscles will protect the biomechanics of the knees and ankles as well as help prevent possible non-contact ACL injuries.*

Much on what I see in the student population related to their biomechanics as they walk across campus is a lot of "collapsing" in the ankle or excessive pronation of the foot which is a precursor to ACL and knee injuries. This collapsing of the ankle while walking usually correlates to a lack of lateral stability in the entire leg due to an under-active Gluteus Medius.

The Gluteus Medius is responsible for stabilizing the leg from the hip downward. It will create enough tension between the pelvis and the femur to help keep the knee aligned with the ankle and hip socket. When this muscle is under active, the ankles tend to roll inwards and down towards the floor. And it collapses due to the weight of the body loading through the joint without the adequate support from the hip above to hold it in place.

ACTIVATION

Over time, the collapsing of the ankle will place additional stress on the knee complex and the infamous ACL. The knee is a designed to track in a precise way. Yet, when there is instability at the hip socket and the ankle is collapsing inwards, the tracking of the knee is skewed and endures angular displacement that compromises its own stability.

This entire process is quietly propagated by specific lifestyle factors that help create an inactive Gluteus Medius. Just looking at the student population at UCLA is a perfect example. They have the unfortunate lifestyle of sitting for a prolonged amount of time, hours upon end in fact, in class or sitting to study. The act of sitting turns off the glutes and also decreases the habitual firing of these muscles, which makes it worse because when they finally get up and walk across the campus they have a lack of force production from the hips!

Another drawback to this sitting culture that coeds and many others around the world endure is that when we sit, our quads and Hip Flexors grow tight and we lose length in our stride. This makes us slower when we walk or run and it also makes us shorter because it is harder to extend through the hip.

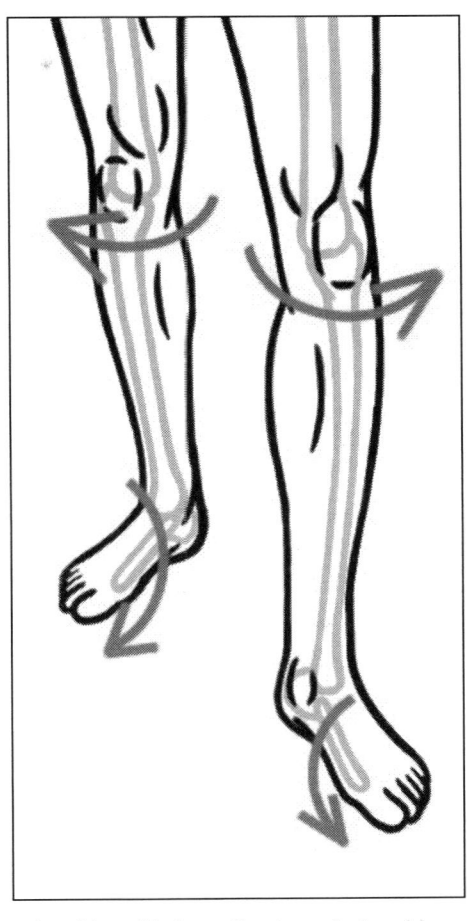

A collapsed ankle will skew the knee's tracking.

The quads and Hip Flexors are the muscles working to keep our spine stable in a sitting position. They respectively attached to hold the pelvis in place and spine vertical. On top of that, these tissues start to refashion and reinforce themselves in a shortened position. In other words they get stronger and tougher to lengthen the longer and the more often that we sit. Conversely, our glutes get weaker due to inactivity the longer we sit. This inverse relationship spells disaster. It's the exact reason a very smart coed can look as if they are sitting while feverishly running laps!

Habitually sitting is one of the most important reasons why we need to develop a practice of activating our glutes on a daily basis, if not even more frequent than that.

Benefits of Hip Activation Routines:

Develop more power and speed
Improve agility and balance
Prevent injuries such as ACL tears

PreHab Exercise Book for Runners

ACTIVATION

CLAMS

This exercise will directly activate the Gluteus Medius, which is one of the muscles that helps to laterally stabilize your knee while running or jumping. Generally speaking, the Gluteus Medius is one of the most under-developed muscles in people's biomechanics. This exercise will surely help activate the Gluteus Medius.

Equipment: You will need a Thera Band for this exercise.

POSITION: Lie on your side with a band wrap around your thighs or shins, just above or below your knees. Bend your knees into 90-degree angles and align your heels with your spine. It's actually more helpful if you perform this exercise with your heels and back up against a wall as it will help you to keep form and alignment.

Start with your knees together and place a hand on your hips to help keep them still once you begin the exercise.

ACTION: Open up your legs and separate your knees while you keep your heels together. Your legs should look like a clam opening its mouth, which is where the name of the exercise comes from.

Separate your knees as far as possible without turning the hips. You should feel muscle activity occur on the sides of each hip right above your hip socket. If you feel it in your back or thighs, stop the rep and start all over again. It's important that you feel the activity in your hips. It may not be easy at first, but stick with it. This is a very useful exercise because the Gluteus Medius is an important muscle to activate.

- *Perform several reps of this exercise with different variations including:*
- *Slow reps- perform the movement on a 3 or 5 count in each direction.*
- *Sustained Rep- perform an isometric hold at the top of the rep for 1-3 seconds.*
- *Pulsate- perform 3-5 extra contraction impulses at the top of the rep.*

ACTIVATION

SINGLE-LEG BRIDGE
This exercise can activate the Gluteus Maximus. It's very important to incorporate into your PreHab routine if you spend much of your day sitting. Sitting lowers the demand for neuromuscular activity to occur in the glutes. However, since the glutes are your prime movers, it is worth taking the time to activate them!

POSITION: Lie on your back with one foot planted on the ground and the other leg pulled tightly into the chest or extended up towards the sky. Bend the knee of the planted leg to a 90-degree angle and make sure that the knee is aligned in a straight line with the shoulder, hip and ankle.

Also, lift the toes as well as the forefoot off the ground. This adjustment will eliminate any strategies of using the ankle or foot for stability and place more responsibility on the hips. Lastly, squeeze the armpits into the rib, park the shoulder blades in the back pockets and pull the shoulders down and away from the ears

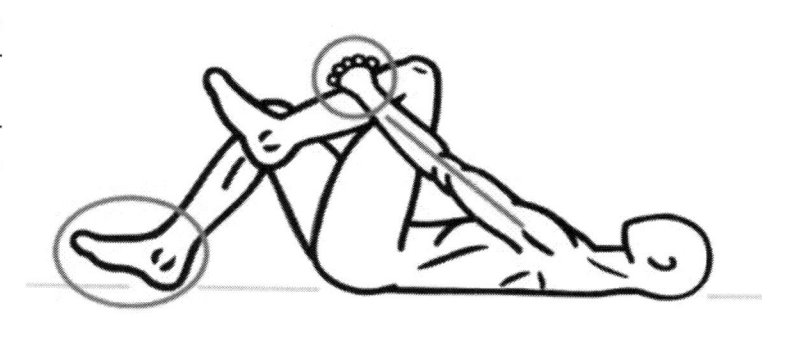

ACTION: Drive your heel into the floor and press your hips up into the sky. Do not arch your back. Stay long through your spine and pull the belly button in towards your spine to engage the abdominals and stabilize the core as you bridge.

Focus on driving the raised knee (or the upheld foot) straight up into the sky as opposed to driving the knee or leg towards your head. Press the hips up until they diagonally align with the shoulders and knee in a straight line when looking at the body from the side.

- *Perform several reps of this exercise with different variations including:*
- *Slow reps- perform the movement on a 3 or 5 count in each direction.*
- *Sustained Rep- perform an isometric hold at the top of the rep for 1-3 seconds.*
- *Pulsate- perform 3-5 extra contraction impulses at the top of the rep.*

ACTIVATION

SIDE PLANK HIP ABDUCTION

POSITION: Start in a side plank position where your shoulders vertically stack over the bottom elbow and the hips are square with the floor at a perpendicular (90-degree) angle. Place one foot on top of the other and align the heels.

Make sure that your bottom hip is aligned in a straight line with your bottom shoulder and ankle when looking at the body from the side view. From a top view, make sure that the hips are aligned with the shoulders and ankles. Do not allow the hips to pike backwards. Press the hips forward and pull the belly button in towards your spine to engage the abdominals and stabilize the core. Also, squeeze the armpits into the ribs, park the shoulder blades in the back pockets and pull the shoulders down and away from the ears.

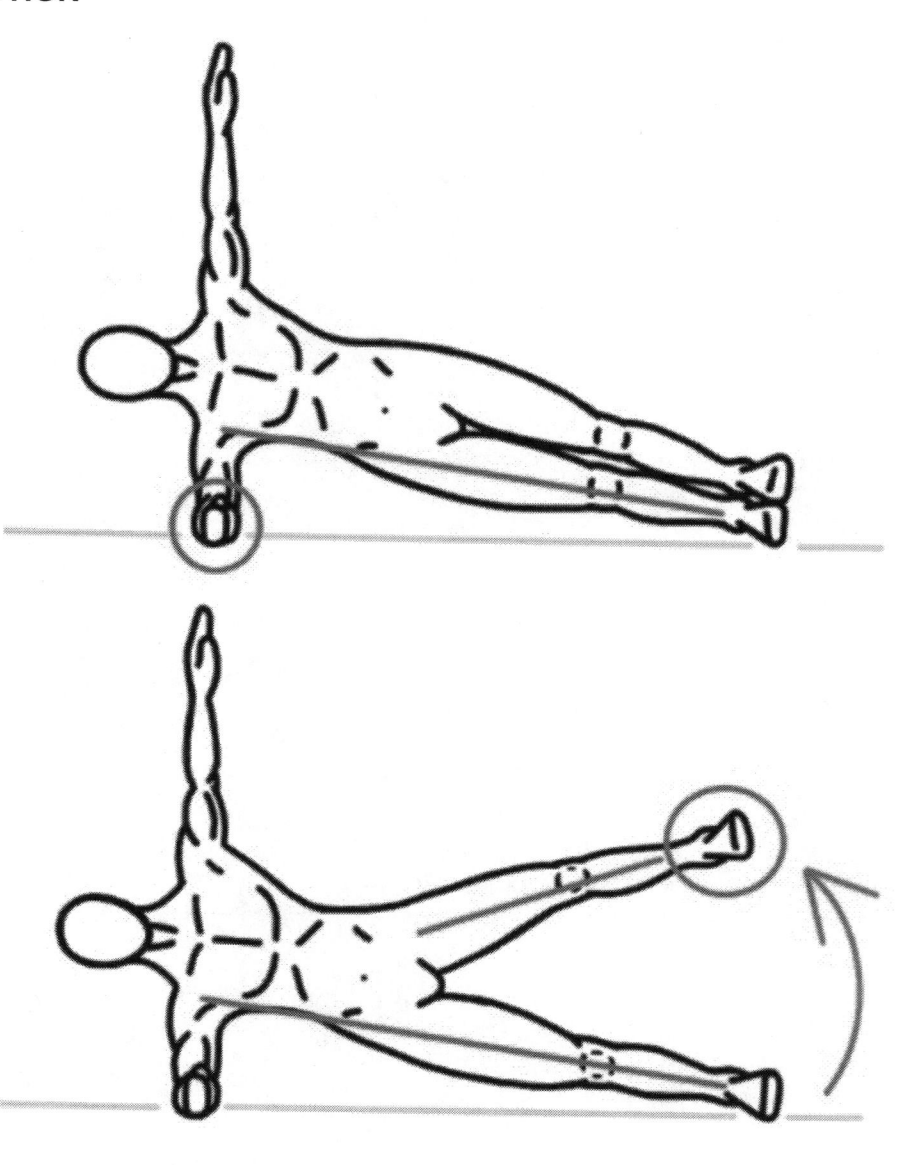

ACTION: Lift the top leg up into the air while maintaining a straight line alignment between the bottom hip, shoulder and ankle. Do not let the hips drop or pike. Instead, press the pinkie toe and heel into the ground as well as the entire forearm in order to help brace for and hold alignment. In a controlled manner, keep the feet parallel as you continue to lift and lower the top leg.

- *Perform several reps of this exercise with different variations including:*
- *Slow reps- perform the movement on a 3 or 5 count in each direction.*
- *Sustained Rep- perform an isometric hold at the top of the rep for 1-3 seconds.*
- *Pulsate- perform 3-5 extra contraction impulses at the top of the rep.*

ACTIVATION

SINGLE-LEG BRIDGE Off of a Roller
As previously mentioned, we can use a single-leg bridge to help activate our Glutes, which are our prime movers. Now, this version of a single-leg bridge will help to activate the deeper muscle fibers and neuromuscular connections that are embedded further down in your hips. Yes, the glutes are a large muscle mass as well as an efficient muscle too.

Performing a bridge off of a foam roller will eliminate any momentum that your glutes can produce when you start a bridge from the floor. That momentum will rob some of the deeper muscle fibers in the glutes from firing in that exercise. Therefore, you can activate more of the fibers in the entire muscle by segmenting the movement pattern and eliminating momentum when you bridge off of a roller.

Equipment: You will need a foam roller or a yoga block for this exercise.

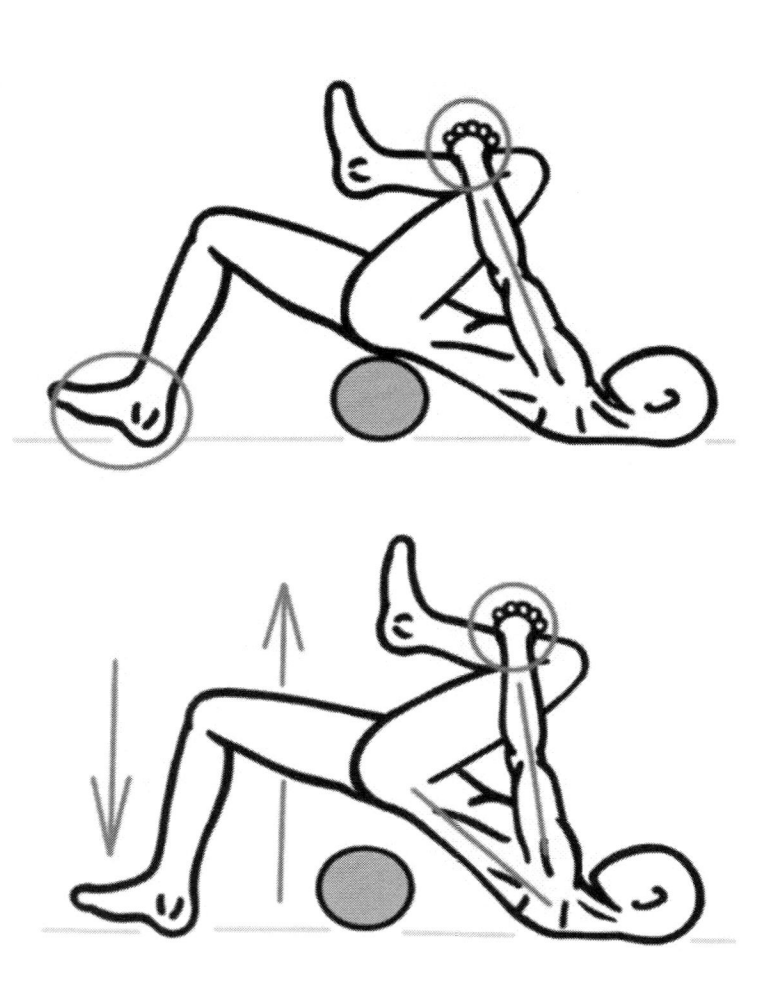

POSITION: Lie on your back with a foam roller directly beneath your pelvis. Have one foot planted on the ground and the other leg pulled tightly into the chest or extended up towards the sky. Bend the knee of the planted leg to a 90-degree angle and make sure that the knee is aligned in a straight line with the shoulder, hip and ankle.

Also, lift the toes as well as the forefoot off the ground as this adjustment will eliminate any strategies of using the ankle or foot for stability and place more responsibility on the hips. Lastly, squeeze the armpits into the rib, park the shoulder blades in the back pockets and pull the shoulders down and away from the ears

ACTION: Drive your heel into the floor and press your hips up into the sky. Attempt to lift the right hip and left hip up off of the foam roller at the same time. This cue will help you to activate the Gluteus Medius in an addition to the Gluteus Maximus and other muscles.

As you bridge, do not arch your back. Stay long through your spine and pull the belly

ACTIVATION

button in towards your spine to engage the abdominals and stabilize the core as you bridge. Focus on driving the raised knee (or the upheld foot) straight up into the sky as opposed to driving the knee or leg towards your head. Press the hips up until they diagonally align with the shoulders and knee in a straight line when looking at the body from the side.

- *Perform several reps of this exercise with different variations including:*
- *Slow reps- perform the movement on a 3 or 5 count in each direction.*
- *Sustained Rep- perform an isometric hold at the top of the rep for 1-3 seconds.*
- *Pulsate- perform 3-5 extra contraction impulses at the top of the rep.*

ACTIVATION

Band Walks

Can you move like a butterfly and sting like a bee? That's what hard-hitting boxer Muhammad Ali said he was going to do to win the title fight against heavyweight champion Sonny Liston. He unloaded a plethora of pre-fight predictions before the fight, calling Sonny a bear and vowing to send him to the zoo after beating the title out of his hands.

Few sided with the Ali at the time, who then went by the name Cassius Clay. But everything changed when he lived up to his promise to move, jab, and dance around the ring. He clobbered Liston with a fury of combination punches and claimed his first heavyweight championship victory within seven rounds.

You may not be vying for a heavyweight title, but having the kind of balance and coordination to move faster, jump higher, and throw with precision has crossed your mind. Or maybe you would like to develop your speed and agility or build power and strength in your squat?

> *Adding this one Activation exercise to your workouts can help you tap into your inner champion. Band Walks will improve lateral stability in your lower body and fire up your glutes before a workout or run.*

Fine-Tuning for Flag Football

When I was 30 years old, I started a flag football league in Hollywood with a bunch of my friends. We'd play every Saturday from 11 a.m. until late afternoon – all year round since it was Los Angeles. And we would have as many as 90 guys show up to play most days. It was truly awesome!

However, our game of flag football wasn't like organized football. We didn't practice during the week, which was a bit problematic in terms of my quarterback play. I found that my accuracy would wane from week to week and hour to hour. After failing to deliver one too many passes, I stopped and looked at the biomechanics of my throw and realized that I was not driving off my back foot enough.

I started to do these Band Walks every Saturday before our games to activate my Gluteus Medius in my push off leg. I would also perform this exercise a couple more times throughout the week to keep the neuromuscular connection fresh.

What I noticed was I developed a lot more lateral stability. It helped me throw more accurately on a consistent basis with more power. The Band Walks also helped me in running routes or playing coverage better as I had quicker change of direction and improved agility. I was "really" on the field every day after I started using a Thera Band to perform Band Walks!

ACTIVATION

> *How to Start*
>
> Thera Bands are the easiest tool for the job, though you can use other kinds of resistance bands or tubing. Whatever type of resistance band you choose to use, you should constantly feel enough pressure from the tube or band to keep your hips engaged and working against the resistance.
>
> Also, don't start off with too much resistance. The goal of this exercise is to create a strong neuromuscular connection over a long duration in order to help provide the lateral stability that you are looking for throughout your run, workout or competition. Look to do this exercise more frequently and for a longer duration before increasing the resistance.
>
> Applying the method of Technical Failure is a great rep prescription for this exercise. In other words, see how many steps you can complete with correct form before looking to increase the resistance.

SAGITTAL BAND WALK (Forward/Backwards Walk)
POSITION: Place the band or tube around the shins, just above the ankles and step your feet out to shoulder width or just slightly wider. Make sure that you can feel tension from the band pressing your legs inward. Next, squat down into an athletic position where your shoulders and knees vertically align over your toes while your hips hinge out behind your heels as you maintain a neutral spine.

ACTION: Keep your feet shoulder width or just slightly wider as you begin to walk forward or backwards. Imagine that your feet are walking on railroad tracks or draw two parallel lines on the floor for you to follow. You will feel resistance from the band or tube that will pull your feet inwards as you walk and as you work against this resistance, you should feel the lateral side of your hips engaging.

Maintain an athletic position as you walk forward and backwards. Keep the shoulders and hips level with the ground. If your hips or shoulders begin to tilt as you walk, it is a sign that your body is compensating for a lack of lateral stability. Also, maintain a neutral spine on each step.

Start with walking 10 steps forward and then 10 steps backwards. Once you can complete this with good form, increase your steps and/or combine your steps with the Lateral Walk for time.

Illustration on next page.

ACTIVATION

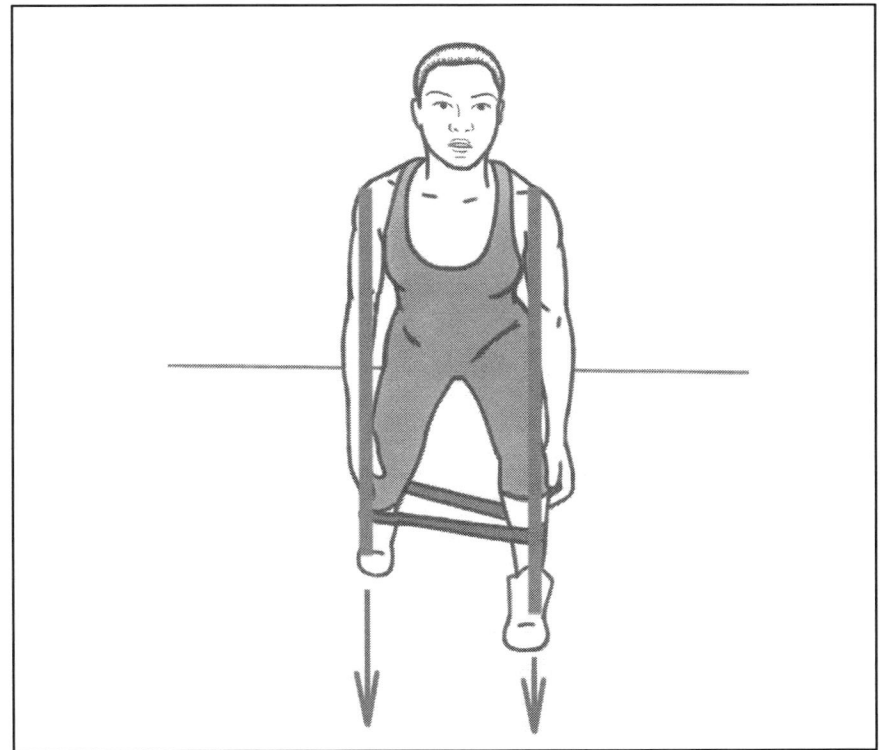

Sagittal Band Walk (Forward/Backwards)

ACTIVATION

LATERAL BAND WALK (Side to Side Walk)
POSITION: Place the band or tube around the shins, just above the ankles and step your feet out to shoulder width or just slightly wider. Make sure that you can feel tension from the band pressing your legs inward. Next, squat down into an athletic position where your shoulders and knees vertically align over your toes while your hips hinge out behind your heels as you maintain a neutral spine.

ACTION: From an athletic position, step out to the side as far as you can while maintaining your shoulders and hips level to the ground. Then step with the trail-leg and bring your feet back to shoulder width or slightly wider before stepping again.

If your hips or shoulders tilt as you step out to the side, it is a sign of compensating for a lack of lateral stability. Allow for a slight tilt of the hips when lifting the lead foot off the floor, but minimize this tilt as much as possible. Again, maintain an athletic position as you walk forward and backwards. Keep the shoulders and hips level with the ground. If your hips or shoulders begin to tilt as you walk, it is a sign that your body is compensating for a lack of lateral stability. Also, maintain a neutral spine on each step.

Start with walking 10 steps forward and then 10 steps backwards. Once you can complete this with good form, increase your steps and/or combine your steps with the Sagittal Walk for time.

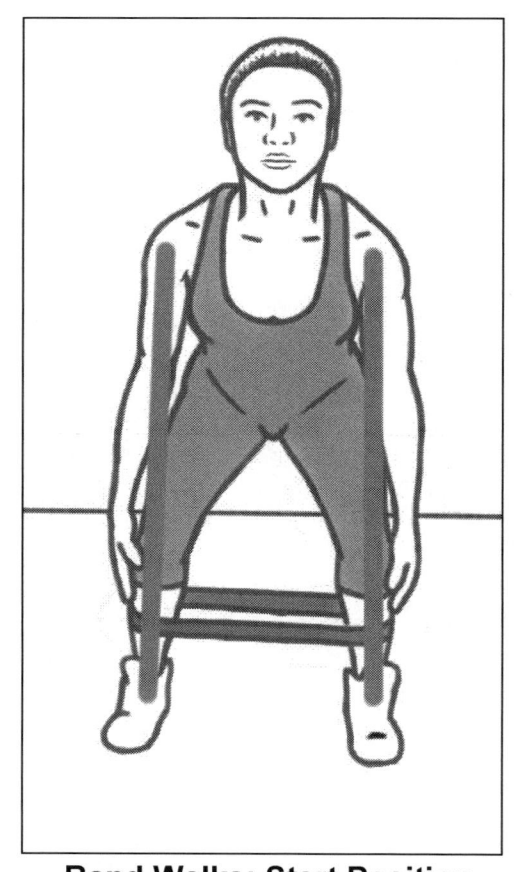

Band Walks: Start Position   **Lateral (Side-to-Side) Walk**

ACTIVATION

AIR SQUATS with a Band
Squatting with a band around the thighs will still elicit a positive neuromuscular response from the muscles that coordinate lateral stability. It is worth using this exercise as a precursor to the Lateral Walks or if you are in a crowded gym and lack enough space to walk.

POSITION: Place the band around the thighs just above or below the knee. This placement around the knees will generate more effective resistance on the legs from a lateral perspective than around the ankles in a stationary squat position – not so in a walking position. The resistance arm (mechanical physical) from a lateral perspective on the leg is greater near the knees in a stationary position because the foot is grounded and acts as a fulcrum. While walking, the foot is not grounded and therefore does not act as a fulcrum. In short, when squatting put the band around the knees and when walking, put the band around the ankles.

ACTION: When squatting, press against the band or tube and make the thighs and knees even wider as you lower down. Thighs will activate the lateral muscles in your hip, especially the Gluteus Medius.

Maintain a neutral spine and keep the shoulders vertically aligned with the toes as you press your hips back behind your knees. Make sure that you are also bending in your ankles – your shins and spine will want to achieve a parallel alignment at the bottom of your squat. If you cannot reach this position, work out your mobility more until you can achieve a good squat position.

Perform 10-15 squats for 1-3 sets before moving on in your workout or run.

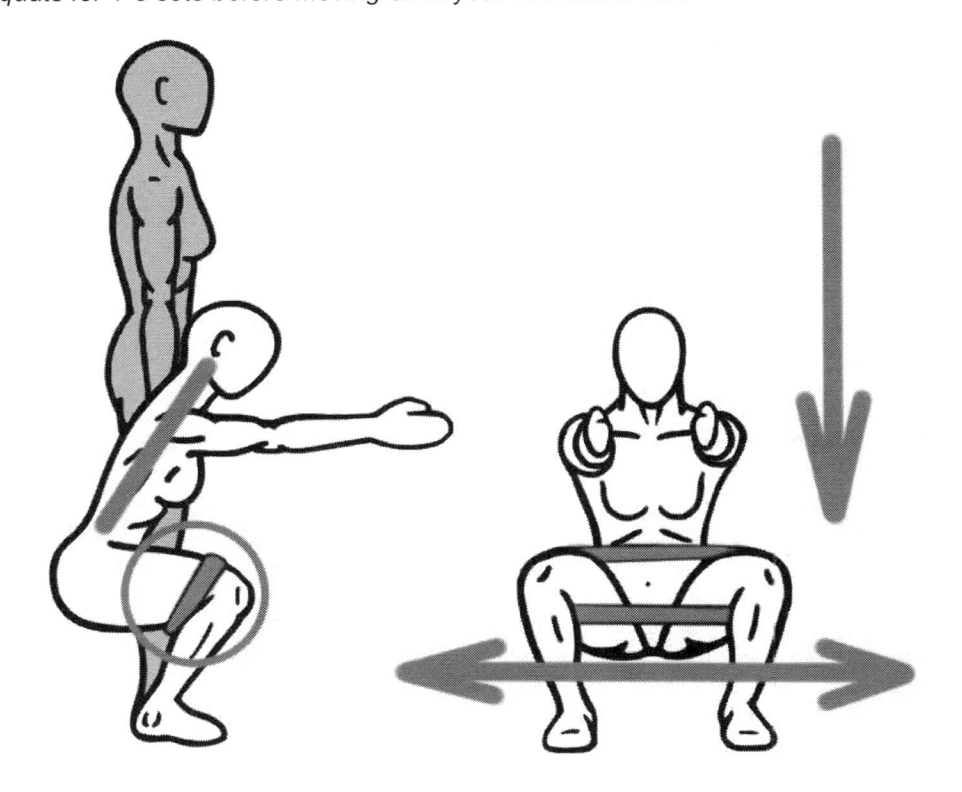

ACTIVATION

Practice Makes Perfect
The more that you integrate these Activation Exercises into your PreHab routines, the more power, strength and coordination you will have when competing and running.

These Activation exercises are great tools that can lead to much better results over time. Master Activation as a technique and you might even begin to move like a butterfly and sting like a bee, or at least throw a football better.

Practice Standing
Once you have developed a sense of what it feels like to activate the muscles of your hips, try to keep the glutes turned on as much as possible – even when just standing!

The more that you practice using this neuromuscular connection, the more facilitated it will become. In other words, the more that you practice squeezing your glutes, the easier it is to recruit them when you go to run, stand up or just move!

And once movement gets easier for you, you will move more often. And that's great in a world where sitting is predominant. So, stand up and get moving!

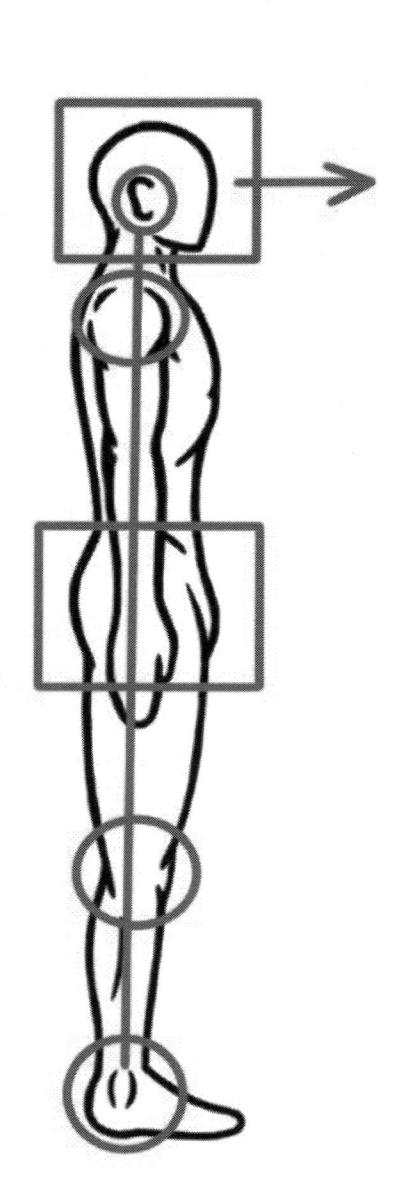

ACTIVATION

Core Activation
Bridging the Hips and Shoulders Together

I remember one summer when I was in college. I was on a mission to have an awesome six-pack. I wanted to look just like the dudes on the cover of the health and fitness magazines that I read. I wanted to upgrade my mid-section and build perfectly sculpted Abdominals and chiseled Obliques. So, I started to do 1,000 crunches a day, thinking that was my ticket to six-pack abs.

I learned a couple of things that summer. One, crunches don't sculpt your abs, no matter how many you do. Two, I got bored fast doing that routine to the point of disgust. When I looked over at the mat area set aside for crunches in the gym, I could hardly stand it

But I wasn't ready to give up. After that summer, I learned how to effectively train my core, and I never went back to crunches! The key to developing your core is optimal movement. It's initiated from the spine out to the limbs. Activating the neuromuscular connections of your core can transform your body, make your workouts more effective, and improve your performance in your chosen sports. Use these PreHab exercises as a basic sequence to activate your Core and take your workout or sport to the next level.

Fire Up Your Abs
I remember the first time I learned how to neurally activate my core. I was in the middle of another fitness workshop. The instructor had us lay on our backs with our arms and legs up in the air. We were told to press our backs, especially the small of our backs, completely flat against the floor so that there was no space whatsoever. Then our workout partners tried to slide their hands under our backs and we had to press down even harder to make sure we blocked their hands. Man, I could feel my abs turn on.

Next, the instructor told us to slowly lower our arms and legs towards the floor while we still blocked our partner's hand.

"Imagine you have a $100 bill under your back, and you don't want your partner to get it," the instructor barked. I pressed my back into the floor even harder. Yet, the more I lowered my arms and legs, the harder it got to keep the small of my back flush to the floor. My abs started to shake terribly, which is when the instructor told us to hold the position for 30 seconds. That was a hard 30 seconds!

However, that one exercise thoroughly activated my Abdominals. I have used it ever since because the using the core is essential to optimizing performance in any movement pattern or exercise. Coincidently, my personal records in lifts and runs improved once I learned to effectively activate my Core before exercising or competing.

ACTIVATION

> **Exercises to Activate Your Core**
> Here is a basic and balanced sequence of PreHab Exercises to activate your core.

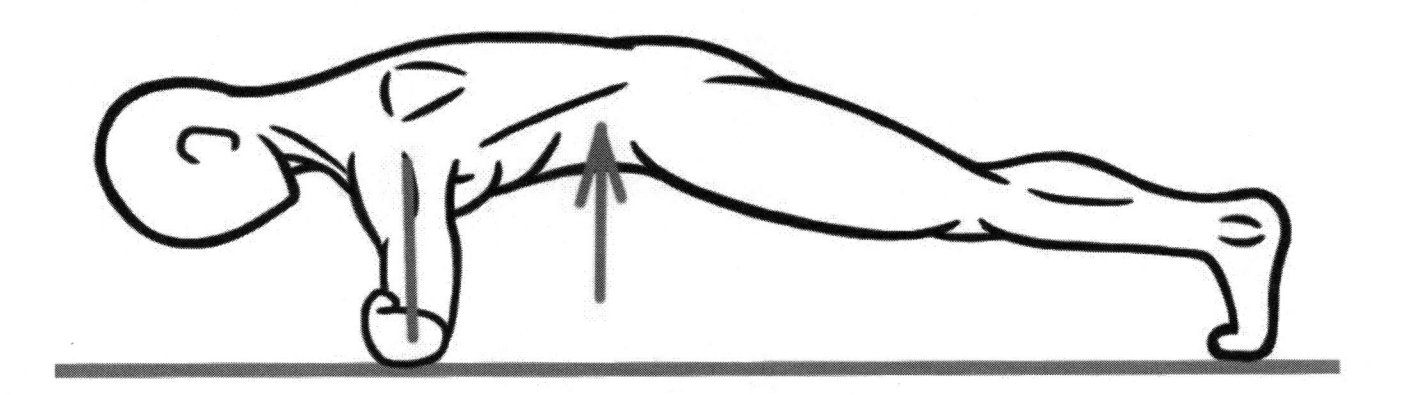

PLANK (ELBOWS) ACTIVATION

POSITION: Lie on your stomach and fold your arms under your chest like a genie. Make sure that your elbows are vertically aligned under your shoulder heads and spread your feet out to shoulder width.

ACTION: Lift up off the ground and form a straight line from ear to ankle. Squeeze the glutes and press the hips towards the floor while pulling the belly button and both kneecaps up to the sky. This will hollow your lumbar spine and activate your Abdominals.

Also, press the heart and Adam's apple up towards the sky while driving the forearms into the floor. Tuck your chin in as if you want to have a double chin and lengthen the back of your neck.

Hold this plank position for 20-60 seconds, depending on your conditioning. Do not sacrifice form for time. Keep good form the entire time and feel your core work to hold the position!

ACTIVATION

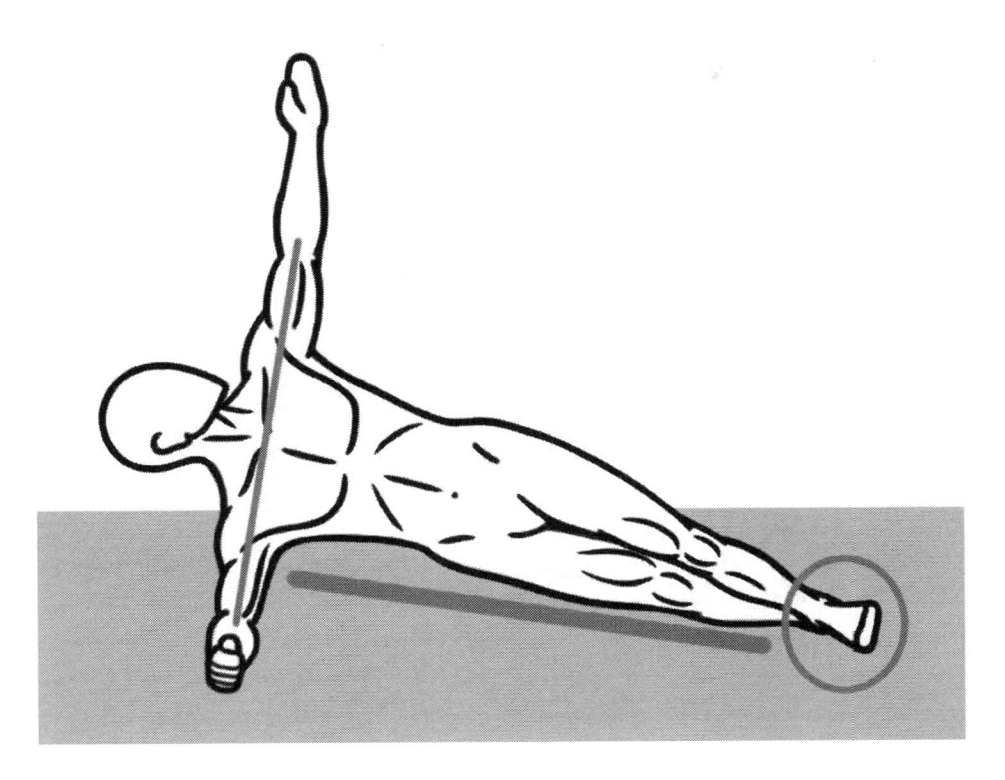

SIDE PLANK (ELBOW) ACTIVATION
The next exercise is a variation of the original plank that will help activate the lateral musculature of your core, namely your obliques and quadratus lumborum.

POSITION: From a plank position, rotate your heels down to the floor and reach one arm up into the sky. Stack the shoulders and hips over one another so they vertically align. Also, squeeze the bottom armpit towards the hips and pull the shoulder head away from the ear in order to stabilize the shoulder girdle.

ACTION: Lift the hips up so they align in a straight line with the bottom shoulder and ankle. Also, make sure your hips align with your shoulders and bottom ankle from a lateral perspective. In other words, do not hinge at the hip or pike in the lumbar-hip complex. Press the hips forward to keep a neutral spine and straight line alignment from bottom ankle to shoulder.

- Now, hold this side plank for 10-60 seconds, depending on your level of conditioning.
- Next, switch over to the other side and repeat the exercise.

Side Plank Symmetry
Lastly, it's important to note on which side of your body that you were able to hold this position with correct form for a longer period of time. The goal is to have each side equal in strength and endurance to help develop more efficient biomechanics in all that you do!

ACTIVATION

SUPERMAN

This PreHab exercise is a progressive version of a back extension on the floor and will help to activate many of the posterior core muscles, namely the Erector Spinae. This exercise compliments the plank and side planks and leads to a synergistic invigoration of the core.

POSITION: Lie on the floor, face down, and tuck the fingers and toes away from one another. Look at the floor and align your face so that it is parallel to the ground. Squeeze the biceps towards your ears and straighten your elbows the best that you can. If you cannot align your arms and legs into straight parallel lines, take more time to work on the mobility around your shoulders and thoracic spine.

ACTION: Reach the hands and feet in opposite directions until they lift up. You want to extend before you lift!

Pull the belly button into the spine and try to lift the chest and thighs up off the ground as the arms and legs reach towards the horizons.

Keep the face parallel to the ground and lengthen the spine as long as possible. You do not want to arch the lumbar spine nor crank the neck. You want to lengthen and lift simultaneously in order to activate all of the musculature on your backside.

Hold the Superman with correct form for 20-60 seconds for 2-3 sets or for as long as possible on one set if pressed for time. In either case, you want to make sure that you can feel the muscles on the posterior side are turned on and are ready for action!

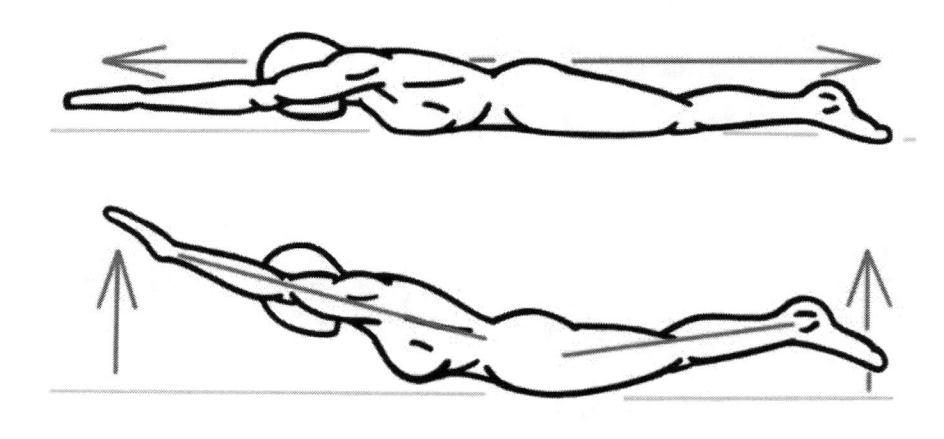

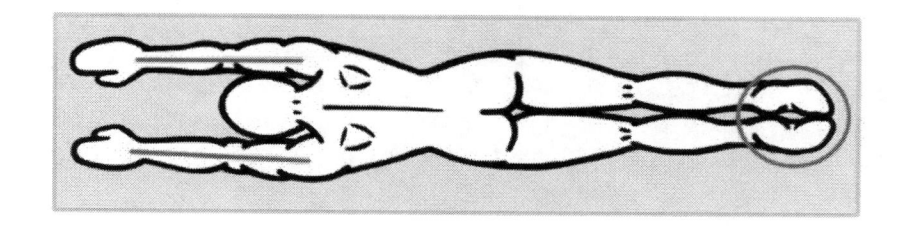

ACTIVATION

> **Dynamic Core Activation**
> In addition to plank rolls, here are a couple of PreHab exercises that will incorporate a more dynamic aspect to your activation sequence.

LEG SCISSORS

POSITION: Lie on your back and place your hands under the small of your back to brace your spine as you lift each foot about 3-6 inches off the ground.

ACTION: Start to crisscross your feet back and forth as you pull your belly button down towards your spine to engage your Abdominals. Press your lumbar spine against your hands while you move your feet.

Scissor your feet for 20-60 seconds and feel your Abdominals become more active. Repeat for additional sets if you choose.

MAT SWIM

POSITION: Lie on your stomach with your arms and legs extended away from one another as far as possible, just like in the Superman exercise.

ACTION: Lift one arm and the opposite leg as your reach towards opposing horizons. Then gently lower down and lift the other arm and leg in the same manner as if you are learning to swim on the ground.

Keep the face parallel to the ground and pull your belly button into the spine to engage the Abdominals. Support your lower back as you try to lift your chest and thigh off the ground.

Mat Swim for 20-60 seconds and feel the posterior side of your core become more activated. Repeat for additional sets if you choose.

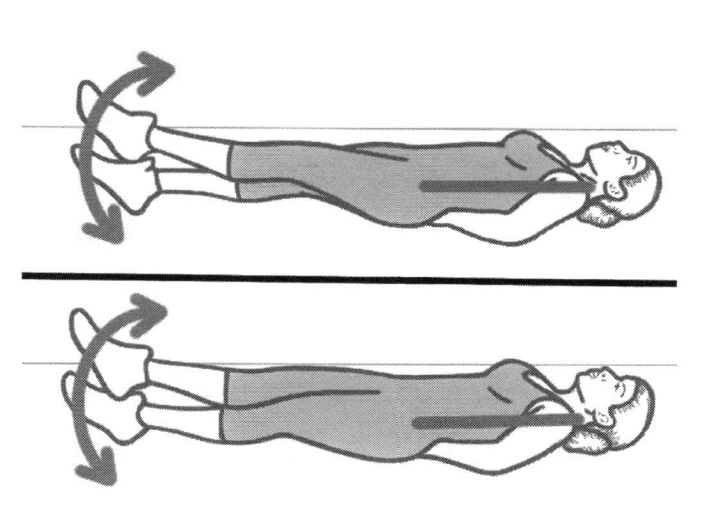

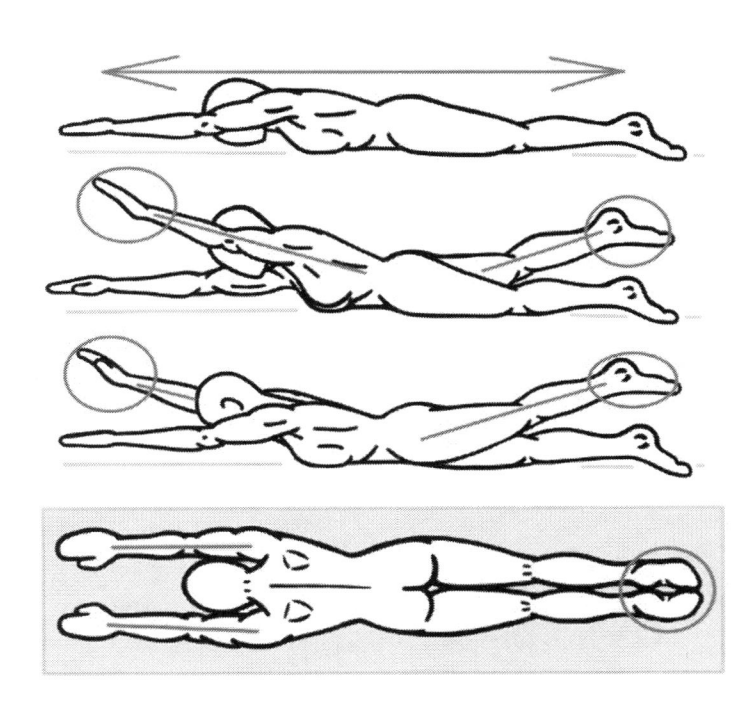

ACTIVATION

JANDA SIT-UP

During his long career as a leading researcher and expert on chronic musculoskeletal pain, Dr. Vladimir Janda discovered a way to activate the core. His technique designed to activate the abdominal muscles without activating the Hip Flexors in a technical sit-up, is a great tool to use for anyone who has tight hip Flexors or spends much of their day sitting.

This exercise employs the body's reciprocal inhibition reflex between the Hip Flexors and Hamstrings as a way to isolate the Abdominals. This exercise is highly recommended for athletes and runners who have tight Hip Flexors and lack abdominal support in core stability. Test your Hip Flexor mobility to see if you are a good candidate to use the Janda sit-up.

POSITION: Lie on your back with your legs propped up on a stability ball or bent in a way that your heels can either hook on the floor or on the back of a fixed object for support. Place the hands behind the head or extend the arms back over head.
ACTION: Curl the heels back towards the hips to activate the hamstrings as you curl up through your spine.

Curl up slowly and smoothly to make sure that your Abdominals engage fully. You can increase your pace once you are sure that you are engaging the Abdominals.

Attempt to look into your belly button as you curl up. This will help your spine curl congruently.

If your arms are extended overhead, keep the biceps next to the ear the entire time. This will create a longer lever arm and provide more resistance or load to the Abdominals.

Do 10-15 sit-ups for 2-3 sets and make sure that you can feel the Abdominals engaged.

ACTIVATION

SOFT ROLLING

Soft Rolling is one of the best core activation exercises because it doubles as a movement evaluation! If you can't roll correctly, your Core is responsible.

POSITION: Lie on your back with your arms and legs extended away from one another as if you are in position for the Supermans, but on your back.

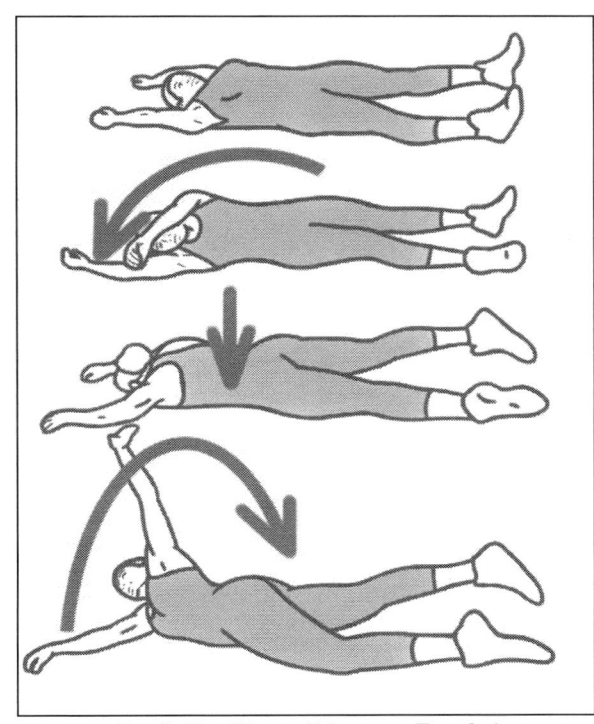

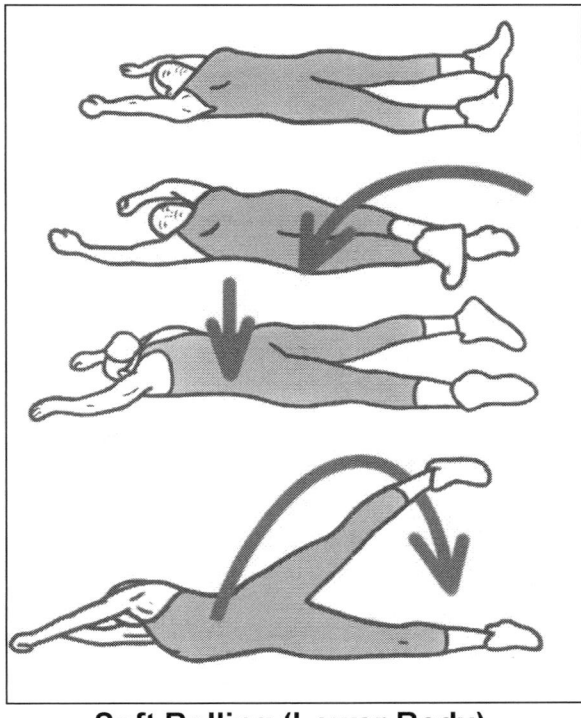

Soft Rolling (Upper Body)   **Soft Rolling (Lower Body)**

ACTION: Take one arm or one leg and reach across your body in an attempt to roll yourself over into your stomach (or back when you return).

Relax the other three limbs completely! Do not use them to push off or to help reach. Keep them completely limp and allow your core to create the roll over all on its own.

Your body will have the tendency to cheat, because it is easy for your prime movers, such as your hips or shoulders, to cheat in this movement and compensate for the lack of core activation.

> *Make your core work!*
> *Keep your other arms and legs relaxed.*

Also, look at where you want to roll towards because your spine and your body will go where your eyes go. So, lift the head and direct your gaze as you roll to look at the spot

ACTIVATION

where your eyes will end up in the finished position.

Once you roll over onto your stomach, attempt to roll back onto your backside using the same arm or leg. Rotate through all four limbs and keep practicing until you know that you can roll over without cheating!

Don't Skip Core Activation

As stated before, all biomechanically, proficient movement starts with Core invigoration. Or in other words, if you really want to move well and improve your performance, your core needs to be ready to fire and support you as you move!

You can lose a lot of power and endurance in how you move if your core is not firing when you need it to fire. For example, if your core is not engaged as you run a 10K, you are losing kinetic energy on every single step, which can add up and make a considerable difference in your performance. Or if you are trying to complete some strength training exercises and your core is not turned on, you will lose stability in your form and therefore lose power in that movement pattern because form equals function.

ACTIVATION

Shoulder Activation
More Important than you may think-

Once you have loosened up your shoulders with the soft tissue therapy and mobility exercises, the next objective is to re-invigorate the neuromuscular system in that area with a variety of activation exercises.

This sequence of PreHab exercises is similar to setting up a tent. You start with mobility work just like you would laying out a tent's canvas on the floor to get started setting it up. The activation exercises represent the act of erecting the tent by fashioning the metal poles under the canvas. Then comes strapping the tent to the poles and grounding the canvas down with spikes to complete the sequence with stability exercises.

Synergy
One of the most important reasons to activate all of the muscles connecting through the shoulder is to re-establish a balanced synergy of forces on the joint. Let's face it, most of us don't use a balanced full range of motion in the shoulders that often. The majority of our days are spent with the arms performing tasks in front of the body (and in an elevated position if you work on a computer or at a desk.) How many times do you reach over head? Behind you? Or how many times are you pushing yourself up onto something as if you were about to sit upon a high wall or even do a dip? Not that much probably. And that's because the average daily lifestyle doesn't command the shoulders to work through all the various directions that they were built for. Instead, we predominantly work in a forward and protracted position, which is not doing much for the integrity of our biomechanics.

***Develop a daily practice of activating the shoulders in a synergy
of directions to help maintain proper biomechanics.***

Top Down Approach
I know it's easy to neglect doing certain exercises, like a shoulder activation sequence because of time, or that you don't think shoulder mobility is important to your sport, such as running. However, don't believe the hype. Neglect is a very slippery slope because every exercise has a direct and indirect effect on your biomechanics.

Be Responsible-
Don't blow off your own responsibility of maintaining your health and fitness – this includes taking the time to manage and address your own biomechanics.

Activating the Shoulders will help you to practice and maintain proper biomechanics. When you move, your arms always play a role, even if it is a secondary role. They still matter and how they move will still affect the larger movement pattern you are practicing.

ACTIVATION

For example, have you ever slipped on a wet surface, like moist grass or even perhaps ice? One of the things that you do right away is to throw your arms out to the side to regain balance. Yet, stop and think for a minute. What if you didn't previously activate all of your shoulder muscles? Well, you would still be able to throw out your arms. You would just do it with bad mechanics.

Now imagine if you go trail running or, worse yet, play soccer for two hours after working on a computer all day without activating all of your shoulders. You would still be flinging your elbows about and using your arms for balance, but you'd be doing it all with bad mechanics. On top of that, you would add more repetitions to compensating movement strategies and probably make your trapezius muscle even tighter and your shoulders more protracted. In the end, it's not worth it to skip over basic maintenance of your entire body.

Your biomechanics are an integrated system and compensation at any joint will affect all the rest. Even if you just run, synergizing the shoulders with some activation exercises will allow your body to practice and further develop sound biomechanics.

> *Where to start?*
> Since the shoulder is so versatile in its movement and so many muscles work through this joint, I recommend a simple exercise that is also very versatile and will activate most of the muscles in the shoulders, including the rotator cuffs.

Rotator Cuff Muscles

You've probably heard of the Rotator cuff muscles before just by talking to friends and family. These four tiny muscles are very popular because many people either injure these muscles or have major faults (dysfunctions) associated with them. The rotator cuff muscles help to articulate finite movements at the shoulder capsule that translate into much larger patterns of the entire arm in space.

For example, if you get down into a push-up position, look at the position of your biceps. Does the belly of your biceps face in towards each other, or do they face away from the toes and forward towards the top of the head? If they face forward, you are engaging the rotator cuff muscles that help create external rotation in the shoulder joint, which is the most stable position for the shoulders. (Yes, you may feel weaker in external rotation if you do not habitually practice the movement. So, practice more and get stronger!)

The Rotator Cuff Muscles
Supraspinatus
Infraspinatus
Teres Minor
Subscapularis

ACTIVATION

> **Push/Pull Series**
> These exercises will help activate the rotator cuff muscles and are very simple to do!
> More importantly, they will help create stability in your shoulders.

The Push/Pull Series is a very effective Activation Exercise because it can be done anywhere and at any time, which in the modern world of computer-based activities, driving in cars many hours a week and years of bag holding, our shoulders need all the help that they can get.

'Frequency' is key in shaping our biomechanics. As biomechanist Katy Bowman says, what we can do more often will yield a larger effect on the integrity of our joints than what we do more intensely or enthusiastically. The Push/Pull then is a power exercise since we can always practice it.

The Push/Pull Concept:
Simpler grasp your hands together and either push or pull the hands against the other to create a moment of resistance. Then relax. Then push or pull and once more relax. Each push or pull is a rep. It's simple to do and can be done anywhere.

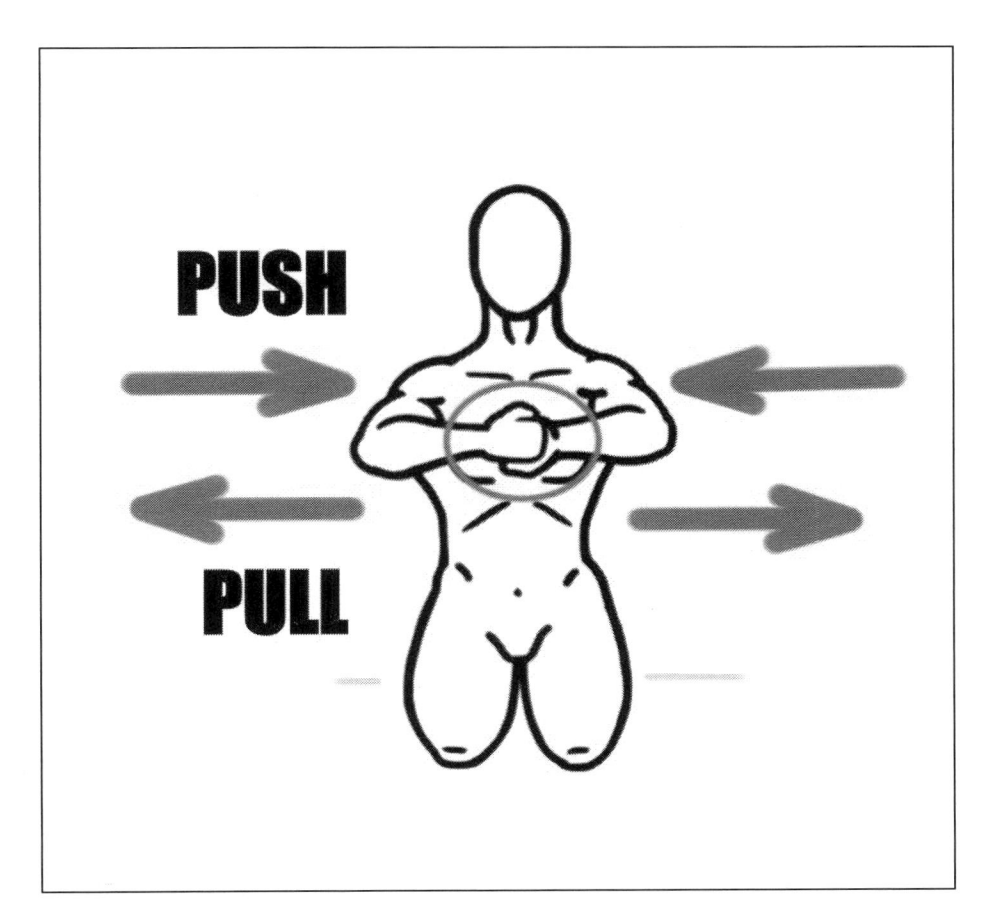

ACTIVATION

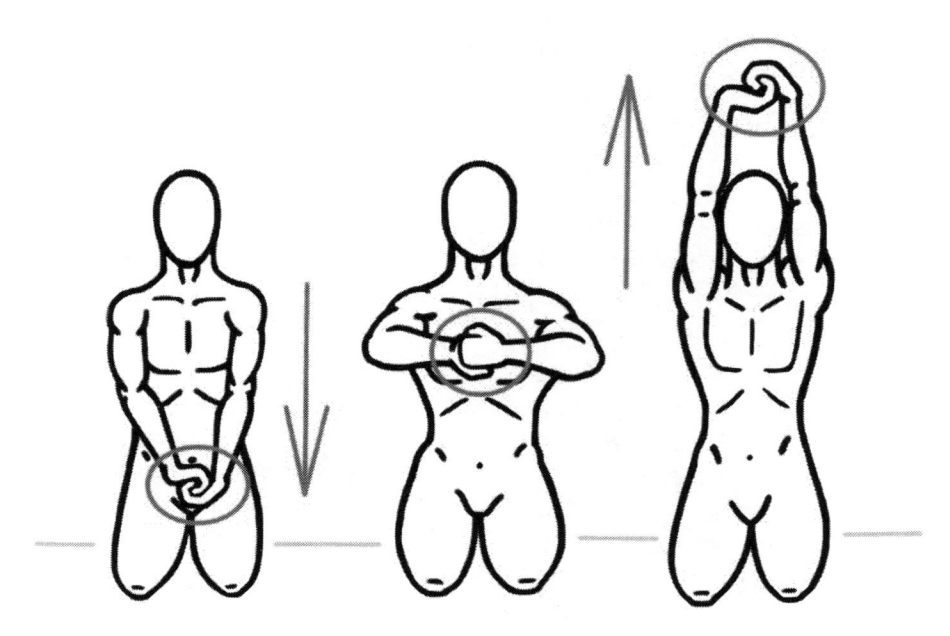

PUSH-PULL - VERTICAL
POSITION: Kneel down or stand with the hips stabilized and hold the hands together with the palms facing each other. Keep the fingers tucked into each other and thumbs aligned on opposite sides of the grasp.

ACTION: Push or pull the hands against one another as the arms vertically extend up to the sky and down to the floor. Then flip hands and switch grips.

- *Pull hands apart several times before switching hand position and repeat.*
- *Next, push together for the same amount of reps in each hand position.*
- *Feel the muscles deep within the shoulder socket become invigorated or "burn" with this exercise.*
-

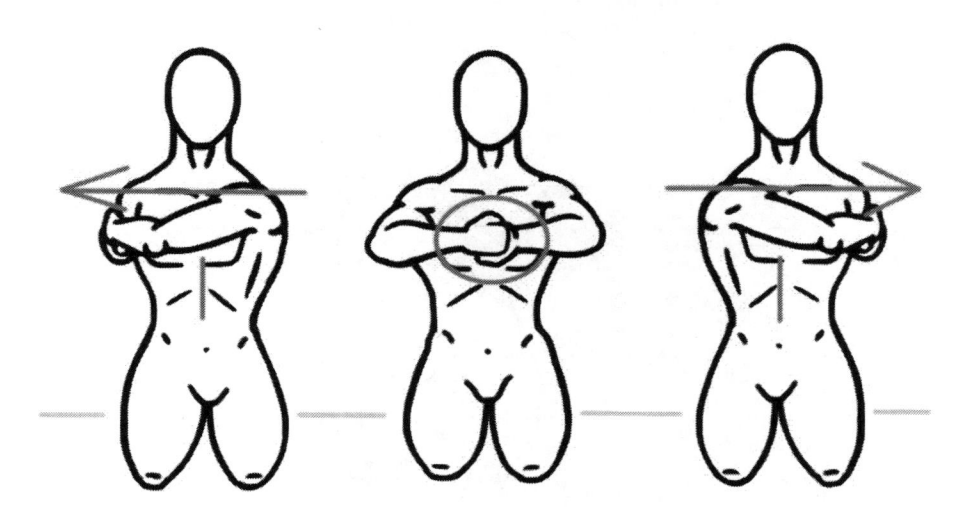

PUSH-PULL - HORIZONTAL
POSITION: Kneel down or stand with the hips stabilized and hold the hands together with the palms facing each other. Keep the fingers tucked into each other and thumbs

ACTIVATION

aligned on opposite sides of the grasp.

ACTION: Horizontally push or pull the hands against one another and keep the arms with the forearms parallel to the floor. Then flip hands and switch grips. Stay tall and keep eyes focused forward.

- *Pull hands apart several times before switching hand position and repeat.*
- *Next, push together for the same amount of reps in each hand position.*
- *Feel the muscles deep within the shoulder socket become invigorated or "burn" with this exercise.*

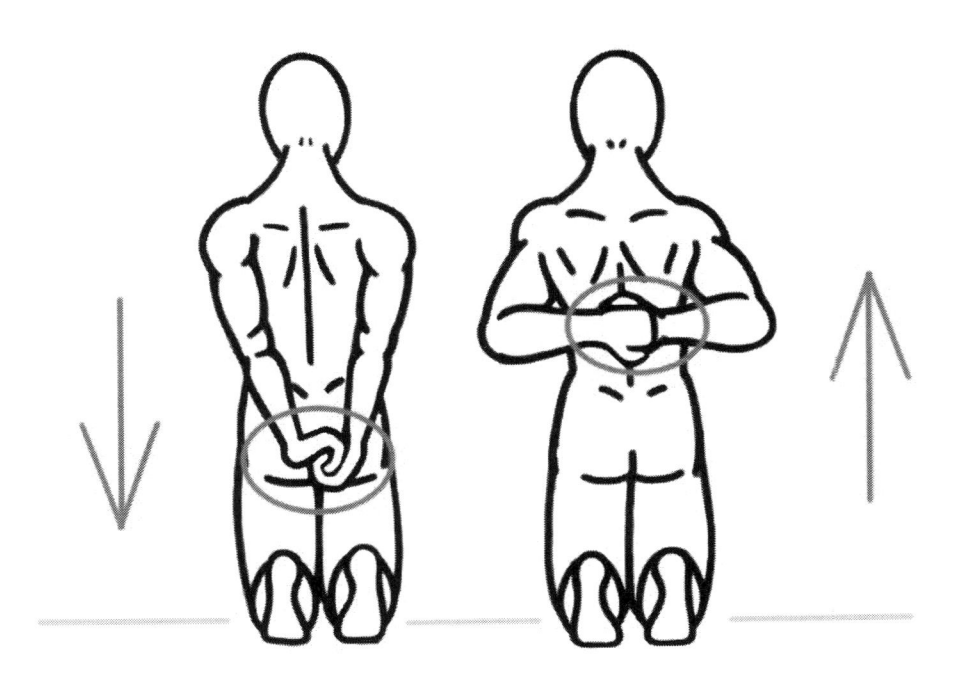

PUSH-PULL - POSTERIOR
POSITION: Kneel down or stand with the hips stabilized and hold the hands together with the palms facing in. Keep the fingers tucked into each other and thumbs aligned on opposite sides of the grasp.

ACTION: Push or pull the hands against one another as the arms climb up the back and press down into the floor. Then flip hands and switch grips.

- *Pull hands apart several times before switching hand position and repeat.*
- *Next, push together for the same amount of reps in each hand position.*
- *Feel the muscles deep within the shoulder socket become invigorated or "burn" with this exercise.*

ACTIVATION

PUSH-PULL – DIAGONAL

POSITION: Kneel down or stand with the hips stabilized and place the hands at one hip. Hold the hands together with the palms facing in. Keep the fingers tucked into each other and thumbs aligned on opposite sides of the grasp.

ACTION: Push or pull the hands against one another as the arms diagonally lift up to the sky over one shoulder and diagonally press down to the floor along the opposite hip. Then flip hands and switch grips.

- *Pull hands apart several times before switching hand position and repeat.*
- *Next, push together for the same amount of reps in each hand position.*
- *Afterwards, switch the hands to the opposite hip and start the entire sequence all over again. Feel the muscles deep within the shoulder socket become invigorated or "burn" with this exercise.*

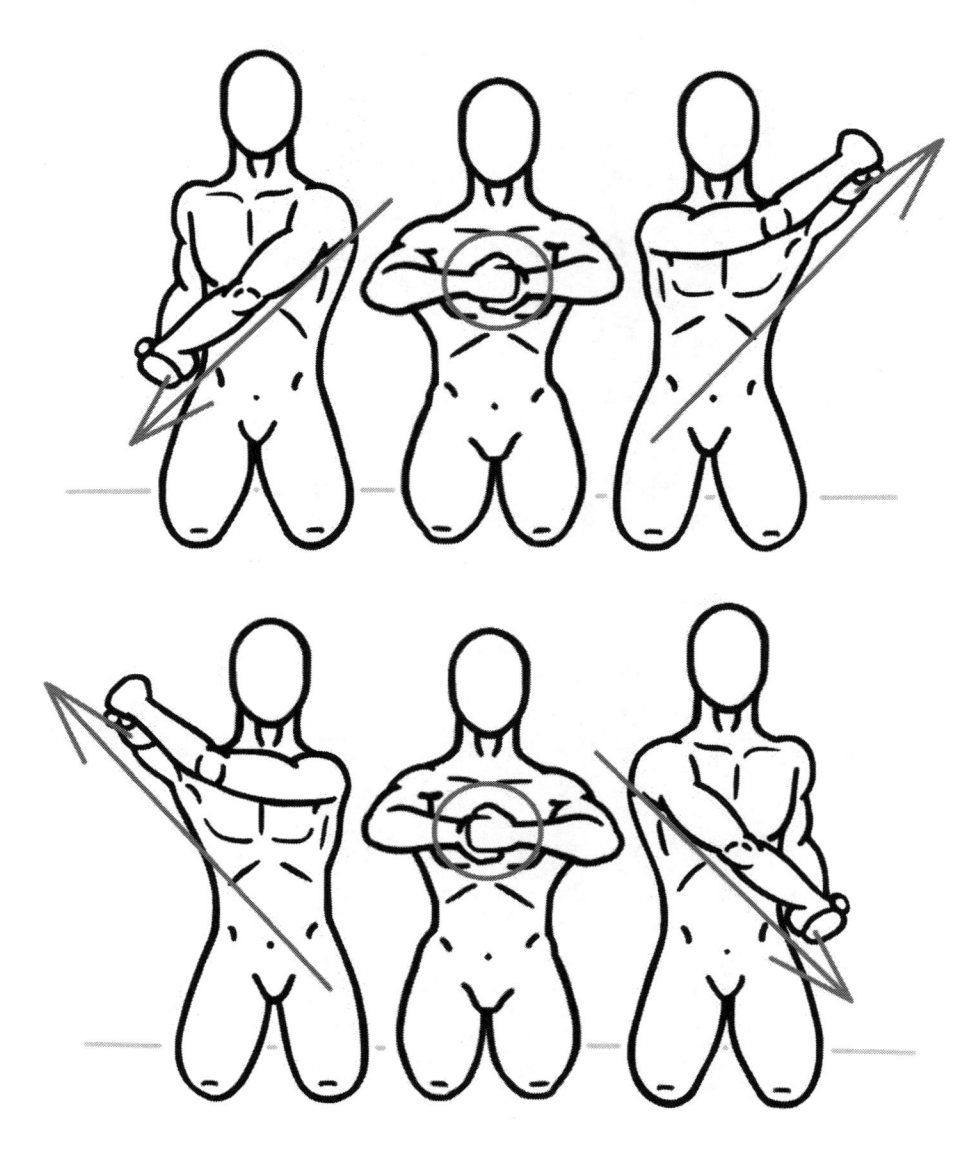

ACTIVATION

Shoulder Girdle Activation

The shoulder joint attaches the arm to the Scapula (shoulder blade), while the shoulder girdle, a mass of musculature covering the ribs and arms, attach the shoulders to the rest of the body.

The Shoulder Girdle muscles:

Latissimus Dorsi (Back)
Levator Scapulae (Neck and Shoulder)
Pectoral muscles (Chest)
Rhomboids (Back)
Serratus Anterior (Rib Cage and Shoulder)
Rotator Cuff Muscles (Shoulder)
Teres major (Back)
Deltoids (Shoulders)
Intercostals (Rib Cage)
Trapezius (Neck, Back and Shoulder)

The following exercises will help activate and strengthen the four major movements of the shoulder girdle. All of these exercises are going to be counter-intuitive to a certain degree. Each exercise will require you to keep your elbows fully extended. However, all of the movements are similar to a bunch of traditional exercises, i.e. push-up, pull-up and dip. Chances are that your body will naturally want to bend the elbows on every rep as the larger muscles in your chest, shoulders and arms will want to do all of the work because they are your prime movers. Don't let the larger muscles do the work. Keep the elbows fully extended and make the shoulder girdle muscle turn on. The intention is to activate the stabilizers and synergists of the shoulder girdle – not to do a push-up or pull-up.

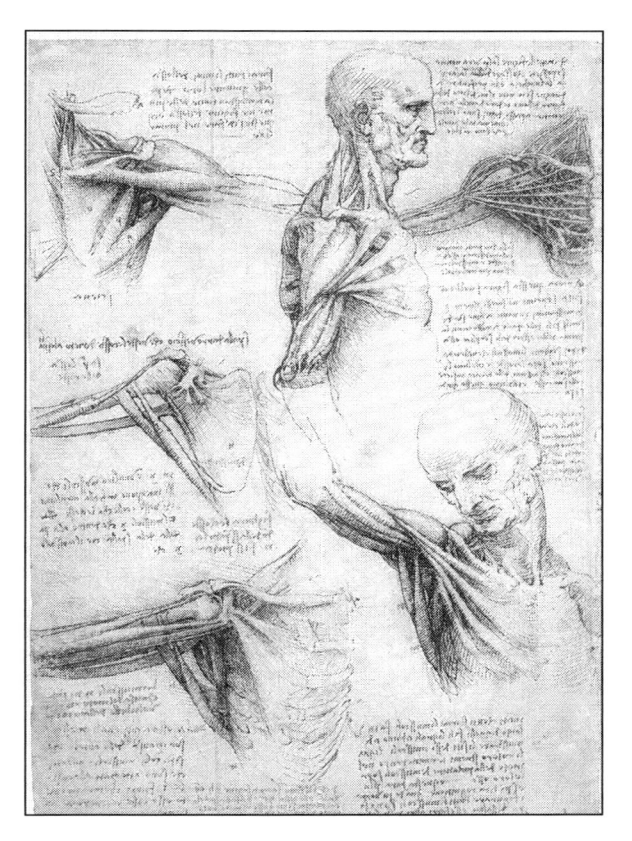

Drawings by Leonardo da Vinci

ACTIVATION

Protraction
Believe it or not, even though a lot people walk around all day with protracted shoulders, many of them are not strong in this movement pattern. People can develop protracted shoulders as a biomechanical default due to their lifestyle. See, being in this position and being actively engaged in this position are two different things. The following exercise is designed to help us to be active and strong while in protraction, which is a fundamental part of many other movement patterns like throwing, pressing and holding.

PLANK PROTRACTION (Faux Push-ups)
Start with the arms at a 90-degree angle to the spine and hold the body straight from head to heels. Engage the abdominals and pull the belly button in towards the spine. Straighten the elbows and knees.

Lower the chest and hips as far as possible to the floor and *keep the elbows straight*. Then press the torso away from the floor as far as possible and keep a straight line through the head, hips and heels. The movement strengthens the muscles of the shoulder girdle, not the arms.

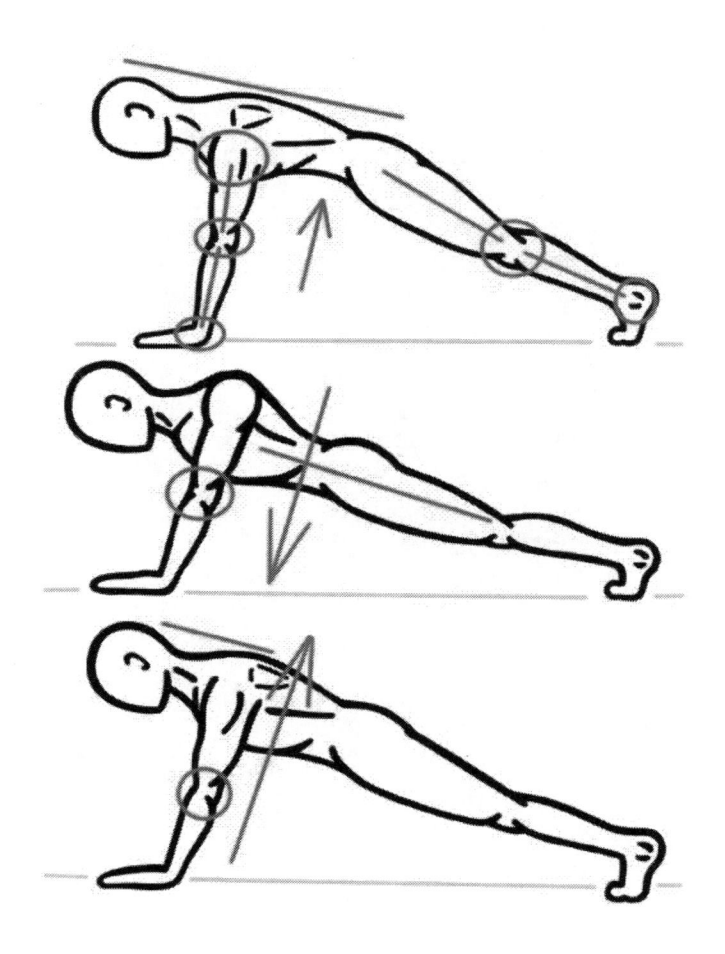

Perform anywhere from 3-10 reps, using any of the activation techniques: slow, sustain, pulsating or regular effort.

ACTIVATION

Retraction
Retraction of the shoulder girdle is a movement that is underdeveloped in many people due to working on a computer, wearing a backpack or by doing too much pressing exercises that work the chest and shoulders. Practicing retraction exercises will ultimately lead to more shoulder stability and improved biomechanics. So, if you struggle with retraction exercises, make them a priority until you feel confidence in your performance of the movement.

INVERTED RETRACTION
Hang from a bar in a horizontal position or use a cable row machine and practice pitching your shoulder blades together. Ask someone to spot you or have them place a finger in the center of your back while you pull. If you touch their finger, then you've retracted through a full range of motion.

Perform anywhere from 3-10 reps, using any of the activation techniques: slow, sustain, pulsating or regular effort.

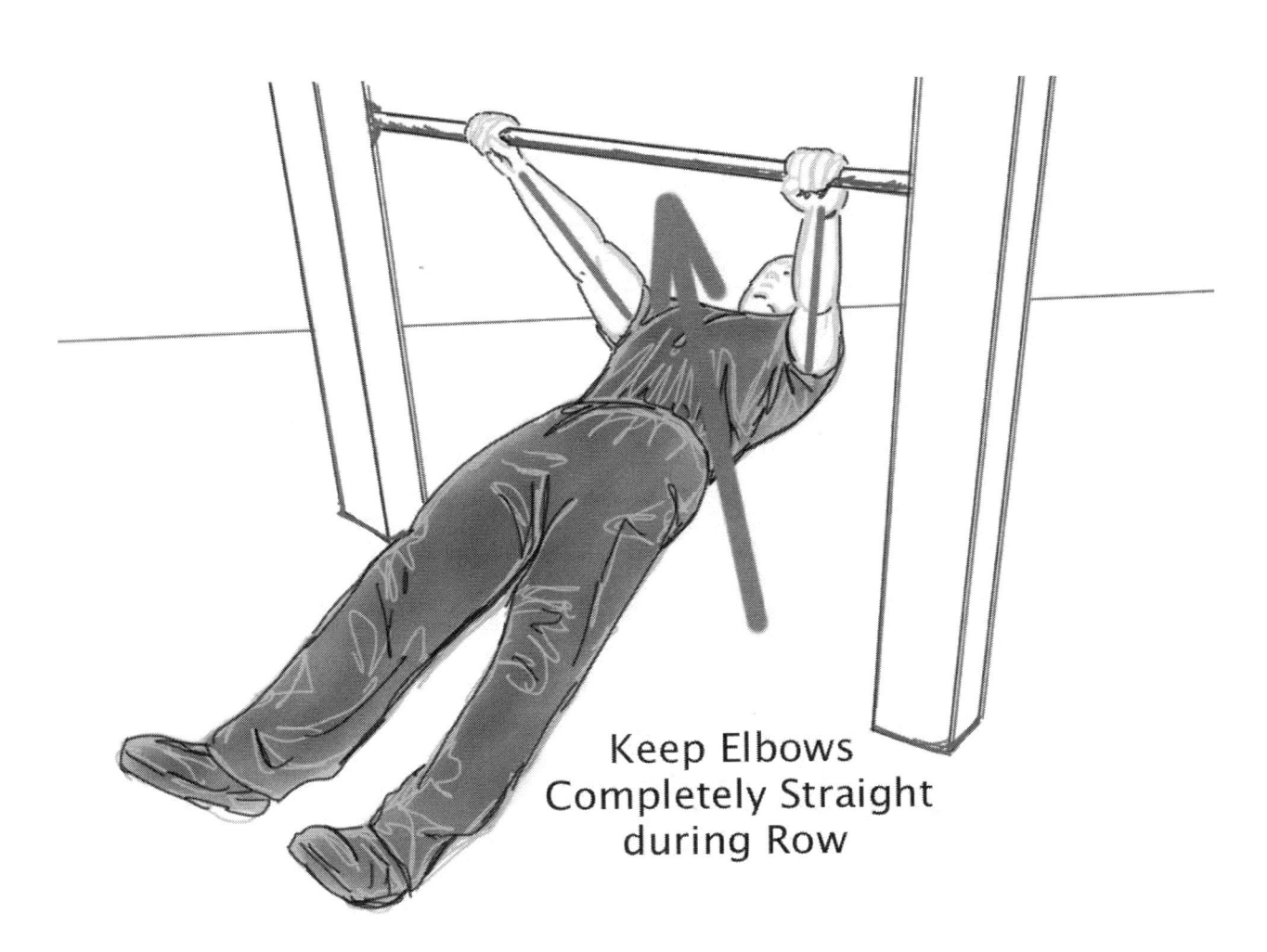

Keep Elbows Completely Straight during Row

ACTIVATION

RETRACTION on a Cable Row
If performing an Inverted Retraction Pull is too difficult for you at this time, substitute the exercise with a Retraction Pull on a Cable Row machine instead. Simply, sit on the row machine and hold the cable with your arms fully extended.

Attempt to squeeze your shoulder blades together until they can touch. Keep the spine straight and pull the shoulders down and away from the ears. Also, squeeze the belly button into the spine to engage the abdominals.

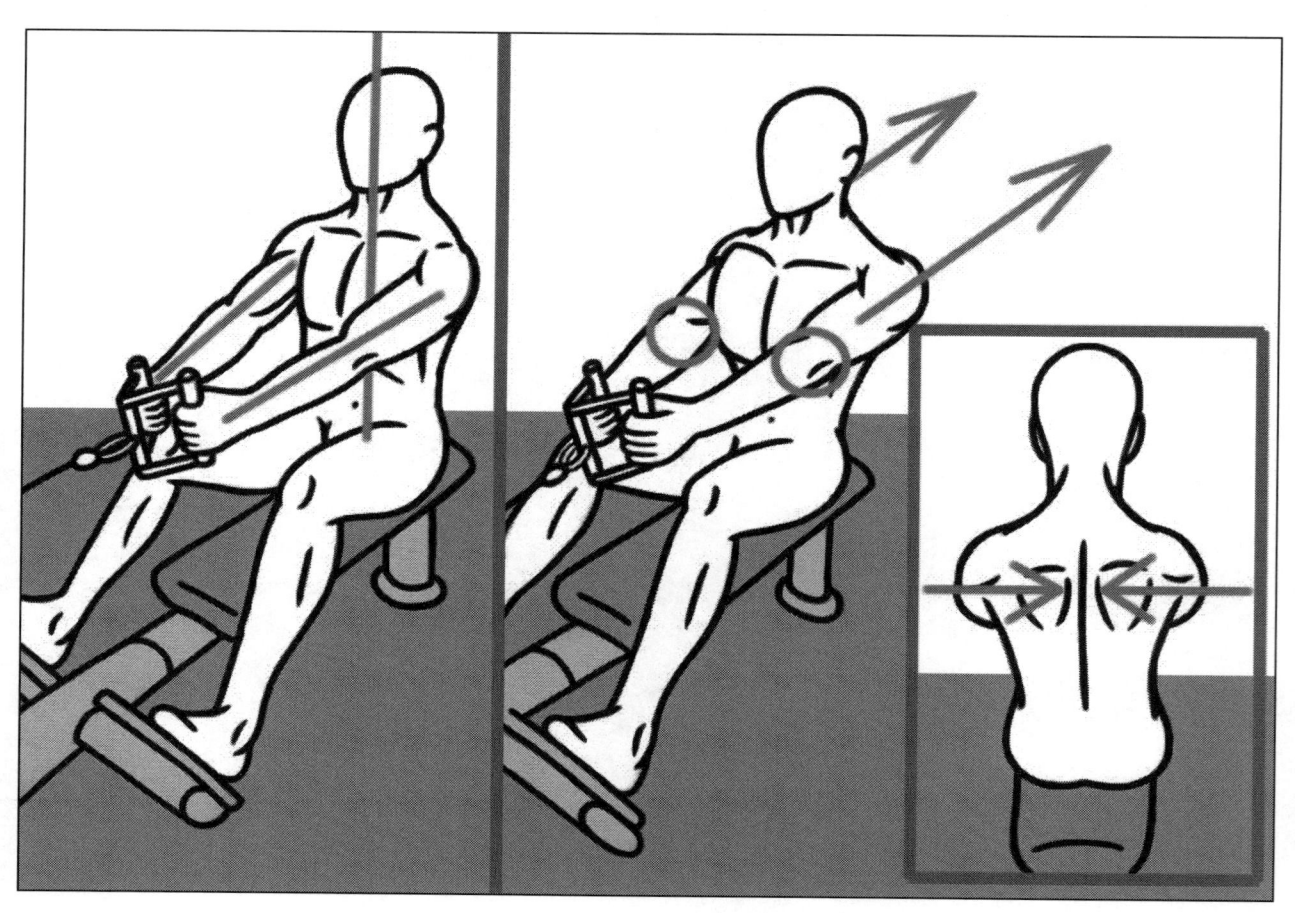

Perform anywhere from 3-10 reps, using any of the activation techniques: slow, sustain, pulsating or regular effort.

ACTIVATION

Depression
Here are two great exercises that will be mentally counter-intuitive. Your body will naturally want to bend your elbows on each rep, but keep the correct form and be intentional at feeling the musculature around your rib cage and under the shoulders start to work on each rep.

THE FAUX PULL-UP

Hang from a pull-up bar, with or without assistance, and attempt to perform a pull-up while keeping the elbows fully extended. That's right; try to do a pull-up with straight elbows- that's the exercise.

This exercise will train your body to depress the Shoulder Girdle. The movement may be minimal at first, but keep working on it until you can really notice an increase in mobility. Eventually, you will want to easily reverse shrug your bodyweight.

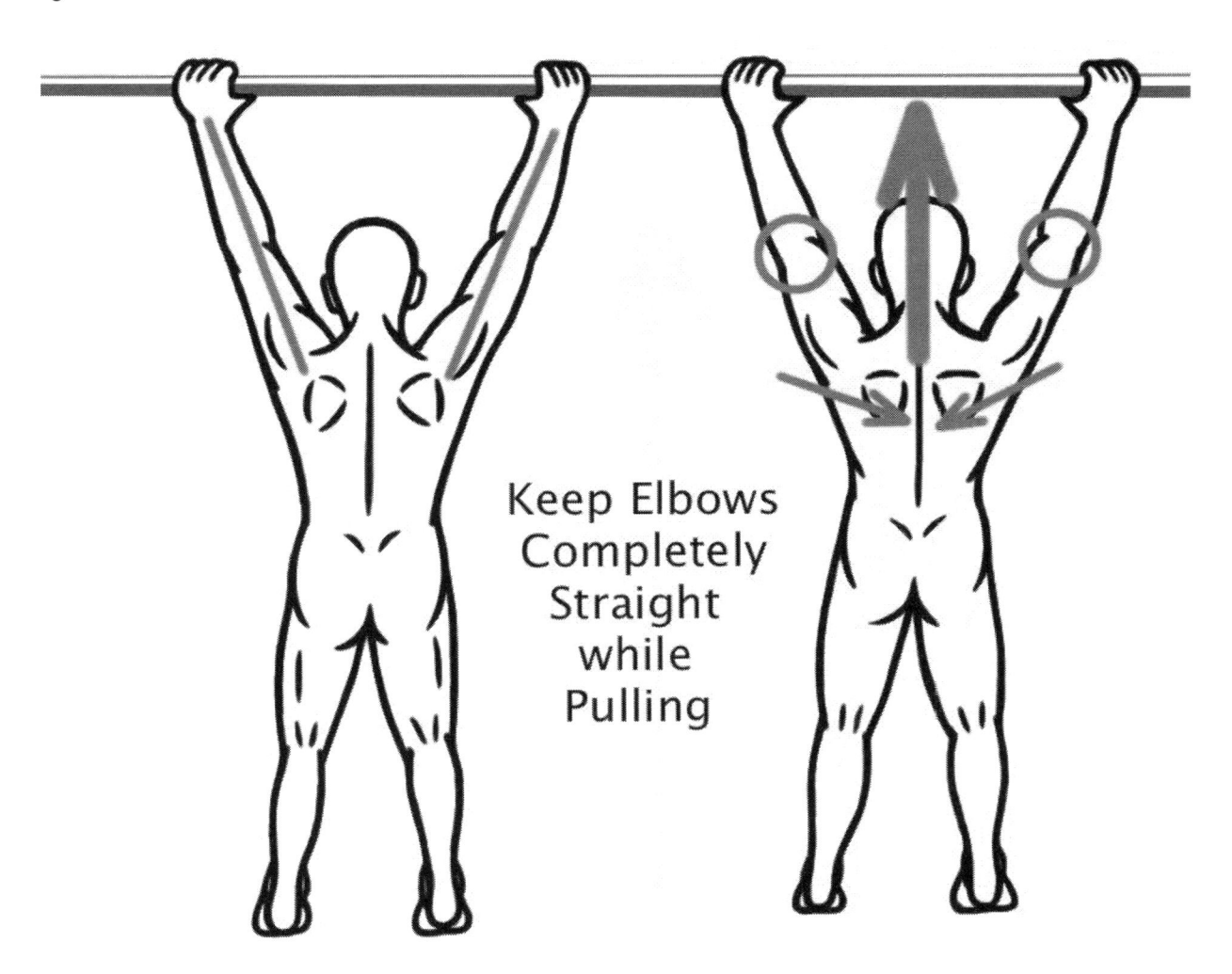

Perform anywhere from 3-10 reps, using any of the activation techniques: slow, sustain, pulsating or regular effort.

Keep Elbows Completely Straight while Pulling

ACTIVATION

Elevation
This exercise will activate the muscles of the shoulder girdle that are responsible for elevation. Even though we will spend much time trying to avoid performing shoulder elevation throughout PreHab because many people have a computer or driving lifestyle that creates a prolong posture of elevation, it is still important to include this exercise to help maintain proper strength and biomechanical synergy throughout all movement patterns.

DOWN-DOG PRESS-UP
Start in the top of a push-up, with your body aligned in a plank position. Make sure your belly button is pulled in towards the spine to engage the abdominals. Keep the hands shoulder-width apart and pull the shoulders down and away from the ears.

Next, press up into a Down Dog position by lifting your hips up to the sky and driving the floor away with your hands and feet. Push your hips up as high as possible and attempt to touch your biceps to your ears as you press your heart back towards your ankles.

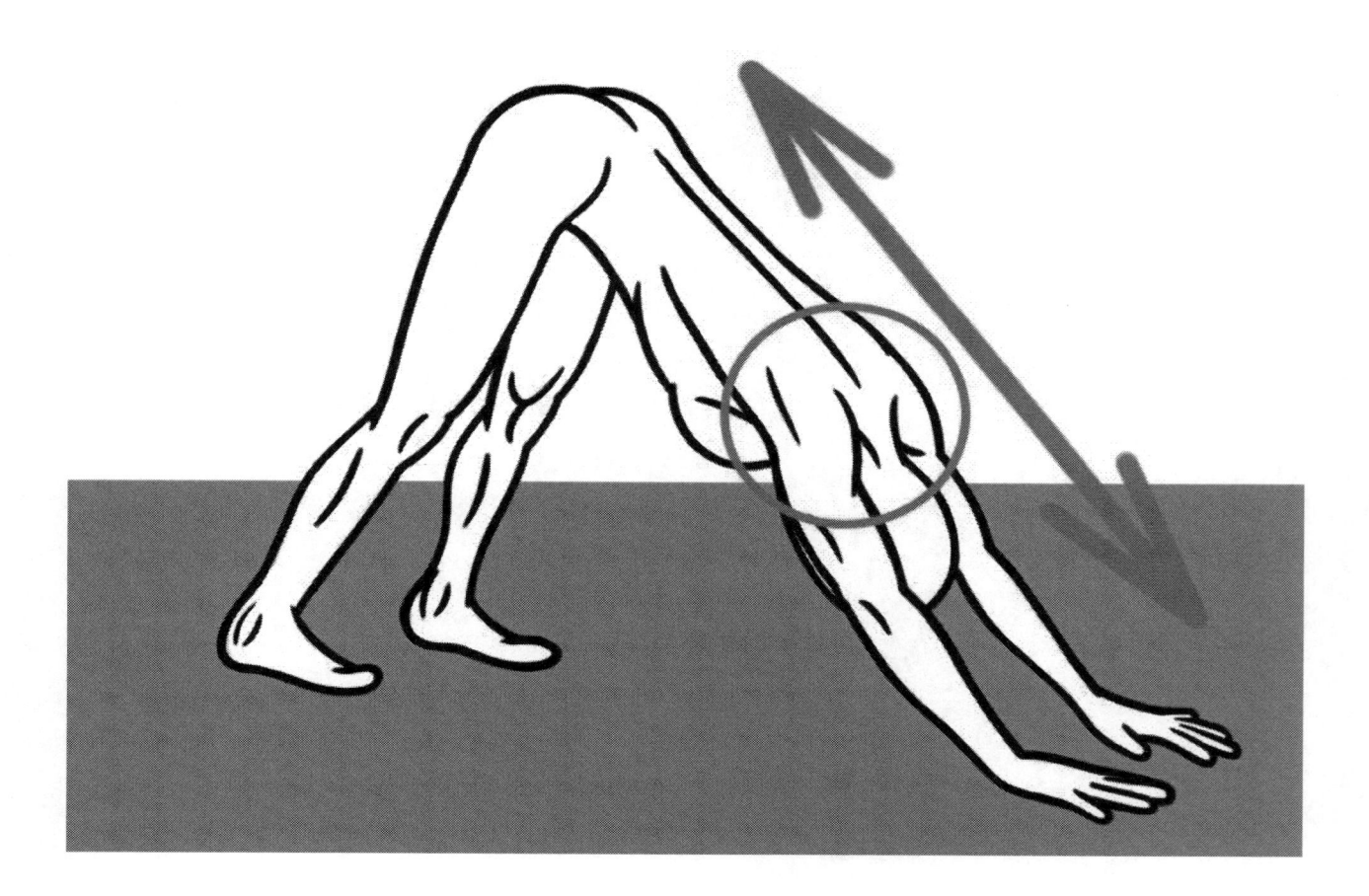

Perform anywhere from 3-10 reps, using any of the activation techniques: slow, sustain, pulsating or regular effort.

ACTIVATION

Band Exercise
The following exercise will help to activate the rotator cuff muscles as well as the shoulder girdle and requires the use of a Thera Band or Resistance Tube.

EXTERNAL ROTATION with Thera Band
Place the Thera Band around the wrists and bend the elbows to 90 degrees while positioning both elbows just in front of the rib cage.

Next, press against the band and attempt to rotate the forearms outward to the sides while holding the elbows stationary alongside of the ribs. Keep the shoulders depressed by squeezing your armpits into your rib cage and pulling the shoulders down and away from the ears.

Attempt to external rotate the forearms to 30 degrees and feel the muscles deep in the lateral side of the shoulder joint become activated.

- *Complete 1-2 sets of 5-10 reps.*
- *Perform anywhere from 3-10 reps, using any of the activation techniques: slow, sustain, pulsating or regular effort.*

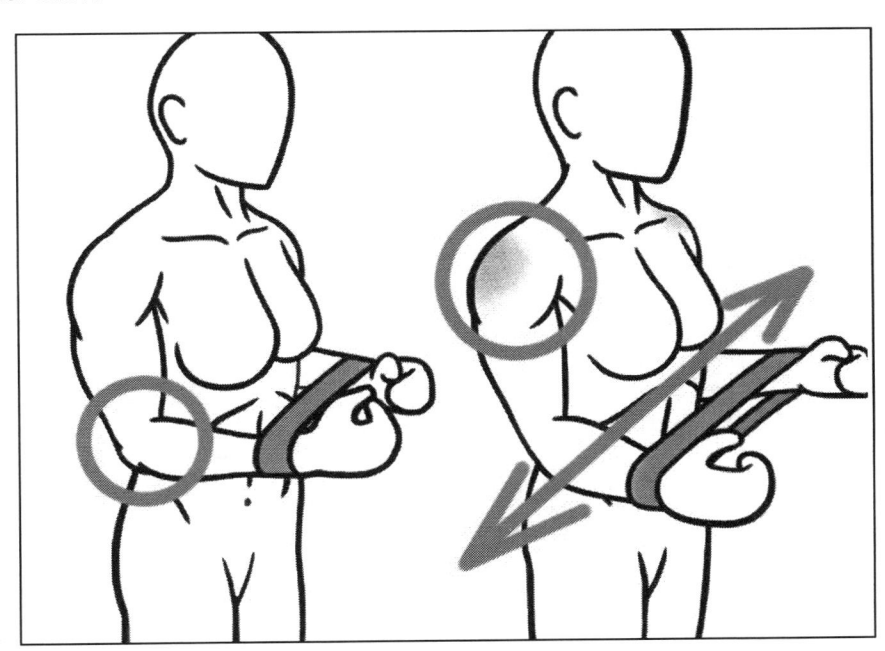

ACTIVATION

Ready to Rock!
Remember the purpose of activating your shoulders before your run is to help eliminate compensations from occurring in your biomechanics. However, the benefits of activating your shoulders on a regular basis will also lead to better alignment and posture in all that you do – like washing your car, typing on your computer, or playing sports! These shoulder activation exercises are just another piece in a larger puzzle. The more your keep plugging away with all this PreHab, the more benefits will come in all that you do.

ACTIVATION

Posterior Chain Activation
Awaken a Massive Neuromuscular System

How far do you want to get ahead in life? I mean, how far do you want to go – literally, because all forward movement is dependent on your posterior chain.

If you are looking to sprint fast, jump high or run long distances, your posterior chain is responsible for creating these movements, which is why spending some time to activate these muscles will lead to better performance. Activation exercises will help to ignite the muscles fibers in your posterior chain, which includes everything from the back of your head down to your toes.

The synchronization and timing of how all of these muscles work together dictates how your body will actually construct the movement and can make a difference between first place and second place.

Compensation Strategies
The posterior chain is ripe for compensation strategies since it is a very expansive neuromuscular system. There are numerous joints in this system:

> **Posterior Chain by the Numbers**
>
> There are 360 joints in the entire body
> 76 joints in your Spine and Pelvis
> Another 62 joints in your legs.
> The Posterior Chain incorporates 138 joints.

The risk of compensating in a movement pattern will multiply with every joint that is included in the applied neuromuscular system.

> That gives you plenty of reasons to mobilize and activate
> your Posterior Chain before you exercise!

Red Flags
If you have ever watched people try to Deadlift in a gym, you've probably seen people performing the exercise with rounded backs or over-arched backs. These are two prevalent ways that people compensate in this one exercise.

Now, take the number of different movements that use the posterior chain, i.e. walking, running, jumping and even standing up. Multiply it by the number of joints in this

ACTIVATION

neuromuscular system, and we get a lot of reasons to carefully train these patterns.

Use the Whole Chain
Compensation occurs in the posterior chain when one segment of this neuromuscular system is not properly firing the muscles fibers at a specific time. Therefore, one of the main objectives to focus on when performing activation exercises is to make sure that all the muscles groups in the posterior chain are engaged and firing.

How to evaluate?
If you understand Mike Boyle's Joint-By-Joint approach, you can easily evaluate any movement of the human body. It is relatively easy to grasp. The more that you look at movement through this kind of lens or filter, the more versed you will be in assessing all human movement.

Spine First
When you are trying to assess a person's alignment in an exercise designed to activates the posterior chain, focus on evaluating the movement of the spine as the first step. The proper alignment of a stable spine will appear as a skinny "S" from the ear hole to tailbone. Yet, in arched maneuvers or extensions, the thoracic spine, which is the spine along the rib cage or the top curve of the skinny "S", will move and change the position of the shoulders and head.

Stable Lumbar
It is important to note that the Thoracic spine is the mobile section of the spine as opposed to the lumbar spine, which is the section of vertebrae that connects the pelvis to the rib cage. When moving, especially in posterior chain exercises, the goal is to keep the lumbar spine supported by engaging the core musculature and maintaining proper alignment between the pelvis and lumbar spine.

Lumbar-Pelvic Alignment
How can we assess if a person is maintaining proper alignment between the lumbar spine and the pelvis? We can use landmarks on the body to help assess this alignment while moving.

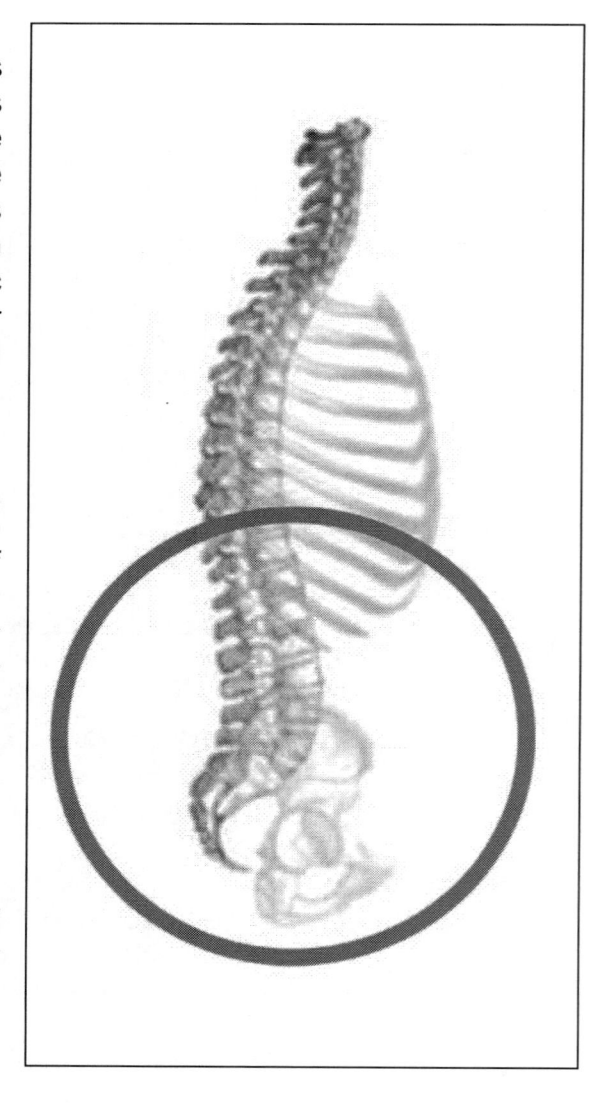

ACTIVATION

Fingers Test

Place your fingers on the anterior superior iliac crest, which are the boney points of your hips that appear in line with your belly button on the front of your body. Next, place your thumbs on the Costal Cartilage at the bottom of your rib cage; the costal cartilage is bone-like structure that connects the ribs to the sternum in the front of the body.

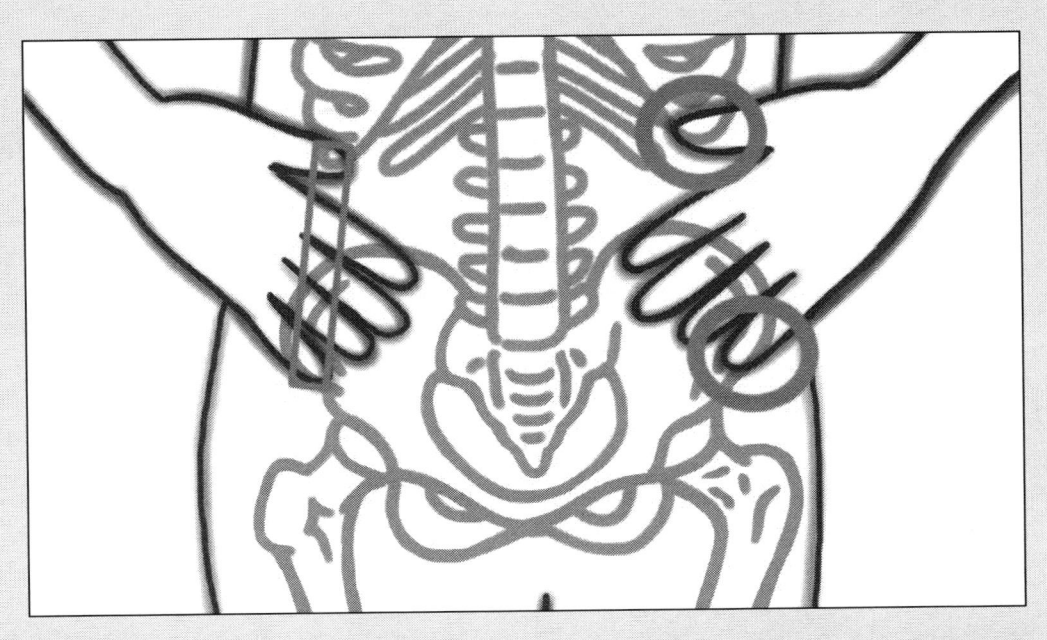

Now, perform several different types of movement while you keep your fingers and thumbs on these landmarks. This will allow you to assess how much movement actually occurs in the lumbar spine, which is not ideal for performing movements with the posterior chain.

Perform the following movements:

> **Squat**
> **Hip Hinge**
> **Bridge**

Can you maintain the same distance between the anterior superior iliac crest and costal cartilage as you perform these movements? If not, spend much more time with Core Activation and Core Stability exercises. You'll want to do this until you can create and maintain a healthy alignment between your lumbar spine and pelvis while performing posterior chain exercises.

ACTIVATION

> ### *Activate, Not Strengthen*
> *The goal of activation exercises, especially with the posterior chain, is to facilitate or turn on the neuromuscular connections within these specific muscles groups. The goal of Activation will precede the process of strengthening and is best to distinguish each objective separately. This approach will help you to train your body to establish alignment and coordination before adding the physiological stress that will create strength and endurance.*

What's the Difference?

The difference between activation and strengthening or stability exercises, is the mode of force application during the sets and reps. Activation exercises do not need a lot of sets or reps. Sometimes one rep is enough, as in performing an isometric hold or a loaded back squat. The goal with activation exercises is that you can feel specific muscles engage and turn on. If you do not, you have not activated those muscles and performing larger movements or exercises will not include the muscles you intended to activate. In other words, you need to feel your muscles get activated.

Conversely, strengthening muscles and creating stability is based on applying an overloaded stimulus or demand of movement in a specific pattern that forces your body to adapt. The stimulus or demand may be moving for an extended amount of time, i.e. performing a number of sets and reps, or moving through a specific amount of resistance or load with weights, momentum or resistance bands.

Strength and stability exercises have the objective of expanding your potential to move through specific patterns with more force, speed or endurance. While activation exercises are a mechanism of recruitment of muscle fibers in order to just establish movement in specific patterns.

> ### Posterior Chain Strength – Exercise Progression
> The opportunity to develop strength and stability in the posterior chain will become very abundant once all of the muscles in this movement system have been activated. That's because so many movements in life, such as walking, running, jumping and even standing up, use the posterior chain. Activate this neuromuscular system, and life becomes a workout!
>
> *Here are several exercises to use in order to activate your posterior chain:*

ACTIVATION

SUPERMAN BACK EXTENSION
When performed properly, this PreHab exercise can excite the entire posterior chain and help leverage a foundation for better posture against the faulting habits of upper and lower cross syndrome, see reference point.

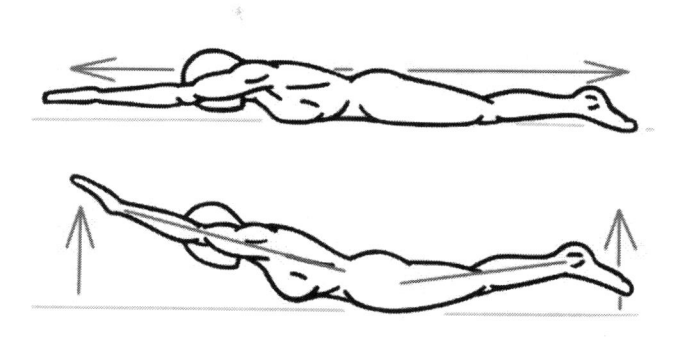

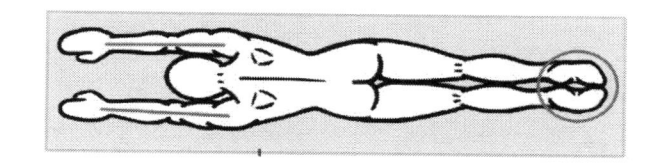

POSITION: Lie on your stomach with your arms extended overhead and parallel with your legs. Avoid cranking your neck back by holding your face parallel with the floor.

ACTION: Reach the toes and fingers towards opposite horizons until the reach becomes a lift. Then continue to reach until the arms, legs and even the chest lift off the ground.

Keep the integrity of your lumbar spine by pulling the lower ribs away from the hips and drawing the belly button into the spine to engage the Abdominals. Continue to keep the neck aligned by holding the face parallel to the floor.
Lift and hold for 20-30 seconds or perform slow and controlled reps.

MATT SWIM
This PreHab exercise is a variation of the Superman Back Extension that helps prep the neuromuscular system for the contra lateral movement patterns that are found in walking, running and even swimming.

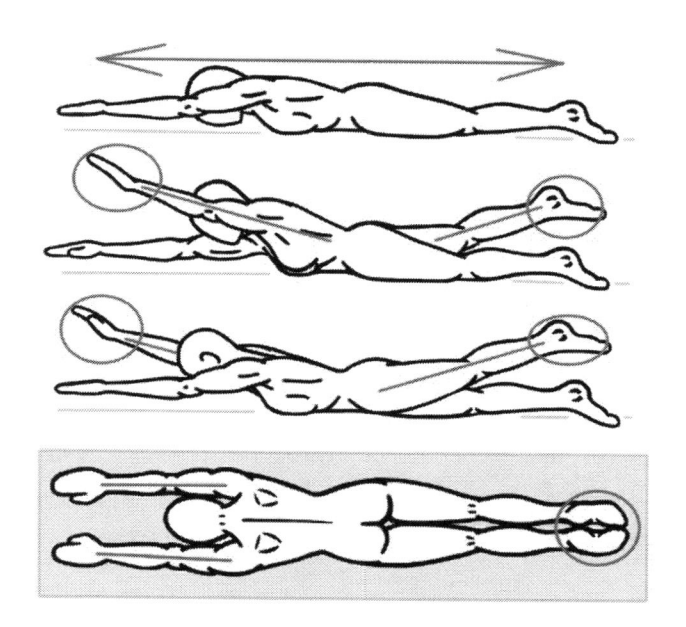

POSITION: Lie on the ground and extend the arms overhead in parallel alignment. Lengthen through the body and reach the fingers away from the toes while touching the feet together.

ACTION: Lift an arm and the opposite leg off the ground as high as possible. Maintain straight elbows and knees. Keep the neck long and the face parallel to the floor. Pull the belly button up into the spine to support the lower back and then alternate between sides.
Lift and hold for 20-30 seconds or perform slow and controlled reps.

ACTIVATION

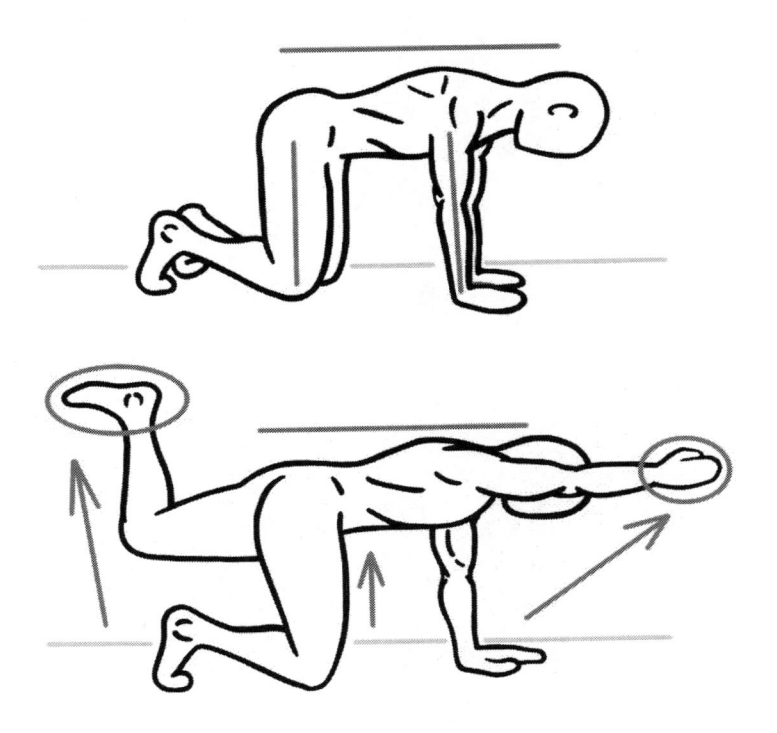

TABLETOP HAND & HEEL LIFT

This PreHab exercise will not only activate the Posterior Chain, it will also activate your shoulders, hips and core as well.

POSITION: Place the wrists under the shoulders and the knees under the hips.

ACTION: Press one heel up to the sky and reach the opposite hand towards the horizon at the same time. Keep a 90-degree bend in the knee and pull the belly button into the spine to engage the abdominals and support a straight spine. Alternate sides and repeat several times.

- Perform several reps of this exercise with different variations including:
- Slow reps- perform the movement on a 3 or 5 count in each direction.
- Sustained Rep- perform an isometric hold at the top of the rep for 1-3 seconds.
- Pulsate- perform 3-5 extra contraction impulses at the top of the rep.

Option to regress this exercise and focus solely on Activating the Glutes with this modification.

272 PreHab Exercise Book for Runners

ACTIVATION

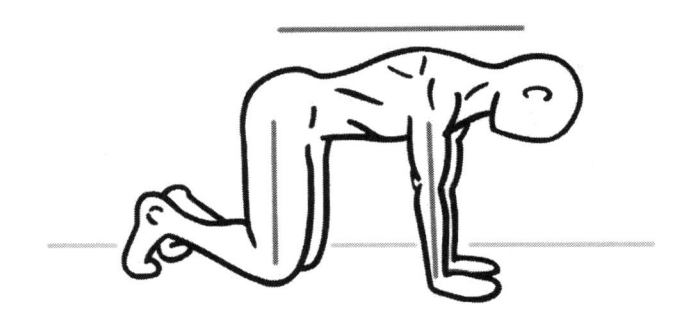

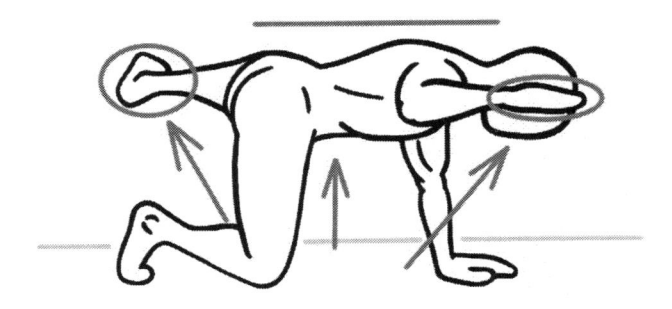

TABLETOP SHOULDER & HIP ABDUCTION

This PreHab exercise will not only activate the Posterior Chain, it will also activate your shoulders, hips and core as well.

POSITION: Place the wrists under the shoulders and the knees under the hips.

ACTION: Slide one knee out to the side towards the horizon and pull the opposite hand off the ground at the same time. Keep 90-degree angles in the knee and elbow and attempt to lift the shin and forearm as high as possible while keeping them parallel to the floor. Keep your spine stable and neutral.

- Perform several reps of this exercise with different variations including:
- Slow reps- perform the movement on a 3 or 5 count in each direction.
- Sustained Rep- perform an isometric hold at the top of the rep for 1-3 seconds.
- Pulsate- perform 3-5 extra contraction impulses at the top of the rep.

Option to regress this exercise and focus solely on Activating the Glutes with this modification.

PreHab Exercise Book for Runners

ACTIVATION

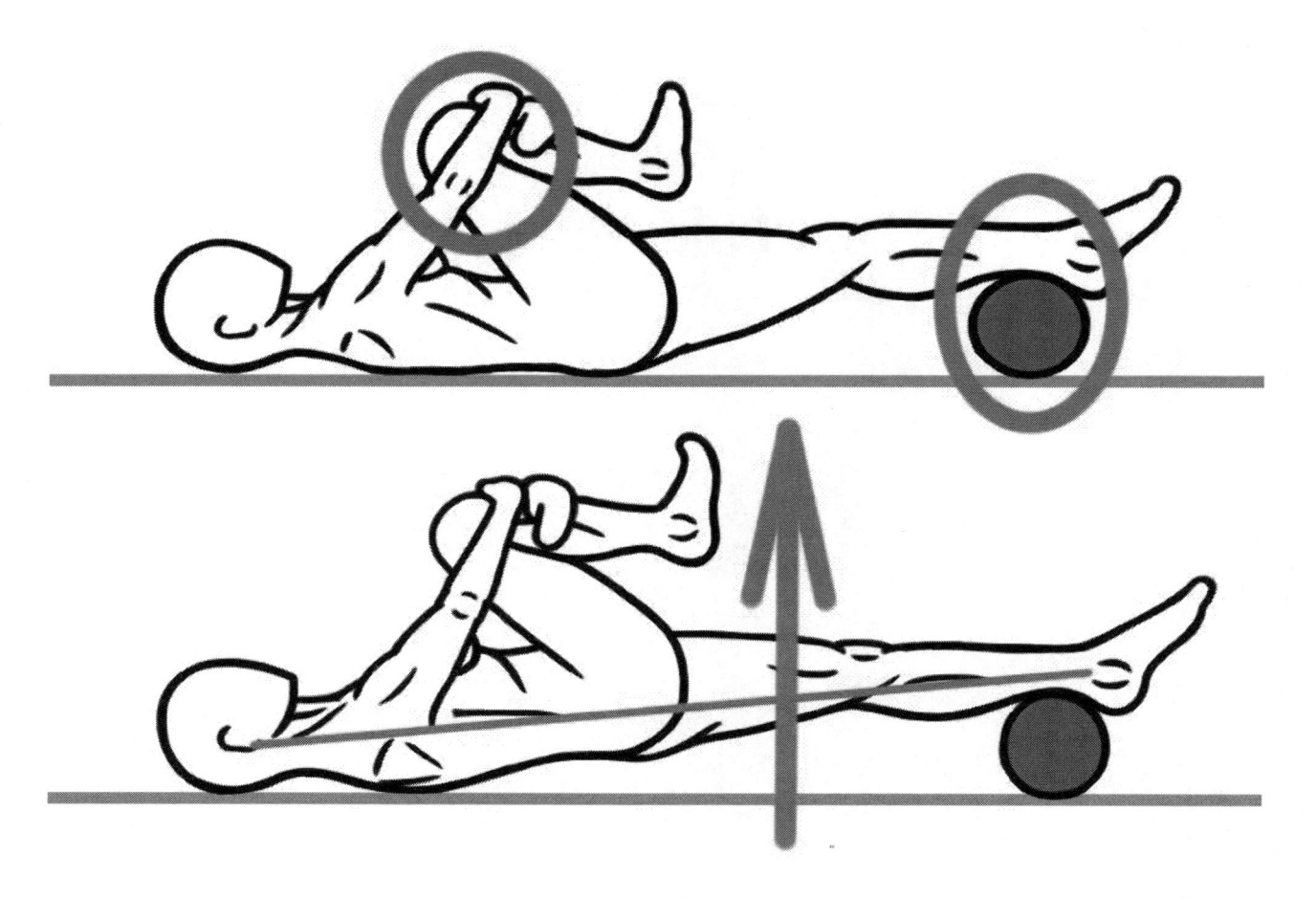

EXTENDED BRIDGE (STRAIGHT-LEG BRIDGE)

This unilateral PreHab exercise will help stimulate the neuromuscular system of the posterior chain within the movement pattern of your gait, i.e. walking or running. It is very useful for two reasons: First, the unilateral aspect of the exercise helps to prep the musculature that will coordinate stability in the gait. Second, the supine positioning helps to negate many strategies in walking or running that use momentum to compensate for biomechanical faults.

POSITION: Lie on your back and place one foot (at the ankle or heel) on a foam roller or a step while squeezing the other leg into your chest. Lengthen your entire body from head to heel and pull the shoulders down and away from the ears.

ACTION: Press your leg into the roller or step and lift your hips up towards the sky while maintaining neutral alignment in your spine as much as possible. Pull the belly button into the spine to engage the Abdominals and tuck the chin in towards your throat to help stabilize your cervical spine.

- *Perform several reps of this exercise with different variations including:*
- *Slow reps- perform the movement on a 3 or 5 count in each direction.*
- *Sustained Rep- perform an isometric hold at the top of the rep for 10-15 seconds.*
- *Pulsate- perform 3-5 extra contraction impulses at the top of the rep.*

ACTIVATION

REVERSE TABLETOP BRIDGE

POSITION: Sit and reach back to place the palms on the floor with straight elbows and the fingers pointing forward. Bend the knees and hips to 90-degrees with feet shoulder-width apart.

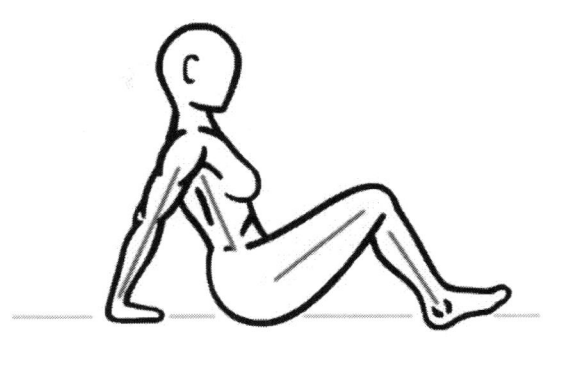

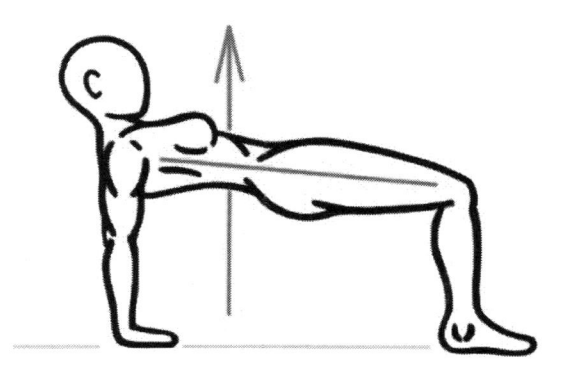

ACTION: Press into the palms and heels to lift the hips up towards the sky. Keep the elbows straight, lengthen the spine and reach the knees towards the horizon in front. Attempt to align the hips with the height of the shoulders and knee before lowering down. Repeat several times.

- *Perform several reps of this exercise with different variations including:*
- *Slow reps- perform the movement on a 3 or 5 count in each direction.*
- *Sustained Rep- perform an isometric hold at the top of the rep for 1-3 seconds.*
- *Pulsate- perform 3-5 extra contraction impulses at the top of rep.*

REVERSE PLANK

POSITION: Sit with an upright spine and reach both arms backwards with straight elbows. Plant the palms on the ground and lean back while extending the legs out in front of the body.

ACTION: Press the palms and heels into the floor to lift the hips up into the sky. Keep the elbows straight and lengthen through the entire body. Attempt to align the hips in a straight line with the shoulders and heels. Lower down and then repeat several times.

- *Perform several reps of this exercise with different variations including:*
- *Slow reps- perform the movement on a 3 or 5 count in each direction.*
- *Sustained Rep- perform an isometric hold at the top of the rep for 1-3 seconds.*
- *Pulsate- perform 3-5 extra contraction impulses at the top of rep.*

PreHab Exercise Book for Runners

ACTIVATION

HIP HINGE
POSITION: Stand tall with the feet aligned under the hip sockets and the arms by the sides.

ACTION: Hinge in the hip socket and drive the hips backwards towards the horizon as the arms extend and reach towards the opposite horizon. Lower the torso down until parallel with the floor. Keep the legs as straight as possible as the tailbone and the top of the head pull away from each other as much as possible. Keep the hips and shoulders level to the floor. Press the hips forward and lift the chest to return to standing. Repeat several times.

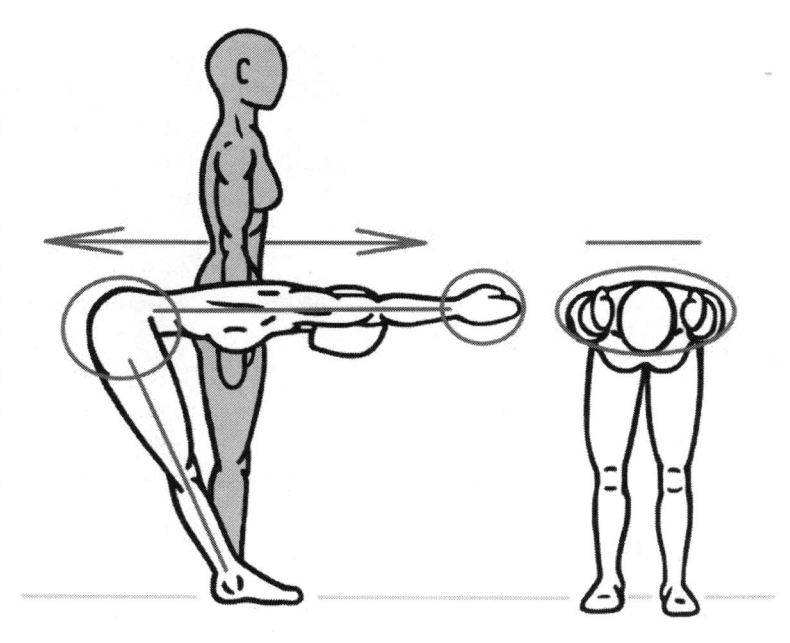

- Perform several reps of this exercise with different variations including:
- Slow reps- perform the movement on a 3 or 5 count in each direction.
- Sustained Rep- perform an isometric hold at the bottom of the rep for 1-3 seconds.

WIDE STANCE ROTATED HIP HINGE
POSITION: Stand in a wide stance with both feet flat on the floor and the knees fully extended.

ACTION: Press the hips back towards the horizon and extend one arm towards the opposite horizon as the other arm reaches to touch the floor directly beneath the starting position of the hips. Stay long through the entire body throughout the movement and attempt to place the palm flat on the floor on each hinge. Alternate sides on each repetition and repeat several times.

- Perform several reps of this exercise with different variations including:
- Slow reps- perform the movement on a 3 or 5 count in each direction.
- Sustained Rep- perform an isometric hold at the bottom of the rep for 1-3 seconds.

ACTIVATION

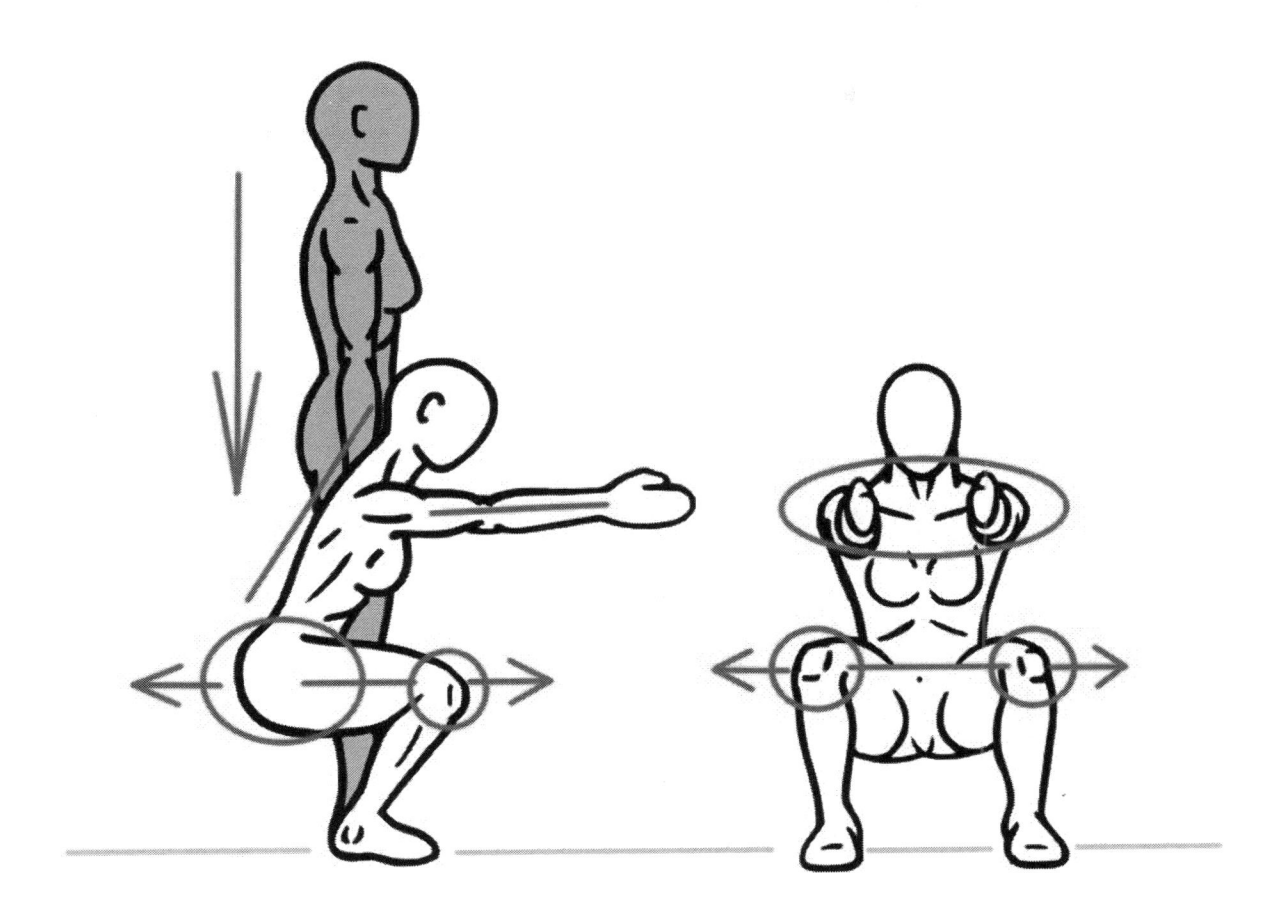

SQUAT

POSITION: Stand with the feet in a comfortable stance that is just a little more than shoulder-width apart. Let the arms hang along the sides of the body as the eyes focus on the horizon.

ACTION: Bend the knees forward and sit the hips backwards. Press the thighs wide and lower the hips to the height of the knees. Reach the arms to the horizon and lengthen the spine. Press the hips forward and drive the top of the head up into the sky to stand up. Repeat several times.

- *Perform several reps of this exercise with different variations including:*
- *Slow reps- perform the movement on a 3 or 5 count in each direction.*
- *Sustained Rep- perform an isometric hold at the bottom of the rep for 1-3 seconds.*
- *Pulsate- perform 3-5 extra contraction impulses at the bottom of the rep.*
- *Load- Hold a weight or use a band to create resistance as your perform this exercise.*

ACTIVATION

LOW-TO-HIGH LUNGE

POSITION: Start in a Low Lunge position with the fingertips aligned on the floor with the toes of one foot and the opposite foot extended as far back as possible. Straighten the back knee.

ACTION: From this position, stand into a High Lunge with both arms reaching into the sky. Focus the eyes onto the horizon and keep the front knee directly over the front ankle. Press the rear heel into the floor and level the hips before lowering down to repeat this movement. Repeat several times on each side.

- *Perform several reps of this exercise with different variations including:*
- *Slow reps- perform the movement on a 3 or 5 count in each direction.*
- *Sustained Rep- perform an isometric hold at the top of the rep for 1-3 seconds.*
- *Pulsate- perform 3-5 extra contraction impulses at the top of the rep.*

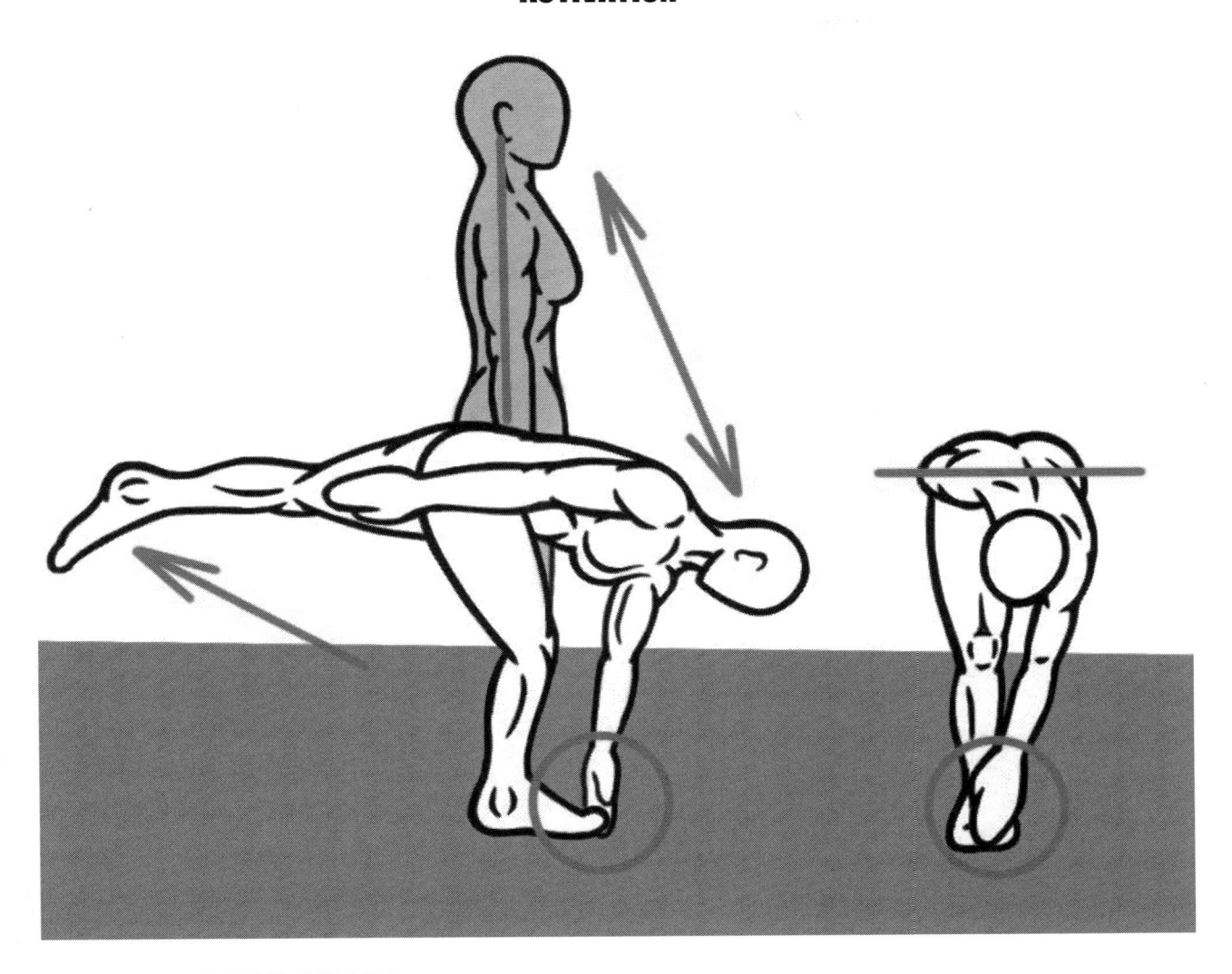

ACTIVATION

SINGLE-LEG TOE TOUCH

POSITION: Start in a tall, standing position with your eyes focused on the horizon. Shift your weight onto one leg in order to easily lift the other leg up into the air.

ACTION: Lower your torso towards the floor and reach for the standing foot with your opposite hand as your extend the back leg straight out towards the horizon behind you. Attempt to lay your torso on top of your standing thigh as you keep your hips level with the floor and maintain balance. Bend your knee slightly.

Touch your toe and then stand up tall once again as you gaze back out at the horizon. Repeat several times on each leg.

- *Perform several reps of this exercise with different variations including:*
- *Slow reps- perform the movement on a 3 or 5 count in each direction.*
- *Sustained Rep- perform an isometric hold at the top of the rep for 1-3 seconds.*
- *Pulsate- perform 3-5 extra contraction impulses at the top or bottom of the rep.*

ACTIVATION

GLUTE-HAMSTRING EXTENSIONS (GHD Machine)
Unfortunately, you will need assistance from a partner or a machine in order to perform Glute Hamstring Extensions. Yet, it is one of the most effective exercises to use.

Just about every gym will have some version of the Glute Hamstring Extension machine. If not, you can always use a massage/stretch table as well as anchoring your heels under some heavy dumbbells or your partner's hands to perform this exercise.

POSITION: Use the lower pad to anchor your heels into position as you lay the front of your thighs against the upper pads. Make sure that your hip is not positioned inline with the upper pad- this will only block your hip hinge and make your body flex your spine instead.

This exercise is to be performed with a neutral spine throughout the entire range of motion. This means no flexing (bending) the spine when you lower and not extending (arching) as you rise up.

ACTION: Simply hinge in the hip socket to fold forward. If you are not sure if you are

ACTIVATION

hinging correctly at the hips while maintaining a neutral spine, practice the Hip Hinge with a pole several times before performing this exercise.

- *Perform several reps of this exercise with different variations including:*
- *Slow reps- perform the movement on a 3 or 5 count in each direction.*
- *Sustained Rep- perform an isometric hold at the top of the rep for 1-3 seconds.*
- *Pulsate- perform 3-5 extra contraction impulses at the top of the rep.*

Different Arm Positions:
The most basic position is crossing your arms over your chest as you flex and extend in the hip socket. More advanced positions of the arms will place a larger resistance load onto the posterior chain as well as help activate the posterior muscles of the arms and thoracic spine.

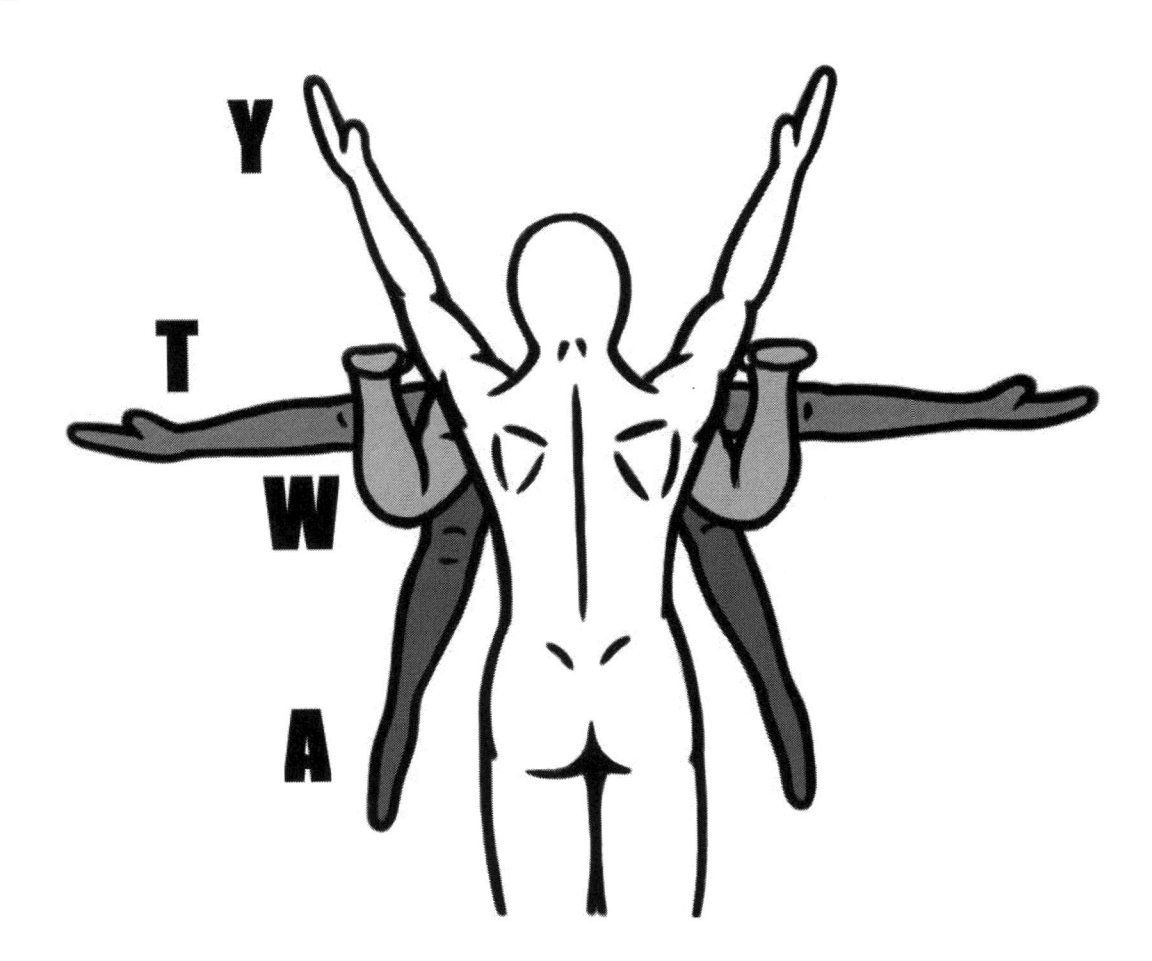

Y-T-W-A's
These arm positions will stimulate more neuromuscular activity in the posterior aspects of your thoracic spine and shoulders, which is ideal for people who suffer from Upper Cross syndrome and poor posture of the upper body.

ACTIVATION

Y-T-W-A Extensions
As you perform the Glute-Hamstring Extension, hold your arms in positions that form the following letters in conjunction with your spine and head.

Y= Arms straight overhead.
T= Arms perpendicular to the spine.
W= Forearms parallel and elbows bent below the height of the shoulders.
A= Arms extending towards hips.

Perform several reps of the Glute-Hamstring Extension with proper form or hold an isometric contraction for 20-30 seconds to help activate the posterior chain.

'Y' Glute-Ham Extension

'T' Glute-Ham Extension

'W' Glute-Ham Extension

'A' Glute-Ham Extension

ACTIVATION

SINGLE-LEG DEADLIFT (SL DL) with Pole

This PreHab exercise will help facilitate or excite the posterior chain in a unilateral movement pattern that requires elevated levels of coordination and stabilizing. This exercise is a very effective exercise to use when activating and prepping for agility and power events, such as football, baseball (hitting and pitching) or Olympic weight lifting.

POSITION: Stand on one leg while holding a pole along your back that expands and touches your head, thoracic spine and pelvis (tailbone). Make sure that all three points are in contact with the pole as you tuck your chin in towards your throat and gaze at the horizon.

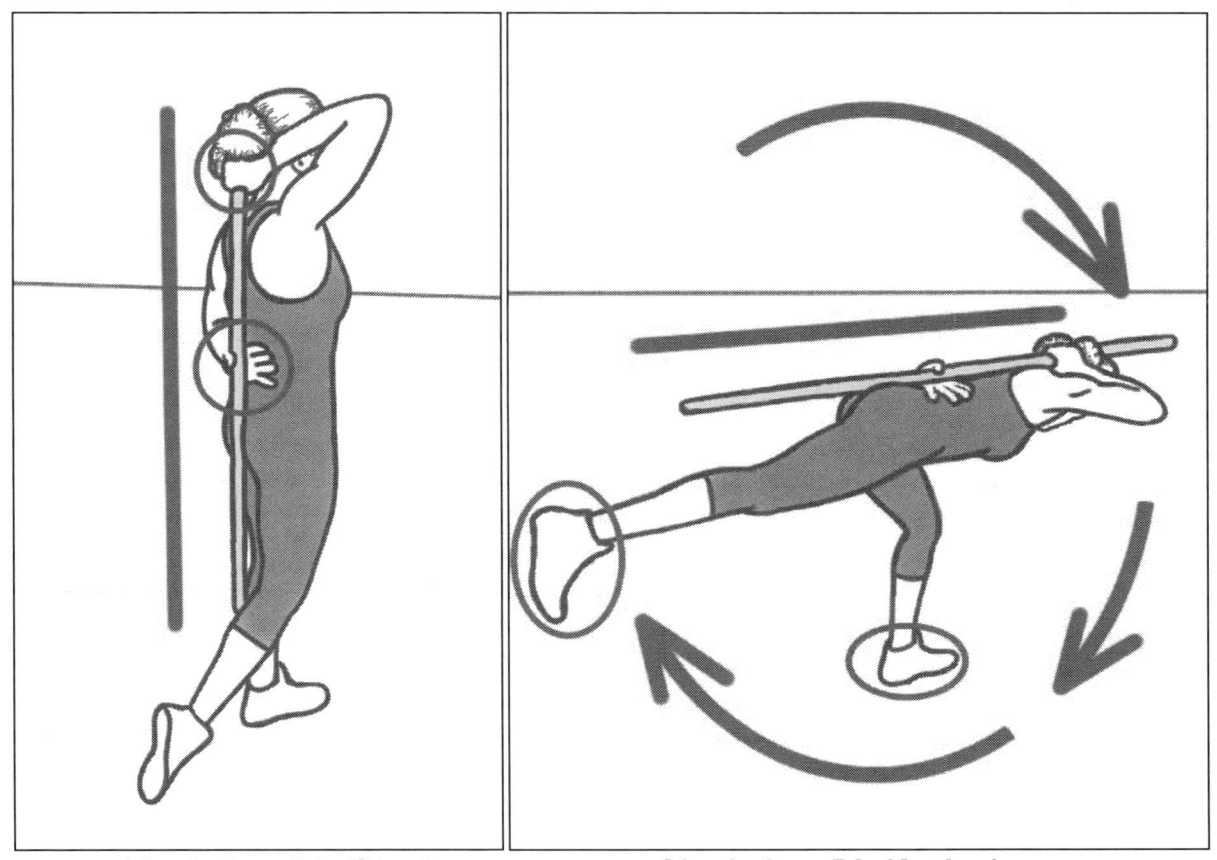

Single-Leg DL (Start)   *Single-Leg DL (Action)*

ACTION: Reach your off leg back towards the horizon in order to lower your chest down towards the ground. Keep the hips square to the floor. Do not let the hips rotate. Instead, focus on how the standing hip socket is allowing the femur (thigh bone) to rotate in the joint.

Keep your head, thoracic spine and tailbone all in contact with the pole as you bend your standing knee and attempt to lay your stomach down on top of your thigh.

Establish balance as you lower and as you stand back up. Press your pinkie toe into the floor as you stand up and return to the starting position. Keep the standing knee

ACTIVATION

vertically behind your toes. Yet, allow the knee to bend as you lower the torso and straighten the knee as you stand up.

Perform these reps as slow as possible and with as much balance and control throughout the movement.

- *Perform several reps of this exercise with different variations including:*
- *Slow reps- perform the movement on a 3 or 5 count in each direction.*
- *Sustained Rep- perform an isometric hold at the top of the rep for 1-3 seconds.*
- *Pulsate- perform 3-5 extra contraction impulses at the top of the rep.*

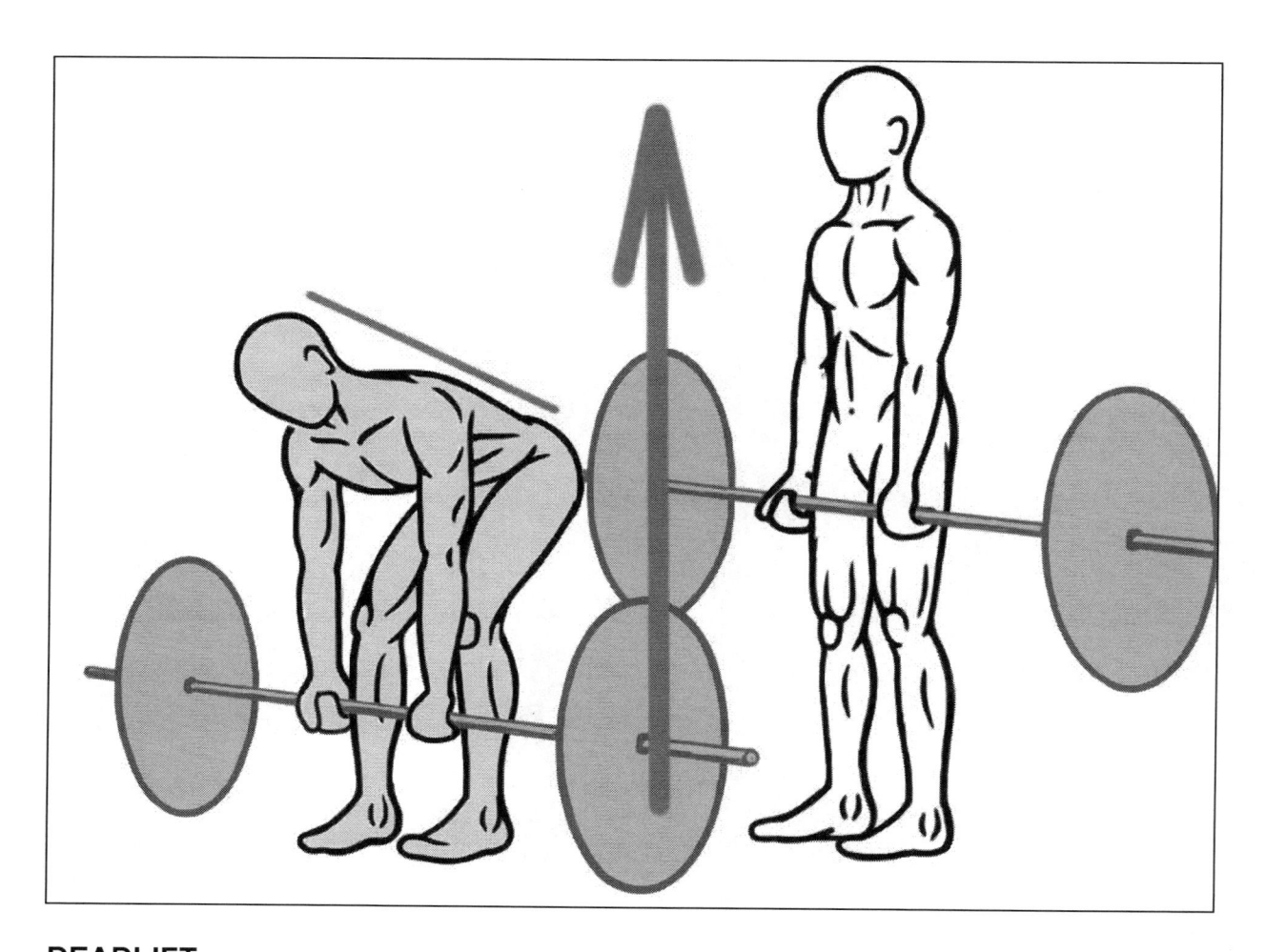

DEADLIFT

This PreHab exercise uses load to activate the neuromuscular connections of the posterior chain. A heavy load will force more neurological motor units to invigorate more muscle fibers, but caution is needed when lifting weights with limited prep time.

Using the Deadlift as an activation exercise will increase neuromuscular power and recruitment, which can help improve performances in a mile sprint, a game of basketball or cycling.

ACTIVATION

Ideally, you will want to perform this lift at 75 to 85 PERCENT of your One Rep Max for the Deadlift. However, reduce the weight if you do not feel that you have had enough prep time and if your body does not feel adequate neuromuscular tension from other PreHab exercises.

POSITION: Stand over a kettle bell or barbell and align the handle with the top of the foot, where your shoelaces would be. Position your feet shoulder-width apart and take hold of the bar with a grip that aligns an inch wider than your thighs.

Tuck your chin into your throat and straighten your spine by reaching the top of your head towards one horizon and your tailbone towards the other horizon. Do not round your back and do not bend your neck to let up. Look at the floor and pull the belly button in toward the spine to engage the Abdominals and stabilize your lumbar spine.

Press your thighs out wide and pull your shoulder heads down and away from your ears. Squeeze your armpits down towards your hip pockets and park your shoulder blades into your back pockets.

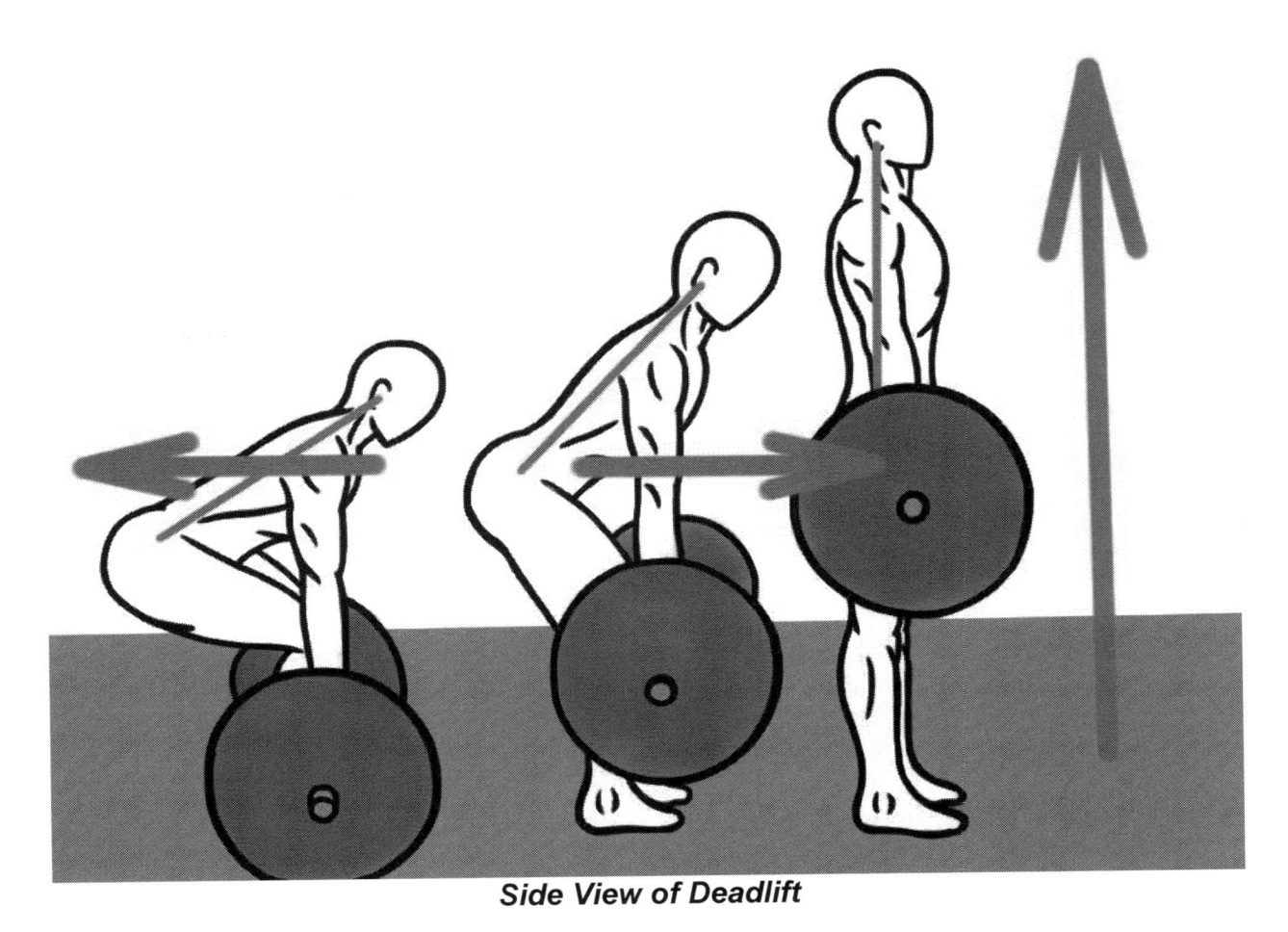

Side View of Deadlift

ACTION: Press into the heels and stand up tall by driving your hips forward into the bar.

PreHab Exercise Book for Runners

ACTIVATION

Do not round or overarch your back. Simply drive your hips forward and reach the top of your head high into the sky while keeping your chin tucked into your throat.

Once you have stood up tall with your ears, hip sockets and ankles all aligned in a straight line, place the weight back down on the ground by pressing your hips back towards the horizon and hinging in the hips to lower the torso and weight.

Perform 1-3 controlled reps. Repeat for an additional set if you wish, but refrain from performing too many sets and reps. This activation exercise is to help invigorate neuromuscular connections, not to build strength. Keep the reps and sets small while performing as a prep exercise.

WALKING AIRPLANE LUNGE
POSITION: Standing tall and gazing at the horizon.

ACTION: Similar to the Single-Leg Toe Touch and Single-Leg RDL, this exercise will have you balancing on one leg, but while walking. Step forward and then lower the torso down until it is parallel to the floor as your reach both hands towards the horizon in front and then extend the back leg towards the horizon behind you. Next, lift the chest up to the sky and gaze back at the horizon as you step forward into another lunge. Keep the hips level with the floor and stay long throughout the entire body.

- *Perform several walking reps of this exercise with different variations including:*
- *Slow reps- perform the movement on a 3 or 5 count in each direction.*
- *Sustained Rep- perform an isometric hold at the top of the rep for 1-3 seconds.*

ACTIVATION

VERTICAL JUMP

This exercise is a quick and easy way to activate a large portion of your posterior chain. However, performing this exercise with good form is important because the risk of compensation in the vertical jump will increase when there is limited prep time.

POSITION: Stand in an athletic position with the nose vertically aligned over the toes, and the spine in neutral alignment parallel with the shins. Do not allow the back to arch or round. Make sure that the hips hinge and bend both the knees and ankles in order to form this athletic stance.

ACTION: Jump straight up as high as possible by sending the hips forward and up while driving the heels into the ground and pressing through the balls of your feet.

Focus on creating and using the full triple extension technique, which refers to combining the three movements of hip, knee and ankle extension into one movement pattern. The goal is to align the toes, kneecaps, hip sockets and spine into one straight line at the height of the jump.

Pull the belly button into the spine to engage the abdominals and support the lumbar spine as you jump.

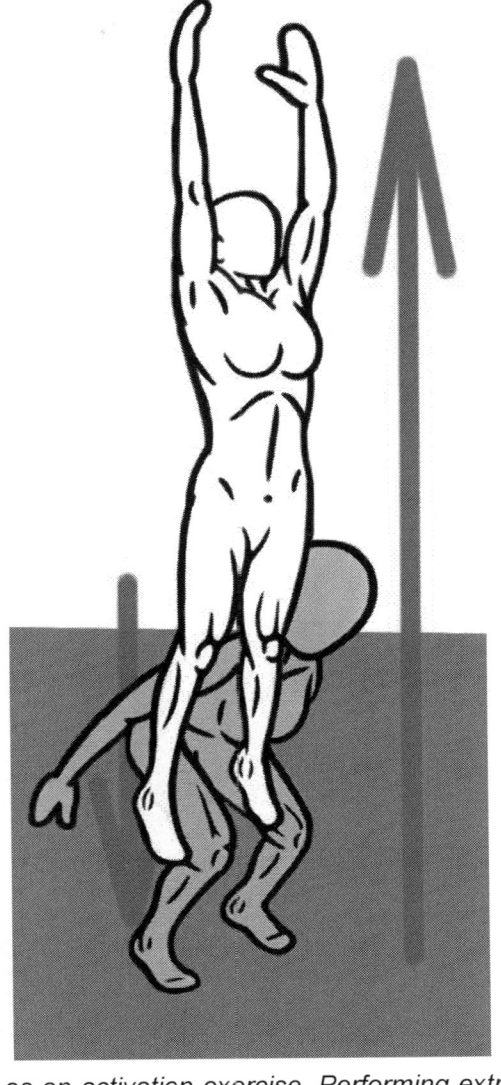

Land softly and repeat this movement 3-5 times when using as an activation exercise. Performing extra sets and reps to develop strength and power should be allocated for a strength and conditioning session. This would include more prep time to help stabilize and coordinate the neuromuscular system to exert higher levels of force and speed.

ACTIVATION

Prevent by Activating

If you want real progress and results to come from your training, take the time to mobilize and activate your posterior chain. The posterior chain generates so much of what you do physically. At the same time, this neuromuscular system is so large that it is easy to "poke holes' in it. In other words, it's easy to compensate in movements that use the posterior chain. Prevent compensation by activating first. There are 138 different joints to manage in this system. Be sure that you take some time before you get moving to synchronize this massive system. If you do, you will see the rewards from your efforts for sure!

ACTIVATION

Combination Exercises for Activation

Practicing exercises that use large movement patterns will incorporate more joints and involve an increased amount of coordination and recruitment of the neuromuscular system. This will accelerate the activation process and help the development of sport-specific or life-activity skills.

Focus Makes a Difference
Whenever I work with a client at UCLA's Drake Stadium, finding parking in Westwood is a mission. Not only are there thousands of other people converging on the campus any day of the week, but there is also street cleaning and two-hour parking limitations to contend with each time. However, every time I go, I get a good parking spot when I am focused on getting a good parking spot.

I know it sounds a bit out there. Yet, it has not failed me yet. As soon as I leave my apartment, I just start thinking about finding an open parking spot on Gayle or Strathmore, right near the stadium. And it works. I end up finding an open spot. I park and I am delighted as I head off to the stadium. And yes, I will admit there have been times that I have either parked blocks away or ended up circling the streets for 20-30 minutes looking for a spot. Coincidentally, I had always been mentally distracted each of those times way before I even started driving towards campus.

When the mind goes, energy will follow-
A meditation maxim

Hitting the Target
What do parking spots have to do with activation exercises? It's a matter of focus. There is an underlying principal that is important to embrace in order to be more effective with these combination exercises.

Place your focus on the areas that you intend to activate while performing these combination exercises to be more effective. These exercises include large movement patterns, which will incorporate more joints and thus increase the risk for compensation in your biomechanics to arise. Limit the potential of compensation and also hit your target by keeping your awareness on the muscle groups you want to activate and the biomechanics patterns you intend to improve.

These combination exercises will help you develop a foundation for efficient movement patterns and improved motor skills while monopolizing less time in your training session. Do not rush through these exercises, and do not concentrate solely on the number of reps. Instead, emphasize correct form and focus on the areas you intend to activate first and foremost. You can gain a lot of benefit from these exercises in less time when you focus on the target.

This sequence of activation exercises will progress in complexity and difficulty.

ACTIVATION

DOG POINTER SERIES

> These exercises will help develop stability in: *Shoulders, Shoulder Girdle, Core & Hips (Rotators).*
>
> Use in PreHab routines for: *Running, Agility, Balance & Ball Skills (Sports).*

DOG POINTER - SAGITTAL

POSITION: Start in a tabletop position with the wrists directly under the shoulders and the knees beneath the hips. Then pull one elbow in to touch the opposite knee while lengthening through the spine.

ACTION: Simultaneously extend the hand and foot towards opposite horizons until the arm and leg are parallel to the floor. Pull the belly button into the spine to engage the abdominals and support the lower back while keeping the spine and face parallel to the floor.
Repeat several times on each side.

ACTIVATION

DOG POINTER – DIAGONAL

POSITION: Start in a tabletop position with the wrists directly under the shoulders and the knees beneath the hips. Then pull one elbow in to touch the opposite knee while lengthening through the spine.

ACTION: Simultaneously extend the hand and foot in a diagonal fashion towards opposite horizons until the arm and leg are parallel to the floor. Pull the belly button into the spine to engage the abdominals and support the lower back while keeping the spine and face parallel to the floor. *Repeat several times on each side.*

ACTIVATION

DOG POINTER – LATERAL

POSITION: Start in a tabletop position with the wrists directly under the shoulders and the knees beneath the hips. Then pull one elbow in to touch the opposite knee while lengthening through the spine.

ACTION: Simultaneously extend the hand and foot laterally out to the side towards opposite horizons until the arm and leg are parallel to the floor. Pull the belly button into the spine to engage the abdominals and support the lower back while keeping the spine and face parallel to the floor.
Repeat several times on each side.

ACTIVATION

WINDSHIELD WIPERS SERIES

This progression of exercises will help to activate your posterior shoulder muscles, the shoulder girdle, and the posterior core musculature as well as the obliques and abdominals. In fact, most people perform these exercises with the intention of strengthening the anterior side of their core, i.e. abs and obliques. However, there is a lot of benefit in using these exercises to help counter Forward Head and Upper Cross postural alignments in addition to adding synergy and balance to the entire shoulder complex.

> These exercises will help activate: *Shoulders (Posterior), Shoulder Girdle & Core.*
>
> Use in PreHab routines for: *Running, Sprinting, Agility, Squatting, Hip Hinging, Lunging, Throwing, Rotation & Spinal Extension.*

The following exercises progress in complexity and difficulty. It is important to select the exercise that is most appropriate with your ability to perform each rep with correct form.

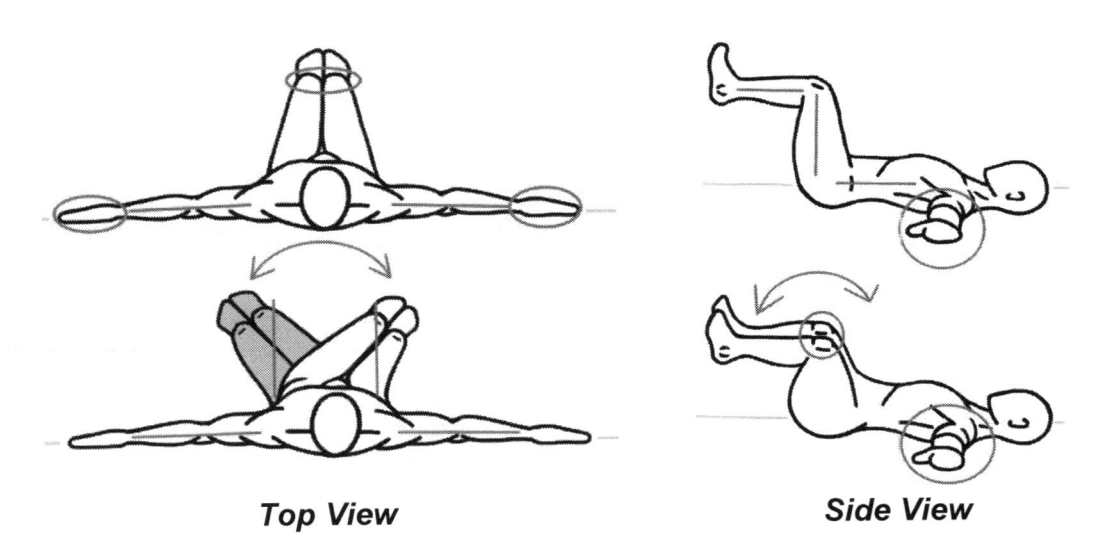

Top View   *Side View*

MODIFIED HALF WINDSHIELD WIPERS

POSITION: Lie down on the floor and hold the arms out into a "T" position with the spine. Lift the legs up in a chair position (90 degrees in the hips, knees and ankles) and squeeze an imaginary "dime" between the knees.

ACTION: Rotate both knees out to one side while pressing the arms into the ground to keep both shoulders flat with the floor. Rotate the hips until the knees reach shoulder-width while squeezing an imaginary "dime" between the knees to keep the legs in alignment with one another. Keep the arms and shoulders in contact with the floor and alternate between sides.
- *Repeat 5-10 repetitions in each direction for 1-3 sets.*
- *Optional: Pause when the knees reach shoulder width and sustain the effort of pressing the arms and shoulders down into the ground as you hold the position for a 1-3 count.*

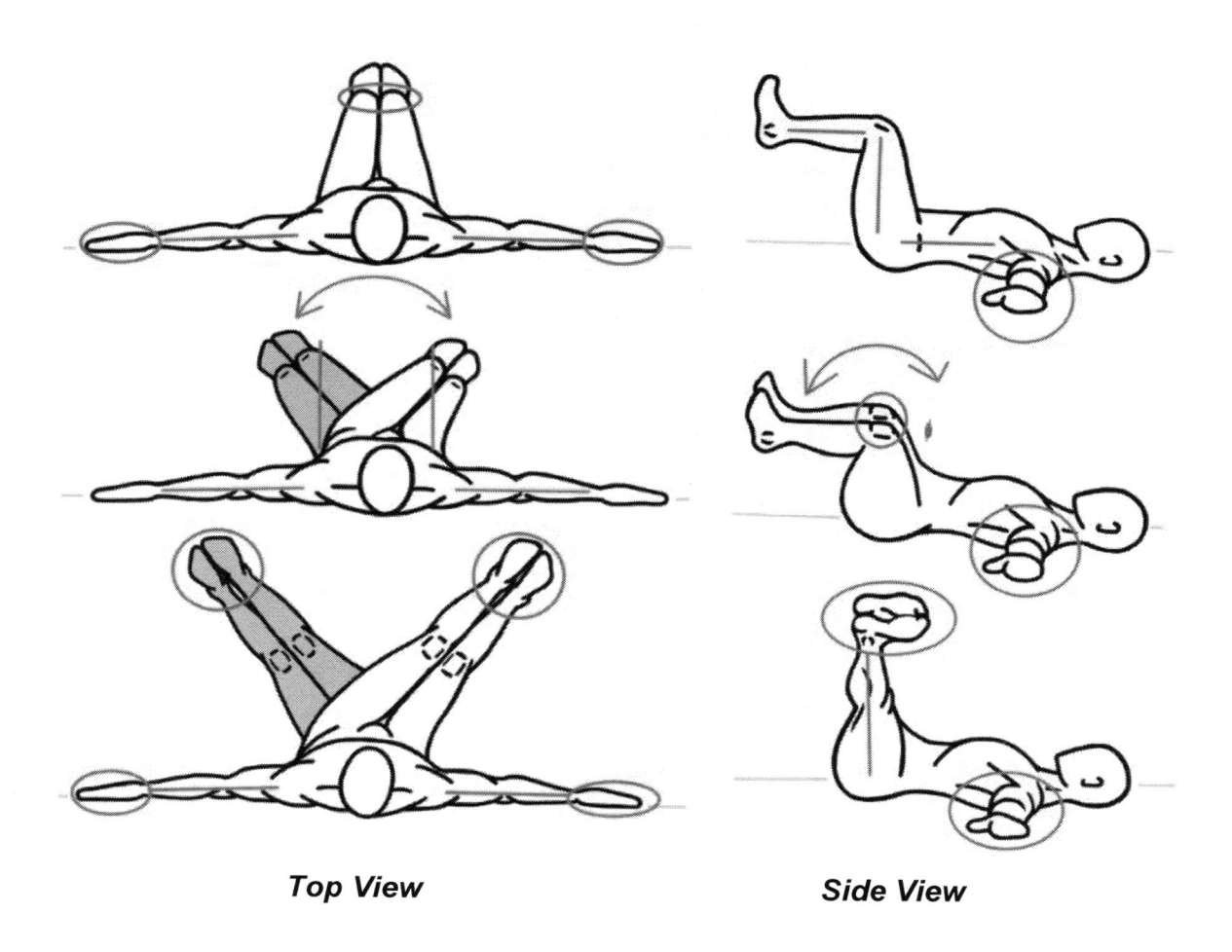

ACTIVATION

Top View *Side View*

MODIFIED WINDSHIELD WIPERS WITH KNEE EXTENSION
POSITION: Lie down on the floor and hold the arms out into a "T" position with the spine. Lift the legs up in a chair position (90 degrees in the hips, knees and ankles) and squeeze an imaginary "dime" between the knees.

ACTION: Rotate both knees to one side while pressing the arms into the ground to keep both shoulders flat with the floor. Rotate the hips until the knees reach shoulder-width and then straighten the legs to full extension in the knees while squeezing an imaginary "dime" between the knees. After which, bend the knees and transition to the other side. Keep the shoulders completely flat to the floor throughout the movement.

- *Repeat 5-10 repetitions in each direction for 1-3 sets.*
- *Optional: Pause before and after your extend the knees when they reach shoulder width and sustain the effort of pressing the arms and shoulders down into the ground as you hold the position for a 1-3 count.*

ACTIVATION

HALF WINDSHIELD WIPERS

POSITION: Lie on the floor and hold the arms out into a "T" formation with the spine. Extend both legs up towards the sky with straight knees and squeeze an imaginary "dime" between the knees.

ACTION: Swing the legs out to one side while pressing the arms into the floor to keep the shoulders in contact with the ground. Rotate the hips until the knees reach shoulder-width and squeeze an imaginary "dime" between the knees. Keep the knees straight and the shoulders pressed into the floor on each rotation.

- *Repeat 5-10 repetitions in each direction for 1-3 sets.*
- *Optional: Pause when the knees reach shoulder width and sustain the effort of pressing the arms and shoulders down into the ground as you hold the position for a 1-3 count.*

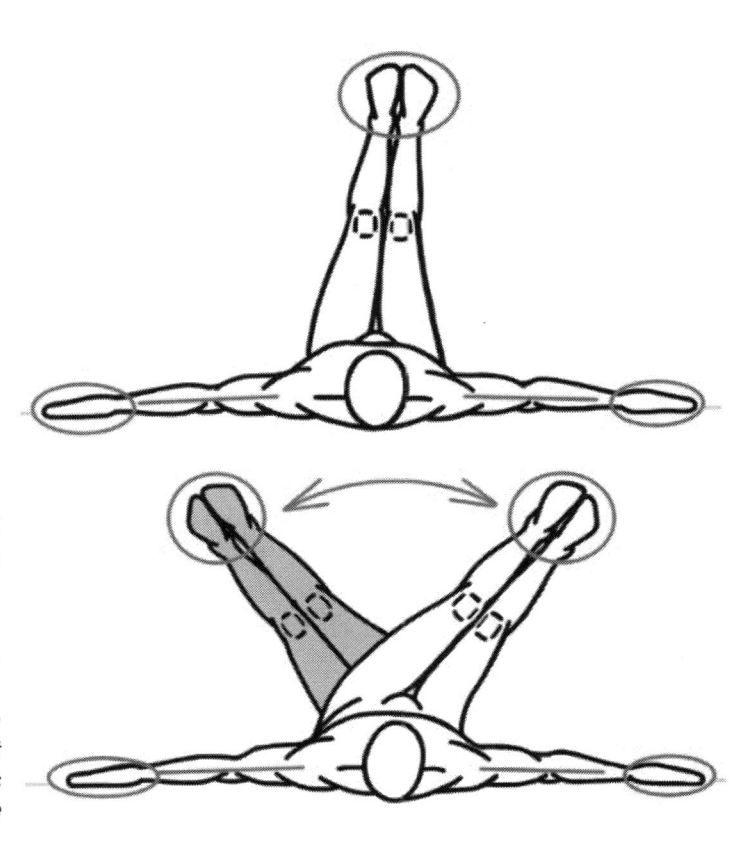

PreHab Exercise Book for Runners

ACTIVATION

FULL WINDSHIELD WIPERS

POSITION: Lie on the floor and hold the arms out into a "T" formation with the spine. Extend both legs up towards the sky with straight knees and squeeze an imaginary "dime" between the knees.

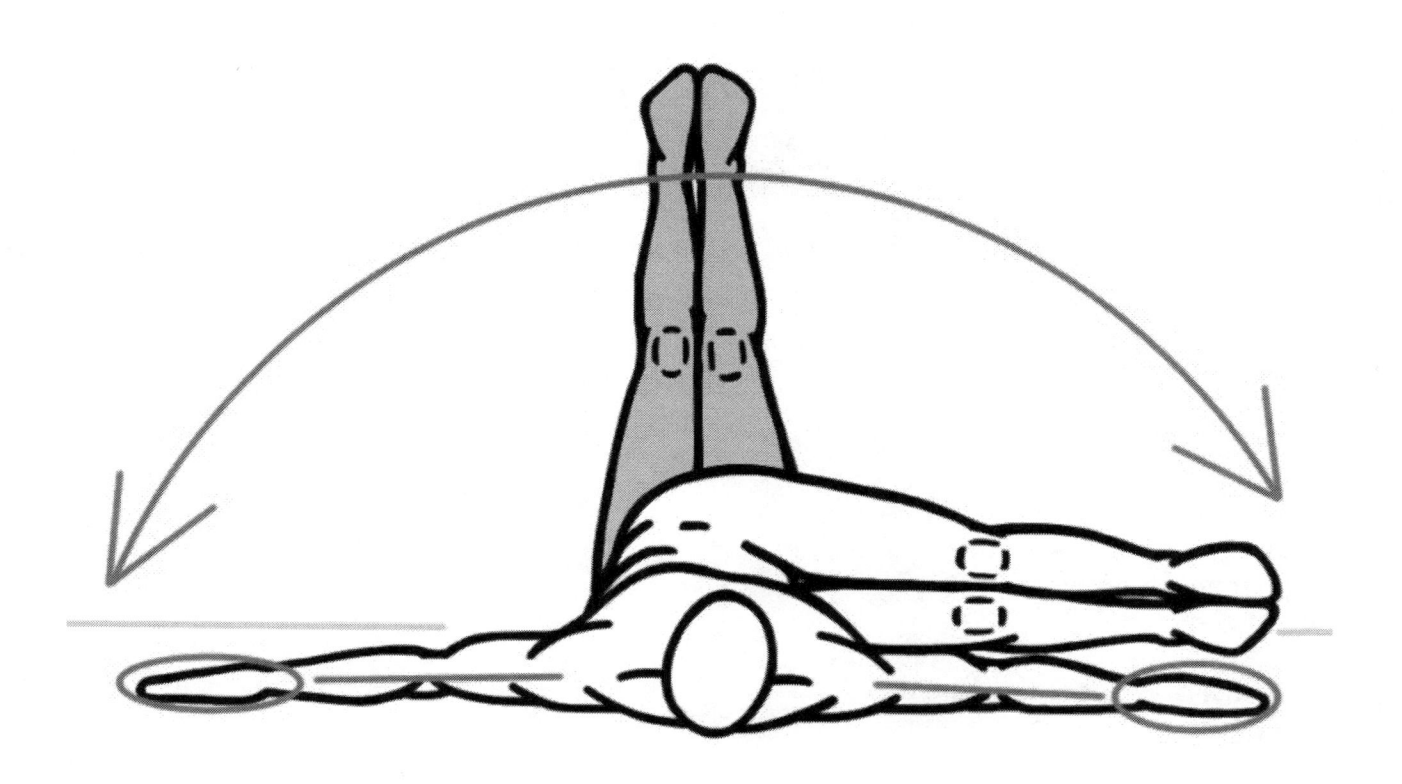

Top View

ACTION: Swing the legs out to one side while pressing the arms into the floor to keep the shoulders in contact with the ground while squeezing an imaginary "dime" between the knees. Attempt to touch the feet to the hands. Keep the knees straight and swing the legs as far as possible while under control and press the shoulders into the floor.

If the shoulders and arms lift off the floor, begin to modify the exercise and limit the distance that the feet will travel from side to side. Stay within a modified range of motion and gradually increase the distance until the shoulders are able to maintain contact with the floor.

- *Repeat 5-10 repetitions in each direction for 1-3 sets.*
- *Optional: Pause when feet are an inch from the ground or in their further range of motion and sustain the effort of pressing the arms and shoulders down into the ground as you hold the position for a 1-3 count.*

ACTIVATION

CRAWL SERIES

The following exercises will help to activate a large portion of your neuromuscular system. These exercises will also help develop coordination of large movements in positions that are not as frequently used in the modern day lifestyle of an average person. Using these crawls and walks allow us to revisit primitive movement patterns that you may not get to while working in your office all day. Remember, we crawled before we ever walked both in our own personal development as a child, but also in an evolutionary sense as well. These activation exercises help us to tap into and awaken the parts of our DNA and biomechanics that made us crawl before we walked.

BEAST WALK (Bear Crawl)

> This exercise will help activate: *Shoulders, Shoulder Girdle, Core (Anterior), Hips & Ankles/Feet.*
>
> Use in PreHab routines for: *Running, Lunging, Throwing & Pressing/Pushing.*

POSITION: Start in Tabletop, with wrist aligned directly under the shoulders and the knees directly beneath the hip sockets. Lift the knees off the floor.

ACTION: Walk forward on all fours while keeping the spine parallel with the floor. Do not allow the knees to touch the ground. Engage the abdominals to support the lower back by pulling the belly button up to the spine. Tuck the chin into the throat and pull the shoulders back away from the ears to release tension on the neck.

Crawl for a predetermined amount of reps, such as 10-20, or for a specific time frame, i.e. 30 seconds. For best results, crawl in a combination of directions, forward, backwards and side-to-side.

ACTIVATION

BEAR CRAWL (Straight-Leg Bear Crawl)

This exercise will help activate: *Shoulders, Shoulder Girdle, Core (Anterior), Hips & Ankles/Feet.*

Use in PreHab routines for: *Running, Lunging, Throwing & Pressing/Pushing.*

POSITION: Start in Down Dog, with both hands and feet on the ground and the hips extended towards the sky. Straighten the arms and legs and lengthen through the spine.

ACTION: Lift opposite arm and leg off the ground and reach them as far as possible forward to begin to crawl. While alternating arms and legs on each stride, continue to press the hips up to the sky and keep the arms and legs straight. Stay long in the spine and engage the abdominals.

Crawl for a predetermined amount of reps, such as 10-20, or for a specific time frame, i.e. 30 seconds. For best results, crawl in a combination of directions, forward, backwards and side-to-side.

ACTIVATION

CRAB WALK

> This exercise will help activate: *Shoulders, Core (Posterior), Hips & Ankles/Feet.*
>
> Use in PreHab routines for: *Running, Squatting, Lunging, Rowing, Pressing/Pushing & Pulling.*

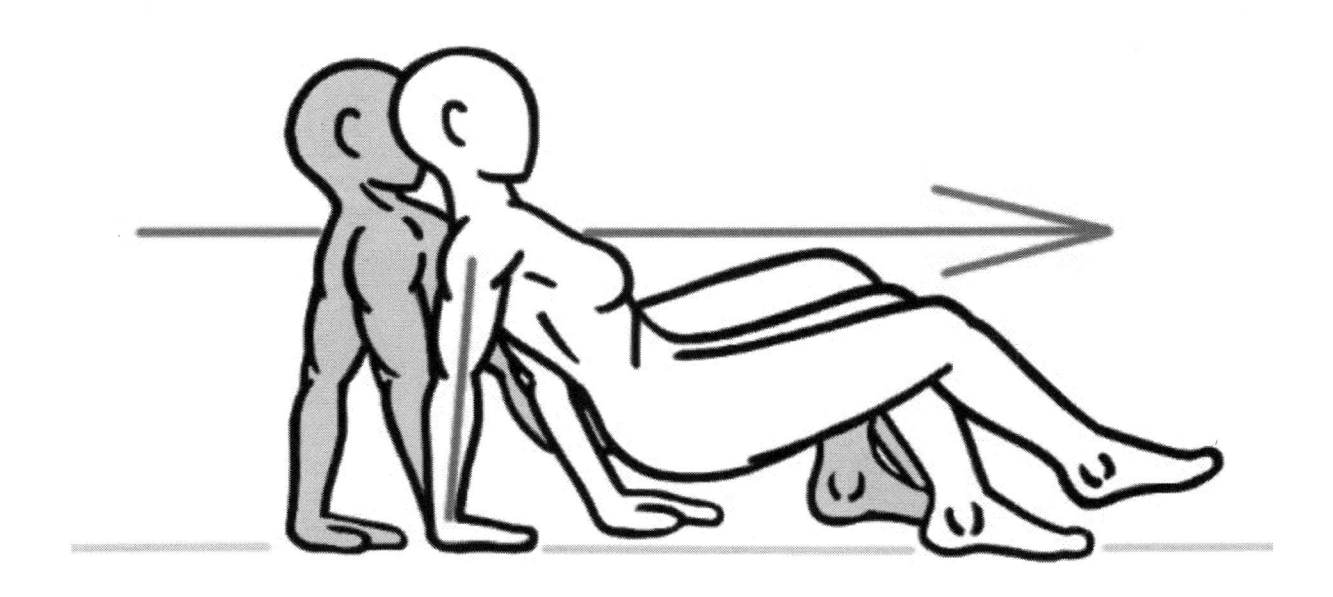

POSITION: Start in a seated position with both hands and feet planted on the ground and knees bent. Press down into the hands and feet and lift the hips off the floor. Keep the arms straight and lift the chest.

ACTION: Walk forward on all fours by lifting the opposite hand and foot and reaching forward. Keep the chest lifted and the arms straight. Pull the shoulders down away from the ears and push the crown of the head into the sky. Do not let the hips touch the ground.

Crawl for a predetermined amount of reps, such as 10-20, or for a specific time frame, i.e. 30 seconds. For best results, crawl in a combination of directions, forward, backwards and side-to-side.

ACTIVATION

CATERPILLAR (Inch Worm)

This exercise will help activate: *Shoulders, Shoulder Girdle, Core (Anterior), Hips & Ankles/Feet.*

Use in PreHab routines for: *Running, Lunging, Throwing & Pressing/Pushing.*

POSITION: Start in a tall, standing position with your eyes gazing at the horizon.

ACTION: Stand tall and then place both hands on the floor. Walk your hands out as far as possible while keeping everything else off the ground. Keep the arms and legs as straight as possible and engage the abdominals to support the lower back. At full extension of the body, start to walk the feet forward until they reach the hands. Then stand up and start the next repetition. This exercise will warm up the shoulders and the abdominals while also stretching the posterior chain of the body (calves, hamstrings and back.) It will also stimulate the neuromuscular system, which is advantageous before running.

Crawl for a predetermined amount of reps, such as 10-20 reps, or for a specific time frame, i.e. 30 seconds.

ACTIVATION

INVERTED ROW (Recline Row)
This exercise will help to activate your Posterior Chain as well as your Shoulders and Shoulder Girdle in the posterior aspect and retraction. This exercise will also help to integrate the two main muscular engines of the body: shoulders and hips.

> This exercise will activate: *Shoulders, Shoulder Girdle, Posterior Chain & Core (Posterior).*
>
> Use in PreHab routines for: *Running, Sprinting, Jumping, Squatting, Hip Hinging, Throwing (Deceleration of the arm), Rowing, Pressing/Pushing, Pulling & Spinal Extension.*

Equipment: A secure and adjustable bar that can hold your body weight.

POSITION: Adjust and secure the bar at a height that matches the bottom of your sternum. Place both hands on the bar just outside shoulder's width.

Next, press your chest to the bar and walk your feet under the bar as far as possible until you are in a recline position (lying backwards). Slowly extend your arms until your elbows are completely straight and align your body in a straight line from your shoulders to your ankles.

ACTIVATION

ACTION: Pull your elbows wide and back. Drive your chest up to touch the bar while you maintain the straight-line alignment from shoulder to ankle. Attempt to touch your chest to the bar and squeeze your shoulder blades towards one another as you row.

Press your heels into the ground and pull the belly button in towards your spine to engage the abdominals and stabilize the core. Make sure that you do not arch in your back. Keep a straight-line alignment from shoulders to ankles as you row.

Also, squeeze the armpits into the ribs, park the shoulder blades in the back pockets, and pull the shoulders down and away from the ears. Do not let your shoulders lift up towards the ears as this fault will create a disproportionate amount of tension in the upper trapezius and Levator Scapulae muscles. Practice good form on each and every rep.

Next, gently lower your body back towards the floor with a straight-line alignment from shoulders to ankles until your arms fully extend before performing another rep.

- *Perform between 5-15 reps with good form depending on your conditioning.*
- *Optional: Sustain your hold in the top position as an isometric contraction for one second on each rep or hold the top position as an isometric contraction for a specific amount of time, such as 15-30 seconds instead of performing reps. Another option is to practice several pulsating contractions at the top position on each rep.*

PUSH-UP

This exercise will help to activate your shoulders and shoulder girdle as well as for your core. It's very beneficial for athletes who use their arms in their sports, even just for counter balance in agility moves, as this exercise will help integrate the shoulders and hips to work as one unit.

> This exercise activates: *Shoulders, Shoulder Girdle & Core (Anterior).*
>
> Use in PreHab routines for: *Sprinting, Agility, Throwing, Rowing, Pressing/Pushing, Pulling & Spinal Flexion.*

POSITION: Lie on your stomach and place your hands alongside your body with the heel of your palm horizontal aligned with the bottom of your chest. Make sure that your fingers point forward, towards the shoulders, and that you squeeze the elbows in towards one another until the forearms press against the rib cage.

Lengthen your entire body from head to heels and tuck your chin into your throat as if you are giving yourself a double chin as you reach the top of your head towards the horizon. This adjustment will help stabilize your neck as you align your head and spine in neutral.

ACTIVATION

The Push-up: Start & Finish

ACTION: Push both hands into the floor and press your body up into the air until your elbows fully extend. As you push, squeeze the armpits into the ribs, park the shoulder blades in the back pockets and pull the shoulders down and away from the ears in order to stabilize the shoulder girdle. Also, attempt to externally rotate your shoulders by attempting to turn your fingers out and the belly of your biceps forward as you push off the floor. Do not expect your hands to actually move. Simply by attempting to externally rotate the arm, the shoulders will develop more stability in the shoulder joint over time.

Additionally, pull the belly button in towards your spine to engage the abdominals and stabilize the core as you push up off the floor. Keep your shoulders, hips and ankle in alignment. Do not allow your hips to pike, or pop up towards the sky as you push up. Squeeze the glutes and brace your core to help maintain alignment throughout the exercise.
Next, gently lower back down until the chest touches the floor with a straight line alignment of the shoulders, hips and ankles.

- *Perform 5-20 push-ups with good form to help activate the shoulders and core.*
- *Optional: Sustain the push effort for an additional second at the top position of the push-up or perform several pulsating contractions in the top position to help create more tension and send more neurological impulses to the shoulders, chest and core. Another optional is to push up and lower down on a 3-5 count and perform several slow reps with good form.*

ACTIVATION

PULL-UP

This exercise will help to activate your shoulders and shoulder girdle as well as your core. It's very beneficial for developing stability and strength in the shoulders and core. It will also help integrate the shoulders and hips to work as one unit.

This exercise activates: *Shoulders, Shoulder Girdle & Core.*

Use in PreHab routines for: *Sprinting, Jumping, Throwing, Rowing, Pressing/Pushing, Pulling & Spinal Flexion/Extension.*

POSITION: Hang from a bar with your hands wider than shoulder width and arms completely straight. An alternate to doing a pull-up would be to perform a set of pull-downs on a cable machine in the gym.

ACTION: Now, pull your body upwards until your chin passes the height of the bar or your chest touches the bar. Forcefully pull your belly button in towards your spine as your pull to engage the core muscles that will help create an upward momentum.

Next, lower back down to hanging position with straight arms to complete the pull-up rep.

Perform anywhere from 3-15 pull-ups depending on your level of conditioning and strength.

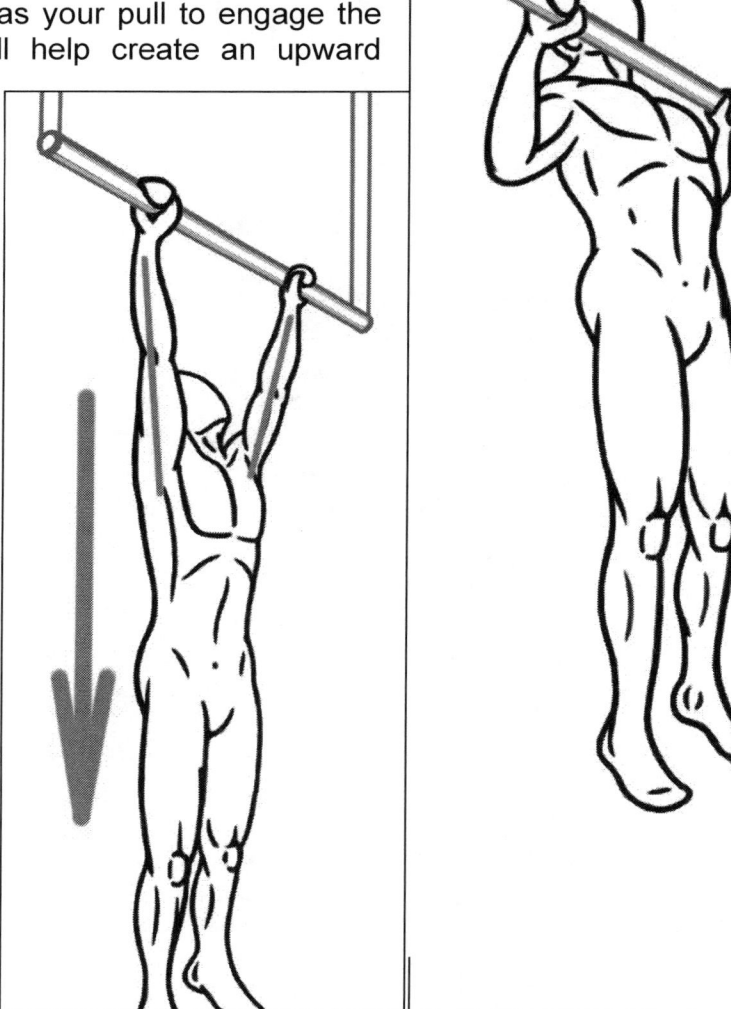

ACTIVATION

TALL CABLE CHOPS

This exercise will help to activate and stabilize the core, shoulder and hips, which is also referred to as the pillar of all movement. In addition to improved stability, this exercise will help a person develop coordinated movements through the pillar and help a person to integrate and use the pillar (core, shoulders and hips) as one unit.

> This exercise will activate: *Core, Shoulders & Hips.*
>
> Use in PreHab routines for: *Running, Sprinting, Lunging, Rowing, Pressing/Pushing, Pulling, Throwing, Rotating, & Spinal Flexion/Extension.*

Equipment: Adjustable Cable machine with Rope extension.

POSITION: Kneel on both knees with hips positioned over the knees with a vertical neutral spine. This position is called "Tall Kneeling."

Slide the rope completely to one side of the cable junction in order to make it as long as possible. Place one hand at either end of the rope. Position yourself far enough away from the machine that the cable will cross your chest on a 45-degree diagonal. Also, make sure that the cable crosses the body in a parallel fashion as the shoulders and hips are perpendicular to the machine.

Start with your arms fully extended on a diagonal up towards the cable insertion on the machine.

ACTION: Pull the cable across the body and down towards the floor on a diagonal pattern. Keep the cable close to the body as it passes the chest and reaches the bottom hand as close to the ground as possible while maintaining a tall, vertical spine.

Lift the chest, squeeze the armpits into the ribs, park the shoulder blades in the back pockets, and pull the shoulders down and away from the ears. Also, pull the belly button in towards your spine to engage the abdominals and stabilize the core.

Return the arms to the starting position in a controlled and smooth motion to complete the rep.

- *Perform 5-15 reps on either side to activate and integrate the core, shoulders and hips.*
- *Vary the exercise by performing the reps very slowly or pausing in the bottom position.*
- *Perform 2-3 sets of 10-15 reps on each side to develop more stability and integrate the core, shoulders and hips.*

Illustration on next page.

ACTIVATION

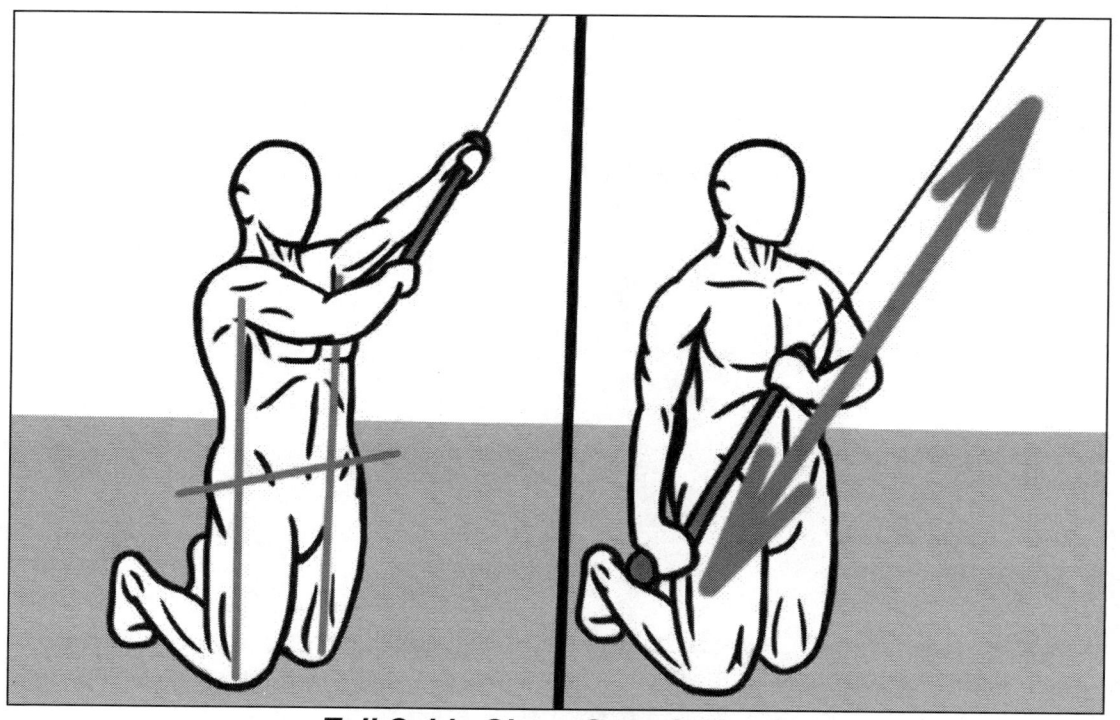

Tall Cable Chop: Start & Finish
Position hips and shoulders directly over the knees and pull across the body in a diagonal down towards the floor.

Medicine Ball Lift: Start & Finish
Reach the Medicine Ball towards the floor and then up to the sky.

ACTIVATION

MEDICINE BALL LIFT (MB Lift or Reverse Wood-Chop)

> This exercise will help activate: *Hip, Ankle, Core & Shoulders.*
>
> Use in PreHab routine for: *Running, Agility, Jumping, Lunging, Throwing & Balance.*

POSITION: Stand with your feet at shoulder-width apart and hold a Medicine Ball (MB) out in front of your body with straight arms. Make sure that the toes are pointed forward and parallel with one another.

ACTION: Squat down and rotate the shoulders to reach the MB down to the floor directly to your side. Push the hips backwards and press your thighs wide in order to lower down as far as possible. Keep both feet flat on the ground.

Reach as far as possible with your arms while you maintain a long spine and keep your chest lifted. Rotate through the torso and aim the MB for a target on the floor that shoulder be perpendicularly aligned with the arch of your feet.

Next, drive your hips forward as you stand up, rotate and reach the MB up to the sky on a large diagonal swing. Pivot the rear foot inwards and lift the heel up off the ground as you rotate the hips and shoulders to follow the MB.

Extend the MB up and away from your body as far as possible while aiming for a target that is perpendicularly aligned with the arch of your foot on the other side. Lengthen the entire body and pull the belly button in towards your spine to engage the abdominals and stabilize the core as you extend your arms. Also, squeeze the armpits into the ribs, park the shoulder blades into the back pockets, and pull the shoulders down and away from the ears to create stability in the shoulders. Gently repeat the entire movement several times on each side.

- *Perform 2-3+ sets of 5-10+ reps on each leg.*
- *Start with a slow pace and gradually increase the speed of the movement.*
- *Important Note: Reduce the speed if you begin to lose balance or alignment while performing the movement.*

Illustration on previous page.

ACTIVATION

SPEED SKATERS

This exercise will activate: *Hips (Lateral Aspect), Ankle/Foot & Core.*

Use in PreHab routines for: *Running, Agility, Jumping, Skiing/Skating, Squatting & Lunging.*

POSITION: Stand in an athletic stance with the feet shoulder-width apart, toes pointing forward, legs in triple flexion (ankles, knees and hips all bent), spine in neutral alignment while sloping forward. Keep your chest high, nose aligned, and your toes and eyes on the horizon. Next, lift one foot up off the ground and extend it backwards towards the horizon as you slide the same side arm forward and slightly rotate the shoulder. Bend the elbows to 90 degrees as if running.

Slide from side to side and align the shoulder and hip over the ankle.

ACTION: Laterally slide to the side in a full stride that is comfortable by driving the outside edge of the opposite foot down into the floor and fully extending that leg in a lateral push.

Keep the hip and shoulder at the same height as you slide and maintain neutral

ACTIVATION

alignment in the spine. Do not round the back or stand up. Stay low.

Plant the raised foot into the ground and quickly decelerate the momentum of your body before laterally pushing off with that foot in order to redirect your body and return to the starting position.

Press into your pinkie toes to produce and absorb the lateral push of the leg. Also, fully extend the ankle, knee and hip (triple extension) of the push leg each time that you slide to a side.
The triple extension is an important biomechanical skill to develop and will help create more power and force in running, jumping and agility drills.

The main objective for using this exercise is to activate the hips, especially the Gluteus Medius, which lies on the outside of the hip and will provide lateral stability as well as help protect the knee.

Pause.

Add a momentary pause (at least a one-count) between each slide as you stand on a single leg. This will help develop single-leg stability and will positively affect the rest of your training or performance.

Perform between 10-20 reps or work for time (15-30 seconds) to help activate the hips.

Align Shoulder and Hip in a straight line with the Ankle on each pause.

ACTIVATION

HANGING ARCH/HOLLOW
This exercise will help to activate the core musculature and the shoulder girdle. This exercise can also help you to integrate the shoulders and hips to perform as one unit especially while throwing, rowing, pressing/pushing or pulling. This exercise will train both Global Flexion and Extension of the spine, which provides more power and economy to every movement.

> This exercise will activate: *Core & Shoulder Girdle.*
>
> Use in PreHab routines for: *Running, Sprinting, Jumping, Squatting, Hip Hinging, Throwing, Rowing, Pressing/Pushing, Pulling & Spinal Flexion/Extension.*

Equipment: A secure bar that will be able to hold your body weight.

POSITON: Hang from a secure bar that supports your body weight with your hands shoulder-width apart or slightly wider. Squeeze your legs together to make the legs feel as if they are one. This adjustment will limit asymmetries in your movement and also help to engage the oblique muscles.

Depress the shoulders and press the top of the head up into the sky as much as possible. In other words, squeeze the armpits into the rib, park the shoulder blades in the back pockets, and pull the shoulders down and away from the ears or reverse shrug your shoulders. This adjustment will help to stabilize and engage all of the muscles in your shoulder girdle.

Tuck your chin into your throat and attempt to give yourself a "double chin" as you press the top of your head up to the sky and gaze at the horizon. Reach the toes down towards the ground and create a straight-line alignment with the head, shoulders, hips and ankles.

ACTION: Forcefully contract your abdominals and pull your sternum down towards your hips and your hips up towards your ribs. Attempt to make your spine go from the natural "S" curve and curl into a large, skinny "C."

Next, reverse the "C" by arching your spine and forcefully contracting your posterior core muscles as if you are attempting to bend over backwards while holding onto the bar.

Now, continue to extend and flex your spine and core into a large, skinny "C" and a reversed large, skinny "C." This is both Global Flexion and Global Extension.

While practicing the Arch/Hollow positions, be sure to keep your chin tucked into your throat; stay long through the spine. Continue to squeeze the armpits into the ribs, park the shoulder blades in the back pockets, and pull the shoulders down and away from the ears. Also, allow your legs to swing back and forth with the Arches and Hollows because the legs are just an extension of this spinal alignment.

ACTIVATION

Practice 10-20 Arches and Hollows or perform reps for time, i.e. 15-30 seconds.

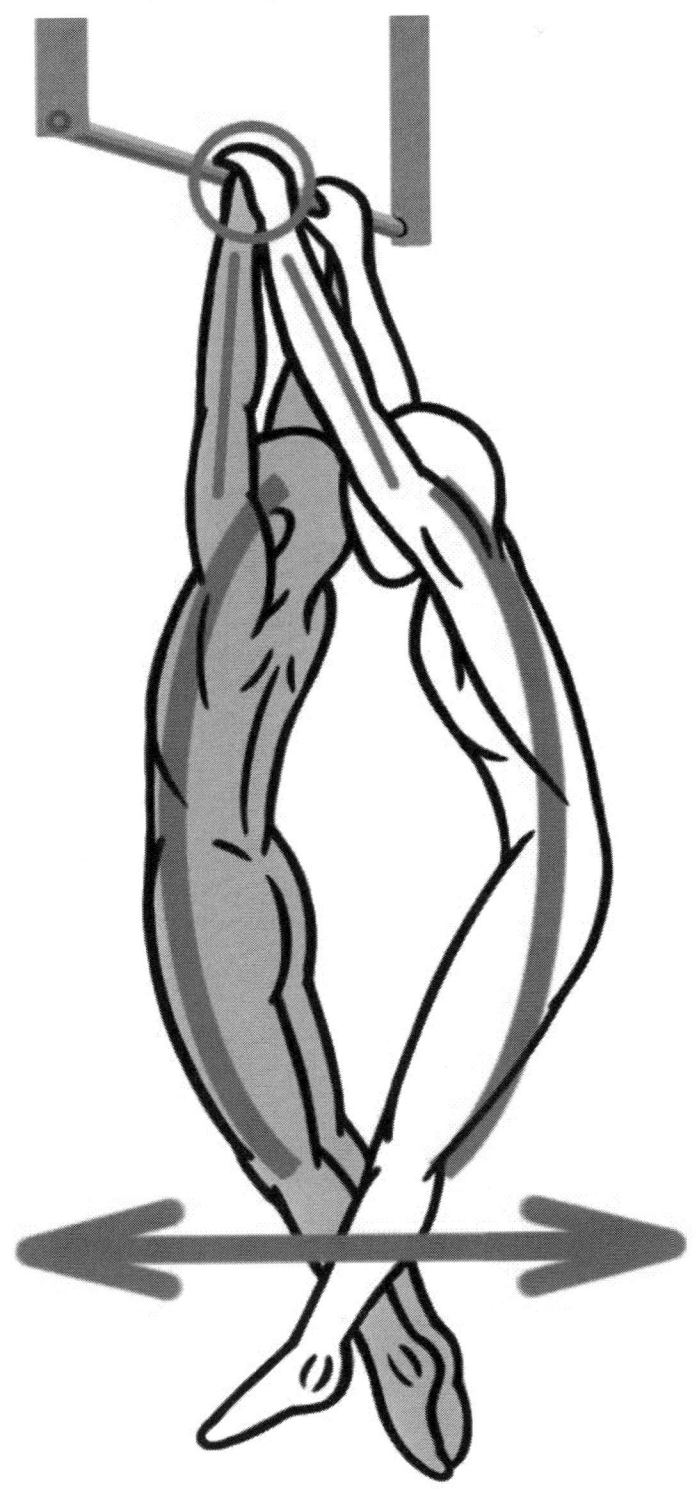

Hanging Arch Hollows

ACTIVATION

TUCK JUMPS

This exercise will help to activate the core musculature and the shoulder girdle. This exercise can also help you to integrate the shoulders and hips to perform as one unit especially while throwing, rowing, pressing/pushing or pulling. This exercise will train both Global Flexion and Extension of the spine, which provides more power and economy to every movement.

> This exercise will activate: *Hips, Ankle/Foot, Posterior Chain & Core.*
>
> Use in PreHab routines for: *Running, Sprinting, Jumping, Squatting, Hip Hinging & Spinal Flexion/Extension.*

POSITION: Stand in tall stance with a vertically aligned spine and your feet shoulder width apart. Do not let your heels touch the ground. Balance on your forefeet with your knees slightly bent and your hips flexed a little bit. Bend your elbows and hold your hand in front of your chest as you gaze at the horizon.

ACTION: Quickly dip your hips and bend your knees as you swing your arms down to the ground to create a downward momentum that will soon be redirected into a jump. Keep your chest lifted and as soon as your elbows straighten to allow your fingers to point at the ground, drive your feet into the ground and pop your hips forwards as you jump straight up.

Vertically jump as high as you can while you keep your body in a straight-line alignment from head to hips to heels. Press the top of your head up into the sky as high as possible as you pull the belly button in towards your spine to engage the abdominals and stabilize the core. Point the toes down to the ground as you jump as this will help you to fully develop your Triple Extension technique, which is simultaneous extension of the ankle, knee and hip.

Now, pull the knees up and into the chest at the height of your jump. This movement will require quick activation of the abdominals as you attempt to press the tops of your thighs into the front of your torso.

Next, quickly extend the legs and reach the toes back down to the ground and land on your forefeet. Bend in your knees and hips as you attempt to land softly on the ground. Also, do not let your heels touch the ground as you land. Instead, attempt to "catch" all of your weight and "stick" the landing on your forefeet.

Landing on your forefeet will help to activate many proprioceptors, the neuromuscular sensory neurons that coordinate movement of the lower leg and feet.

- *Perform 3-5 Tuck Jumps in a set for activation.*
- *Optional, pause and re-establish balance on your forefeet in between each Tuck Jump.*

Illustration on next page.

ACTIVATION

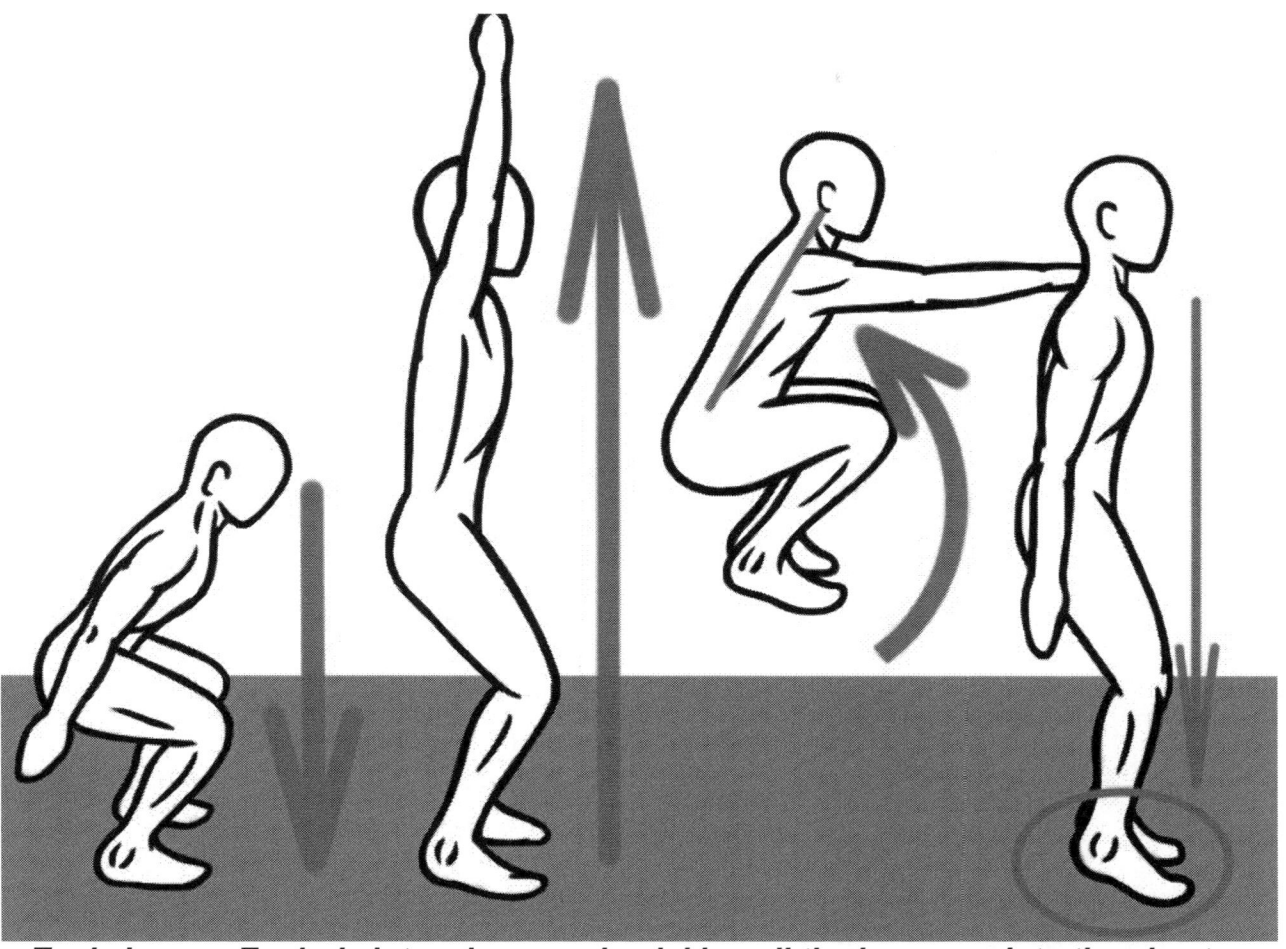

Tuck Jumps: Explode into a jump and quickly pull the knees up into the chest.

HANGING KNEE TUCKS

This exercise will help to activate your core (anterior) and shoulder girdle muscles. It will also help you to develop the Global Flexion movement pattern. It provides elevated levels of intensity (power and load) for the core muscles, which is beneficial for athletes who throw, pull, row, press/push, or brace against great resistance such as in boxing, wrestling or football.

> This exercise will help activate: *Core (Anterior) & Shoulder Girdle.*
>
> Use in PreHab routines for: *Running, Sprinting, Agility, Jumping, Throwing, Pulling & Spinal Flexion.*

POSITON: Hang from a secure bar that supports your body weight with your hands shoulder-width apart or slightly wider. Squeeze your legs together to make the legs feel as if they are one. This adjustment will limit asymmetries in your movement and also help to engage the oblique muscles.

ACTIVATION

Hang with straight arms and legs before tucking the knees into the chest.

Depress the shoulders and press the top of the head up into the sky as much as possible. In other words, squeeze the armpits into the ribs, park the shoulder blades in the back pockets, and pull the shoulders down and away from the ears or reverse shrug your shoulders. This adjustment will help to stabilize and engage all of the muscles in your shoulder girdle. Reach the toes down towards the ground and create a straight-line alignment with the head, shoulders, hips and ankles.

ACTION: Smoothly curl your spine into forward flexion as you roll the thighs up to the front and attempt to tuck the knees to your chest. Forcefully pull the belly button in towards the spine and squeeze your legs together.

Keep the elbows straight and continue to pull the shoulders down and away from the ears to depress the shoulder girdle. If you cannot maintain this shoulder position, reduce the number of reps that you are performing or regress to another exercise to activate your core.

Once the knees reach their highest height, gently return them back to the starting position and extend the legs towards the floor.

- *Perform several reps of this exercise with good form.*
- *Optional: Hold the legs at the top position and sustain an isometric contraction for a designated amount of time, i.e. 1-10 seconds, or perform several pulsating contractions while in the top position. Another option is to perform each rep on a 3-5 count in slow contractions.*

ACTIVATION

SKIPPING

This exercise will help to activate the foot, ankle, hip and the rest of the posterior chain. It's a good way to practice triple extension (extending the ankle, knee and hip in a coordinated power movement) before performing jumps, agility moves or sprinting.

> This exercise will help activate: *Posterior Chain, Hips, Ankle & Foot.*
>
> Use in PreHab routines for: *Running, Sprinting, Jumping, Squatting, Hip Hinging & Lunging.*

POSITION: Stand on one foot with the opposite knee raised to knee height, which will help produce more force in the downward "stab" of the skip and create a larger rebound effect in the up phase of the skip.

ACTION: Drive the upheld foot down into the ground in a "stabbing" motion as you thrust the standing knee into the air. Swing the arms through to help create momentum as you begin your skips.

Stab the forefoot into the ground and attempt to keep the heel from touching the ground. This adjustment will generate more elastic energy to be used by the legs as you launch your body forward and up on each skip. Do not be slow with your stab either. Strike the forefoot down forcefully and try to flick the ground back behind you as far as possible.
Pull the belly button in towards your spine to engage the abdominals and stabilize the core as you skip. This will create more power in the hips. Also, powerfully swing your

ACTIVATION

arms so that your hands travel from cheek to cheek, face-cheek, and butt-cheek.

Keep your chest lifted and stay long through your spine as you skip. Tuck your knee up to hip height each time and make sure that you fully extend through your jumping ankle, knee and hip, which is triple extension.

Skip for either 10-20 reps, a designated distance, i.e. 20 yards, or specific time frame, i.e. 20-30 seconds.

Perfect Practice

There's a saying, "practice makes perfect." However, there is a flaw with this simple principal. What if you are practicing incorrect form? Would you be improving? Would you eventually be perfect? The answer is no.

I have spent years watching people move with compensation strategies in their biomechanics as they exercise. And there is no way that they would ever reach "perfect" if they kept moving that way. That's partly why they come to me for coaching in the first place. They realize that they are not improving and that "perfect" is just a word, not a reality.

The first step towards perfection is interrupting imperfections, namely the different ways that you compensate in your biomechanics and how you move. This is where these activation exercises come into the program – interrupting the old, in order to create the new.

So, what does perfect look like in an activation exercise? This is a great question to ask because looks may be deceiving too.

The goal of these activation exercises is to ignite certain muscles groups that will generate specific biomechanical functions. You will be able to feel if the corresponding neuromuscular system has been facilitated or "activated." You will know if your muscles have been turned on. You will feel the difference, which will put you on to the road to perfection, which heads right through to "stability.'

Stability
Control in Movement

When high winds rolled into northwestern Washington State on a cold November day in 1940, no one expected anything other than a passing windstorm. But in Tacoma, Washington, 30 miles south of Seattle, the 40-mile-an-hour winds revealed a major design flaw in the stability of the Tacoma Narrows Bridge.

The wind whipped the cable-suspended bridge around like waves in the ocean. And there was no way that the bridge could withstand the powerful oscillating movements. Within a few hours, the bridge ripped apart and plunged into the Puget Sound below. Fortunately no one died in the accident, but a pet dog went down with a vehicle and was never found. And it was 10 years before a better bridge was built after the collapse.

Your bones, muscles, ligaments, and joints are a lot like the structural design of a bridge. If they're stable and balanced, your movements will be smooth and efficient. And even if an unexpected force is working against you like a linebacker trying to tackle you or the high impact of running, your body can maintain balance and stability. But if there's a weakness or flaw in your biomechanics an injury is imminent, and you may not even realize it. Proper stability is the key to staying active and injury-free.

Photo by Chris Connelly

What is stability?
As mobility is your ability to execute specific movement patterns, stability is the degree in which you can control your movement through those patterns.

STABILITY

One way to look at your Stability is through the lens of accuracy. In other words, how precise are your movements? How good is your balance? How accurate is your hand or foot coordination? And how good are all three when you're on the move?

> **Why is Stability important?**
> Drawing an analogy to profit margins is a great way to illustrate the overall affect Stability will have on your performance and fitness throughout your lifetime.

The Business Model of Movement
Let's say that your body is a factory and the product is movement. Then your Stability is the efficiency rating of your assembly line that produces movement. Now, if your assembly line (your Stability) is very inefficient, i.e. high labor costs, malfunctions, hold-ups, strikes, etc., then your costs to produce movement will rise, which is not ideal for your profit margin – if you still have any at this point!

However, if your factory's assembly line, aka your body's Stability, is very efficient, you instantly lower the cost of every movement you make and increase your profit margins while also providing a solid fiscal foundation for the longevity of your business.

> ***The more that you improve your body's Stability, the longer you can remain active in life!***

Stability will help you to maintain better alignment in your body mechanics over time and also improve the execution and function of each movement pattern you use.

Furthermore, developing Stability will lead to better performance in anything. The more that your body can increase the efficiency in movement, the less energy and time will be lost or wasted when fulfilling a task.

For example, if you can increase the hip stability in your running form, you will create a shorter and more efficient stride. The positive gain in efficiency is then multiplied by every stride taken, which can really add up when considering the number of strides in a 5K, 10K and even a 26.2-mile marathon! Soon enough, small improvements in Stability can lead to large improvements in performance.

> Essentially, Stability reduces the risk of injury and creates greater performance when you're running, lifting weights, playing sports or even doing ordinary activities like working in your garden or wrestling with the kids.

STABILITY

How to Improve Stability-
The first step is to recognize where you are instable. You want to look at specific joints, such as the ankle, hip and shoulders, and you want to look at specific movement patterns. I know that sounds a bit overwhelming, which is why I have included the following exercises to test your Stability with reference to the joints and body mechanics involved in the movements.

> ***Test your Stability with these Exercises***
> Single-Leg Heel Lift – *Ankle & Hip*
> Single-Leg Rotation – *Ankle & Hip*
> Hip Hinge – *Core & Spine*
> Single-Leg Stand-Up – *Ankle, Knee & Hip*
> Extended Plank Up – *Core & Shoulders*
> Ipsilateral Stability Test – *Shoulders, Core & Hip*

STABILITY ASSESSMENT: Single-Leg Heel Lift
This test will demonstrate how stable your ankle is when producing movement and absorbing force in the Sagittal Plane (Front-to-Back). If you have difficulty with this move, practice it every day until you can master this movement.

POSITION: Lift one knee to hip height and stand with arms parallel to the ground with palms pressed together. Focus the eyes on the horizon and lengthen the spine.

ACTION: Press into the forefoot and lift the standing heel off the ground while maintaining focus on the horizon. If the heel comes off the ground without losing balance, then you have a good level of stability in this movement pattern.

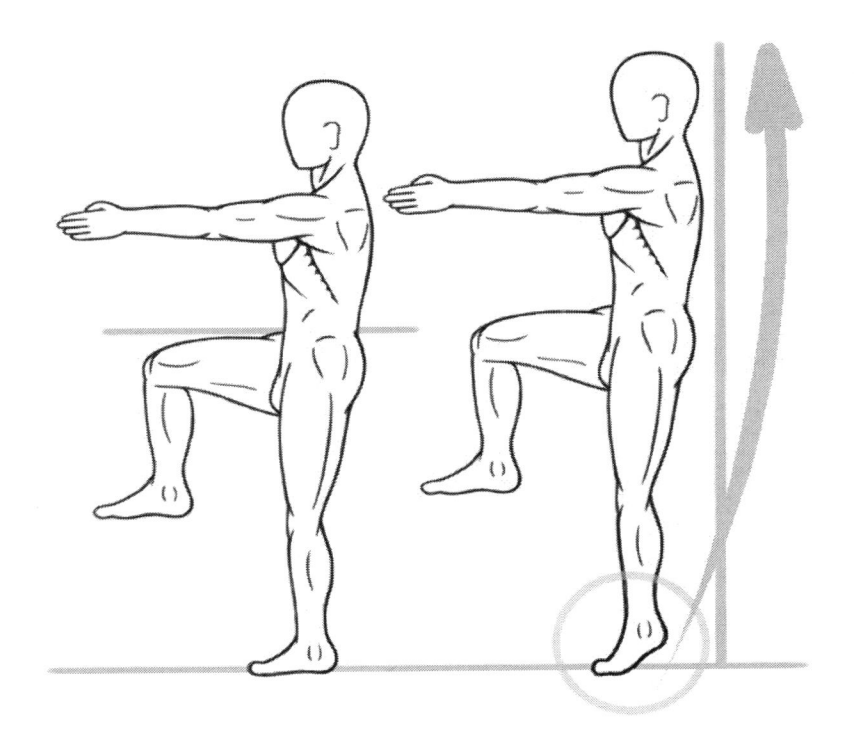

PreHab Exercise Book for Runners

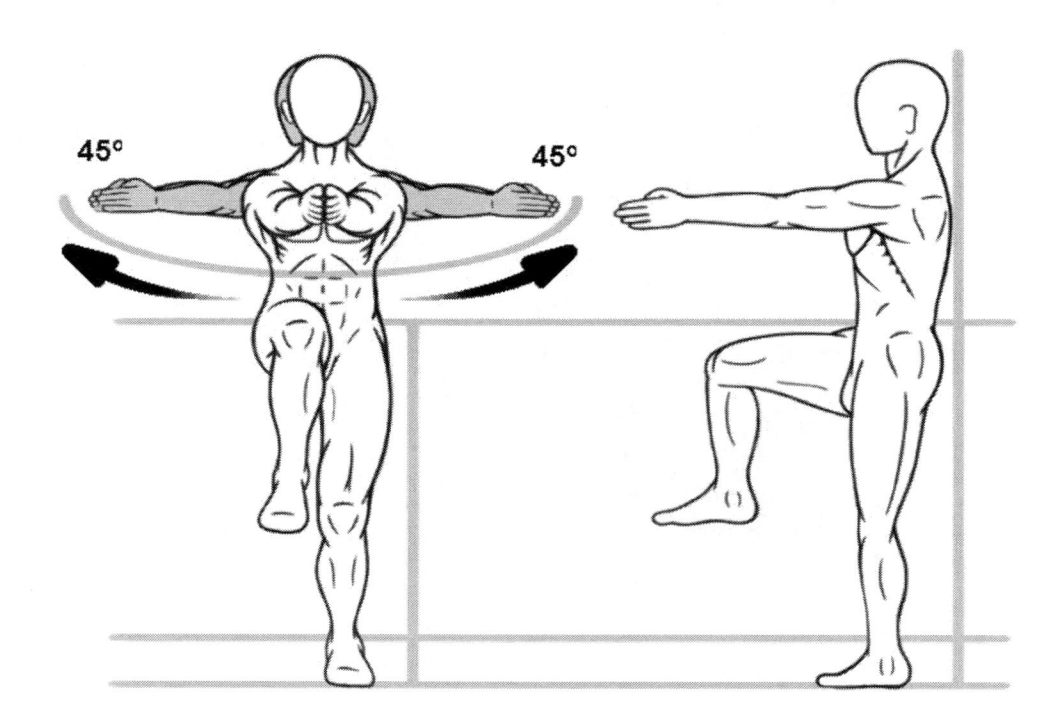

STABILITY

STABILITY ASSESSMENT: Single-Leg Rotation
This test will let you know how well your ankle and hip can stabilize when dealing with rotational forces, which is prevalent in many movements, especially running.

POSITION: Stand on one leg with arms parallel to the ground and palms pressed together. Lift the opposite knee to hip height and establish balance. Focus the eyes on the horizon and lengthen the spine.

ACTION: Rotate the arms 45 degrees to the left and right while maintaining a focus on the horizon. If the arms can successfully reach 45 degrees or more to the right and left without losing balance, then you have a good level of stability in this movement pattern.

STABILITY ASSESSMENT: Hip Hinge
If you Powerlift or go heavy with your weightlifting, this test will clearly tell you if you are able to do your lifting with a stable spine, which is important for safety and performance. If you can pass this test, you have the ability to align your spine and use it as one massive lever. If you cannot pass this test, it means that you are not using your spine as one complete level, but instead you are using your spine as 22 individual joints and you are losing leverage in your lift. It doesn't mean you can't get the weight off the ground. It simply means that you are losing power and kinetic efficiency when it comes to your spine.

STABILITY

POSITION: Stand with feet together and grasp the pole behind the back with two hands. One hand is placed at the small of the back with the palm facing out while the other hand is placed directly behind the neck with the palm facing the body. Next, align the body against the pole so that the head, the spine (just between the shoulder blades) and the hips are all in contact with the pole.

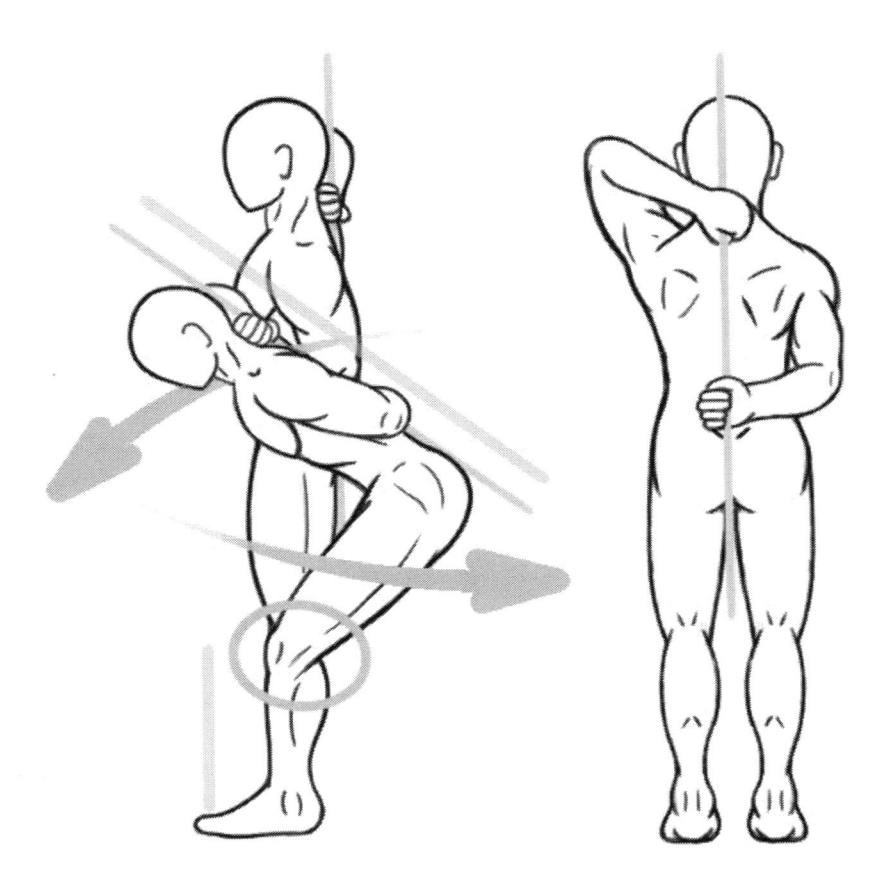

ACTION: Now, slide the hips directly backwards while bending at the knees, keeping the hips, spine and head in contact with the pole. Keep the shins vertical to the floor. The primary movement in this exercise is the flexion in the hip socket, not a flexion or bending of the spine. Attempt to align the thighs and torso into a 90-degree angle or smaller while maintaining the head, spine and hips in complete contact with the pole.

ALIGN HEAD, UPPER BACK AND HIPS AGAINST POLE
KEEP SHINS VERTICAL
PRESS HIPS BACK
LOWER TORSO FORWARD
MAINTAIN 3 POINTS OF CONTACT WITH POLE
MAKE 90-DEGREE ANGLE WITH TORSO AND THIGHS

If all requirements are met, then you have a good level of stability in this movement pattern.

STABILITY

STABILITY ASSESSMENT: Single-Leg Box Squat
This test will let you see how well your hip and ankle can protect your knee. Common faults in this test are: loss of balance and uncontrollable side-to-side movement of the knee while attempting to stand.

POSITION: Sit on a bench that matches the height of the knee and lift one foot off the ground. Hold the arms parallel to the ground at shoulder width and lengthen the spine. Use a mirror or have a partner watch the knee tracking over the foot.

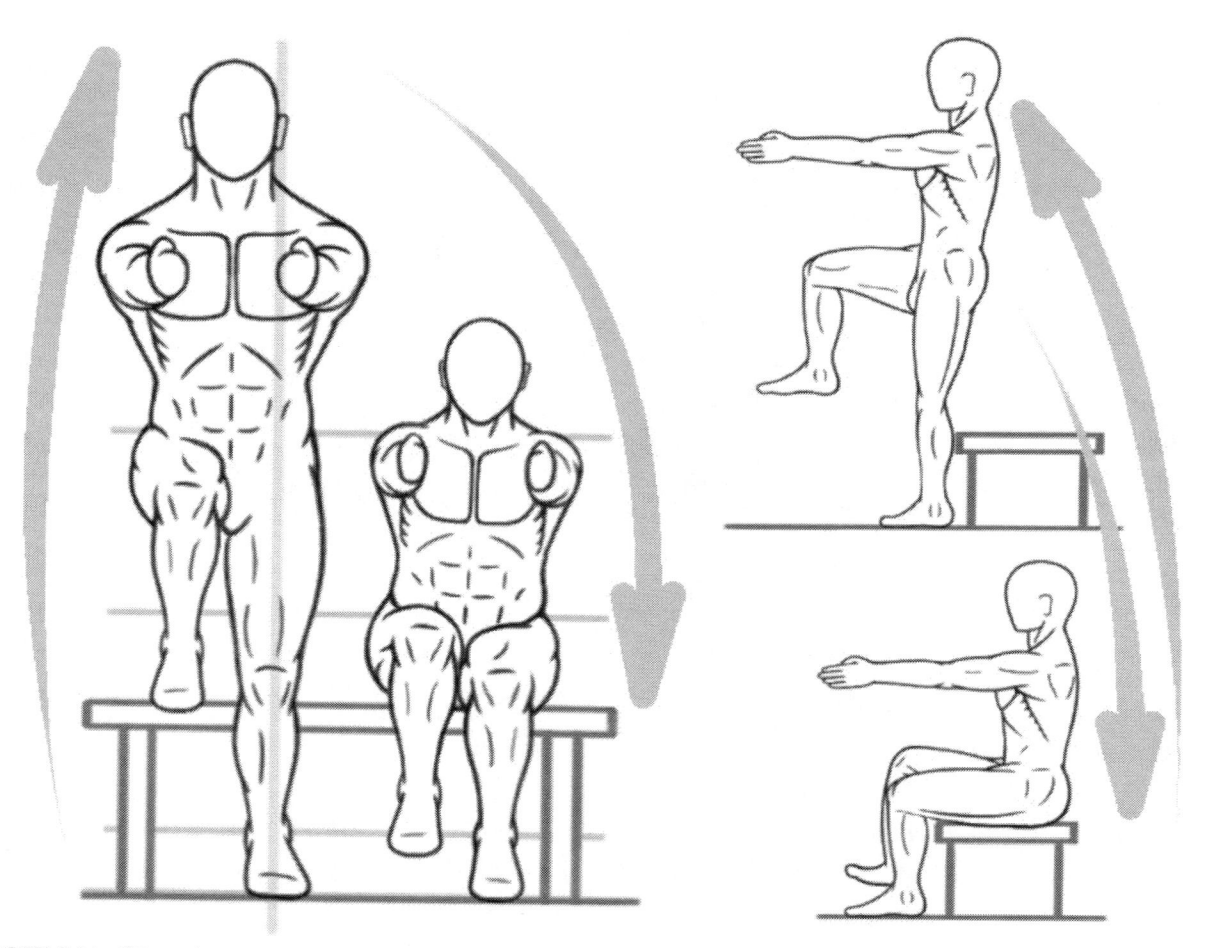

ACTION: Stand up onto one leg while maintaining balance. Make sure that the standing knee tracks over the foot by keeping the kneecap within the width of the standing foot. See diagram's insert.

**SIT WITH HIPS AT KNEE HEIGHT
STAND UP ONTO ONE LEG
TRACK THE KNEECAP OVER THE FOOT
MAINTAIN BALANCE**

If all requirements are met, then you have a good level of stability in this movement pattern.

STABILITY

STABILITY ASSESSMENT: Lateral Lunge to Single-Leg Balance
This test will also evaluate how stable you are on only one leg. Yet, this exercise will also include a bias of lateral directions in its movement pattern, which differs from the Sagittal (Front-to-Back) pattern of the Single-Leg Stand-Up.

POSITION: Stand in wide stance (feet elbow-width apart) and lower down into a deep lateral lunge where the hips are as low as the knees and the ankle, knee, hip socket and shoulder all vertically align with one another. Keep the other leg straight and the spine straight by lifting the chest.

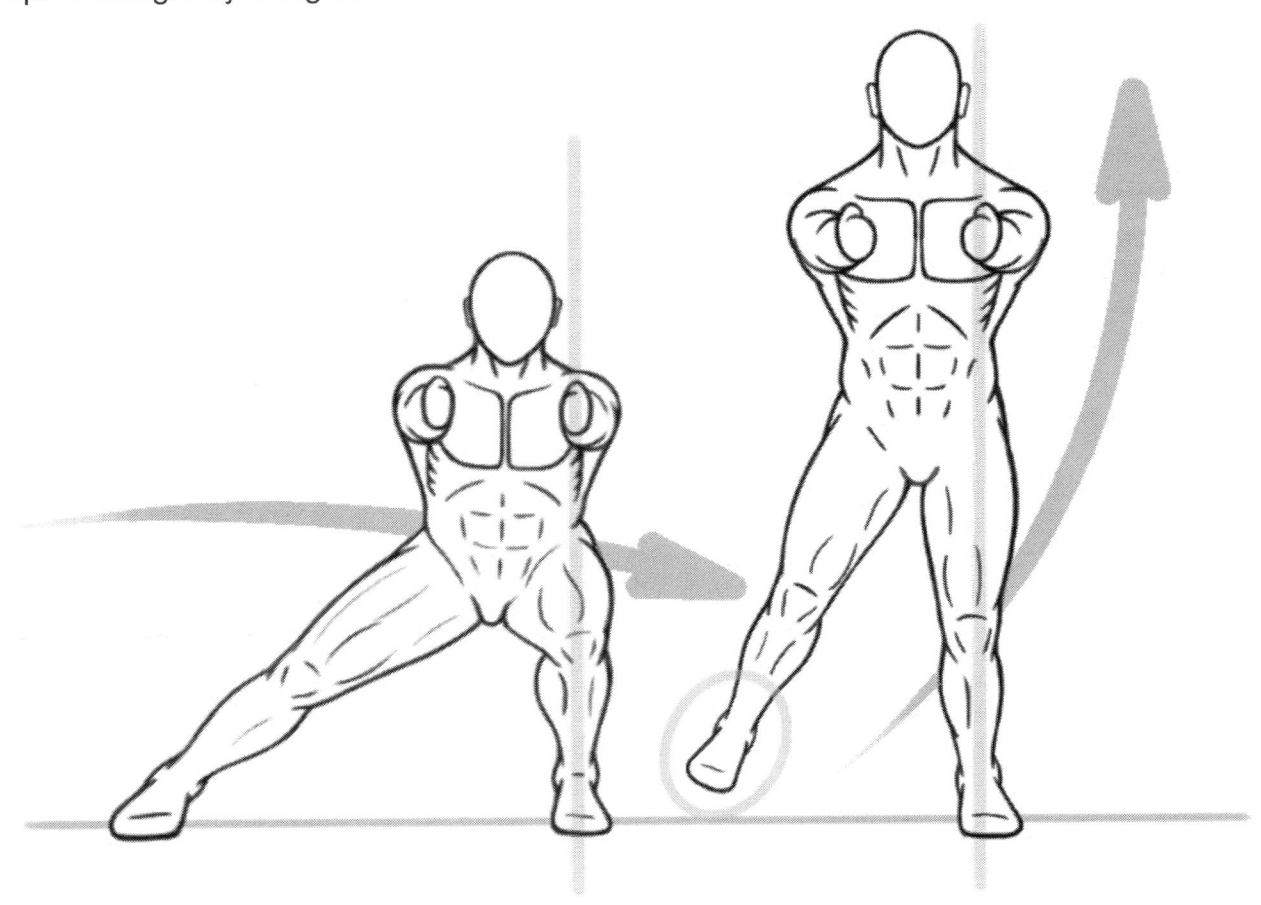

ACTION: Lift the trail leg (the straight leg) off the ground and stand up onto one leg. Press the top of the head up into the sky and maintain balance on only one leg while standing.

    LOWER HIPS TO KNEE HEIGHT
    LIFT TRAIL LEG OFF GROUND
    STAND UP ONTO ONE LEG
    MAINTAIN BALANCE

If all requirements are met, then you have a good level of stability in this movement pattern.

STABILITY

STABILITY ASSESSMENT: Trunk Stability Push-up
This Test will evaluate how well your Shoulders, including the Shoulder Girdle, and Core muscles can support the Spine in a Stabilized position as you push. Common faults in this test are: Hip Hinging (or piking the hips) and elevating the shoulders (squeezing the shoulders up towards the ears). If you notice either fault, visit to the Shoulder and Core Stability sections.

POSITION: Lie down on the floor with the hands shoulder-width apart with the heel of each palm aligned in a straight line with the top of the forehead.

ACTION: Push up into a plank position by extending elbows and engaging the abdominals. Press the entire body (chest, stomach, thighs and knees) to come up off the ground at the same time in straight alignment.

PLACE HANDS SHOULDER-WIDTH APART
ALIGN PALMS WITH TOP OF FOREHEAD
LIFT ENTIRE BODY OFF GROUND
FULLY EXTEND ELBOWS

If all requirements are met, then you have a good level of stability in this movement pattern.

STABILITY

STABILITY ASSESSMENT: Ipsilateral Rotary Stability Test
This Test will put the spotlight on your rotary muscles in both your shoulders and your hips, in addition to challenging how well the core can link together your upper body and lower body.

POSITION: Start in a tabletop position with the wrist directly under the shoulder joints and kneecaps directly under the hip sockets. Bring an elbow to touch the same side kneecap underneath the torso and establish balance.

ACTION: Simultaneously extend the arm and leg towards opposite horizons and keep the hips and shoulders level (parallel to the floor). Maintain balance throughout the movement and align extended arm and leg in a straight line.

- **WRISTS UNDER SHOULDERS & KNEES UNDER HIPS**
- **SAME SIDE ELBOW AND KNEE TOUCH**
- **EXTEND ARM AND LEG TO THE HORIZON**
- **KEEP SHOULDERS AND HIPS LEVEL TO FLOOR**
- **MAINTAIN BALANCE**

If all requirements are met, then you have a good level of stability in this movement pattern.

STABILITY

> **PreHab Exercises to Improve Your Stability**
> *There are several ways to improve your stability. This book will provide a series of exercises that focuses on specific joint action first and then will provide more exercises that will incorporate larger movement patterns and utilize multiple joint actions simultaneously.*

How to Improve-
- Start performing these exercises SLOWLY in order to learn the pattern and develop control throughout the entire movement.
- *Add SPEED as long as you can maintain ACCURACY and CONTROL in the movement.*
- Increase the number of sets and reps as your body develops more strength and stamina in these movements.

Stability exercises are desired for you to increase your control in the way that you move in order to provide a solid foundation for all of your movements.

STABILITY

Shoulder Stability

Since every joint in the body is connected, it's advantageous to include shoulder stability exercises into your PreHab routine, even if you are a long distance runner. Yet, if you're an athlete who runs in your sport or competes in triathlons, shoulder stability exercises should be considered mandatory in your preparation drills.

Caught by Surprise
When I learned I had shoulder instability, my jaw hit the floor. I was in the middle of a Continuing Education seminar when the instructor stuck her fingers underneath my shoulder blades and said, "This is dangerous."

The muscles that were responsible for securing my shoulder blades to the posterior side of my rib cage were grossly underdeveloped in relationship to my chest. I had spent so much time doing pushing/pressing exercises that the size and strength of my chest dwarfed the strength of my upper back muscles, namely the Rhomboids and lower Trapezius muscles. It was a recipe for disaster.

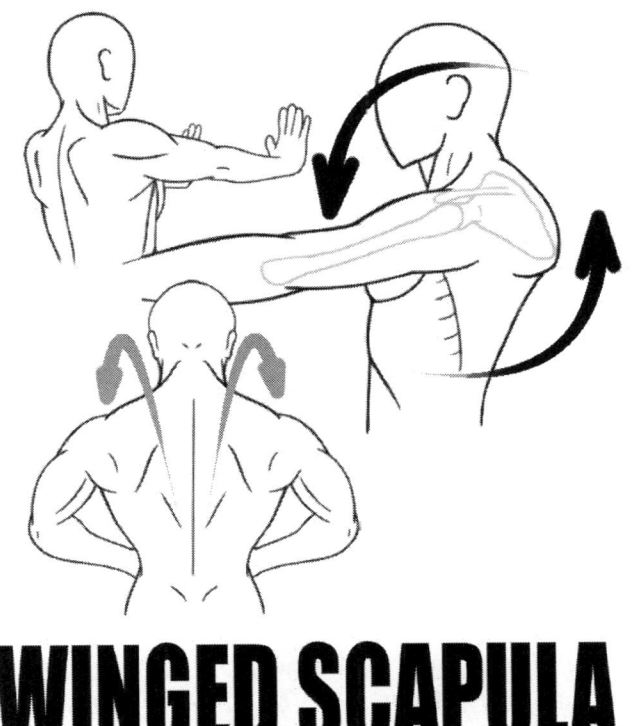

WINGED SCAPULA

"There is no way that I should be able to place my fingers in between your shoulder blades and rib cage," she said. "Your shoulders don't have the stability that they need, especially if you're going to keep working out as you do."

I used a heavy bag in my garage growing up and I did a lot of different kinds of bench presses and dumbbell presses. Looking back, I realized that my shoulder alignment and stability had been compromised. However, I was still shocked to discover this during class.

Corrective Measures
I suddenly found myself on a mission to stabilize my shoulders. The first step I needed to take was just activating all of the muscles of my shoulder girdle to help secure my scapulae to my rib cage and create a stable platform to operate upon. The next step I took was to develop more stability around the actual shoulder joint by strengthening the rotator cuff muscles with a variety of exercises, including:

STABILITY

> ## Shoulder Stability Exercises
>
> *Internal & External Rotation*
> *Push/Pull Progressions*
> *Plank Variations*
> *Y-T-W-A's with Resistance Tube*

Together, the synergy of forces produced by these exercise will develop stability at the shoulder joint, where the Humerus (arm bone) inserts into the shoulder capsule on the scapulae. It's a multi-directional joint, which is very beneficial because the arm uses numerous movement patterns through a very expansive range of motion.

The last step of my shoulder stability protocol was to integrate the action of the shoulder joint with the shoulder girdle. I wanted to explore the full range of motion and numerous movement patterns of the arm with control.

Establishing control over how the body moves
is an effective barometer of stability.

Be in Control
When performing all of these stability exercises, continuously ask yourself if you are truly controlling the movement or if momentum is taking over. It's okay if you start out using these exercises without complete control of the movements, but you want to intentionally work towards having control. If you lose control, even the slightest, you increase the risk of compensation and invite the possibility of leaking power in your movement.

Stability in movement leads to efficiency
in force production and biomechanics.

Improvements on the Bench Press
One of the improvements I found from adding all of these Shoulder Stability exercises into my training was that I was able to bench press more weight for more reps in a single workout.

> ### Stability Sequence for Rotator Cuffs & Shoulder Girdle
> The following sequence of exercises will help develop more stability in the shoulder complex by first addressing the Rotator Cuff muscles and then including movements that will integrate the shoulder Girdle muscles as well.

STABILITY

EXTERNAL ROTATION with Resistance Tube
This exercise will target the external rotators of the shoulders, a movement pattern that is underdeveloped in many people. This will help to secure the Humerus (arm bone) into the shoulder joint.

Equipment: A resistance tube or Thera Band and a rolled-up towel, about 3 inches in diameter.

POSITION: Hold the rolled-up towel between your rib cage and your upper arm, just above the elbow. Slide your elbow forward until it is aligned with the front of your rib cage. This will allow you to stabilize the shoulder blade onto the rib cage. It also place the emphasis of the movement onto the rotator muscles as opposed to the Deltoid (shoulder) and compensating with abduction.

Attach the resistance tube or Thera Band to a secure piece of equipment or pole and position your body at a distance that will place an adequate amount of tension in the tube or band. Make sure that your hips and shoulders are aligned with the tube or band in a parallel manner.

Bend your elbow to a 90-degree angle and squeeze the armpits into the ribs. Park the shoulder blades in the back pockets and pull the shoulders down and away from the ears.

ACTION: Rotate in the shoulder capsule and pull your knuckles away from the anchored point of the tube or band as your elbow remains in the same place. Make sure that the forearm rotates and the upper arms continue to squeeze in against the towel. The forearm and hand should extend at least outside the width of your shoulder.

Do not turn the shoulders or hips as you perform this movement. You will want to feel a muscular sensation deep within the shoulder. If you press into your shoulder with your opposite hand to feel when the Humerus intersects into the shoulder capsule, you should be able to feel the muscles on the posterior and lateral side of this joint become activated.

Perform 5-10 reps for 1-3 sets.
Be strict with your form and feel the muscles activate deep within the shoulder joint.

Illustration on next page.

STABILITY

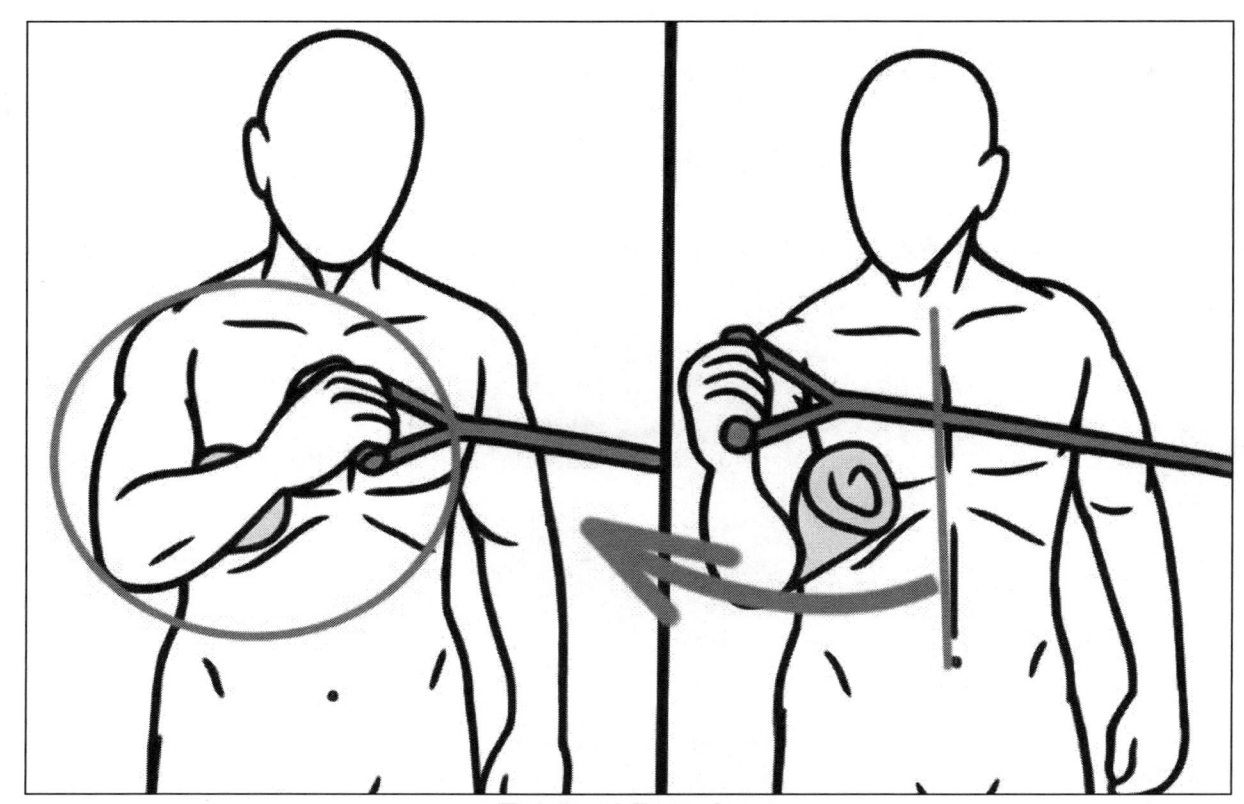

External Rotation

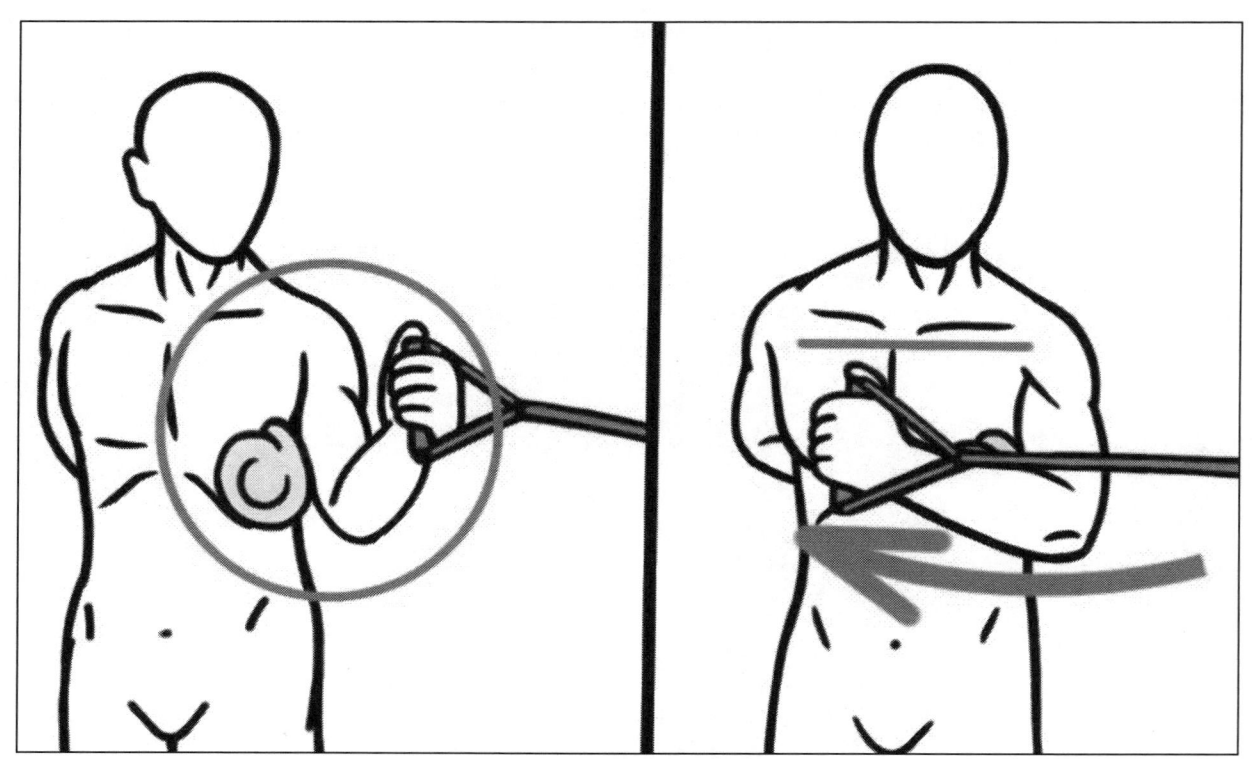

Internal Rotation

STABILITY

INTERNAL ROTATION with Resistance Tube
This exercise will target the internal rotators of the shoulders and will help to secure the Humerus (arm bone) into the shoulder joint.
Equipment: A resistance tube or Thera Band and a rolled-up towel, about 3 inches in diameter.

POSITION: Hold the rolled up towel between your rib cage and your upper arm, just above the elbow. Slide your elbow forward until it aligns with the front of your rib cage. This will allow you to stabilize the shoulder blade onto the rib cage. It helps place the emphasis of the movement onto the rotator muscles as opposed to the Deltoid (shoulder) and compensating with abduction.

Attach the resistance tube or Thera Band to a secure piece of equipment or pole and position your body at a distance that will place an adequate amount of tension in the tube or band. Make sure that your hips and shoulders are aligned with the tube or band in a parallel manner.

Bend your elbow to a 90-degree angle and squeeze the armpits into the ribs. Park the shoulder blades in the back pockets and pull the shoulders down and away from the ears.

ACTION: Rotate in the shoulder capsule and pull your knuckles away from the anchored point of the tube or band as your elbow remains in the same place. Make sure that the forearm rotates and the upper arms continue to squeeze in against the towel. The forearm and hand should rotate inwards and align with your sternum.

Do not turn the shoulders or hips as you perform this movement. You will want to feel a muscular sensation deep within the shoulder. If you press into your shoulder with your opposite hand to feel when the Humerus intersects into the shoulder capsule, you should be able to feel the muscles on the posterior and lateral side of this joint become activated.

Perform 5-10 reps for 1-3 sets.
Be strict with your form and feel the muscles activate deep within the shoulder joint.

Illustration on previous page.

STABILITY

EXTERNAL ROTATION with Thera Band
A quick and easy alternative to performing External Rotation with a Resistance Tube is to use a Thera Band placed around both wrists simultaneously. A common fault on this exercise is that the Deltoids (Shoulder muscles) initiate shoulder Abduction to compensate for External Rotation. You can tell if this is occurring by watching the elbows. If they move away from the rib cage, then the Deltoids are compensating for a lack of External Rotation. Simply press the elbows into the ribs and continue.

POSITION: Place the Thera Band around the wrists and bend the elbows to 90 degrees while positioning both elbows just in front of the rib cage.

ACTION: Press against the band and attempt to rotate the forearms outward to the sides while holding the elbows stationary alongside of the ribs. Keep the shoulders depressed by squeezing your armpits into your rib cage and pulling the shoulders down and away from the ears.

Attempt to external rotate the forearms to 30 degrees and feel the muscles deep in the lateral side of the shoulder joint become activated.

Complete 1-3 sets of 5-10 reps.

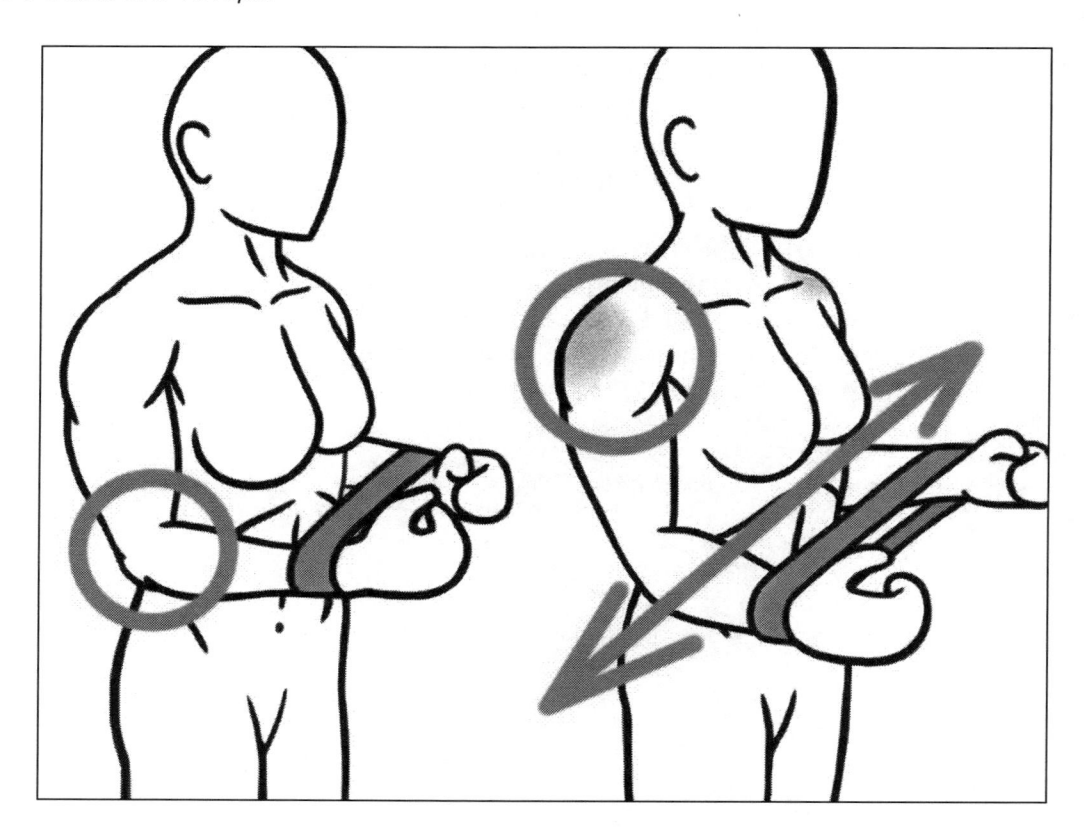

STABILITY

PLANK PROTRACTION

POSITION: Start with the arms at a 90-degree angle to the spine and hold the body straight from head to heels. Engage the abdominals and pull the belly button in towards the spine. Straighten the elbows and knees.

ACTION: Lower the chest and hips as far as possible to the floor and *keep the elbows straight*. Then press the torso away from the floor as far as possible and keep a straight line through the head, hips and heels. The movement strengthens the muscles of the shoulder girdle, not the arms.

Repeat 10-15 times for 1-3 sets.

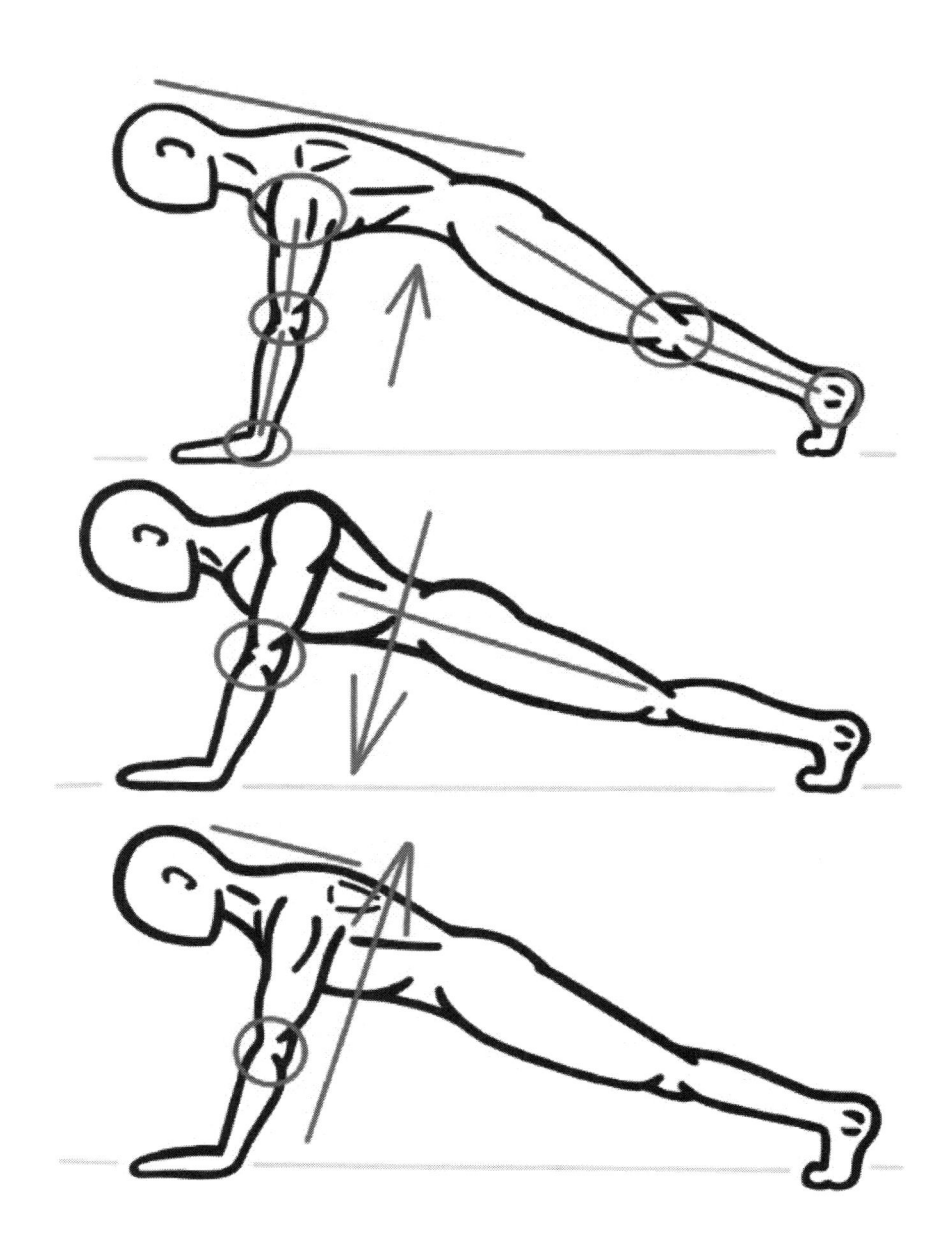

STABILITY

PLANK LATERAL SHIFT
POSITION: Start with the arms at a 90-degree angle to the spine and hold the body straight from head to heels. Engage the abdominals and pull the belly button in towards the spine. Straighten the elbows and knees.

ACTION: From center, shift the shoulders laterally to one side as far as possible. Attempt to align the heart of each thumb while keeping head to heel alignment and engaging the abdominals. Keep both elbows fully extended throughout the movement.

Repeat 10-15 times over each side for 1-3 sets.

PLANK SAW
POSITION: Start with the arms at a 90-degree angle to the spine and hold the body straight from head to heels. Engage the abdominals and pull the belly button in towards the spine. Straighten the elbows and knees.

ACTION: From center, shift the body forward as far as possible before switching direction and shifting backwards. Keep both elbows fully extended and stay aligned from head to heel. Roll over the toes going forward and drive into the heels when shifting backwards.

Repeat 10-15 times for 1-3 sets.

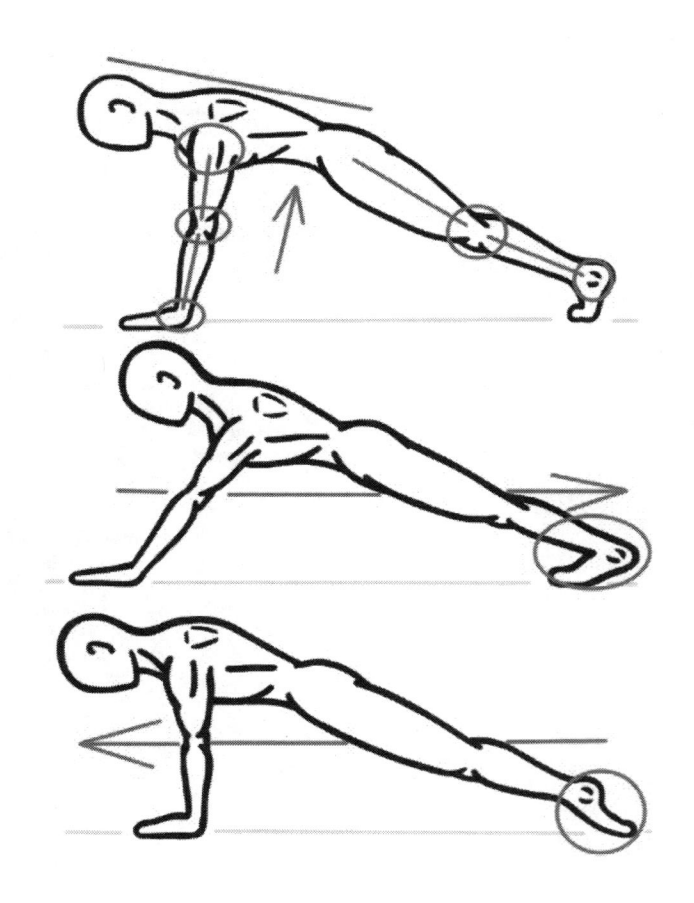

STABILITY

> **Plank Variations**
> These plank variation exercises will prominently develop stability and strength in a push or pressing movement pattern, such as push-ups, crawls, bench pressing and more.

PLANK SHOULDER TAP

POSITION: Start in a plank position with the arms on a 90-degree angle with the spine, hands at shoulder-width distance, and both elbows and knees fully extended. Pull the belly button in towards the spine to engage the abdominals and lengthen throughout the entire body.

ACTION: Lift a hand and tap the opposite shoulder with the palm while keeping the hips and shoulders level with the floor.
Alternate hands and repeat for 10-20 repetitions per side.

PLANK REACH

POSITION: Start in a plank position with the arms on a 90-degree angle with the spine, hands at shoulder-width distance, and both elbows and knees fully extended. Pull the belly button in towards the spine to engage the abdominals and lengthen throughout the entire body.

ACTION: Extend an arm forward and reach for the horizon while keeping the hips and the shoulders level with the floor.
Alternate between arms and repeat for 10-20 repetitions per side.

STABILITY

PLANK WALLET TOUCH

POSITION: Start in a plank position with the arms on a 90-degree angle with the spine, hands at shoulder-width distance, and both elbows and knees fully extended. Pull the belly button in towards the spine to engage the abdominals and lengthen throughout the entire body.

ACTION: Lift a hand and touch the same-side-hip where a person may hold their wallet. Keep the hips and shoulders level with the floor as you reach your hand to touch your wallet.
Alternate hands and repeat for 10-20 repetitions.

PLANK ROTATED REACH

POSITION: Start in a plank position with the arms on a 90-degree angle with the spine, hands at shoulder-width distance, and both elbows and knees are fully extended. Pull the belly button in towards the spine to engage the abdominals and lengthen throughout the entire body.

ACTION: Reach an arm out to the side and up to the sky while rotating the shoulders and keeping balance. Reach as high as possible by pulling the hands away from one another and pressing hard into the floor.
Alternate the arms and repeat for 10-20 repetitions on each side.

STABILITY

Y-T-W-A's

These exercises will prominently develop stability and strength of the shoulder in flexion, extension and abduction movement patterns. Increasing strength with these exercises is very helpful in "pulling" exercises, throwing motions and also provides more stability to all pushes or presses.

These exercises are also very helpful in integrating the shoulders and arms with the posterior chain as well as a way to help reduce or eliminate a Forward Help and Upper Cross postural alignment.

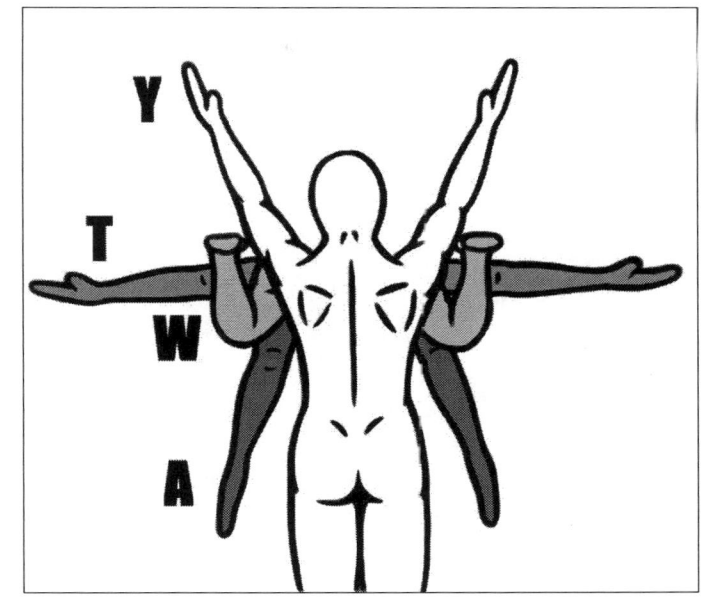

Equipment: Resistance tubes or Thera Bands

POSITION: Anchor the tube or band onto a secure piece of equipment or pole at the height of your shoulders. Then extend the arms parallel to the ground and step back until there is an adequate amount of tension in the band or tube.

'Y' ACTION: Extend both hands up towards the sky with straight arms and form a "Y" with your spine. Keep your spine in a neutral position while you extend your arms. Do not sway or arch your back as you lift your arms. Instead, pull the belly button in towards your spine to engage the abdominals and stabilize the core.
Return to the starting position.

"Y" Pull: Start & Finish

PreHab Exercise Book for Runners

STABILITY

"T" ACTION: Extend both hands out to the side and keep the arms parallel to the floor. Expand your chest as you reach your arms wide and squeeze your shoulders blades towards one another behind your heart in a retraction movement. Do not let your shoulders elevate or lift upwards in this movement. Be sure to squeeze the armpits into the ribs. Park the shoulder blades in the back pockets and pull the shoulders down and away from the ears.

'T' Pull: Start & Finish

Keep your spine in a neutral position while you extend your arms. Do not sway or arch your back as you lift your arms. Instead, pull the belly button in towards your spine to engage the abdominals and stabilize the core.
Return to the starting position.

'W' Pull: Start & Finish

"W" ACTION: Deeply bend each elbow and pull the hands directly away from the anchor point of the tube or band. Your arms will form a "W" with your head and hands as the upper points and the elbows as the lower points. This movement will strengthen external rotation, as well as retraction of the shoulder blades. Reach the fingertips back towards the horizon behind you as you squeeze the shoulder blades to touch one another behind your heart. Do not let your shoulders elevate or lift up towards your ears.

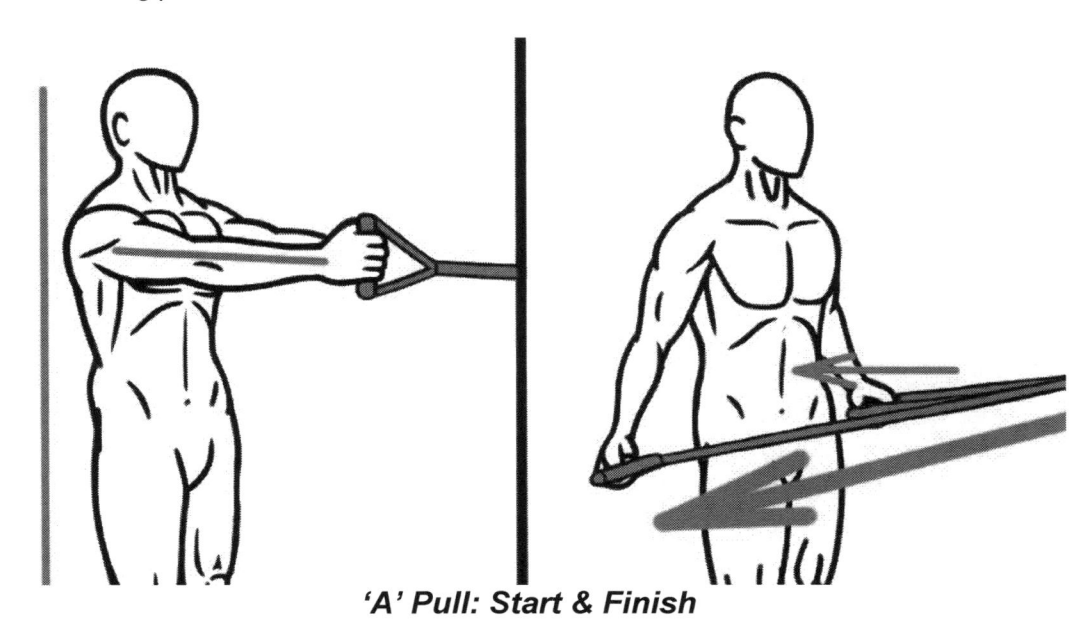

STABILITY

Instead, squeeze the armpits into the ribs. Park the shoulder blades in the back pockets and pull the shoulders down and away from the ears. Also, pull the belly button in towards your spine to engage the abdominals and stabilize the core.
Return to the starting position.

'A' Pull: Start & Finish

"A" ACTION: Extend both hands down to the ground and behind the body as if you are forming an "A" with the arms. Keep your chest lifted and reach your fingers for the ground as you extend backwards to create the largest range of motion in your shoulders and chest.

As you extend your arms, squeeze the armpits into the ribs, park the shoulder blades in the back pockets and pull the shoulders down and away from the ears. Also, keep your spine in a neutral position while you extend your arms. Do not sway or arch your back as you lift your arms. Instead, pull the belly button in towards your spine to engage the abdominals and stabilize the core.
Return to the starting position.

D1 & D2 PULLS with Resistance Band
These two exercises will help stabilize and strengthen the shoulder in two different diagonal movements. These exercises are very helpful to incorporate into your training, as they will help integrate the shoulder girdle and rotator cuff muscles. This is a movement pattern that we utilize a lot in life, but do not intentionally train in many exercises. Yet, once you incorporate this exercise in your training, you will feel more Mobility and Stability in the shoulders.

Equipment: A resistance tube of TheraBand.

STABILITY

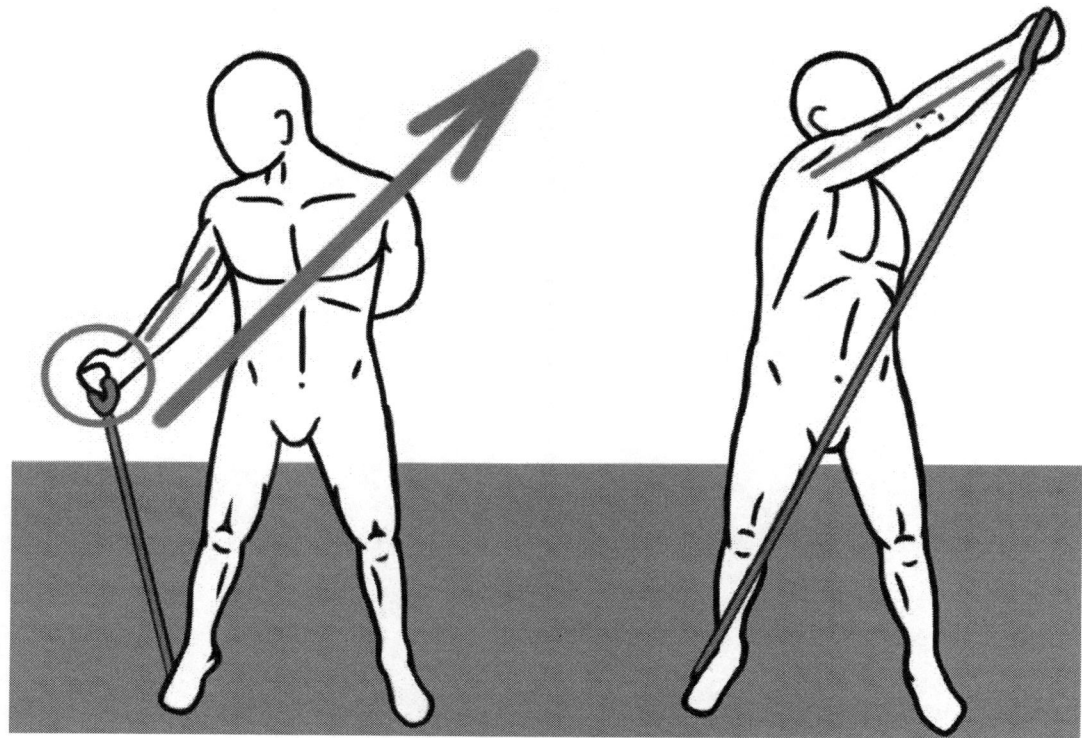

D1 Pulls: Start & Finish

POSITION: Place one foot on the end of the resistance tube or Thera Band as you stand with your feet shoulder-width apart. Hold the other end of the tube or band with one hand that you have positioned at your same side hip for D1 and the opposite for D2.

D1 ACTION: Reach your hand on a diagonal over the opposite shoulder as your keep your hips stationary. Pull the belly button in towards your spine to engage the abdominals and stabilize the core as you extend your hand up into the sky as far as possible. Attempt to touch your elbow to the ear on the opposite of your head as a way to help coordinate the D1 pattern.

Also, squeeze the armpits into the ribs. Park the shoulder blades in the back pockets and pull the shoulders down and away from the ears as your reach your arm on a diagonal. Then gently return the arm to the starting position.

D2 ACTION: Pull your arm up and away from your hip as your hand back over your same side shoulder on a diagonal. Your lifted arm and opposite leg should approximately align in a straight line. Attempt to stretch the tube or band across your heart as your lift up and back.

Do not let your shoulder lift up as you reach. Instead, squeeze the armpits into the ribs. Park the shoulder blades in the back pockets and pull the shoulders down and away from the ears.

STABILITY

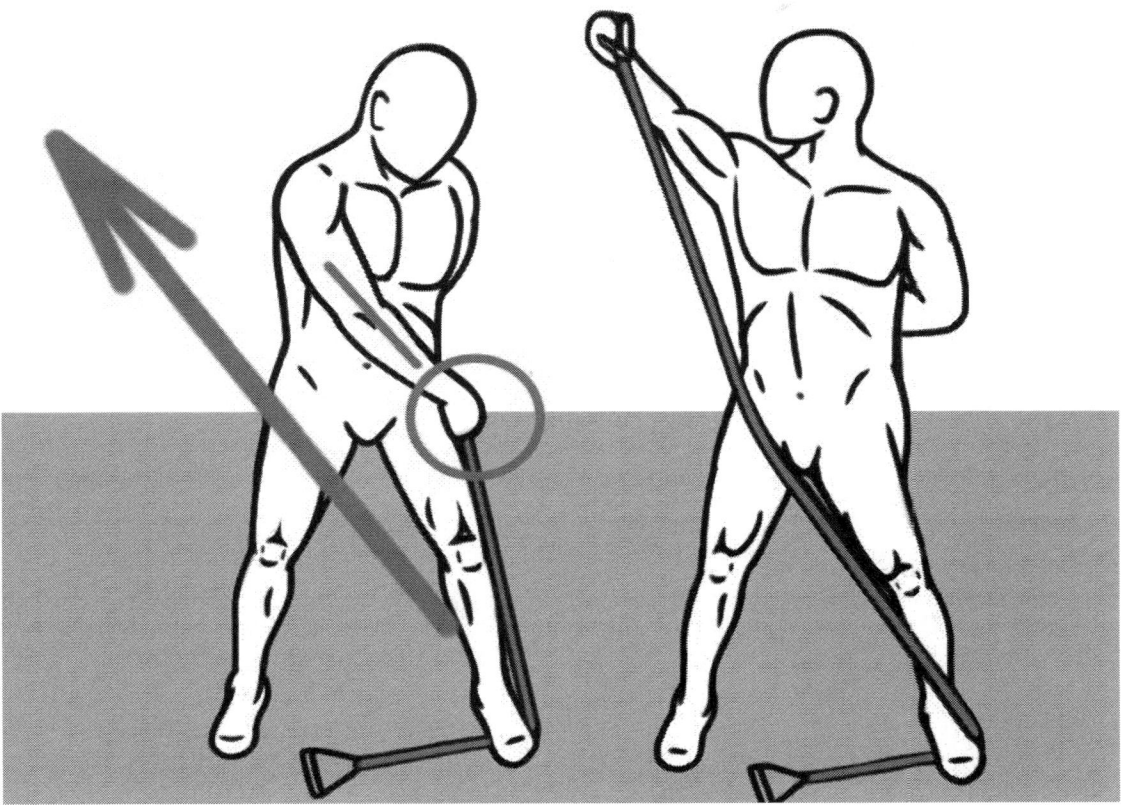

D2 Puls: Start & Finish

Also, do not let your hips or shoulder twist as you perform this movement. Pull the belly button in towards your spine to engage the abdominals and stabilize the core. Then gently return the arm to the starting position.

Perform 1-3 sets of 5-10 reps on each arm.

STABILITY

Train more than just your legs!

Even though running may be your thing, it's very beneficial to train your body in a holistic way. Your body is a very integrated tensegrity structure and compensation or poor mechanics in any one of your 360 joints will lead to a ripple effect that can be reduced, if not eliminated, with training the whole body evenly.

So, it may be counterintuitive to spend time with these shoulder exercises if you are looking to get faster with your feet. But in the long run, all pun intended, it's a smart move to maintain good biomechanics throughout your entire body.

STABILITY

Core Stability
More than just a Six-Pack

Core Stability will help protect your spine and build a foundation for proper biomechanics. Investing time in developing Core Stability will also help you to use your own energy more efficiently.

Core Stability Equals Spinal Stability
Despite what popular culture might tell you, Core Stability is not defined by having six-pack abs or a nice set of obliques. In fact, there are many people out there in the world who have chiseled abs and no stability in their core.

Core Stability is really about how the core of your body and spine behave, especially during physical activity. Another way to think of Core Stability is spinal stability.

Energy Dump
Have you ever taken out the trash and found out that there was a hole in the bag? I have. I once took the trash out from my apartment, walked all the way down the hall to the trash chute. Then, after I dropped the bag through the chute's trap door, I turned and saw that the bag had been leaking the whole time.

This same phenomena can happen when you run too! Without you ever knowing, you may be dropping a lot of power and energy out of your kinetic chain because your core is not stable.

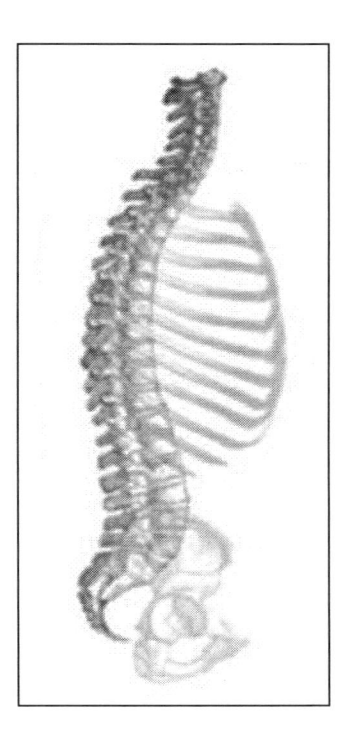

Your core can dump energy in a variety of ways such as breaking spinal alignment, rotating the pelvis or constricting the rib cage. Conversely, creating and utilizing a stable core will conserve energy and streamline force production.

One Powerful Lever
When the spine moves as one complete unit, it can transmit a massive load of kinetic energy in a particular direction. In other words, the spine can act as a powerful lever and this occurs in three positions: global Flexion, global extension and stable neutral.

Global Movements
There are 23 vertebrae in the spine connected by 22 joints. When they all move together in a synchronized fashion, the movements are powerful. We use the term "global" because every joint/vertebrae equally shares the load of the movement, which allows the total output of power to become multiplied. In other words, the spine is a perfect example of how a complete, whole unit outweighs the sum of its parts.

PreHab Exercise Book for Runners

STABILITY

Broken Chain
Whenever one vertebrae is flexing proportionally more than the others, the spine is not in global Flexion, global extension or stable, neutral alignment. Consequentially, there is an uneven distribution of force/load on the vertebrae and the kinetic chain through the spine is broken. When this happens, you are losing energy in your movement.

The good thing is that human beings are pretty amazing! We can perform at a very high level even when we have a broken kinetic chain and are losing energy. Just because you are not maintaining global Flexion and extension, does not mean you can't accomplish your goal.

I can still take the trash out even if there is a hole in the bag. It just means that I will be making a mess as I do it. And we can still perform in sports or run marathons with misalignments in the spine. It just means we will also be making a biomechanical mess that we will need to clean up later.

The following exercises will strengthen the core muscles in a variety of ways and help develop core and spinal stability by providing you the opportunity to use the spine as one unit.

"Golden Rule"
Since there are thousands of different exercises out there today for core strength, here is a rule to follow when training for core and spinal stability. Ask if you are working with your entire spine, from the base of skull to the tailbone, in an even and united fashion as you perform the movements of the exercises. Follow this simple rule and you will be able to further develop Core Stability in anything that you do!

Sequence of exercises
The following PreHab exercises form a basic sequence for Core Stability that translates into running rather well.

DEAD BUGS
This exercise will help develop enough strength on the anterior (front) side of your body for Core Stability. Since the exercise is rather demanding, a modification of knees bent is provided. Also, there are two versions of this exercise: Contralateral (Opposite Arm and Leg) and Ipsilateral (Same Side Arm and Leg).

STABILITY

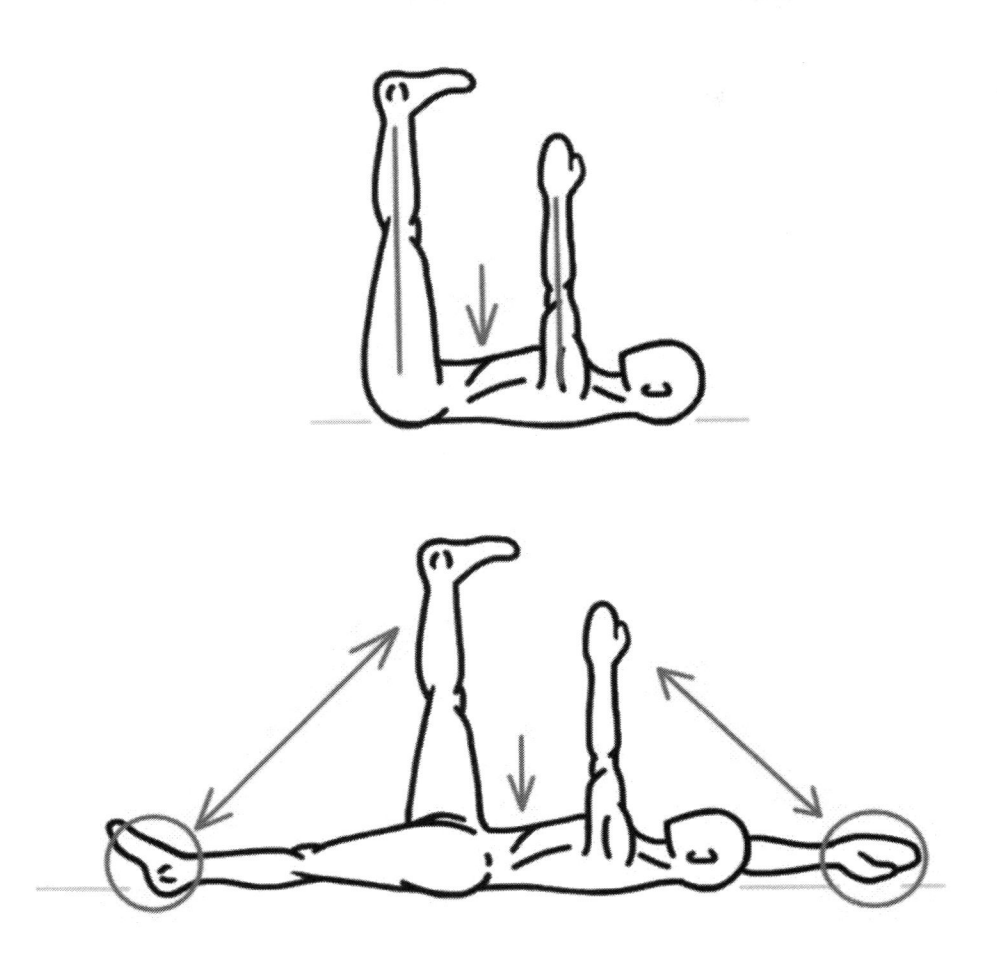

Contralateral Dead Bugs: Side View

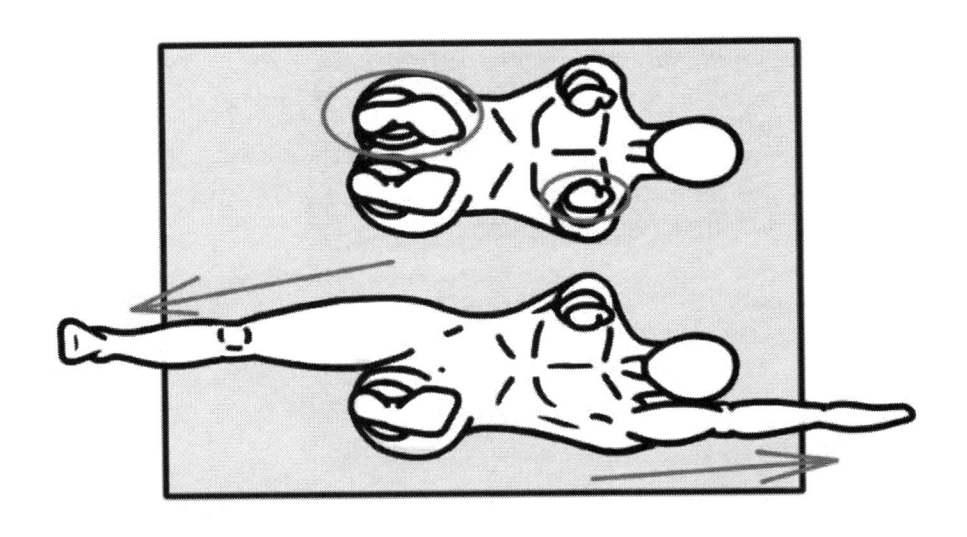

Contralateral Dead Bugs: Top View

STABILITY

CONTRALATERAL DEAD BUGS-
POSITION: Lie on the floor and extend the arms and legs straight up to the sky. Pull the belly button into the spine to help flatten the lower back completely to the floor. Straighten the elbows and the knees completely.

ACTION: Inhale and lower the *opposite* arm and leg to the floor. When lowering, reach the hand and the heel away from one another as far as possible and straighten the knee. Continue to pull the belly button into the spine to keep the lower back flat against the floor. Touch the hand and heel to the floor.

Next, exhale and simultaneously pull the arm and leg back to the original starting positions and then alternate sides.
Repeat 5-15 times on each side for 1-3 sets.

Illustration on previous page.

IPSILATERAL DEAD BUGS
POSITION: Lie on the floor and extend the arms and legs straight up to the sky. Pull the belly button into the spine to help flatten the lower back completely to the floor. Straighten the elbows and the knees completely.

ACTION: Inhale and lower the *opposite* arm and leg to the floor. When lowering, reach the hand and the heel away from one another as far as possible and straighten the knee. Continue to pull the belly button into the spine to keep the lower back flat against the floor. Touch the hand and heel to the floor.

Next, exhale and simultaneously pull the arm and leg back to the original starting positions and then alternate sides.
Repeat 5-15 times on each side for 1-3 sets.

Illustration on next page.

STABILITY

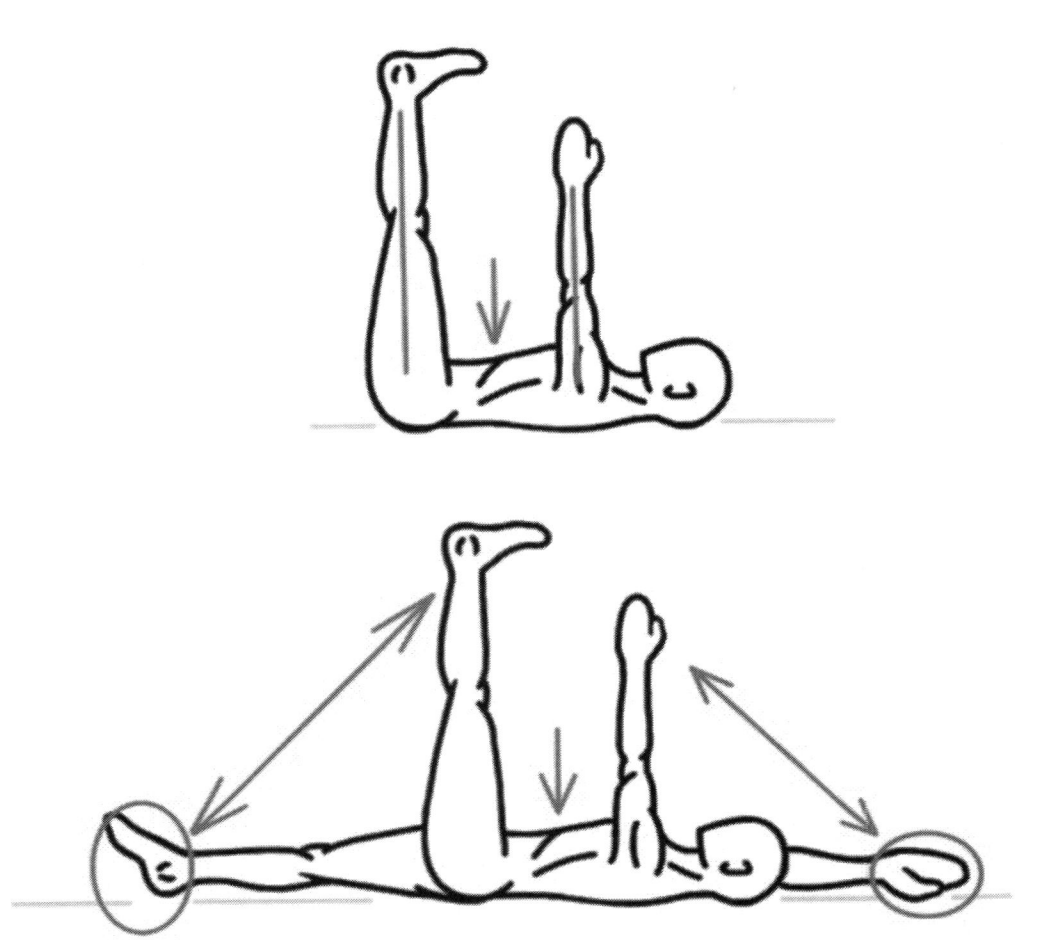

Ipsilateral Dead Bugs: Side View

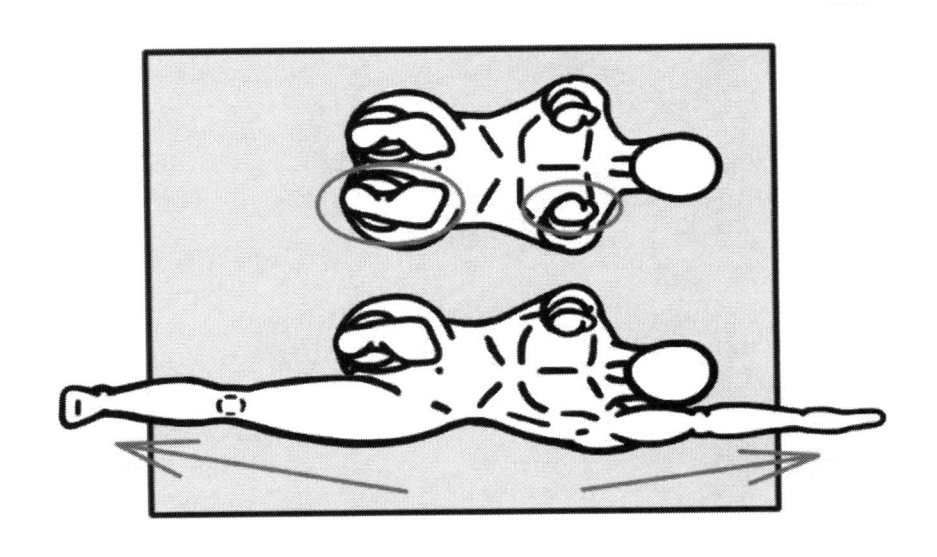

Ipsilateral Dead Bugs: Top View

STABILITY

MODIFIED DEAD BUG - CONTRALATERAL
POSITION: Lie on the floor and lift the legs up into a chair position (90-degree angles in the hips and knees) while extending both arms straight up to the sky. Pull the belly button into the spine to help flatten the lower back completely to the floor.

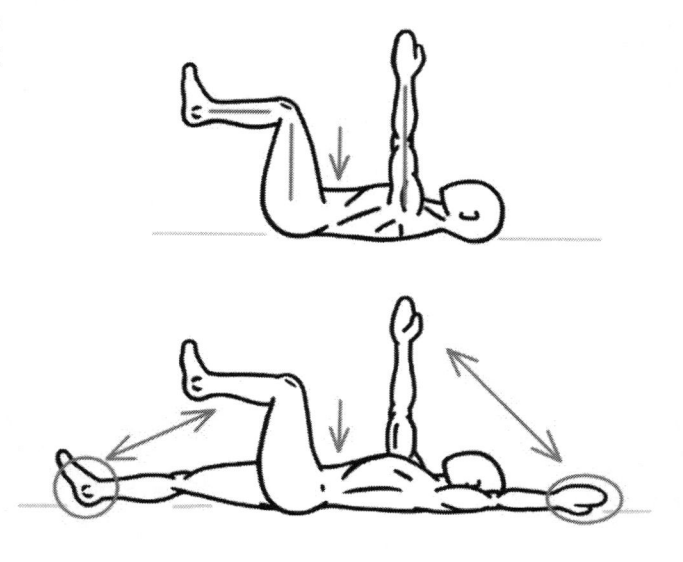

ACTION: Inhale and lower the *opposite* arm and leg to the floor. When lowering, reach the hand and the heel away from one another as far as possible and straighten the knee. Continue to pull the belly button into the spine to keep the lower back flat against the floor. Touch the hand and heel to the floor.

Next, exhale and simultaneously pull the arm and leg back to the original starting positions and then alternate sides.
Repeat 5-15 times on each side for 1-3 sets.

MODIFIED DEAD BUG – IPSILATERAL
POSITION: Lie on the floor and lift the legs up into a chair position (90-degree angles in the hips and knees) while extending both arms straight up to the sky. Pull the belly button into the spine to help flatten the lower back completely to the floor.

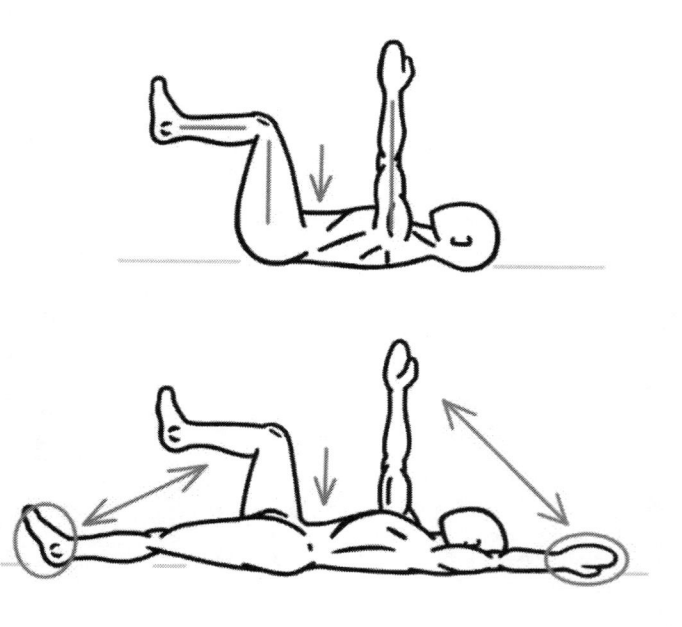

ACTION: Inhale and lower the *same side* arm and leg to the floor. When lowering, reach the hand and the heel away from one another as far as possible and straighten the knee. Continue to pull the belly button into the spine to keep the lower back flat against the floor. Touch the hand and heel to the floor.

Next, exhale and simultaneously pull the arm and leg back to the original starting positions and then alternate sides.
Repeat 5-15 times on each side for 1-3 sets.

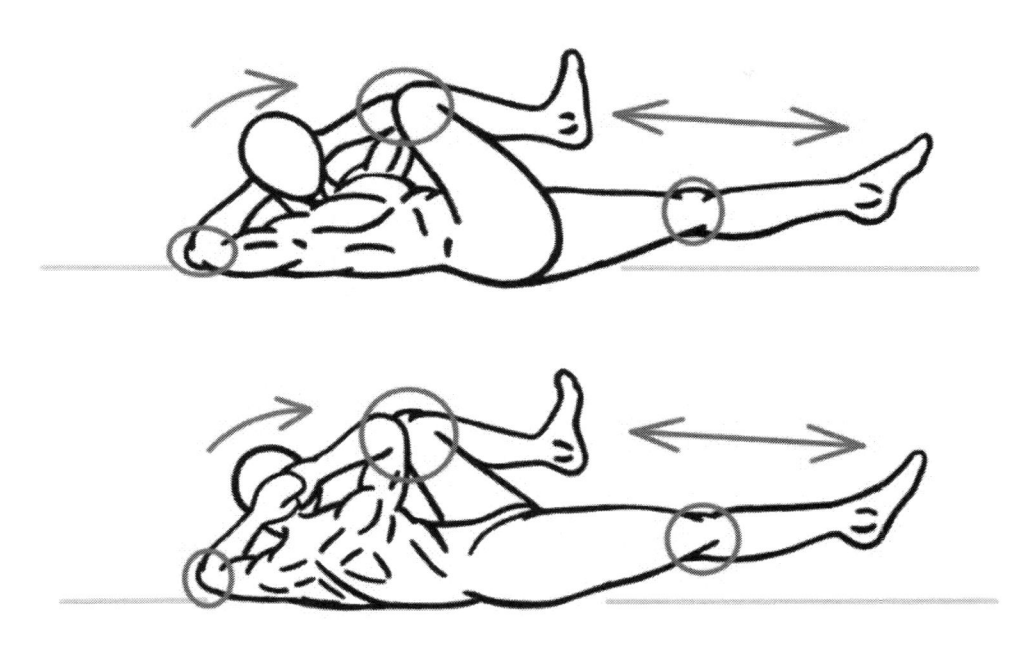

STABILITY

BICYCLE CRUNCH
POSITION: Start on the floor with one elbow touching the opposite knee. Extend the opposite leg towards the horizon and lift it off the ground.

ACTION: Simultaneously, switch arms and legs and touch the opposite elbow and knee together. Reach the other leg towards the horizon and keep it lifted in the air while the other elbow drops towards the floor. Stay long through the entire body and alternate sides.
Repeat 5-15 times on each side for 1-3 sets.

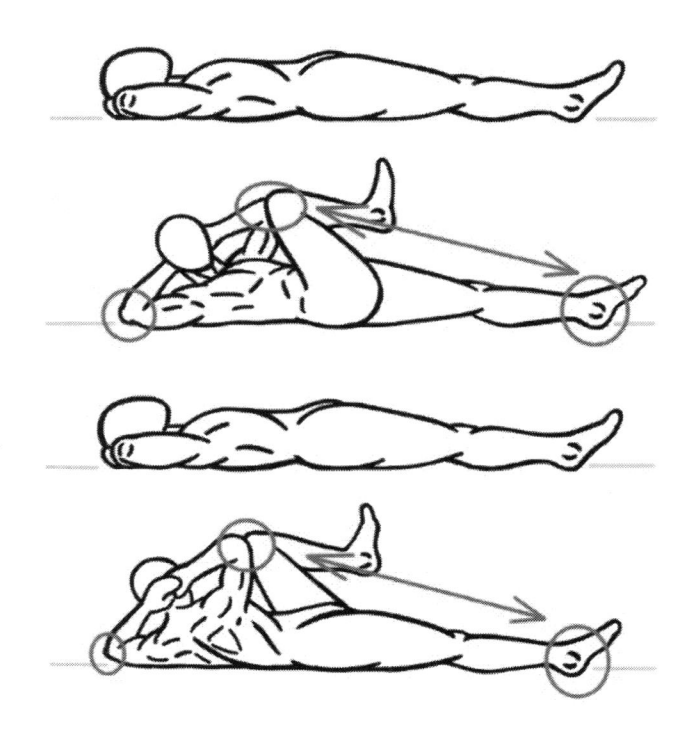

MODIFIED BICYCLE CRUNCH
POSITION: Lie on the ground with the legs extended straight out on the floor and the hands interlaced behind the head.

ACTION: Curl up and tuck a knee up towards the chest. Touch the knee to the opposite elbow and then lower back down to the floor under control. Maintain length through the entire body and alternate between sides while exhaling on each crunch.
Repeat 5-15 times on each side for 1-3 sets.

PreHab Exercise Book for Runners

STABILITY

SUPINE TOE TOUCH
POSITION: Lie on the ground with both legs extended up into the sky, directly over the hips and the arms stretched out over top of the head on the ground. Keep arms and legs straight.

ACTION: Curl up through the spine, attempting to touch the toes with the hands while keeping the legs straight and still. Then roll back to the ground with control and start again.
Repeat 5-15 times for 1-3 sets.

SINGLE-LEG SUPINE TOE TOUCH
POSITION: Lie on the ground with one leg extended up into the sky and the arms spread out into a "T" formation with the spine. Keep the arms and legs straight.

ACTION: Curl up to touch the toes with the opposite arm. Then lower back down to the ground under control. Keep the opposite arm and leg fully extended while staying long through the spine. Exhale when curling up and inhale when lowering back down to the floor.
Repeat 5-15 times on each side for 1-3 sets.

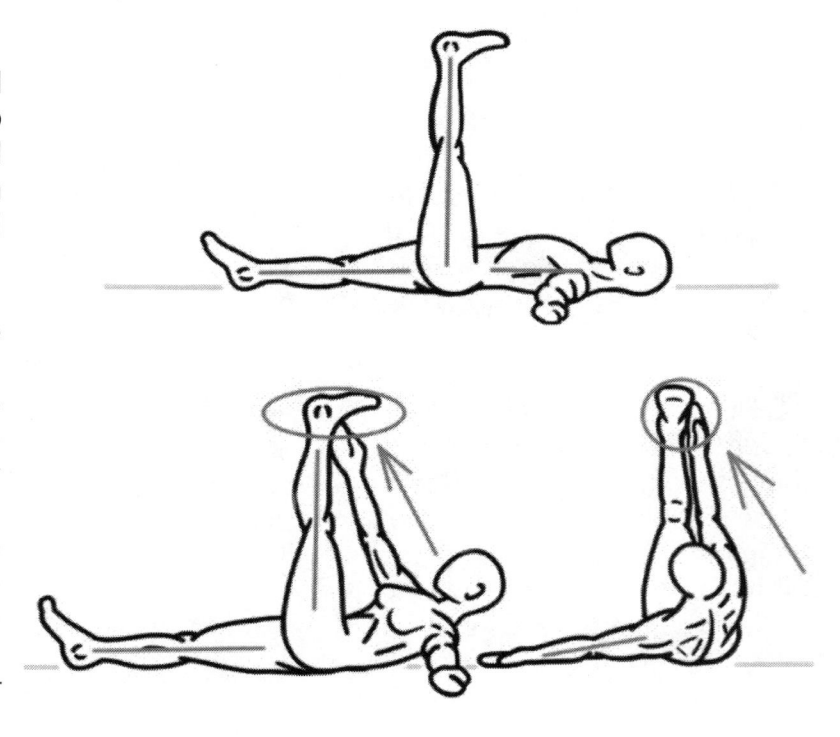

STABILITY

BACK EXTENSION SERIES
Even though many people perform abdominals exercises when they are targeting their core, you also need to include exercises for the posterior side of the torso, which is also the core. These muscles will primarily extend the spine backwards or in an arched position. Just remember to focus on the "Global" mechanics of the core and spine when performing these back extensions.

PRONE BACK EXTENSION
POSITION: Lie on the floor with the arms by the sides and the feet together.

Lengthen through the entire body from head to toes.

ACTION: Lift the chest and legs off the ground by lengthening through the whole body. Reach the top of the head away from the toes. Keep the back of the neck long and straight. Engage the abdominals to support the lower back by pulling the belly button up into the spine.
Repeat 10-15 times for 1-3 sets

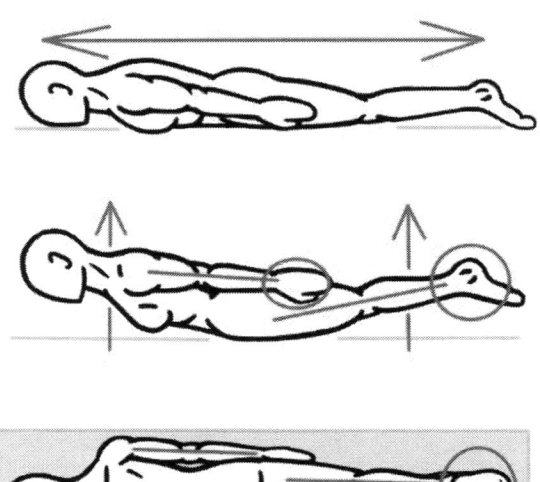

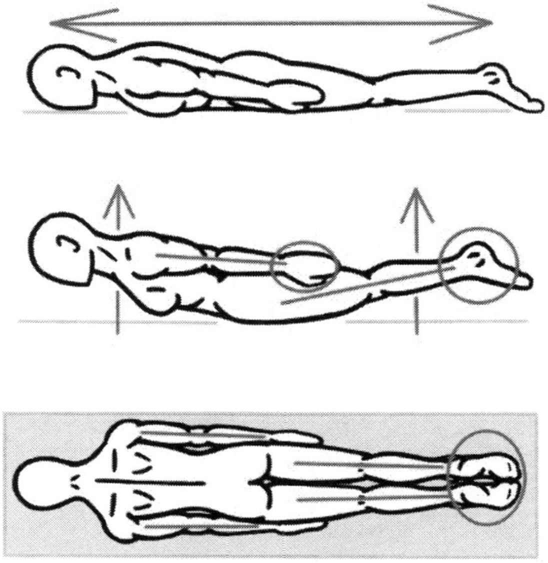

STARFISH BACK EXTENSION
POSITION: Lie on the floor with the feet separated far apart and the arms held out into a "T" formation with the spine. Keep arms and legs straight.

ACTION: Lift the chest and legs off the ground by lengthening through the whole body. Reach the top of the head away from the tailbone while extending the fingers and toes further away from the shoulders and hips. Keep the back of the neck long and straight and engage the abdominals by pulling the belly button up into the spine to support the lower back.
Repeat 10-15 times for 1-3 sets.

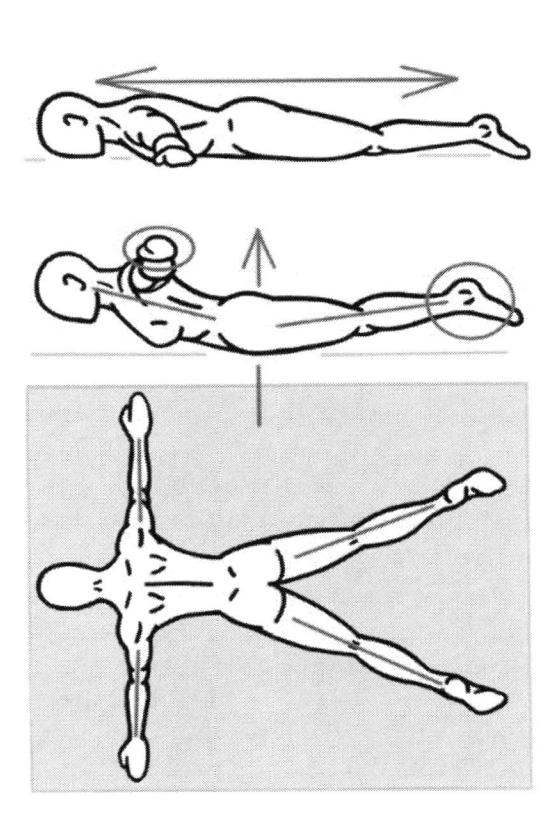

STABILITY

SUPERMAN BACK EXTENSION
POSITION: Lie on the ground and extend the arms overhead in parallel alignment. Lengthen through the body and reach the fingers away from the toes while touching the feet together.

ACTION: Lift the chest and legs off the ground by lengthening through the body and reaching the hands away from the feet. Keep the neck long and the face parallel to the ground. Pull the belly button up into the spine to engage the abdominals and support the lower back.
Repeat 10-15 times for 1-3 sets.

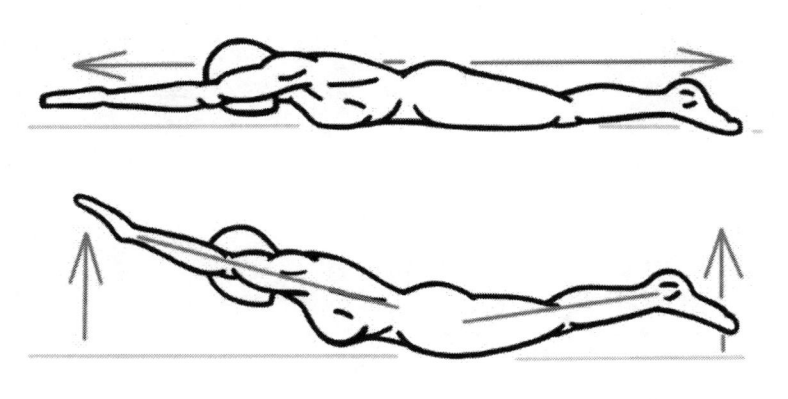

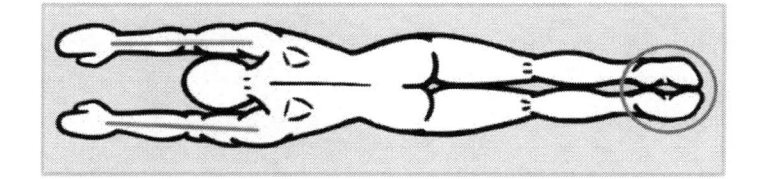

PLANK SERIES
Even though we use designated Planks as Activation Exercises, we can revisit them in order (and build off of them) to help develop more Core Stability.

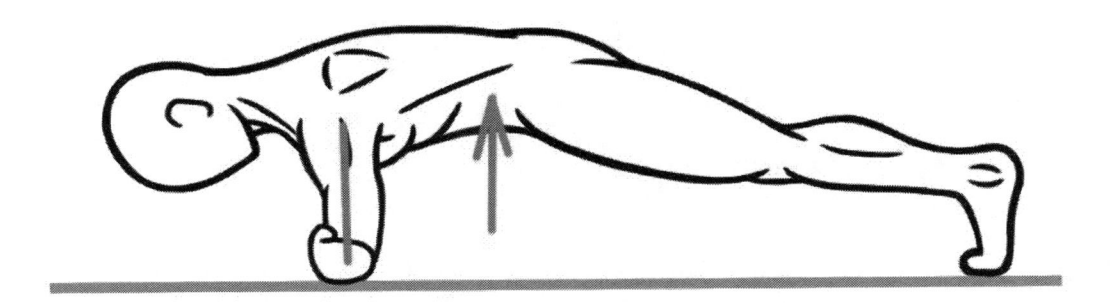

PLANK (ELBOW) for Stability
POSITION: Lie on your stomach and fold your arms under your chest like a genie. Make sure that your elbows are vertically aligned under your shoulder heads and spread your feet out to shoulder width.

ACTION: Lift up off the ground and form a straight line from ear to ankle. Squeeze the glutes and press the hips towards the floor while pulling the belly button and both kneecaps up to the sky. This will hollow your lumbar spine and activate your abdominals.

STABILITY

Also, press the heart and Adam's apple up towards the sky while driving the forearms into the floor. Tuck your chin in as if you want to have a double chin and lengthen the back of your neck.

Hold this plank position for 20-60 seconds in a series of sets or for as long as you possibly can. Yet, do not sacrifice your form for time. Keep good form the entire time and feel your core work!

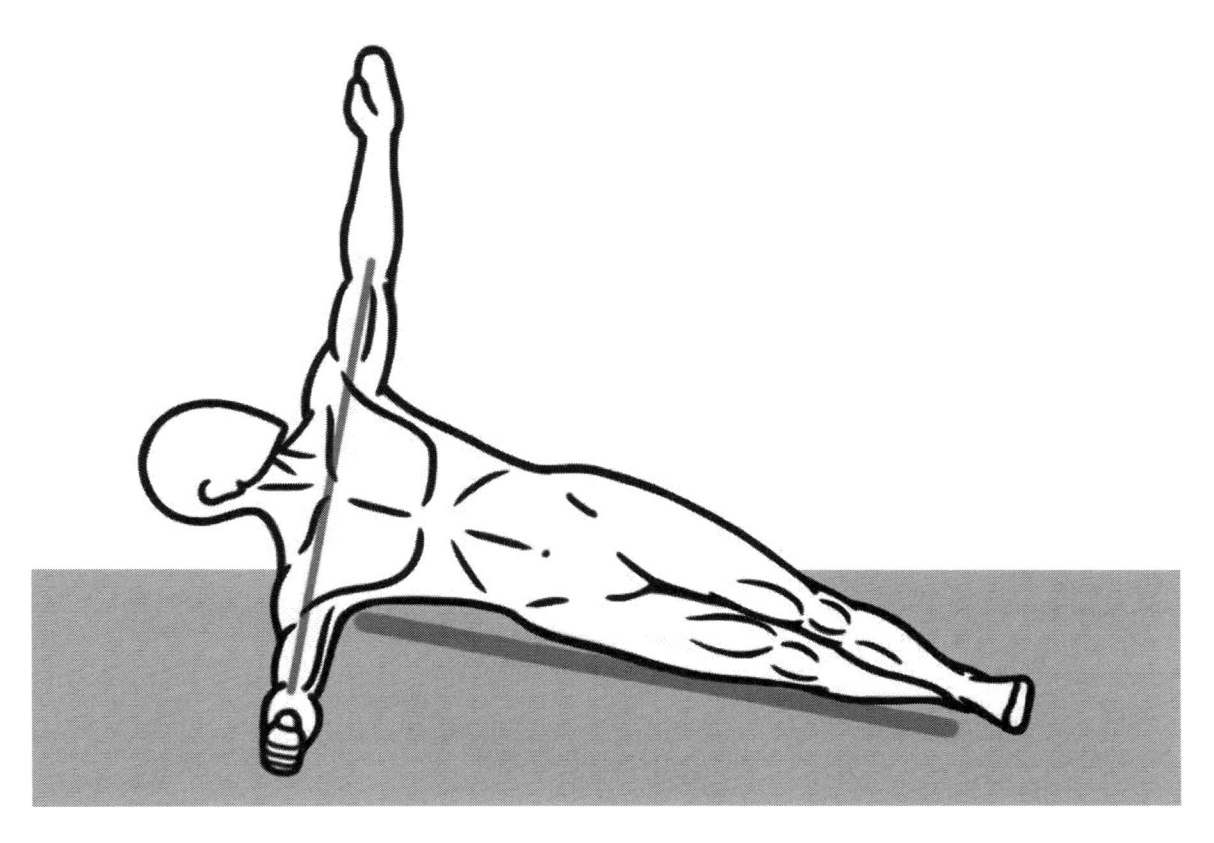

SIDE PLANK (ELBOW) for Stability
The next exercise is a variation of the original plank that will help activate the lateral musculature of your core, namely your obliques and quadratus lumborum.

POSITION: From a plank position, rotate your heels down to the floor and reach one arm up into the sky. Stack the shoulders and hips over one another so they vertically align. Also, squeeze the bottom armpit towards the hips and pull the shoulder head away from the ear in order to stabilize the shoulder girdle.

ACTION: Lift the hips up so they align in a straight line with the bottom shoulder and ankle. Also, make sure your hips align with your shoulders and bottom ankle from a lateral perspective. In other words, do not hinge at the hip or pike in the lumbar-hip complex. Press the hips forward to keep a neutral spine and straight line alignment from bottom ankle to shoulder.

Now, hold this side plank for 10-60 seconds in a series of sets on each side. Do not sacrifice your form for time. Keep good form!

STABILITY

PLANKS with LOWER BODY VARIATIONS
Now, we will take your Planks to a higher level. First, we will change the form from an elbow plank to a push-up or full plank. Next, we will add in some lower body variations that emulate many of the biomechanics of running.

PLANK LEG PEDAL
POSITION: Start with the arms at a 90-degree angle to the spine and hold the body straight from head to heels. Engage the abdominals and pull the belly button in towards the spine. Straighten the elbows and knees.

ACTION: Drop one knee down to the floor and drive back into the opposite heel while pressing the floor away with full extension through the shoulders and arms. Alternate back and forth between legs and keep the shoulders level to the floor.
Repeat 10-15 times per leg for 1-3 sets.

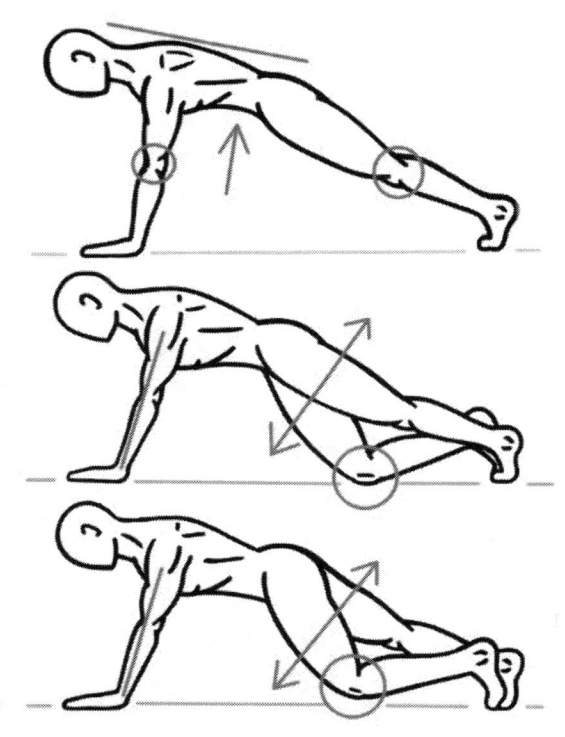

PLANK HEEL TOUCH
POSITION: Start with the arms at a 90-degree angle to the spine and hold the body straight from head to heels. Engage the abdominals and pull the belly button in towards the spine. Straighten the elbows and knees.

ACTION: Lift one foot off the ground and tap the toes on the opposite heel while pressing the floor away with full extension through the shoulders and arms. Maintain length from head to heels and stabilize the hips. Alternate between legs while keeping the shoulders level to the floor.
Repeat 10-15 times per foot for 1-3 sets.

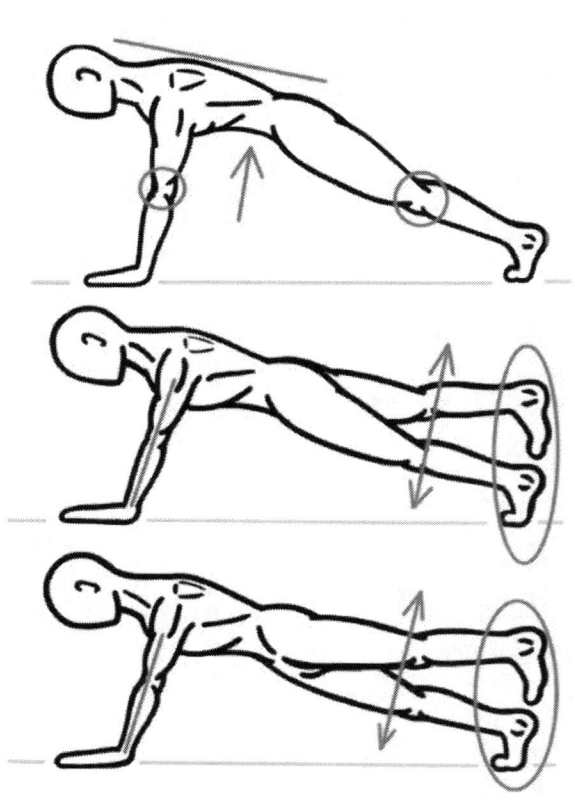

STABILITY

PLANK LEG CURL

POSITION: Start with the arms at a 90-degree angle to the spine and hold the body straight from head to heels. Engage the abdominals and pull the belly button in towards the spine. Straighten the elbows and knees.

ACTION: Curl one heel up towards the hips while pressing the floor away with full extension through the shoulders and arms. Maintain length from head to heels and stabilize the hips. Alternate between legs while keeping the shoulders level to the floor.
Repeat 10-15 times per leg for 1-3 sets.

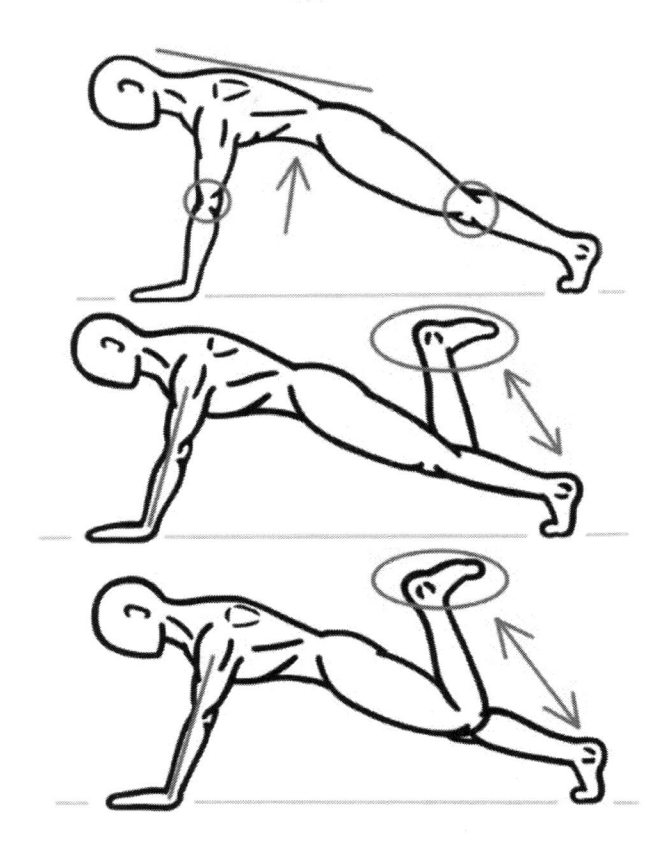

PLANK HIP ABDUCTION

POSITION: Start with the arms at a 90-degree angle to the spine and hold the body straight from head to heels. Engage the abdominals and pull the belly button in towards the spine. Straighten the elbows and knees.

ACTION: Step one foot out to the side with a straight leg and tap the toes on the floor while pressing the floor away with full extension through the shoulders and arms. Keep the shoulders still in the exercise and attempt to stabilize the spine over a target or a line on the floor.
Repeat 10-15 times per leg for 1-3 sets.

PreHab Exercise Book for Runners

STABILITY

PLANK TUCK

POSITION: Start with the arms at a 90-degree angle to the spine and hold the body straight from head to heels. Engage the abdominals and pull the belly button in towards the spine. Straighten the elbows and knees.

ACTION: Tuck one knee up into the chest as high as possible while driving back into the opposite heel and pressing the floor away with full extension through the shoulders and arms. Lengthen through the spine and maintain the straight-line alignment of the shoulder, hips and rear heel.
Repeat 10-15 times per side for 1-3 sets.

PLANK TUCK - ABDUCTION

POSITION: Start with the arms at a 90-degree angle to the spine and hold the body straight from head to heels. Engage the abdominals and pull the belly button in towards the spine. Straighten the elbows and knees.

ACTION: Tuck one knee to the outside of the same side arm while driving back into the opposite heel. Aim to touch the triceps with the knee. Lengthen through the spine and maintain the straight-line alignment of the shoulder, hips and rear heel.
Repeat 10-15 times per side for 1-3 sets.

STABILITY

PLANK TUCK – ADDUCTION
POSITION: Start with the arms at a 90-degree angle to the spine and hold the body straight from head to heels. Engage the abdominals and pull the belly button in towards the spine. Straighten the elbows and knees.

ACTION: Tuck one knee to the opposite elbow while driving back into the rear heel. Attempt to touch the knee to the elbow. Lengthen through the spine and maintain the straight-line alignment of the shoulder, hips and rear heel.
Repeat 10-15 times per side for 1-3 sets.

PLANK BIRD DOG
POSITION: Start with the arms at a 90-degree angle to the spine and hold the body straight from head to heels. Engage the abdominals and pull the belly button in towards the spine. Straighten the elbows and knees.

ACTION: Simultaneously lift one arm and the opposite leg off the floor and reach the hand and foot towards opposite horizons. Maintain the straight-line alignment of the head, hips and rear heel while also keeping the shoulders and hips level to the floor. Fully extend both arms and legs.
Repeat 5-15 times on each side for 1-3 sets.

STABILITY

> ### *Global Flexion/Extension Exercises*
> *Even though we may not utilize a Global Flexion or Extension position in running-related sports, it's still beneficial. Putting the body into these positions help trains the neuromuscular system to coordinate movement with the spine, acting as one unit as opposed to 23 individual parts. Remember, the spine is one powerful lever when it moves as one unit!*

HOLLOW ROCKS

This exercise will help strengthen the anterior core muscles and create a stabilized spine in a flexed position.

POSITION: Lie on your back with the arms and legs pointed away from each other. Have the hands and feet touching as you lift the arms and legs off the ground. As you lift the arms and legs, curl your spine by pulling your sternum towards your hips and your back, bottom, and ribs away from the pelvis. Your body should look like a skinny "C" on its side. Now, try to stabilize the position by trying to look at your belly button as you pull the belly button in towards the spine.

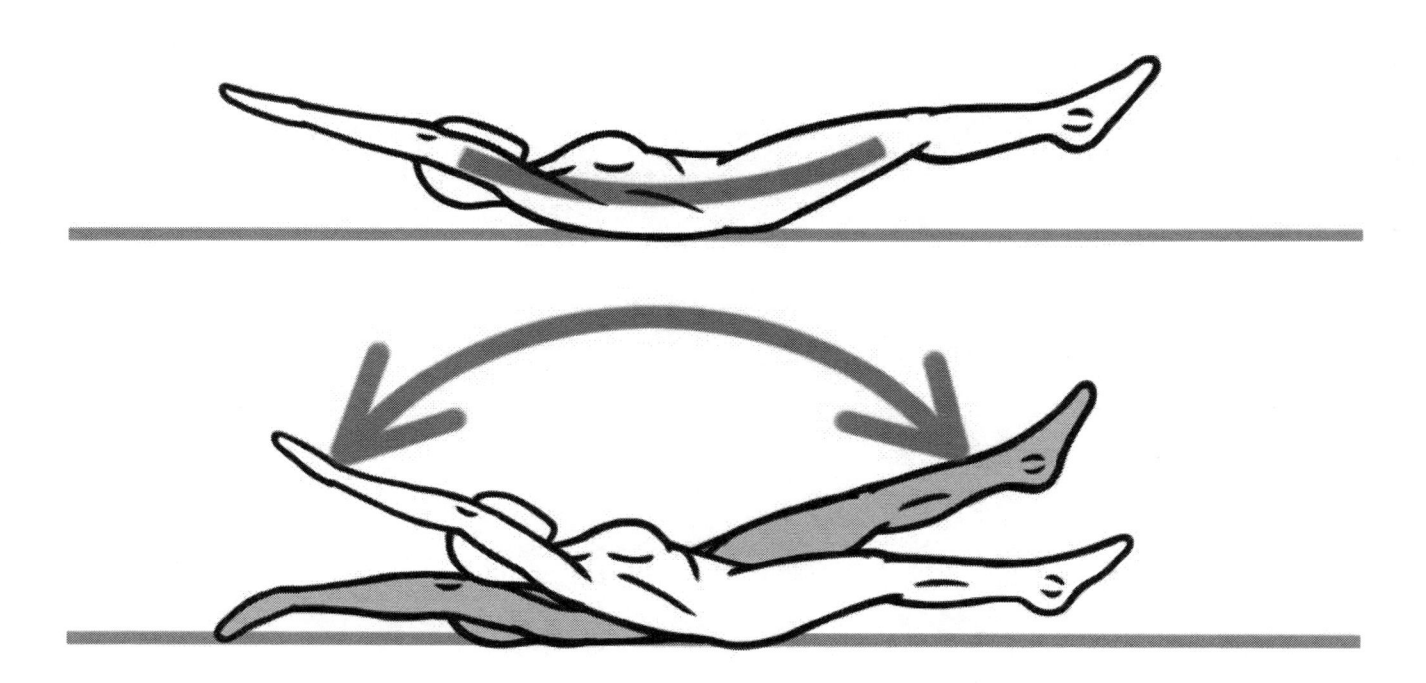

ACTION: Now, keep this skinny "C" position as you gently begin to rock. Start with small rocks and allow the momentum to grow, which will make the rocks bigger. As you rock back and forth, you want to feel your shoulder blades and hips come off the ground in an alternating fashion.

Rock continuously for either time, i.e. 20-30 seconds, or for 10-15+ reps.
Combine with Arch Rocks and complete 2-3 sets.

STABILITY

ARCH ROCKS
This exercise will help strengthen the posterior core muscles and create a stabilized spine in the extended position.

POSITION: Lie on your stomach with the arms and legs pointed away from each other. Have the hands and feet touching as you lift the arms and legs off the ground. As you lift the arms and legs, curl your spine by pulling your shoulder blades down towards your hips and lifting the chest as well as the thighs off the floor. Your body should look like a skinny "C" on its side.

Tuck your chin into your throat and do not overarch your neck. Your ears should be aligned with your biceps if you have good shoulder mobility. And the back of your neck needs to be long and straight.

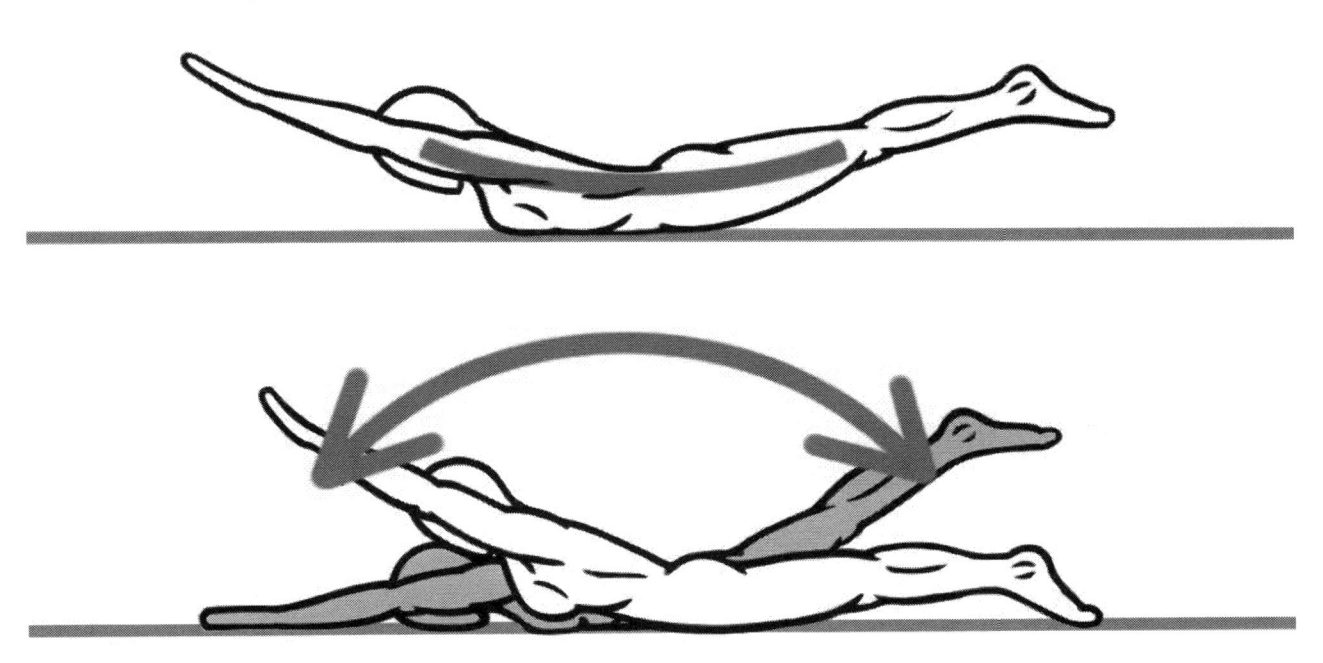

ACTION: Now, keep this skinny "C" position as you gently begin to rock on your stomach. Start with small rocks and allow the momentum to grow, which will make the rocks bigger. As you rock back and forth, you want to feel your chest and pelvis come off the ground in an alternating fashion.

Rock continuously for either time, i.e. 20-30 seconds, or for 10-15+ reps.
Combine with Hollow Rocks and complete 2-3 sets.

Be Powerful
As mentioned before, the main purpose of developing Core Stability is to create more power in your movements. These exercises help you to use the spine as one powerful lever as opposed to 22 individual joints and will help prevent you from dumping out energy with inefficiencies in your movement patterns.

STABILITY

STABILITY

Hip Stability
Don't Run Without It!

Simply put, stability increases ability. In other words, if you are stable in your biomechanics, your ability to perform specific movements will multiply.

Illustrating an Example
Here's a factoid that you may not know: I draw all of the exercise illustrations in my books and on my blog myself, each and every one. I will sit down (though for not too long because I know what sitting does to my body) and I will sketch out each movement as specific as I possibly can. On top of that, one of the simple joys that I have is going to a local cafe in the mid-morning to draw some of these exercise illustrations and listen to some music. However, it isn't always easy.

On a few occasions I have sat down in a cafe to draw and have been thwarted by a table that isn't stable. You know the kind that wobbles when you press down on a corner and it pops back up when you let go. Well, imagine what it's like to draw detailed pictures on a table that won't stay still – it's frustrating and nearly impossible. Of course, an obvious solution is to switch tables or to stick something under one of the legs to create stability. It's ironic to get one of those wobbly tables when I'm there to draw exercises and images to promote stability.

Need for Hip Stability
If you are working out or playing a sport, there is a necessity to develop hip stability. You need stability to provide for the best possible results in any sport, and it's important to remember the Glutes are your prime movers. The coordination, timing and balance of every movement depend on how stable you are in each joint. Any weakness or compensation will influence the production of all of your movements. Yet, the hips generate more power and are more responsible for the mass of your movements when compared with the rest of the body. Ensuring stability in this joint complex will greatly benefit the rest of your biomechanics.

Increased Control
Since your hips play a major role in your movement, stability in this joint would also have an impact. Stability is the degree of manageable control of the forces that pass through a joint. Or in other words, will you control the forces that run through your joints or will momentum and torque control and influence how your body moves? Ideal stability is the ability to hold a joint in a specific position despite the external forces acting on it. You control the joint's positioning.

STABILITY

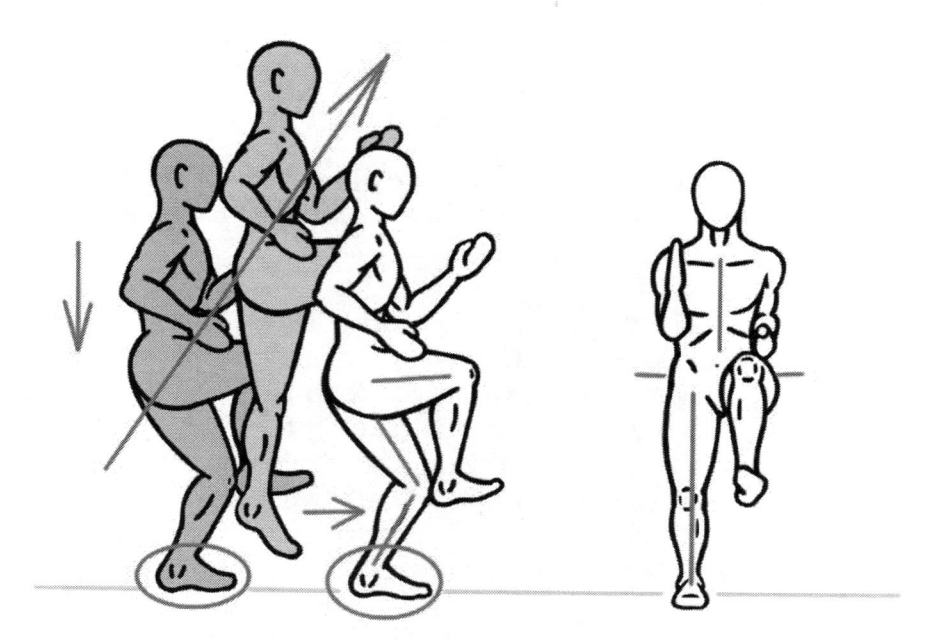

Hip Stability Test: 'Stick the landing.'

HIP STABILITY TEST
Here is a very simple way to gauge where you rank in hip stability. All you need is a mirror or a partner to watch you perform a basic hop on one leg.

POSITION: Stand in front of a mirror in order to observe the movement of your hips as you hop. You will need to clearly define the iliac crests on each hip by either visually displaying it, meaning no baggy shirts covering your hip bones, or by placing your hands on your hips to mark the position of the iliac crests.

ACTION: Gently hop and land on only one leg as you watch the hips. Note if the hips tilted when you landed. Did one hip drop closer down towards the floor than the other hip? If your hips tilted, then you have a certain lack of hip stability on your landing leg.

The goal of this test is to determine how much training and development your hips need in regards to stability. Hip stability is extremely beneficial to runners and athletes who run because the hop in this test correlates to the unilateral loading the hips experience on every single stride. The easier it is to "stick" the landing in this simple hop test, the more control and stability you have in your hips while you run.

Hop and "stick" the landing. If you can do this, it means you have enough neuromuscular control to keep your hips parallel once you make contact with the ground.

Where to Start?
There are many different exercises to choose from when looking to improve and develop hip stability. Here is a progression of different PreHab exercises to start with.

STABILITY

BRIDGE MARCH
This exercise will help create stability of the hips as well as help train you to maintain proper lumbar-pelvic alignment. This is where the spine connects with the pelvis and is a place where many people experience lower back pain.

POSITION: Lift up into a bridge position with the hips in line with the shoulders and knees. Walk the feet out until there is a 90-degree bend in your knees and reach your fingers towards your heels. Also, squeeze the armpits into the ribs, park the shoulder blades in the back pockets and pull the shoulders down and away from the ears.

ACTION: Lift up one foot and reach the knee towards the sky as you begin to march in place with both legs. Keep the hips level with the floor and maintain the same height as you march. Also, pull the belly button in towards your spine to engage the abdominals and stabilize the core. *March in place for either time (i.e. 30 seconds) or sets of 10-30 reps.*

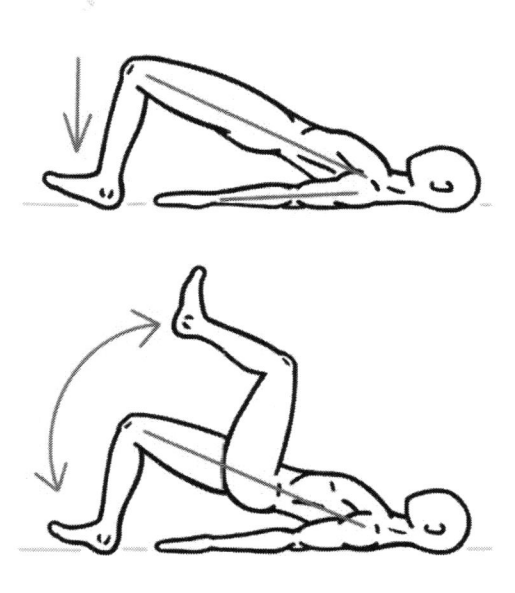

HIP HIKE
This exercise will help to strengthen the lateral hip muscles, including the Gluteus Medius, which will help protect your knee when you run, jump or squat.

POSITION: Lay on your side with your legs out straight and place your elbow directly beneath your shoulder. Square off your shoulders and hip to the ground on a 90 degree angle and stack one foot on top of the other. Also, squeeze the armpits into the rib, park the shoulder blades in the back pockets and pull the shoulders down and away from the ears.

ACTION: Lift your hips up into a side plank position by driving your forearm and foot into the floor. Keep your shoulders and hips perpendicular to the ground and pull the belly button in towards your spine to engage the abdominals and stabilize the core. Lift the hips up until they form a straight line with the bottom shoulder and ankle. Gently lower back down to the floor and repeat the movement. *Hike the hip up for either time (i.e. time) or perform 1-3 sets of 5-15 reps.*

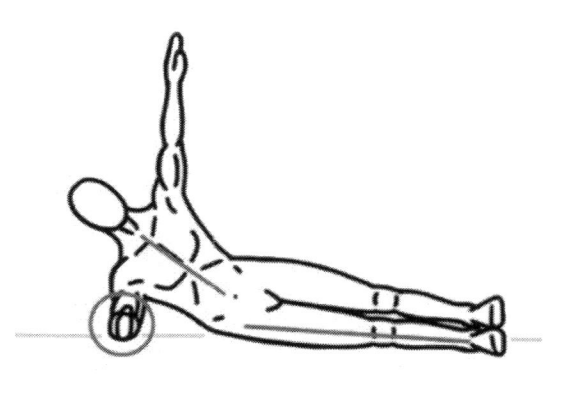

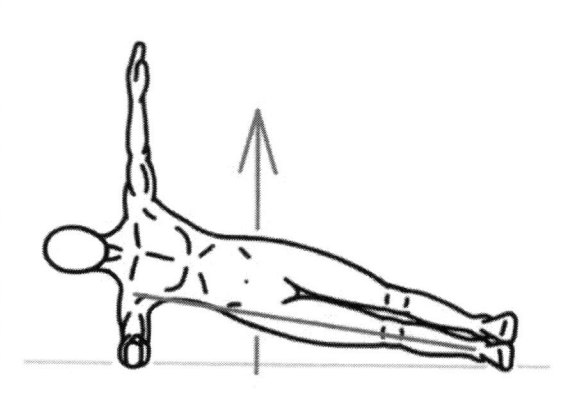

STABILITY

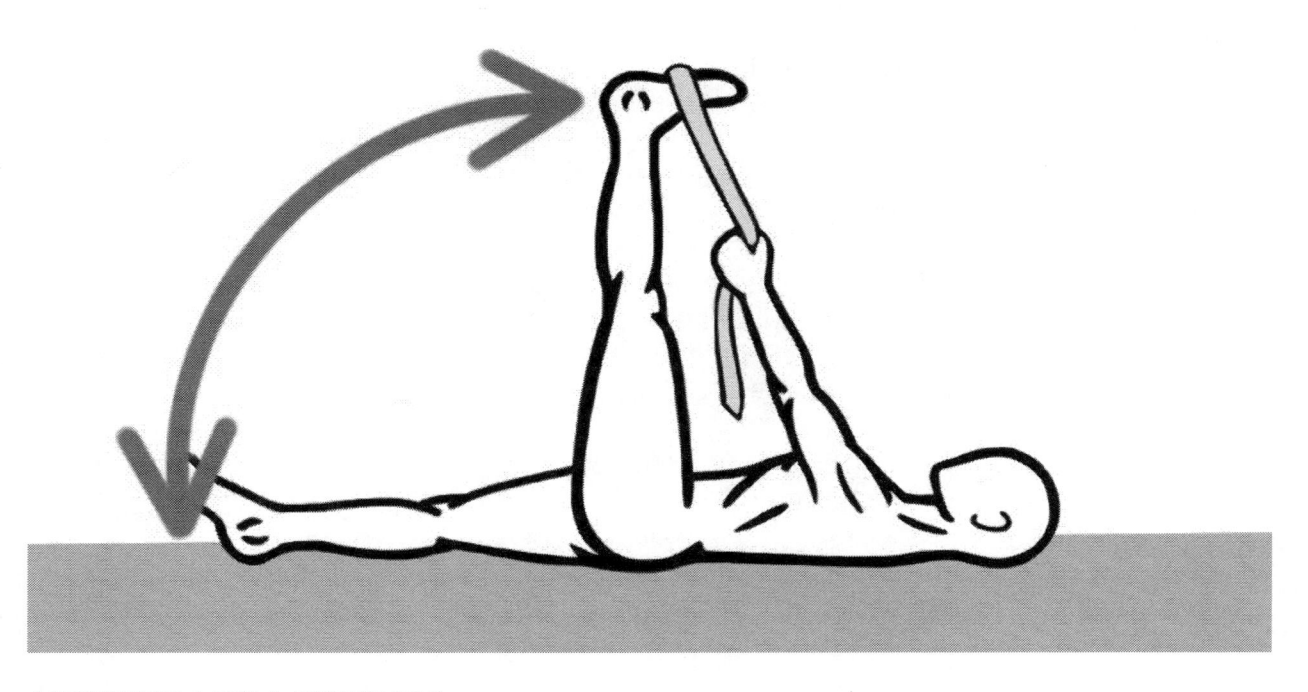

ASSISTED LEG-LOWERING
This exercise will help you to stabilize your hip in the swing phase of your gait, which is when you pull your leg forward for another stride, and it will also develop the proper biomechanics of the hip hinge that can help improve your Deadlift and jumping ability.

POSITION: Lie on your back and wrap a strap or towel around on foot as you lift both legs straight up over the hips. Make sure both legs are straight and that your lower back is flat on the floor as you hold the strap tight. Also, squeeze the armpits into the ribs, park the shoulder blades in the back pockets and pull the shoulders down and away from the ears.

ACTION: Lower the free leg down to the floor as you hold the other leg in place with the strap. Keep the legs completely straight and touch the ground with the heel. Then pull the belly button in towards your spine to engage the abdominals and stabilize the core as you lift the leg up and return it to the starting position.

Repeat this movement several times for each leg. Aim for 1-3 sets of 5-15 reps. Also, feel free to include some variations in the sets, such as an isometric hold with the foot an inch off the ground, or perform the rep very slowly on a five-count.

STABILITY

SINGLE-LEG BRIDGE (Two Versions)
In addition to a version of this exercise being used to activate the Glutes, this exercise will help stabilize the hips and build strength in any single leg position such as lunging or running.

POSITION: Lie on your back with one foot planted on the ground and the other leg pulled tightly into the chest or extended up towards the sky. Bend the knee of the planted leg to a 90-degree angle and make sure that the knee is aligned in a straight line with the shoulder, hip and ankle.

Single-Leg Bridge with Heel Reach

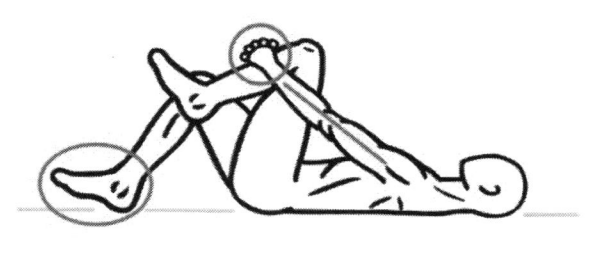

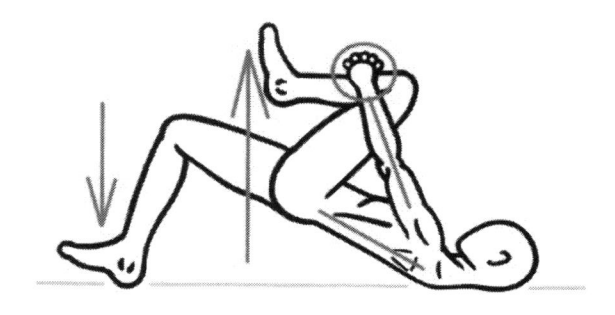

'Locked' Single-Leg Bridge

Also, lift the toes as well as the forefoot off the ground. This adjustment will eliminate using the ankle or foot for stability and place more responsibility on the hips. Lastly, squeeze the armpits into the rib, park the shoulder blades in the back pockets and pull the shoulders down and away from the ears

PreHab Exercise Book for Runners

STABILITY

ACTION: Drive your heel into the floor and press your hips up into the sky. Do not arch your back. Stay long through your spine and pull the belly button in towards your spine to engage the abdominals and stabilize the core as you bridge.

Focus on driving the raised knee (or the upheld foot) straight up into the sky as opposed to driving the knee or leg towards your head. Press the hips up until they diagonally align with the shoulders and knee in a straight line when looking at the body from the side.

Repeat this movement several times for each leg. Aim for 1-3 sets of 5-15 reps. Also, feel free to include some variations in the sets, such as an isometric hold at the top of a rep, three to five pulses at the top or perform the rep very slowly on a five-count.

SIDE PLANK HIP ABDUCTION
This exercise will help develop the lateral aspect of hip stability, which is essential in all single leg movement patterns, such as lunging or running.
Personally, I use this exercise as a barometer of an individual's readiness to run. If one of my clients or players cannot complete 10 reps of this exercise with perfect form, I view it as a red flag for an increased risk of faults on compensations in their mechanics.

POSITION: Start in a side plank position where your shoulders vertically stack over the bottom elbow and the hips are square with the floor at a perpendicular (90-degree) angle. Place one foot on top of the other and align the heels.

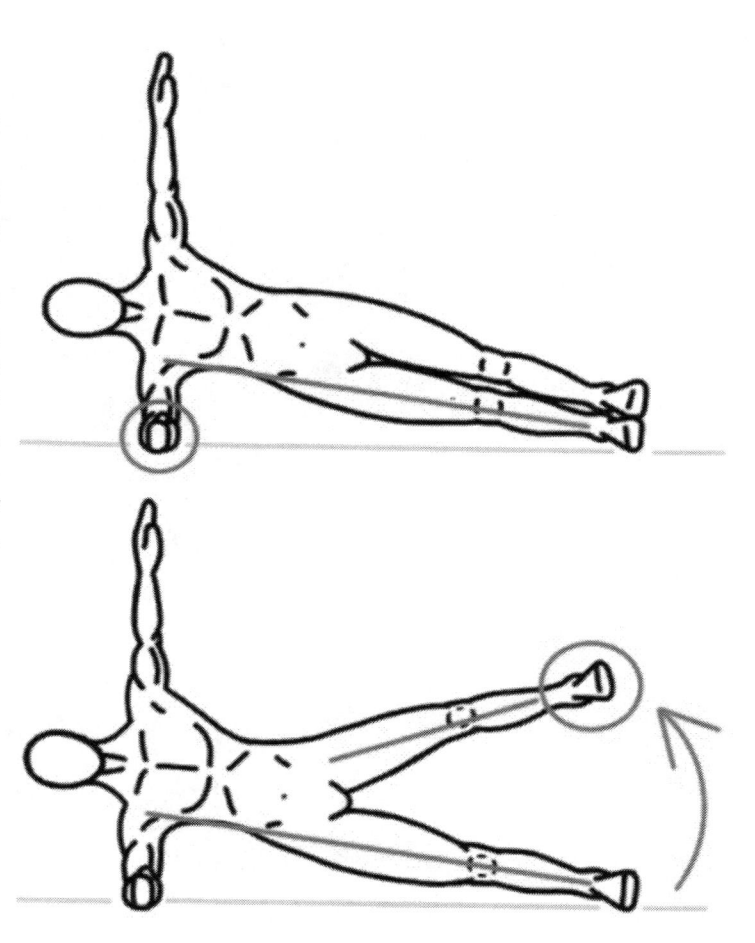

Make sure that your bottom hip is aligned in a straight line with your bottom shoulder and ankle when looking at the body from the side view. From a top view, make sure that the hips are aligned with the shoulders and ankles. Do not allow the hips to pike backwards. Press the hips forward and pull the belly button in towards your spine to engage the abdominals and stabilize the core. Also, squeeze the armpits into the ribs, park the shoulder blades in the back pockets and pull the shoulders down and away from the ears.

STABILITY

ACTION: Lift the top leg up into the air while maintaining a straight line alignment between the bottom hip, shoulder and ankle. Do not let the hips drop or pike. Instead, press the pinkie toe and heel into the ground as well as the entire forearm in order to help brace for and hold alignment. In a controlled manner, keep the feet parallel as you continue to lift and lower the top leg.

Repeat this movement several times for each leg. Aim for 1-3 sets of 5-15 reps. Also, feel free to include some variations in the sets, such as an isometric hold at the top of a rep, three to five pulses at the top or perform the rep very slowly on a five-count.

LEG-LOWERING
This exercise will help you to stabilize your hip in the swing phase of your gait, which is when you pull your leg forward for another stride, and it will also develop the proper biomechanics of the hip hinge that can help improve your Deadlift and jumping ability.

POSITION: Lie on your back with both legs extended straight up into the sky and your arms alongside of your body. Make sure that your lower back is completely flat against the ground and that your knees are as straight as possible.

Press your palms into the floor as you squeeze the armpits into the ribs park the shoulder blades in the back pockets and pull the shoulders down and away from the ears. Lastly, pull the belly button in towards your spine to engage the abdominals and stabilize the core.

ACTION: Lower one leg all the way down to the ground as you brace your core and keep your lower back flat on the ground. Press the arms into the ground to support the movement and touch the heel to the floor with a straight knee.

Next, lift the leg up and return to the starting position. Stay long in the spine and keep the head on the floor. If you have difficulty with this exercise, revert back to the Assisted Leg Lowering to develop your strength and mechanics.

Repeat this movement several times for each leg. Aim for 1-3 sets of 5-15 reps. Also, feel free to include some variations in the sets, such as an isometric hold with the foot an inch off the ground, or perform the rep very slowly on a five count.

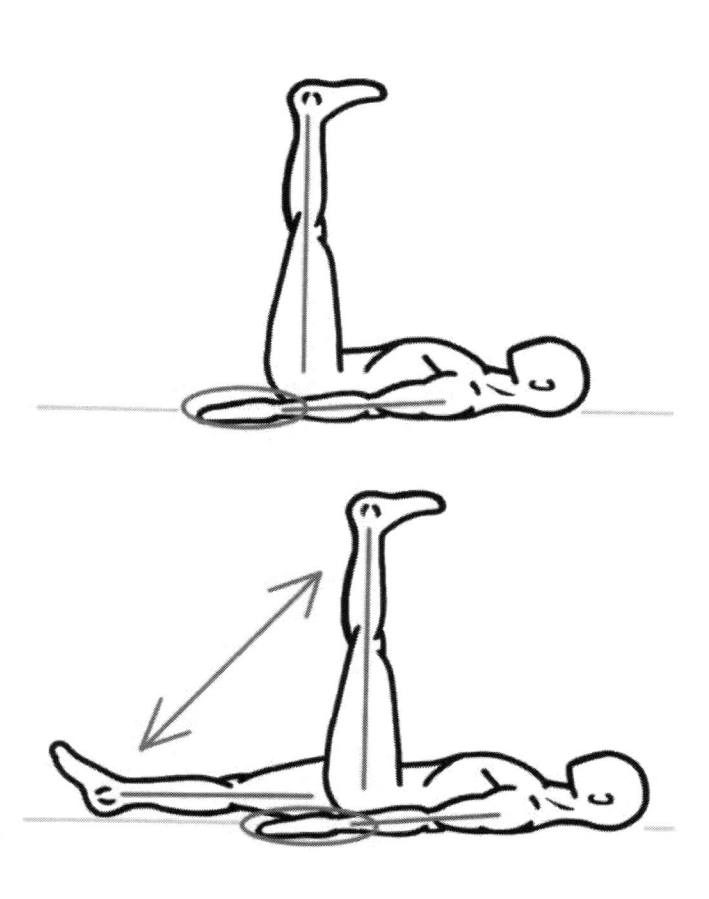

STABILITY

LATERAL SQUAT WALK
This exercise will help develop hip stability in lateral movements as well as a deep-flexed position such as squatting, jumping or changing direction. This exercise can also be used as an activation exercise due to the amount of neuromuscular recruitment it can elicit.

POSITION: Sit down into a squat and attempt to align the hip with the height of the knees. Keep the feet, at least the big toes, parallel with one another and lift your chest up to the sky like Superman. Lengthen your torso and tuck your chin as you maintain neutral alignment of the spine.

ACTION: Laterally step out as wide as possible while staying in a squat position. Do not let your hips pop up or your shoulders drop. Keep your chest lifted as you walk sideways in a squat. Drive into the heel and pinkie as you step to the side and then attempt to bring the feet close together as much as you possibly can when you step together.

Either squat walk sideways for 5-15 reps or alternate stepping from side to side in place. If you choose to work in the alternating fashion, it's more effective to draw a line on the floor or use a cone as a marker and make sure that you clear the line/cone on each and every step. Also, feel free to vary the speed and perform some slow reps.

Lateral Squat Walk: Add Bands for Resistance
Another variation for this exercise is to use a Thera Band wrapped around your thighs or shins by your knees. Bands will provide more resistance that will recruit more neuromuscular activity on each step.

STABILITY

ASSISTED CURTSY LUNGE
This exercise will help create more stability in the hip across two major movement patterns, hip extension and abduction. Additionally, this exercise will help develop power of the hips that can easily translate to the movements of running, jumping and changing directions.

POSITION: Hold on to a pole or railing with both hands as you stand with your feet together. Make sure that the pole or railing can support all of your body weight. You need a solid pole or railing to focus on how your hip and femur (thigh bone) interact. Use this exercise as an opportunity to clean up the mechanics at the hip socket. You will want to develop a smoothness of movement in this joint throughout its full range of motion by gradually lessening the assistance that you create with the pole or the railing.

ACTION: Step one leg back behind and out to the side of the standing leg. Try to touch the knee down on the outside of the standing heel as you keep your shoulders and hips squared off forwards.

Press the hip of the standing leg backwards on a diagonal as if you are pressing your back pocket far away from the pole. Also, deeply flex the hip, knee, and ankle in order to lower the hips down as far as possible and touch the opposite knee to the floor.

Next, drive into the standing heel and press the hip forward on a diagonal back to the starting position. Keep the chest lifted throughout the entire movement and do not arch in your lower back. If you cannot sit your hips down to the height of your knee, go back and do more mobility exercises for the hip.

Repeat this movement several times for each leg. Aim for 1-3 sets of 5-15 reps. Also, feel free to include some variations in the sets, such as an isometric hold with the knee an inch off the ground, or perform the rep very slowly on a five-count.

PreHab Exercise Book for Runners 369

STABILITY

AIRPLANE LUNGE

This exercise is very beneficial to runners and athletes because it offers the opportunity to develop hip stability with a large load. When performed correctly, one individual hip socket will be responsible for organizing position and balance of the entire body, which can translate into better body control, more agility and stable gait.

POSITION: Stand with feet together and the arms raised overhead. Reach the top of the head up towards the sky and lengthen the spine. Pull the belly button in towards your spine to engage the abdominals and stabilize the core. Touch the biceps to your ears and keep them there throughout the entire movement.

ACTION: Slide one leg backwards and reach the foot towards the horizon as you lower your chest towards the floor and reach the arms towards the opposite horizon.
Hinge in the standing hip socket and keep the hips level with the floor. Do not let the hips rotate towards a side. Stay square in the hips and allow the standing knee to bend as you lower the torso. Attempt to touch your stomach to the thigh of your standing leg as you work to hold your arms and back leg parallel to the floor.

Next, drive the hips forward and lift the chest like Superman as you return to the starting position. Reach the top of the head and the fingers up into the sky as you stand to keep neutral alignment in the spine.

Repeat this movement several times for each leg. Aim for 1-3 sets of 5-15 reps. Also, feel free to include some variations in the sets, such as an isometric hold in the airplane position, or perform the rep very slowly on a five-count.

Ready, Set, Go!
With good hip stability, you should be ready for anything – especially any running. You will gain more power, speed, agility and longevity with stable hips. So, don't rush yourself. Get yourself ready and stable. Then go. *It's worth it! Especially, in the long run.*

STABILITY

Ankle Stability
Make the Cut!

Developing the stability of your ankle is essential in running, especially if you are attempting to improve your speed and agility or looking for longevity in this sport.

Our ankles are responsible for absorbing and redirecting forces up to six times our body weight on every single step, which is a hefty responsibility. At the same time, the landing phase in running can happen so quick, that we do not realize just how much stability we have or do not have in our ankles. Yet, we can easily keep running because we have so much forward momentum that we may never be the wiser to even check on how our ankles are holding up.

Penalty Flag
NFL coaches and scouts scrutinize every potential player's ankle stability before they draft that player or trade for them because it is a good predictor of future ACL injuries. So, before an NFL team invests possibly millions in a player, they will discuss what they see in that player's ankle biomechanics, which is certainly a good reason to practice a few stability exercises to say the least.

> ***The probability of non-contact ACL injuries is inversely related to the stability of your ankle.***

Make the Cut
In addition to a football player's attempt to make the final roster, ankle stability plays an important role in your agility. When you cut and change direction, your ankle is responsible for absorbing and redirecting all of your body weight and more – possibly six times more depending on your speed. If your ankle cannot control the momentum of your body due to any weakness or lack of stability, you will not be able to change direction.

> ***The level of your agility is dependent on the level of stability in the ankle.***

Take Control
If you want to reduce the risk of an ACL injury or you want to have a high level of agility, you will want to incorporate stability exercises for your ankle.

STABILITY

Eye Test
Grab a friend and perform the eye test on your ankles as you run. It's simple and can be very informative. You can also do this test by yourself if you have a treadmill and a camera.

Have your friend run in front of you at various speeds and watch what happens at the ankle. Does the ankle stay aligned with the heel and the knee, or does it collapse in or fall out? If your ankle is not staying in line with the heel and the knee, your ankle stability needs to be addressed.

Grab a friend and take turns watching each other's ankles while you run.

Watch the Heel in relation to the Achilles Tendon and Calf Muscles. Determine whether the Ankle will:

Pronate
Supinate
Remain in Neutral

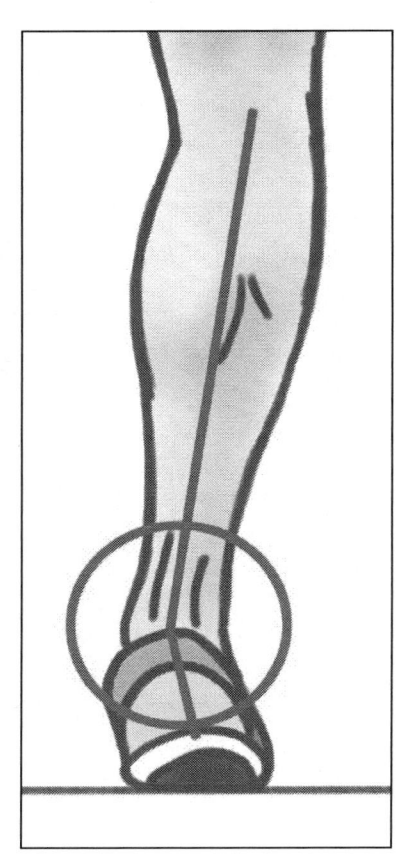

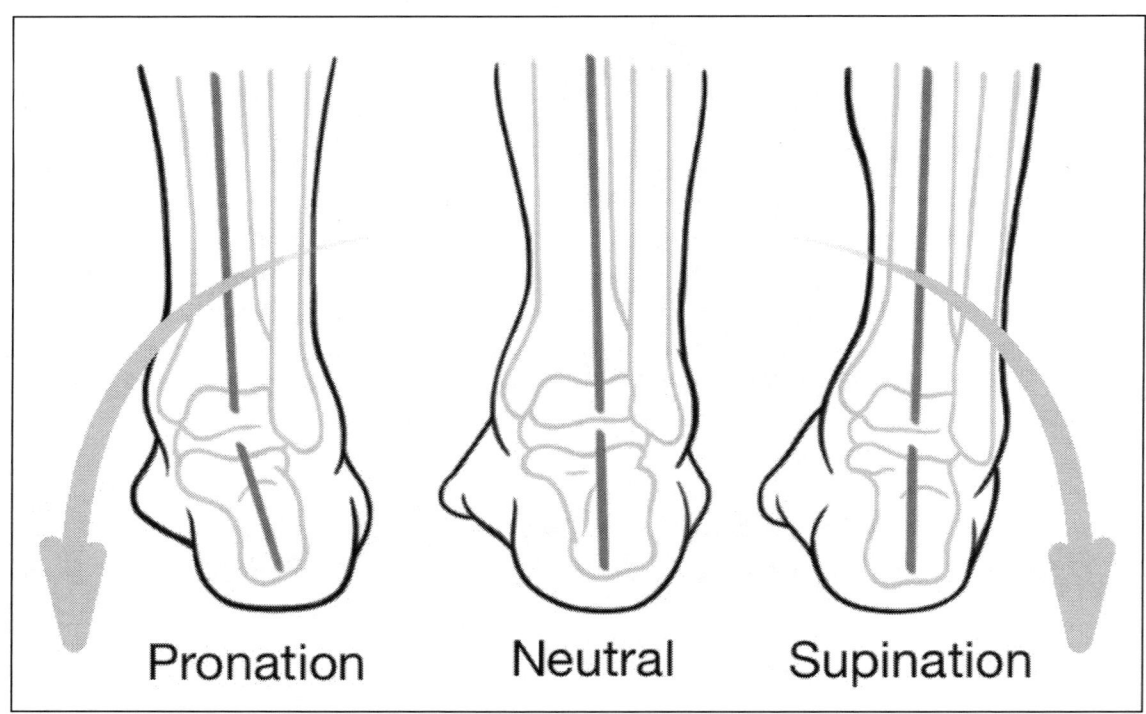

Pronation   Neutral   Supination

Eye Testing the Ankle: Multiple Choice Answers
Rolls In (Pronation) – Remains Aligned (Neutral) – Rolls Out (Supination)

STABILITY

ANKLE PLANTAR FLEXION with Thera Band
This exercise will help you to develop stability throughout the full range of motion of the ankle in flexion. This movement pattern differs from other exercises because it provides resistance without using your full body weight, which helps you to progress through different levels of strength at the joint.

Equipment: Thera Band, Resistance Tube or Towel.

POSITION: In a seated position, wrap a Thera Band around the underside of your foot at the forefoot. You can substitute the Thera Band with a Resistance Tube or Towel, though a Thera Band is preferred since it is more secure than a tube and a towel does not have an elastic quality to it.

Start with the ankle in a dorsiflexed position. Then simply pull the toes back towards the shin and straighten the knee completely as you hold onto the band.

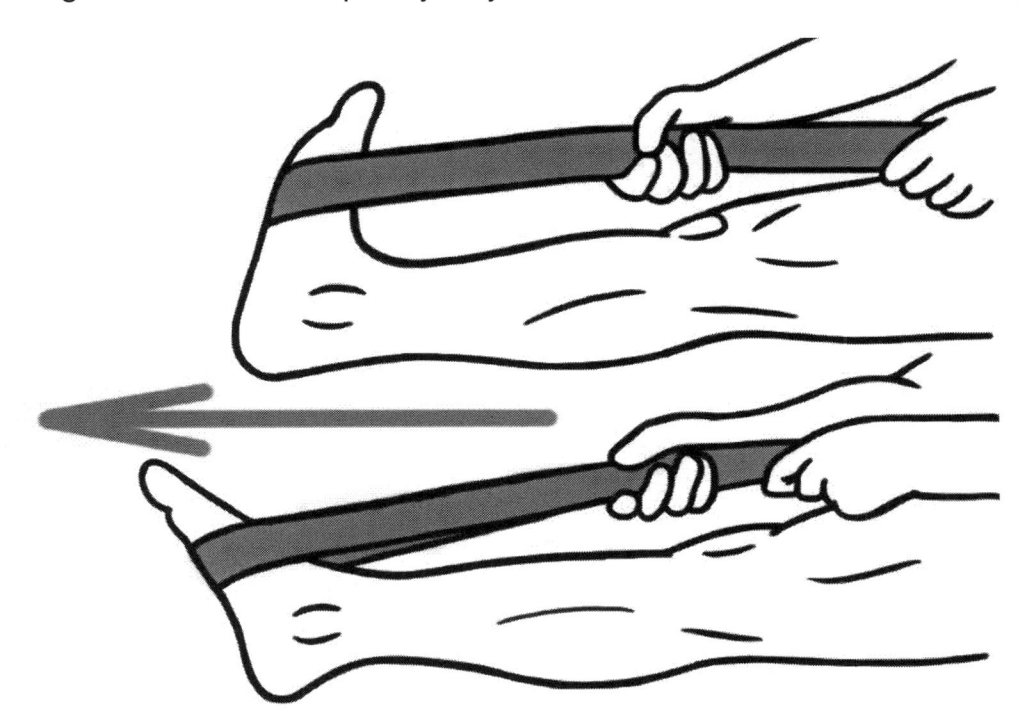

ACTION: Point the toes and press the forefoot away from the shin as far as possible while keeping the ankle in neutral. In other words, make sure that the big toe and pinkie toe are even as you point the toes away from the body.

Keep the knee straight as you reach the foot and start to imagine that you are pulling the heel back towards your hips when you reach the end of your range of motion. Then gently return the foot back to the starting position.

Perform 8-12 reps for 1-3 sets on each ankle.
As you hold the band, adjust the tension in order to make your Perceived Effort (PE) be at a 7+ on a scale of 1-10 throughout the entire movement.

PreHab Exercise Book for Runners

STABILITY

ANKLE DORSIFLEXION with Thera Band
This exercise will contribute to your ankle stability by strengthening the muscles that create the Dorsiflexion and provide full range of motion at the ankle in all activities.

Equipment: Thera Band, Resistance Tube or Towel.

POSITION: Anchor the Thera Band to a secure piece of equipment or pole in front of you as you sit on the ground. You can substitute the Thera Band with a resistance tube, but a band is preferred because it is more secure.

Point the toes and hold the ankle in Plantar Flexion as you slide back from the anchor point and create some tension on the Band.

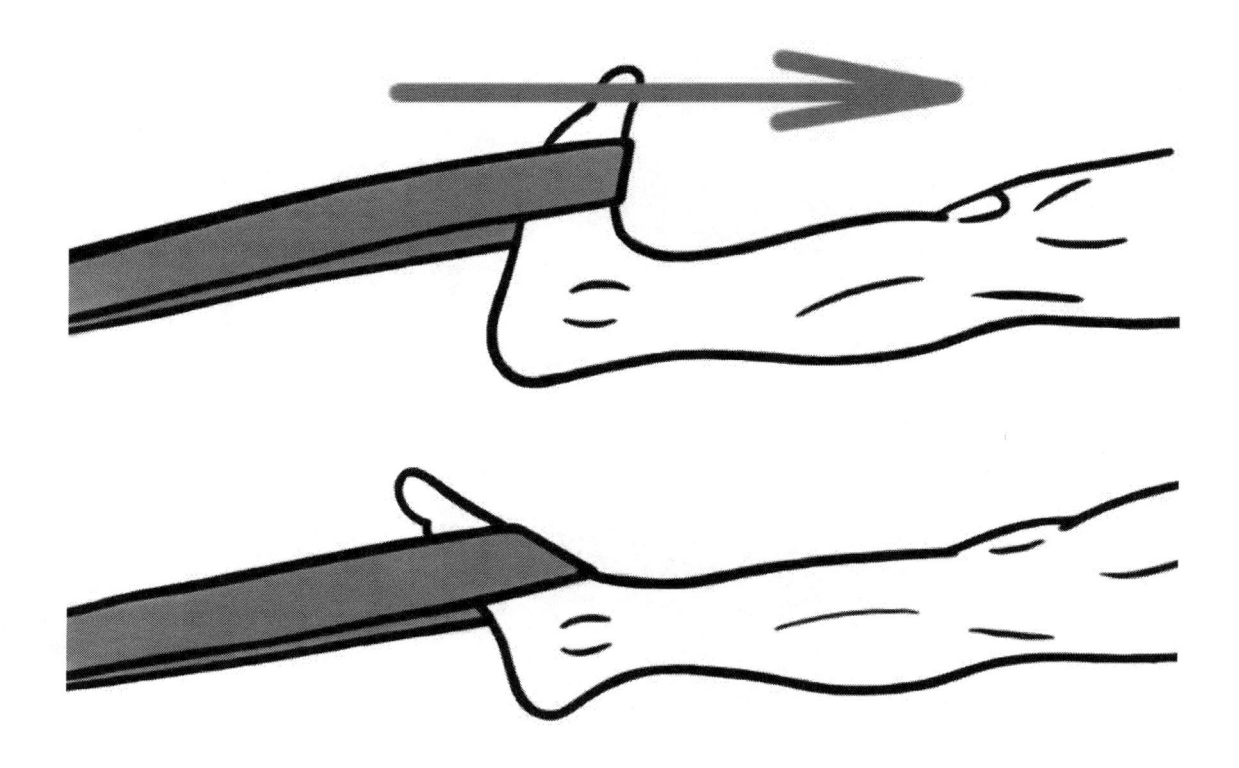

ACTION: Pull the toes back towards your shin as far as you can as you hold your knee straight. Flex the ankle in neutral alignment and avoid inversion or eversion by keeping the big toe even with the pinkie toe as you pull the forefoot back towards the shin.

Perform 8-12 reps for 1-3 sets on each ankle.
As you hold the band, adjust the tension in order to make your Perceived Effort (PE) be at a 7+ on a scale of 1-10 throughout the entire movement.

STABILITY

ANKLE EVERSION with Thera Band
This exercise will help develop strength and stability in the lateral or side to side direction of your ankle, which will help to keep your ankle from collapsing inwards while you run and possible protect you from an ACL injury somewhere down the road. It will also facilitate improvements in one's agility.

Equipment: Thera Band, Resistance Tube or Towel. A Thera Band is preferred due to the elastic quality and also because it can wrap around the foot in a secure position.

POSITION: Wrap the Thera Band around the underside of your forefoot and then snake the outside portion of the band over the front of your shin. Combine it with the other portion of the band as you pull it around the back of your calf and hold it on the outside of you knee. This spiral positioning of the strap should pull your pinkie toe up towards the front middle of your shin.

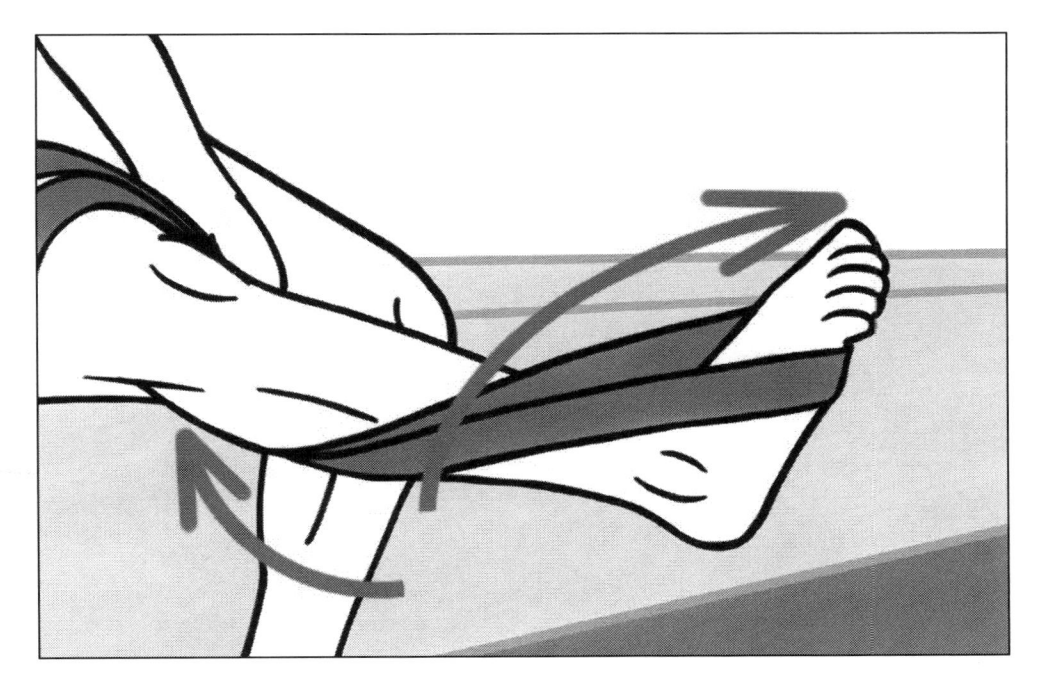

ACTION: Plantar flex the ankle and point the toes away from the shin. Focus on extending through the big toe while rotating the sole of the foot out towards the outside of the body (away from the midline), as that will produce the eversion action at the ankle.

Keep the knee straight as you reach the foot and start to imagine that you are pulling the heel back towards your hips and the outside edge of your foot towards the inside of your ankle when you reach the end of your range of motion. Then gently return the foot back to the starting position.

Perform 8-12 reps for 1-3 sets on each ankle.
As you hold the band, adjust the tension in order to make your Perceived Effort (PE) be at a 7+ on a scale of 1-10 throughout the entire movement.

STABILITY

ANKLE INVERSION with Thera Band
This exercise will help develop more ankle stability and facilitate improvements in one's agility in a lateral direction as well. Limitations or weakness in eversion of the ankle is not as common as in inversion. However, performing stability in both directions will help create balance at the ankle joint.

Equipment: Thera Band, Resistance Tube or Towel. A Thera Band is preferred due to the elastic quality and also because it can wrap around the foot in a secure position.

POSITION: Wrap the Thera Band around the underside of your forefoot and then snake the inside portion of the band over the front of your shin and combine it with the other portion of the band as you pull it around the back of your calf and hold it on the inside of you knee. This spiral positioning of the strap should pull your big toe up towards the front middle of your shin.

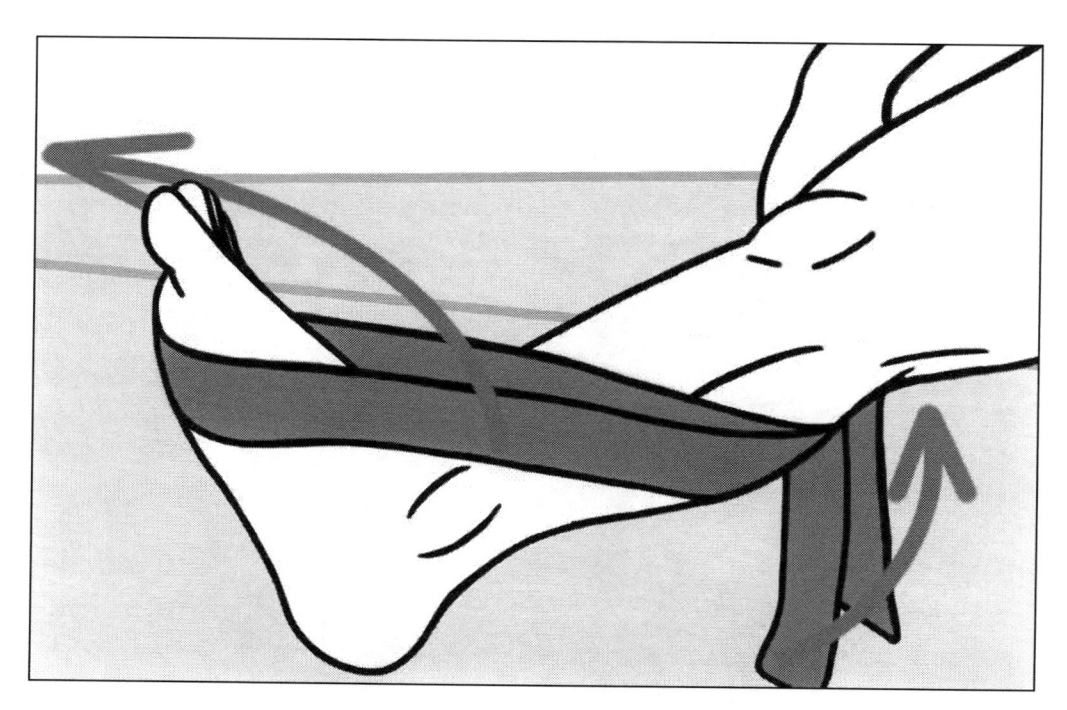

ACTION: Plantar flex the ankle and point the toes away from the shin. Focus on pointing the little toe as much as possible as you rotate the sole of the foot in towards the middle of the body. This will produce the inversion action at the ankle.

Keep the knee straight as you reach the foot and start to imagine that you are pulling the heel back towards your hips when you reach the end of your range of motion. Then gently return the foot back to the starting position.

Perform 8-12 reps for 1-3 sets on each ankle.
As you hold the band, adjust the tension in order to make your Perceived Effort (PE) be at a 7+ on a scale of 1-10 throughout the entire movement.

STABILITY

Unstable Surfaces

Another way to develop more stability at the ankle is by performing movements on an unstable surface. This technique will introduce more instability in the mechanics of the ankle joint and quickly stimulate a host of Proprioceptors throughout the entire ankle and foot complex that will help the body to coordinate movement with more balance and control.

These exercises intentionally activate the Proprioceptors of the lower leg and foot. These sensory neurons are continuously monitoring the body's position in space and relaying reflexive messages throughout the neuromuscular system in order to coordinate movement.

Equipment and Techniques
Now, there are many different ways to create unstable surfaces as well as just increasing the perceived instability of the body. The most important element in this type of training is safety first and foremost, followed by effectiveness and practicality. So, always make sure that you are working out in a safe environment and take the correct precautions before attempting these exercises.

Eyes Closed- simply closing your eyes as you move will force your body to coordinate balance, stability and movement without the visual component of your motor control unit in your brain. This variation in itself will facilitate a lot more communication among your Proprioceptors and neuromuscular system. Yet, it also increases your risk of falling or bumping into objects as you move.

Balance Pad- this square foam pad works very well to activate your Proprioceptors. The texture of this pad will absorb much of the ground reaction forces that your body is accustomed to using when coordinating movement. The pad essentially interferes with a feedback loop of your body and the environment and will force your body to send more messages through your neuromuscular system via the proprioceptors that will train your body to communicate faster and more creatively.

Stability Disc- this inflatable disk plays a very similar role to that of the Balance Pad. It will interfere with the neuromuscular system's ability in coordinating movement, and force it to create new strategies and perform faster communication within itself.

STABILITY

Towels - probably the easiest "unstable surface" to create. Simply fold up a towel until it reaches approximately 1-2 inches in height and you have a very similar effect to that of the Balance Pad and Stability Disk. The main disadvantage is that the towel is not built with the same level of reflexive or reactive texture to that of the Balance Pad and Stability Disk.

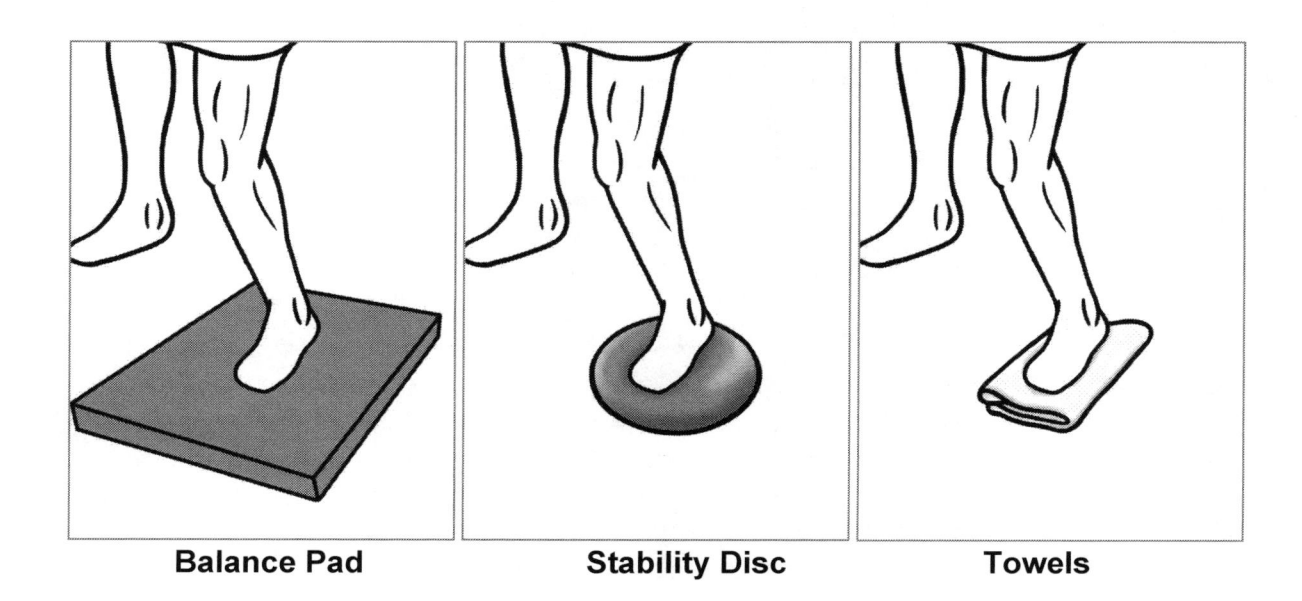

Balance Pad **Stability Disc** **Towels**

Integrating Instability into Exercises

We can integrate a level of instability into just about any exercise we choose. Yet, when it comes to developing more ankle stability, there are four exercises that we can focus on and gain a lot of benefit from. They are:

- **Single-Leg Heel Lift**
- **Single-Leg Rotation**
- **Single-Leg Toe Touch**
- **Compass Reaches**

Before you perform any of these exercises on an unstable surface or with your eyes closed, make sure that you can perform these movements with correct form and under control.

STABILITY

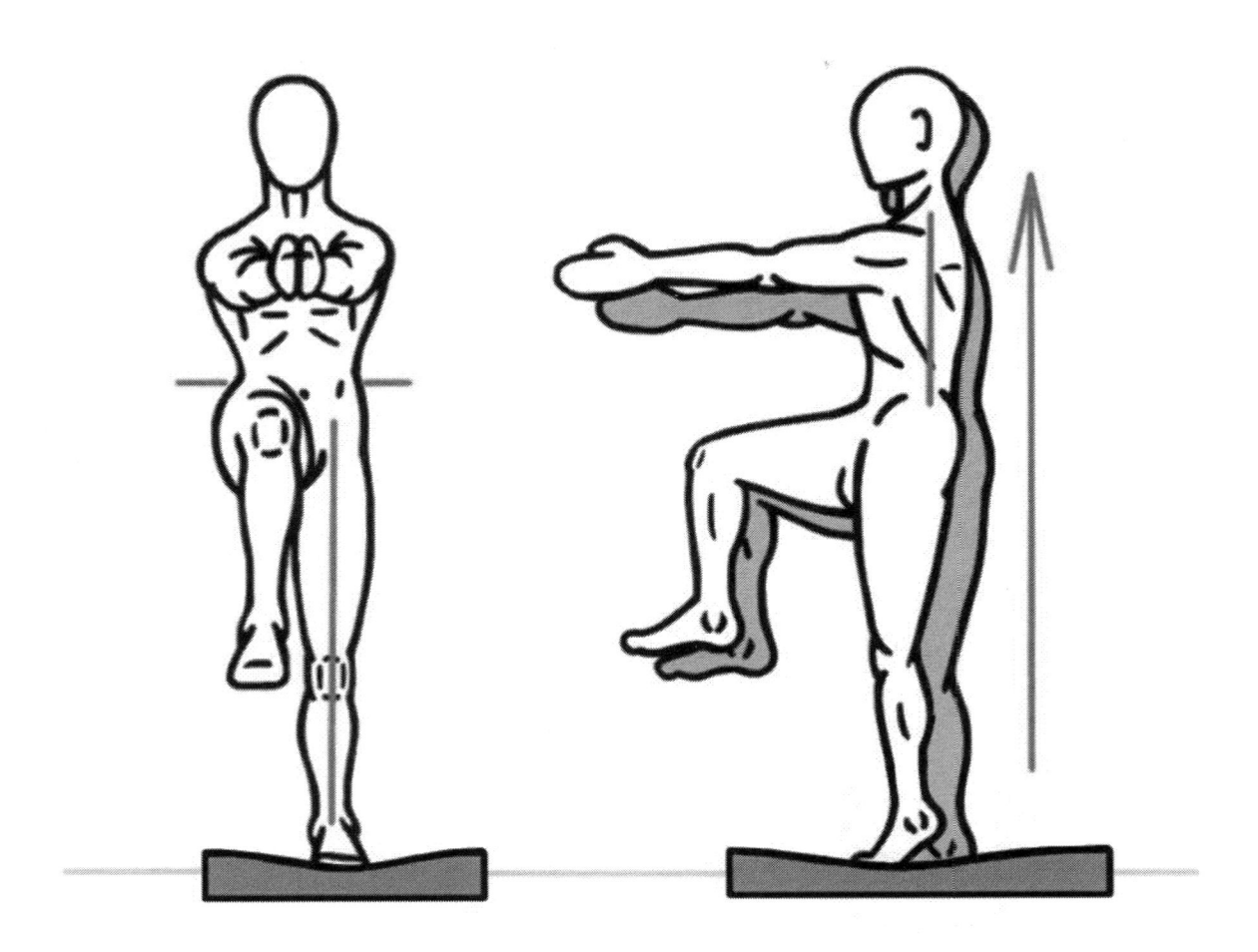

SINGLE-LEG HEEL LIFT (Unstable Surface)
POSITION: Lift one knee to hip height and stand with arms parallel to the ground with palms pressed together. Focus the eyes on the horizon and lengthen the spine.

ACTION: Press into the forefoot and lift the standing heel off the ground while maintaining focus on the horizon. Drive the top of your head straight up into the sky and pull the belly button in towards the spine to engage the abdominals and maintain alignment over the standing heel.

Perform between 10-15 reps for 2-3 sets on the floor with correct form before progressing to unstable surfaces or the closed eyes techniques. When you have progressed to this next level, reduce the reps to 3-8 reps per set until you feel proficient at the movement. Then progress to a higher amount of reps.

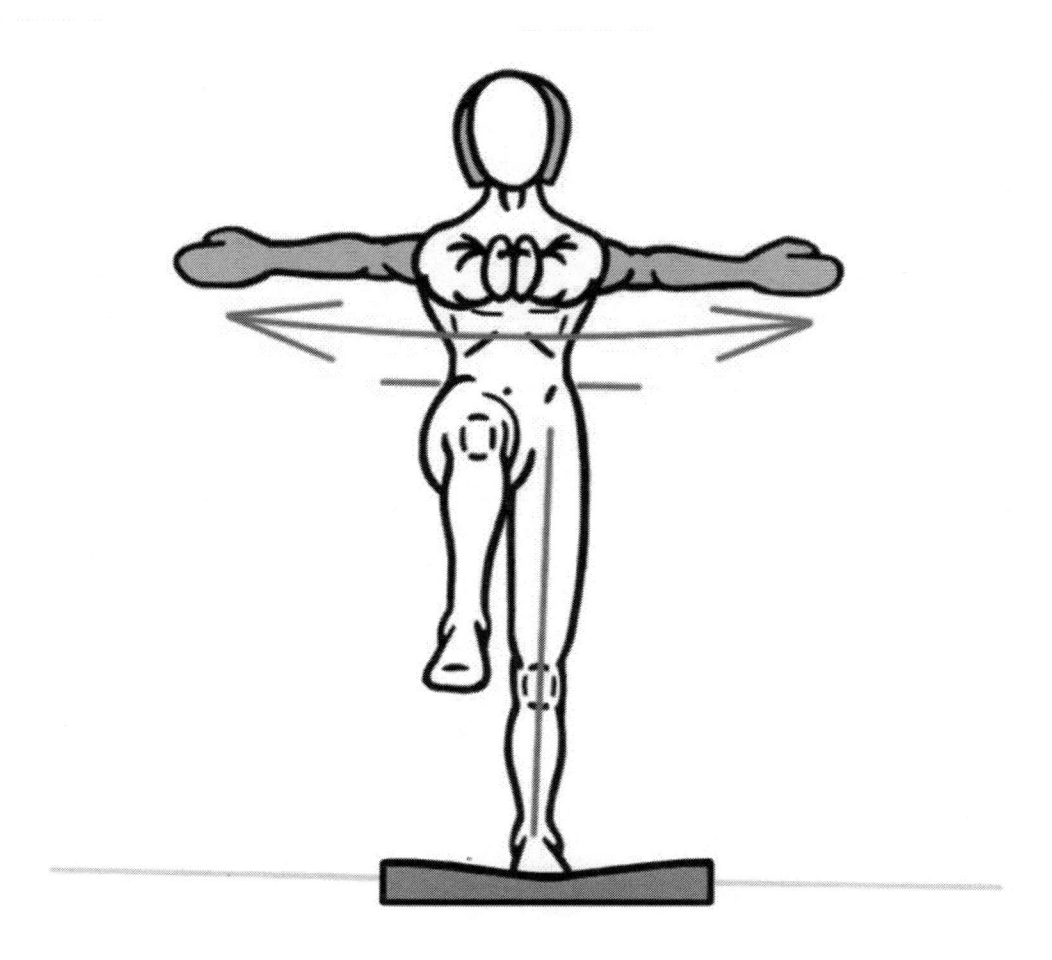

STABILITY

SINGLE-LEG ROTATION (Unstable Surface)
POSITION: Stand on one leg with arms parallel to the ground and palms pressed together. Lift the opposite knee to hip height and establish balance. Focus the eyes on the horizon and lengthen the spine.

ACTION: Rotate the arms 45 degrees to the left and right and keep your eyes on your hands throughout the entire movement. Pull the belly button in to engage the abdominals and attempt to maintain neutral alignment over the standing heel. Do not protract your shoulders forward. Relax your trapezius muscles and turn your sternum towards each side as you rotate. Also press your pinkie toe into the ground to help create more lateral stability in the standing leg.

Perform between 10-15 reps for 2-3 sets on the floor with correct form before progressing to unstable surfaces or the closed eyes techniques. When you have progressed to this next level, reduce the reps to 3-8 reps per set until you feel proficient at the movement. Then progress to a higher amount of reps.

STABILITY

SINGLE-LEG TOE TOUCH (Unstable Surface)
POSITION: Stand on top of an Airisks Pad, Dyno Disk or Towel with one foot lifted up into the air.

ACTION: Extend the lifted leg back towards the horizon in order to lower your opposite hand down to touch your standing toes or a spot on the floor near your standing foot. Keep the standing knee vertically behind your toes. Allow the knee to bend as you lower the torso and straighten the knee as you stand up. Also, stay long through your spine and attempt to touch your stomach to the top of your standing thigh as you balance on one foot.

Imagine that you can press evenly into the four corners of your foot:

Big Toe
Pinkie Toe
Inside Heel
Outside Heel

STABILITY

Next, drive the hips forward and lift the chest as you stand up. Be sure to pull the belly button into your spine to engage the abdominals and stabilize the core as you press the top of your head up into the sky.

Perform between 8-10 reps for 2-3 sets on the floor with correct form before progressing to unstable surfaces or use the closed-eyes techniques. When you have progressed to this next level, reduce the reps to 3-5 reps per set until you feel proficient at the movement. Then progress to a higher amount of reps.

COMPASS REACHES (Unstable Surface)
With the right training exercise, you can improve your own level of fitness, agility, and running mechanics. The Compass Reach is a perfect exercise for anyone who is lacking hip and ankle stability, and wants to step up their game.

POSITION: Stand on one foot and imagine you are at the center of a large compass. It is helpful to have actual lines on the ground to indicate the different directions: north, south, east, west, northeast, southeast, northwest and southwest.

ACTION: Slowly reach your raised foot in each direction while maintaining balance on one leg. Do not touch the ground with the reaching leg. Lower down into a squat in order to reach out as far as possible.

Keep your shoulders square to the front and aligned over your standing toes. Reach your foot in each direction while maintaining balance and then switch legs.

Perform at least one round of Compass Reaches on the floor before progressing to an unstable surface or using the closed-eyes technique. Then perform anywhere from 3-6 rounds on each leg.

STABILITY

Reach: South

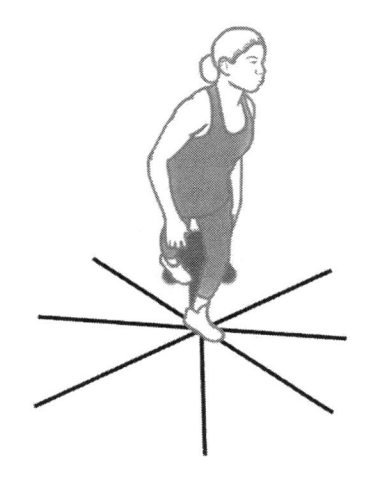

Reach: Southwest

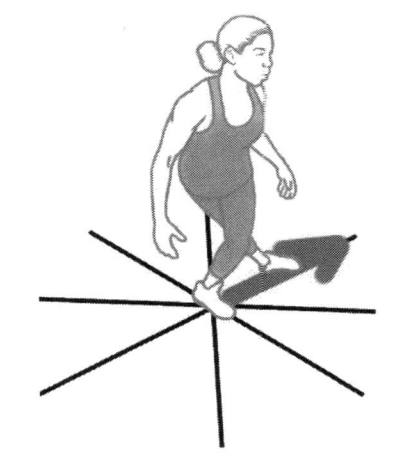

Reach: West

Reach: Southeast

COMPASS REACHES

All EIGHT DIRECTIONS

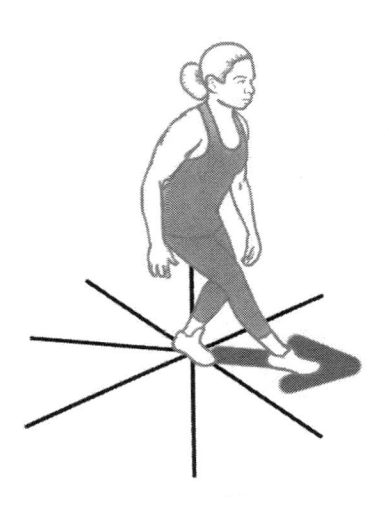

Reach: Northwest

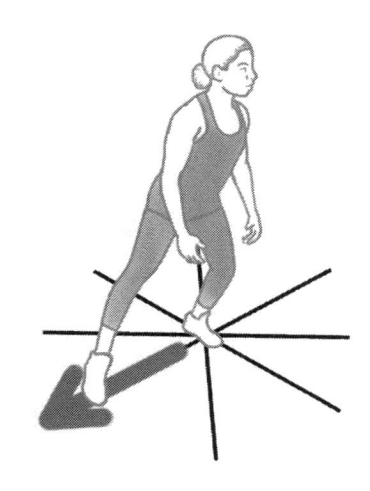

Reach: East

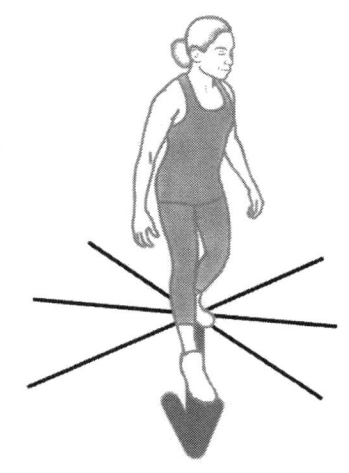

Reach: Northeast

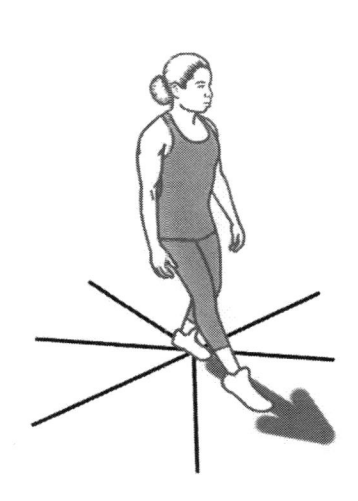

Reach: North

PreHab Exercise Book for Runners

STABILITY

Instant Replay

Ankle stability is very important to your longevity in running, especially if you are an athlete who also wants to perform with a high level of agility. Therefore, an additional tool that you can use is video.

You can benefit a lot from video recording yourself during exercise and watching how your ankle responds and stabilizes itself through all of these exercises. Having visual evidence will give you a more accurate perspective on exactly how stable of a foundation you have while running or playing your sport.

As they say, a picture is worth a thousand words and you can make some of those words be: agility, stability, longevity, speed, quickness, cutting, alignment, biomechanics, and more.

STABILITY

Combination Exercises for Stability

Developing the ability to stabilize the entire body throughout the full range of motion in larger movement patterns will enhance your performance in any work out, sport or life activity.

The following Combination Exercises provide the opportunity for the neuromuscular system to develop stability in large movement patterns and create more control in task-orientated activities that you may perform in your training or sport.

In other words, these exercises will challenge your body's ability to create controlled movement that will help you to perform at your highest level, achieve better results or reach specific goals in your training collectively.

Master Lock by Zoo Fari

"Golden Rule"
Evaluate each complete movement and assess the performance of every joint involved to accurately make adjustments and address specific faults or dysfunctions in your biomechanics.

Stability Progression
This sequence of exercises will gradually progress in the level of difficulty.
Use the exercises that are appropriate for your level of Stability.

STABILITY

SIDE PLANK ROTATION

This exercise will help develop stability in: *Shoulders/Shoulder Girdle, Core, Hips (Lateral Aspect) & Ankle (Lateral Aspect).*

Use in PreHab Routines for: *Running, Agility, Throwing & Rotation.*

POSITION: Bridge off the ground in a side plank on the elbow with the shoulders and hips vertically square to the floor and the bottom ankle, hip and shoulder all aligned in a straight line. Place the top hand behind the head.

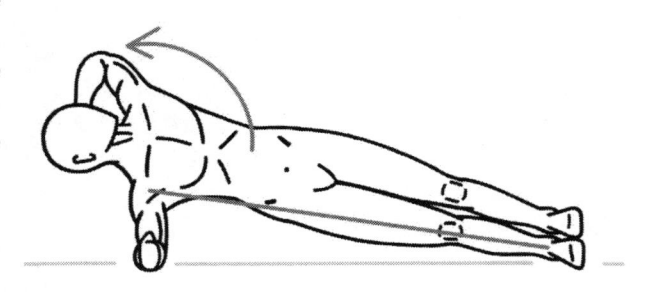

ACTION: Rotate the top elbow towards the horizon behind the body and then rotate down to touch the bottom hand with the top elbow while maintaining a straight-line alignment of the bottom ankle, hip and shoulder.

Perform 2-3+ sets of 5-10+ reps on each side.
If you cannot perform controlled reps of this exercise with proper form, either reduce the number of reps and sets or regress to another stability exercise that will target the intended areas.

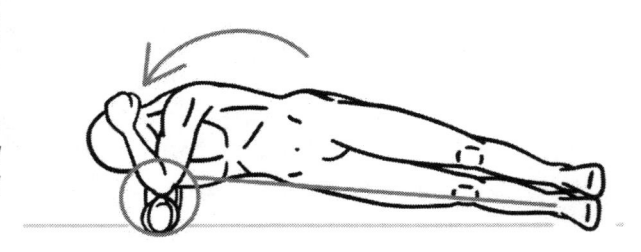

SIDE PLANK (ELBOW) ROTATED REACH

POSITION: Bridge off the ground in a side plank on the elbow with the shoulders and hips vertically square to the floor and the bottom ankle, hip and shoulder all aligned in a straight line.

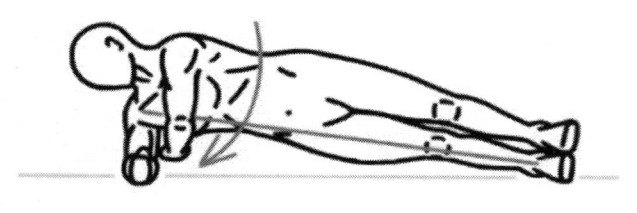

ACTION: Rotate the torso and reach the top arm under the bottom armpit as far as possible before reversing the rotation and extending the top arm over the body, reaching the hand towards the horizon behind the body. Maintain a straight-line alignment of the bottom ankle, hip and shoulder.

Perform 2-3+ sets of 5-10+ reps on each side.
If you cannot perform controlled reps of this exercise with proper form, either reduce the number of reps and sets or regress to another stability exercise that will target the intended areas.

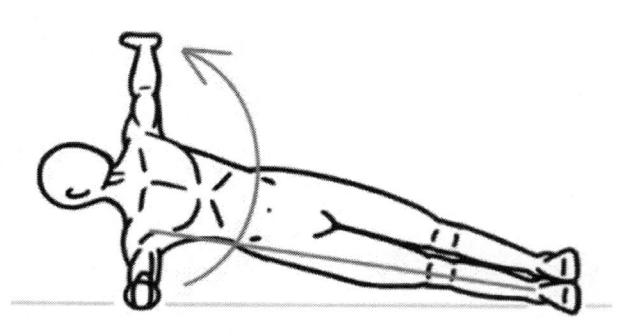

STABILITY

SIDE PLANK HIP ABDUCTION

This exercise will help develop stability in: *Hips, Ankle (Lateral Aspect), Core (Lateral Aspect) & Shoulders/Shoulder Girdle.*

Use in PreHab routines for: *Running, Agility, Balance & Lunging.*

POSITION: Bridge off the ground in a side plank on the elbow with the shoulders and hips vertically square to the floor and the bottom ankle, hip and shoulder all aligned in a straight line.

ACTION: Lift the top leg up towards the sky with the feet parallel to one another. Also, keep the shoulders and hips vertically square to the floor throughout the movement to maximize work in the top hip.

Perform 2-3+ sets of 5-10+ reps per leg. If you cannot perform controlled reps of this exercise with proper form, either reduce the number of reps and sets or regress to another stability exercise that will target the intended areas.

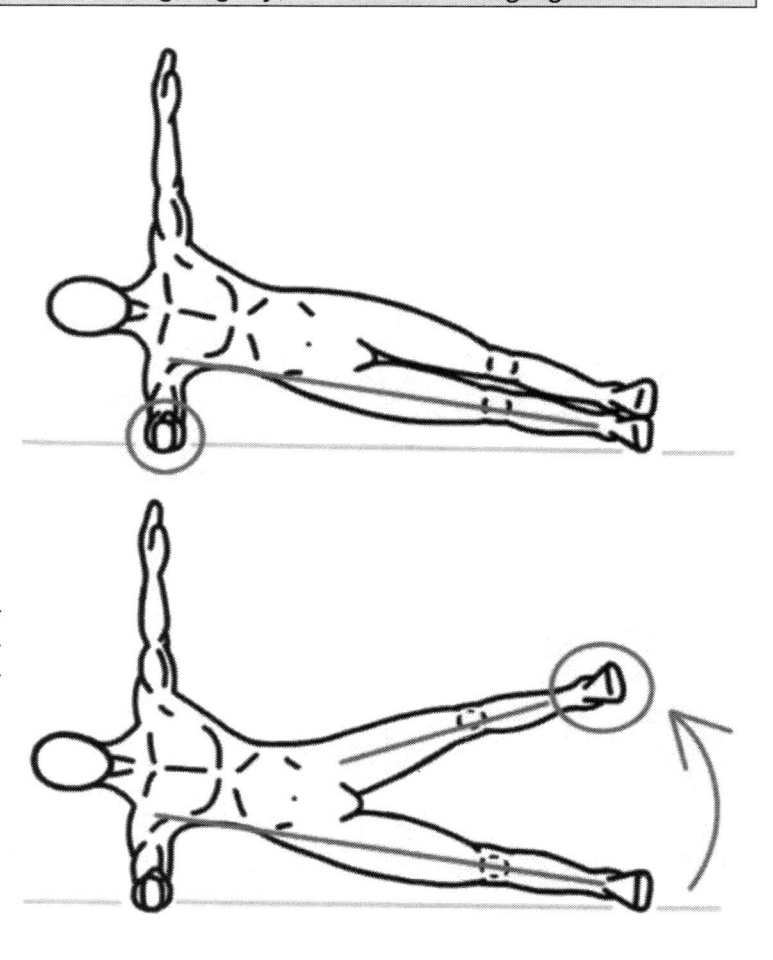

TALL CABLE CHOP

This exercise will help to activate and stabilize the core, shoulder and hips, which is also referred to as the pillar of all movement. In addition to improved stability, this exercise will help you develop coordinated movements through the pillar and help you to integrate and use the pillar (core, shoulders and hips) as one unit.

This exercise will help develop stability in: *Core, Shoulders & Hips.*

Use in PreHab routines for: *Running Sprinting, Lunging, Rowing, Pressing/Pushing, Pulling, Throwing, Rotating & Spinal Flexion/Extension.*

Equipment: Adjustable Cable machine with rope extension.

POSITION: Kneel on both knees with hips positioned over the knees with a vertical neutral spine. This position is called "Tall Kneeling."

STABILITY

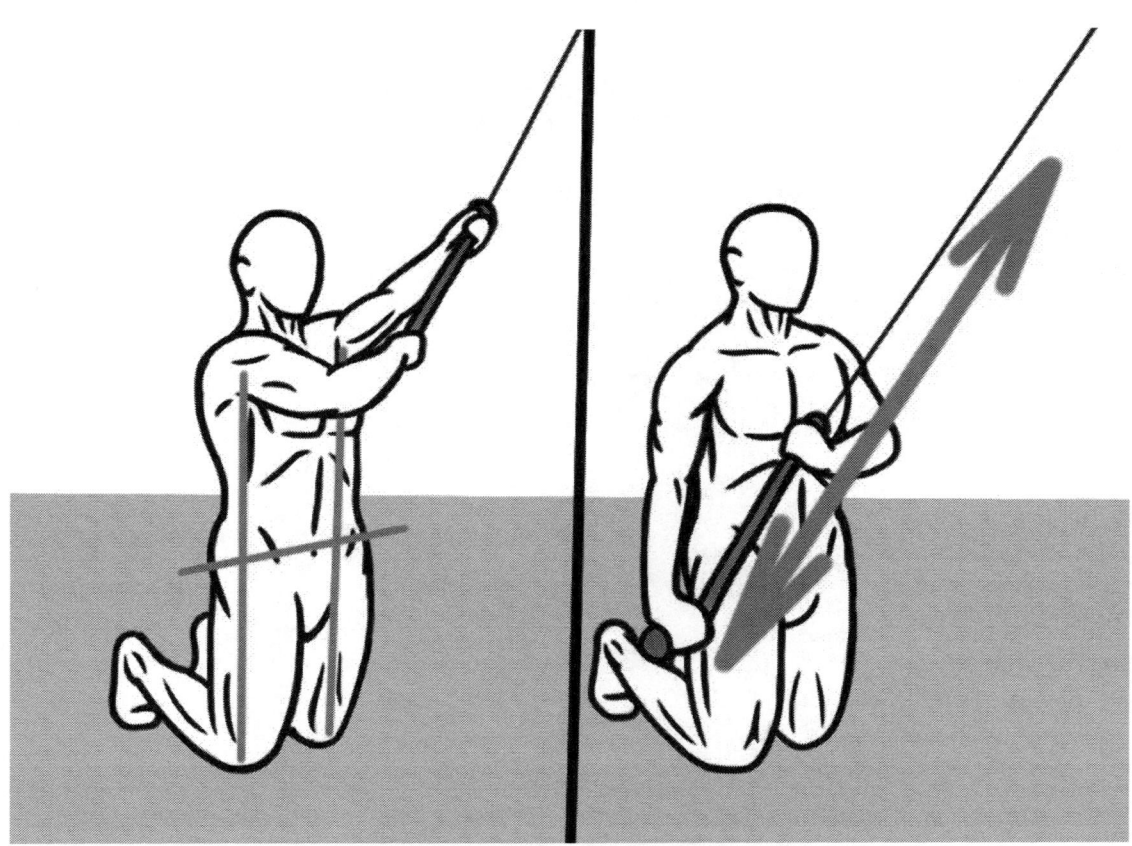

Tall Cable Chop: Start & Finish

Slide the rope completely to one side of the cable junction in order to make it as long as possible. Place one hand at either end of the rope.

Position yourself far enough away from the machine that the cable will cross your chest at a 45-degree diagonal. Also, make sure that the cable crosses the body in a parallel fashion with the shoulders and hips are perpendicular to the machine. Start with your arms fully extended on a diagonal-up towards the cable insertion on the machine.

ACTION: Pull the cable across the body down towards the floor on a diagonal pattern. Keep the cable close to the body as it passes the chest and reach the bottom hand as close to the ground as possible while maintaining a tall, vertical spine.

Lift the chest and squeeze the armpits into the ribs. Park the shoulder blades in the back pockets and pull the shoulders down and away from the ears. Also, pull the belly button in towards your spine to engage the abdominals and stabilize the core.
Return the arms to the starting position in a controlled and smooth motion to complete the rep.

- *Perform 5-15 reps on either side to activate and integrate the core, shoulders and hips.*
- *Vary the exercise by performing the reps very slowly or pausing in the bottom position.*
- *Perform 2-3 sets of 10-15 reps on each side to develop more stability and integrate the core, shoulders and hips.*

STABILITY

MEDICINE BALL LIFT (MB Reverse Wood-Chop)

This exercise will help develop stability in: *Hip, Ankle & Core.*

Use in PreHab routine for: *Running, Agility, Jumping, Lunging, Throwing & Balance.*

POSITION: Stand with your feet at shoulder-width apart and hold a Medicine Ball (MB) out in front of your body with straight arms. Make sure that the toes are pointed forward and parallel with one another.

ACTION: Squat down and rotate the shoulders to reach the MB down to the floor directly to your side. Push the hips backwards and press your thighs wide in order to lower down as far as possible. Keep both feet flat on the ground.
Reach as far as possible with your arms while you maintain a long spine and keep your chest lifted. Rotate through the torso and aim the MB for a target on the floor that shoulder be perpendicularly aligned with the arch of your feet.

Next, drive your hips forward as you stand up, rotate and reach the MB up to the sky on a large diagonal swing. Pivot the rear foot inwards and lift the heel up off the ground as you rotate the hips and shoulders to follow the MB.

Extend the MB up and away from your body as far as possible while aiming for a target that is perpendicularly aligned with the arch of your foot on the other side. Lengthen the

STABILITY

entire body and pull the belly button in towards your spine to engage the abdominals and stabilize the core as you extend your arms. Also, squeeze the armpits into the ribs. Park the shoulder blades in the back pockets and pull the shoulders down and away from the ears to create stability in the shoulders. Gently repeat the entire movement several times on each side.

- *Perform 2-3+ sets of 5-10+ reps on each leg.*
- *Start with a slow pace and gradually increase the speed of the movement.*
- *Important Note: Reduce the speed if you begin to lose balance or alignment while performing the movement.*

ELEVATED SPLIT SQUAT

This exercise will help develop stability in: *Hip, Ankle & Core.*

Use in PreHab routines for: *Running, Agility, Balance, Coordination, Lunging & Jumping.*

POSITION: Stand and extend one leg backwards to place the foot on a bench or box with sole of foot facing up. Stand at a distance that will allow the back leg to be almost straight while you keep the hips aligned squarely with the shoulders and bottom foot.

ACTION: Squat with the standing leg and rotate through the torso as if running. Press the hips backwards and bend deeply in the standing hip, knee and ankle to create Triple Flexion.

Reach the back knee down towards the floor as you press the top of your head up to the sky and keep the chest lifted. Also, pull the belly button in towards your spine to engage the abdominals and stabilize the core as you rotate and squat. Next, drive the hips forward and lift the chest as you return to standing. Make sure that the hips align directly under the shoulders and above the standing ankle. Press the top of the head up into the sky as high as possible.

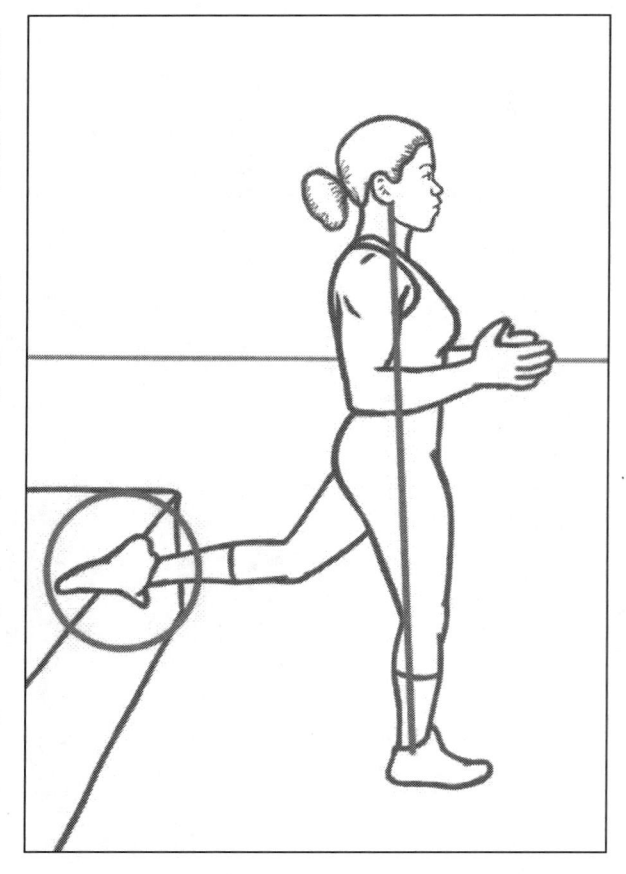

STABILITY

Press your pinkie toe into the floor to help create more balance while standing and keep your eyes on the horizon as much as possible when performing this movement.

Gently repeat this movement several times on each side.

- *Perform 2-3+ sets of 5-10+ reps on each leg.*
- *Start with a slow pace and gradually increase the speed of the movement.*
- *Important Note: Reduce the speed if you begin to lose balance or alignment while performing the movement.*

PreHab Exercise Book for Runners

STABILITY

HIGH LATERAL LUNGE

This exercise will help develop stability for: *Posterior Chain, Hip & Ankle.*

Useful in PreHab routines for: *Running, Agility, Jumping, Squatting, Hip Hinging (Deadlifts) & Lunges.*

POSITION: Extend your arms out to the side and parallel to the ground to measure your foot position. Step each foot out and vertically align them with your elbows. Next, turn both feet parallel with one another and point the toes forward.

Weight Option: Hold a dumbbell vertically in one arm.

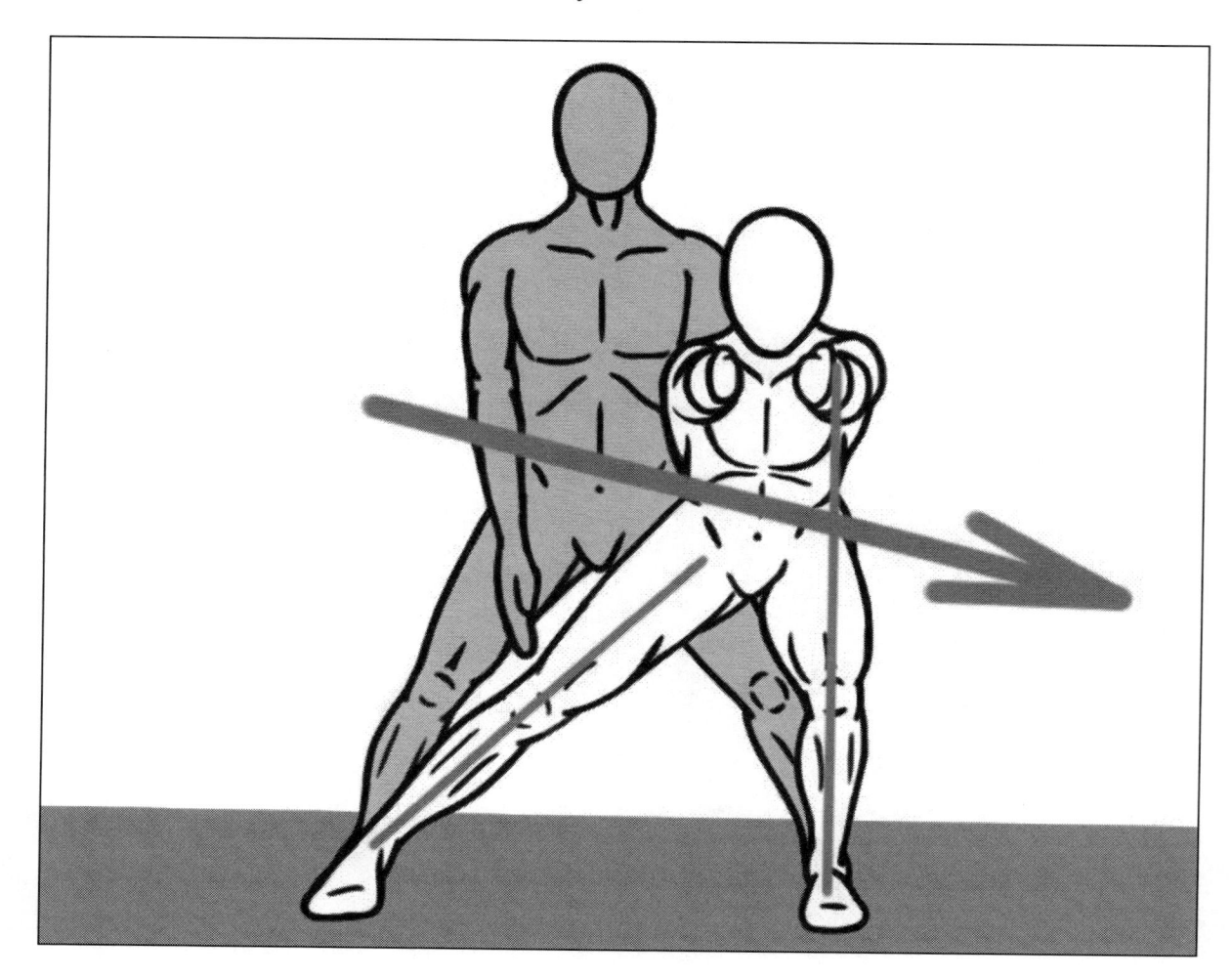

ACTION: Bend one leg and slide the hips backwards and to that side as you hold a dumbbell in one hand. Press the hips back towards the horizon as you bend your knee. Lower the hips down until you reach 90-degree angles in your hip and knee. Do not let your knees press out in front of you toes as it will create more stress on the kneecap. Instead, drive the hips backwards towards the horizon behind you and press the thigh out laterally to help create more depth. Keep the chest lifted and the spine in neutral alignment. This will strengthen the Thoracic spine.

STABILITY

Attempt to align the shoulder, hip and ankle of the lunging side all in the same vertical plane. Use a mirror or a partner to spot you on this alignment.

Next, press your foot into the ground and drive your hips forward to return to the starting position.
- *Perform between 8-10 reps for 2-3 sets on the floor with correct form before adding a load (i.e. using a barbell or other weight.)*
- *If not perfect with form, reduce the reps to 3-5 reps per set until you feel proficient at the movement. Then progress to a higher amount of reps.*

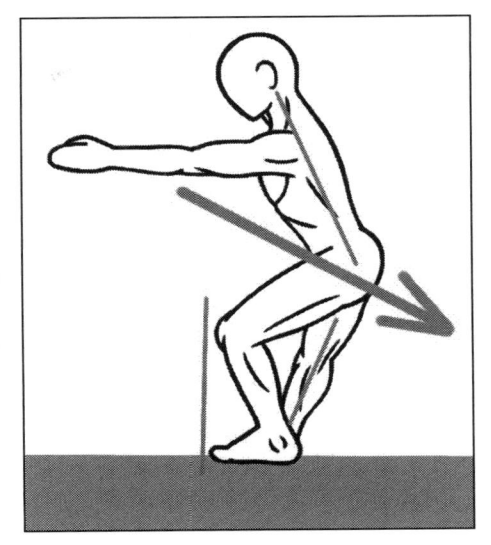

SINGLE-LEG BOX SQUAT

This exercise will help develop stability for: *Posterior Chain, Hip & Ankle.*

Useful in PreHab routines for: *Running, Agility, Jumping, Squatting, Hip Hinging (Deadlifts) & Lunges.*

POSITION: Sit on a bench that matches the height of the knee and lift one foot off the ground. Hold the arms parallel to the ground at shoulder-width and lengthen the spine.

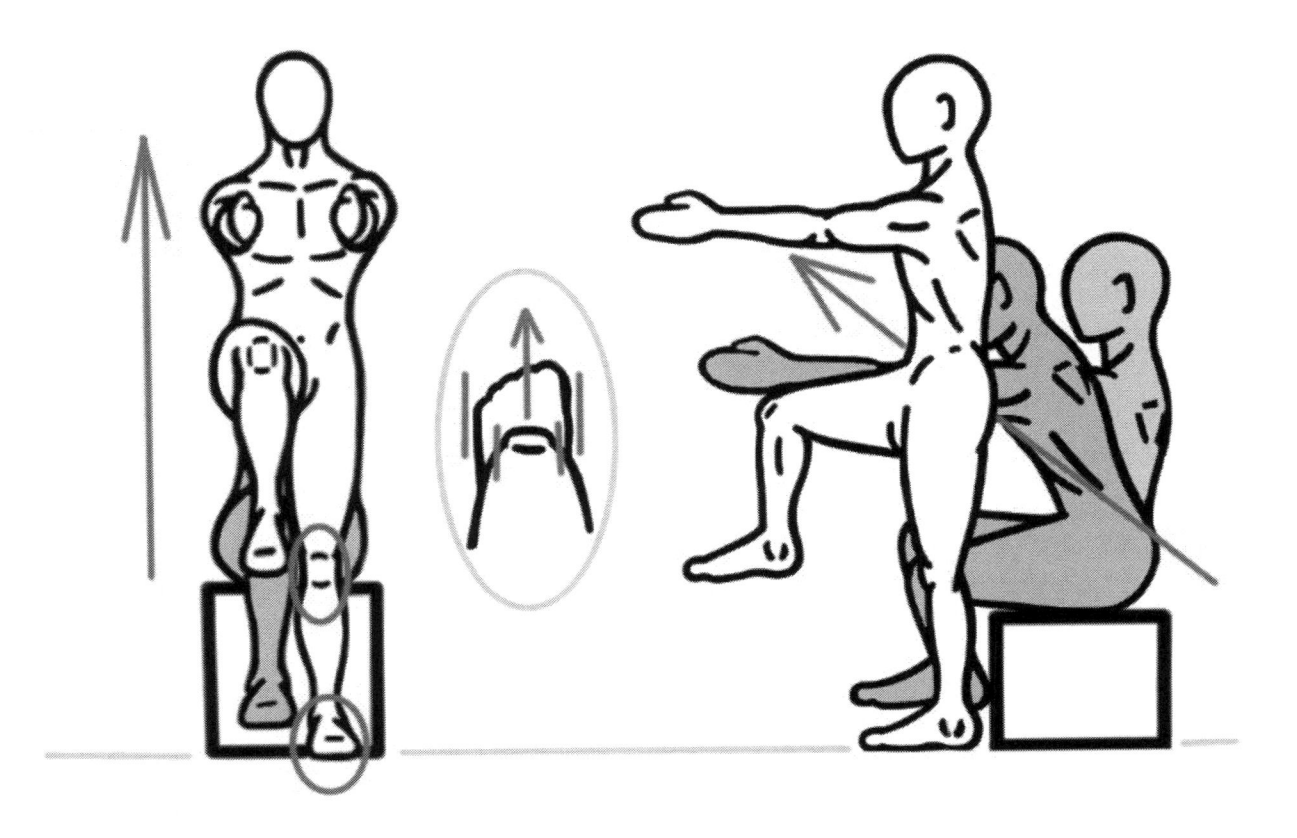

PreHab Exercise Book for Runners

STABILITY

ACTION: Stand up onto one leg while maintaining balance. Make sure that the standing knee tracks over or to the outside of the foot as this will help protect the ACL and knee joint from extra stress. Keep the chest lifted and extend the arms for counter balance. Press the hips forward until they vertically align with the head, spine and standing ankle.

Weight Option: Hold a dumbbell against the chest with both hands.

The goal of this exercise is to practice the squat mechanics on a single-leg in order to develop more stability in the hip and ankle. These are the main guidelines to follow:

LOWER HIPS TO KNEE HEIGHT
DO NOT LET KNEES PASS IN FRONT OF TOES
SQUAT ON SINGLE-LEG WHILE KEEPING BALANCE.
DO NOT LET THE KNEE COLLAPSE INSIDE THE FOOT

- *Perform between 8-10 reps for 2-3 sets on the floor with correct form before adding a load (i.e. using a barbell or other weight.)*
- *If not perfect with form, reduce the reps to 3-5 reps per set until you feel proficient at the movement. Then progress to a higher amount of reps.*
-

Alternative Position: Stand on top of a box or bench with one leg hanging off to the side in order to perform a single-leg squat or a modified pistol squat.

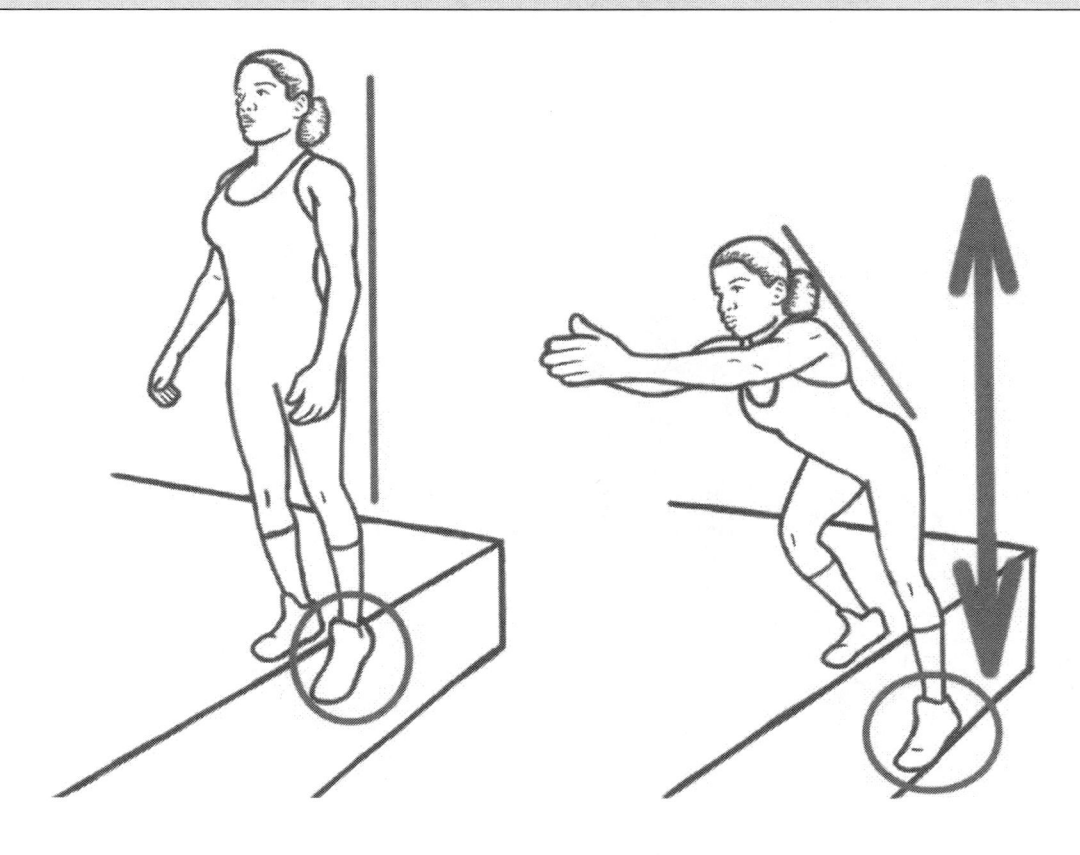

STABILITY

ACTION: Lower down into a single-leg squat by reaching the hang foot down towards the floor. Reach the arms forward for counter balance and pull the belly button in towards the spine to engage the abdominals and help maintain a stable spine. Then drive the box down into the floor with the squat-leg and stand up tall. Use the same rep prescription as above.

SINGLE-LEG TOE TOUCH

| This mobility exercise will help develop stability for: *Posterior Chain, Hip, Ankle & Core.* |
| Useful in PreHab routines for: *Running, Agility, Jumping, Squatting, Hip Hinging (Deadlifts) & Lunges.* |

POSITION: Start in a tall, standing position with your eyes focused on the horizon. Shift your weight onto one leg in order to easily lift the other leg up into the air.

ACTION: Lower your torso towards the floor and reach for the standing foot with your opposite hand as your extend the back leg straight out towards the horizon behind you. Attempt to lay your torso on top of your standing thigh as you keep your hips level with

STABILITY

the floor and maintain balance. Bend your knee slightly.

Touch your toe and then stand up tall once again as you gaze back out at the horizon. Repeat several times on each leg.

Repeat this movement several times for each leg. Aim for 1-3 sets of 5-15 reps.
Advanced versions: Perform reps on Unstable Surfaces, such as a Balance Pad, or increase your speed on each rep while still maintaining balance and accuracy.

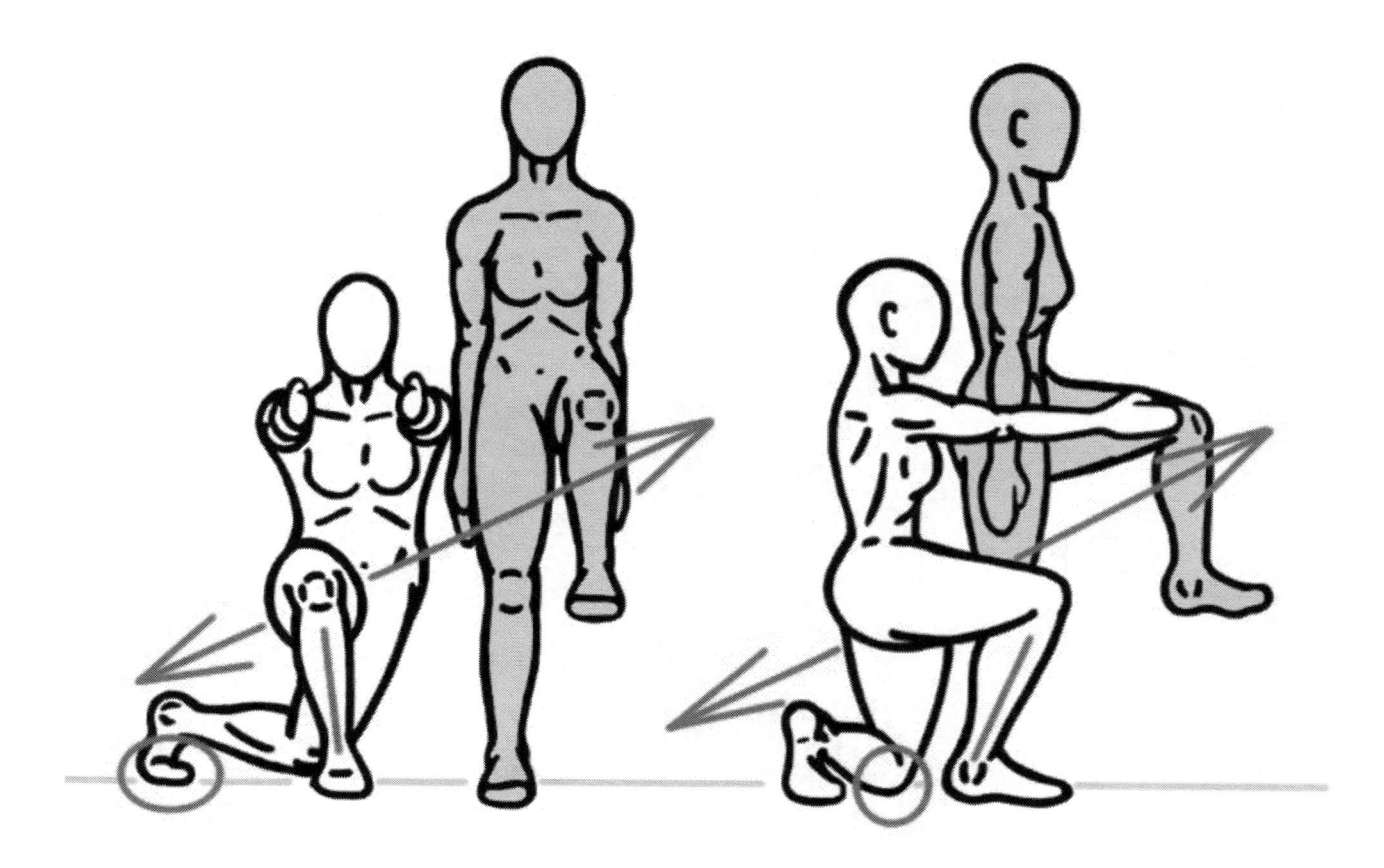

CURTSY LUNGE

This mobility exercise will help develop stability for:
Posterior Chain, Hip, Ankle & Core.

Useful in PreHab routines for: *Running, Agility, Jumping, Squatting, Hip Hinging (Deadlifts) & Lunges.*

POSITION: Stand tall on one leg with the opposite knee tucked to hip height.

ACTION: Step the raised leg back and behind the standing leg while sliding the hips directly backwards and reaching for the horizon with both arms. Lift the chest, sit at the hips and bend the knees. Then drive the hips forward and come back to the original

STABILITY

standing position on one leg, quickly establishing balance before starting the next lunge. This exercise will develop more lateral stability in each leg.

Weight Option: Hold a dumbbell against the chest with both hands.

- *Perform between 8-10 reps for 2-3 sets on the floor with correct form before adding a load (i.e. using a barbell or other weight.)*
- *If not perfect with form, reduce the reps to 3-5 reps per set until you feel proficient at the movement. Then progress to a higher amount of reps.*

DEEP LATERAL LUNGE

> This mobility exercise will help develop stability for:
> *Posterior Chain, Hip, Ankle & Core.*
>
> Useful in PreHab routines for: *Running, Agility, Jumping, Squatting, Hip Hinging (Deadlifts) & Lunges.*

POSITION: Extend your arms out to the side and parallel to the ground to measure your foot position. Step each foot out and vertically align them with your elbows. Next, turn both feet parallel with one another and point the toes forward.

Weight Option: Hold a dumbbell vertically in one arm.

ACTION: Bend one leg and slide the hips backwards and to that side as you hold a dumbbell in one hand. Press the hips back towards the horizon as you bend your knee.

STABILITY

Lower the hips down until they reach the height of your knee. This is more difficult and requires more mobility that the High Lateral Lunge. At the same time, you will develop more strength and coordination throughout a large range of motion in this lateral movement pattern, which will help develop more stability and improve agility and jumping abilities.

Do not let your knees press out in front of you toes as it will create more stress on the kneecap. Instead, drive the hips backwards towards the horizon behind you and press the thigh out laterally to help create more depth.

Keep the chest lifted and the spine in neutral alignment. This will strengthen the Thoracic spine.

Attempt to align the shoulder, hip and ankle of the lunging side all in the same vertical plane. Use a mirror or a partner to spot you on this alignment.

Next, press your foot into the ground and drive your hips forward to return to the starting position.

- *Perform between 8-10 reps for 2-3 sets on the floor with correct form before adding a load (i.e. using a barbell or other weight.)*
- *If not perfect with form, reduce the reps to 3-5 reps per set until you feel proficient at the movement. Then progress to a higher amount of reps.*

SINGLE-LEG DEADLIFT (SL DL)

This exercise will develop stability for: *Hip, Ankle & Core.*

Use in PreHab routines for: *Running, Sprinting, Jumping, Squatting & Hip Hinging.*

POSITION: Stand tall while holding dumbbells or a barbell (optional) and lift one foot off the ground. Make sure that your spine is in neutral alignment and is vertically stacked over your hip and standing ankle. Tuck your chin into your throat to stabilize your neck and keep your head in neutral position as you perform this exercise.

Also, pull the belly button in towards the spine to engage the abdominals and stabilize the spine as you squeeze the armpits into the rib cage. Park your shoulder blades into your back pockets and pull the shoulders away from the ears to stabilize the shoulder girdle.

ACTION: Extend the lifted leg back towards the horizon in order to lower your opposite hand down to touch your standing toes or a spot on the floor near your standing foot. Keep the standing knee vertically behind your toes. Allow the knee to bend as you lower the torso and straighten the knee as you stand up. Also, stay long through your spine

STABILITY

and attempt to touch your stomach to the top of your standing thigh as you balance on one foot.

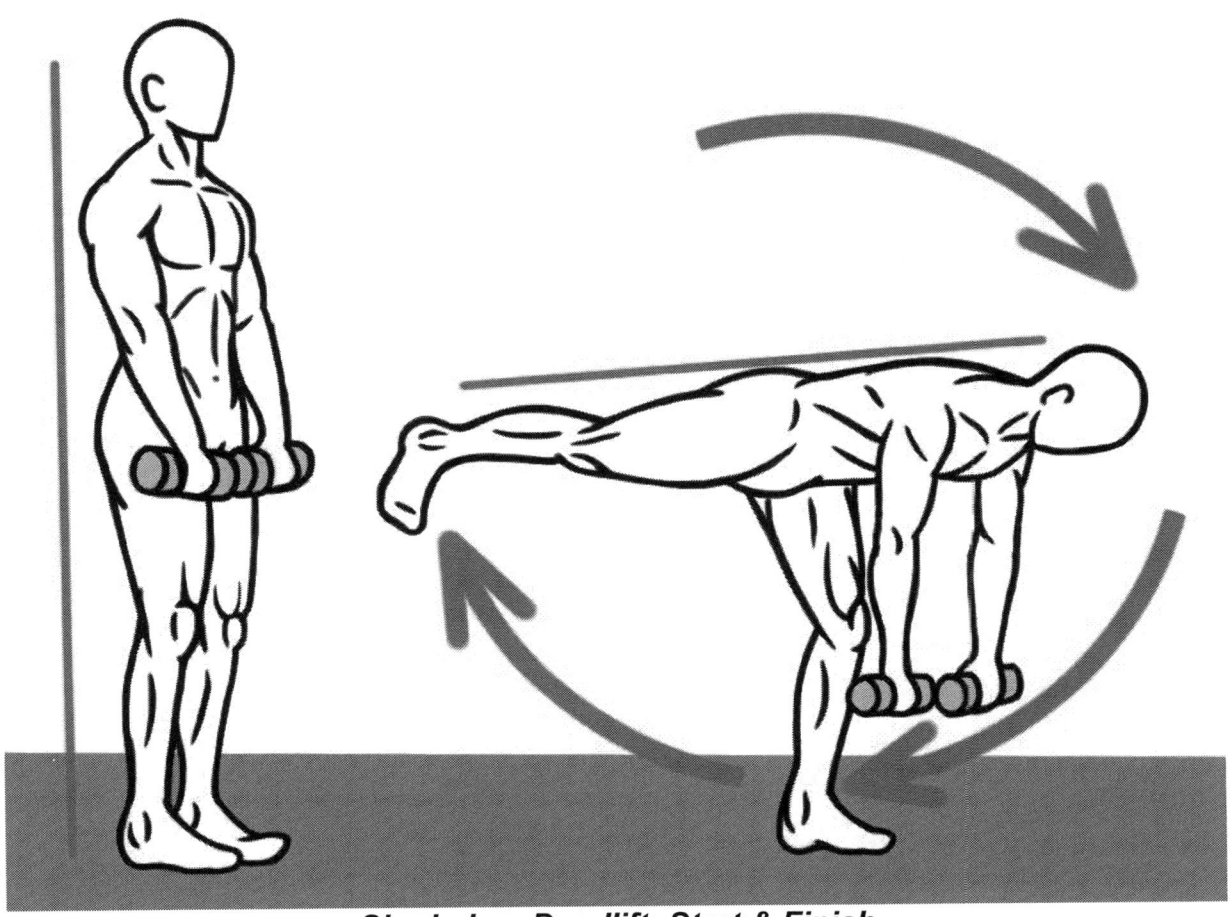

Single-Leg Deadlift: Start & Finish

Direct the barbell down towards your toes in a straight vertical line. Do not let it swing out in front or in towards your body. Also, keep the barbell level to the ground and stop lowering down when the barbell reaches the approximate middle of your shin.

> *Imagine that you can press evenly into the four corners of your foot:*
> **Big Toe**
> **Pinkie Toe**
> **Inside Heel**
> **Outside Heel**

Next, drive the hips forward and lift the chest as you stand up. Be sure to pull the belly button into your spine to engage the abdominals and stabilize the core as you press the top of your head up into the sky.

PreHab Exercise Book for Runners

STABILITY

- *Perform between 8-10 reps for 2-3 sets on the floor with correct form before adding a load (i.e. using a barbell or other weight.)*
- *If not perfect with form, reduce the reps to 3-5 reps per set until you feel proficient at the movement. Then progress to a higher amount of reps.*

SPEED SKATERS

This exercise will develop stability for: *Hips (Lateral Aspect), Ankle/Foot & Core (Lateral Aspect).*

Use in PreHab routines for: *Running, Agility, Jumping, Skiing/Skating, Squatting & Lunging.*

POSITION: Stand in an athletic stance – feet shoulder-width apart, toes pointing forward, legs in triple flexion (ankles, knees and hips all bent). Keep the spine in neutral alignment while sloping forward, chest high, nose aligned with the toes and eyes on the horizon.

Next, lift one foot up off the ground and extend it backwards towards the horizon as you slide the same side arm forward and slightly rotate the shoulder. Bend the elbows to 90 degrees as if running.

ACTION: Laterally slide to the side in a full stride that is comfortable by driving the outside edge of the opposite foot down into the floor and fully extending that leg in a lateral push.

Keep the hip and shoulder at the same height as you slide and maintain neutral alignment in the spine. Do not round the back or stand up. Stay low.

Plant the raised foot into the ground and quickly decelerate the momentum of your body before laterally pushing off with that foot in order to redirect your body and return to the starting position.

Press into your pinkie toes to produce and absorb the lateral push of the leg. Also, fully extend the ankle, knee and hip (triple extension) of the push leg each time that you slide to a side.

STABILITY

The triple extension is an important biomechanical skill to develop and will help create more power and force in running, jumping and agility drills.

> **Pause.**

Add a momentary pause (at least a one-count) between each slide as you stand on a single leg. This will help develop single-leg stability and will positively affect the rest of your training or performance.

Perform 2-3 sets of 10-20 reps with pauses between each slide to develop more stability in the hips.

Speed Skaters: Start & Finish

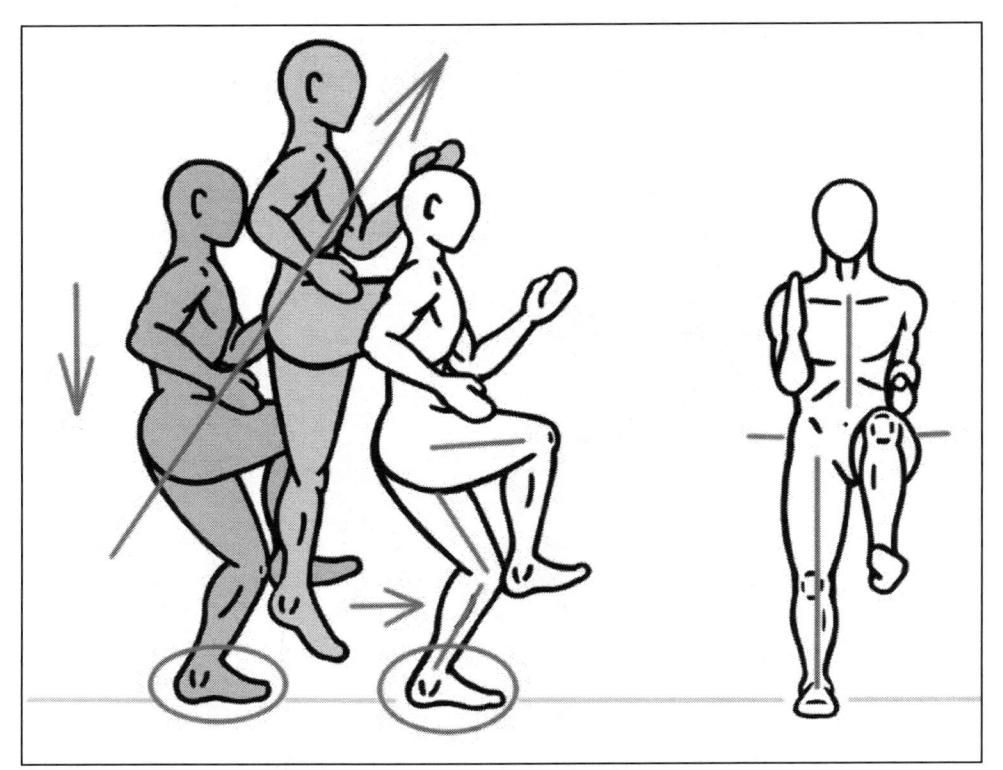

STABILITY

Single-Leg Hop: Start & Finish

STABILITY

SINGLE-LEG HOP

> This exercise will help develop stability for: *Hip, Posterior Chain, Ankle & Core.*
>
> Use in PreHab routines for: *Running, Agility & Jumping.*

POSITION: Start in an athletic stance – feet shoulder-width apart, toes pointing forward, legs in triple flexion (ankles, knees and hips all bent). Keep the spine in neutral alignment while sloping forward, chest high, nose aligned with the toes and eyes on the horizon.

Next, lift one foot off the ground and lift the knee up to hip height as you shift your body weight over to the other leg. Align your belly button and nose in a vertical line with your big toe, but do not allow the knee to collapse inwards. Keep the knee vertically aligned with the pinkie toe.

ACTION: Quickly lower the hips about 1-3 inches and explosively push off the ground into the air by driving the floor down and behind you. Use the triple extension technique when hopping. You should be fully extending through the ankle, knee and hip when pushing off the ground while forcefully pulling the belly button in to engage the abdominals and stabilize the core.

Drive the top of the head up into the sky and forward when hopping to help create a neutral spine. Keep a vertical alignment from head to heel to maximize your force output in the hop.

Perform this movement with speed and swing the arms for assistance in generating power to push off. Keep the chest lifted and do not let the standing knee collapse inwards when hopping. Use a mirror or have a partner observe the mechanics of your knee.

Gently land on the *same* leg. "Stick" the landing by quickly establishing balance on the single leg and returning to the starting position with as little derivation in stability or control as possible.

Press into your pinkie toes to produce and absorb the lateral push of the leg. Also, fully extend the ankle, knee and hip (triple extension) of the push leg each time that you slide to a side.

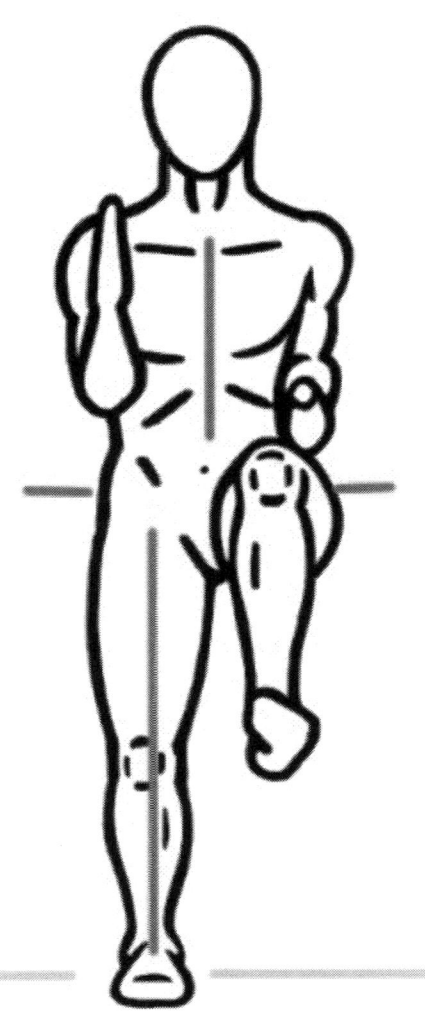

'Stick' the landing with 'Level' Alignment.

STABILITY

The triple extension is an important biomechanical skill to develop and will help create more power and force in running, jumping and agility drills.

> **Pause.**

Add a momentary pause (at least a one-count) between each slide as you stand on a single leg. This will help develop single-leg stability and will positively affect the rest of your training or performance.

Perform 2-3 sets of 3-8 reps with pauses between each slide to develop more stability in the hips, ankle and core.

Take the Lead

Let's use a metaphor real quick. Your performance, whether it's going for a run or running while you play a sport, is a dance. There are steps you take and moves that you make where timing and energy define all of the movements. Additionally, many times you are dancing with a partner and creating momentum.

In this dance of yours, momentum, many times, is leading you. Whether it's as you glide through your stride in a 10K or when you turn the corner to drive to the hoop. Sometimes, it's momentum that leads you through all of your moves, especially those unfortunate ones where you may fall or go too wide on your turn.

The goal is not to let momentum cramp your style. Work on your stability in large movement patterns and be the one who leads this performance or dance each and every time!

Strength Training for Runners

There are mainly two reasons that runners need to strength train: increased longevity and improved performance.

Strength training will help to fortify your soft tissue and bones, as well as positively stimulate your hormonal system. And you need both to combat the stress of running.

Repetitive Stress
Just as the tires on your car get wore out from driving, your body endures wear and tear when running. The only difference is that your body is designed to naturally heal itself if given the right conditions. Unfortunately, repetitive stress hampers the body's ability to rejuvenate itself.

Repetitive stress syndrome and repetitive stress injuries, such as a stress fracture, occur when there is a chronic overload of stress on the body that continually surpasses the body's ability to heal itself. In other words your body does more "work," such as running, than it is designed to handle.

Photo by Michael Pereckas

RUNNING DRILLS

The application of repetitive stress is just as important as the frequency of stress, meaning how the body experiences stress in terms of movement patterns has a major impact. Highly repetitive movement patterns, such as your gait or stride in running, will create imbalances of stress and tightness throughout the body. These imbalances will warp your biomechanics over time that will lead to compensation strategies and possible injuries somewhere down the road.

Strength training can help to balance out the body and minimize the effects of repetitive stress. The exercises recommended in this section will help biomechanically counter-balance the effects of running as well as train the body to become powerful and efficient in other patterns that are essential for natural movement.
Additionally, strength training can create an environment of positive stress that leads to proper healing and adaption of the soft tissue and bones. Plus, these training adaptations build resistance to the effects of repetitive stress.

Art History
Have you ever taken an art history class? If you have not, I am sure you can imagine how much emphasis and discussion goes into examining the texture of certain paintings, especially how the angle and thickness of the brush strokes help to define the painting.

In strength training, the loading pattern of each exercise carries just as much importance of each brush stroke from van Gogh or Gauguin. Your body will adapt in the direction resistance, i.e. load, weight and stress, is placed on the body through movement patterns. In other words, the bones of your leg grow more dense and stronger when you Back Squat because of the vertical displacement of stress in the body.

Portrait of van Gogh

> **Running places stress on the body in only one specific direction and pattern.**
>
> **Strength training can help balance out the predictable adaptions by placing stress on the body in other directions.**

No Bulk
Many times when I am giving advice to women about strength training, one of the first things they tell me is that they do not want to bulk up. I completely understand their concern, and I smile as I tell them that strength training will not bulk them up. How they eat, sleep, move and think are the culprits to bulking, not strength training.

RUNNING DRILLS

Perceived Exertion (PE)
Perceived Exertion is an important measure to use when strength training. It represents the amount of effort that you are using during a movement. Are you maxing out and using everything that you've got? That would be a 10 on a scale of 1-10. Are you kind of pushing it? That's a 4. Use PE to estimate where you are with your strength.

PE is an estimation of how much effort you use while strength training that helps track and regulate your progress.

Effective strength training approximately requires an effort level above a 7 on a PE scale of 1-10 in a set of 5-8 repetitions. If your PE is below a 7 when strength training that will allow you to perform more reps. Sets with high rep schemes (10+) help promote muscular growth (size) and endurance, which may be welcomed by many. However, runners looking to avoid bulk will want to stay away from the mid-rep range (8-12) and reduce overall volume (the amount of weight x sets and reps) in a strength-training program.

Use a simple 1-10 Scale for Perceived Exertion (PE) where 10 equals Max Effort.

Then attempt to complete all sets of Strength Training exercises at a 7 or 8 of PE in order to appropriately stress the muscles, tendons and bones for positive strength adaptions.

Maintain Strength
One of the best ways to limit bulk while strength training is to use the PE scale. Strength training is designed to keep you (as well as your bones and soft tissue) strong. It's important to note that your body can naturally maintain its current level of strength for 7-14 days.

Aim to schedule strength training per movement pattern at least once every 7-14 days.

Gain Strength
Conversely, runners looking to gain strength and speed will benefit from strength training with a high frequency among sessions. The one pitfall to avoid is overtraining or not recovering enough between training sessions. Ideally, you will want to give your body 48 hours to recover from strength training in a particular movement pattern. This time frame will allow the body's inflammation and protein synthesis cycles to complete. Yet, it is possible to continue strength training in other movement patterns while recovering.

RUNNING DRILLS

> **Major Movement Patterns**
>
> *Here are eight archetypal movement patterns to incorporate into your strength training program.*
>
> **Hip Hinge**
> **Squat**
> **Lunge**
> **Carries**
> **Pull**
> **Push (Core Integrated)**
> **Row (Horizontal Pulls)**
> **Press (Shoulder Stability)**

A list of strength training exercises that correlate with each of these movement patterns will be provided at the end of this section.

Programming

I habitually walk around the gym and ask people "what are you working on?" And most of their answers are either body parts or muscles such as arms or quads. And sometimes I just get a blank stare, as if I were speaking to them in gibberish.

I ask people what they are working on in order to understand their training program and gauge their progress. However, more often than not, it seems that people work out without a program, which is kind of like driving your car on vacation without a GPS.

Training programs are the maps to your progress and improvement. They guide you to where you want to go and also give you a barometer on how your training is going. Randomly working out will bring you results, but they may not be the results you're looking for. The random approach to strength training is kind of like me hopping on the 405 in Los Angeles to head to San Francisco without realizing I am heading south towards San Diego instead.

How to Program

There are numerous different ways to design a training program. In fact, program design is half science and half art. As long as science can support your art, anything you come up with is plausible.

Essentials

Aside from knowledge of biomechanics and functional movement patterns, the main ingredient to an effective training program is an understanding of force and energy applications. You should be able to discern, in your program and for each exercise, if you are training for size, speed, strength or endurance.

RUNNING DRILLS

In other words, you want to be clear what changes you want to create in your physiology. Do you want to run faster? Run longer? Do you want to look good at the pool this summer? These are all legit questions to ask. And they all have scientifically-supported answers that can bring you the tangible results you want!

> ### Prescription (Rx) for Sets and Reps
> Once you know what physiological changes you want to make, the next step is to develop a firm understanding the set and reps schemes that will bring about the results that you are after.

Here are the basic Set and Rep Schemes:

- 1-5 Reps for **Power (Strength and Speed)**
- 5-8 Reps for **Strength**
- 8-12 Reps for **Size and Conditioning**
- 12+ Reps for **Stamina and Endurance**

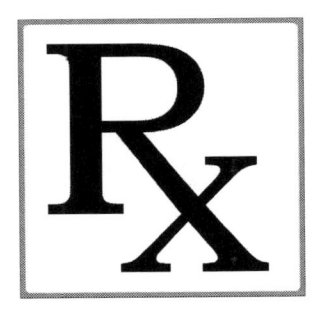

Use these Set/Rep schemes in conjunction with the goals of your training program and you will be more effective each time you walk into your gym.

Periodization

Another program-design tool that you can use is the Periodization template. This approach divides your training calendar into a timeline of sections designated to focus on specific themes and objectives while working towards one main goal, such as running a marathon.

> *Periodization programs contain planned progressions to raise the effectiveness of the training, such as an eight-week phase of training for strength before a training phase for power since strength is a prerequisite for power production.*

Most training programs for long-distance running events, such as a marathon or a 10K, follow a Periodization progression and divide up weekly workouts based on specific goals and themes, i.e. long run, recovery, speed day and more.

Macro Objectives

In traditional Periodization programs, the training calendar will be sectioned off to focus on the broad objectives that are linear prerequisites for the main goal, i.e. an event or competition or the start of a new season.

RUNNING DRILLS

> **Progression of Macrocycles-**
> *Designated periods of a training program, usually 6-16 weeks, focusing on specific sequential goals.*
>   *Macrocycle One:* **Hypertrophy**
>   *Macrocycle Two:* **Strength**
>   *Macrocycle Three:* **Power**
>   *Macrocycle Four:* **Endurance**
>   *Macrocycle Five:* **Competition (Event or start of season)**

A Periodization schedule using Macrocycles usually follows a yearly or seasonal timeline and is broken down in smaller segment that delineate and address other goals in training.

Microcycle

Chances are you've seen or heard of a training program's Microcycle. They commonly come in weekly forms, such as Monday: Weights; Tuesday: Yoga; Wednesday: Run, etc.

> *Microcycles are smaller segments of a program design that help integrate and balance out additional aspects of training. For example, a Microcycle can include a day of sprints to help maintain speed and power during the Endurance Macrocycle.*

Day Specific

Using the Microcycle format allows you to deepen your focus by choosing training themes for each workout or training session. Many training programs at all levels, from high school to the Olympics, follow this approach because it makes the entire program easier to manage and organize.

> ***Example of a Day-Specific Microcycle:***
>
>   Monday- **Power (Strength Training)**
>   Tuesday- **Active Recovery (Run)**
>   Wednesday- **Speed (Run)**
>   Thursday- **Endurance (Strength Training)**
>   Friday- **Stride Technique (Run)**
>   Saturday- **Distance (Run)**
>   Sunday- **Recovery (Yoga/Massage)**

RUNNING DRILLS

Use of the Microcycle format helps you to incorporate different training aspects on a continual basis, which will positively contribute to the progress of your program. Additionally, the spacing between repeating the same training aspect, such as speed or stride technique, will actually help you to 'learn' and improve in that focus according to Peter Brown, author of 'Make It Stick.'

> ### *Patterning*
> *Human Beings respond to patterns. Both our minds and our bodies are constantly looking for patterns in everything, which is why creating a pattern in your training program will yield positive results. Periodization is just a complex pattern, but one that your neuromuscular system can and will recognize if you keep to it.*

Sets: The Power of Three
Three is a useful number in strength training. It provides a constructive structure for physiological adaption and progression. In fact, many rep schemes use a three-set formula to help the body recognize and adapt to the patterned stimulus of strength training.

> ### **Three Set Formula for Strength Training**
>
> *Set One:* Introduction
>
> *Set Two:* Improvement
>
> *Set Three:* Mastery

In this format, the neuromuscular system has an opportunity to optimize its movement patterns and force production mechanisms through comparing its performance in the first set to the second set and adjusting for the third set based on pattern recognition.

Additional Sets, Lower Reps
Performing additional sets will provide more opportunities for the neuromuscular system to make adjustments, which is very beneficial when working on Power Days as the reps remain low per set. However, making too many corrections in your form from set to set without the advice of a coach or spotter can be problematic. That's because this can create unintentional adjustments in your biomechanics, just as Confucius said that too much thinking without learning can create problems in your life.

RUNNING DRILLS

Mesocycles
Within the Periodization structure, Macrocycles can be divided into Mesocycles, where Microcycles can be constructed in a patterning sequence similar to sets and reps. In other words, your Microcycles can also experience the evolutionary progression outlined in the Three Set Formula.

Repeating a Microcycle will provide an opportunity for your neuromuscular system to recognize the patterns among the different workouts and create adjustments to become more efficient and optimize performance. In other words, your body can learn how to manage its resources more effectively to deal with the stresses of the week's workout. Thus, creating Mesocycles in your training program will help to progress your training more and deliver more results. As your mastery of a Microcycle develops, your performance will also develop.

Law of Diminishing Returns
Why not just do the same routines every single week? This seems like a very logical answer to ask. I only wish more people would ask it, because the answer appears to be counter-intuitive based on what we just discussed about pattern recognition and performance enhancement.

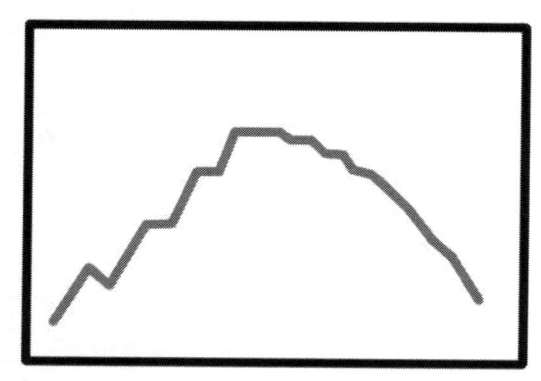

The Law of Diminishing Returns is an economic principal that applies rather fittingly to training. Essentially, the principal states that the reward from one specific action will diminish in volume or effectiveness each time that action is performed. And it could even become a negative reward if the action is pursued too many times. In other words, the first time you bench press, you will gain the most reward from this action. Yet, the more you bench press, the less you will gain from it. And if you end up bench pressing every single day, you will eventually start to develop negative consequences such as limited range of motion in your shoulders and imbalances in your biomechanics.

Change Things Up
Mesocycles are a perfect way to help change up the patterning of your workouts and limit the Law of Diminishing Returns in your training program. To do this, limit the number of Microcycles in a Mesocycle in such a way to create a pattern that your body can adjust to without losing too much reward by repeating in a prolonged manner.

Month-to-Month Program Cycles
Mesocycles of 3-4 Weeks will help develop pattern recognition among all of your workouts within your training program while limiting the Law of Diminishing Returns.

RUNNING DRILLS

Varying Exercise Sequences
One easy way to manage variables among Mesocycles in a training program is to change up the sequences of exercises used in each workout. Your body will recognize patterns in terms of intensity, volume and movements. In other words, your body can 'learn' what exercises follow one another and begin to 'cheat' out possible gains. At the same time, the different themes and objectives of the Macrocycles are mainly addressed in terms of intensity and volume - i.e. power to endurance as opposed to movements. Consequentially, changing the sequence of exercises (movements) every 3-4 weeks will help provide variability among Mesocycles and thus limit the possible effects of Diminishing Returns in your training program.

Designing your Program
Now, that you've received a whole bunch of information concerning sets, reps, Perceived Effort, movement patterns, Macrocycles, Mesocycles and Microcycles, it's time to put everything together and design your own program.

Step One: Clarify your Goal
Are you looking to just develop longevity because you want to continue to run for decades to come? Are you looking to compete in a specific event? Is running part of your fitness routine to lose weight and manage stress? These are all great goals to have because they present clear intention.

On the other hand, if you're not clear on what your goal is, then take some time to figure it out. Mark a day in your calendar, perhaps a week or two away, and set a deadline for yourself to come up with a goal. Don't worry, you can always change it. However, training without a clear goal will only bring about unclear results.

If you have a clear goal, it is easy to create a clear path to achieve it.

Step Two: Outline your Progress
Reverse engineering is a very impactful way to strategize any plan and relatively easy to do. Simply, use your imagination to see what it looks like to accomplish your goal: What race did you just finish? Did you win? Or in terms of longevity, how old do you see yourself still running? How fast and agile are you? In terms of losing weight, how much do you weigh now? How do you look? How do you feel? What other activities are you doing in life? Questions like these will help you know what you need to do in your program.

Do you need to develop speed? Then you need to create a Macrocycle for power! Are you looking to complete a marathon? Well, you need a Macrocycle for endurance! How much time do you have before your event? You need to plan your program schedule accordingly.

RUNNING DRILLS

K.I.S.S.
Keep It Simple, Sam. Don't get too complicated with your first time programming. Remember, your body is a pattern-seeking sponge. If you just focus on the basic themes of strength, power and endurance in a few simple Macro, Meso and Microcycles, your body will respond.

Step Three: Selecting Exercises
The last step will be the easiest step if you use exercises that represent the seven archetypal movement patterns. Simply, strategize how you can incorporate these seven movements into your Microcycle and rearrange the sequence between Mesocycles.

Example Microcycle A:

Program Goal: Increase Speed for 5K

Macrocycle: Progresses to Power Cycle
   3 Week Block

Microcycle – Day Specific

   Monday- Strength Train
      Hip Hinge 5 Sets 5 Reps
      Pull 5 Sets 5 Reps
      Lunge 3 Sets 8 Reps
      Press 3 Sets 8 Reps
   Tuesday- PreHab and Active Recovery
      Steady Pace Run – 5 miles
      PreHab Exercises: Core Stability and Gait Efficiency
   Wednesday- Strength Train
      Carries 4 Sets for 50ft
      Squat 4 Sets 6 Reps
      Push 4 Sets 6 Reps
      Row 4 Sets 6 Reps
   Thursday- PreHab and Run (Stride Focus)
      400m Repeats
      PreHab Exercises: Lateral Hip and Core Activation
   Friday- PreHab and Sprints
      200m Repeats
      PreHab Exercises: Crawl Progression
   Saturday- Long Distance Run
      8 Mile Paced
   Sunday- PreHab and Active Recovery
      4 Mile Jog
      PreHab Exercises: Full Body Mobility

RUNNING DRILLS

Example Microcycle B:

Program Goal: Longevity

    Macrocycle: Progresses to Endurance Cycle
        3 Week Block

Microcycle Format – Day Specific

    Monday: PreHab and Run - Stride Focus
        4 Mile Run
        PreHab Exercises: Core Activation and Gait Efficiency
    Tuesday:
        Carries 3 Sets for 50ft
        Squat 3 Sets 12 Reps
        Press 3 Sets 12 Reps
        Hip Hinge 3 Sets 12 Reps
        Lunge 3 Sets 12 Reps
    Wednesday: PreHab and Long-Distance Run
        8 Mile Run – Paced
        PreHab Exercises: Hip and Ankle Activation
    Thursday: Strength Training
        Carries 3 Sets for 50ft
        Lunge- 3 Sets 15 Reps
        Push- 3 Sets 15 Reps
        Row- 3 Sets 15 Reps
    Friday: PreHab and Run - Speed Focus
        800m Repeats
        PreHab Exercises: Core & Shoulder Stability
    Saturday: PreHab and Long Distance
        12 Mile Run – Paced
        PreHab Exercises: Recovery Circuit
    Sunday: Yoga or PreHab and Light Run
        PreHab Exercises: Full Body Mobility

RUNNING DRILLS

Strength is Ability
All of these strength-training exercises will help you run longer and run faster. They will help restore your biomechanics and are important to practice, because the more that you run, the more your body is exposed to patterns of repetitive stress. Strength training will help to combat the effects of repetitive stress and keep your "ability' to run at an all-time high!

Running Drills

Strength Exercises

Here are a series of exercises for you to incorporate into your training program. These exercises cover the seven basic movement patterns and will help to balance out your biomechanics. However, you do not need to limit yourself to only these exercises or even the strength-training principals presented previously in this section.

There are many more exercises, techniques and training principals that you can employ to help you achieve the results that you want – especially, if you are looking to take on other activities besides just running. Yet, if running is your main focus, the following exercises will provide a good foundation of strength that you can build off of to help your running.

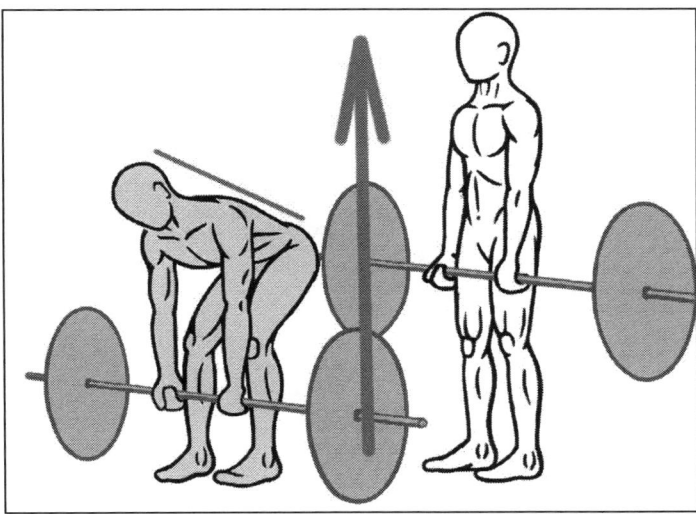

DEADLIFT (DL) - Hip Hinge
This strength training exercise is very beneficial to runners as part of a PreHab routine because it can stimulate and condition the posterior chain through a large range of motion. The DL will help develop power and provides a foundation for stability and speed.

Equipment: For a basic level DL, you can use a barbell, kettlebell or dumbbell.

POSITION: Stand with your feet shoulder-width apart and align the arch of your foot (where your shoelaces are) with the barbell, handle of the kettlebell, or the center of a dumbbell in a tall, upright position.

Sit back with your hips and bend your knees as you reach down to take hold of the barbell with your hands. Keep your shins as vertical as possible and do not let your knees pass out in front of your toes. Press your thighs out wide to provide more room

for your torso to lower down towards the floor.
Hold onto the barbell with your hands shoulder-width apart. Conversely, if you are using a kettlebell or a dumbbell, your arms will be inside your thighs.

Make sure your back is in neutral alignment, the skinny "S." If you cannot establish a neutral spine in the starting position of this lift, go back and perform more mobility exercises for your hips, ankles and posterior chain. It is very important to perform this exercise with a neutral spine and that includes the neck. Do not crank the neck. Instead, tuck your chin and create a neutral alignment in your neck. Your head should be looking at the floor when you are in the starting position.

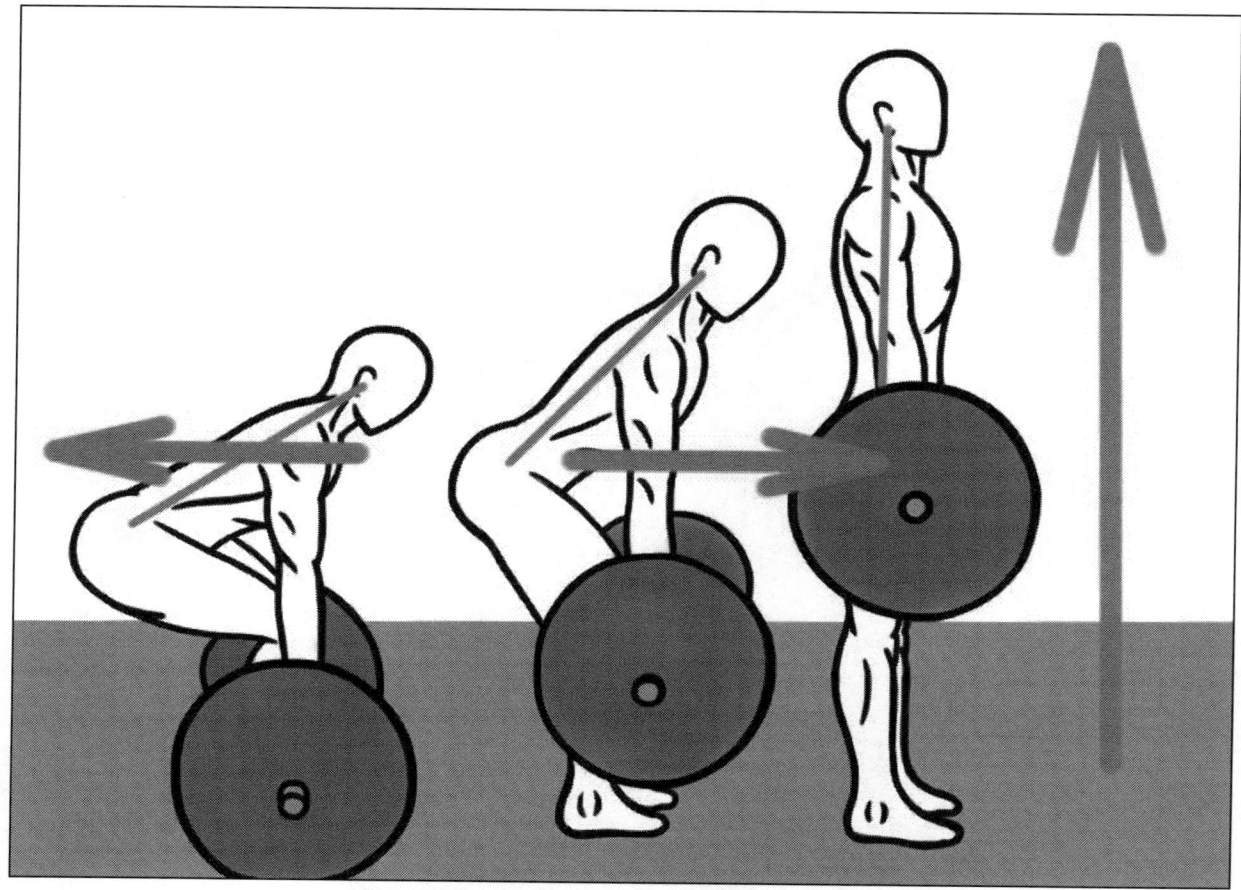

Deadlift: Start & Finish (Side View)

ACTION: In one smooth movement, drive your hips forward and stand up with the weight. Lift your chest high like Superman, but do not arch in your lower back. Maintain the natural "S" curve of your spine as you stand up, this includes tucking in your chin to keep you neck in alignment.

Press your hips forward until they vertically align with your ears and ankle. Pull your belly button in towards your spine to engage the Abdominals and brace your lumbar spine. Reach the top of your head up into the sky and pull the shoulders down away from the ears as you squeeze the shoulder blades together.

RUNNING DRILLS

Next, smoothly press your hips backwards and keep a neutral spine as you lower the weight back down to the floor. Press your thighs wide as you lower to make room for the torso and tuck your chin in towards your throat.

- *Repeat the lift several more times in based on the rep scheme for your workout. Your PE level when finished should be a 7 or higher.*

SQUAT
This strength training exercise is very beneficial as the resistance load will help fortify the soft tissue and bones against the stress of running. Additionally, this exercise will also help develop more coordination and power throughout the neuromuscular system, which will contribute to increases in speed and agility.

RUNNING DRILLS

Equipment: For a basic Squat, you can use either a barbell or dumbbells.

POSITION: Stand with your feet shoulder-width apart and your hips vertically aligned with your ankles and ears. You can either hold a barbell along the back of your shoulders and trapezius or hold a dumbbell with both hands in a vertical position against your chest, this is called a Goblet position.

Pull your belly button in towards your spine to engage your Abdominals and tuck the chin in towards your throat to hold a neutral spine with the natural "S" curve of your spine.

ACTION: Sit your hips down towards the floor as you keep your chest lifted high into the air. Bend your knees and keep your shins as vertical as possible. Do not let your knees pass in front of your toes. Press your thighs wide to make room for your torso to lower towards the floor.

Lower your hips to the height of your knees or lower if possible while maintaining a neutral spine. Do not arch your lower back. Keep your tailbone pointing out backwards to avoid a "butt wink" when the pelvis rotates down and under during a squat. Keep the spine long and the chest high as you sit as low as possible.

Next, drive the heels into the ground and press the hips forward to come back to standing. Keep the chest lifted and maintain a neutral spine.

Return to the starting position where the hips are vertically aligned with the ankles and ears.

- *Repeat the lift several more times based on the rep scheme for your workout. Your PE level when finished should be a 7 or higher.*

PULL-UP (Pull)

This strength training exercise will help runners maintain a balanced symmetry between upper body and lower body. This will stimulate and develop a large portion of musculature on the torso, arms and shoulder girdle including the Latissimus and core. Many runners suffer from asymmetries above and below the waist due to the repetitive nature of running and the affect it has on the soft tissue and bones. Developing strength in the upper body that is comparable to the lower body's development will help maintain proper biomechanical alignment and the ability to create functional movements.

Equipment: A Pull-up bar that will support your weight and allow you to fully hang with straight arms and not touch the ground.

POSITON: Hang from a bar with your hands outside shoulder width. Make sure that your elbows are fully extended and that your arms are straight.

RUNNING DRILLS

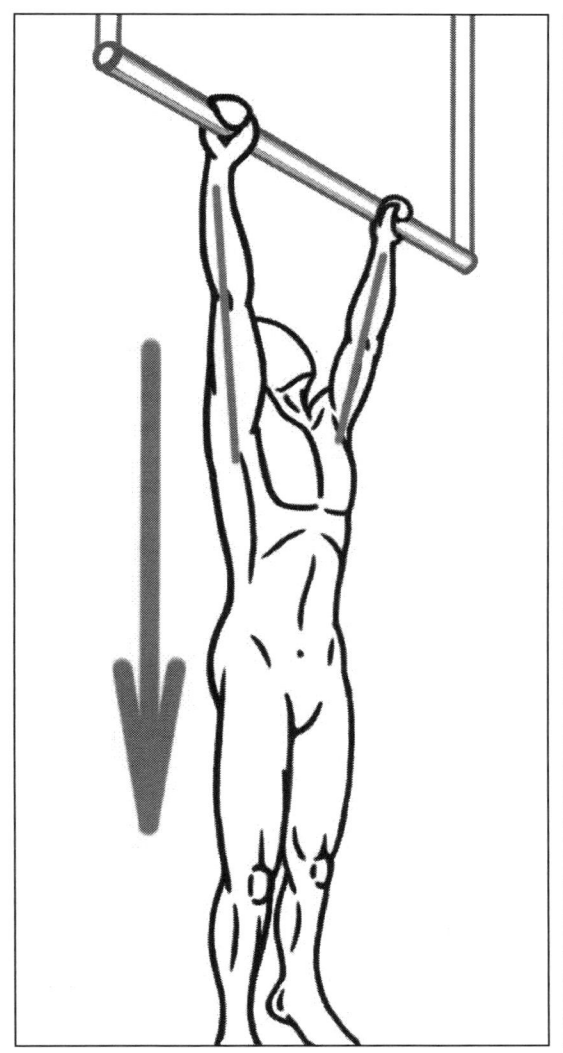

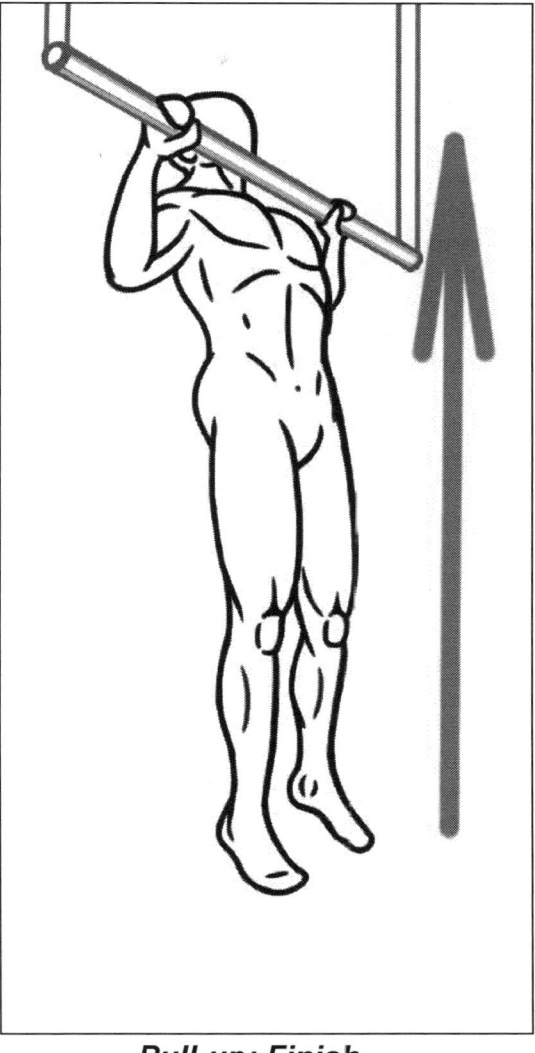

Pull-up: Start *Pull-up: Finish*

ACTION: To pull yourself up to the bar, the first objective is to create stability in the shoulder girdle and core. This is accomplished by forcefully pulling your belly button in towards your spine to engage the abdominals and stabilize your core. At the same time, reverse shrug (or depress) your shoulders by squeezing your armpits down towards your pockets and pulling your shoulder heads away from your ears.

Once you have engaged the core and the shoulder girdle, pull yourself up towards the bar by forcefully retracting your arms and squeezing your shoulder blades towards one another. Bend your elbows as you press your chest forward like Superman.

Attempt to clear the height of the bar with your chin or touch the bar with your chest below, lowering back down to the start position.

- *Repeat the lift several more times based on the rep scheme for your workout. Your PE level when finished should be a 7 or higher.*

RUNNING DRILLS

PUSH-UP (Push)
Another strength exercise that helps runners maintain symmetry between the upper and lower portions of their bodies is the push-up. This exercise also helps to integrate the core in movements while developing strength and stability in the upper body.

POSITION: Start by lying down on the floor on your stomach. Place your hands alongside of your body with the fingers pointing up towards your head. Align the heel of your palm with the bottom of your chest and squeeze your elbows towards one another so that your forearms touch your rib cage. Lengthen your entire body from heel to head and tuck your chin in towards your throat to establish a neutral spine and neck.

ACTION: Before you push yourself away from the floor, the first objective is to create stability in the shoulder girdle and core. This is accomplished by forcefully pulling your belly button in towards your spine to engage your abdominals and stabilize your core. You also want to reverse shrug (or depress) your shoulders by squeezing your armpits down towards your pockets and pulling your shoulder heads away from your ears.

Next, press your palms into the floor and drive your body away from the floor. Make sure that you keep neutral alignment in your body as you perform this movement. This means that your hips should be in a straight line with your ears and ankles as you push yourself up from the floor. Fully extend your arms and protract your shoulders forward at the top of the push-up position.

RUNNING DRILLS

Then, when you lower down towards the floor, squeeze your elbows in towards one another to keep the elbows aligned with the shoulders and wrists. Make sure that you lower all the way down as well. This means that your chest, stomach and thighs all should touch the floor at the bottom of your push-up.

- *Repeat the lift several more times based on the rep scheme for your workout. Your PE level when finished should be a 7 or higher.*

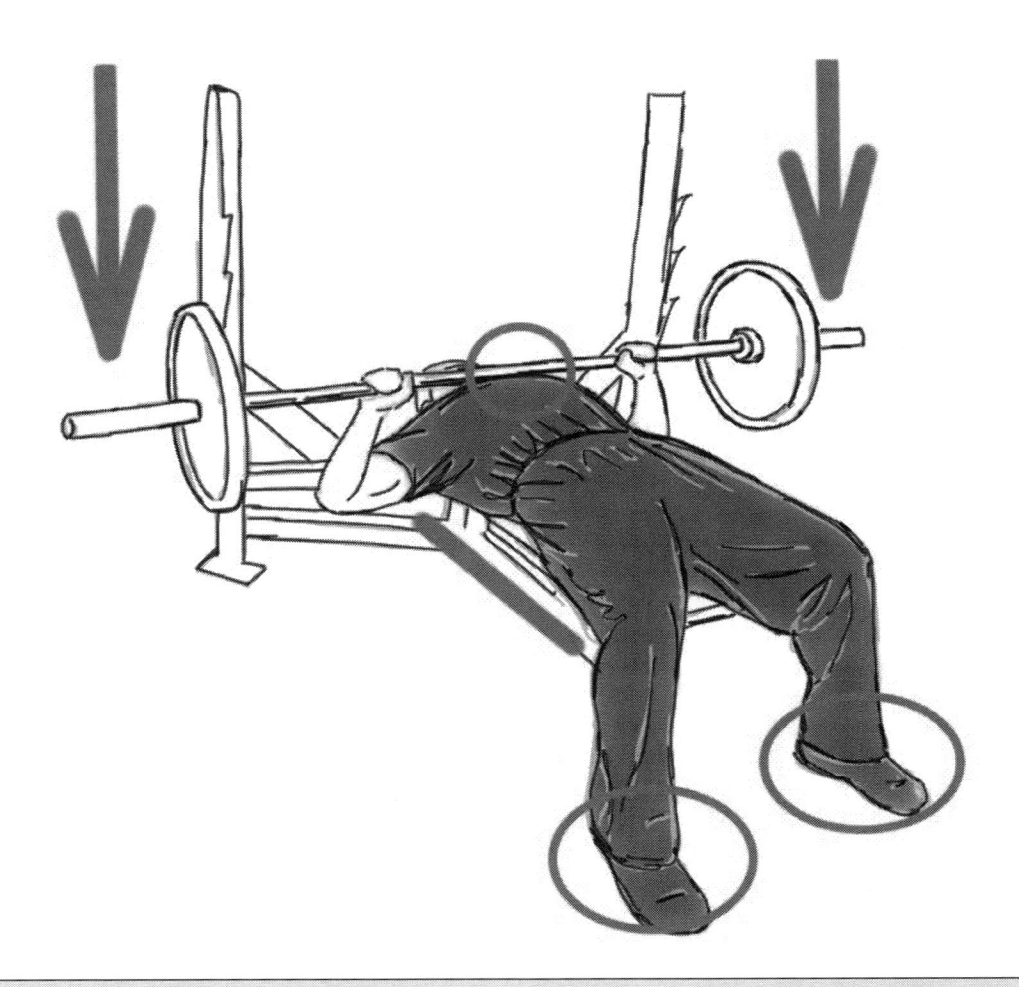

BENCH PRESS (Press)
This strength exercise is similar to that of the Push-up (Push), but has a slight difference. A push involves more core integration, as the body is moving away from an object or surface. However, a Press integrates more shoulder stability because this type of exercise focuses on moving an object away from the body. Practicing both types of exercises will help to develop core and shoulder stability in these dominant upper body movements.

Equipment: A standard weight lifting bench and barbell rack.

PreHab Exercises for Runners

RUNNING DRILLS

POSITION: Lie on the bench face up and position your eyes directly under the barbell. Place your hands on the barbell about one hand's length outside shoulder width. Do not hold the bar too wide as that will limit the range of motion that you will work through in regards to your shoulders and shoulder girdle. Lastly, place both feet on the floor outside shoulder width to help stabilize your body on the bench.

ACTION: Lift the barbell off the rack and position it directly over your heart as you squeeze your armpits down towards your pockets and pull the shoulders away from the ears to stabilize the shoulder girdle. Now, lower the barbell all the way down and touch your chest with the bar as your bend your arms and drive your elbows wide and down towards the floor.

Next, press the bar back up over the heart as you pull the belly button in towards the spine to engage the abdominals and stabilize your core. Keep your hips on the bench and do not arch your lower back as you press up. Straighten your arms and fully extend your elbows at the top of the lift as you continue to squeeze your armpits down towards your pockets.

Bench Press: Finish

RUNNING DRILLS

Also, you want to add external rotation of the shoulders as you press the barbell up towards the sky. To engage external rotation of the shoulders, think about turning your thumbs out to the side as your press up and twist the belly of your biceps to face up towards your shoulders.

- *Repeat the lift several more times based on the rep scheme for your workout. Your PE level when finished should be a 7 or higher.*

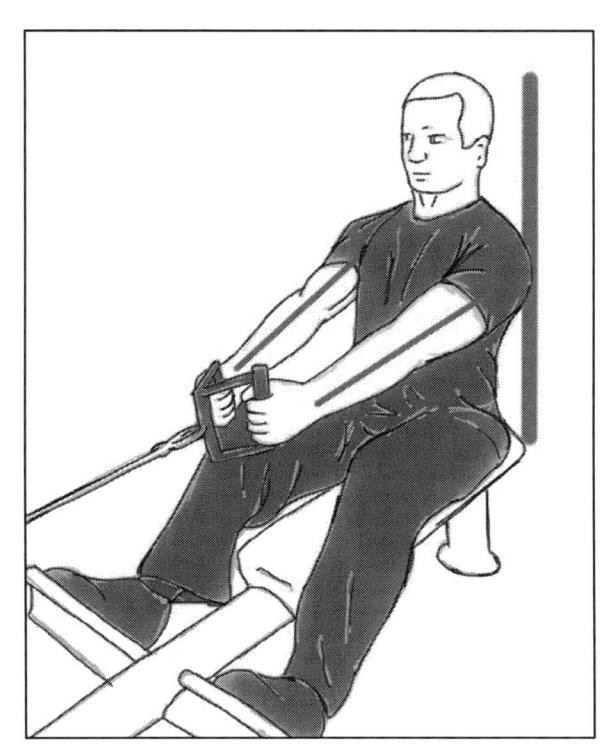

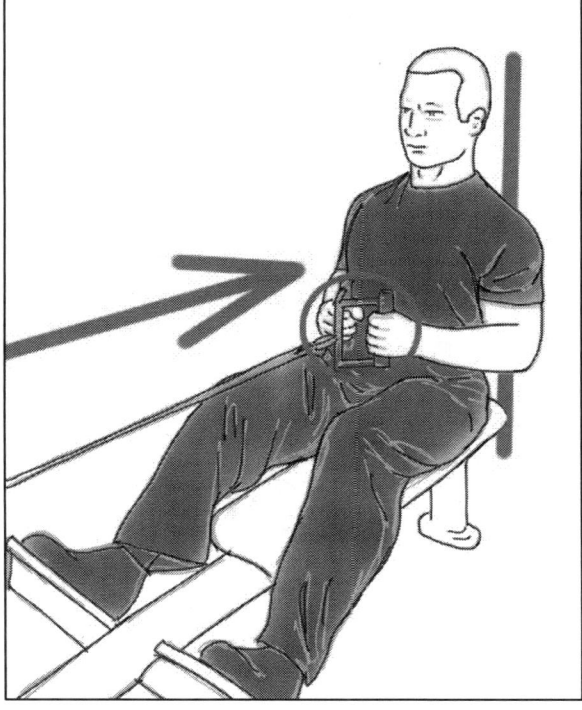

SEATED CABLE ROW (Row)
This strength exercise will help develop stability in the shoulder girdle and core when performed correctly. It is a complementary exercise to any Push or Press exercise.

Equipment: A cable row machine is the most preferred piece of equipment to use, because it allows more freedom in movement compared with other weighted row machines in a gym. You can also substitute this exercise with a dumbbell row if needed.

POSTION: Sit on the machine with a tall, upright and neutral spine as your hands hold the handle of the cable with straight arms. Make sure that your pelvis is also vertically aligned. Do not let the pelvis tilt forwards or backwards, as it will affect the alignment of your spine.

ACTION: Before you start the row, the first objective is to create stability in the shoulder girdle and core. This is accomplished by forcefully pulling your belly button in towards your spine to engage your abdominals and stabilize your core. At the same time, reverse shrug (or depress) your shoulders by squeezing your armpits down towards your pockets and pulling your shoulder heads away from your ears.

Now, pull the cable in towards your body and direct your pinkies towards your belly button as you keep the shoulders depressed. Retract the shoulder girdle as much as you possibly can by squeezing the shoulder blades towards one another. Pull the belly button in towards the spine to engage the abdominals and stabilize your core while also pressing into your feet to integrate the lower body into the movement.

Next, straighten the arms and fully extend the elbows as you return the cable's handle back to the starting position. Keep neutral alignment of your spine throughout the entire exercise.

- *Repeat the lift several more times based on the rep scheme for your workout. Your PE level when finished should be a 7 or higher.*
-

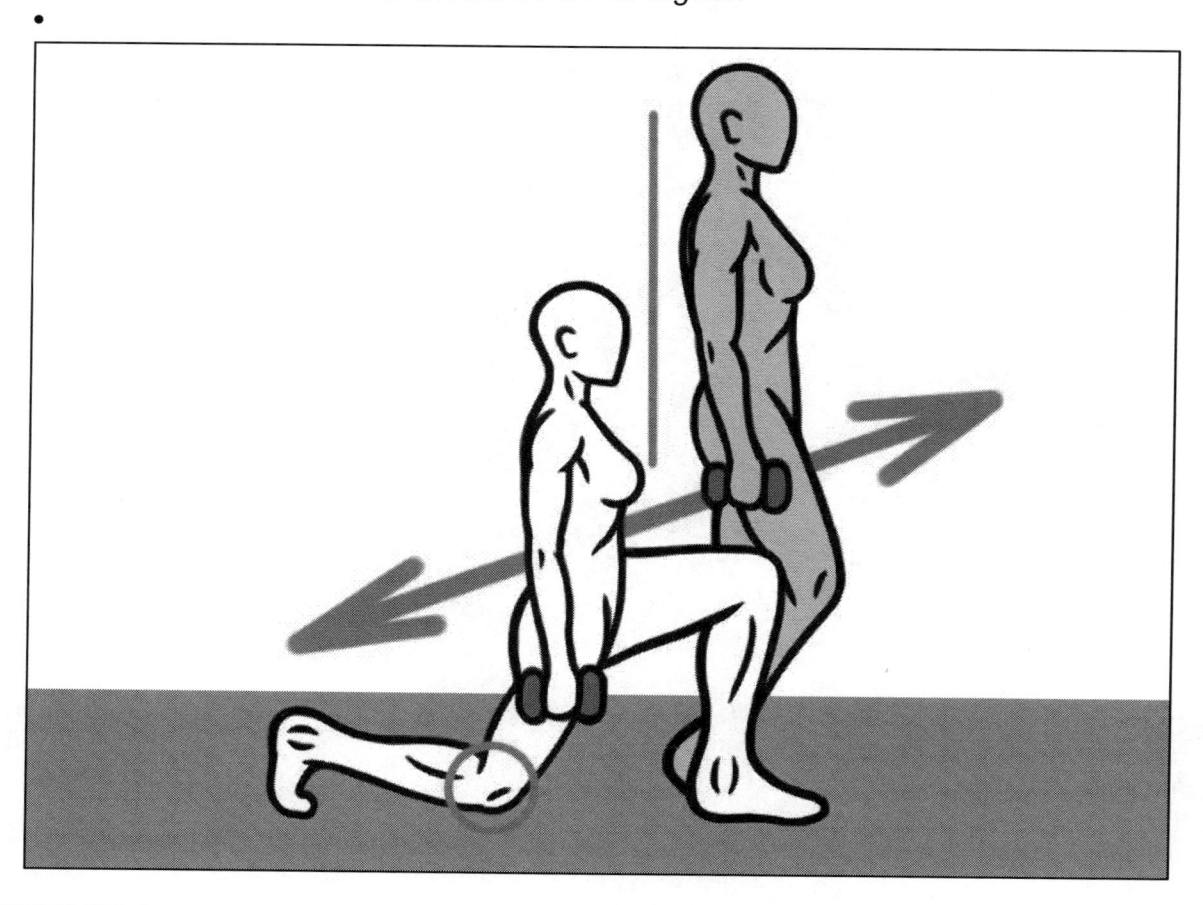

REVERSE LUNGE (Lunge)
This strength exercise is an important exercise for runners as it helps develop hip and ankle stability. It also enhances coordination and efficiency in your gait or stride.

RUNNING DRILLS

Equipment: You can add more resistance (load) to this movement by holding a pair of dumbbells or a medicine ball.

POSITION: Stand in a neutral position with your feet together- weights by your side with straight arms if you choose to load this exercise.

ACTION: Step backwards and lower the back knee towards the ground as if you are kneeling in front of a king or queen. Do not let your knee touch the ground though. Protect your kneecap by stopping just about the ground.

As you step backwards, slide your hips back and keep your chest lifted high into the sky as if you are as proud as Superman. Tuck the back toes under when you step back.

Next, drive the hips forward and return to standing by pressing both feet into the ground and pushing the top of your head up into the sky. Keep a neutral spine as you stand, even if you tilt forward a bit. Do not let your shoulders or chest collapse forward. Keep the chest lifted.

Also, make sure your knees track in line with your toes. Do not let them buckle in or fall out to the side. Pay close attention to where your knees are as you lunge and stand.

Once you return to a standing position, switch legs and perform a lunge on the other side.

- *Repeat the lift several more times based on the rep scheme for your workout. Your PE level when finished should be a 7 or higher.*

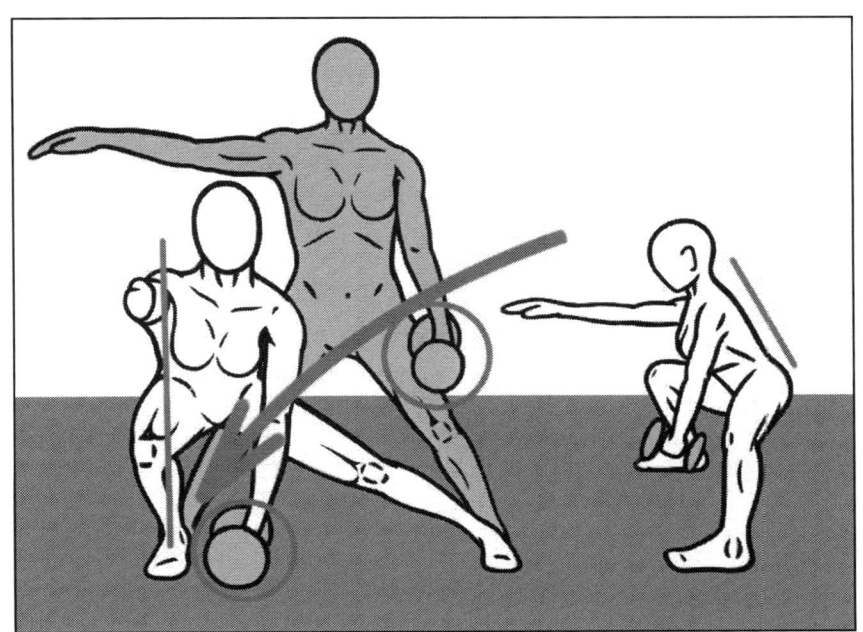

Also, feel free to substitute the Retro Lunge with a Deep Lateral Lunge instead.

PreHab Exercises for Runners

RUNNING DRILLS

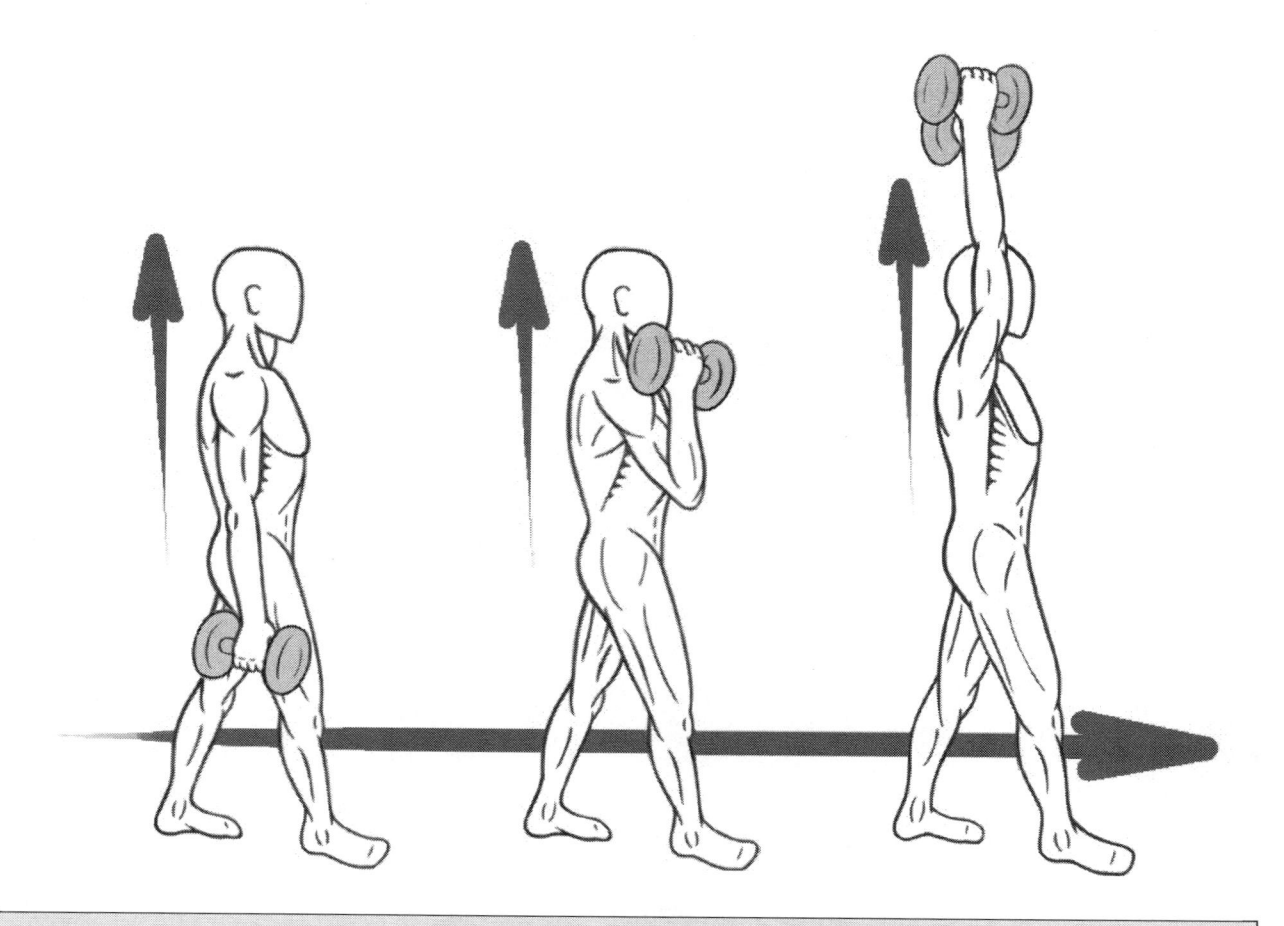

CARRIES – Farmer's Carry, Rack Carry & Overhead Carry

This strength exercise will develop Core Stability and help integrate the Hips, Core and Shoulders in regards to Movement Efficiency. More importantly, this Strength Exercise allows the individual to increase their resistance to overall 'stress,' which will positively condition the body and make the cells more resistance against repetitive movements and repetitive stresses.

POSITION: Stand Tall while holding weights in hands at the Hips (Farmer's Carry), at the Shoulders (Rack Carry) or extended overhead (Overhead Carry).

ACTION: Walk forward for a predetermined distance while maintaining an upright posture. Do not shrug the shoulders or bend the elbows. Press the crown of the head up into the sky, focus the eyes on the horizon and keep the shoulders over the hips.

Carries can be performed for a set distance, such as 50 feet or for a specified amount of time, which is commonly referred to as 'Time Under Tension.' Both techniques will strengthen the body from head to toe.

- *Choose weights and distances that require a PE level of 7 or 8 each set and progress each variable over the course of training.*

RUNNING DRILLS

RUNNING DRILLS

RUNNING DRILLS

Gait Efficiency Drills

The mechanics of your stride, also referred to as your Gait, are extremely important in determining how fast and how long you can walk or run. They also act as a barometer for future injuries to your ankles, knees, hips or back.

The goal of these exercises is to help develop efficiency in your Gait and align the mechanics of your stride in order to produce more speed and longevity while reducing your risk of injury.

Grand Reasons
In 2011, I paid a visit to the Grand Canyon and hiked all the way to the river and back in six hours with relative ease too. I followed Hermit's Trail, which is an 18-mile journey with an additional mile descent and ascent tacked on to it. Of course, I was warned by a Park Ranger not to attempt a journey to the river and back in a single day. Then again, he had no one idea that I had been practicing these Gait Efficiency drills religiously.

All in all, the hike was amazing! I stopped and took many pictures along the way and explored several nooks and crannies of the canyon. I also passed many other hikers along the way and just enjoyed the beautiful playground of the canyon. This hike was by far one of my favorite hikes that I have ever done in my life. And I do not think I would have enjoyed it as much as I did if my stride was not as powerful and efficient as it was. I literally felt as if I was just taking a stroll through the park.

Hiking the Grand Canyon: Hermit's Trail is an 18-mile round trip that also has a mile ascent and descent.

Math in Sports and Running
If you are competing as an athlete, even with yourself, the efficiency of your stride mechanics or Gait will largely determine the end result of your performance. It is simple math:

For every step you take, the inefficiencies of your stride or Gait are multiplied and will negatively subtract from your overall performance and energy.

If you want to perform your best each time you run or compete, give yourself a mechanical advantage by using these exercises to develop efficiency in your Gait and maximize the output from each and every stride you take!

90 Steps
x.75 Gait Efficiency
─────────
67.5
Actual Work Completed
22.5
Net Loss per 90 Steps

RUNNING DRILLS

Exercise Progression
These Gait Efficiency drills are organized in a progression that will increase in complexity and intensity along the way. It's recommended that you start at the beginning and continue to work through the sequence of drills while focusing on establishing good form in each exercise.

If you cannot complete the entire sequence with good form, use the *Joint-By-Joint Approach* and have a partner help you recognize where your faults or limitations arise in your biomechanics. Then prioritize correcting these faults as you continue to perform this sequence over the course of your training.

> *Always prioritize establishing proper biomechanics in basic movement patterns before training with larger, complex movement patterns.*

COMPASS REACHES
This exercise will forces your hip, ankle and foot to all work together when producing movement and ultimately will develop better balance and stability.

POSITION: Stand on one foot and imagine you are at the center of a large compass. It is helpful to have actual lines on the ground to indicate the different directions: north, south, east, west, northeast, southeast, northwest and southwest.

ACTION: Slowly reach your raised foot in each direction while maintaining balance on one leg. Do not touch the ground with the reaching leg. Lower down into a squat in order to reach out as far as possible.

Keep your shoulders square to the front and aligned over your standing toes. Reach your foot in each direction while maintaining balance and then switch legs.

Perform anywhere from 3-6 rounds on each leg.

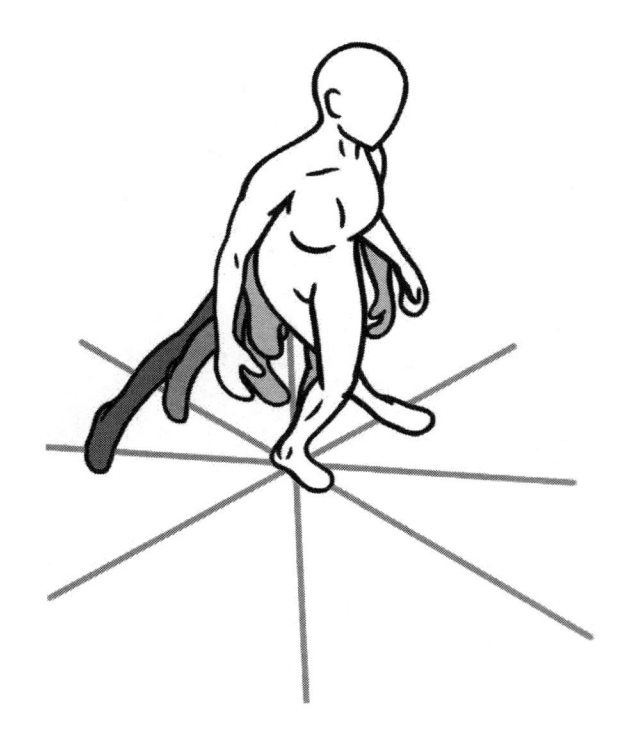

RUNNING DRILLS

Reach: South

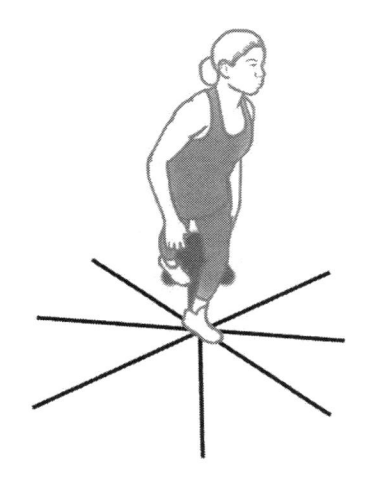

Reach: Southwest

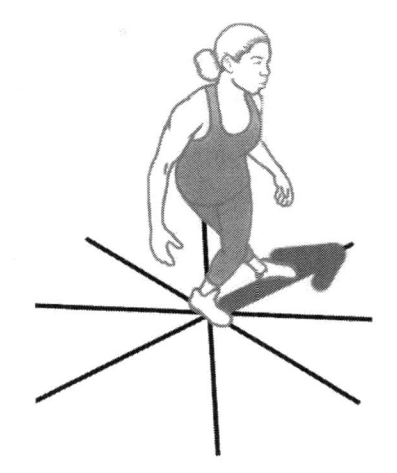

Reach: West

Reach: Southeast

COMPASS REACHES

All EIGHT DIRECTIONS

Reach: Northwest

Reach: East

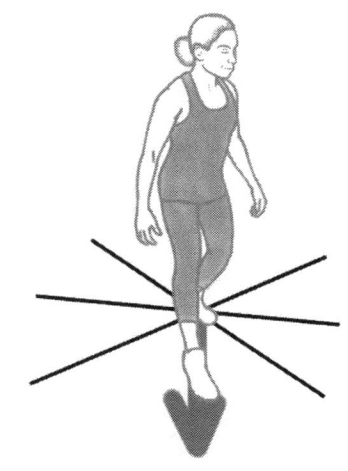

Reach: Northeast

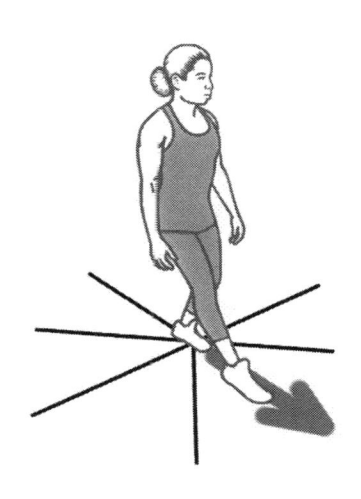

Reach: North

HEEL MARCH

ACTION: Standing tall, focus the eyes on the horizon and walk forward. Stab the heels into the ground while flexing the ankles and pulling the toes up towards the nose. Lift the chest and swing the arms. Pull the belly button into the spine to help engage the abdominals and fully extend back through the legs to powerfully drive the floor back and away. This exercise will help develop length in the stride by strengthening the hip's extension.

Repeat 10-20 steps for 1 or 2 sets.

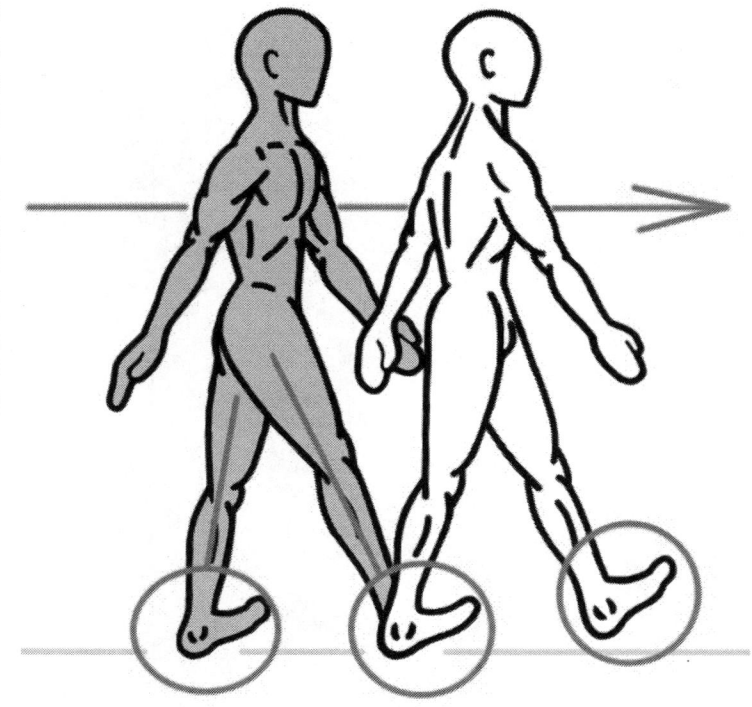

TOE MARCH

ACTION: Standing tall, focus the eyes on the horizon, and walk forward using only the forefoot to make contact with the ground. Fully extend through the ankles, lift the chest and swing the arms as the heels stay lifted off the ground. Also, pull the belly button in towards the spine to engage the abdominals and reach the top of the head up to the sky to lengthen through the spine. This exercise will help develop proper forefoot position when running.

Repeat 10-20 steps for 1 or 2 sets.

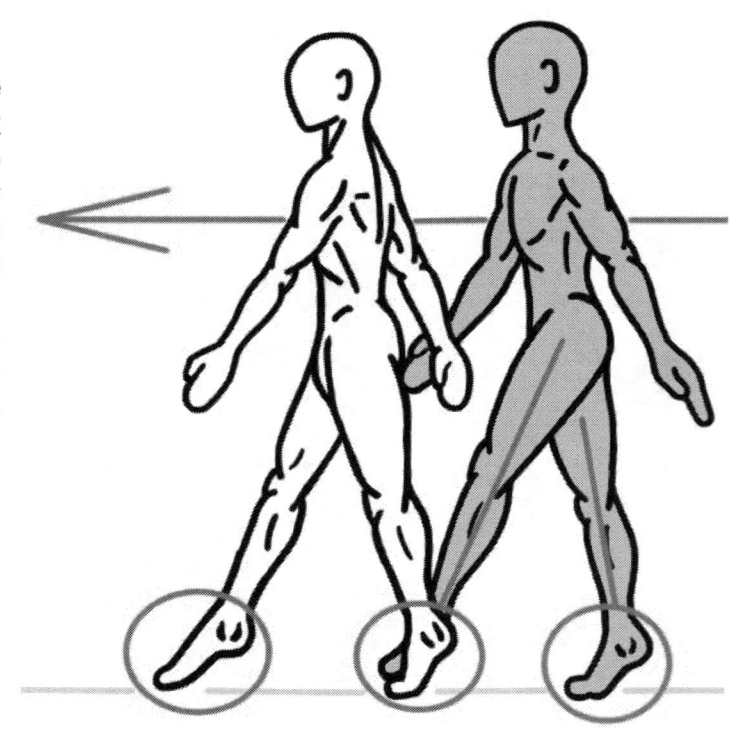

RUNNING DRILLS

KNEE-HUG MARCH

ACTION: Step forward and pull one knee up into the chest with both arms while pressing the floor back and away with the standing leg. Lift the chest, lengthen through the spine and focus the eyes on the horizon. Drive the body forward and lift the standing heel up off the ground on each step. Relax as much as possible while pressing the top of the head into the sky and finding balance on the forefoot during each step. This exercise will help provide the mobility to tuck the knee forwards and develop a full range of motion in the stride.

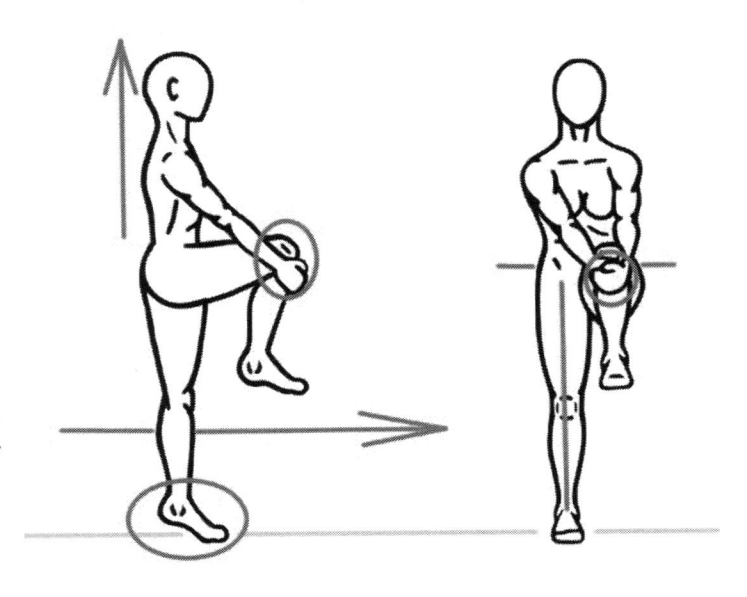

Repeat 10-20 steps for 1 or 2 sets.

HEEL-PULL MARCH

ACTION: Step forward and pull one heel up towards the hips with the same side hand as the opposite arm reaches for the sky. Drive the floor back and away with the standing leg while lifting the heel off the ground and balancing on the forefoot. Pull the belly button in towards the spine to engage the abdominals and don't allow the lower back to arch. Relax as much as possible while pulling the heel into the hips and find balance on the forefoot during each step. This exercise will help provide the mobility to extend the leg backwards and develop a full range of motion in the stride.

Repeat 10-steps for 1 or 2 sets.

RUNNING DRILLS

STRAIGHT-LEG MARCH

ACTION: Step forward and swing one foot forward with a straight-leg while driving into the floor with the standing leg. Keep the chest lifted, lengthen through the spine and pull the standing heel up off the ground so the body balances on the forefoot. Reach the opposite hand out front to touch the foot if possible and keep the eyes on the horizon. Relax the leg as it swings forward. This exercise will help provide the mobility to swing the leg forward and develop a full range of motion in the stride.

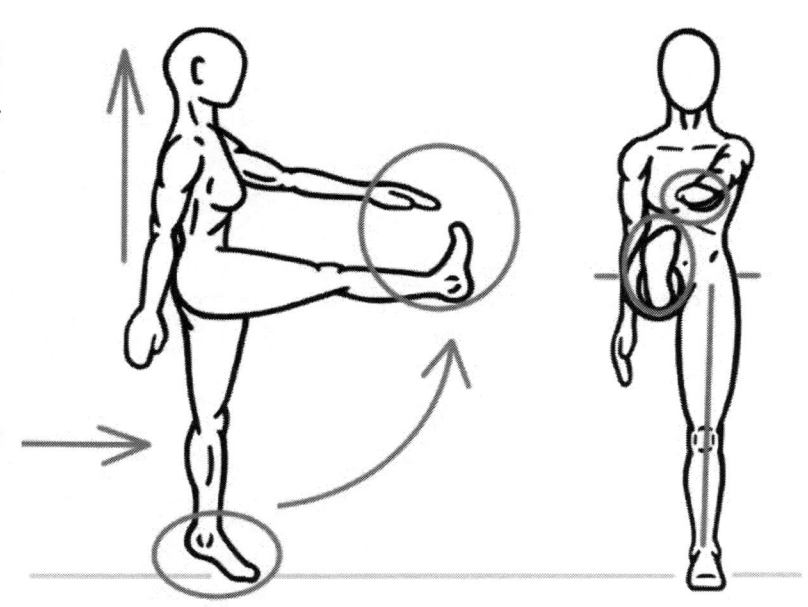

Repeat 10-20 steps for 1 or 2 sets.

LEG-CRADLE MARCH

ACTION: Step forward and pull a shin up into the belly with both arms as the standing leg drives into the floor. Lift the chest, lengthen the spine and focus the eyes on the horizon as one hand holds the knee and the other catches the heel. Press the top of the head into the sky and pull the standing leg's heel off the ground as the arms cradle the shin. Relax as much as possible and find balance on the forefoot in each step. This exercise will help open the hip while developing stability.

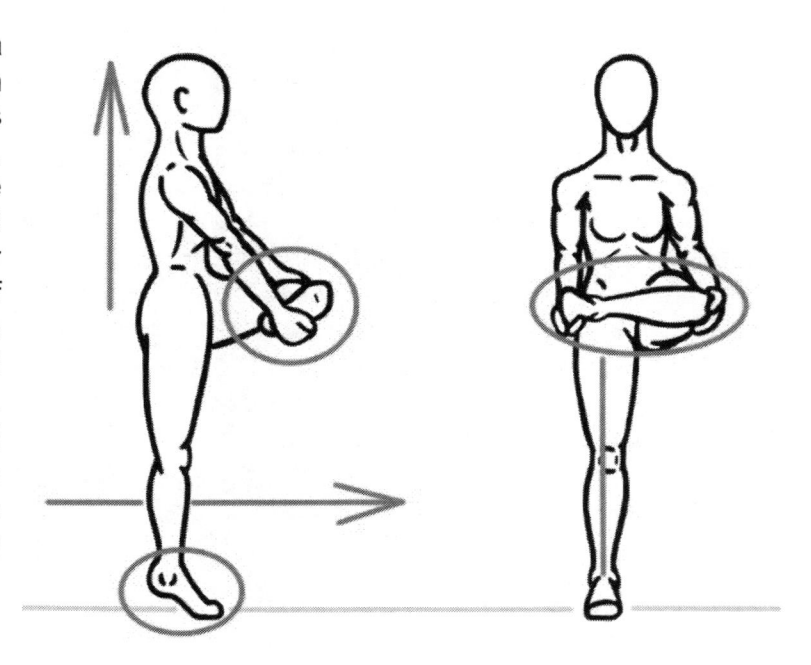

Repeat 10-20 steps for 1 or 2 sets.

RUNNING DRILLS

CROSS-LEGGED MARCH
ACTION: Step forward and cross the leg over the other leg. Then push the hips backwards and fold the torso over the legs, reaching the arms towards the floor. Keep both legs fully extended and lengthen through the spine while hinging in the hips and keeping balance. Lengthen the back of the neck straight by tucking the chin into throat and relax the shoulders. Press into both heels and drive the hips forward to stand up. Then step forward with the foot that is folded over in front first and then swing the rear leg through for the next cross over. This exercise will help open the hips and release tension in the IT Band.

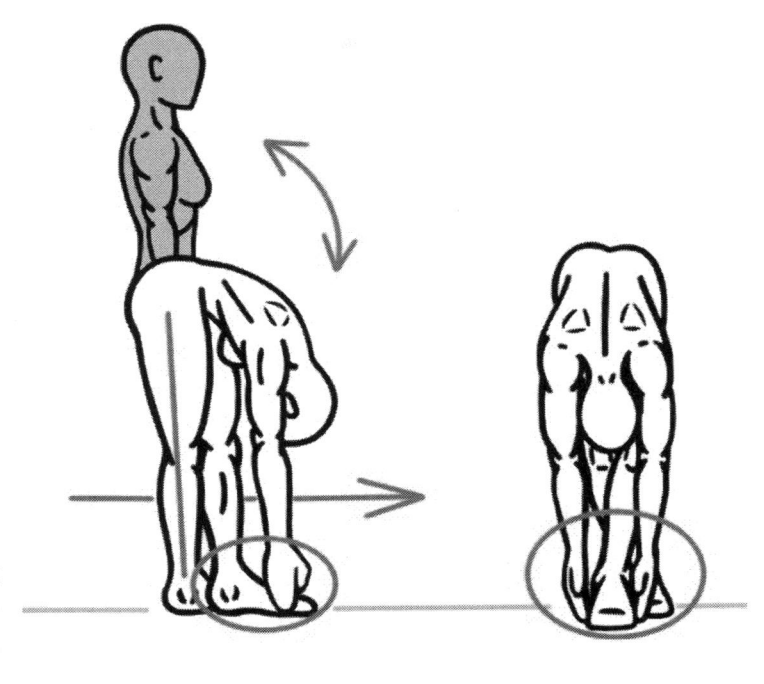

Repeat 5-20 steps for 1 or 2 sets.

SIT-BACK MARCH (LEG SWEEP)
ACTION: Step forward and plant the heel into the ground with the toes off the ground. Next, slide the hips back towards the horizon and reach the arms forward in the opposite direction. Sit back as far as possible and lift the chest to keep the spine long. Point the front toes up to the nose as the eyes focus on the horizon. Press into the standing heel and drive the hips forward to stand up tall before taking the next step. This exercise will help release tension in the posterior chain (Glutes, Hamstrings and Calves) and strengthen the posture of the upper body.

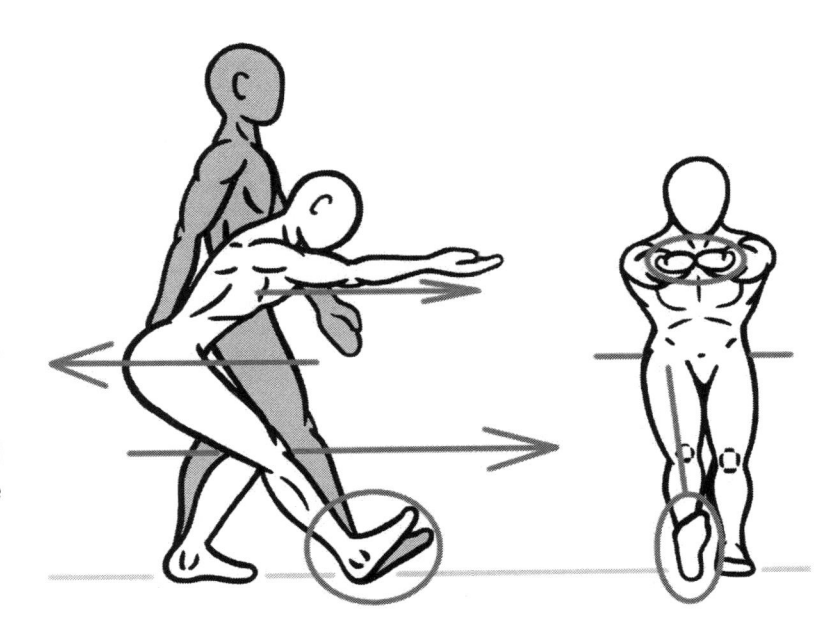

Repeat 5-20 steps for 1 or 2 sets.

RUNNING DRILLS

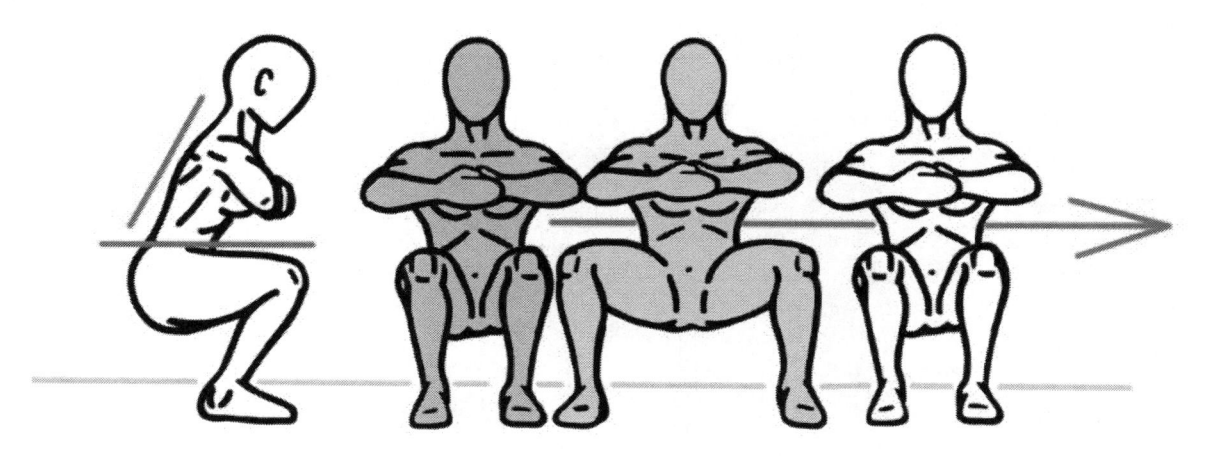

LATERAL SQUAT WALK
ACTION: Lower into a squat, dropping the hips below the height of the kneecaps. Then step out to the side as far as possible while maintaining the same height. Continue walking in a lateral direction and keep the chest lifted while focusing the eyes on the horizon. Relax as much as possible to help the hips to sink deeper into the squat. This exercise will introduce larger loads onto the leg muscles, which will prepare the body for the increased amount of stress when running.

Repeat 5-20 times in each direction for 1 or 2 sets.

WALKING LUNGE & REACH
ACTION: Step forward into a lunge and reach both arms up and back as the rear knee almost touches the floor. Fully extend the arms and keep the thumbs touching throughout the reach. Also, make sure that the kneecaps track over the width of the front toes when lunging. Drive into the front heel and push off with the back forefoot to come forward into a standing position. Then switch legs and repeat the movement. This exercise will introduce a larger load to each individual leg and will prepare the body for the increased amount of stress when running.

Lunge 5-20 times per leg for 1 or 2 sets.

438 PreHab Exercises for Runners

RUNNING DRILLS

LATERAL LUNGE

POSITION: Start in a comfortable wide-stance position or step into a comfortable wide stance from a neutral standing position as an advanced version.

ACTION: Lunge to one side by sitting the hips backwards and keeping one leg completely straight. Attempt to lower the hip onto the heel of the bending leg while tracking the kneecap over the toes. Reach the arms towards the horizon to lift the chest and straighten spine. Either return to start or step through into a walk, which is more advanced.

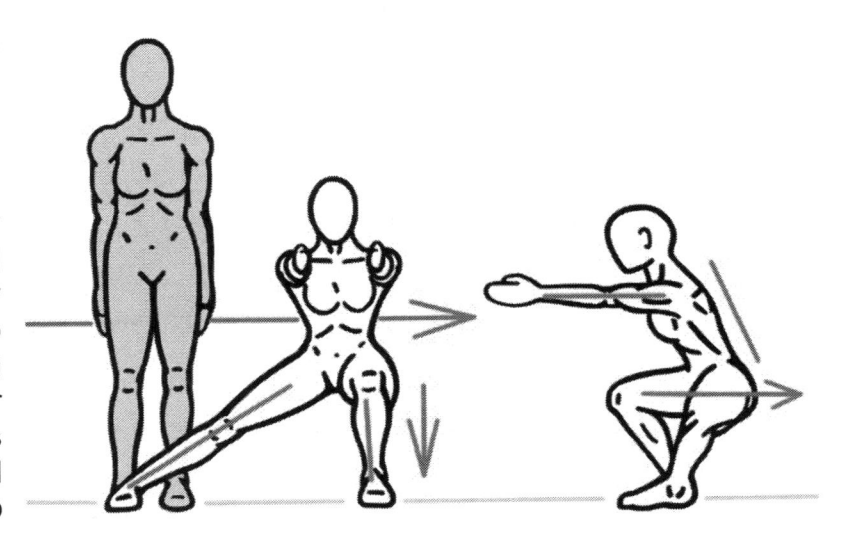

Repeat 5-20 times on each leg for 1-3 sets.

WALKING LUNGE & ROTATE

ACTION: Step forward into a lunge and almost touch the floor with the rear knee as both arms reach up and over to the side. Rotate the arms towards the leg that is in front and fully extended the elbows while keeping the thumbs touching. Again, track the kneecap of the front leg over the toes on each step. Drive into the front heel while pushing off the rear forefoot to come forward into a standing position and switch sides. This exercise will introduce a larger load and a higher demand for more stability on each individual leg that will prepare the body for the increased amount of stress when running.

Lunge 5-20 times on each leg for 1 or 2 sets.

PreHab Exercises for Runners

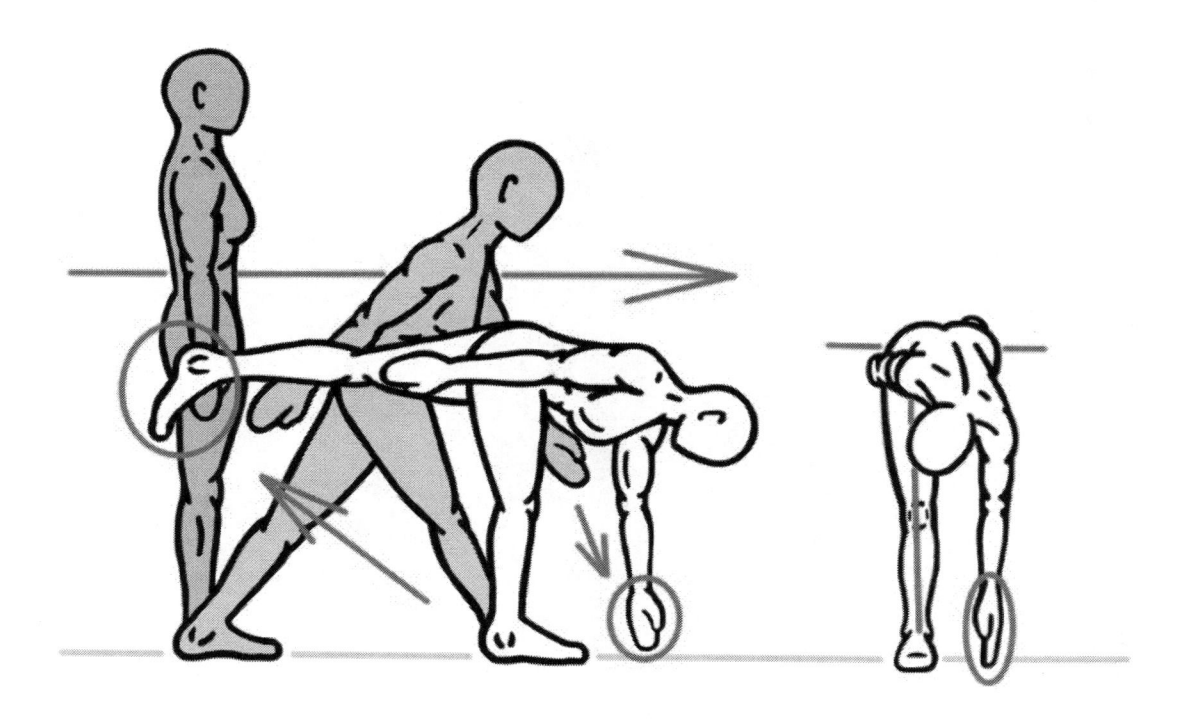

RUNNING DRILLS

SINGLE-LEG LUNGE with CONTRALATERAL REACH
ACTION: Step forward onto one foot and reach the opposite hand to the ground by lifting the trail leg up to the sky. Pull the belly button in towards the spine to engage the abdominals to support the lower back while also lengthening the spine. Raise the trail leg parallel to the ground and keep the hips square to the standing leg. Drive the hips forward and lift the chest to come to standing. Switch legs and repeat movement. This exercise introduces higher demands for stability, balance and coordination.

Repeat 5-20 times on each leg for 1-3 sets.

RUNNING DRILLS

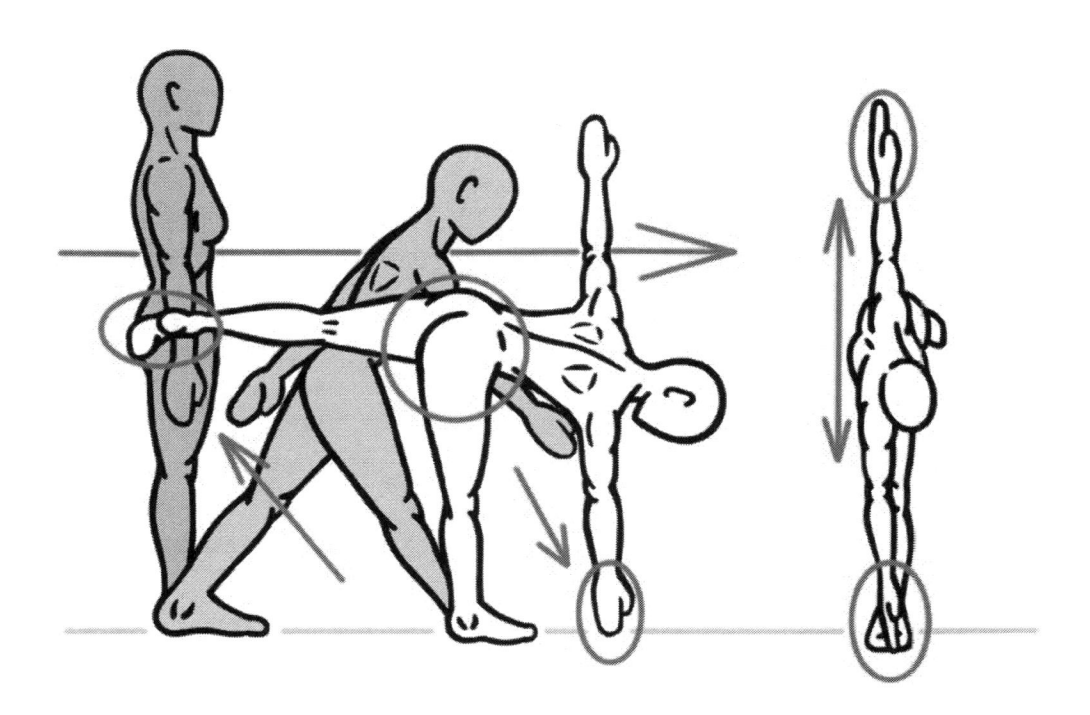

SINGLE-LEG LUNGE with IPSILATERAL REACH
ACTION: Step forward onto one foot and reach the *same-side* hand to the ground by lifting the trail leg up to the sky. Pull the belly button in towards the spine to engage the abdominals to support the lower back while also lengthening the spine. Raise the trail leg parallel to the ground and roll the hips open while also rotating the torso until the chest faces the horizon and the shoulders are stacked over one another. Drive the hips forward and lift the chest to come to standing. Switch legs and repeat movement. This exercise will develop more lateral stability and test balance and coordination.

Repeat 5-20 times on each leg for 1-3 sets.

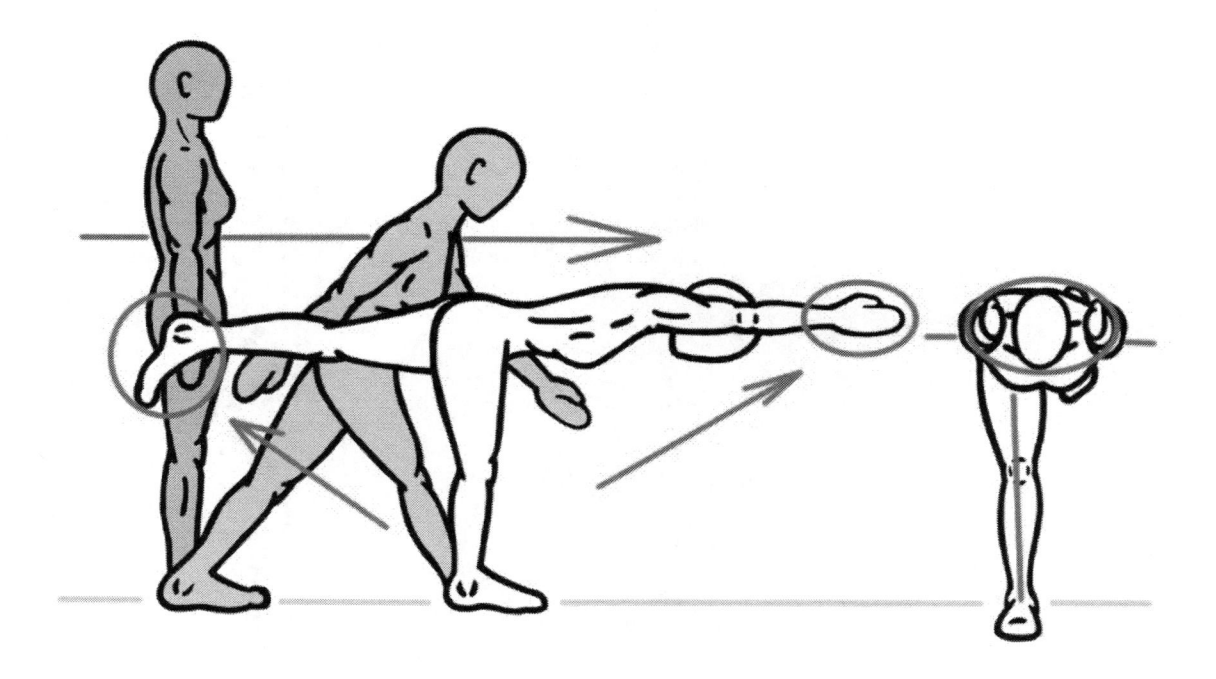

RUNNING DRILLS

SINGLE-LEG AIRPLANE LUNGE
ACTION: Step forward onto one foot and extend both arms overhead towards the horizon while lifting the trail leg up to the sky. Pull the belly button in towards the spine to engage the abdominals to support the lower back while also lengthening the spine and reaching the hands towards the horizon. Lift the trail leg parallel to the ground and keep the hips square to the standing leg. Then drive the hips forward and lift the chest to come to standing. Switch legs and repeat movement. This exercise continues to test balance, stability and coordination of each individual leg.

Repeat 5-20 times on each leg for 1-3 sets.

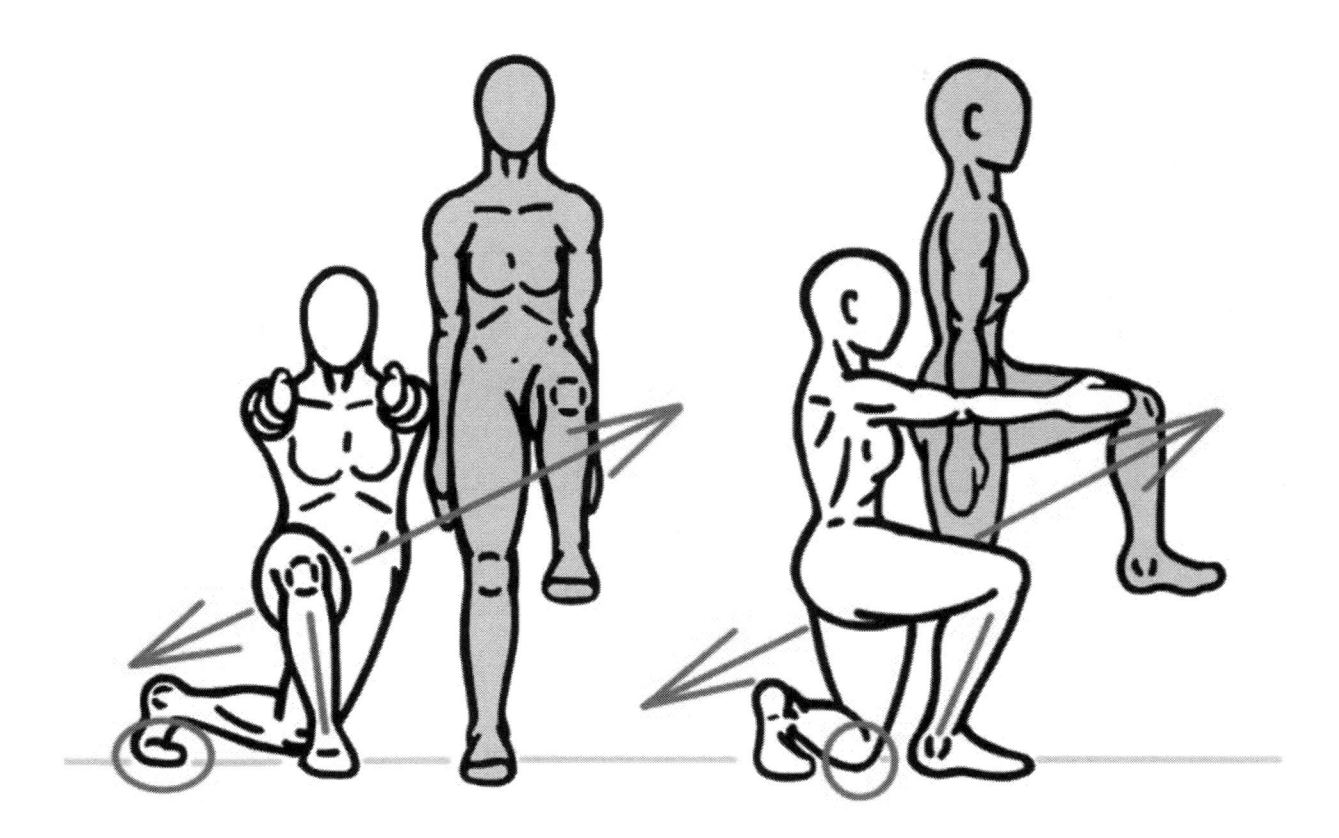

RUNNING DRILLS

STATIONARY CURTSY LUNGE

POSITION: Stand tall on one leg with the opposite knee tucked to hip height.

ACTION: Step the raised leg back and behind the standing leg while sliding the hips directly backwards and reaching for the horizon with both arms. Lift the chest, sit at the hips and bend the knees. Then drive the hips forward and come back to the original standing position on one leg, quickly establishing balance before starting the next lunge. This exercise will develop more lateral stability in each leg.

Lunge 5-20 times on each leg for 1 or 2 sets.

RUNNING DRILLS

Time to Shine

If you want to perform your best and set some personal records, efficiency is essential no matter what arena you are competing in. Guts and heart may get you through the tough spots, but your best performance is simple math.

Personal Records are made when you maximize output and minimize inefficiency.

When it comes to running, the more that you can maximize the output of your gait, the further and faster you can go with every single step!

It's simple math.
So, practice perfecting your form and you will make new records for yourself.

RUNNING DRILLS

Running Technique

So, you want to run faster or go farther? Or perhaps both? If running is your thing or you are just an athlete who runs a lot, developing proper biomechanics and practicing good form will help you to run farther and run faster – at the same time.

Improve your Technique
You may wonder what technique can do for you. Well, I used to believe in "no pain, no gain." I imagined that success as a runner and an athlete came down to how much I wanted it, which is why I love many movie montages such as the ones in all of the Rocky movies. Then I saw how technique was also a key to success.

> *Heart, determination and grit will help pave a path to success.*
> *So will technique.*

5K Challenge
In my evolution to becoming a PreHab advocate, I had some doubts that I categorize as healthy skepticism. A part of me believed in "form equals function," and therefore I saw power in technique. At the same time, I didn't like listening to other trainers say form is everything, especially when they themselves had bad form, let alone bad posture.

I decided to put form and technique to the test when I created my 5K Challenge. It simply was a 30 Day Training Program for a 5K in which I did not run once. I only did PreHab Exercises, in which I focused specifically on mobility, activation, stability and running technique. I did no conditioning at all. Well, more specifically, I did no metabolic or aerobic conditioning. I believed that these PreHab exercises would improve my biomechanics were a critical component of running, and I wanted to prove it.

Challenge Summary
During my 30-day PreHab Challenge, I dramatically improved my biomechanics and running technique. And it led to a reduction in my 5K time by over three minutes – all without running once. Not even one day.

After this 5K Challenge, I was sold on the notion that technique and form are very important. I was also convinced that I had a lot of room for improvement in regards to my own biomechanics. That's when I chose to take on the mission of eliminating biomechanical compensation for myself and others and became an advocate for PreHab.

Run Better
Now, many runners have been practicing some of the following exercises without calling them PreHab exercises and that's fine with me. I am not too sure where the term "PreHab" originated, I just know that Tim Ferriss helped to popularize the term in his

RUNNING DRILLS

book, *The 4-Hour Body: An Uncommon Guide to Rapid Fat Loss, Incredible Sex, and Becoming Superhuman*. The most important thing about PreHab exercises is that if you're a runner or an athlete who runs, doing these exercises will improve your running technique.

Ground Contact
Let's take a moment and look at how you make contact with the ground when you run. Yes, your foot makes contact with the ground but what part of your foot is a different question.

> *When you run, you will either use a Heel Strike, Mid-Foot Strike or a Forefoot Strike.*

Not all styles are biomechanically equal. And if you are looking to increase your running speed, endurance and longevity, the way that you make contact with the ground makes a huge difference.

Heel Strike - Oh, no!
The Heel Strike is the least biomechanically advantageous way to run for two main reasons. First, when you heel strike, your foot is hitting the ground in front of the center of gravity of your body. This will actually slow you down as you run.

> **When you run with a heel strike, you create a braking mechanism in your running technique.**

The mechanics of a heel strike are similar to that of the pole vault. When the pole is driven into the ground (in front of the athlete), it creates a large braking mechanism. Yet, the momentum of the athlete running does not stop. Instead, it coils up into the bending of the pole and ultimately changes directions to lift the athlete up and over the bar.

When running with a Heel Strike, you are constantly "pole vaulting" over your front leg on each step. The Heel Strike creates a braking action to your forward momentum. It forces you to apply additional power to overcome or vault over this lead leg, which ultimately tires you out and will slow you down.

Ideally, when running for speed or distance, you want to use forward momentum as a driving force in your stride. The goal is to eliminate all mechanics that diminish or interrupt your momentum.

The second reason that the Heel Strike negatively contributes to your running technique is its biomechanical effect on your legs and hips. As mentioned before, the Heel Strike is a braking mechanism just like the pole is in a pole vault. The only difference is that the pole used in the pole vault is designed to bend, which stores the force of the

RUNNING DRILLS

athlete's momentum in the pole until the energy is redirected and the athlete is launched over the pole. Our legs and hips are not designed like those poles.

When you Heel Strike, all of the forward momentum of your running gets stopped by your leg, which is solid and sturdy. The force of your momentum needs to go somewhere because energy cannot be destroyed, according to the Newtonian principal. Consequentially, the Heel Strike makes your own body unnecessarily absorb the force of your momentum because it redirects the energy up your leg, through your knees and thighs, right into your hip sockets and even your lower back. You are literally pounding your legs, hips and spine with your momentum every step you take when you Heel Strike.

Heel Striking unnecessarily redirects your momentum back into your body and forces your legs, hips and spine to absorb even more force with each step you take while running.

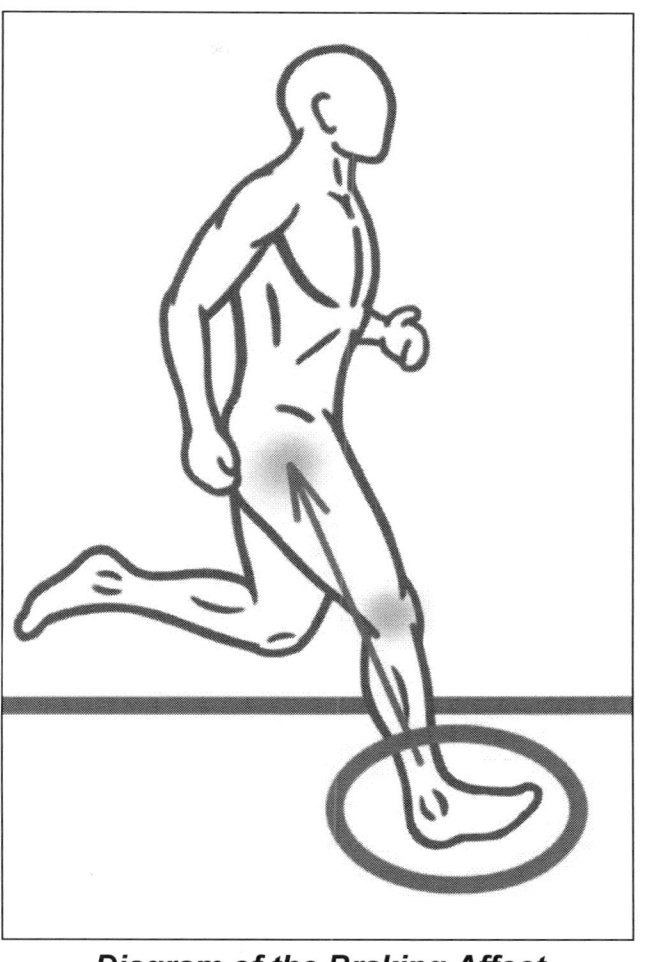

Diagram of the Braking Affect In a Heel Strike

Causes of the Heel Strike

Habitual sitting is one of the major reasons why people start to run with a heel strike. As mentioned before in this book, sitting for long periods of time, especially over the course of years, will eventually remold your soft tissue and biomechanics. Prolonged sitting will create tightness in the Hip Flexors and the quadriceps, while also helping to deactivate the Glute muscles, which are the body's prime movers.

Sitting affects your running – Photo by Christopher Sessums

RUNNING DRILLS

Eventually, the tightness developed in the Hip Flexors and quadriceps from sitting will reduce the output of force in your push off leg while running because the mobility of your hip extension becomes restricted. At the same time, the desire to run faster can make a person start to over stride and extend the foot farther out in front of the body in an attempt to gain more ground. However, over striding will include a Heel Strike and the braking mechanism that goes along with it. This can also overstress the mechanics of your posterior chain muscle groups and possibly cause a pulled hamstring.

Set Yourself Apart
If you really want to make waves as a runner, work on your technique and develop the biomechanics that will help you to do more with less! As noted, the Heel Strike is a common compensation strategy in running. Many people don't know they do it because it's not very easy to watch yourself run. Yet, there is a simple way to start running with a more economic running technique.

Spend more time barefoot in order to stop yourself from habitually Heel Striking.

Take your shoes off!
Test yourself by running with no shoes on. Start on soft grass and then work your way to a more solid surface over time. You will be surprised by what you find!

You cannot Heel Strike when you run if you do not have cushioned-soled shoes on your feet!

Now, I am not recommending that you start barefoot running if that is not for you. I am simply giving you a very good drill to use to help change your running technique and eliminate heel striking for good.

RUNNING DRILLS

Minimalist Shoes

If you want to be an avid runner with good biomechanics, you will at some point (soon) convert to minimalist shoes, aka shoes with a negative heel. Any heel in your shoe, no matter the height, will change your biomechanics over time. A heel in your shoe creates an inclined platform or slope on which all of your movement is created. Eventually this will shorten your calf muscles, add more stress to your knees, and make your quadriceps do more work that your Glutes are biomechanically designed to do.

In short, running in minimalist shoes is a step in the right direction when it comes to your biomechanics.

Meanwhile, a positive-heeled shoe can actually cause you to develop a heel strike. The highly-cushioned sole allows you to make contact with the ground, heel first. Worse yet, most shoes today are made with a cushioned sole and a positive heel. So, it's easy to develop a Heel Strike merely by walking into a shoe store!

Need more proof for minimalist shoes? Pick up Katy Bowman's books, *Alignment Matters* and *Every Woman's Guide to Foot Pain Relief*. Katy is a biomechanist and coach who examines ideal alignment in movement and posture as well as its effects on biological function. In other words, Katy looks to see what diseases can and will result from specific compensations in human alignment. She also notes a study that shows the calf muscles shorten by an average of 18 percent in women who habitually wear high heels over the course of 20 years. Still need reasons to switch to minimalist shoes?

RUNNING DRILLS

Stepping in the Right Direction
After discussing the negative consequences of the Heel Strike technique and positive heels in shoes, let's change focus to running techniques that work for your body. There are two different techniques that can help you to run faster and run further. They are the Mid-Foot Strike and Forefoot Strike in combination with the Forward Lean.

Strike Techniques

Mid-foot Strike

Forefoot Strike

RUNNING DRILLS

Forward Lean
The ideal alignment of a person standing stacks the ear over the shoulder, over the hip socket, and over the ankle. The Forward Lean follows the same ideal alignment – just on a slant. The Forward Lean is used to create forward momentum when you run. It is basically a controlled fall, meaning that the lean creates a "fall," which is movement caused by gravity. This fall is controlled in terms that the fall never grows too large because the next step in your run stops it. In addition, because of the forward slant of your alignment, the fall is continuously reinvented with every single step.

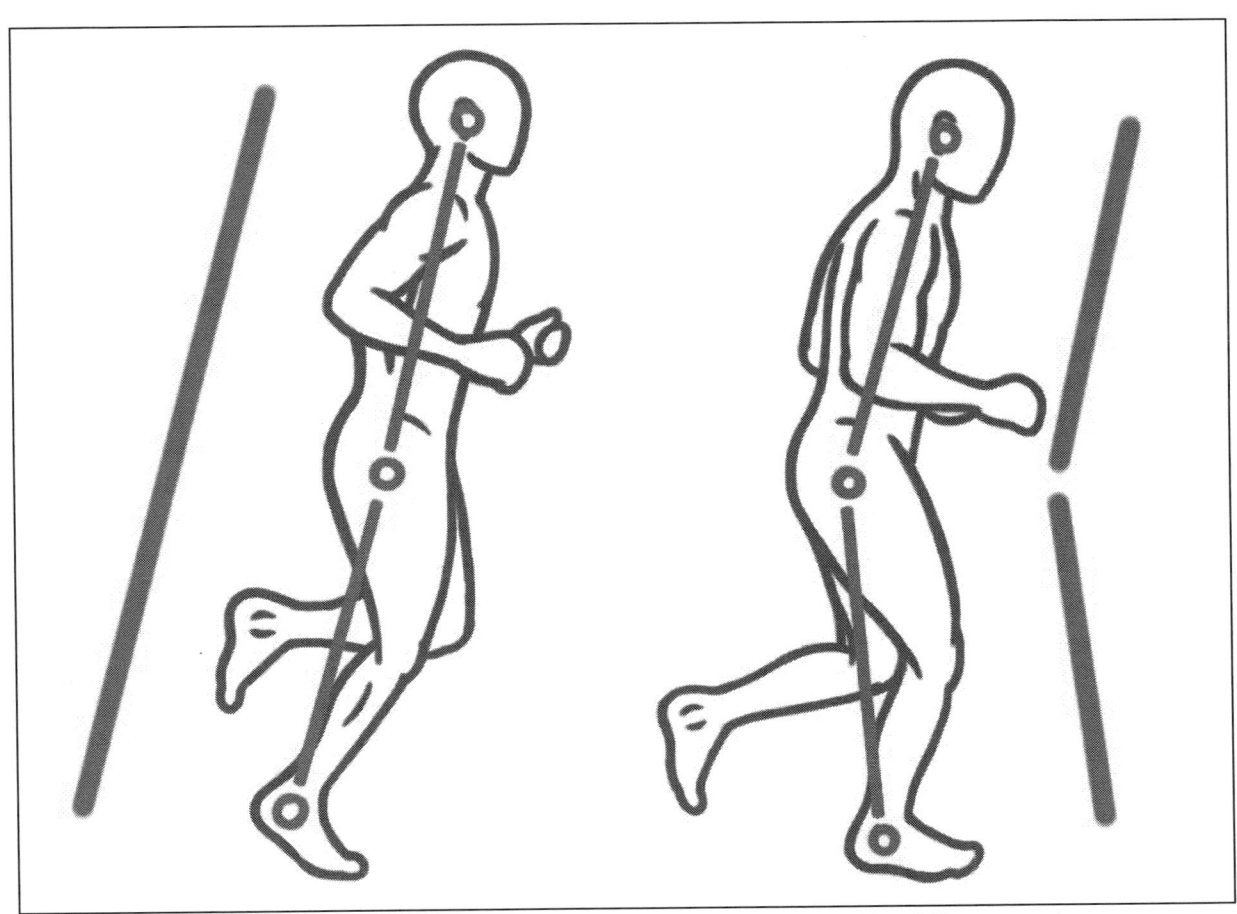

The Forward Lean Alignment vs. a Hinged Hip Alignment

Essentially, the Forward Lean produces a controlled fall where gravity creates momentum because of a slanted alignment. The generated momentum is then used to propel the running technique forward.

Ride the Fall
The Forward Lean essentially allows you to run farther using less energy. All you need to do is to "break" the controlled fall by planting a foot on the ground. The closer you plant that foot at or behind your center of gravity, the easier it is to continue creating that controlled fall for the next step. Soon enough, your running form begins to become: Fall - Plant - Fall - Plant - Fall - Plant...

RUNNING DRILLS

Constructing the Forward Lean

Stand in front of a wall at arm's length away and place both hands on the wall. Now, start to lean forward and use your arms to support you. As you lean forward, maintain a straight-line alignment between your ankle, hip socket and ear hole.

Stability is an important factor in effectively using the Forward Lean approach. You need to make sure that your head, spine and hips are stabilized in proper alignment. There are a host of common faults in these areas. They frequently show up as Forward Neck, Upper Cross syndrome of the Shoulders and Thoracic Spine, Lower Cross syndrome of the Hips and Lumbar spine, as well as too much tightness between the pelvis and thighs that can cause a lack of mobility called a Muted Hip.

Visit the previous exercise sections, Stability and Gait Efficiency, in order to help establish the necessary stability needed for the Forward Lean.

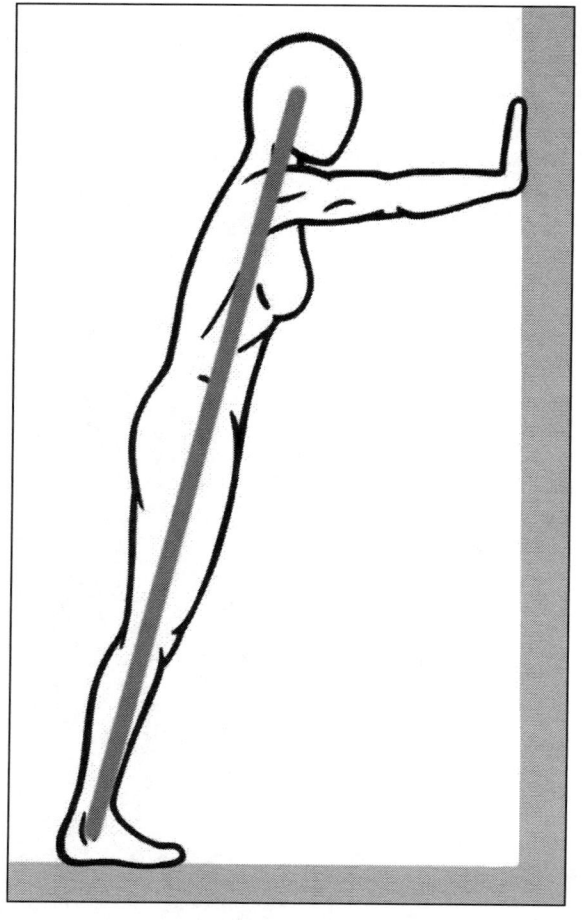

Use a wall to develop the Forward Lean

Striking Position

Where your foot strikes the ground in relation to your center of gravity is also vitally important to the effectiveness of the Forward Lean. If you strike the ground in front of your center of gravity, you will be creating support that breaks your fall too early. This premature action will lessen the amount of forward momentum available to propel you forward. Ideally, you will want to keep this fall seamlessly going from step to step to really economize your energy and running form.

Note that your center of gravity is different from the bottom of the slanted ear-hip-ankle alignment. You will usually find your center of gravity directly beneath your hips if you are well stabilized and aligned in a Forward Lean. Knowing where your center of gravity is important because it will help you accurately manage your foot striking position on each step. Simply aim for the ground directly beneath or behind your hips.

RUNNING DRILLS

Slope and Speed

The degree of your Forward Lean will also correspond to the Speed in wish you want to run. The faster that you want to go, the more of a Forward Lean you will want to have. Just look at a Sprinter, who literally launches herself forward out of the starting blocks. If you are a long distance runner, the slope of your Forward Lean will be much less with well-deserved reason too. However, the steeper the slope, the more force and energy it takes to break your fall and keep you going forward as opposed to falling flat on your face. Therefore, if you are running a marathon, you want to minimize your forward lean as much as possible without killing off the controlled fall.

The degree to which you lean forward when you run will correlate to the amount of speed and acceleration that you intend to employ. Faster speeds and acceleration will have steeper slopes to their leans.

Explosive Acceleration employs a steep Forward Lean

Speed and Acceleration in Sports

Many sports require the players and athletes to change direction as well as change speed. Acceleration is a huge part of sports like football, baseball, lacrosse, soccer and many more. The Forward Lean aids acceleration immensely. Practicing different degrees of slope while running will help athletes build more speed control and acceleration while playing in their sport.

For example, a skilled wide receiver in football will heavily lean forward when starting their route. This will help them try to break away from a defender and increase to reach top speed. A lacrosse player may also use this lean technique to help quickly change direction to outmaneuver a defender. No matter the direction of the lean, an extravagant slope will provide more momentum that the athlete can use to increase his speed.

RUNNING DRILLS

PreHab in Sports
When we look at the sports that require high levels of agility and acceleration, such as basketball, soccer, football and lacrosse, to name a few, an effective PreHab routine needs to address a couple of key concepts in order to fully prepare the athlete for practice and competition.

> **Essential PreHab Exercise Progressions for Improved Agility & Acceleration:**
>
> **Ankle Mobility**
> **Posterior Chain/Hip Activation**
> **Hip Stability**
> **Core Stability**

Ideally, athletes should work through every phase of PreHab, including mobility, activation and stability, for each joint complex, but that is not always possible. There is only so much time allotted for practice for team sports, which means that everything cannot be covered in each practice. When time is a factor, it's important to focus on the following four PreHab concepts as part of practice. Focus on these four techniques and have athletes incorporate the other PreHab concepts on their own as much as possible.

These four PreHab concepts will provide support to proper biomechanics and help develop efficient movement patterns before athletes practice the skills and timing of their sport. It is not the best that you can do, but it is the least that you can do. Forget better results over time, use the Joint-By-Joint approach to evaluate how the athlete is moving and analyze where limitations exist in their biomechanics. Then attempt to incorporate PreHab exercises and techniques to address any faults in future training sessions or practices.

> **Determining your Strike**
> In addition to the faulty Heel Strike, there are two other foot positions to use when running: the Mid-Foot Strike and the Forefoot Strike.

Forefoot Strike
The Pose Method by Dr. Nicholas Romanov made the Forefoot Strike very popular because of its effectiveness in creating speed. Nicholas was a running coach who worked with Russian Sprinters in the 1970s and noticed that the longer an athlete's foot remained in contact with the ground, the slower that athlete ran. So, he started to instruct his sprinters to only touch the ground with the balls of the feet and keep the heel, as well as the mid-foot, off of the ground.

RUNNING DRILLS

Helps Sprinting
The Forefoot Strike and the Pose Method are very effective at maximizing your running speed due to the biomechanics. When the foot strikes the ground and you intentionally keep the heel from touching down, the musculature and fascia of the foot and calf, as well as the rest of the posterior chain, quickly absorb a large amount of kinetic energy. This energy is quickly and reflexively redirected back out through the body as soon as the foot transitions into the "push-off" phase.

The biomechanics of a forefoot strike is similar to that of dribbling a basketball. The basketball is made of an elastic material, rubber, and filled with air. When you bounce the ball on the floor, the elastic properties of the ball quickly absorb and redirect the kinetic energy. Conversely, if you throw a sandbag against the floor, it sticks. There is no bounce because there are no elastic properties to absorb and redirect the kinetic energy. Your soft tissue, the musculature and fascia, has an elastic element to it that allows it to absorb and redirect energy.

Forefoot Strike

Key: Heels Off the Ground
Another important biomechanical factor that affects the speed produced from the Forefoot Strike is not allowing the heels to touch the ground. When a runner can keep the heels from touching the ground, this action creates an additional lever system. This allows the ankle joint to catch and redirect kinetic energy. In essence, the entire posterior chain, from toes to spine, is absorbing and redirecting kinetic energy with each step. This maximizes the amount of energy that can be generated and controlled.

The major drawback to using the Forefoot technique is the amount of stress that the body endures, especially the soft tissue of the calves and feet. Since the calves and feet are at the bottom of the kinetic chain, the amount of stress is compounded on each step by the weight of the entire body. In fact, the amount of stress absorbed by the body while sprinting is estimated at six times one's body weight.

Since the Forefoot Strike creates large amounts of stress on the body, it is very important to include large amounts of soft tissue therapy in a training program.

RUNNING DRILLS

Mid-Foot Strike
Danny Dreyer's book, *Chi Running: A Revolutionary Approach to Effortless, Injury-Free Running*, has helped increased people's understanding and application of the mid-foot strike. Danny is an ultra-endurance athlete who teaches and uses the mid-foot strike as part of his method with incredible results.

The mid-foot strike uses the most amount of surface space while running in comparison to the other two foot positions. When the foot touches down on the ground, it uses the entire foot, except for the inner arch, as support.

Benefits of the mid-foot strike:
- Less acute stress is absorbed by the foot and lower leg.
- More surface space during contact allows for more stability.

The Long Haul
The mid-foot strike is very useful for long distances as it will help economize your effort throughout the run. More stability and less stress will allow runners to save energy for more strides at the far end of the run. That's because there is less physiological breakdown of the soft tissue as well as less neuromuscular activity to support balance, coordination and timing with the mid-foot strike.

Comparisons between mid-foot and forefoot
There are advantages to each of these two running techniques. The forefoot strike can provide more elastic energy and power on every single step, but also creates more stress on the body, specifically the soft tissue of the lower leg and foot. Conversely, the mid-foot strike offers more stability and less stress in comparison. However, the mid-foot strike will allow for more drag fiction due to the larger amount of surface space of the foot that contacts the ground. It also lessens the amount of elastic energy that can biomechanically be used on each stride.

Mid-foot Strike

In short, the forefoot strike is a very useful technique for sprinting and speed work because of the increased power potential. While the mid-foot strike offers an economic advantage in distance running and jogging. However, you do not need to just choose one technique. You can practice both techniques as a way to expand your skill set and maximize your running potential.

RUNNING DRILLS

Practice
Even if you get it right the very first time that you try either one of these techniques, be intentional and continue to practice your running technique and drills, because life will get in the way – literally and figuratively. Remember your biomechanics are always shifting and remolding around what you do on a daily basis. So, if you set aside the time to practice these drills and focus on your technique, your body will remember and use good form when running.

See for yourself-
As part of a mental exercise, go down to a track and watch how people run. Specifically look to see how their foot makes contact with the ground. Notice which part of the foot actually makes contact with the ground first and where the foot is in relation to the rest of the body. Is the foot in front of the body, behind the body or under the body? Is there a Heel Strike, Mid-Foot Strike or Forefoot Strike?

This mental exercise will help you to recognize the different mechanics of running and give you an intrinsic understanding of your own technique as well.

Form Running Drills

This sequence of exercises will help develop the biomechanics that fuel a healthy and fast stride. The sequence progresses in complexity and intensity as it will also assimilate the physical demands of running.

RUNNING DRILLS

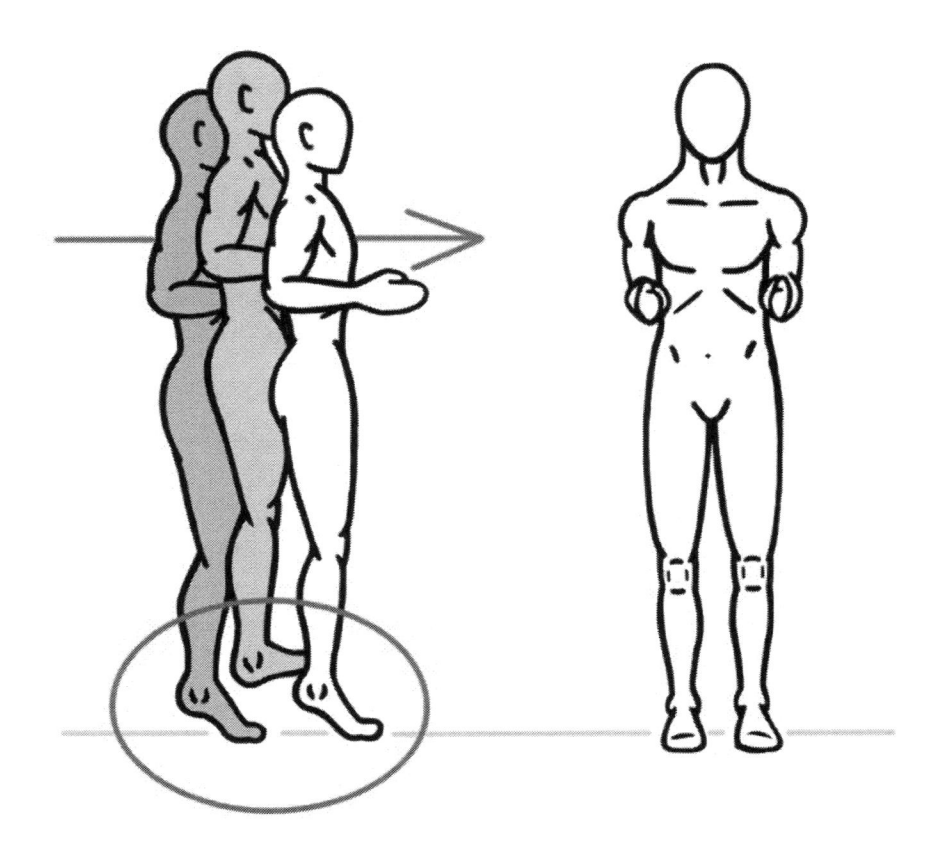

ANKLE HOP

POSITION: Stand with the pelvis in neutral, the abdominals engaged, spine tall, the shoulder blades pulled towards the hips, eyes focused on the horizon, and the heels off the ground while balancing on the forefoot.

ACTION: Hop forward using only the ankles. Forcefully extend through the ankles to push the ground down and away. Land only on the forefoot and keep the heels off the ground while engaging the abdominals, staying tall through the spine with the eyes focused on the horizon.

- *Perform these Ankle Hops in varying directions: Forward, Backwards and Laterally.*
- *Perform 10-30 times for 1-3 sets*

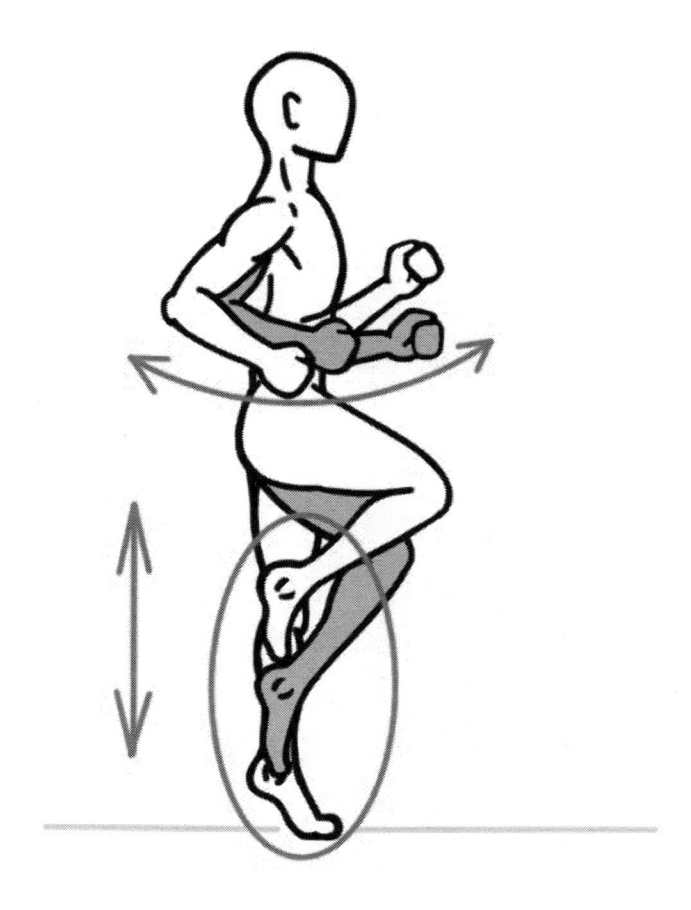

RUNNING DRILLS

HEEL STRIDE

POSITION: Stand with the pelvis in neutral, the abdominals engaged, spine tall, the shoulder blades pulled towards the hips, eyes focused on the horizon, and the heels off the ground while balancing on the forefoot.

ACTION: Run in place or run forward while quickly pulling the heels directly up towards the hips. Spend as little time as possible with the forefoot in contact with the ground and keep the knees in front of the body. Do not confuse this exercise with Heel Pull Strides (Buttkickers).

- *Perform these Heel Strides in varying directions: Forward, Backwards and Laterally.*
- *Perform 10-50 strides for 1-3 sets.*

RUNNING DRILLS

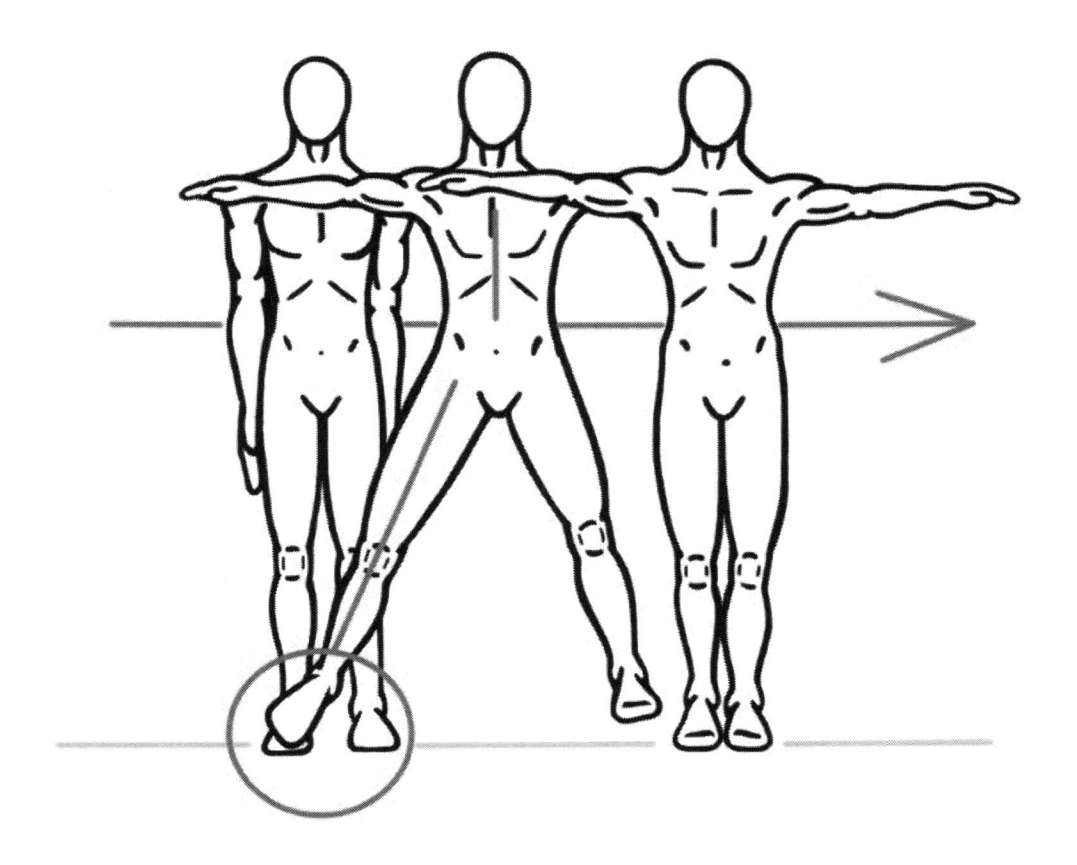

LATERAL SHUFFLE

POSITION: Stand with the pelvis in neutral, the abdominals engaged, spine tall, the shoulder blades pulled towards the hips, eyes focused on the horizon, and the heels off the ground while balancing on the forefoot.

ACTION: Step out to the side and laterally push off with the trail leg to start the traveling. Land on the forefoot and quickly pull the trail leg to meet the lead leg before stepping out and laterally driving to the side again. Stay long in the spine and extend through each push off as much as possible.

- *Shuffle 10-30 strides in each direction for 1-3 sets.*

RUNNING DRILLS

KNEE TUCK STRIDE (HIGH KNEES)
POSITION: Stand with the pelvis in neutral, the abdominals engaged, spine tall, the shoulder blades pulled towards the hips, eyes focused on the horizon, and the heels off the ground while balancing on the forefoot.

ACTION: Run forward and over-emphasize tucking the knees high on each stride. Keep the chest high and the heels off the ground as the arms freely swing and the forefoot drives into the ground. Lengthen the spine and engage the abdominals.

- *Perform these Knee Tucks in varying directions: Forward, Backwards and Laterally.*
- *Perform 10-50 strides for 1-3 sets.*

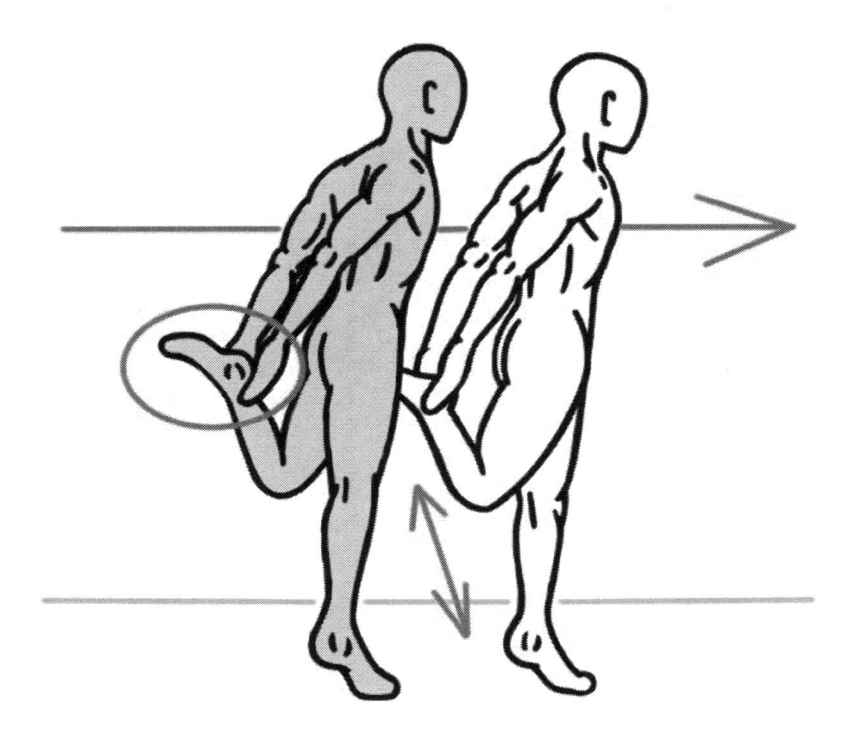

HEEL PULL STRIDE (BUTT KICKERS)

POSITION: Stand with the pelvis in neutral, the abdominals engaged, spine tall, the shoulder blades pulled towards the hips, eyes focused on the horizon, and the heels off the ground while balancing on the forefoot.

ACTION: Run forward and kick the heels back up to touch the hips or hands. Quickly return the foot to the ground on each stride, only making contact with the forefoot. Keep the heels off the ground, lean forward through the chest and stay long through the spine.

- *Perform these Heel Pulls in varying directions: Forward and Laterally.*
- *Perform 10-50 strides for 1-3 sets.*

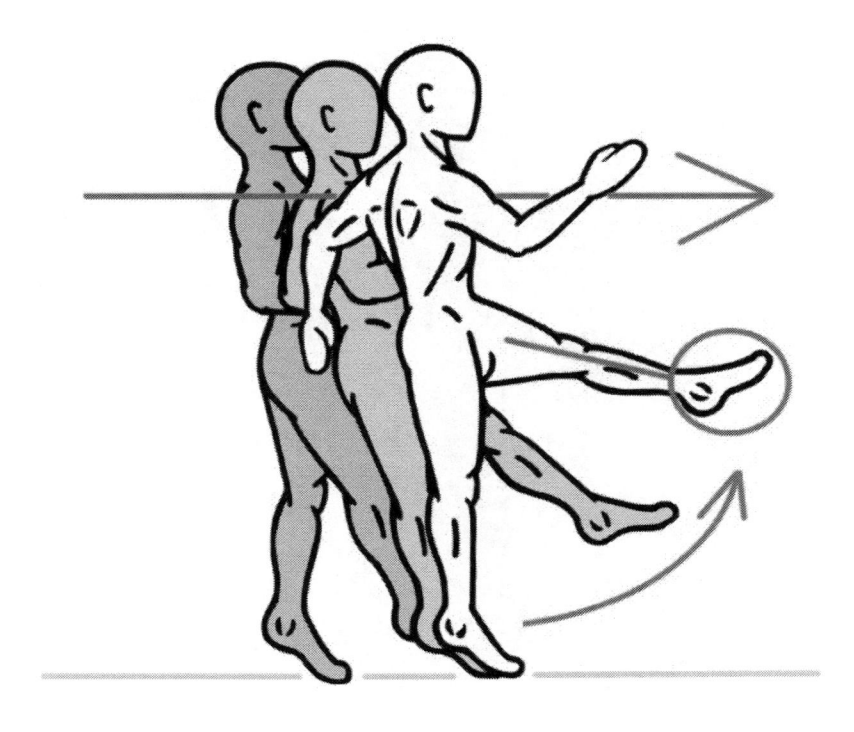

RUNNING DRILLS

STRAIGHT-LEG STRIDE
POSITION: Stand with the pelvis in neutral, the abdominals engaged, spine tall, the shoulder blades pulled towards the hips, eyes focused on the horizon, and the heels off the ground while balancing on the forefoot.

ACTION: Run forward with straight legs, kicking the toes towards the horizon and quickly stabbing the forefoot down into the ground on each stride. Drive the ground down and backwards and swing the arms. Stay long in the spine and focus the eyes on the horizon.

- *Perform 10-50 strides for 1-3 sets.*

RUNNING DRILLS

BACKPEDAL

POSITION: Stand with the pelvis in neutral, the abdominals engaged, spine tall, the shoulder blades pulled towards the hips, eyes focused on the horizon, and the heels off the ground while balancing on the forefoot.

ACTION: Run backwards by reaching each foot behind the body as far as possible on each stride. Strike the ground with the forefoot and swing the arms while staying tall through the spine and driving the ground down and forward.

- *Perform 10-50 strides for 1-3 sets.*

RUNNING DRILLS

CARIOCA

POSITION: Stand with the pelvis in neutral, the abdominals engaged, spine tall, the shoulder blades pulled towards the hips, eyes focused on the horizon, and the heels off the ground while balancing on the forefoot.

ACTION: Step out to the side and then pull the trail leg across the body to continue running laterally while swinging the arms and rotating back and forth through the hips. Keep the heels off the ground and the chest lifted as the forefoot makes contact with the ground on each stride.

- *Perform 10-30 strides in each direction for 1-3 sets.*

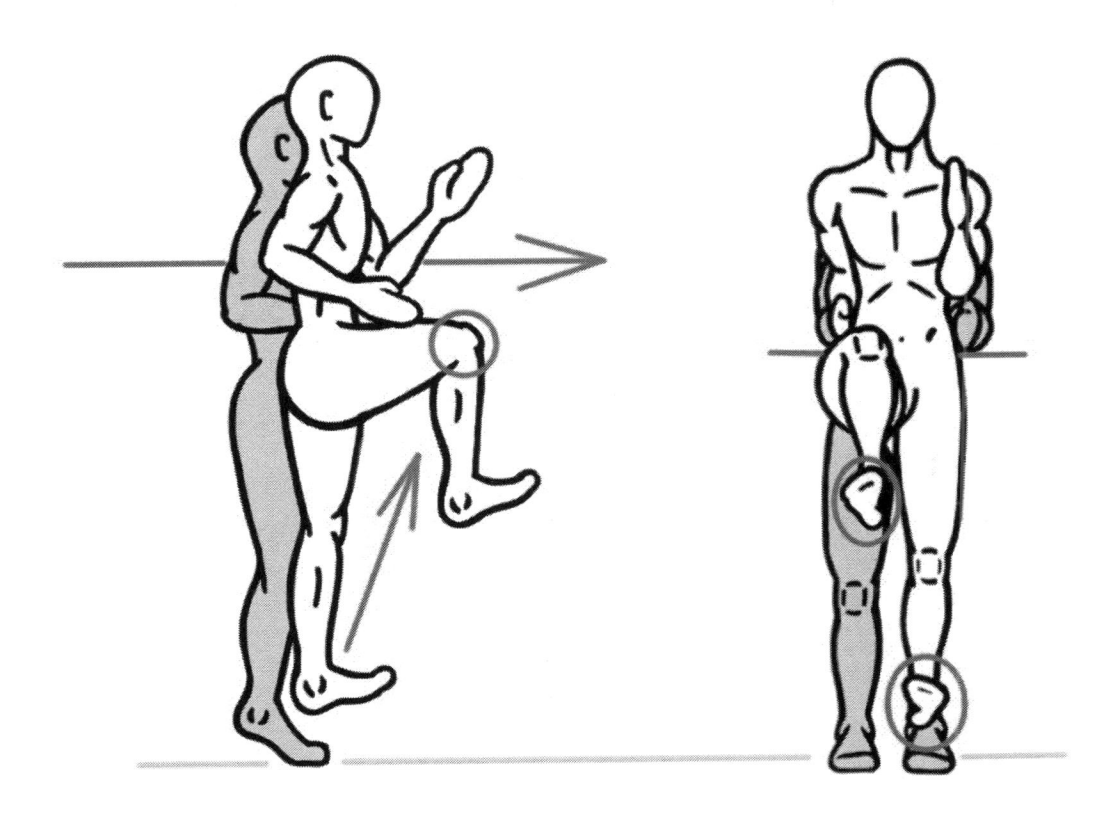

RUNNING DRILLS

A-SKIP
POSITION: Stand with the pelvis in neutral, the abdominals engaged, spine tall, the shoulder blades pulled towards the hips, eyes focused on the horizon, and the heels off the ground while balancing on the forefoot.

ACTION: Start with an ankle hop before tucking one knee and the opposite arm in skip fashion. Quickly return to an ankle hop before skipping on the other side. Keep the chest high, heels off the ground and land on the forefoot.

- *Perform these A-Skips in varying directions: Forward, Backwards and Laterally.*
- *Perform 10-30 skips on each side for 1-3 sets.*

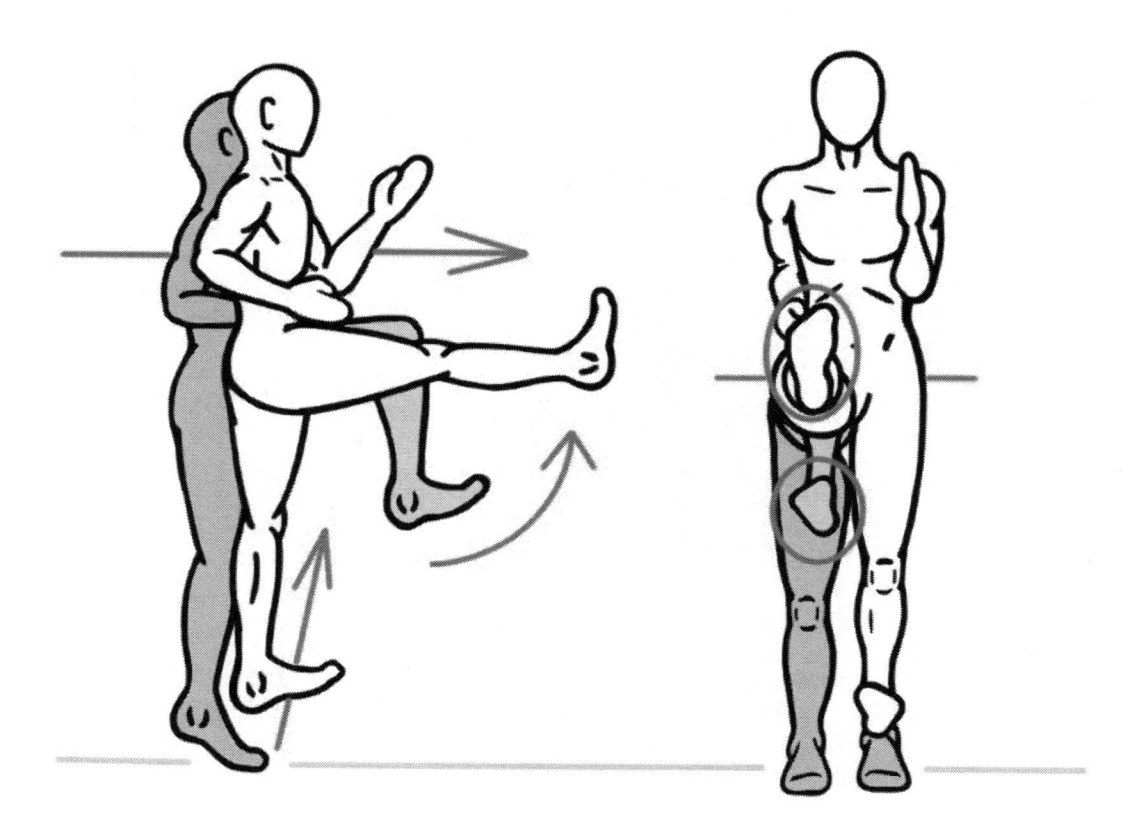

RUNNING DRILLS

B-SKIP

POSITION: Stand with the pelvis in neutral, the abdominals engaged, spine tall, the shoulder blades pulled towards the hips, eyes focused on the horizon, and the heels off the ground while balancing on the forefoot.

ACTION: Start with an ankle hop before tucking one knee and the opposite arm in skip fashion. At the top of the skip, kick the heel out towards the horizon with a straight leg. Quickly return to an ankle hop before skipping on the other side. Keep the chest high and land on the forefoot.

- *Perform 10-30 skips on each side for 1-3 sets.*

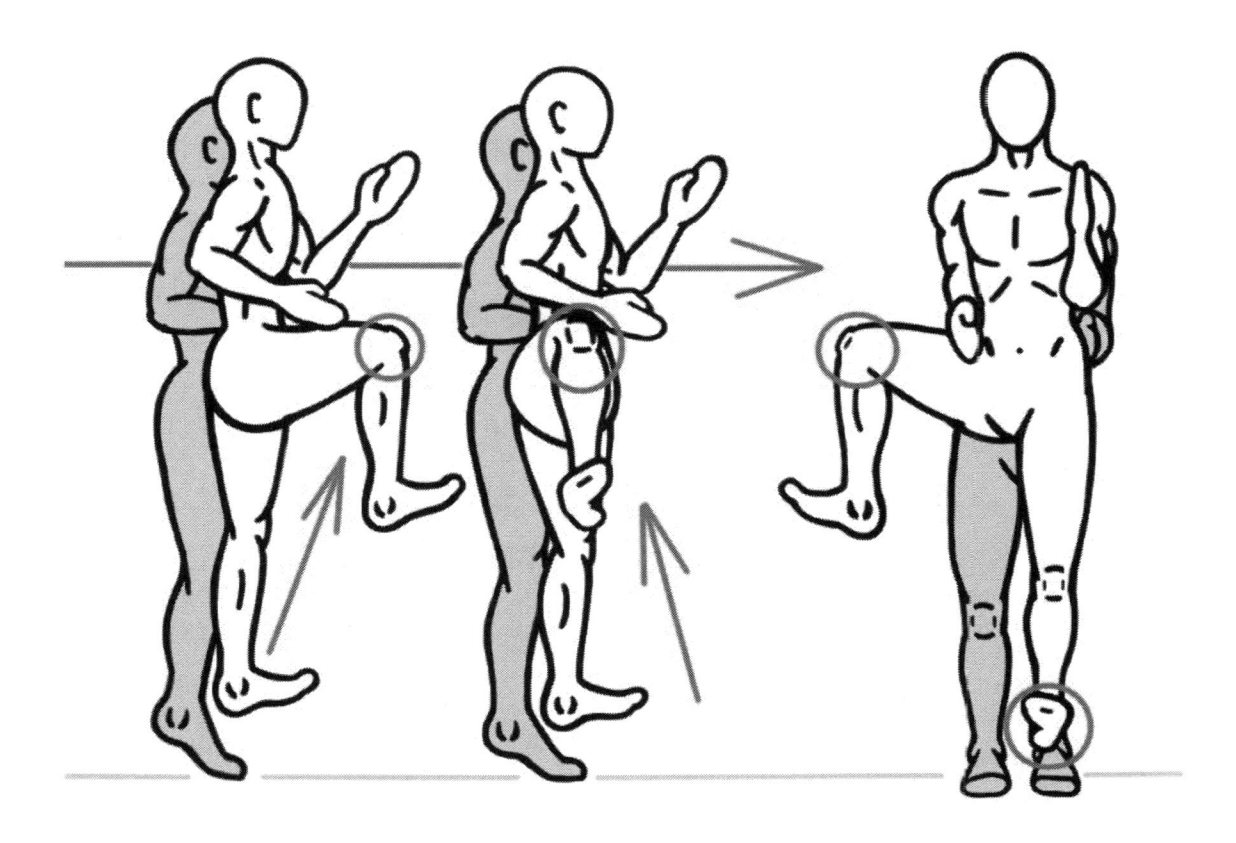

RUNNING DRILLS

TRIPLE A-SKIP

POSITION: Stand with the pelvis in neutral, the abdominals engaged, spine tall, the shoulder blades pulled towards the hips, eyes focused on the horizon, and the heels off the ground while balancing on the forefoot.

ACTION: Start with an ankle hop before tucking one knee and the opposite arm in skip-fashion. Repeat the skip with very the same leg out to the side and once more forward in a three-count sequence before returning to an ankle hop and switching sides. Keep chest high and land on the forefoot.

- *Perform 10-30 skips on each side for 1-3 sets.*

RUNNING DRILLS

ALTERNATING BOUNDING SKIP
POSITION: Stand with the pelvis in neutral, the abdominals engaged, spine tall, the shoulder blades pulled towards the hips, eyes focused on the horizon, and the heels off the ground while balancing on the forefoot.

ACTION: Start with a few ankle hops before launching into a series of bounding skips. On each skip, forcefully drive the ground back and away with an intention of skipping for height or distance. Alternate legs on each skip while keeping the chest high and the heels off the ground.

- *Skip for Distance and the skip for Height.*
- *Perform 10-30 skips on each side for 2-4 sets.*

RUNNING DRILLS

FORWARD LEAN POSITIONING

POSITION: Stand with the pelvis in neutral, the abdominals engaged, spine tall, the shoulder blades pulled towards the hips, eyes focused on the horizon, and the heels off the ground while balancing on the forefoot.

ACTION: Tuck one knee to hip height and lean forward with a straight spine until the lean becomes a "fall." Quickly, stab the forefoot into the ground and start running. Keep the forward "fall" occurring on each stride while running to create a momentum that economizes total energy expenditure.

- *Repeat 5-10 times on each leg.*

Get Out and Run!

You've gotten a lot of information about different techniques in running as well as the elements of an effective PreHab practice. Now, the next step is to start running again!

Remember, Rome was not built in a day. Shifting your technique and developing your practice will take time and effort. Yet, it is worth it.

If you intentionally keep a certain level of dedication in your training, the sky is the limit for you, and I am very happy for you too!

So, get out there and run now.

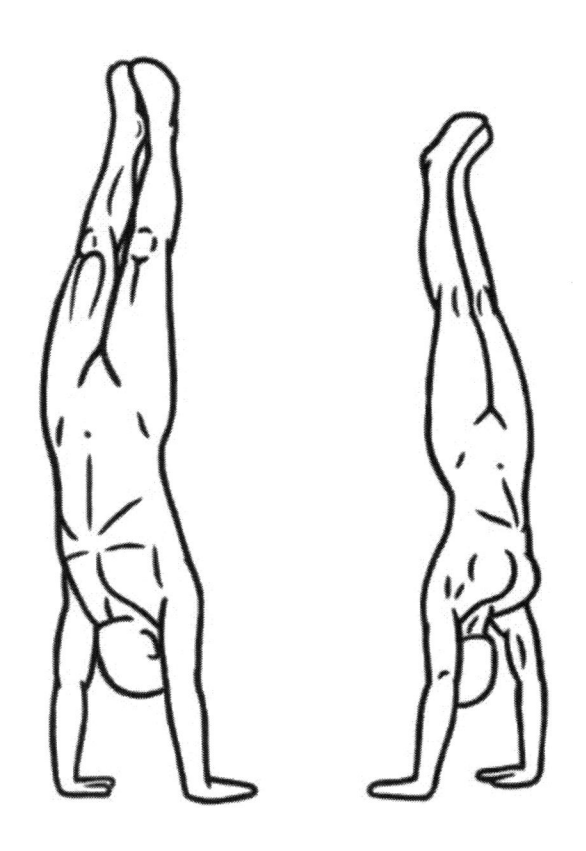

Recovery

RECOVERY

RECOVERY

Yoga
One of the original forms of PreHab

Walk into any gym or health club, and you'll probably see some yoga classes on the schedule taught by ultraflexible and ultrafit instructors. Look a little harder, and you'll find boutique yoga studios around town with a cult-like following. But this form of exercise is far from a popular fitness trend.

As far back as 5,000 years ago, people practiced yoga. Bend over backwards. Contort the body into in hundreds of different asanas (poses). This is what early yogis did, all with the simple intention of preparing for meditation. Not to be more flexible. Not to look better in yoga pants. Yoga was originally practiced to help people cultivate a meditative state of mind.

I'm sure you can relate to how this all came about.
I know I can.

Seeking Enlightenment
I first tried to meditate in high school. I had learned about Confucius, Buddhism and Bushido in a humanities class and instantly I wanted to master the art of Zen. I believed that Zen would focus my power and help me succeed in everything I did. From football to school work to masterfully flirting with the girl I had a crush on, I thought that a little Zen meditation would solve my problems.

When I first sat down to meditate, I could not sit still at all. To make matters worse, the more I tried to empty my mind, the more things I instantly thought about. I was aiming for nirvana and I arrived at frustration and annoyance. Instead, I was victim of my own 'Monkey Mind,' a Zen term describing the restlessness or unsettling of one's mind, and I was not experiencing the focus and personal power that I sought. I would later discover yoga, Kung Fu and other movement arts that would point me in the right direction. I am sure that the original yogis had a similar experience. I imagine that they were trying to deal with their own problems back in the day and sought out clarity of the mind. However, I can only fathom that they ran into some difficulty along the way. Luckily, they persisted and started to incorporate movement to help steady the mind.

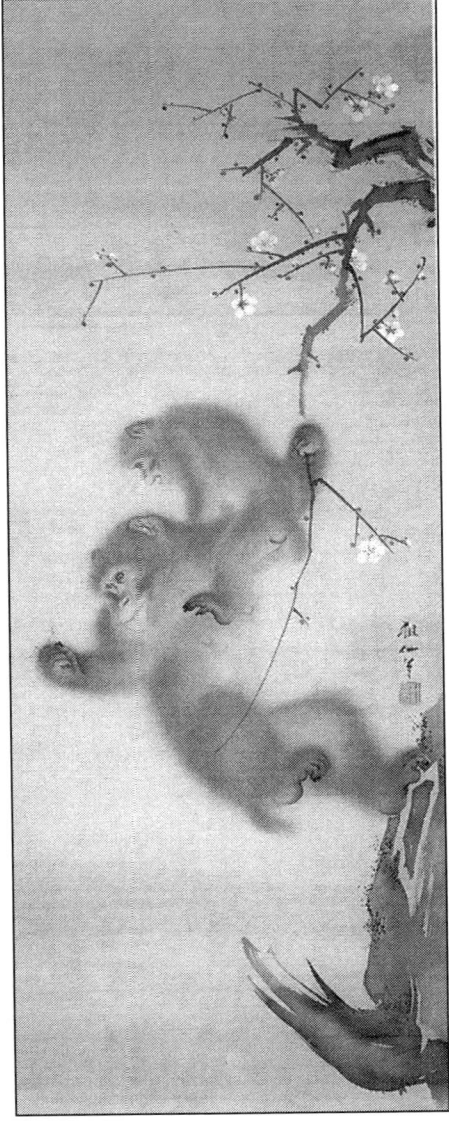

RECOVERY

Monkeys in a Plum Tree By Mori Sosen

Preparing to Meditate
The chief purpose of practicing the physical form of yoga is to prepare the body to meditate. The asanas and sequences are intentionally designed to align the body, specifically the spine, and release unnecessary tension in the body that can create distractions from within. In the end, your mind is left to contemplate purpose and explore bliss.

The Practice of Yoga
It's been a while since the early days of yoga. Now the practice of yoga has grown and developed in numerous ways to heal the body, grow the spirit, and steady the mind. There are many different forms of yoga, from a Vinyasa Flow to Bikram to Power Yoga and more. They all offer the benefits of a physical workout as well as the gifts of meditation and introspection.

Defining "Practice"
A practice is the repetitive action of a sequence of activity to improve a specific skill, such as a basketball team practicing to become a more skillful team.

A practice is also the repetitive action of an activity or skill in order to improve as a person, such as a meditation practice.

In either context, yoga is a practice akin to PreHab. You can further improve your health and fitness by practicing yoga. But it's not just for those in search of a Zen-state-of-mind. Yoga is a proven way of training and conditioning that can also further your skills as an athlete or runner. Just look at the Stanford Cardinals football team.

Yoga in College Football
In 2014, *The New York Times* reported on the unique training methodology for the Stanford University football team. With a winning 11-3 season as an NCAA Division 1 team, their training strategy carried them all the way to the Rose Bowl.

Here's how yoga fits into their program. Head Strength Coach Shannon Turley has his players take yoga to help improve their flexibility and alignment along with doing other mobilization techniques and PreHab exercises. And it seems to work. Not only is Stanford a nationally-ranked team, the number of season-ending injuries on the team is very low – only three in the last two years (2012-2013), which is pretty darn amazing.

Yoga can help athletes perform better and longer!

RECOVERY

Yoga is also a great practice for learning to control your mind and become a better person. When I return to my yoga mat, I set an intention for that day's practice. Sometimes I practice to be present. Sometimes I practice to give up my complaints. Simply, I set the context to define the way I want to improve myself, and I keep that intention with me as I make my way through all of the poses.

Even psychology studies agree, practicing yoga with the intention of becoming a better person truly works if you believe it does.

> **Common Benefits of Practicing Yoga**
>
> *Increases Mobility*
> *Activates Dormant Muscles*
> *Improves Stability*
> *Develops Awareness*
> *Creates more Stamina*
> *Steadies the Mind*

Breathing in Yoga
In correlation to the asanas or poses, there is a simple system to follow when it comes to your breathing. Inhale as you arch, and exhale as you fold.

- *Inhale while Arching*
  Stand up and lift up your chest and inhale deeply. You can feel your spine arching backwards and naturally making more room in your torso as you breathe.

- *Exhale while Folding*
  Now, empty all of the air out of your lungs as you fold forward to touch your toes. Can you feel how easy it is to fold forward while exhaling? There is no air in your torso to impede your fold.

Duality in Yoga
As a whole, the art of yoga truly embraces the masculine and feminine dualistic laws of the universe. With each expanding and contracting pose, your body responds. It's the yin- and-yang affect that helps your body and your mind find its center. Corresponding your breath to each asana is part of this art as it will help to fulfill the intention of each pose.

Yet, don't stress yourself out too much over how you are breathing at first. Remember, yoga is a practice, meaning that it is a process where you can strive for continual improvement and progress over time. Coordinate your breath to the poses when you are ready.

RECOVERY

Breathing to Energize and Calm

When I train people, I watch how they breathe during the exercise because I learn so much about them. Recognizing breathing patterns tells me if a person is comfortable, aligned or supported in their movement. And that has a huge impact with how they perform the exercise. Usually, I find that everyone can improve how they perform an exercise, let alone move in general, when they pay more attention to the way they breathe.

There are many different breathing techniques out there that could fill a book all by itself. Here are basic breathing techniques that I encourage people to use:

Inhale to Energize – Exhale to Relax

Simply by taking a few deep breaths in, you create a more Sympathetic tone in your Neurology, which provides you with more energy. The Sympathetic Nervous System is the Fight or Flight mechanisms in your body. It heightens your awareness, releases Adrenaline and stimulates the heart rate. In other words, it will energize your body.

Conversely, exhaling will create a more Parasympathetic tone of your Nervous System, which will helps you to calm down, release tension and relax. The Parasympathetic Nervous System is the train tracks for your body's natural recovery cycle.

Breathing Cues:

Inhale to Energize

Exhale to Relax

Practice 10 deep inhalations or 10 deep exhalations to see the difference that these breathes make on your physiology as well as your mind.

RECOVERY

Fire Breathe for Activation
This yogic breathing technique is easy to do and extremely effective. First, stand or sit with a neutral spine and close your mouth. Press your tongue up against the roof of your mouth and either place your palms over your belly or hold the arms by your side. Also, feel free to close your eyes if you wish.

Next, start to breathe in short, forceful exhalations through your nose with quick inhalations. Powerfully use your abdominals to create these staccato exhalations and continue to breathe in rapid cycles for approximately 30 seconds or a count of 30 breaths.

Pause and repeat again if necessary.

Yogic Fire Breathe

Yoga Sequence

There were a couple of reasons that I kept returning to yoga when I first started, despite being able to develop a sustainable stillness in my mind for meditation. I routinely came back to yoga classes because I found all of the asanas and poses really helped me to recover from all of my runs.

Here is a sequence of yoga poses that will help runners recover faster-

RECOVERY

LATERAL BEND

POSITION: Place the feet together and press the palms overhead with straight arms.

ACTION: Keep the hips square. Stretch both arms up and over the top of the body and reach the hands out to the side as far as possible. Maintain length throughout the entire body and squeeze both legs together. Breathe deeply and relax.

Hold for 30+ seconds or for 10 deep breaths.

NECK FLEXION

POSITION: Place a hand directly on top of the head and reach opposite arm out to the side and down.

ACTION: Gently pull the top of the head towards one shoulder with the hand while squeezing the opposite arm into the rib cage and lengthening the neck. Keep the face square with the shoulders. Breathe deeply and relax.

Hold for 30+ seconds or for 10 deep breaths.

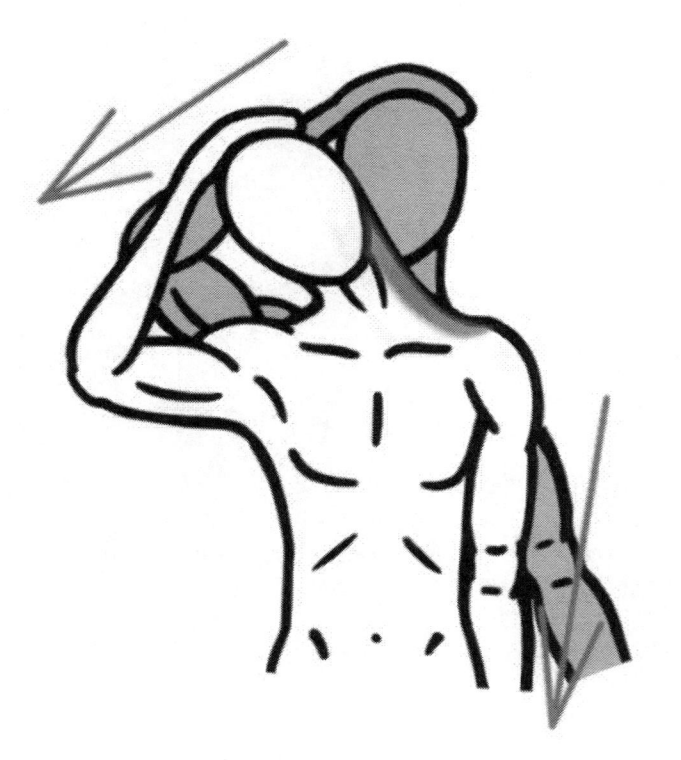

RECOVERY

FORWARD FOLD

ACTION: Stand with the feet together and then circle the arms up and back as you reach for the horizon behind you. Next, fold forward by hinging in the hip sockets and lower the torso over the legs while lengthening the spine and reaching the top of the head away from the tailbone. Allow the knees to bend softly and lay your torso over your thighs. Breathe deeply and relax.

Perform 3-5 Forward Folds as well as perform a Forward Fold throughout the entire Yoga Sequence.

Alternate RX: Hold for 30+ seconds or for 10 deep breaths throughout the Yoga Sequence.

ROTATED NECK FLEXION

POSITION: Place a hand directly on top of the head and tuck the opposite arm behind the back.

ACTION: Gently pull and rotate the head down towards the shoulder. Attempt to stick the nose into the armpit while threading the opposite arm further back around the rib cage. Lengthen through the neck and keep the spine straight. Breathe and relax.

Hold for 30+ seconds or for 10 deep breaths.

RECOVERY

STANDING HEEL-PULL

POSITION: Stand tall on one foot with the hips and shoulders square to one another. If needed, place one hand on a wall for balance.

ACTION: Lift up one foot and pull the heel in towards the hips with the same side hand. Keep the hips square and the chest lifted while lengthening through the spine and attempt to touch the heel to the hips. Breathe deeply and relax.

Hold for 30+ seconds or for 10 deep breaths.

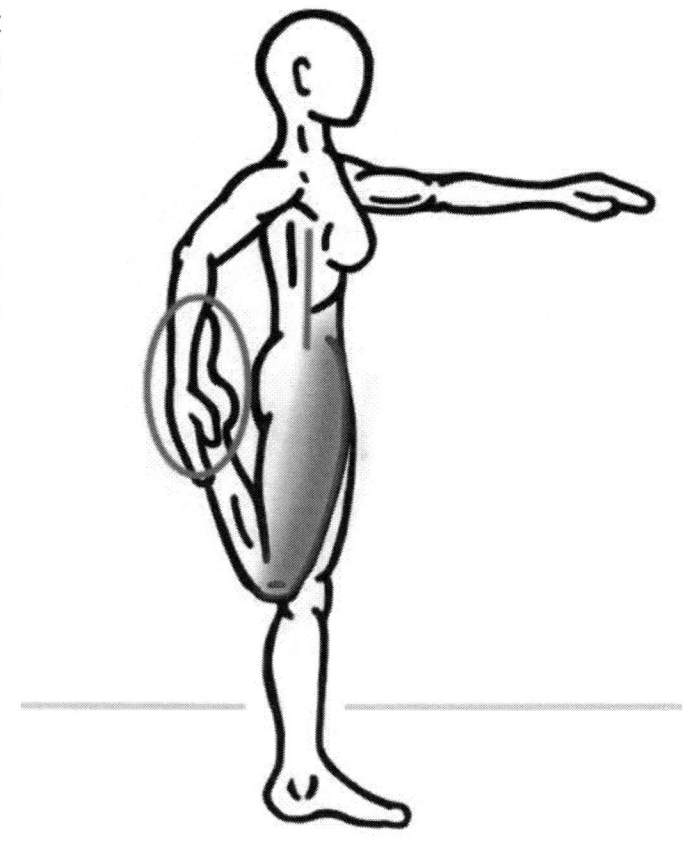

FORWARD BEND WITH INTERLACED HANDS

POSITION: Stand with feet at shoulder width and interlace hands behind the back.

ACTION: Fold the torso forward over the legs while reaching the hands up towards the sky. Let the head loosely hang and straighten the arms. Squeeze the shoulder blades towards each other and open up the chest. Breathe deeply and relax.

Hold for 30+ seconds or for 10 deep breaths and then alternate the interlacing of the fingers.

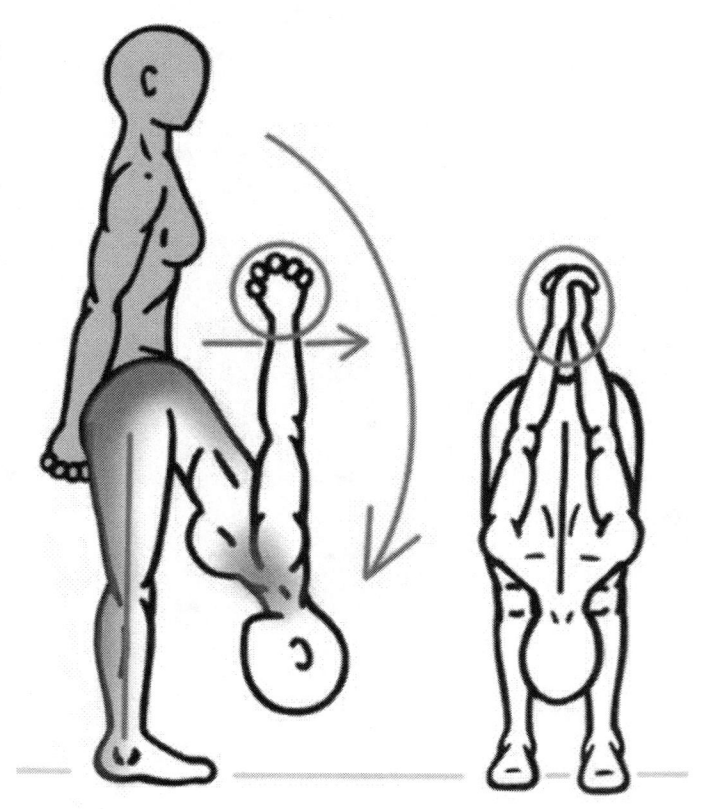

RECOVERY

WIDE STANCE LATERAL FLEXION

POSITION: Stand with the feet comfortably separated as far apart as possible and hold the spine tall in neutral alignment.

ACTION: Extend one arm up and over the head and reach laterally towards the horizon with the hand. As the other arm circles under and across the rib cage, reach laterally for the opposite horizon. Lengthen through the spine with each breath and deepen the stretch as much as possible.

Hold for 30+ seconds or for 10 deep breaths in each direction.

WIDE STANCE ROTATION

POSITION: Stand with the feet separated as far apart as possible and the spine in neutral alignment. Place one hand on top of the opposite shoulder, covering the shoulder joint with the palm and thread the other hand around the back.

ACTION: Rotate through the spine and look backwards over the shoulder that is covered with the hand. Lengthen the spine and press the top of the head up into the sky while twisting deeper into the rotation with each breath.

Hold for 30+ seconds or for 10 deep breaths in each direction.

RECOVERY

WIDE STANCE ROTATED FORWARD FOLD

POSITION: Stand with the feet comfortably separated as far apart as possible.

ACTION: Fold the torso forward over one leg and reach both hands towards the foot. With each breath, reach further into the stretch and attempt to touch the forehead to the kneecap while aligning the spine over the thigh. Keep both legs as straight as possible while pressing the tailbone up towards the sky. Relax and release the tension in the shoulders and arms.

Hold for 30+ seconds or for 10 deep breaths over each leg.

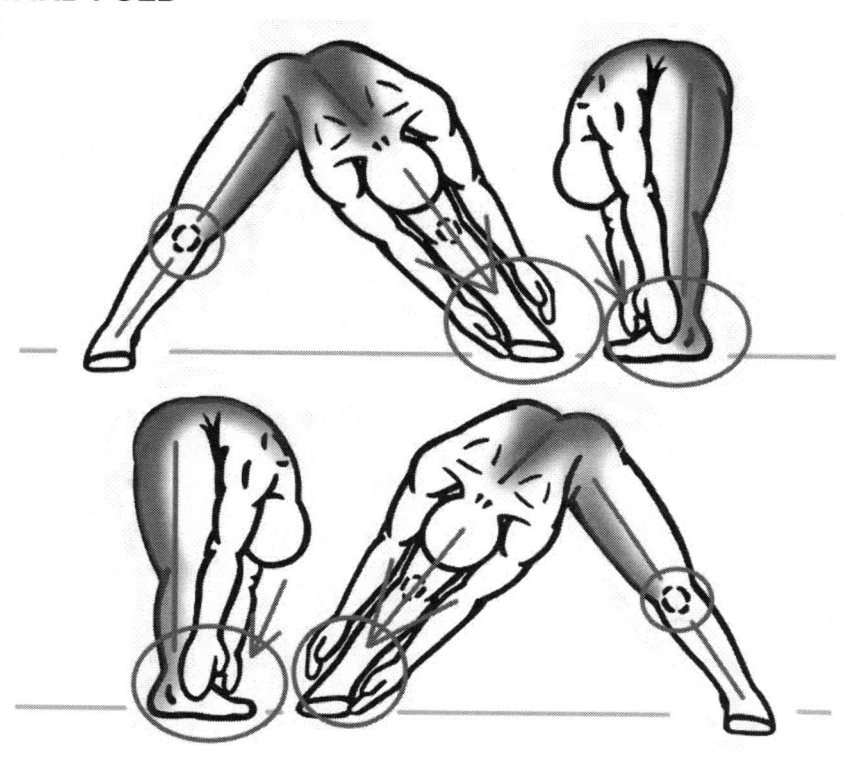

PYRAMID

POSITION: Step back into a split stance with both legs straight and feet planted on the floor. Square the hips off with the legs at 90-degree angles.

ACTION: Hinge forward at the hips with neutral alignment of the spine. If the hands do not touch the ground, place the hands on the thigh or shin and hold. Keep both legs straight and lengthen the spine, pulling the top of the head away from the tailbone as far as possible. On each exhale, attempt to lower the torso closer to the ground by hinging in the hips.

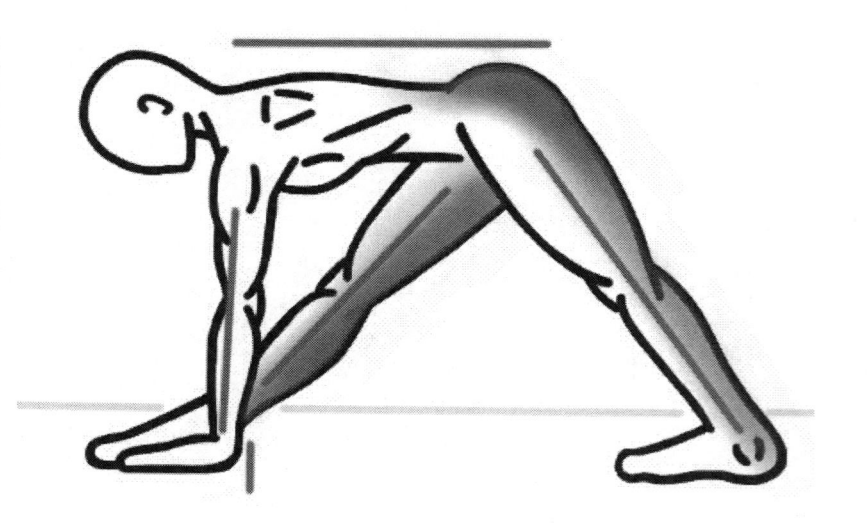

Hold for 30+ seconds or for 10 deep breaths over each leg.

RECOVERY

REVOLVED PYRAMID
POSITION: Step back into a split stance with both legs straight and feet planted on the floor. Square the hips off with the legs at 90-degree angles.

ACTION: Hinge forward at the hips with neutral alignment of the spine. Place the hand opposite of the forward leg on the ground or modify using the thigh or shin. Next, rotate the shoulders and reach the other arm up to the sky. Keep both legs straight and twist deeper into the rotation with every breath as the eyes gaze up at the sky.

Hold for 30+ seconds or for 10 deep breaths over each leg.

EXTENDED PYRAMID
POSITION: Step back into a split stance with both legs straight and feet planted on the floor. Square the hips off with the legs at 90-degree angles.

ACTION: Hinge forward at the hips with neutral alignment of the spine and pull the top of the head away from the tailbone. Next, reach both arms overhead towards the horizon and pull the belly button into the spine to support the lower back by engaging the abdominals. Lengthen through the spine and reach the hands for the horizon while breathing deeply.

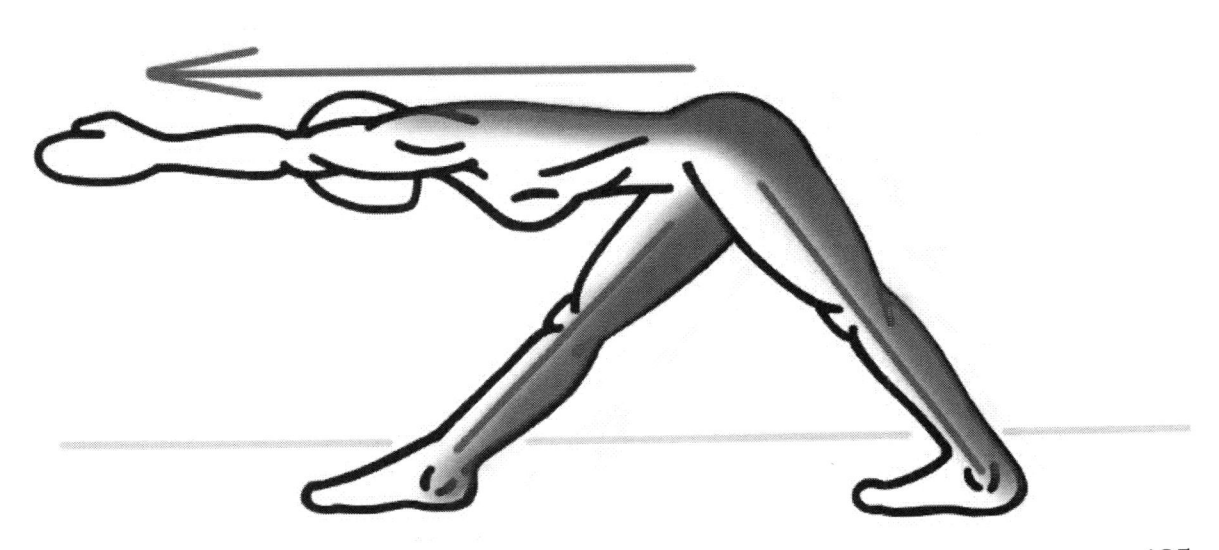

Hold for 30+ seconds or for 10 deep breaths over each leg.

RECOVERY

WARRIOR ONE POSE

POSITION: Start in a high-lunge position with the front knee aligned directly over the ankle and the rear foot extended out in a 45-degree angle.

ACTION: Reach up overhead with parallel arms while reaching the top of the head towards the sky and focusing eyes on the horizon. Pull the shoulder blades down the back and extend through the fingers. Next, square the hips off to the front and pull the belly button in towards the spine to engage the abdominals. Press the rear heel into the floor and breathe.

Hold for 30+ seconds or for 10 deep breaths over each leg.

RECOVERY

TRIANGLE POSE

POSITION: Start in a high-lunge position with the front knee aligned directly over the ankle while the rear foot is rotated out to a 90-degree angle.

ACTION: Fully straighten both legs and then reach the front arm towards the horizon by hinging at the hips and tilting the pelvis. Place the front hand on the ground or on the shin while reaching the opposite hand up to the sky. Lengthen the spine, rotate the shoulders and open the chest as the eyes gaze to the sky. Pull the head away from the tailbone and breathe.

Hold for 30+ seconds or for 10 deep breaths over each leg.

REVOLVED TRIANGLE POSE

POSITION: Start in Triangle Pose with both legs straight and hands reaching in opposite directions.

ACTION: Keeping both legs as straight as possible, rotate through the torso and place the opposite hand on top of the front foot while the other arm reaches for the sky and the shoulders twist. Lengthen the spine and pull the top of the head and tailbone away from one another as the eyes gaze to the sky.

Hold for 30+ seconds or for 10 deep breaths over each leg.

PreHab Exercises for Runners

RECOVERY

LOW-LUNGE EXTENSION

POSITION: Kneel on the ground and place both hands on the front knee.

ACTION: Slide the rear knee backwards as far as possible and straighten both arms to lift the chest towards the sky. Keep the front knee aligned over the front ankle. Breathe deeply and relax.

Hold for 30+ seconds or for 10 deep breaths on each leg.

LOW-LUNGE WITH LATERAL FLEXION

POSITION: Kneel on the ground and slide the rear knee as far backwards as possible while keeping the front knee aligned directly over the ankle.

ACTION: Use the arm on the same side of the front leg to take hold of the opposite arm at the wrist. Next, pull the arm over top of the head as far as possible towards the horizon. Keep the shoulders square with the hips and both elbows straight. Lengthen through the spine and breathe deeply.

Hold for 30+ seconds or for 10 deep breaths on each leg.

RECOVERY

REVOLVED LUNGE

POSITION: Step back into a lunge position with the rear leg straight and the front knee over the ankle. Keep feet parallel.

ACTION: Next, place the opposite elbow on the outside of the front thigh while rotating the torso and pressing the palms together in prayer position. Keep reaching the front knee forward and drive into the rear heel as the eyes look up towards the sky. Keep the spine long and comfortably twist a little deeper with each breath. Stay relaxed in the pose.

Hold for 30+ seconds or for 10 deep breaths over each leg.

CAMEL POSE

POSITION: Kneel down with the knees shoulder-width apart and tuck the toes under.

ACTION: Place a hand over top of the heel while extending the opposite arm up and back. Keep a long spine and breathe deep. Next, lower the raised arm to cover the other heel if possible and lengthen through the spine. Breathe deep and relax. To get out of the pose with little strain, gently sit the hips down onto the heels.

Hold for 30+ seconds or for 10 deep breaths in the appropriate variation.

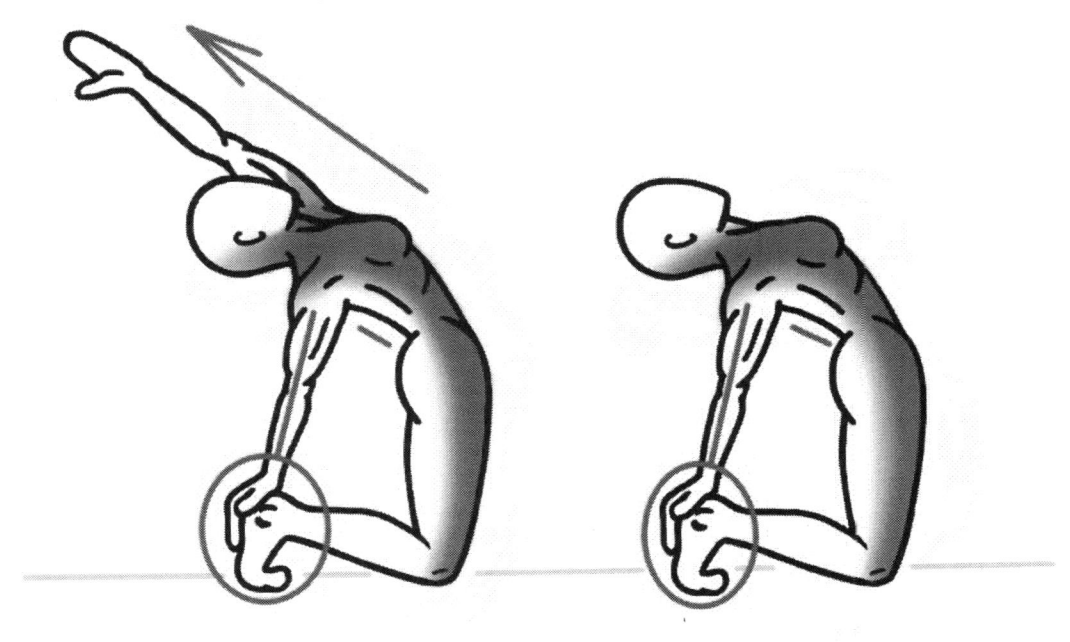

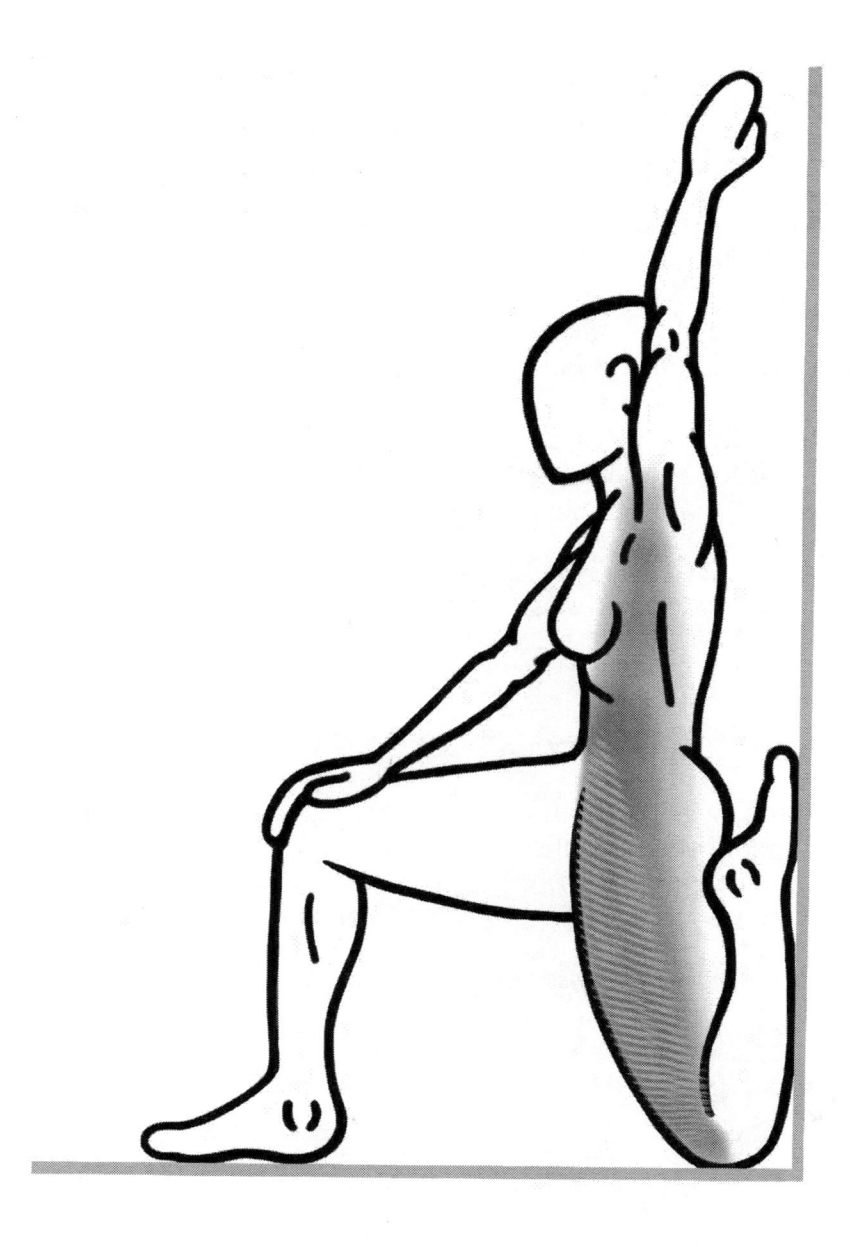

RECOVERY

COUCH STRETCH
POSITION: Kneel on the ground with the rear shin pressed against a wall.

ACTION: Place both hands on the forward knee and gently slide the rear knee closer to the wall. Press against the front knee with both hands and press the hips back towards the wall, attempting to touch the rear heel. Once the hips are back far enough, take the arm that is on the same side of the braced knee, and reach up to touch the wall. Breathe deeply and relax.

Hold for 30+ seconds or for 10 deep breaths in the appropriate variation.

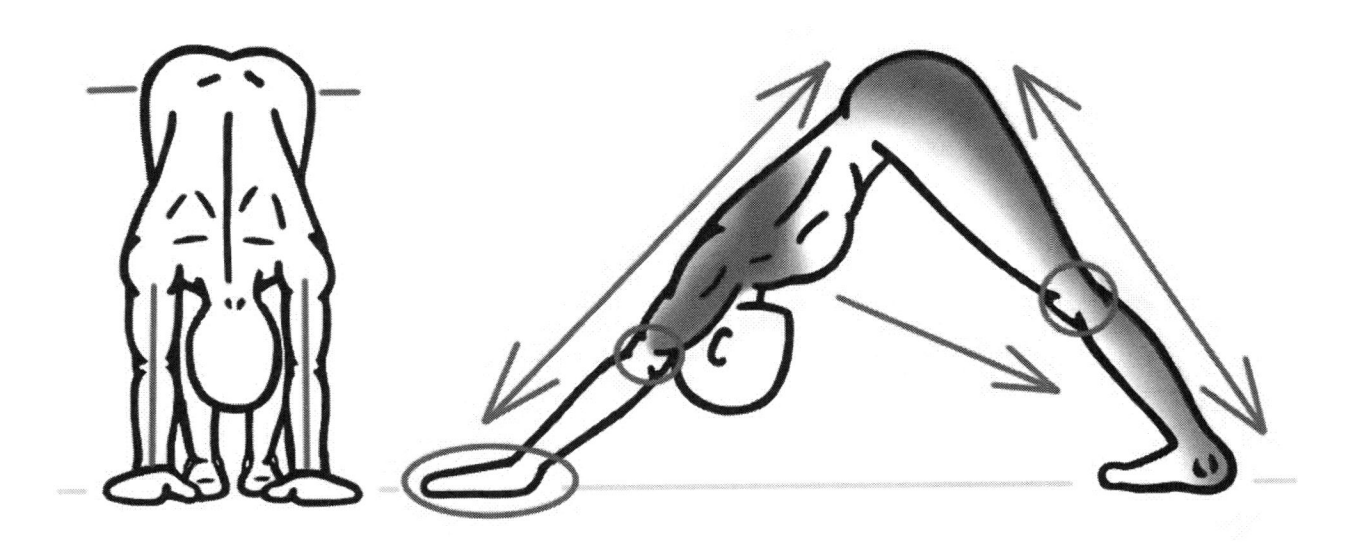

RECOVERY

DOWN-DOG
POSITION: Place both the feet and hands at shoulder width on the ground in a plank position while aligning the middle fingers parallel with one another and fully extending the elbows and knees.

ACTION: Press into the hands and feet and drive the hips straight up to the sky. Pull the shoulders away from the ears to free up the neck and press the heart towards the ankles while lengthening through the spine and leg.

Hold for 30+ seconds or for 10 deep breaths. Repeating this pose 1-3 times is recommended. Remember to breathe deeply and relax.

PIGEON POSE
POSITION: From a plank position, fold one leg under the torso so that the shin is as close to a 90-degree angle with the spine as possible and then sit the hips down on the floor while keeping the chest lifted.

ACTION: Next, walk the hands forward as far as possible and gently lower the torso over the folded leg. Make any and all adjustments needed if discomfort arises. Keep the pose pain free and relax into the stretch.

Hold for 30+ seconds or for 10 deep breaths over each leg.

PreHab Exercises for Runners

BOW POSE

POSITION: Reach back with both hands and take hold of the ankles. If the hands are unable to reach, use a towel wrapped around the ankles.

ACTION: Hold the ankles and gently kick the hands and feet up towards the sky, lifting the chest and thighs off the ground. Keep the spine long and squeeze the thighs together as the chest and shoulders open up. Breathe deeply and stay relaxed through the entire body.

Hold for 30+ seconds or for 10 deep breaths. Repeating this pose 1-3 times is recommended. Avoid any discomfort in the back or knees.

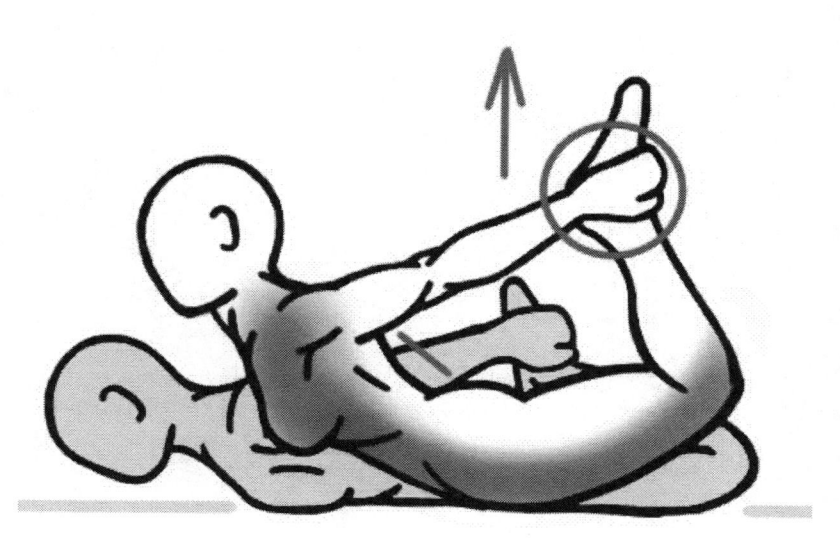

SEATED ROTATION

POSITION: Sit on the ground with both legs extended straight out in front of the body.

ACTION: Place one foot on the outside of the opposite knee and then position the opposite elbow against the outside raised thigh. Lengthen the spine and take a deep breath in. Exhale and use the arms to help rotate the torso to look directly behind the body. Gently press the elbow into the raised knee to rotate deeper with each breath. Be gentle in the twisting and keep lifting the crown of the head up to the sky.

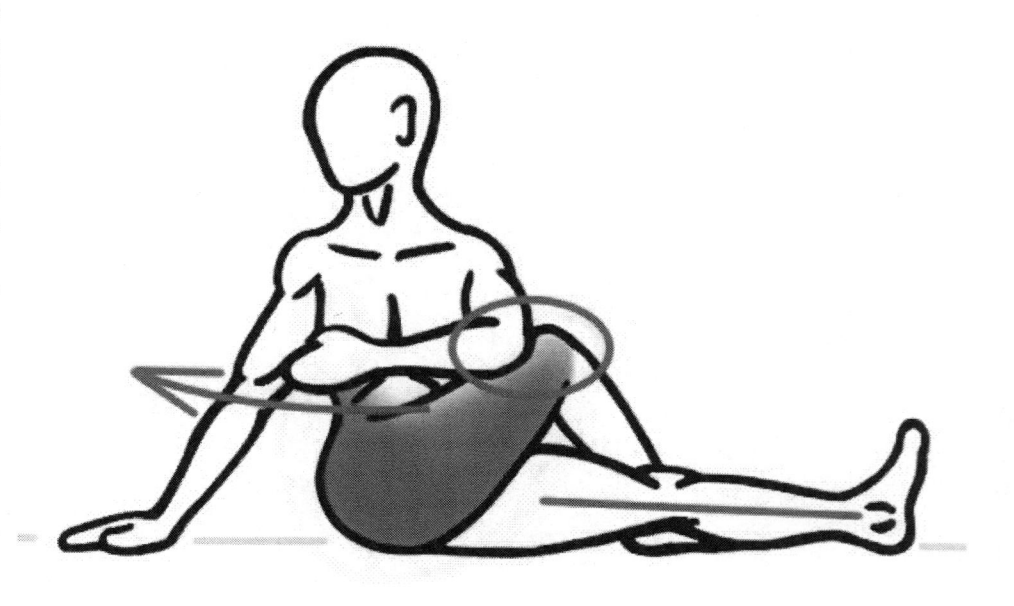

Hold for 30+ seconds or for 10 deep breaths on each side.

WHEEL POSE

POSITION: Lie down on the floor with the feet and hands shoulder width apart. Tuck the heels close into the hips. Turn the hands so that the fingers are facing the shoulders and squeeze the elbows towards one another.

ACTION: Simultaneously, press into the hands and feet to drive the hips up towards the sky. Lengthen through the arms, legs and spine and press the heart forward towards the horizon. Breathe and relax.

Hold for 30+ seconds or 10 deep breaths or what feels comfortable. Repeat this pose 1-3 times if there is no discomfort at all.

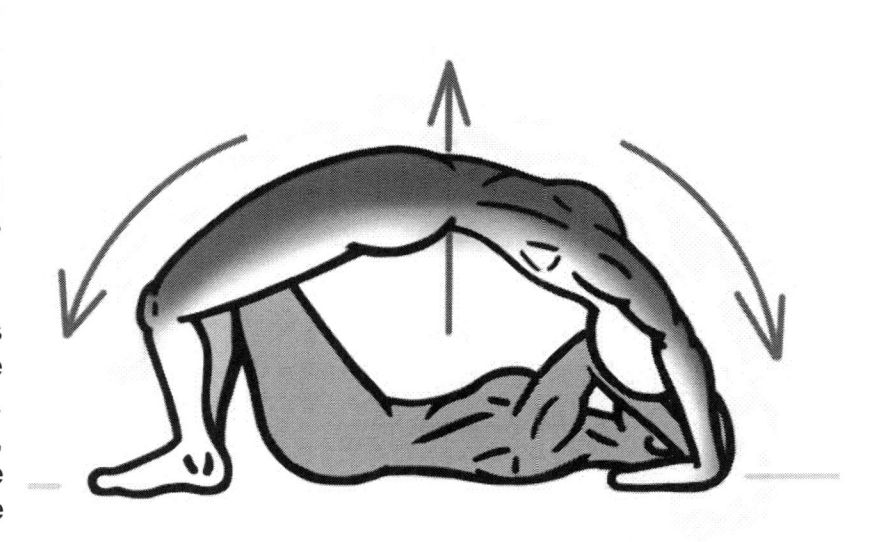

SPINAL TWIST

POSITION: Lie on the floor with the arms held out in a "T" formation with the spine and the legs lifted into "chair" position (90-degrees in the ankles, knees and hips.)

ACTION: Gently twist the torso and lower both legs over to one side of the body while keeping the arms completely flat in the ground. Relax and breathe deeply into the lower torso allowing the body to release deeply and start recovery.

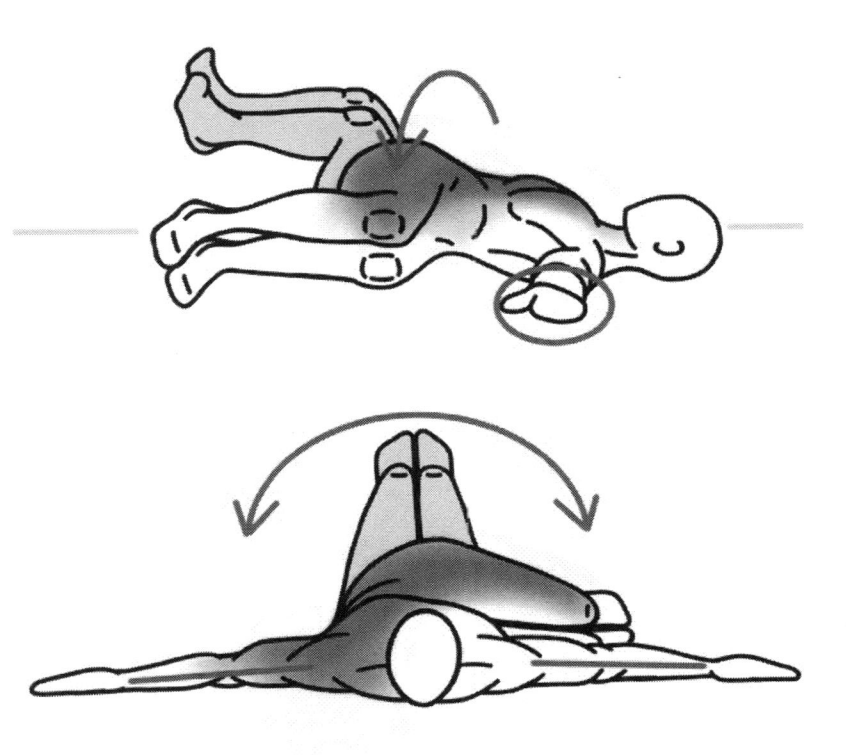

Hold for 30+ seconds or for 10 deep breaths on each side.

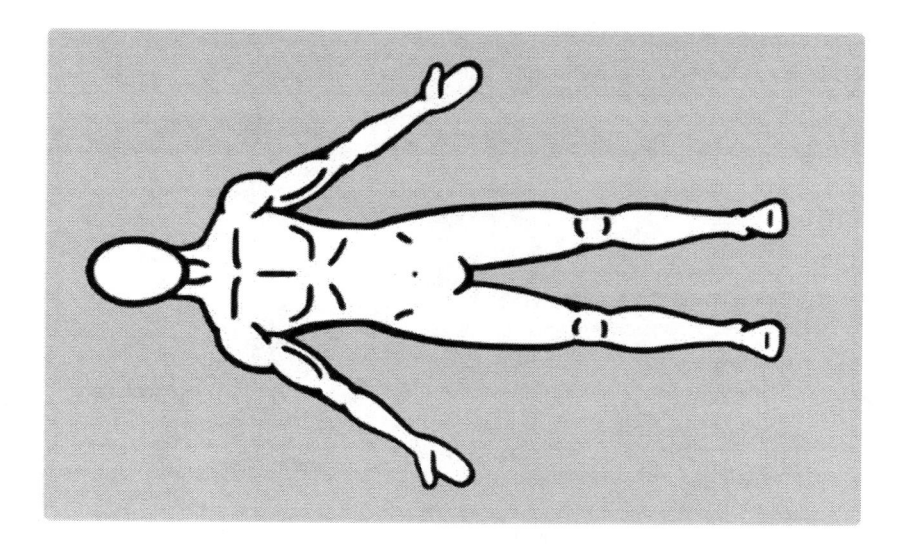

RECOVERY

CORPSE POSE
POSITION: Lie on the floor with arms and legs fully extended out on the floor. Lengthen through the spine and reach the top of the head away from the tailbone. Tuck the chin slightly into the throat to release the back of the neck. Reach the heels away from the hip sockets and the fingertips away from the shoulders. Then allow the breath to easily enter the body and fill up the entire torso – including the belly. Lastly, relax and give all the weight of the body over to the floor. *Perform this exercise in a safe and secure place.*

Rest for 60 seconds to five minutes or more. Set a timer if possible to allow for complete relaxation.

The Shavasana Test for Pain and Stress
Lie down on the floor in this Corpse Pose and breathe for one minute - use a timer, don't guess. As your body rests on the floor, pay attention to any pain that arises. Try not to move, as that will only obstruct the pain signals from flowing through your neurological system. If you start to feel any pain, start to address it in your training.

If you fall asleep, make sure to get more sleep and do more active recovery work as your body's work-to-rest ratio is unbalanced. If you do not feel asleep or start to feel any pain, use this time lying on the floor to visualize the achievement of your next goal- and if you don't have a goal, make one.

RECOVERY

Yoga

Note before you go-

You can either follow this entire sequence or just work with a few poses. It is up to you! There is no right or wrong in yoga. Yoga is a combination of mastering your body, your state of mind, and your breathing. Do what you are able to do and allow your practice to grow.

Yoga is far more than a meditative practice first used more than 5,000 years ago. Incorporate yoga into your training and you will:

Improve Alignment and Posture
Cultivate Energy and Calmness
Increase Mobility and Flexibility
Develop Stamina
Assist Recovery
Steady the Mind

Just remember that yoga is a practice, something to get better at and something that will make you a better person too.

Namaste.

RECOVERY

RECOVERY

Inversions

Another effective tool to help runners and athletes recover is getting turned upside-down with inversions.

From handstands, to headstands to wall drains, inversions will help remove metabolic waste that build up in your soft tissue while you run and reduce overall stress on the body.

Every biochemical reaction that your body uses to create energy will also create byproducts of metabolic waste. These residual wastes are not immediately impactful – even lactic acid takes time to reach a detrimental threshold point. Yet, over time, the accumulation of metabolic waste in your soft tissue will eventually slow you down if left in your system long enough.

Fortunately, your body has a natural removal process for this metabolic waste, which is quite amazing. However, this system is not completely efficient and not always effective, especially when you may be pushing yourself very hard and training beyond your current means.

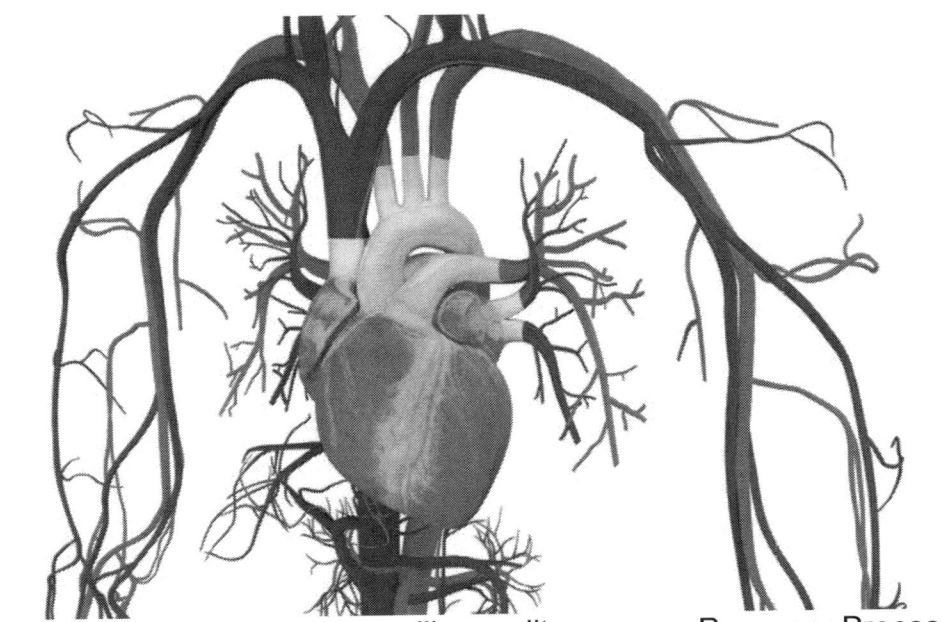

Helping our Circulatory System will expedite our own Recovery Process
Photo by Bryan Brandenburg

Consequentially, inversions offer a simple remedy to the build-up of metabolic waste in your body during training and throughout life. Reversing the pull of gravity by going upside-down in an inversion will help to literally unclog pooled up blood in the lower extremities that can simply carry lingering pieces of metabolic waste back to you main organs, like the liver, kidneys and intestines to expedite their final removal.

RECOVERY

Additionally, this passive drainage technique of inversions helps the body's rejuvenation process as well. Blood is re-oxygenated and also filled with nutrients that are carried back to rebuilding cells throughout the whole body. Proteins, glucose, minerals, antioxidants and more are all distributed back into the soft tissue that previously was saturated with metabolic waste.

Inversions assist with cellular regeneration and renewal.

Inversions also help to de-stress and condition the body. The upside-down positioning will reverse the pull of gravity on the body and reduce the pressure on the bones and soft tissue as well as reduce the stabilizing demands of the articulating components of each joint. This reduction in physiological stress and pressure helps the cartilage and tissues to expand. It also allows the cartilage and tissues to realign the formation of their cells. Given the right conditions, your bones, fascia, muscles and tendons all have an opportunity to remodel the alignment and structure of their cells as a way to adapt and fortify against all the demands of your training as well as your life.

Inversion Progression
Here is a sequence of inversions that progress in difficulty and effort. Choose the inversion that is most appropriate for your energy level and experience.

LEG DRAIN
This exercise will create a restful physiological state while having the legs positioned over the heart. This allows for the blood to drain from the legs and return to your major organs for re-oxygenations and removal of metabolic waste.

POSITION: Lay on the ground with your legs placed up against a wall. Position the hips as close to the wall as possible and lengthen your spine along the floor.

ACTION: Rest in this position for 5-10 minutes and focus on breathing with long exhales as this will help elicit a greater parasympathetic tone of your nervous system and enhance recovery on a cellular level.

The Leg Drain performed against a wall.

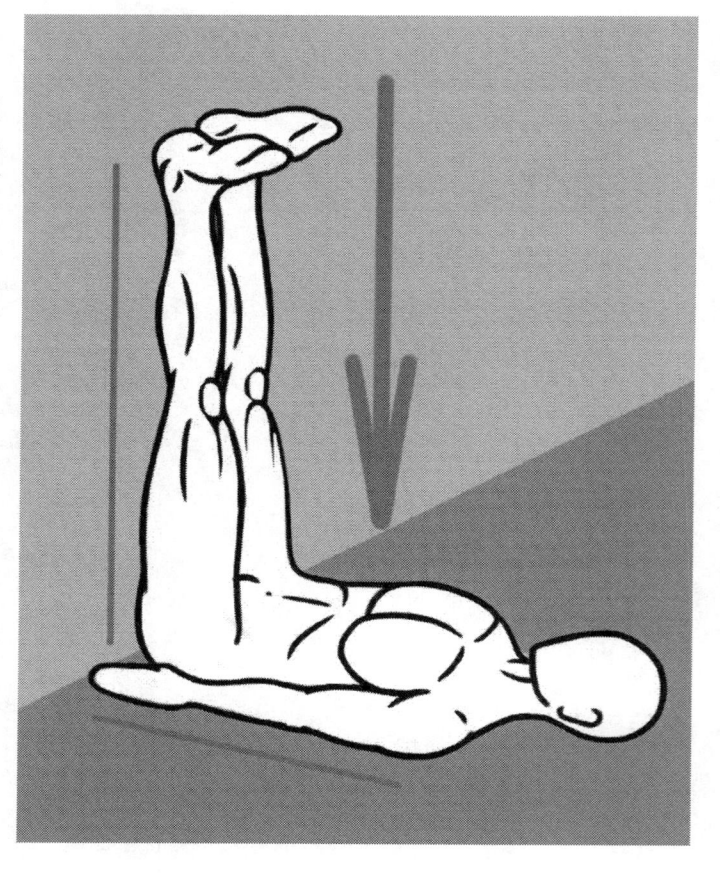

RECOVERY

HEAD STAND

This exercise will invert the entire body, which will help pull blood from the legs as well as the hips and torso back towards the heart to be re-oxygenated and replenished with nutrients. This exercise also reverses the pull of gravity on the body and will help to condition the spine and relieve the lower body's joints and tissue from accumulative pressure.

POSITION: Place the top of your head and your hands on the floor to form a triangle. Keep the hands at shoulder-width apart and position the top of your head approximately six inches from the wall.

ACTION: Walk your feet in towards your hands as you press your hips up over your shoulders. Lengthen through your spine and pull your chin in towards your throat to stabilize your neck. Press your hands into the floor and pull your belly button in towards your spine to engage the abdominals and brace your core.

Next, lift the feet off the ground and pull the knees in towards the elbows as you squeeze your thighs into your torso. Establish balance here before extending the feet up towards the sky.

RECOVERY

Reach your heels up as high as you can and lengthen through the entire body. Use the wall for support and press into the hands to help balance. Attempt to align the ankles over the hips over the shoulders.

Breathe and relax.

- *Hold the Head Stand for as long as you feel comfortable and supported.*
- *Start with a goal of 15 seconds and gradually increase the hold the more that you perform this exercise.*

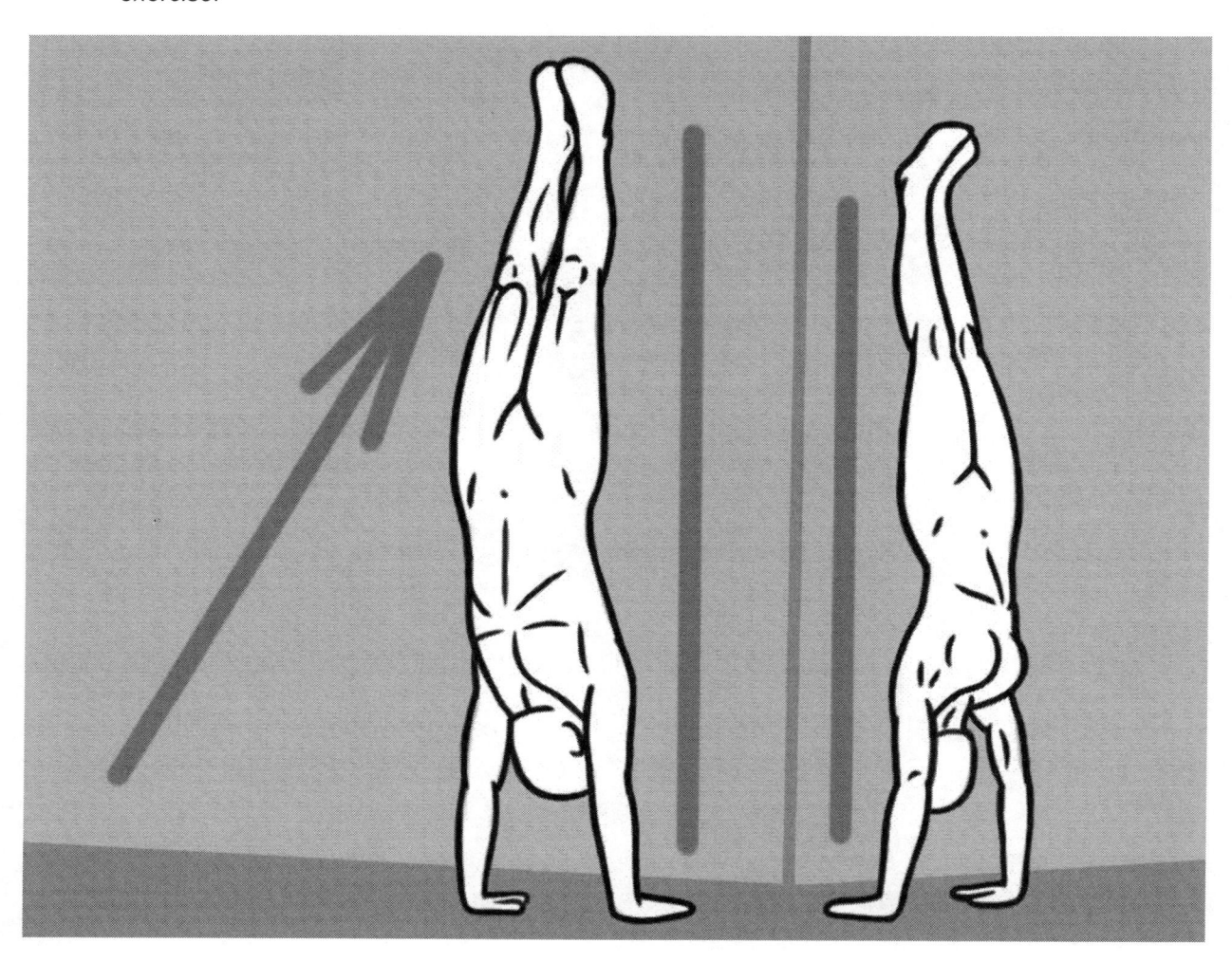

HAND STAND

This exercise will help drain blood from the lower extremities while also conditioning and strengthening the upper body, namely shoulders and spine. This exercise requires much more effort to perform than the other two inversion exercises, Leg Drain and Head Stand. Do not attempt this exercise if you are tired or feel physically exhausted.

POSITION: Place the hands shoulder-width apart on the floor about 3-6 inches from the wall. Straighten the arms completely and walk the feet in towards the wall until you are in a Down Dog position: hips elevated into the sky with both arms and legs completely

RECOVERY

straight.

ACTION: Lift one foot off the ground and gently hop with the other foot. Gradually increase the effort of the hop and practice kicking the other leg up towards the wall. Once you feel practiced enough, hop and kick both legs up to the wall as you hold yourself with straight arms.

Use the wall to help balance as you support your body with your arms. Press your hands into the floor and fully extend your elbows as you push the floor away. Spread your fingers and externally rotate the shoulders for more stability.

Pull the belly button in towards your spine and squeeze your glutes to stabilize your core and hips respectively. Press your feet together until your two legs feel as if they are one.

Tuck your chin into your throat and gaze at the horizon as you vertically align your spine perpendicular to the floor. Do not arch your back and look at the floor. Instead, keep neutral alignment of the spine and stack the hips over the rib cage and head.

To come down from the Hand Stand, gently step one leg back to the floor as you keep your arms straight. It's important to step one leg down at a time in order to reduce the force of impact when your feet hit the ground.

If new to Hand Stands and Head Stands, it best to start this practice under the supervision of an experienced partner.

- *Hold the Hand Stand for as long as you feel supported and maintain correct form.*
- *If you are new to inversions and Hand Stands, hold this position for 10-20 seconds and gradually increase the time throughout your training.*

Step Back to Go Forward
Even though it may seem counterintuitive to focus on recovery when trying to maximize your results in training, it is actually a key ingredient to success. Training hard will break down your body and reduce your strength and ability over time if there is not enough repair time between sessions. This recovery time is very important for your cells to do the physiological work that they need to rebuild and adapt to higher thresholds of stress. In other words, don't neglect your recovery time, because you will not physically grow and repair the wear and tear of training.

Treat your recovery as an essential part of your training and you will see much better results!

RECOVERY

RECOVERY

Sleep

*To sleep, perchance to dream-
Aye, there's the rub.
         -William Shakespeare*

Leave it to the most prolific writer in history to help people rationalize sleep deprivation. Yet, if you do not wish to go crazy as Hamlet did, you will make sleep a priority as part of your training as well as part of your life.

Now, I know that there are millions of articles, blog posts, books and even podcasts that talk about the importance of sleep for your training as well as your health. So, I would rather just reiterate a couple of key points to keep in mind regarding sleep.

First, sleep is the most important recovery tool that you can ever use. It is the physiological state in which cellular repair and protein synthesis occurs the most. So, if you are spending hours breaking down your body as you run and run and run – then you need to sleep and sleep and sleep in order to rebuild your body on a cellular level.

The more you run, the more you want to prioritize sleep.

Second, try to get 7-8 hours of sleep every night, especially if you are training hard. If you are getting less than seven hours a night, your training is going to take a hit because your body is going to start to compensate in a lot of different ways in order to conserve energy. Your mobility or stability or strength or endurance or something will take a hit because you are not allowing enough recovery into your training.

Worse off, the more that you cut into your sleep, the more your training will suffer to an exponential degree.

In other words, if you want to perform your best and maximize your potential, you will honor your body and give it the recovery it needs by sleeping.

Lastly, sleep will help you to age less and age slower. So, if you have aspirations to stay active for many years to come, do yourself a favor and get in those Zzzz's!

RECOVERY

INDEX

INDEX

INDEX

5K Challenge- 87, 445

Achilles Tendinitis- 46
ACL Injuries- 371
    Redflags- 232
Activation- 211
    Abdominal- 218
    Ankle & Foot- 223
    Combination Exercises– 289
    Core- 245
    Dynamic Core- 249
    Glute- 232
    Holding Technique - 216
    Modes of Contractions- 216
    Plank- 246
    Posterior Chain- 267
    Shoulder- 253
    Side Plank- 247
    Techniques- 215
Active Flexibility Exercises- 168, 181
Address Pain First- 27
Adhesions- 95
Alignment- 21, 30 & 59
    Diagrams- 66
    Evaluating- 66
    Exercise- 61
    Lumbar–Pelvic- 268
    Modern Day- 117
    Plank- 69
    Shoulder- 131
    Side Plank- 70
Alternating Bounding Skip- 470
A.M.A.S.S. - 21
Ankle
    Box Hop- 228
    Dorsiflexion with Thera Band- 374
    Eversion with Thera Band- 375
    Hops- 459, 470
    Inversion with Thera Band- 376
    Matrix- 170
    Plantar Flexion with Thera Band- 373
    Single-Leg Box Hop- 229
    Sprains- 54
Ankle Circles
    Rotated- 184
    Standing- 172
    Supine- 182
Arch Rocks- 359
Aristotle- 7

Arm- 83, 86
    Twist- 143
Arm Circles
    on Foam Roller- 134
    (Shoulder Dislocates)- 142
    Side-Lying- 134
Arm Swing- 131
    Interlaced- 135
    Reverse-Palm-137
Atlas Joint- 81

Backpedal- 465
Balance Pad- 377
Balls- 97
Band Walks- 38, 239, 242
Barometer of Strength- 55
Beast Walk (Crawl) - 297
Becoming a Supple Leopard- 73
Bekele, Kenenisa- 87
Bench Press- 328, 423
Bicycle Crunch- 349
    Modified- 349
Big Toe Test- 164
Biomechanical Cost- 112
Biomechanics- 1, 19
Biotensegrity- 99
Bow Pose- 128, 492
Bowman, Katy- 5, 27, 60, 255, 449
Boyle, Michael- 79, 268
Breathing- 95
    Yoga- 477
Bridge March- 40, 363
Bridges- 74, 217, 219, 235, 269
    Extended- 274
    Reverse Tabletop- 275
    Single-Leg- 40, 74, 217, 219, 235, 237, 365
Butt Wink- 145

Cable Row, Seated - 425
Calves- 107
    Standing Calf Stretch- 169
Camel Pose- 489
Carioca- 466
Carries- 408
Cat–Cow- 127
Caterpillar (Inch Worm) - 300
Cellular Regeneration- 498
Certified Strength & Conditioning Specialist- 10
Cervical Spine- 81
Cheek-to-Cheek- 132
Chest- 104
Chest Expansion, Side-Lying- 124

Chi Running- 456
Circulatory System- 497
Clams- 40, 234
Combination Exercises–
    Activation- 289
    Mobility- 195
    Stability- 385
Common Injuries- 33
Compass Reaches- 378, 432
    Single Leg Rotation-44
    (Unstable Surface)-382
Compensation- 203
    Re-Train- 106
    Strategies- 267
Contract/Relax- 177
Cook, Gray- 7, 15, 23, 73, 75
Corpse Pose- 494
Crab Walk- 299
Crawl
    Bear- 298
    Series- 297
Cross-Legged March- 437
Cross-Train- 28

D1 and D2 Pulls- 339-340
Day-Specific- 410, 414-415
Dead Bugs- 344-348
    Contralateral- 346
    Ipsilateral- 346
    Modified- 348
Deadlift (DL) – 284, 417
    Single Leg- 42, 44, 51, 398
    Single Leg with Pole- 283
De-conditioned- 52
Defining 'Practice'- 476
Depression- 263
Designing Your Program- 413
Dog Pointers- 290-292
Dorsiflexion- 46, 167, 374
Down-Dog- 188, 491
    Foot Pedal- 188
    Press-Up- 264
    with Ankle Touch- 189, 207
    with Hip Extension- 189
Dreyer, Danny- 36, 456
Duality- 477
Duhigg, Charles- 24

Elbow- 86
Elevation- 264
Emphasized Turn Over Run- 230
Energy Dump- 343
Equinox Fitness Training Institute- 10, 13
Exhale- 478
Extended Plank-Up Test- 319

INDEX

Extension
    Global Flexion- 357
    Glute-Hamstring- 280
    Hip- 45, 145, 231, 527
    Low-Lunge- 488
    Prone Back- 351
    Shoulder- 138
    Starfish Back- 351
    Superman Back- 271, 352
    Supine Leg-Locked Knee- 182
    Supine Rotated Knee- 183
Eye Test- 372
Eyes Closed- 377

Fascia- 94
Ferriss, Tim- 6, 445
Fingers Test- 269
Fire Breathe for Activation- 479
Foam Rolling- 96, 100, 146, 149
Foot Perspective- 13, 63, 163
Forefoot March- 227
Forefoot Strike- 35, 446, 450, 454, 455
Forward Bend- 124
    Wide-Stance- 190
    Wide-Stance Rotated- 190
    with Interlaced Hands- 482
Forward Fold- 481
    Wide-Stance Rotated- 484
Forward Head- 110
Forward Lean- 35, 451
    Constructing- 424
    Positioning- 471
Front-to-Back- 131
Functional Movement Screen- 10, 15, 75

Gait Efficiency Drills- 431
Global Flexion/Extension Exercises- 357
Global Movements- 343
Glute-Hamstring Extensions (Machine)- 280
Ground Contact- 446
Grounded Windshield Wipers- 152

Habilis- 6
Habit- 7
    building- 24
    interrupt bad- 216
    of Preparation- 24
Hamstring Pulls- 34
Handstand- 497
Hanging Arch/Hollow- 310-311

Headstand- 497
Heel March- 434
Heel-Pull
    March- 435
    Standing- 482
    Stride (Butt Kickers) - 463
Heel Lift
    Single Leg- 51, 226, 319, 378, 538
    Single Leg (Unstable Surface) - 379
Heel Stride- 460
Heel Strike- 34-36, 446
    Causes of- 447
Hip- 80
    Activation- 231
    Extension- 45, 145, 231, 527
    Extension— Range of Motion- 45
    Hike- 39, 41, 363
    Hinge- 276, 320, 408
    Hinge, Wide Stance Rotated- 276
    Hinge with pole- 525
    Matrix Variations- 199-202
    Mobility- 144
    Socket- 67
    Stability- 361
    Stability Test- 362
Holding (Activation Technique) - 216
Hollow Rocks- 358
Human Pretzel- 209
Hydration- 95, 99

Iliotibial Band Syndrome- 39
Inhale- 477-478
Injury Prevention- 23
Inversions- 497
Inverted
    Retraction- 261
    Row (Recline Row) - 301

Janda Sit-Up- 250
Joint-by-Joint Approach- 79
Juris, Paul- 10

Kick stand- 198
Knee-Hug March- 435
Knee Hug, Supine Double- 152
Knee Tuck- 529
    Hanging- 313
    Stride (High Knees) - 462
Knots- 95, 98, 99

Lateral Bend- 480
Lateral Shuffle- 461
Lateral Squat Walk- 368, 438
Lateral Walk- 38
Lats- 107
Law of Diminishing Returns- 27, 412
Leg- 267
Leg-Cradle March- 436
Leg Drain- 498
Leg Lift, Supine- 181
Leg Lowering- 367
    Assisted- 364
Leg Scissors- 249
Leg Swing
    Lateral- 192
    Sagittal- 192
    Transverse- 193
Li, Aaron- 73, 97
Liberson, Craig- 76
Loaded- 216, 219
Lumbar Spine- 80
Lunge
    Airplane- 370
    Assisted Curtsy- 369
    Curtsy- 396
    Deep Lateral- 397
    Kneeling Lunge & Contralateral Reach- 154
    Kneeling Lunge & Ipsilateral Reach- 154
    Kneeling Lunge & Lateral Reach- 155
    Kneeling Lunge & Reach- 74
    Kneeling Lunge & Vertical Reach- 153
    Kneeling Sequence- 153
    Kneeling Stretch- 217
    High Lateral Lunge- 392
    Lateral Lunge- 41, 439, 532
    Lateral Lunge and Reach- 197
    Lateral Lunge Test- 323
    Low-Lunge- 488
    Low-Lunge and Rotation- 187
    Low-Lunge Extension- 488
    Low-Lunge with Lateral Flexion- 488
    Low-to-High- 278
    Reverse- 426
    Revolved- 489
    Single-Leg Airplane- 442

INDEX

Single Leg with Contralateral Reach- 440
Single Leg with Ipsilateral Reach- 441
Spiderman with Touch and Reach- 203-205
Stationary Curtsy- 443
Walking Airplane- 286
Walking Lunge and Reach- 438
Walking Lunge and Rotate- 439

Macro Objective- 409
Major Movement Patterns (Strength Training) - 407
Massage- 97, 120
Math in Sports and Running- 431
Mat Swims- 249
McDougal, Chris- 110
Medicine Ball Lift (Reverse Chop) - 306-307, 389
Mesocycles- 412
Microcycle- 410
Mid-foot Strike- 34, 446, 450, 456
Minimalist Shoes- 65, 448
Mobility
    Ankle & Foot- 163
    Combination Exercises– 195
    Hip- 144
    Mobility WOD- 92
    Posterior Chain- 173
    Shoulder- 130
    Supine Sequence- 181
    Thoracic Spine- 118
Movement
    Correcting- 23
    Counter- 28
    Evaluations- 73, 510
Muscle
    Contractions- 216
    Facilitated (Turned-On)- 212
    Inhibited (Turned-Off)- 212
Myofascial Stick- 113

Neck- 101, 514
    Flexion- 480
    Mobility & Alignment- 110
    Range of Motion- 114
    Rotated Flexion- 481
    Stability Exercises- 89
NFL- 87, 371

Oscillate- 102, 119

Pain- 26, 30
Parracino, Lenny- 13, 63, 163
Patterning- 411
Pelvis- 54
Perceived Exertion- 90, 407
Performance- 214
Periodization- 409
Personal Journey- 9
Pigeon Pose- 491
    with Contralateral Reach- 157
    with Ipsilateral Reach- 157
Piriformis- 105
Plank- 352
    Activation- 246
    Alignment- 69
    Bird Dog- 357
    for Stability- 352
    Heel Touch- 354
    Hip Abduction- 355
    Lateral Shift- 334
    Leg Curl- 355
    Leg Pedal- 354
    Protraction (Faux Push-Up) – 260, 333
    Reach- 335
    Reverse- 275
    Rolls-
    Rotated Reach- 336
    Saw- 334
    Shoulder Tap- 335
    Tuck- 356
    Tuck – Abduction- 356
    Tuck – Adduction- 357
    Variations- 328, 335
    Wallet Touch- 336
Plantar Fasciitis- 48
Pose Method- 454
Positioned- 219
Power-173
PreHabilitation- 16
    Challenge- 17, 88, 445
    in Sports- 454
    Training & Development Goals- 21
    Preparation Techniques for Training-16
Programming- 408
Protraction- 260
Pull-Up- 304, 420-421
    Faux- 84, 263
Pulsating- 216
Push/Pull- 254-258
    Progressions- 328

Push-Up- 302, 422
Pyramid- 484
    Extended- 485
    Revolved- 485

Quadriceps- 106, 180, 447

Range of Motion
    Ankle- 524
    First Toe- 523
    Shoulder- 515
    Spine- 514, 519
Reach
    Compass- 378, 432
    Contralateral- 154
    Plank- 335
    Plank, Rotated- 336
    Quadruped Pigeon- 199
    Rotated- 126, 140, 386
    Side Plank Rotated- 386
Recovery- 473
Retraction- 261
    Inverted- 261
    on Cable Row- 262
    Recline Pull- 85
    Scapula Exercise- 85
Ribcage Peel- 125
Rice, Jerry- 87
Romanov, Dr. Nicolas- 35, 454
Rotation
    Compass Reach Single Leg- 44
    Compass Reach (Unstable Surface)- 382
    External- 328, 330
    External with Resistance Tube- 329
    External with Thera Band- 265, 332
    Internal- 328, 330
    Internal with Resistance Tube- 331
    Low-Lunge- 187
    Seated- 492
    Side Plank- 218, 386
    Single Leg- 226, 320, 378, 537
    Single Leg (Unstable Surface)- 380
    Standing- 122
    Supine Locked- 183
    Wide-Legged- 186
    Wide-Stance- 483
    Wide-Stance Hip Hinge- 276
Rotator Cuff

INDEX

Muscles- 254, 259
Stability- 328
Runner's Knee- 37
Running
    Drills- 429, 458
    Technique- 445
Rx for Sets & Reps- 409

Sagittal Walk- 38
Scapula- 83
Scar Tissue- 98
Scorpion- 158
    Reverse- 159, 185
    Shoulder Roll- 208
Self-Myofascial Release Techniques (SMR) – 96, 100
Sets: Power of Three- 411
Shavasana Test for Pain & Stress- 494
Shin Splints- 52
Shoulder
    Alignment- 131
    Extension- 138
    Flexion- 139
    Girdle Activation- 259
    Girdle Muscles- 259
    Girdle Stability- 328
    Horizontal Abduction- 138
    Joint- 67, 86, 259
    Mobility- 130
    Stability- 218, 327
Side Plank- 70
    Activation- 247
    Alignment- 70
    Hip Abduction- 39, 41, 236, 366, 387
    Hip Hike- 39
    Rotated Reach- 386
    Rotation- 218, 386
    Stability- 353
Single-Leg
    Bridge off Roller- 74, 219
    Deadlift- 42, 44, 51, 398
    Deadlift with Pole- 283
    Heel Lift- 51, 226, 319, 378, 538
    Heel Lift (Unstable Surface) - 379
    Hop- 403
    Lunge with Contralateral Reach- 440
    Lunge with Ipsilateral Reach- 441
    Rotation- 226, 320, 378, 537
    Rotation (Unstable Surface)-380
    Squat off a Box- 43, 75, 322, 393
    Stand-Up- 319, 323
    Supine Toe Touch- 350
    Toe Touch- 279, 395
    Toe Touch (Unstable Surface) - 381
Sit-Back March- 437
Sitting- 447
Skip- 315
    A- 467
    Alternating Bounding-470
    B- 468
    Triple-A- 469
Sleep- 503
Sliding Filament Theory- 94
Slope & Speed- 453
Slow- 218
Soft Rolling- 251
Soft-Tissue Therapy- 49, 93, 97, 100, 107, 112, 133, 146, 165
    Techniques- 96
    Types of Balls- 150
    Types of Rollers- 147
Speed
    and Power- 173
    and Slope- 453
Speed Skaters- 308, 400
Spiderman- 156
    Lunge with Touch and Reach- 203-205
Spinal Twist- 493
Squat
    Air- 76
    Air with Band- 243
    and Reach- 206
    and Rotate- 195
    Barbell Back- 220
    Elevated Split - 390
    Single-Leg off a Box- 43, 75, 322, 393
    Wall- 90, 530
Stability- 22
    Ankle- 371
    Combination Exercises– 385
    Core- 343, 454, 525, 527
    Disc- 377, 378
    Hip- 361
    Improving- 319
    Ipsilateral Test- 319
    Plank- 352
    Rotator Cuff- 328
    Shoulder- 218, 327
    Shoulder Girdle- 328
    Side Plank- 353
    Spinal- 343
Standing- 244
Standing Lateral Flexion- 123
Stand-Up Desks- 62, 146
Stanford University- 16, 87, 476
Star Wars- 211, 215
Starrett, Kelly- 6, 73, 92
Sternoclavicular Joint- 83
Straight-Leg March- 436
Straight-Leg Stride- 464
Stretch
    Couch- 160, 490
    Kneeling Calf with Pole- 168
    Kneeling Lunge- 217
    Neck- 82
    PNF Calf- 224
    PNF Contract/Relax- 177
    Standing Calf Stretch- 169
    Supine Adductor- 180
    Supine Sagittal- 178
    Supine Transverse- 179
Strength
    Exercises- 417
    Training- 22, 30, 54, 57
    Training for Runners- 405
Stress
    Fracture- 54
    Repetitive- 405
    Repetitive Stress Syndrome- 26
Superman- 247
    Back Extensions- 271, 352
Sustained- 217
Synergy- 253

Tabletop Hand & Heel Lift- 272
Tabletop Shoulder & Hip Abduction- 273
Tacoma Narrows Bridge- 317
Tall Cable Chop- 305, 387
Tensegrity Model- 98
Thoracic Expansion on Roller- 122
Thoracic Spine- 81, 102, 118
    Mobility- 118
Toe March- 434
Toe Touch- 350
    Progression- 224
    Single-Leg- 279, 395
    Single-Leg Supine- 350
    Single-Leg (unstable surface)- 381
    Supine- 350
    Wall-Assisted- 191

INDEX

Top-Down Approach- 110, 118, 132, 253
Towels- 378
Towel Scrunch- 227
Trapezius- 101, 259
Triangle Pose- 487
    Revolved- 487
Trigger Points- 102
    Tools- 97
Tuck Jumps- 312

Turley, Shannon- 16, 87, 476

Unstable Surfaces- 377
US Men's Soccer- 174

Vertical Jump- 287

Wall Slides- 89, 132
Warrior One Pose- 486
Wheel Pose- 493

Wide-Legged Hand Walk- 186
Wide-Stance Lateral Flexion- 483
Windshield Wipers- 152, 293-296
Wrist- 86

Yoga- 475
Yoga Recovery Sequence- 479
Y-T-W-A's - 281-282, 337

BASIC ASSESSMENTS AND MOVEMENT EVALUATIONS

BASIC ASSESSMENTS & MOVEMETN EVALUATIONS

STATIC POSTURE

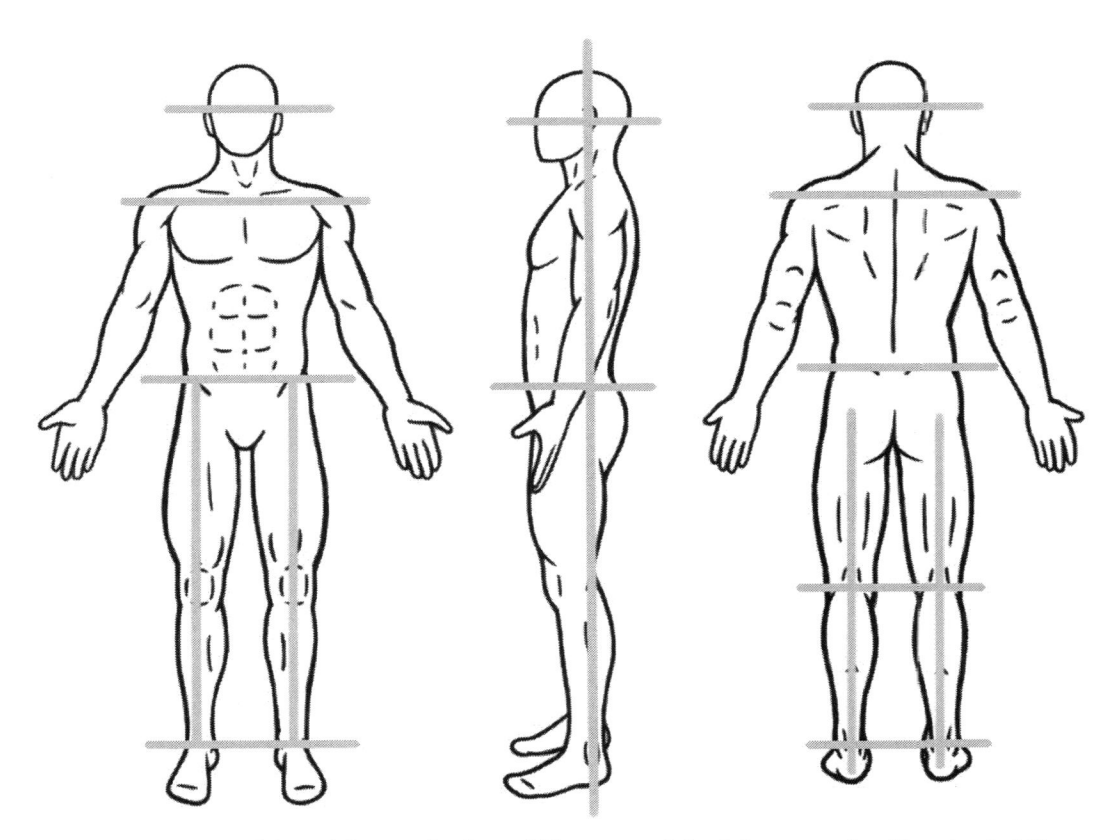

Assess if the Head, Shoulders, Spine, Hips, and Ankles are in Neutral Alignment.

ANTERIOR (FRONT)
- Are the Ears parallel with the floor?
- Are the Shoulders parallel with the floor?
- Are the Hips parallel with the floor?
- Do the Knees align with the Hip Socket and center of the Ankles?
- Do the Ankles collapse in towards the Midline of the body?

LATERAL (PROFILE)
- Is the Head level?
- Are the Hips level with the floor?
- Do the Ears align over the Shoulders, Hips, and Ankles?
- Look for Forward Head Posture, Rounded Shoulders, excessive curvature of the Spine, and a tilted Pelvis (Hips).

POSTERIOR (BACK)
- Are the Ears parallel with the floor?
- Are the Shoulders parallel with the floor?
- Are the Hips parallel with the floor?
- Do the Knees align with the Hip Socket and center of the Ankles?
- Do the Ankles collapse in towards the Midline of the body?

Incorporate PreHab Exercises, starting with Mobility training, for each region (Neck, Shoulders, Hips, Ankles) that fails to exhibit Neutral Alignment.

PreHab Exercise Book for Runners

BASIC ASSESSMENTS & MOVEMETN EVALUATIONS

SPINAL ALIGNMENT – HEAD & NECK

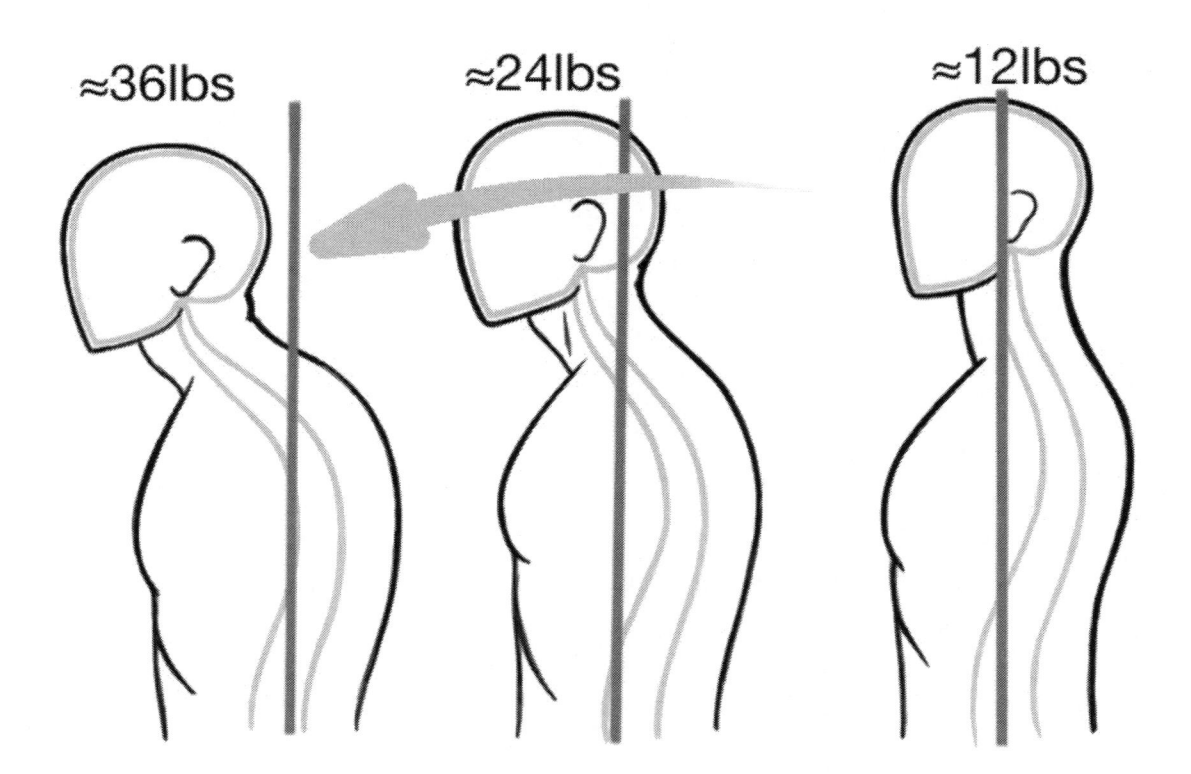

≈36lbs ≈24lbs ≈12lbs

Assess if the Head and Neck (Spine) are in Neutral Alignment.

HEAD & NECK ALIGNMENT

- *Does the Ear vertically align over the Spine and Hips?*
- *Does the Thoracic Spine or Lumbar Spine exhibit excessive curvatures?*
- *Does the Head protract forward beyond the vertical alignment of the Spine and Hips?*

PREHAB EXERCISES

- *Soft Tissue Therapy (Mobility) for the Neck and Shoulder muscles, especially the Upper Trapezius and Chest Muscles.*
- *Stretch (Mobility) the Head, Neck, and Shoulders.*
- *Activate Core and Shoulder Muscles, especially the Deep Neck Flexors, Shoulder Girdle, Abdominals, and Oblique muscles.*
- *Practice Stability exercises for the Shoulders and Core.*

Start with Mobility exercises and progress to Activation and Stability exercises for these regions if the Head and Neck (Spine) fail to exhibit Neutral Alignment.

BASIC ASSESSMENTS & MOVEMETN EVALUATIONS

CERVICAL SPINE RANGE OF MOTION
HEAD & NECK

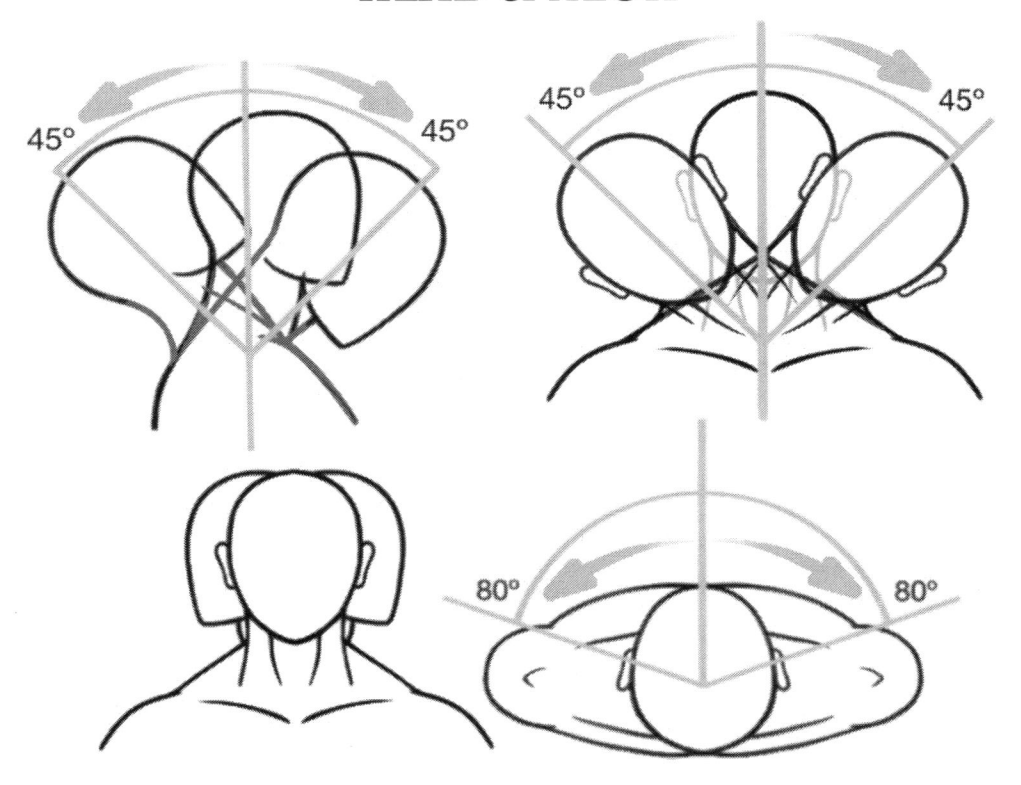

Assess the Range of Motion of the Cervical Spine - Head and Neck.

HEAD & NECK RANGE OF MOTION
- *FLEXION & EXTENSION:* Can the Head 'nod yes' with a Range of Motion of 45° in each direction?
- *LATERAL FLEXION:* Can the Head tilt from Left to Right with a Range of Motion of 45° in each direction?
- *ROTATION:* Can the Head 'nod no' or turn from Left to Right with a Range of Motion of 80° in each direction?

PREHAB EXERCISES
- Soft Tissue Therapy (Mobility) for Neck and Shoulder muscles, especially the Upper Trapezius and Chest Muscles.
- Stretch (Mobility) the Head, Neck, and Shoulders.
- Activate Core and Shoulder Muscles, especially the Deep Neck Flexors, Shoulder Girdle, Abdominals, and Oblique muscles.

Start with Mobility exercises and progress to Activation and Stability exercises if the Head and Neck (Spine) fail to exhibit a full Range of Motion.

PreHab Exercise Book for Runners

BASIC ASSESSMENTS & MOVEMETN EVALUATIONS

SHOULDER RANGE OF MOTION

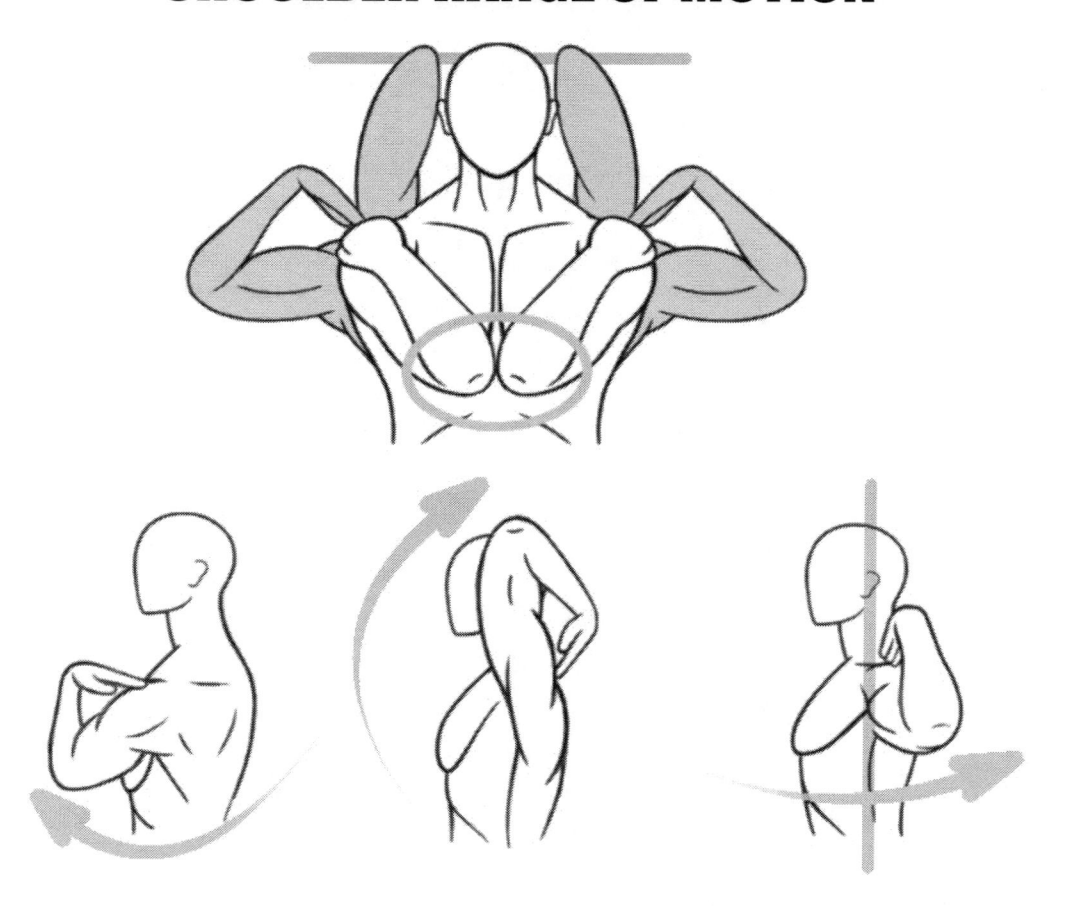

Assess the Range of Motion of the Shoulders.

SHOULDERS RANGE OF MOTION
- ADDUCTION: Can the Elbows touch each other in front of the Heart with the middle finger touching the Shoulder?
- FLEXION: Can the Elbows extend over the top of the Head with the middle finger touching the Shoulder?
- ABDUCTION: Can the Elbows reach backwards behind the Spine and Ears (Midline of the Body) with the middle finger touching the Shoulder?

PREHAB EXERCISES
- Soft Tissue Therapy (Mobility) for Neck, Shoulders, Chest, and Back muscles, especially the Upper Trapezius (Shoulder), Pectorals (Chest), and Latissimus Dorsi (Back) Muscles.
- Stretch (Mobility) the Neck, Shoulders, Chest and Back muscles.
- Activate Core and Shoulder Muscles, especially the Shoulder Girdle and Rotator Cuff muscles.

Start with Mobility exercises and progress to Activation and Stability exercises if the Shoulders fail to exhibit a full Range of Motion.

BASIC ASSESSMENTS & MOVEMETN EVALUATIONS

SHOULDER RANGE OF MOTION

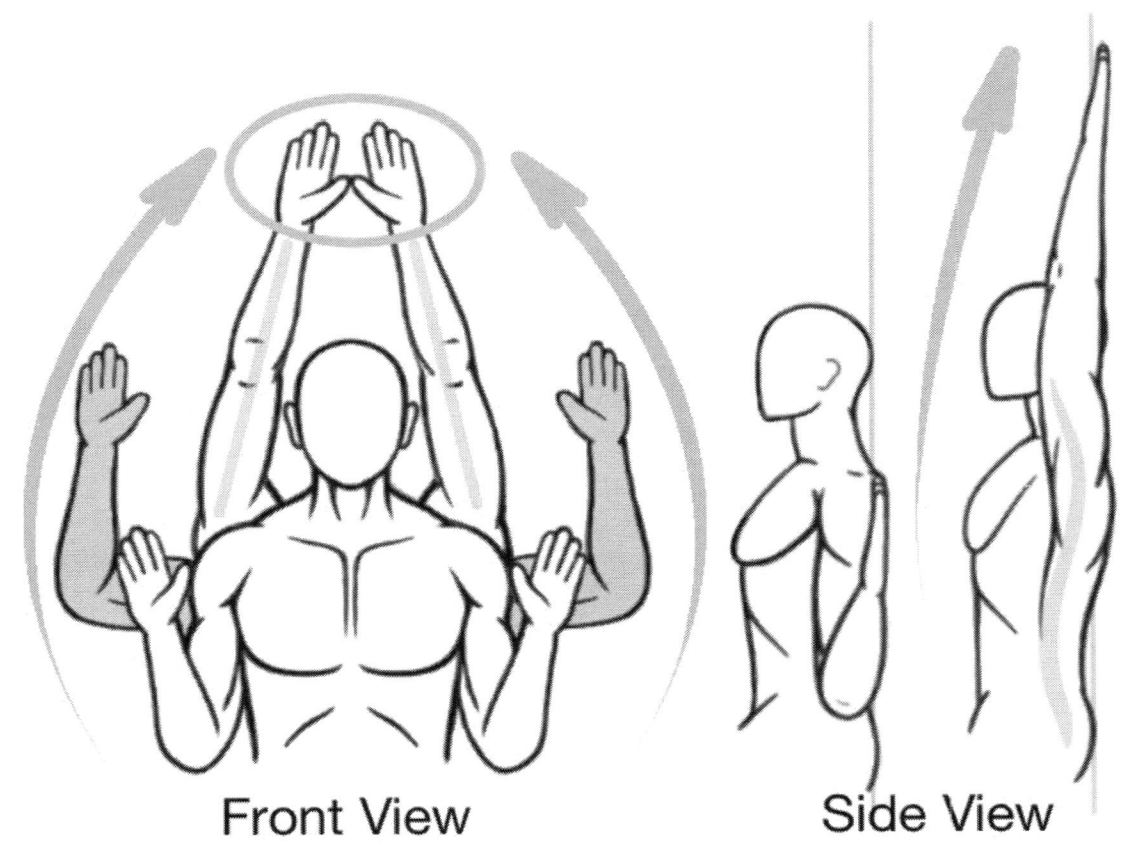

Front View   Side View

Assess the Range of Motion of the Shoulders.

SHOULDERS RANGE OF MOTION
- *Position the Head, Torso, and Hip against the wall in Neutral Alignment.*
- *Hold the Hands out to the side with the Forearms in a vertical position and the backs of the Hands and Elbows pressing into the Wall if possible.*
- *Slide the Arms up overhead until the Elbows fully extend (straighten) and the Thumbs touch as the backs of the Hands press into the Wall.*
- *Maintain Neutral Alignment in the Spine throughout the movement.*

PREHAB EXERCISES
- *Soft Tissue Therapy (Mobility) for Neck, Shoulder, Chest, and Back muscles, especially the Upper Trapezius (Shoulder), Pectorals (Chest), and Latissimus Dorsi (Back) Muscles.*
- *Stretch (Mobility) the Neck, Shoulder, Chest, and Back muscles.*
- *Activate Core and Shoulder Muscles, especially the Shoulder Girdle, Rotator Cuff, and Anterior Core (Abdominals and Oblique) muscles.*

Start with Mobility exercises and progress to Activation and Stability exercises if the Shoulders fail to exhibit a full Range of Motion.

BASIC ASSESSMENTS & MOVEMETN EVALUATIONS

SPINAL RANGE OF MOTION – FLEXION & EXTENSION

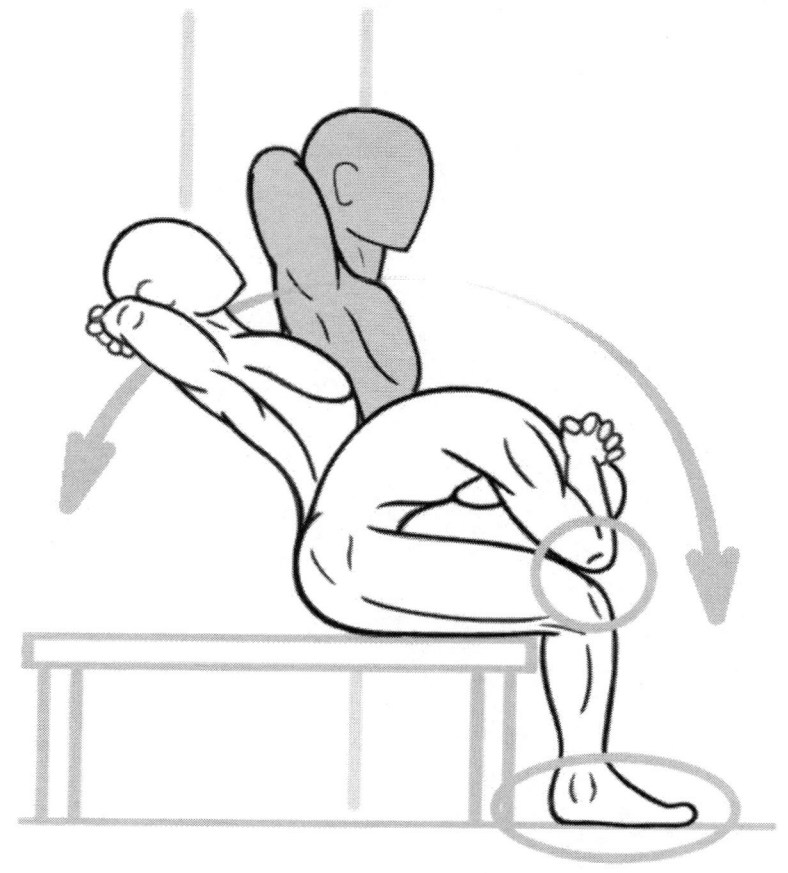

Assess the Range of Motion of the Spine.

SPINAL RANGE OF MOTION
- POSITION: Sit on a bench with Feet firmly on the floor and Hands interlaced behind the Head.
- SPINAL FLEXION: Fold forward and attempt to touch the Elbows to the Kneecaps, not the Thighs, while Feet remain firmly on the floor.
- SPINAL EXTENSION: Lean backwards with the Shoulders and Head and attempt to gaze up at the sky (180°) while the Feet remain firmly on the floor.

PREHAB EXERCISES
- *Soft Tissue Therapy (Mobility) for Chest and Back muscles, especially the Upper Trapezius (Shoulder), Pectorals (Chest), and Latissimus Dorsi (Back) Muscles.*
- *Stretch (Mobility) the Neck, Shoulder, Chest, and Back muscles.*
- *Activate Core and Shoulder Muscles, especially the Shoulder Girdle, Rotator Cuff, and Anterior Core (Abdominals and Oblique) muscles.*

Start with Mobility exercises and progress to Activation and Stability exercises if the Spine fails to exhibit a full Range of Motion.

BASIC ASSESSMENTS & MOVEMETN EVALUATIONS

FOOT & ANKLE ALIGNMENT

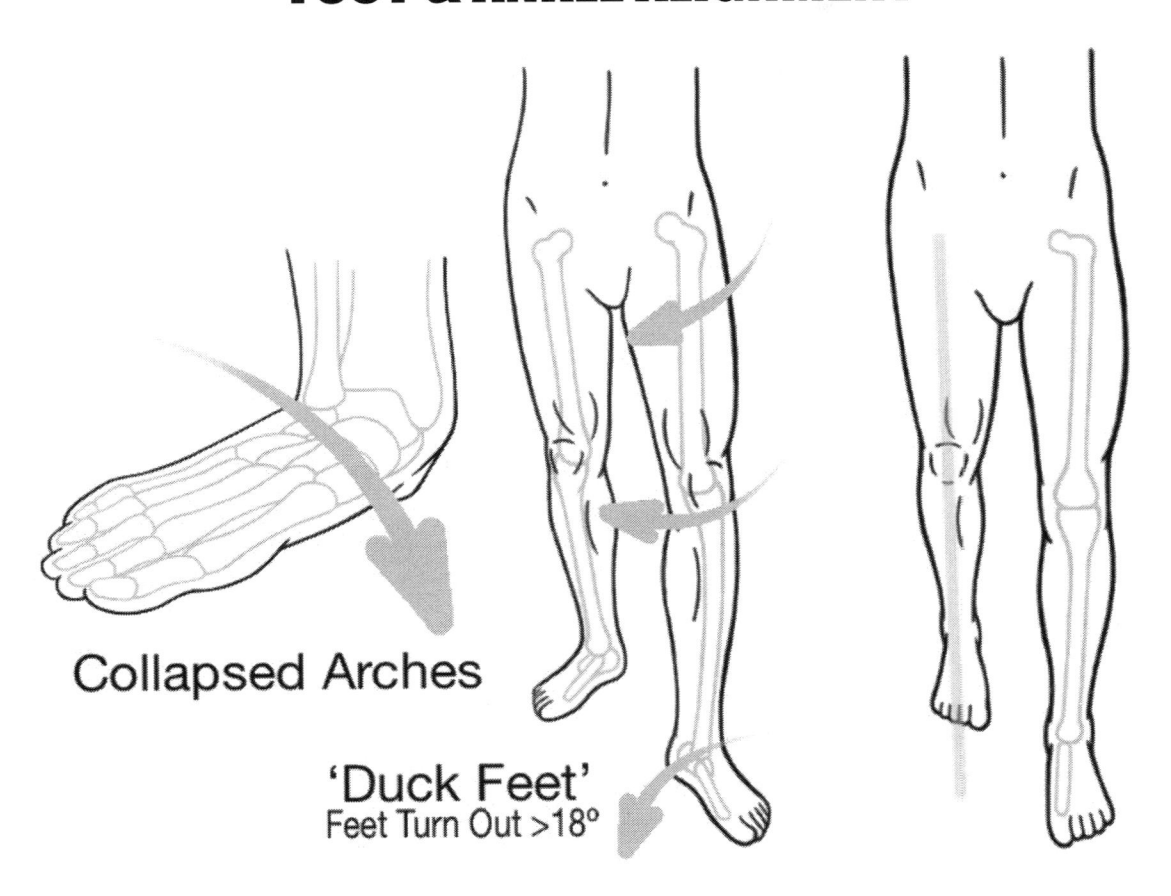

Collapsed Arches

'Duck Feet'
Feet Turn Out >18°

Assess if the Foot and Ankle are in Neutral Alignment.

FOOT ALIGNMENT
- *Do the Toes point forward?*
- *Does the Foot 'turn out' or point out to the sides by an angle greater than 18° of Abduction (away from center)?*
- *Does the Arch of the Foot 'collapse' or drop towards the floor?*

PREHAB EXERCISES
- *Soft Tissue Therapy (Mobility) for the Intrinsic Foot Muscles, Plantar Fascia, Calf Muscles, and Adductors (Groin) Muscles.*
- *Stretch (Mobility) the Foot, Calf, and Ankles.*
- *Activate the Foot, Ankle, and Hip Muscles, especially the Calf and Lateral Hip muscles.*
- *Practice Stability exercises for the Ankle, Hip, and Posterior Chain.*

Start with Mobility exercises and progress to Activation and Stability exercises for this region if the Foot and Ankle fail to exhibit Neutral Alignment.

BASIC ASSESSMENTS & MOVEMETN EVALUATIONS

ANKLE ALIGNMENT

Pronation   Neutral   Supination

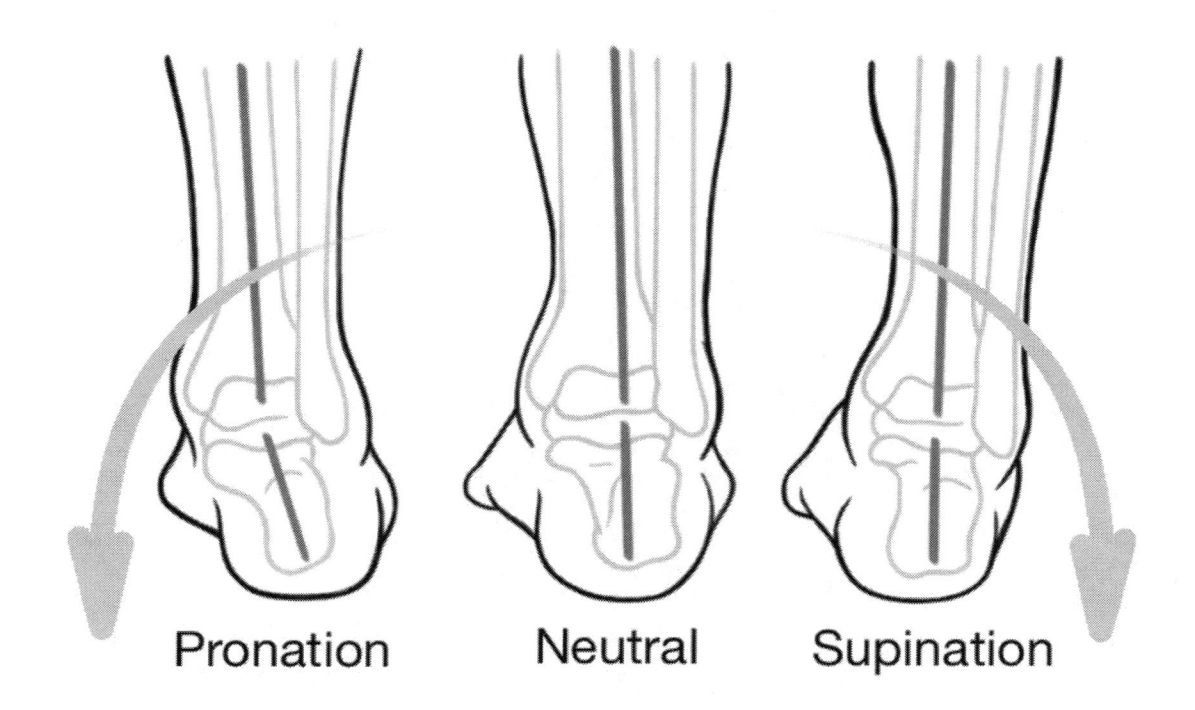

Assess the Alignment of the Ankle.

ALIGNMENT CUES
- Viewing the Ankle from the front or back, observe the Anklebones and draw an imaginary line down the Achilles Tendon to the Heel.
- If the Ankle rolls or 'collapses' in towards the Midline of the body, the Ankle is in Pronation. If the Ankle rolls out away from the Midline of the body, the Ankle is in Supination.
- Note: Any malalignments (Pronation or Supination) in the Ankle create compensation patterns in an individual's running technique.

PREHAB EXERCISES
- Soft Tissue Therapy (Mobility) for the Foot, Ankle, Leg, and Hip Muscles.
- Stretch (Mobility) the Foot, Ankle, Leg, Hip, and Posterior Chain with isolated and Combination Mobility Exercises.
- Activate the Foot, Ankle, Hip, and Posterior Chain Muscles with isolated and Combination Activation Exercises.
- Stabilize the Ankle and Hips with isolated and Combination Exercises.

Start with Mobility exercises and progress to Activation and Stability exercises if the individual fails to exhibit an adequate amount of Stability.

BASIC ASSESSMENTS & MOVEMETN EVALUATIONS

ARCH OF THE FOOT

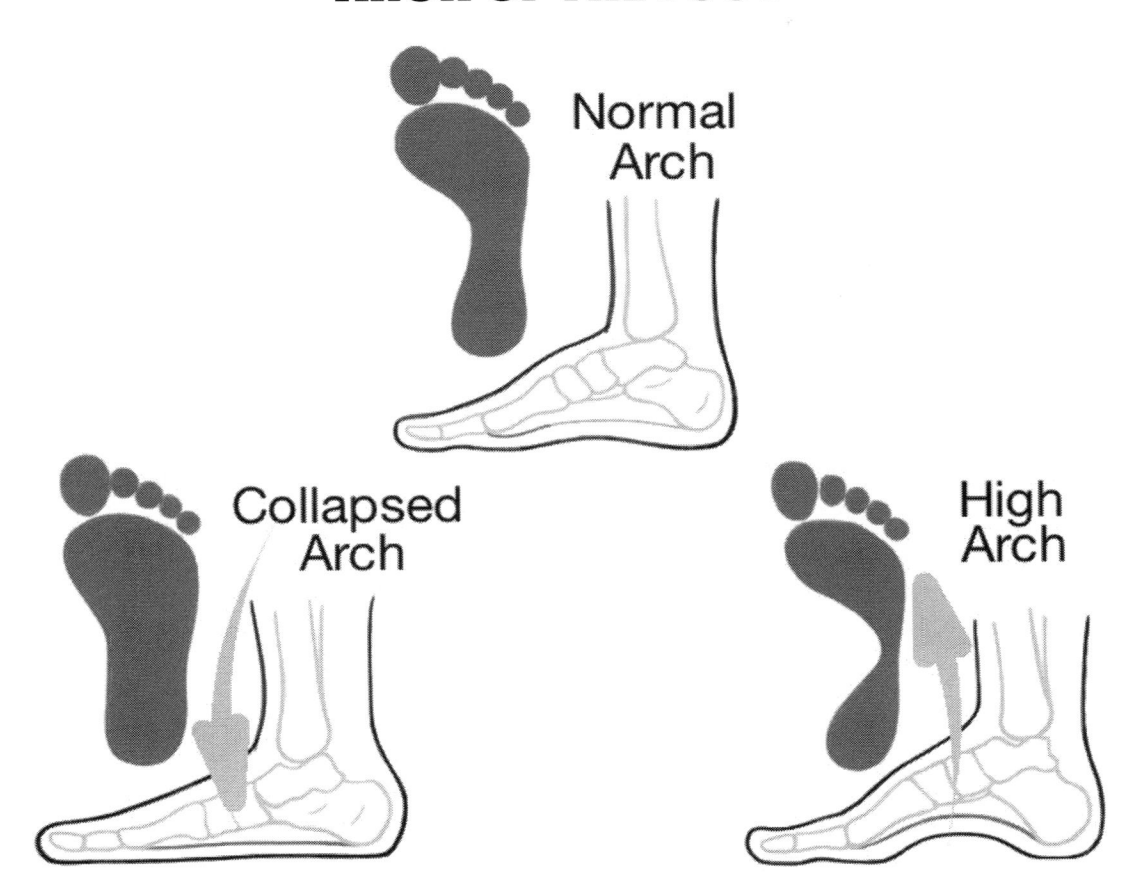

Assess the Arch of the Foot.

ALIGNMENT CUES
- *Viewing the Foot from the inside and observing the type of Footprint, assess the Arch of the Foot.*
- *A 'Collapsed' Arch creates a wide Footprint and a 'High' Arch creates a thin Footprint. A 'Normal' Arch creates a slender Footprint.*
- *Note: Any malalignments (High or Collapsed Arches) in the Foot create compensation patterns in an individual's running technique.*

PREHAB EXERCISES
- *Soft Tissue Therapy (Mobility) for the Foot, Ankle, Leg, and Hip Muscles.*
- *Stretch (Mobility) the Foot, Ankle, Leg, Hip, and Posterior Chain with isolated and Combination Mobility Exercises.*
- *Activate the Foot, Ankle, Hip, and Posterior Chain Muscles with isolated and Combination Activation Exercises.*
- *Stabilize the Ankle and Hips with isolated and Combination Exercises.*

Start with Mobility exercises and progress to Activation and Stability exercises if the individual fails to exhibit an adequate amount of Stability.

BASIC ASSESSMENTS & MOVEMETN EVALUATIONS

FIRST TOE RANGE OF MOTION

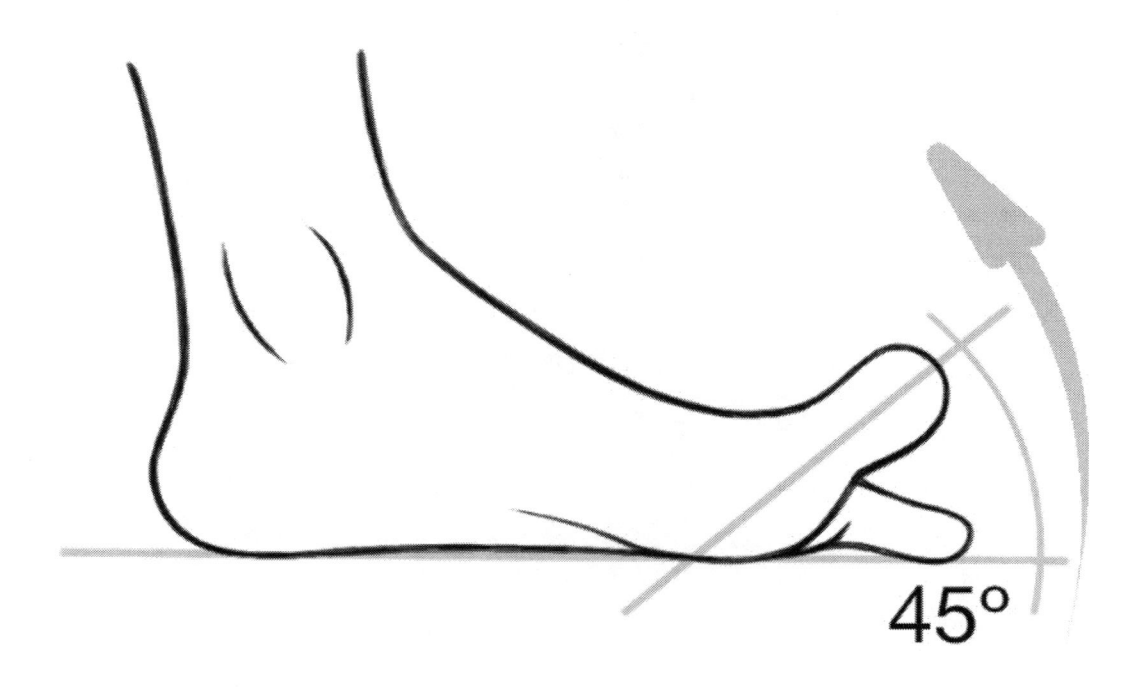

Assess the Range of Motion of the First Toe.

ALIGNMENT CUES
- Place Foot on the floor and lift the First Toe (Big Toe) up towards the sky as high as possible.
- The optimal Range of Motion for the First Toe is 45° or more.
- Note: Any limitation in the First Toe's ROM (Range of Motion) disrupts an individual's Gait Pattern and creates compensation patterns in his/her running technique.

PREHAB EXERCISES
- Soft Tissue Therapy (Mobility) for the Foot, Ankle, and Calf.
- Stretch (Mobility) the Foot, Ankle, and Posterior Chain with isolated and Combination Mobility Exercises.
- Activate the Foot, Ankle, Hip, and Posterior Chain Muscles with isolated and Combination Activation Exercises.
- Stabilize the Ankle and Hips with isolated and Combination Exercises.

Start with Mobility exercises and progress to Activation and Stability exercises if the individual fails to exhibit an adequate amount of Stability.

PreHab Exercise Book for Runners

BASIC ASSESSMENTS & MOVEMETN EVALUATIONS

ANKLE RANGE OF MOTION

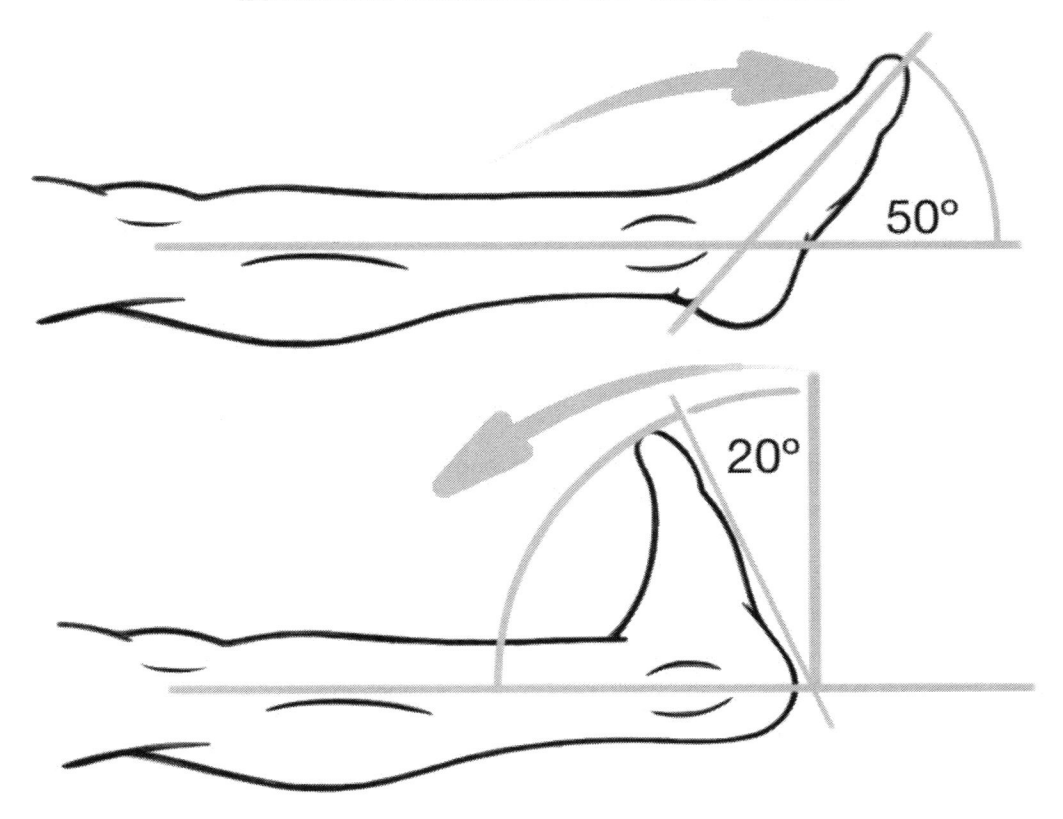

50°

20°

Assess the Range of Motion of the Ankle.

ALIGNMENT CUES

- Point the Toes away from the Shin (Plantar Flexion) and then pull the Toes back towards the Shin (Dorsiflexion).
- The optimal Range of Motion for Plantar Flexion (Toes Point Away) is 50° or more.
- The optimal Range of Motion for Dorsiflexion (Toes Point Towards) is 20° or more.
- Note: Any limitation in the Ankle's Range of Motion creates compensation patterns in an individual's running technique.

PREHAB EXERCISES

- Soft Tissue Therapy (Mobility) for the Foot, Ankle, and Calf.
- Stretch (Mobility) the Foot, Ankle, and Posterior Chain with isolated and Combination Mobility Exercises.
- Activate the Foot, Ankle, Hip, and Posterior Chain Muscles with isolated and Combination Activation Exercises.
- Stabilize the Ankle and Hips with isolated and Combination Exercises.

Start with Mobility exercises and progress to Activation and Stability exercises if the individual fails to exhibit an adequate amount of Stability.

BASIC ASSESSMENTS & MOVEMETN EVALUATIONS

HIP HINGE WITH POLE
HIP MOBILITY & CORE STABILITY

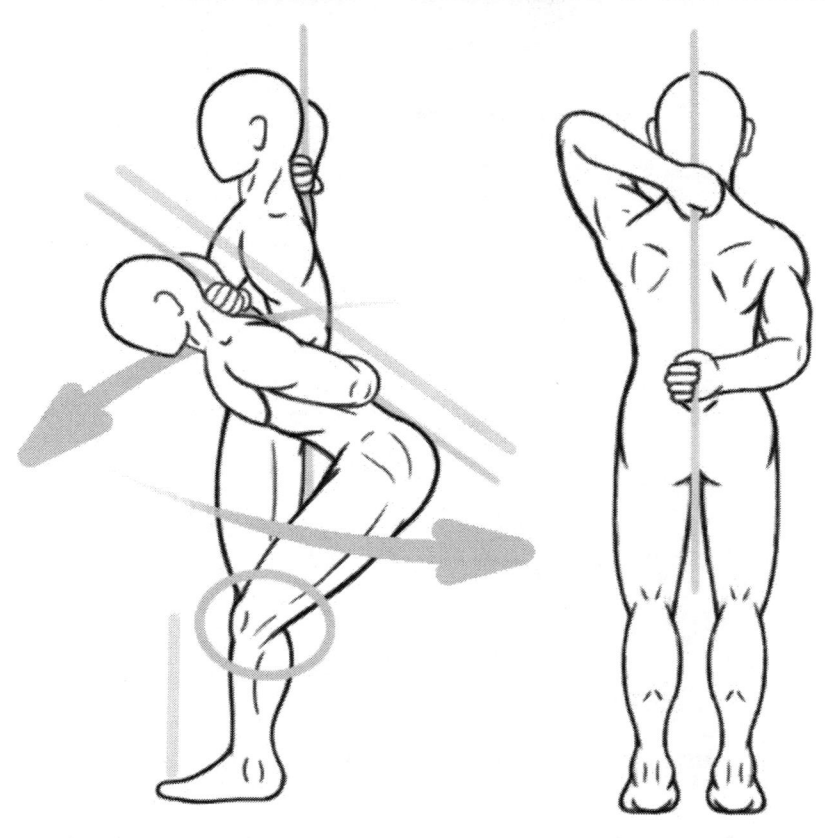

Assess the Range of Motion of Hip Flexion and Core (Spinal) Stability.

HINGE RANGE OF MOTION

- *POSITION: Stand with Feet Hip-width apart and hold a pole along the Back (Spine) with Hands behind the Neck and Low Back as the Head, Heart, and Hips all touch the Pole.*
- *HINGE: Simultaneously bend the Knees and Hips while leaning forward with the Torso, keeping the Chest over the vertical Shins.*
- *ALIGNMENT: Attempt to flex the Hips to 90° while keeping the Head, Heart, and Hips touching the pole.*

PREHAB EXERCISES

- *Soft Tissue Therapy (Mobility) for Hips, Legs, and Back muscles, especially the Glutes (Hips), Hamstrings (Legs), and Latissimus Dorsi (Back) Muscles.*
- *Stretch (Mobility) the Hips, Leg, and Back muscles.*
- *Activate Core Muscles, especially the Anterior Core (Abdominals and Oblique) muscles.*
- *Practice Core, Hip, and Combination Stability exercises.*

Start with Mobility exercises and progress to Activation and Stability exercises if the individual fails to exhibit a full Range of Motion in the Hip Hinge.

BASIC ASSESSMENTS & MOVEMETN EVALUATIONS

HIP EXTENSION WITH POLE
HIP MOBILITY & CORE STABILITY

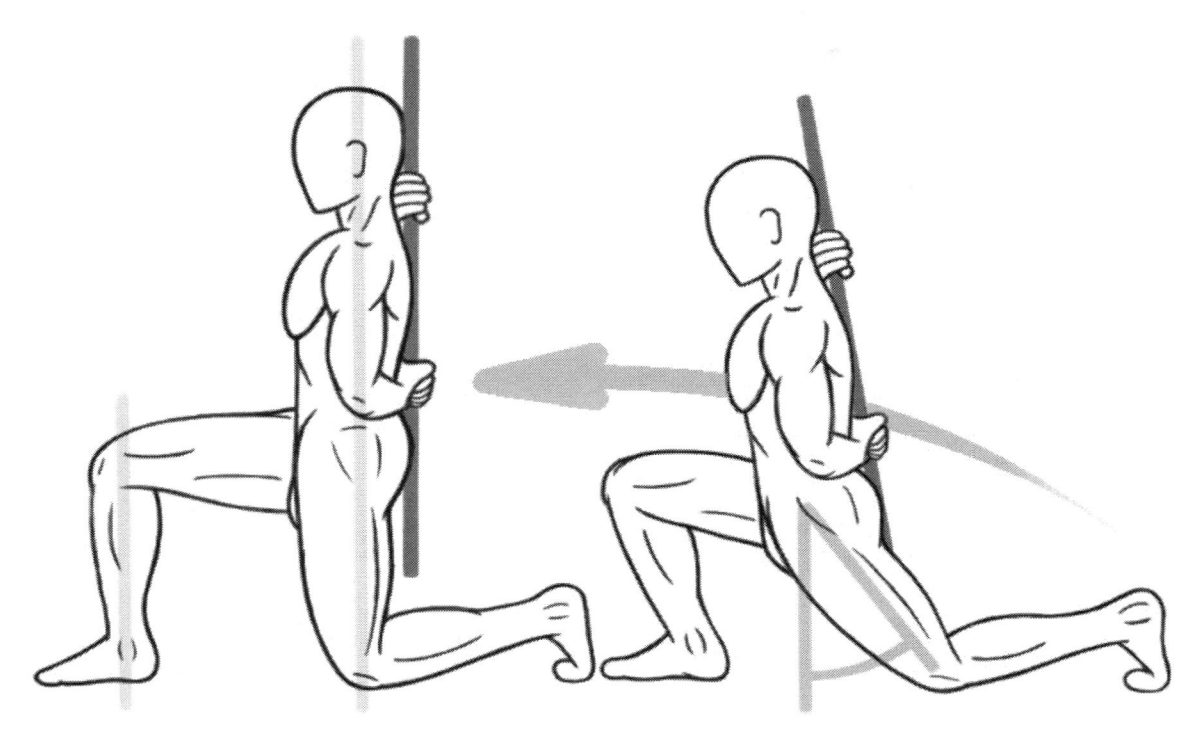

Hip Extension - Optimal Range of Motion: 30°

Assess the Range of Motion of Hip Extension and Core (Spinal) Stability.

LUNGE RANGE OF MOTION
- POSITION: Kneel on one Knee and hold a pole along the Back (Spine) with Hands behind the Neck and Low Back as the Head, Heart, and Hips all touch the Pole.
- LUNGE: Smoothly lunge forward with the Hips as far as possible while keeping the Head, Heart, and Hips touching the pole.
- HIP EXTENSION: Attempt to lunge forward with a Neutral Spine into a Hip Extension of 10° (Minimum) to 30° (Optimal).

• *PREHAB EXERCISES*
- *Soft Tissue Therapy (Mobility) for the Hips, Legs, and Back muscles, especially the Glutes (Hips), Hamstrings (Legs), and Latissimus Dorsi (Back) Muscles.*
- *Stretch (Mobility) the Hips, Leg, and Back muscles.*
- *Activate Core Muscles, especially the Anterior Core (Abdominals and Oblique) muscles.*
- *Practice Core, Hip, and Combination Stability exercises.*

Start with Mobility exercises and progress to Activation and Stability exercises if the Hips fail to exhibit a full Range of Motion.

BASIC ASSESSMENTS & MOVEMETN EVALUATIONS

STANDING KNEE TUCK
HIP FLEXION & SINGLE-LEG STABILITY

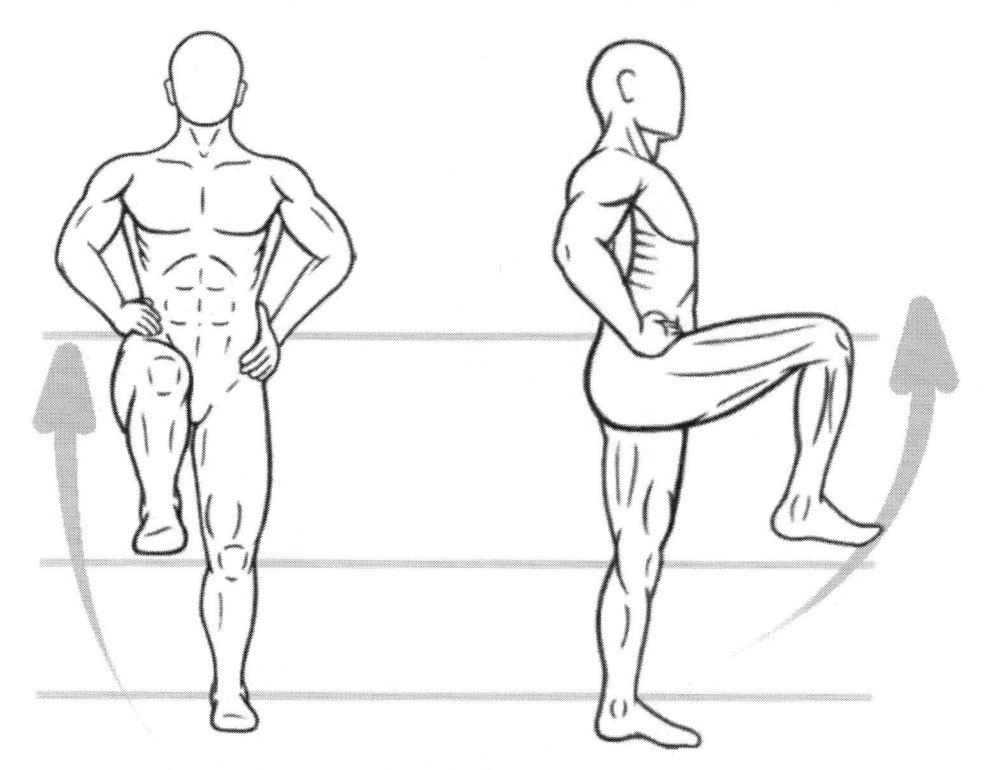

Assess the Range of Motion of Hip Flexion and Single-Leg Stability.

STANDING KNEE TUCK
- POSITION: Stand tall with Feet together and Hands on Hips.
- KNEE TUCK: Lift one Knee up to match the height of the top of the Hips or higher. The Foot should clear the height of the Opposite Knee.
- SINGLE-LEG STABILITY: Attempt to keep the Hips level with the ground and maintain neutral alignment of the Standing Leg, i.e. Hip, Knee, and Ankle in vertical alignment without a collapsed Arch in the Foot.

PREHAB EXERCISES
- Soft Tissue Therapy (Mobility) for the Hip, Leg, and Foot muscles, especially the Glutes (Hips) and the Hamstrings (Leg) Muscles.
- Stretch (Mobility) the Glutes (Hips) and Hamstring (Leg) muscles.
- Activate Hip, Leg, Foot, and Core Muscles, especially the Hip Flexors, Gluteus Medius (Lateral Hip), Intrinsic Foot, Calf, and Core (Abdominals and Oblique) muscles.
- Practice Core and Single-Leg Stability Exercises.

Start with Mobility exercises and progress to Activation and Stability exercises if the individual fails to exhibit a full Range of Motion or Stability.

BASIC ASSESSMENTS & MOVEMETN EVALUATIONS

WALL SQUAT

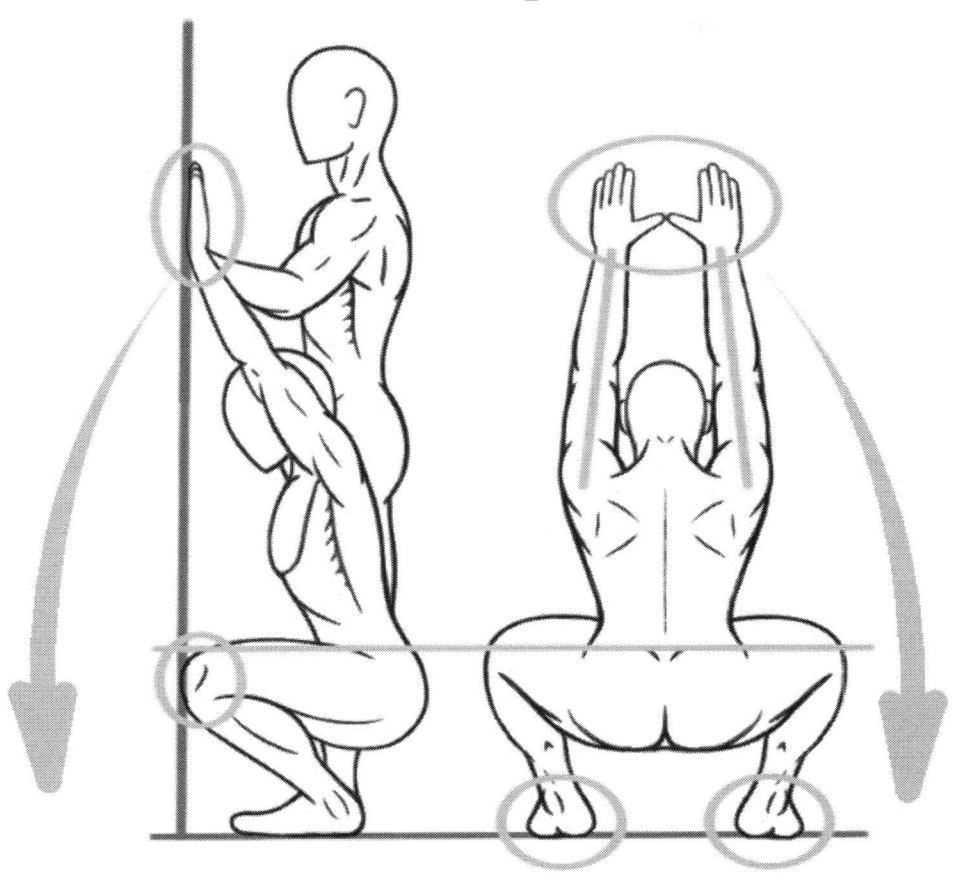

Assess the combined Mobility of the Ankle, Hip, Thoracic Spine, and Shoulders.

ALIGNMENT CUES

- *Squat with Feet shoulder-width apart, Toes pointing forward, Heels flat on the floor. (Ankle Mobility)*
- *Place Hands on the wall, Thumbs touching and Elbows straight. (Shoulder and Thoracic Spine Mobility)*
- *Kneecaps touch the wall with Knees pressed out (Abduction). (Hip Mobility and Activation)*
- *Hips should be at or below the height of the Knees. (Ankle, Hip, & Posterior Chain Mobility)*

PREHAB EXERCISES

- *Soft Tissue Therapy (Mobility) for the Foot, Ankle, Hip, Thoracic Spine, Shoulders, and Posterior Chain.*
- *Stretch (Mobility) the Ankles, Hips, Thoracic Spine, and Shoulders with isolated and Combination Mobility Exercises.*
- *Activate the Core, Hip, and Posterior Chain Muscles with isolated and Combination Activation Exercises.*
- *Stabilize the Ankle, Core, Hip, and Posterior Chain with isolated and Combination Exercises.*

Start with Mobility exercises and progress to Activation and Stability exercises if the individual fails to exhibit a full Range of Motion in the Wall Squat.

BASIC ASSESSMENTS & MOVEMETN EVALUATIONS

LATERAL LUNGE

Assess the combined Mobility and Stability of the Ankle, Hip and Posterior Chain.

ALIGNMENT CUES
- *Stand with Feet 1½ Shoulder Width.*
- *Lunge to one side until the Shoulder and Hip vertically align over the Foot.*
- *Next, Lift the Trail Leg (Back Foot) off the ground.*
- *Stand up onto a Single-Leg and maintain vertical alignment of the Shoulder, Hip, and Foot.*

PREHAB EXERCISES
- *Soft Tissue Therapy (Mobility) for the Feet, Ankles, Legs, Hips, and Posterior Chain.*
- *Stretch (Mobility) the Ankles, Hips, and Posterior Chain with isolated and Combination Mobility Exercises.*
- *Activate Ankle, Hip, and Posterior Chain Muscles with isolated and Combination Activation Exercises.*
- *Stabilize the Ankle, Hip, and Posterior Chain with isolated and Combination Exercises.*

Start with Mobility exercises and progress to Activation and Stability exercises if the individual fails to exhibit a full Range of Motion in the Lateral Lunge.

BASIC ASSESSMENTS & MOVEMETN EVALUATIONS

SINGLE-LEG BOX SQUAT

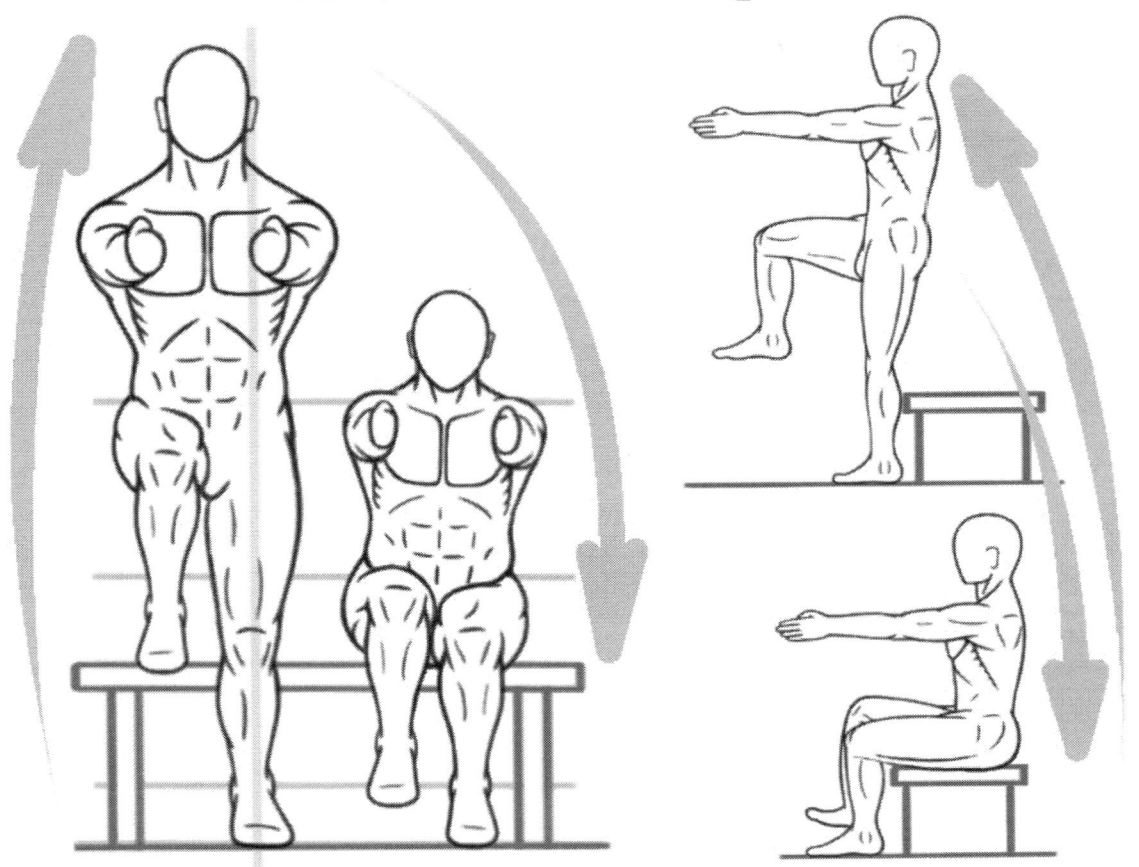

Assess the combined Stability of the Ankle, Hip, and Posterior Chain.

ALIGNMENT CUES
- Stand on one Foot (Single-Leg) with Arms extended for counterbalance and Knee tucked to Hip height.
- Next, sit down on a Knee height box/bench in a controlled manner. Do not flop or drop down.
- Then, with control, stand back up onto one Foot (Single-Leg) while maintaining vertical alignment of the Shoulder, Hip, and Foot.
- Watch for any involuntary or shaky movements, especially at the Knee.

PREHAB EXERCISES
- Soft Tissue Therapy (Mobility) for the Feet, Ankles, Legs, Hips, and Posterior Chain.
- Stretch (Mobility) the Ankles, Hips, and Posterior Chain with isolated and Combination Mobility Exercises.
- Activate Ankle, Hip, and Posterior Chain Muscles with isolated and Combination Activation Exercises.
- Stabilize the Ankle, Hip, Posterior Chain, and Single-Leg positions with isolated and Combination Exercises.

Start with Mobility exercises and progress to Activation and Stability exercises if the individual fails to exhibit a full Range of Motion in the Lateral Lunge.

PreHab Exercise Book for Runners

BASIC ASSESSMENTS & MOVEMETN EVALUATIONS

IPSILATERAL ROTARY STABILITY

Assess the combined Stability of the Shoulders, Core, and Hips.

ALIGNMENT CUES
- Start in Quadruped, i.e. on 'All Fours' or on 'Hands and Knees'.
- Reach same-side (ipsilateral) Hand and Foot towards the horizon.
- Touch same-side (ipsilateral) Elbow and Knee under the Torso.
- Re-extend same-side Hand and Foot towards the horizon before returning to Quadruped or All Fours.
- Maintain balance throughout the entire movement.

PREHAB EXERCISES
- Soft Tissue Therapy (Mobility) for the Hips, Shoulders, and Posterior Chain.
- Stretch (Mobility) the Hips, Shoulders and Posterior Chain with isolated and Combination Mobility Exercises.
- Activate the Hips, Core, and Shoulder Muscles with isolated and Combination Activation Exercises.
- Stabilize the Hips, Core, and Shoulders with isolated and Combination Exercises.

Start with Mobility exercises and progress to Activation and Stability exercises if the individual fails to exhibit a full Range of Motion and Stability.

BASIC ASSESSMENTS & MOVEMETN EVALUATIONS

TRUNK STABILITY PUSH-UP

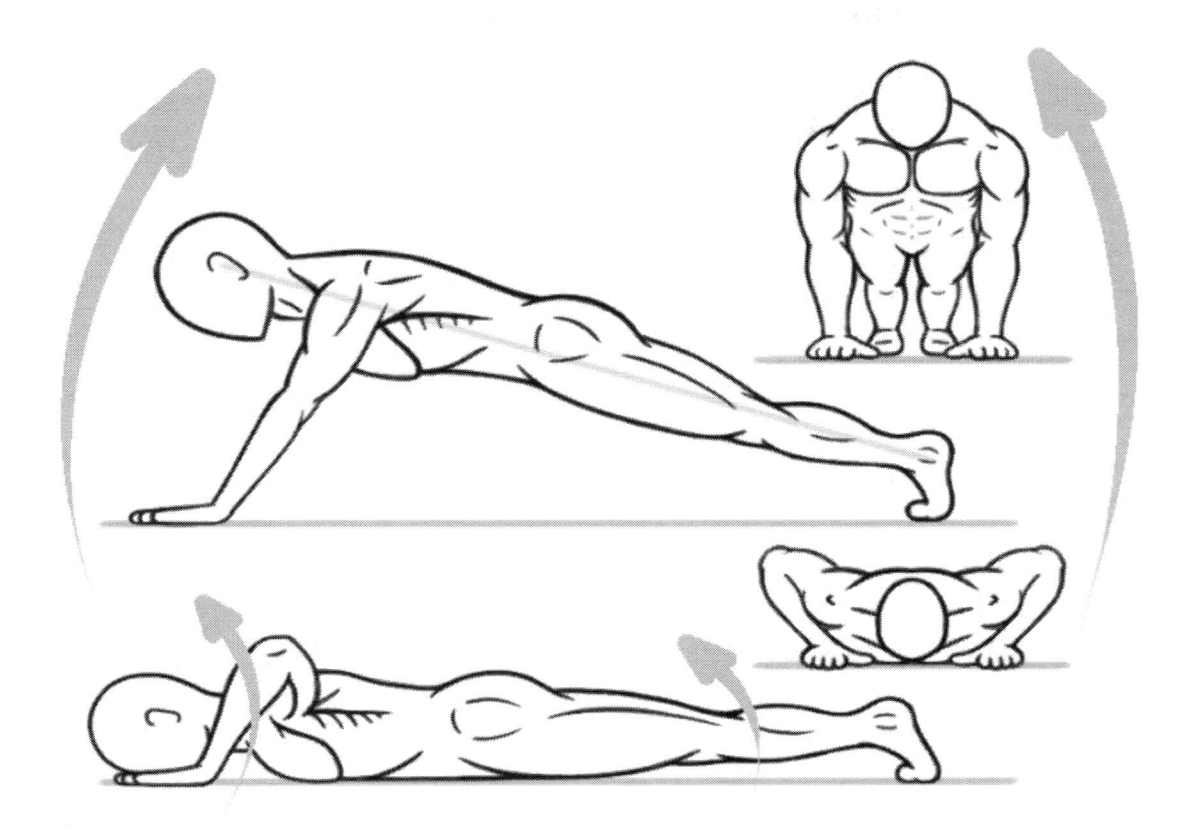

Assess the combined Stability of the Shoulders, Core, and Hips.

ALIGNMENT CUES
- *Lie on the floor with Hands placed Shoulder-Width apart, aligned with the Forehead (advanced) or Chin (intermediate).*
- *Lift the Elbow and Knee off the floor.*
- *Push-up into a Plank Position in one smooth motion while maintaining a straight-line alignment from Ear to Hip to Knees to Ankle.*

PREHAB EXERCISES
- *Soft Tissue Therapy (Mobility) for the Shoulders and Chest.*
- *Stretch (Mobility) the Shoulders and Thoracic Spine with isolated and Combination Mobility Exercises.*
- *Activate the Core, Shoulders, and Hip Flexor Muscles with isolated and Combination Activation Exercises.*
- *Stabilize the Core, Shoulders, and Hips with isolated and Combination Exercises.*

Start with Mobility exercises and progress to Activation and Stability exercises if the individual fails to exhibit an adequate amount of Stability.

BASIC ASSESSMENTS & MOVEMETN EVALUATIONS

SINGLE-LEG ROTATION

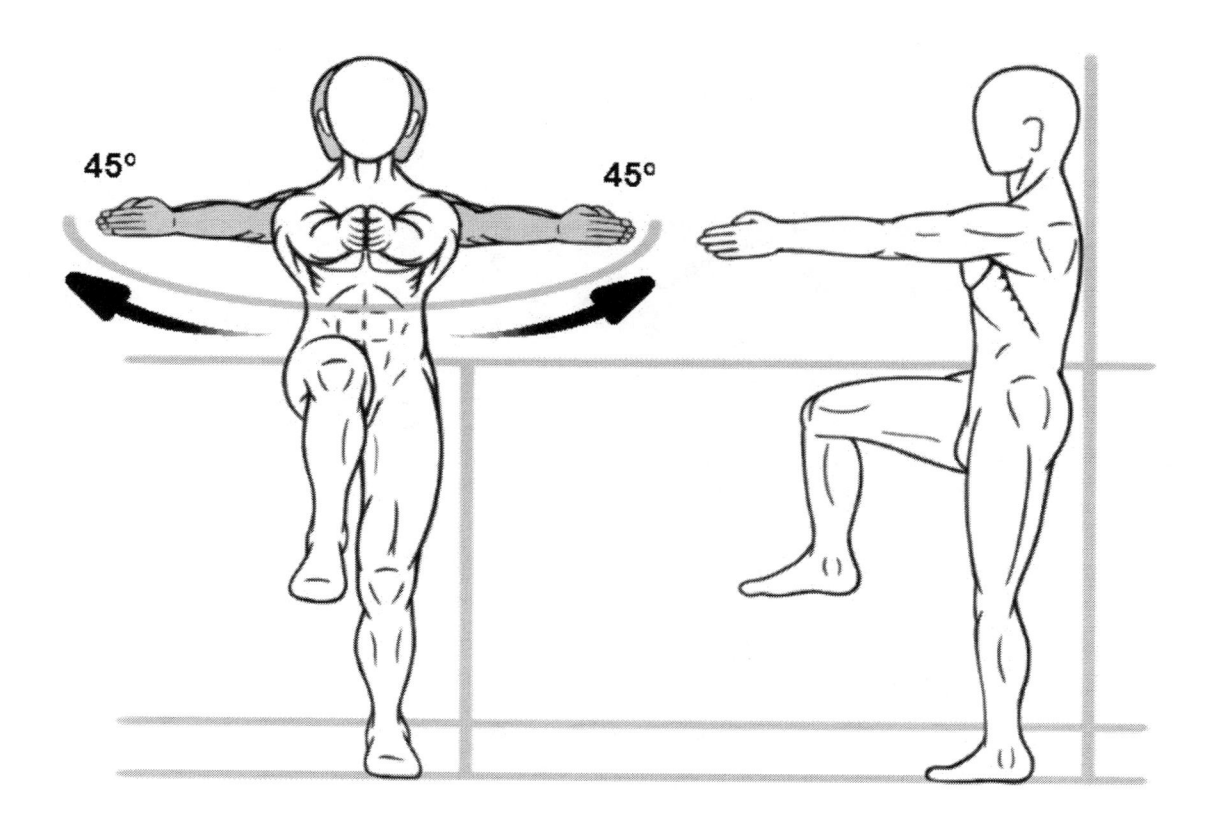

Assess the combined Stability of the Ankle, Foot, and Hips.

ALIGNMENT CUES

- Stand on one leg (Single-Leg) with the opposite Knee tucked to Hip Height and both Arms extended to the horizon, parallel to the floor.
- Rotate the Shoulders to point the Arms to each side at a 45° angle before returning to the start position.
- Attempt to maintain balance in a relaxed manner with the Eyes watching the Hands throughout the entire movement.

PREHAB EXERCISES

- Soft Tissue Therapy (Mobility) for the Foot, Leg, and Hip.
- Stretch (Mobility) the Foot, Ankle, Hip, and Posterior Chain with isolated and Combination Mobility Exercises.
- Activate the Foot, Ankle, Hip, and Posterior Chain Muscles with isolated and Combination Activation Exercises.
- Stabilize the Ankle and Hips with isolated and Combination Exercises.

Start with Mobility exercises and progress to Activation and Stability exercises if the individual fails to exhibit an adequate amount of Stability.

BASIC ASSESSMENTS & MOVEMETN EVALUATIONS

SINGLE-LEG HEEL LIFT

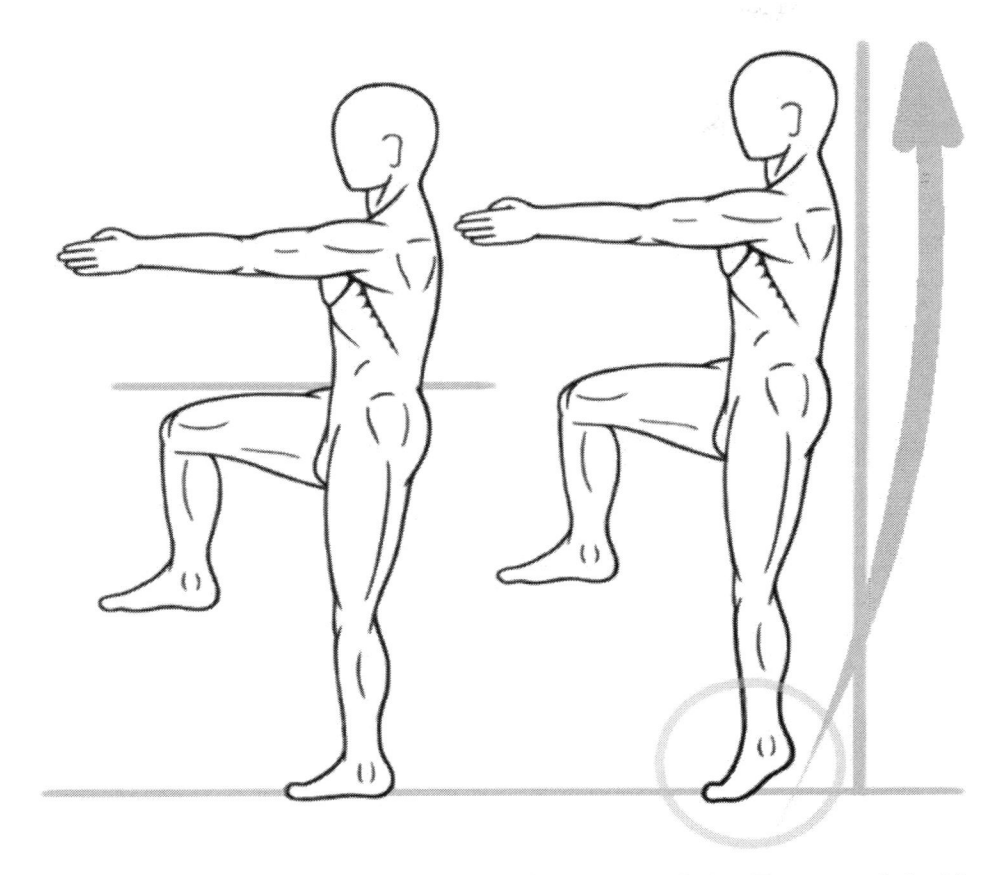

Assess the Range of Motion and Stability of the Foot and Ankle.

ALIGNMENT CUES
- Stand on one leg (Single-Leg) with the opposite Knee tucked to Hip Height and both Arms extended to the horizon, parallel to the floor.
- Lift the standing Heel off the floor while maintaining balance.
- Attempt to extend the Ankle into 50° of Plantar Flexion.

PREHAB EXERCISES
- Soft Tissue Therapy (Mobility) for the Foot, Leg, and Hip.
- Stretch (Mobility) the Foot, Ankle, Hip, and Posterior Chain with isolated and Combination Mobility Exercises.
- Activate the Foot, Ankle, Hip, and Posterior Chain Muscles with isolated and Combination Activation Exercises.
- Stabilize the Ankle and Hips with isolated and Combination Exercises.

Start with Mobility exercises and progress to Activation and Stability exercises if the individual fails to exhibit an adequate amount of Stability.

BASIC ASSESSMENTS & MOVEMETN EVALUATIONS

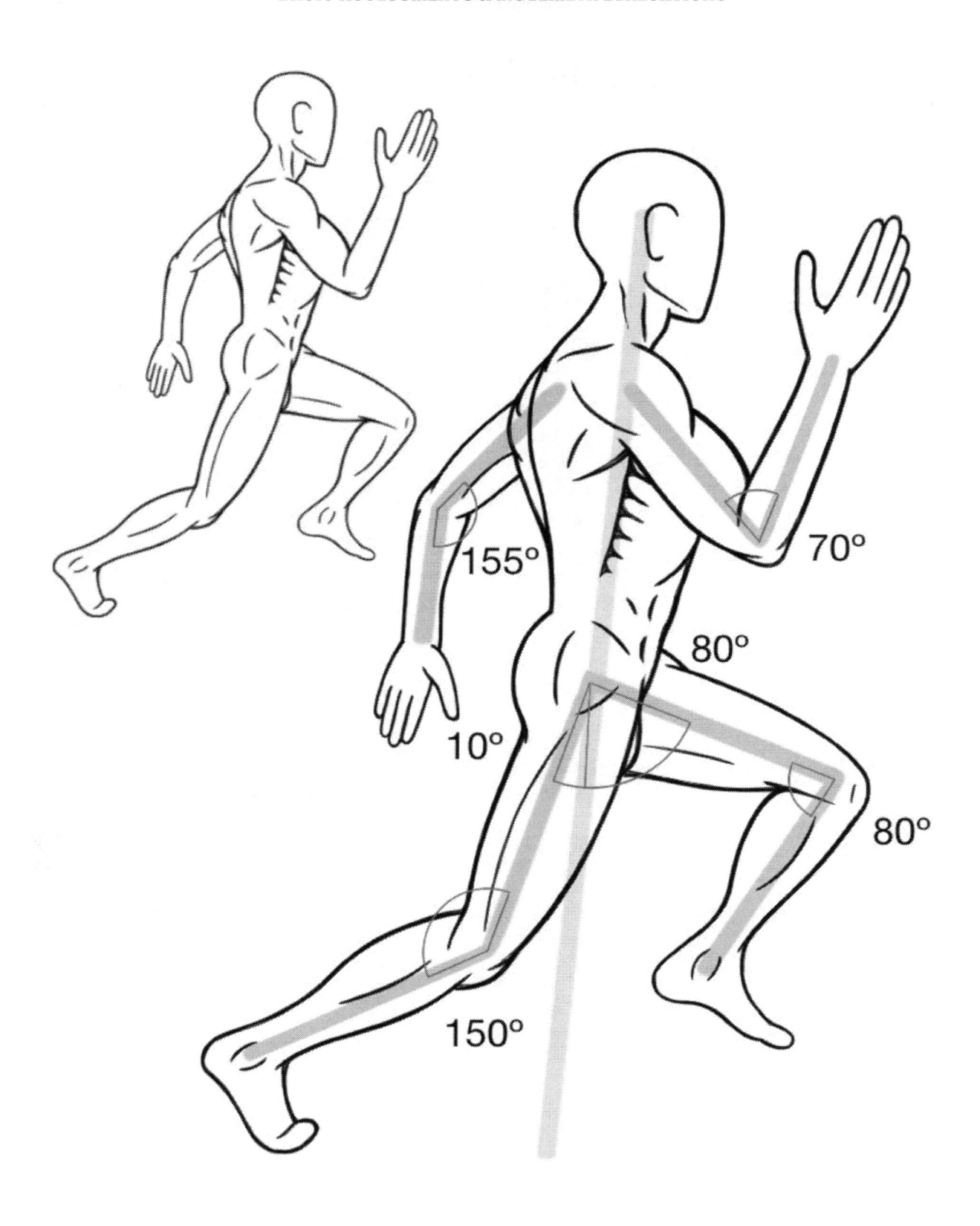

BASIC ASSESSMENTS & MOVEMETN EVALUATIONS

Running Technique
TOE-OFF POSITION

Assess the Runner's Alignment in the Toe-Off Position.
Toe-Off Position: the point where the Back Foot is making final contact with the ground.

ALIGNMENT CUES

- *Front Arm: Elbow is approximately flexed (bent) to 70° and makes a 'short lever arm' in regards to distance of hand from the mid-line of the body (Spine), which decreases any braking momentum in the stride.*
- *Back Arm: Elbow approximately extends to 155° and makes a 'long lever arm,' which helps shuttle kinetic energy backwards to propel the runner forward.*
- *Hip Extension of the 'Stance' Leg (Back Leg) should approximately open to 10° of extension, which helps to lengthen the stride and drive the runner forward.*
- *Knee Extension of the 'Stance' Leg (Back Leg) should approximately open to 150° of extension.*
- *Hip Flexion of the 'Recovery' Leg (Front Leg) should approximately open to 80° and create a relatively 'short lever arm' of the Front Leg in relationships to the midline of the body, which helps to reduce the braking forces in the stride.*
- *Knee Flexion of the 'Recovery' Leg (Front Leg) should approximately open to 80° to help create the mechanically desired 'short lever arm' of the front leg.*

PREHAB EXERCISES

- *Soft Tissue Therapy (Mobility) for the Foot, Leg, and Hip.*
- *Stretch (Mobility) the Foot, Ankle, Hip, and Posterior Chain with isolated and Combination Mobility Exercises.*
- *Activate the Foot, Ankle, Hip, and Posterior Chain Muscles with isolated and Combination Activation Exercises.*
- *Stabilize the Ankle and Hips with isolated and Combination Exercises.*
- *Strengthen the body in order to develop the amount of force needed to push the ground backwards and drive through the 'Toe-Off' Position.*
- *Practice the Gait Efficiency and Form Running Drills, as well as the Forward Lean exercises, to help develop the 'skill' to continuously achieve optimal alignment of this Toe-Off Position.*

Start with Mobility exercises and progress through Activation, Stability and Strength exercises as part of PreHab and training. Then practice both the Gait Efficiency and Form Running Drills to improve Running Technique.

BASIC ASSESSMENTS & MOVEMETN EVALUATIONS

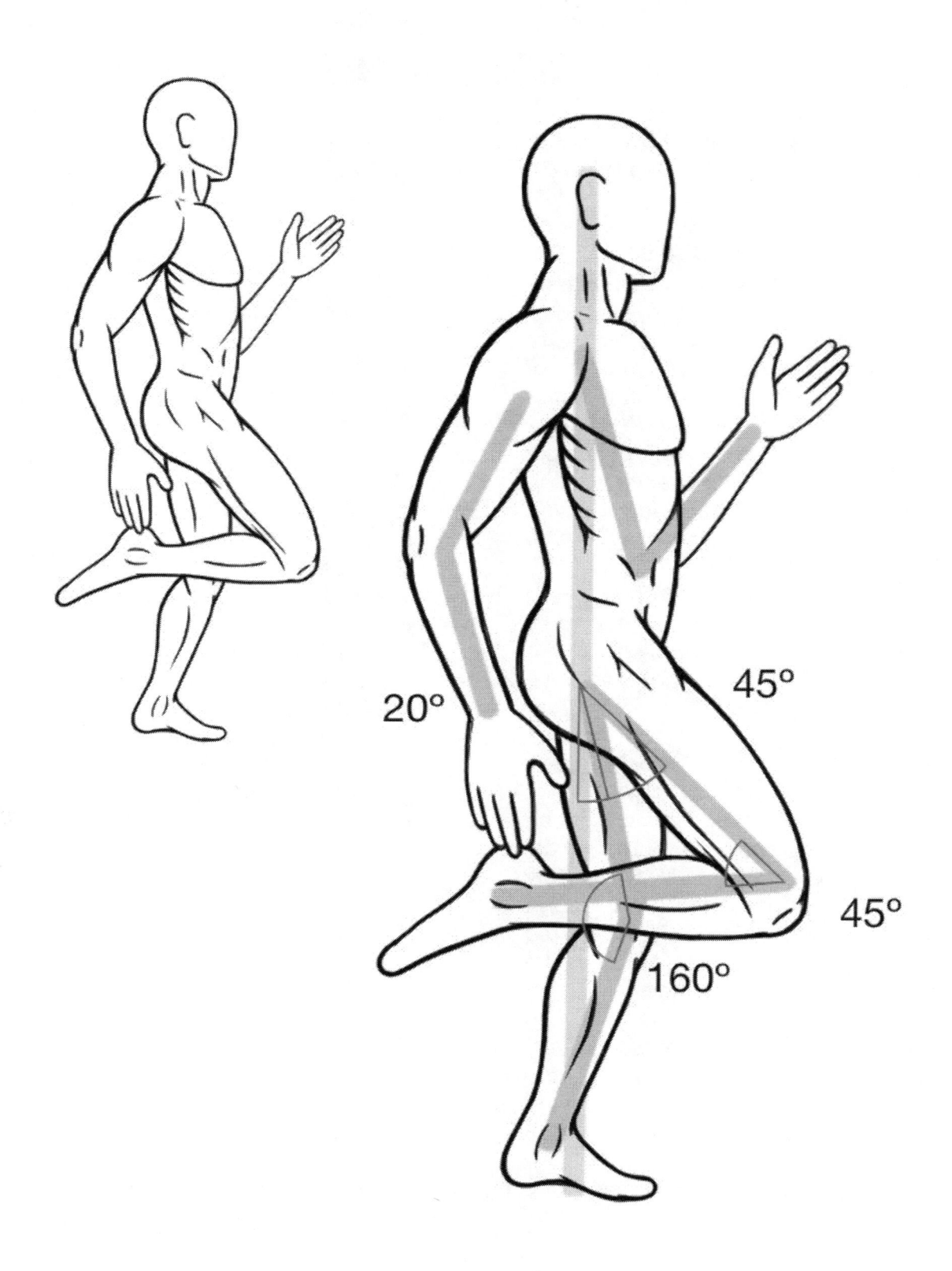

20°

45°

45°

160°

538 PreHab Exercise Book for Runners

BASIC ASSESSMENTS & MOVEMETN EVALUATIONS

Running Technique
FIGURE-FOUR POSITION

Assess the Runner's Alignment in the Figure-Four or Stance Position.
Figure-Four Position is the position where the Stance Foot is fully weight bearing and completely supporting the body.

ALIGNMENT CUES

- *Hip Extension of the 'Stance' Leg (Back Leg) should approximately open to <20° of extension, which offers the optimal 'Length-Tension Relationship' of the Hip and Leg muscles.*
- *Knee Extension of the 'Stance' Leg (Back Leg) should approximately open to <160° of extension.*
- *Hip Flexion of the 'Recovery' Leg (Front Leg) should approximately open to 45° and create a relatively 'short lever arm' of the Front Leg in relationships to the midline of the body.*
- *Knee Flexion of the 'Recovery' Leg (Front Leg) should approximately open to 40° to help create a 'short lever arm' of the front leg and allow for a fast turn-over in the stride.*
- *Midline of the body should align over the 'Stance' Foot. Many times, an individual will strike the ground with the heel in front of the midline, which will create a 'braking' force and slow the runner.*

PREHAB EXERCISES

- *Soft Tissue Therapy (Mobility) for the Foot, Leg, and Hip.*
- *Stretch (Mobility) the Foot, Ankle, Hip, and Posterior Chain with isolated and Combination Mobility Exercises.*
- *Activate the Foot, Ankle, Hip, and Posterior Chain Muscles with isolated and Combination Activation Exercises.*
- *Stabilize the Ankle and Hips with isolated and Combination Exercises.*
- *Strengthen the body in order to develop the ability to support the body over top of one foot with ideal alignment and keep in mind that the downward force on the stance leg can equal 2x bodyweight while jogging and up to 6x bodyweight while sprinting.*
- *Practice the Gait Efficiency and Form Running Drills, as well as the Forward Lean exercises to help develop the 'skill' to achieve the optimal alignment of this Figure-Four Position and reduce the likelihood of running with a Heel Strike.*

Start with Mobility exercises and progress through Activation, Stability and Strength exercises as part of PreHab and training. Then practice both the Gait Efficiency and Form Running Drills to improve Running Technique.

The A.M.A.S.S. Method of PreHab

A simple method of creating an effective PreHab Program that keeps individuals running longer, further, and faster.

ASSESS

First, use Basic Assessments, Movement Evaluations, and Observations to assess the Biomechanical Efficiency and Movement Quality of the individual.
Discover the necessary areas of focus for PreHab.

MOBILIZE

Next, use Soft Tissue Therapy and various Stretching techniques to improve Mobility. Work to improve the individual's Flexibility, Alignment, and Range of Motion.

ACTIVATE

Then, use various exercises to stimulate specific Neuromuscular Connections and Activate targeted Muscle Groups essential to executing Movement Patterns with proper form and alignment.

STABILIZE

After accomplishing the previous steps, use various exercises and increased sets/reps/load schemes to challenge the Neuromuscular System to improve Balance, Coordination, and Body Control.

STRENGTHEN

Finally, further enhance the individual's 'ability' to produce, absorb, and resist Force by developing Strength in various Movement Patterns and through a full Range of Motion.

PreHab. Run. Recover.

(Repeat)

Made in the USA
Columbia, SC
12 July 2025